BREAD

The Ultimate Cookbook

Bread: The Ultimate Cookbook

13-Digit ISBN: 978-1-40034-845-9
10-Digit ISBN:1-40034-845-5

This book may be ordered by mail from the publisher. Please include $5.99 for postage and handling.
Please support your local bookseller first!

Books published by Cider Mill Press Book Publishers are available at special discounts for bulk purchases in the United States by corporations, institutions, and other organizations. For more information, please contact the publisher.

Cider Mill Press Book Publishers
"Where good books are ready for press"
501 Nelson Place
Nashville, Tennessee 37214

cidermillpress.com

Typography: Adobe Garamond, Brandon Grotesque, Lastra, Sackers English Script

Printed in Malaysia

26 27 28 PJM 5 4 3

First Edition

BREAD

The Ultimate Cookbook

CONTENTS

INTRODUCTION

When flour is combined with water, something really special happens. Technically, the molecules in flour become "hydrated." Practically, we are now in the presence of a substance that did not exist before. The flour and water have, in fact, become a dough, which can be kneaded, folded, stretched, rolled, shaped, filled, or left to ferment. Subsequently, the dough can be cooked, boiled, fried, or baked, and the resulting flour-based product will be called bread, bagel, pizza, or any of the millions of terms that we have used over time.

Before starting with the methods and the recipes, we recommend an in-depth incursion into the history of bread (see page 19), which will make you better appreciate the incredible heritage that comes with every single loaf you bake. It will also help you not take for granted all the amazing technological advancements humanity has made, moving away from dense unleavened breads cooked on a griddle to achieve the well-risen loaves we enjoy today.

We would surely not have managed to produce such loaves without learning to master fermentation. In the Fundamentals of Bread chapter, you will be introduced to the fermentation of dough and have a chance to get accustomed to the friendly microorganisms that make our bread rise.

Even if you have never baked a single loaf, *Bread* will teach you the basics and beyond, enough for you to make authentic artisan bread at home.

Loaves are ambitious bakes, but flatbreads and pizzas also have appeal. From pita bread to injera, focaccia to a high-hydration pizza dough, there is no limit to what a pair of skilled hands can produce.

In approaching your first bakes, or in taking on more challenging ones, be aware that you do not need special powers or tools to become a skilled baker. Most of the necessary tools are probably already in your kitchen and, if not, they are quite inexpensive and accessible.

While you do not need special powers, you do need to master two fundamental skills: to gain a feel for dough and to trust your instincts. Despite what is commonly believed, there is indeed nothing overly scientific about baking bread. Although it is true that every minimal aspect of the art of bread making has been analyzed and made into a seemingly exact science, it does not have to be so.

Too many numbers, too many rules. Numbers, like those used to weigh ingredients and measure dough temperature, are surely useful tools. However, numbers are not necessary, and not even sufficient, to turn you into a good baker. Many skilled professional bakers would agree that the best bakers ever were the moms and grandmas traditionally in charge of baking bread for their community. They had no knowledge of numbers and owned no sophisticated tools to help them turn out those beautiful breads that linger in memory.

Nonetheless, those women surely knew what counts most. They knew that you need to really feel and observe the dough in order to discover how to tame it. The recipe is, in fact, nothing more than a roughly written script, which can get you started until you develop your own version. Only you will know what is required to complete this personalized script on a specific occasion.

With this in mind, feel confident in using

the various methods and techniques suggested in this book, as they will be the perfect complement to your own creativity. Know that you are building on more than 10,000 years of baking tradition and that, through your skilled hands, every recipe has the chance to come back to life.

Baking bread is indeed a very important piece of our heritage as human beings, and something we have a responsibility to carry forward. Feel free to be humbled by this rich tradition but do not be scared: working with dough is so ingrained in us that you just need to listen to your inner baking mojo.

As you start to listen, you will see that your dough will start to speak up, and that synergy will create magic that will nourish you in ways you would not have expected.

THE FUNDAMENTALS OF BREAD

There is something wondrous about making your own bread, in your own kitchen, with your own hands. It makes one feel like some sort of magician when, from simple and apparently inert ingredients like flour, water, and salt, one manages to create a food as complete, delectable, nourishing, beautiful, and alive as bread.

To make the simplest bread, one does not even need a rising agent. It is enough to combine flour with water to create something completely new, which we call dough. If you then add some salt, shape the dough into small rounds, and bake it in a hot oven, you have bread. While simplistic in its approach, the quality of what results even from this crude dough may surprise you.

If you repeat the same procedure, adding baker's yeast or sourdough starter to your dough and give it time to rise, violá: you will end up with a bread that more closely resembles your idea of the archetypical loaf.

When you feel confident enough to start experimenting with variations of the type or percentages of the basic ingredients (flour, water, salt, yeast, and time), you will realize that the shapes, textures, and flavors of bread are virtually infinite.

Later on, when you venture into adding other ingredients to your basic doughs, you will feel like a full-blown wizard. However, between your first creations and the many, incrementally improved versions to follow, there will be less variance in the process than you may think.

ESSENTIAL INGREDIENTS

FLOUR

To, most people flour is just a powdery substance sold in a paper package.

However, to professional and home bakers alike, flour is akin to the colors on a painter's palette.

In that paper package lies a whole world. As an apprentice home baker, you will soon realize that a big part of your baking successes and failures resides in the type of flour you use. You will find out how each flour affects the bread you make. Soon, hunting for a particular flour will become just as natural as hunting for the ripest fruits at the grocery store.

Technically, flour derives from the grinding of seeds, nuts, or roots. The most commonly used flour in bread making comes from wheat, but flours from other grains, or cereals, are also very common.

Wheat is the world's most widely grown cereal. One good reason for the supremacy of wheat over other cereals is its superior baking properties. Wheat seeds possess an inner body mostly composed of the large starchy endosperm and the oily germ, all enclosed in an outer layer of bran. Fibers are mostly concentrated in the bran, while the endosperm is where the starches and most of the proteins are stored. Fats are stocked in the germ of the wheat kernel.

Wheat and other cereals can be ground into flours with different degrees of fineness. The level of fineness of the grinding will give us flours that can be coarse, like semolina flour, best suited for pasta making, or fine, like the widely used all-purpose flour.

The fineness of flour is an important quality for bread baking. If you want to make a bread or pastry with a featherlight texture, you will need to look for superfine flour, which has a silky sensation to the touch and confers special powers to your dough.

Laboratory research comparing flours of different fineness shows that wheat flour's ability to absorb water increases with a reduction in particle size. Required time to let the dough develop and the stability of the dough increase along with fineness of the flour. These increases are due to the tendency of flour proteins to be more available in the finest fractions of milled flour. A dough made with finer flour is also more extensible, allowing for easier shaping. In the end, the result of these fine flours is a beautiful-looking bread with higher volume, lighter texture, and better color as compared with bread made with a coarser flour.

Although fineness is desirable in breads that are meant to develop much in terms of volume and have a very light crumb, there is no shortage of breads where different qualities are desirable, and thus do not call for a fine or superfine flour. For example, there are many breads made with the coarse, but delicious, semolina flour, and whole rye breads, which are not supposed to be light nor high in volume. A coarser flour is also the preferred option in several traditional flatbreads.

The white color of flour is a quality that has been associated with wheat for a very long time. In fact, the origin of the very term *wheat* is related to the color white. *Wheat* comes from the old German word weizzi, which derives from the word hwīta, meaning white. The association of wheat and white may be due to the color of wheat flour compared to flour made with other cereals, such as barley, rye, and oats.

The superior baking properties of wheat also confer to whiter bread made with wheat, as compared to breads made with other grains. In order to obtain an even lighter and airier consistency in wheat bread, the bran is partially or totally eliminated or sifted out. Bran removal has been done since antiquity, utilizing increasingly sophisticated milling and sifting techniques.

Based on the level of whiteness in wheat flour (i.e., the relative amount of bran present in the milled flour), different labels are applied, such as: whole wheat, sifted, unbleached white, and white (i.e., bleached white).

Whole wheat flour is obtained when all of the bran contained in the wheat kernel is included in the milled flour. Not all whole wheat flours are the same, however. Most store-bought whole wheat flours are not made by grinding the whole seed at once, but rather by adding the bran, which was previously removed, back in to the refined flour. The resulting flour, even if it's called whole wheat (or, on occasion, whole meal), will not truly include the whole ground wheat kernel, but only the endosperm and bran fractions. In fact, the vitamin- and essential fats-rich wheat germ is not included in most industrial whole wheat flours.

Sifted flour is obtained by sifting flour that has been derived by milling the whole wheat kernel at once. In general, the sifting process is intended to remove the bran, leaving the endosperm and wheat germ in the flour. Both milling and sifting can be achieved via different methods. Different degrees of sifting can produce flours with varying percentages of bran, or ashes. Depending on the level of bran content, the resulting flour will feature different degrees of whiteness. The wheat germ, however, will always remain in the flour, if the kernel is truly milled whole.

Unbleached white flour is obtained by using roller mill technology. This sophisticated method involves mechanically isolating the endosperm from the bran and the wheat germ, in order to mill just the endosperm. This process produces a finer, whiter flour compared to sifted flour. Such flour is extremely versatile and has a long shelf life. The term *unbleached* means that no bleaching agent is added to the flour to increase its whiteness. Unbleached, however, does not mean that the flour is necessarily free from chemical additives. A very common additive that can be found in unbleached flour is sodium bromate, which improves the baking performance of the flour. However, this additive has been linked to unfavorable health outcomes, and is banned in several countries outside the United States. Therefore, you may want to check that your unbleached white flour is also unbromated before purchasing.

A flour branded as "white flour" may indicate that the flour has been bleached. Bleaching is done to increase whiteness, but also to improve baking properties. Through bleaching, the flour is oxidized, which can mimic the natural aging process of flour.

Other Commonly Used Flours

Pastry flour refers to superfine white wheat flour with a protein content that is relatively low, making it ideal for pastries. Soft wheat is the main grain used here.

Graham flour refers to a coarse, 100 percent whole wheat flour.

Bread flour refers to white flour with a high protein content, which is ideal for bread baking. It is generally obtained from hard wheat.

All-purpose flour refers to white flour that can be used for all sorts of baking purposes. It is generally a combination of hard and soft wheats.

Stone-milled flour refers to flour that has been milled via the traditional milling technique of grinding the whole kernel between stones.

Authentic stone-milled flour can be sifted or unsifted, but can never be white, or superfine. It is very common, however, to find stone-milled flours in which stone milling is only one part of the milling process, with the remaining milling carried out with more sophisticated techniques. These flours resemble roller-milled flours.

Locally Milled or Store-Bought?

Not so long ago, there were thousands of mills in the United States. With the advent of modern milling techniques in the second half of the nineteenth century, large milling plants gradually took over the work done by small and less technologically advanced gristmills, making industrial, mass-produced flour the norm all across the globe.

The last decade, however, has seen a revival of local artisan mills, and the availability of flour milled without the use of advanced technology is increasing. However, local mills are still too few and too scattered to provide a significant proportion of the flour used in baking, as access to a large distribution channel is limited for these local mills. The best way to buy flour from a local mill is online.

Most contemporary artisan mills use the ancient technique of stone milling. This technology is as old as agriculture, although important developments in the approach have occurred. In particular, the source of power that makes the stones rotate against each other to grind the kernels has considerably changed over time: from hand-operated mills, ancient Rome's water mills, and medieval windmills to today's modern electricity-powered stone mills.

Even with these notable differences, the basic mechanisms that make stone mills effective have changed little, particularly when compared to their eighteenth-century relatives. Consequently, genuine stone-milled flours are, in all likelihood, similar to preindustrial flours. With flour produced via today's local stone mills, one can experience a bread that holds the charm of something lost in time, evoking ancestral memories.

The flours commonly found in grocery stores are processed in highly automated roller mill plants, where the mills break open the kernel and scrape the endosperm away from the bran and germ. Following a run through sifters and purifiers, these mills produce a completely refined wheat flour, which contains only the finely ground endosperm.

Sifters and purifiers are used in most local mills, too, but if the kernel is ground whole—as in stone milling—it is not possible to later filter out all of the bran from the flour. Similarly, the fats contained in the wheat kernel's germ are released into the flour during milling when the kernel is broken. These fats end up coating the particles of flour, making them stick together more and affecting their ability to absorb water during dough development.

This is why, when using flours produced in an authentic stone mill, one should not expect the superfine, powdery, white substance you probably grew up calling flour. Similarly, the breads made with the darker, coarser stone-milled flours will never share the characteristics of the breads made with standard white flours. Bread volume will most likely be affected, as well as crumb density and crust color.

Still, there are small artisan mills that use more advanced technology and can offer whole flours that provide better baking performance compared to what would be produced by traditional stone mills. The main point of artisan mills is not to revive old technology, but rather to offer a more wholesome flour.

When deciding if it is better to use flour from local artisan mills or a store-bought variety, one should first answer this question: What is most important to me? If your aim is to learn to bake an awe-inducing and feathery-light baked good to compete with an award-winning bakery, industrial flours are the way to go. If you instead value taste and nutrition over appearance and consistency, local mills have much more to offer.

Finally, if you find yourself wanting it all, then you must have a variety of different flours at hand and learn to combine them in a manner that can give you an uncompromised, aesthetically pleasing bread.

IT'S IN THE WATER

Water is a key ingredient in making bread dough. Adding water to flour hydrates the molecules, which have a strong affinity for this solvent. In addition to hydrating the flour, water allows for the formation of the gluten that regulates enzymatic activity, gives life to yeast, hydrates starch granules during baking, allows gelatinization, and does important work to incorporate other dough ingredients, such as glucose, sucrose, and salt.

The first condition for the water you use for your dough is that it is suitable for human consumption. In other words, the water you use in your bread needs to be reasonably clean, and therefore drinkable.

You may have heard claims that a certain bread or food cannot be made in any place other than its original geographical area, because the real secret for the recipe's success is "in the water." Neapolitan pizza is a good example. It is often claimed that an authentic Neapolitan pizza can only be made in Naples, because of the water there. This may actually be an exaggeration, as it was noticed that New York's tap water is not so dissimilar from the mystical water of Naples, and so are other waters.

Nonetheless, local differences are sometimes truly relevant and can explain the failure in replicating a particular recipe.

Once the question of drinkability has been resolved, there are three more characteristics of water that should be considered in bread baking:

Water Hardness

In the baking industry, water is classified according to its hardness, which depends on its concentration of mineral salts, especially calcium and magnesium. These minerals interact with proteins, affecting the dough development in different ways. Specifically, a very soft water can collapse a dough, while water that is too hard results in poor production of gasses, reduces the activity of yeast, and creates a tighter gluten net, which requires prolonged proofing. Information on water hardness is often made available by municipalities. If you plan to use your tap water, you may want to check this information and evaluate if you need to dilute your tap water with bottled water to reach the right balance of minerals. Water filters may also come in handy if your water is too hard.

Water pH

A neutral solution has a pH of 7, a basic pH is greater than 7, and an acidic solution has a pH less than 7. For bread dough, it is generally preferable to use a slightly acidic water, with a pH around 5 to 6, but Neapolitan pizza likes a higher pH of 7. If your tap water inclines toward basic, you may consider diluting it with bottled water with a lower pH. Testing for pH is very easy nowadays, thanks to the availability of home kits.

Water Temperature

Professional bakers consider having control over the internal temperature of their doughs to be fundamental to achieving a successful, repeatable result. Water is a very smart way to easily achieve desired dough temperature, as it is easy to warm up or cool down water before combining it with flour. There are plenty of formulas, of various levels of complexity, to calculate the ideal water temperature based on desired dough temperature. They all consider the room and/or flour temperature and/or pre-ferment temperature; desired dough temperature; and estimated added temperature generated by mixing the dough (including hand mixing). These formulas can be useful, but they are always an approximation. A good way to easily get the correct water temperature is to consider the ambient temperature in your kitchen. If your kitchen temperature is high, you can still obtain a lower dough temperature by adding cold water, although not below 40°F. If your kitchen temperature is cold, you can achieve a higher desired dough temperature by adding warmer water, though not warmer than 77°F. Finally, if you are using a mixer and know that it tends to warm the dough considerably, cooling your water before adding it to the dough is a good idea.

SALT

Contrary to popular belief, the primary reason for adding salt to a dough is not for taste. Although salt does improve the taste of bread considerably, its other functions in bread making are far more important.

Have you ever tried baking bread without adding salt? The result will be a flat and pale loaf, so far away from the rustic beauty you were likely envisioning. The presence of salt in dough slows down the activity of the yeasts and bacteria as well as the activity of the enzymes, so that there will still be sugars remaining to be transformed when the loaf is baked, allowing for good oven spring and browning of the crust. This is particularly important for rye bread, which has a very high enzymatic activity.

Thanks to its ability to impede bacterial activity, salt also functions like a natural disinfectant, inhibiting the proliferation of potentially harmful bacteria, both during fermentation and after baking, working as an effective antimolding agent. Of course, good bacteria are also partially inhibited by salt's presence, with a consequent reduction of acidity in the final loaf.

In addition, salt aids bread with developing a good structure by making the gluten net more resistant and more effective at keeping the gasses in, resulting in a loaf that is higher in volume and possesses a more open crumb.

Salt absorbs water; thus, a dough containing salt will be drier and more elastic, and will be less sticky during handling and shaping. On the contrary, a dough without salt is sticky and difficult to work with.

Salt also stiffens the dough, and this is why it is generally added during the last phases of mixing rather than at the beginning, so as not to toughen the dough too early in the proceedings.

Too much salt can, however, negatively affect dough development. In most recipes, the ideal amount of salt is a mere 2 percent of the total amount of flour (2 grams per 100 grams).

ENZYMES

Enzymes are molecules, generally proteins, which bring about biochemical reactions. In bread baking, amylases are the class of enzymes we most care about. The amylases present in wheat flour help reduce starch and fructose to simpler sugars. In particular, the amylose and amylopectin bonds in wheat starch need to be broken, producing dextrin and maltose, which are easily fermentable sugars. These sugars can then be "eaten" by yeast cells, and the resulting fermentation process will produce carbon dioxide, which is what makes a dough rise. Proper enzymatic balance in flour is also essential for the color and flavor of the final loaf.

MILLING AT HOME

One important advantage of milling at home is the reappropriation of our long-lost relationship with grains. Having the ability to access whole grains, and learn about their different shapes, colors, smells, and hardnesses, brings a different approach to the practice of baking. The milled grains become the real stars, giving a distinctive character to each and every bake. You will also become aware of the value and importance of quality grains, surely much more than when buying industrially milled flours at the grocery store.

The best argument for home milling is the freshness of the flour. With the easy-to-use home mills available nowadays, one can grind just enough flour for a bake and use it immediately after milling. The advantage of this practice is to preserve the nutrients contained in the grain, as the quality and concentration of both vitamins and essential fats start to decrease soon after milling. Thus, being able to make your own flour will give you the most nutrient-packed bread you could possibly eat.

It is important to note, though, that there can be some drawbacks to these home mills. The main defect is that some of them overheat flour in a way that commercial mills may not. Heat, like time, is another born enemy to nutrient-rich flour. Therefore, a local mill could be the best option if your primary concern is a nutrient-packed flour.

A BRIEF HISTORY OF BREAD MAKING

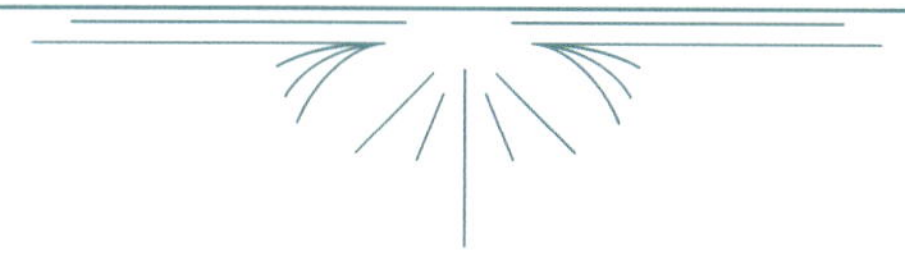

THE FERTILE CRESCENT: WHERE WHEAT GREW WILD

The origins of bread are inseparable from the origins of wheat cultivation. Wheat cultivation began in the Middle East, in an area called the Fertile Crescent, which today includes Syria, parts of Turkey, Iraq, and Iran.

Long before the actual cultivation of common wheat, grains closely related to it once grew wild and abundant in the Fertile Crescent. Barley and emmer, as well as einkorn and rye, were all present in different areas of this large region. There was something special about the seeds from these grasses: they were big and full of starches, easy to reach, and easy to store. The oldest seeds that have been discovered so far date back 33,000 years. These seeds, found in Mount Carmel in northern Israel, were identified as emmer, a close relative of modern wheat.

In the beginning, these wild relatives of wheat were presumably crossed or ground, combined with water, and then cooked. The resulting preparation likely resembled porridge or polenta.

Between 10,000 and 12,000 years ago, humans began domesticating wild cereals and agriculture was born. The wild grains were progressively selected to promote richer harvests, and soon they mutated in a way that made them incapable of surviving without the human hand. The bounty provided by this mutation also made humans heavily dependent on these domesticated grains. The advent of agriculture and the increased availability of stored grains also brought new ways of eating cereals, and thus was bread born.

First came unleavened flatbreads. The mixture of ground grain and water was cooked, first on a griddle and then in rudimental ovens, rather than being boiled.

EGYPT: THE BREAD THAT BUILT THE PYRAMIDS

The first historical documents reporting the existence of leavened bread date back to the second millennium BCE. At that time, the Egyptians had possibly the most advanced culture in the world, thanks to their highly developed agriculture.

The ancient Egyptians grew emmer and barley—emmer for bread and barley for beer and yeast. While it is unclear how the leavening process was discovered, it was likely by accident. Perhaps there was an establishment that was both bakery and brewery, and some yeast-rich beer foam spilled on a dough and made it rise magically. It is likely that the ancient Egyptians also used authentic sourdough cultures, made by wild yeasts and bacteria present in the air and in the flour.

Another debt that the modern world owes to the ancient Egyptians is the considerable progress they made in regards to the oven. Egyptian ovens were conically shaped, had an opening in the front, and the baking chamber was coated with tiles, a trio of qualities that aided in heat being conducted and retained.

The ancient Egyptians used communal bakeries to sustain and give salaries to the workers, including the clerical class; a common salary at that time included two pounds of bread made from emmer a day. Considering all of this, it would not be out of line to suggest that the pyramids were built thanks to leavened bread.

GREECE: THE MANY SHAPES OF BREAD

The ancient Greeks learned the art of leavening from the Egyptians. In the Greece of fifth and fourth century BCE, cereals and bread were elevated by politicians, writers, and philosophers. Bread came in several different shapes and flavors, but it was not abundant, as Greece was not Egypt or the Fertile Crescent—Greek soil was not optimal for agriculture, and the ancient Greeks needed to import most of their wheat from their colonies, such as Sicily.

Due to the scarcity of wheat, bread in ancient Greece was mostly reserved for the higher social classes, and was offered to commoners only on festive occasions.

While the ancient Greeks did not make huge advancements in terms of bread making, it is thanks to their bakers that leavened bread became known to the ancient Romans, who made considerable progress.

ROME: BREAD AS WE KNOW IT

It is hard to believe what happened after early Romans (fourth century BCE) "discovered" bread baking. Within less than two centuries from that moment, leavened bread flourished like never before, in any civilization. Wheat became central to Rome's economy, and new territories were often annexed to the Republic, and later to the Empire, because of the need to import as much wheat as possible.

In Rome, bread was not a luxury reserved for the nobles as it had been in Greece. And at the apex of the Roman Empire, plebeians (the poor of Rome) did not have to work for their bread, as the ancient Egyptians did. Fragrant loaves from the state-owned bakeries were dispensed free of charge to the multitudes in order to keep them at bay and prevent insurrections.

Outside the empire's capital, plebeians did not have the right to free bread, but they could always access a public oven and bake their own bread there. Not surprisingly, given the importance attributed by Romans to bread, by the middle of the second century BCE, Rome had instituted a bakers' guild, and bakers had become highly specialized; there were the bread bakers, the sweets bakers, the milk bakers, and the pastry bakers. The bakers were freedmen, unlike other workers, who were typically slaves. There were rules regarding the role of bakers: they were not allowed to leave the profession of their fathers, in an attempt to ensure that the skills, then considered so vital, would never be lost.

Romans, who had "a thing" for water and were highly skilled hydraulic engineers, invented the water mill. Water mill technology has been used ever since, and some water mills are still up and running in both the United States and Europe.

Roman ovens were modeled after the conically shaped ovens used by the Egyptians, and, stunningly, these ovens were so advanced that no substantial changes to the oven occurred from Roman times to the twentieth century.

As if that were not enough in terms of advancing bread making, the Romans are responsible for the establishment of wheat as the world's supreme cereal. Early Romans made bread mostly out of einkorn and later with emmer, like the Greeks and Egyptians. During the first century BCE, though, a new type of wheat started to take over: common wheat had landed in Roman harbors and quickly won over the hearts (and stomachs) of Romans thanks to its superior baking properties. The new wheat became the most desired and widely grown cereal in the Roman Empire.

EUROPE: THE BREAD OF LORDS AND THE BREAD OF PEASANTS

The fall of the Roman Empire coincided with a recession in terms of bread making and wheat availability. Imports stopped and wheat circulation across Europe became more difficult. Agricultural techniques also went backward, making harvests all over the continent poorer and more unpredictable.

Famines and plagues became frequent, and the sultry white bread of the late Romans became a memory of a long-lost golden age. However, in monasteries, the monks continued to cultivate top-notch grains.

Later on, when feudalism was instituted, the peasants worked the lands of feudal lords, receiving a part of the harvest and the right to bake bread in the lords' ovens in return. The lords were served white bread made with the sifted flour, and peasants ate black bread made with the bran discarded after sifting and a small amount of sifted flour.

Where wheat did not grow, common people ate bread made with grains other than wheat, such as barley and oats in Scandinavian countries and rye in Eastern Europe, France, and Northern Italy. Millet was also used to make bread, and in Mediterranean areas durum wheat was the staple cereal. All of these grains were considered of poorer quality and lower nutritional value compared to common wheat. This is probably because they produced a bread that was denser and took a long time to bake.

Nobility and royalty, however, could afford to buy wheat from merchants, even in areas where wheat did not grow, so the aristocracy continued to have white and light loaves on the table all through the Middle Ages.

Often, common people did not have enough of any type of grain to make bread, and needed to make flour from whatever source was readily available—anything to produce a loaf that could quell their hunger. Examples include tree bark in Nordic countries, chestnuts in Southern Europe, and even acorns. Legumes were also used, and later on potatoes—and the list of alternatives is much longer. These replacements for grain ended up characterizing European bread in peculiar and fascinating ways, and it is thanks to these ingenuous means of producing bread that a very important part of Europe's culinary and bread making heritage was born.

The Middle Ages were prolific in terms of giving birth to countless different local breads, but they did not produce any substantial technological progress in bread baking, with the exception of the of the windmill's advent in the seventh century. Windmills, which have Persian origins, were used to grind grains and operate field irrigation pumps. However, written evidence supports that the use of windmills did not reach Europe until at least the twelfth century.

During the Renaissance, and starting in Italy, commerce flourished again, and wheat's exchange and distribution became easier. White

bread was no longer associated with the noble rank, though it was still a sign of wealth. The urbanite middle classes could buy bread from local bakeries, and well-off peasants could bake it in their ovens.

Around this time, yeast derived from beer was reintroduced into the baking process. This was a relative of modern baker's yeast and had been long lost since the Roman Empire, where it was often used as an alternative leavening agent to sourdough. Once reintroduced, yeast quickly became favored over sourdough, because it could produce lighter bread. It is said that Marie de Medici made baker's yeast popular again. The Tuscan noblewoman, who eventually became queen of France, apparently brought her crew of Italian bakers to Paris, and it is said that the contemporary superiority of French luxury bread and pastries started there.

After the various military successes of Napoleon across the continent, wheat-based breads and pastries became more popular in Northern and Eastern Europe, as these were what was enjoyed by the ruling court, and the citizens who inhabited the capital of the empire, Paris.

NORTH AMERICA: INDUSTRIAL WHEAT AND FLOURS

Wheat was introduced to North America by the colonists, but it took a while for it to become the primary grain. Initially rye, oats, and corn were much more popular cereals than wheat, but French influence was strong in the young United States, and thus the cultivation of wheat was driven forward. However, it was not until the midnineteenth century that substantial progress occurred in American wheat breeding and milling techniques.

There were two major events that shaped wheat farming and distribution in North America. The first event occurred in Canada. A Canadian farmer, David Fife, was not pleased with the performance of his wheat. So he asked one of his workers, a native of Scotland, to return home and find him another variety of wheat. The worker returned home, went to the harbor, and found a ship full of wheat.

He bought a small amount of it and sent it on to Mr. Fife in Canada, who, unfortunately, sowed the wheat immediately. As this was a winter wheat and needed to be sown in the fall rather than in the spring, the first harvest was, according to legend, disastrous, producing just one stalk of wheat, from which a few seeds were saved. Fortunately, these were then sown at the proper time, and in a few years, the seeds of this mysterious wheat, Red Fife, had multiplied and produced fantastic harvests. Red Fife is a hard wheat and produces a flour that allows bread to rise higher, which made it immediately popular among bakers. Soon this wheat was being grown in most of the United States, and other high-performing hard wheats followed, like Turkey Red and Marquis.

The second major moment for North American wheat concerns the search for solutions to the problems that arose around the milling of Red Fife. As this wheat has superior baking properties, bakers wanted it to be as refined as possible. However, stone mills struggled with its hardness, and as a result the flour could not be properly sifted. To make matters worse, the stones of the mills wore down faster when milling hard wheats like Red Fife and Turkey Red. These issues caused the milling industry to pursue different techniques of milling, and in a few decades roller mills were born.

Roller mills were made from metal, rather than stone, and could separate the endosperm from the bran through purifiers. Later, extractors were able to isolate the wheat germ from the endosperm. The levels of fineness and whiteness obtained by these mills were unprecedented, and soon the United States began to export large amounts of white flour to Europe.

As wheat became so important in the United States, sizable investments were made in researching the cereal. Wheat was studied in increasingly sophisticated laboratories, where it was bred, crossbred, and directly modified. This continues to be done with the aim of selecting plants with improved baking properties, as well as improved resilience to pests, drought, and weather. The result is wheat varieties which provide immensely productive harvests without need of much care from the farmer.

THE REDISCOVERY OF ARTISAN BREAD AND LOCAL WHEAT VARIETIES

In the twentieth century, the availability of high-performing and cheap white flour resulted in its massive use for baking and cooking. And the spread of mass-produced flour was quickly followed by mass-produced bread. Thanks to the use of high-speed mixers, and chemical dough conditioners and improvers, the rising process could be sped up like never before. At the same time, machines were capable of substituting for humans in every stage of the baking

process, so that thousands of loaves of bread could be baked at once. The advantages in terms of productivity and cost are clear.

But as this mass-produced, cheap bread started to become the only kind that people were familiar with, nostalgia for the artisan breads of the past began to rise. Starting in the 1970s, this feeling fully bloomed in the '90s, and it hasn't faded since.

The term "artisan bread" generally refers to a bread made either at home or in a nonindustrial bakery. In an authentic artisan bakery, the baker has full control over the final product; in other words, the process of making bread is not fully automated. As opposed to quick-rising packaged bread, artisan bread is expected to have undergone a proper, longer fermentation and to be free from chemical additives. Today, small artisan bakeries inspired by the European bread tradition are successfully opening in every corner of the world, including, curiously, Asia, where there was never a tradition of bread making. At the same time, more and more households are learning to bake their own bread, regaining control over its quality.

Paralleling the revival of artisan bread, scientists, farmers, and wheat lovers started to hunt for old wheat varieties. Sources were mostly seed banks, where original seeds from different regions of the world were stored. Other important sources were isolated pockets of farmland where growers have continued to use local wheat varieties, rather than converting to the dominant, modern strains. Sometimes old seeds were rediscovered by pure chance, in the attic of an elderly relative, or a disused barn.

This is good in many ways. First of all, there is the big advantage of preserving biodiversity. As agronomists tell us, we cannot foresee all of the climatic changes to come, and biodiversity in our wheat is a guarantee that we will have bread on our table for a long time to come. Foodies also appreciate having a wide array of different grains and wheat varieties because as with cheese and wine, different local varieties present a rich array of different flavors for consumers. Finally, there are also health-related benefits to reintroducing old wheat varieties in our diet. It has been argued that modern wheat has undergone excessive change, or that this change occurred too fast for our biology to adapt. It is indeed true that older varieties of wheat have been consumed for a longer amount of time, and they have already passed the test as reliable food staples. Studies tend to confirm that older wheat varieties are superior to newer ones in terms of digestibility, and often in their nutritional profiles, too.

Thanks to all of these considerations and to the contagious enthusiasm of wheat "archeologists," old varieties are becoming the next big thing in bread baking. As an example, in California the cultivation of wheat almost became a memory from the past, but interest in heritage wheat varieties has revived the local grain economy, and now more and more land is being converted to wheat agriculture.

Similar phenomena can be observed in Sicily, which was once the cradle of wheat, and has now been reborn as a heritage wheat paradise. France is also rediscovering its many precious local wheat varieties, and so on. These are still just pockets compared to the vastly dominant conventional wheat farming that rules the market. However, the number of these pockets is growing exponentially.

EQUIPMENT & TOOLS FOR BAKING BREAD

To start making bread, you do not need any special tools. You can manage to bake your first bread using only what is commonly found in the average home kitchen. However, if you want to become a skilled bread baker, having the right tools at hand will make bread baking more enjoyable and may greatly improve the quality of your loaves.

ESSENTIALS

SCALE

A scale will be your best friend through your bread baking endeavors. Your scale, along with your oven, is one appliance you should learn to know and love. The international bread baking language runs on weights, rather than volume measurements, and the best recipes will contain both. There are several good reasons why measurements expressed in weights are preferable to volumetric ones. Flour can vary in volume

depending on its fineness. A coarser flour has a smaller volume compared to a more finely ground one. Therefore, the weight of a cup of flour varies according to the type of flour. Other ingredients, like water, need to be scaled based on the total amount of flour, something that is easily done using weights. If you are unfamiliar with your kitchen scale, start by weighing volumes you are used to (like a cup, a teaspoon, etc.) so that you start getting the grip of the new system. In no time, you will become very fond of your scale. Just trust that it will make bread baking infinitely easier. You absolutely do not need a high-tech scale. Choose based on your budget, and know that almost any scale will serve the purpose of bread making. There are bakeries that still use decades-old analog scales and have no intention of swapping them out for the newest one.

You will need to measure everything from a pinch of salt to a few pounds of flour, so make sure that your scale can reliably handle weights in this range. In case your scale is not reliable for the lower end, you can always buy an additional scale that is dedicated to weighing small amounts.

You also need to consider the dimension of your scale, meaning both the actual dimensions of the scale and the scale's weighing surface. The actual dimension needs to properly fit the space available in your kitchen. Even more important than this is the size of the scale's weighing surface. In order to be able to comfortably weigh a big piece of dough, you need a large weighing surface on your scale.

ASSORTED CONTAINERS

You will need several containers of different sizes to mix ingredients and allow your dough and pre-ferments to rest and rise.

The size of your containers depends on the amount of dough you prefer to work with. Always consider that both your pre-ferments (yeast- or sourdough-based) and your dough need to have enough space in order to triple in volume. Dough and pre-ferments generally double in volume, but you do not want to be unprepared for the days when your leavening agents are unusually active.

Containers with straight walls are preferred, as they are easy to keep clean with sticky dough. A lid that can effectively seal the container is also preferable to a looser one. Alternatively, you can always use the mixing bowls that you surely already have in your kitchen, and cover them with plastic wrap or with a pan lid that fits the bowl.

RUBBER SPATULA

You will not be able to keep the walls of your containers tidy and remove sticky dough without a rubber spatula. A clean container is key to consistent bread making, as clean means an unfavorable ground for the proliferation of unwanted microorganisms.

PROOFING BASKETS

It is possible to make bread without using proofing baskets, but once you start using them, you will realize that they make the process much easier. With your shaped loaf in the basket, you can easily move the dough around your kitchen without disturbing the dough. This will be particularly handy when baking at home, where kitchen space is not exclusively dedicated to bread. Bread proofing baskets come in different shapes and materials, and nowadays are very reasonably priced and easy to get. To start, considering purchasing a couple of round baskets and a couple oval-shaped ones.

KITCHEN TOWELS

It is always good to have clean kitchen towels at hand. You can use any clean piece of cloth made of cotton or linen. The lighter the better. They can be very useful, especially when working with wet doughs or when you need to line a proofing basket. If properly dusted with flour,

they will ensure that the dough won't stick to the basket or the towel.

BENCH SCRAPERS

These come in different materials and shapes, and you will want to have at least two on hand. One should have round edges and be used to detach your dough from the container where you are mixing or proofing it. The other essential type of scraper has a blade with a straight edge, and the best ones are made of stainless steel. The metal scraper will enable you to easily cut your dough, as well as help you to scrape dough off of your work table. In fact, the metal bench scraper could become one of your most important bread making tools, as a good one will enable you to cut risen dough without deflating it, and can also help you shape very wet doughs. So do not skimp when shopping for bench scrapers, and make sure they are not too small, so that they can handle large pieces of dough.

WORK SURFACE

This is another fundamental aspect of your little home bakery. Check your kitchen for a work surface that has a good height for you. It could be a corner of your countertop, your kitchen table, or a kitchen island. Also check that, whatever the surface, it gives stable support. In the bread making process, you may need to punch your dough (literally) or slap it around, and in order to do either, stability is a must. If you have a choice of materials to work on, there are different possibilities. Both marble and wood are good. Stainless steel is not considered optimal by many—yet that is what most professional bakers have to use, because of hygienic regulations. The reason why both stone and wood are preferred is that they are not as cool as stainless steel. In other words, they will not affect dough temperature. Stainless steel instead will cool down the dough slightly, creating an extra variable to take into account. Wooden surfaces are also generally good to work with because the uneven texture of wood is an advantage when

shaping medium-hard doughs. Marble, on the other hand, is easier to keep clean, and its smoothness may be the best surface for very wet and sticky doughs. Yet, ultimately, the material you work on depends on what feels best to you.

BAKING THERMOMETER

As with your scale, you will quickly become very fond of your baking thermometer, as it will prove an invaluable tool in helping you control one of the most important variables in bread baking: temperature. You do not need to get the most technological device on the market and you do not need all of the extra functions some thermometers offer—unless you prefer them. All you need is a sensor that can easily penetrate doughs and liquids and accurately determine their temperature. Simple multipurpose kitchen thermometers are nowadays easy to find and quite inexpensive—get one immediately.

ASSORTED LOAF PANS

It is essential to have a few loaf pans of different sizes. You will need them for quick breads and breads with a high percentage of whole grains and seeds, which require the dough to be very wet and do not have the strong gluten structure necessary to keep their shapes without the loaf pan.

PARCHMENT PAPER

Good parchment paper always comes in handy. It can make loading the loaves in the oven a much easier job, especially when you are just starting out. Just make sure that your parchment paper can tolerate temperatures up to 500°F or higher.

OVEN

This is one appliance you surely cannot do without in bread baking. However, keep in mind that in case of necessity, there is also the possibility of making bread on a stove—such as flatbreads. Like any other essential baking tool, your oven does not need to be high-tech, so do not assume that you will have to trade an old oven for a new one to become a bread master. Your old oven may hold some good surprises—just as your brand-new one could. The most important thing is to know your oven, and use it at its full potential.

If you need to buy an oven for your kitchen, one important aspect to check is the maximum temperature. Both breads and pizzas love a very hot oven, so make sure to invest in an oven that can reach at least 500°F. If it can go above this, so much the better. If you can also find a kitchen oven that is good at retaining steam, that is a bonus. There are some rather new kitchen ovens designed for the most ambitious home chefs that can generate steam. Buying one of these could be the best option, but the steam control must be effective. In other words, you need to make sure that your advanced oven with steam function can be used for bread baking. In order for this to be possible, it is necessary to have full control of when to release steam, and for how long.

In the most common scenario of having to adapt your kitchen oven to your new passion, some tips follow.

Heat: to generate and retain heat are the main characteristics of any oven. Unfortunately for home bakers, common kitchen ovens are not made to reach and retain the high temperatures preferred by bread. Luckily, there are a few tricks that can make your oven more efficient, both in terms of generating and retaining heat. For instance, you can use baking stones and place them on the middle and bottom racks of the oven. Remember, however, that baking stones absorb and release heat slowly and this is why they and the oven should undergo a long preheat—1 to 1½ hours is a good amount of time for this method. A baking steel is also a valid option and it is more efficient than a baking stone, as it warms up faster, giving similar or even better results. If you have cast-iron pans or Dutch ovens, they can also be used to improve heat absorption. To use cast iron, just place the implement on the bottom of the oven when you start preheating.

Steam: Steam is naturally released from the loaf when the heat of the oven makes water contained in the dough evaporate. In a traditional wood-fired oven, the steam generated by the baking process is not efficiently dispersed outside of the oven, which is good for bread. In the absence of ambient steam, the loaf quickly forms a crust and the loaf's inner gasses are no longer able to make the bread expand further. The resulting bread will have a smaller volume, be denser, and take longer to bake. It is then clear why in modern ovens, with more efficient ways to disperse fumes and steam, we need to add steam during baking in order to compensate. This is most important in the initial stages of baking. Later on, when the crust has already formed, it is good to let all of the steam out and let the loaf bake in a dry oven.

There are several ways to create steam in your home oven. The first may sound strange, but ice cubes are a very effective means of creating steam, because they vaporize slower than water. To utilize ice cubes, place a baking sheet on the bottom of your oven when you start preheating. Then you will just need to throw a few ice cubes on the pan when you insert the loaves on the upper oven rack.

Lava stones are a very effective way to increase the oven's temperature and create steam. They are easily found in shops that sell grilling supplies. And they are easy to use: place the lava stones on a baking sheet or cast-iron skillet and set the pan on the bottom of the oven when you preheat it. When you load your loaves into the oven, pour a glass of water over the hot stones.

The old-fashioned way to generate steam in a home oven is to place a small pot with water in the bottom of the oven. However, this system is not preferred, because the resulting steam tends to be concentrated in only one part of the oven, and risks creating asymmetry in the baked loaves. It is better to pour a cup of hot water directly on a hot baking sheet or a cast-iron pan placed in the bottom of the oven. Another way to add water to the oven and generate steam is to use a spray bottle and spray the walls of the oven soon after loading the loaves, and then repeating a few minutes later.

BAKING STONE/STEEL

Purchasing one or more baking stones and using them to bake will drastically improve the quality of your bread. With a baking stone, you can obtain crusts that resemble those of breads baked in a wood-fired oven. There are several types of baking stones available, made of different materials, and overall, they will all be efficient. However, some characteristics make one baking stone superior to another. One aspect to consider is the thickness of the stone. A good bread baking stone should be at least ½ inch thick. Also, be aware that rectangular stones are more useful than round ones, as they cover more oven surface. Ideally, your stone should cover the entire oven rack, leaving just a slim margin on all sides for air circulation.

There are now very practical and efficient baking steels available. A baking steel heats more rapidly than a baking stone and it is easier to store away when not needed, but gives similar results in terms of improved oven spring. As such, they are worth considering.

DUTCH OVEN

Not as essential as a baking stone, but a Dutch oven can help you make bakery-perfect loaves. A Dutch oven is any ovenproof pot or pan with a lid. You may already have one at home; look through your collection of pots and pans and you may be surprised. If you buy one, a deep cast-iron skillet with a lid is the best choice for bread. The advantage of using a Dutch oven is that the lid helps retain the natural steam gener-

ated by the baking loaf. It is common to remove the lid halfway through the baking time, so that the steam can be released and the crust can get some color. The small dimensions of the Dutch oven also maximize oven temperature by creating an oven within the oven. Remember that if using this method, the pot should be placed in the oven upon starting to preheat. The limits of this method are that the shape and dimension of the breads you bake are conditional to the shape of the pot or pan used. As such, this method can be used when baking specific types of breads, but surely not all of them.

PEEL

A baker's peel is essential to load a delicate, fully risen dough into the oven without deflating it. It is also helpful in removing baked breads from the oven without burning oneself. Peels can be made out of wood or metal. Both materials do the job, and the ultimate choice is up to the baker. As to the dimension, it depends, again, on the baker. If you prefer to load one loaf at a time, then a narrow peel will be the best. If you like to load multiple loaves at once, then the peel should be almost as wide as the inside of your oven. Always remember to sprinkle some coarse semolina or cornmeal on the peel before placing an unbaked loaf on it—it will help significantly.

OVEN GLOVES

Considering that in bread making you need to work with a very hot oven, good protective gloves are essential, and imperative when working with the Dutch oven method. When choosing, I prefer gloves that allow for fine hand movements, as ordinary mitten-style gloves may not. Remember, when searching for gloves, that you will need to move your hands quickly to get the best out of your oven. It is also important to choose long gloves, because it is common to get burns on the forearms when reaching into the oven while wearing normal-length gloves.

LAMES/BLADES

It is common, but not always necessary, to score your loaves before baking them. Scoring a loaf of bread allows the crumb space to fully expand during baking without being held back by the external layer of the loaf, which generally hardens and dries slightly during the last stages of proofing, and will continue to harden during baking. If the growth in volume, called oven spring, is accentuated, the external layer could also spontaneously break, altering the look of the bread in undesirable ways. This is why scoring needs to be precise in order to make the bread expand in a harmonious fashion. An exception to this is very wet dough, where the external layer does not generally dry enough to restrain expansion. There are different types of scoring tools. Some use a lame to score their loaves, others prefer razor blades, either held in the hand or mounted on a blade holder. Those bakers who are perfectionists change their blades frequently to ensure a clean cut.

ADDITIONAL TOOLS

MIXER

There are a variety of machines used to mix and work dough. Although commercial bakeries would have a hard time without such machines, they are not essential to the home baker. When amounts of dough are as small as the ones made at home, hand mixing and kneading are perfectly viable options. It is, however, useful to have a mixer, especially when handling sweet doughs, which can be very sticky and require intense kneading. The type of mixer generally available to the home baker is the stand mixer, also called the planetary mixer. There are several reasonably priced models on the market. For bread baking, you want to select a machine with a good dough hook, a powerful motor, and a large bowl. Having several speeds is another important characteristic. Bread dough likes a gentle, slow mixing in the first stages, but can benefit from shorter, medium-high speed mixing in later stages of the process. Sweet bread doughs often require more vigorous mixing.

MILL

As with the mixer, owning a mill is not a necessity in bread making, but it can be a very pleasant addition to one's kitchen. The aroma of freshly milled grains is indeed quite addictive, and you may quickly become fond of your home mill. Nowadays, there are plenty of different types and brands to choose from, such as countertop electric stone mills. This type of mill is a miniature version of the modern stone mills used by commercial artisan mills. They can look very appealing on the kitchen countertop, and can produce coarse to relatively fine flour, although not as fine as the flour produced in commercial facilities. Small stone mills also tend to overheat flour, unlike commercial models.

Countertop electric mills are another type that is available, and these use metal plates instead of stone to grind the grains. They are less attractive, but just as effective as stone mills. Some models can produce finer flour than others and can also overheat the flour, so look into these aspects before purchasing.

Countertop manual mills use either stone or metal plates and are run on manual, rather than electric, power. Operating one will give you a full workout, but it may be worth it. The big advantage of manual over electric mills is increased control over grain grinding. Manual mills offer the possibility to vary the intensity of the grinding based on the feedback from the grains. In other words, with practice, the home miller develops a "feel" for milling and understands when the grains need a gentler action. This will benefit the flour by damaging the grains as little as possible during the milling process.

If you already have a mixer, there might be an option to purchase a milling attachment. Before choosing an attachment instead of a countertop mill, look into the quality of what's available for your mixer, focusing on how fine the flour it produces is, and the level of overheating when the mill is set on its finest gear.

FERMENTATION IN BREAD MAKING

The term "fermentation" derives from the Latin fervere, which means "to burst."

Fermentation is a metabolic process performed by microorganisms that extracts energy from carbohydrates, releasing a series of by-products, among which is carbon dioxide. Carbon dioxide, the main agent responsible for the increase in volume in bread dough, stays in the dough only if entrapped by a tight gluten net. In the absence of this characteristic, the carbon dioxide is released into the environment. In bread baking, we have two main types of fermentation: alcoholic fermentation and lactic fermentation.

ALCOHOLIC FERMENTATION

Yeasts are single-celled microorganisms classified as fungi. They are special, because they're capable of obtaining energy under both anaerobic and aerobic conditions. Anaerobic processes evolved first in the very beginning of life on Earth, when oxygen was not yet available. Later on, yeast cells developed mechanisms to obtain energy in the presence of oxygen. In bread making, the dominant type of yeast fermentation is anaerobic. In such conditions, yeasts obtain energy through alcoholic fermentation. In short, during dough fermentation yeast cells multiply in number, and break down starches and sugars that naturally occur in flour to produce energy for their survival. This process is called glycolysis, which is aimed at providing energy to the yeast cells, and, in alcoholic fermentation, generates as by-products such as alcohol and carbon dioxide. The carbon dioxide makes the dough rise, while the alcohol tends to slowly evaporate from the dough.

LACTIC FERMENTATION

This type of fermentation is not performed by yeast cells, but is instead the result of the proliferation and life maintenance functions of another type of microorganism, lactic acid bacteria. The basic mechanism is the same as in alcoholic fermentation. Lactic acid bacteria, just like yeasts, are capable of carrying out glycolysis. This complex series of biochemical reactions is performed in the absence of oxygen, and aimed at extracting energy from starches and sugars. The difference is the by-product. In lactic fermentation, the main by-product is lactic acid, followed by carbon dioxide, alcohol, and acetic acid. The latter molecules can, however, only be produced by specific types of lactic acid bacteria.

BAKER'S YEAST

The result of the discard made during beer production, baker's yeast resides in the froth that evolves during brewing, which is commonly called barm.

Used since antiquity to leaven bread, baker's yeast is today produced through industrial multiplication and processing of isolated cultures of one single type of yeast cell, *Saccharomyces cerevisiae*, which is the anaerobic yeast most commonly found in traditional beer brewing.

There are different types of packaged yeast, all containing live cultures of *Saccharomyces cerevisiae*. Active dry yeast is the most easily found baker's yeast, and it consists of almost completely dried yeast cells. It needs to be activated before use by combining it with warm water and letting it sit for a few minutes. It does not like the cold, so you should never combine it with cold water.

Instant yeast is made of partly dried yeast cells. It is more "alive" than active dry yeast, and lasts for a much shorter time after it has been exposed to air. You can easily distinguish the two just by looking at the granules that comprise these commercial yeasts. Instant yeast granules are bigger. Instant yeast does not require activation in water, so it can be sprinkled on the dough at any time during the mixing process.

Fresh yeast, also known as cake yeast, is not easy to find in the United States nowadays. It needs refrigeration, and lasts for only two weeks. Like instant yeast, it does not need to be activated, and can simply be crumbled and added to the dough during mixing. It is less concentrated than the other two types of commercially sold yeasts, and, therefore, you will need about three times more of it to achieve the same leavening effect. This amount could affect the taste of the baked bread, giving it a pronounced yeasty flavor.

FERMENTATION WITH BAKER'S YEAST

This type of fermentation is carried out by a single type of microorganism and relies only on the alcoholic fermentation processes. As a by-product, the yeast cells will supply plenty of carbon dioxide, but no lactic acid. There are two main methods that can be followed when fermenting dough with baker's yeast: the direct and the indirect method.

The direct method simply means that yeast is added to the mixture of flour and water directly, i.e., while all of the ingredients are being combined. Recipes using the direct method are faster, but this also means that the fermentation process is over faster. Consequently, some of the biochemical reactions that take place in a long-fermented dough simply do not happen, or are reduced. Industrial bread is based on the direct method, because of obvious advantages in terms of production rate.

The indirect method refers to bread recipes that require the preparation of a pre-ferment before the actual mixing of the final dough. While there are several types of yeast-based pre-ferments, what is common to all of them is that they require fermenting part of the flour and water called for in the recipe ahead of time.

Poolish is a liquid pre-ferment that, as suggested by the name, was first developed in Poland. It is made with equal amounts of water and flour, and so can also be referred to as a 100 percent hydration pre-ferment. The amount of yeast added to a poolish varies according to the desired leavening time of the pre-ferment. Less yeast is added to the pre-ferment for longer leavening times, while more yeast is added to speed up the process.

For example: ⅓ lb. (150 g) flour and ⅓ lb. (150 g) water is fermented with 1½ teaspoons (4 g) of active dry yeast for a fast-rising pre-ferment, 3 hours at room temperature, versus ⅓ teaspoon (1 g) of active dry yeast being used for a longer rise of 12 hours at room temperature.

Biga is another pre-ferment, first developed in Italy. Its name evokes an ancient Roman's carriage, perhaps to signify the role that the pre-ferment has in carrying forward fermentation. Unlike poolish, biga is a stiff pre-ferment and is generally made with half as much water as flour. Like poolish, the relative amount of yeast added determines the length of the fermentation needed for a biga.

For example: ⅓ lb. (150 g) flour and 2.6 oz. (75 g) water is fermented with ½ teaspoon (1.5 g) of active dry yeast for a faster rise of 3 hours at room temperature, versus ⅓ lb. (150 g) flour and 2.6 oz. (75 g) water fermented with ⅕ teaspoon (0.6 g) of active dry yeast for a longer rise of 22 to 24 hours at room temperature.

SOURDOUGH FERMENTATION

This type of fermentation is accomplished by a culture containing several populations of microorganisms that thrive in a regularly fed mixture of water and flour. Both yeasts and lactic acid bacteria are commonly found in sourdough cultures. There can be substantial variations between one culture and another, especially if the cultures originated in different geographical areas, due to the varied natures of wild yeasts and lactic acid bacteria that can populate a sourdough culture.

Thanks to the rich microcosmos of living fungi and bacteria, making sourdough bread includes both alcoholic and lactic fermentation processes. The baked breads will differ considerably in terms of volume, texture, and flavor depending on the specific type of sourdough culture used and the way the culture is kept. When a sourdough culture is stable and capable of leavening a dough, it is called sourdough starter. When a sourdough starter is heavily neglected, yeast populations become very small and the type of lactic acid bacteria that produces acetic acid will become prevalent, giving us a very sour bread with poor volume development. On the other hand, a sourdough culture that pullulates yeast and has a predominance of helpful lactic acid bacteria will reward our careful attention by producing a well-developed loaf with ideal volume and texture, and a flavor that is complex but not acidic.

Different types of bread recipes call for different types of sourdough starters. They can vary based on the kind of grain used or on the whiteness of the flour (or flours) used. Starters are also classified based on the relative proportion of water to flour contained in the mixture. Here are some examples: 100 percent hydration, also called a liquid starter, refers to a sourdough starter in which the proportion of water to flour is 1:1 in terms of weight. This level of hydration is most commonly used by American, German, and Scandinavian bakers.

Eighty percent hydration refers to a soft sourdough starter in which the proportion of water to flour is 0.8 to 1, or 8 to 10. In other words, there is 80 percent as much water compared to flour. The same math applies to a 70 percent or 60 percent hydration starter, and so on. These medium-stiff starters were traditionally preferred by French bakers. A stiff starter features 50 percent hydration and is the type of starter commonly found in Italian sourdough bread recipes, where it is called pasta madre.

All bread that uses sourdough as the leavening agent is based on the indirect method. To use sourdough in a dough, one needs an active sourdough starter that has been recently fed water and flour. As with yeast-based pre-ferments, the fermentation time in sourdough-based baking will be determined by the relative amount of starter added to the mixture of flour and water ahead of adding it to the final dough.

For example: 7 oz. (200 g) flour and 7 oz. (200 g) water fermented with 2 tablespoons (35 g) of 100 percent hydration sourdough

starter allows for a slow rise of 12 to 16 hours at room temperature, while a much larger amount of starter can produce a pre-ferment that is ready to be added to the final dough in only 3 to 4 hours.

Scientific evidence shows bread made with sourdough is more digestible as compared to bread made with baker's yeast (though yeasted breads using pre-ferments have some of the same beneficial qualities of sourdough). This is due to time and lactic fermentation. Regarding time, fermentation with sourdough is generally longer than for a yeast-based one, because in sourdough baking it is neither possible to use the direct method, nor to shorten final fermentation time below a minimum of 3 to 4 hours. Lactic fermentation, while it does not help the dough rise, does plenty to make it more gut-friendly. The processes involved are complex, but the main point is simple: lactic fermentation is superior to alcoholic fermentation in terms of catabolizing proteins such as gluten which are potentially problematic for our digestive systems.

HOW TO MAKE A SOURDOUGH STARTER

Making your own starter is a highly rewarding endeavor that you do not want to miss. Once a stable starter has been created, it can be maintained indefinitely, given the right care. There are several ways to create a starter. The most straightforward method is to make use of the many wild yeasts and good bacteria naturally occurring in flour and in the air, and let time do the rest. Here is a recipe for a 100 percent hydration starter.

DAY 1 —MORNING

Mix ¼ cup (56.75 g) lukewarm water (around 85°F) and a scant ½ cup (56.75 g) all-purpose flour together and place the mixture in a clean container, making sure that the mixture takes up no more than one-third of the container. Put the lid on (if you are using a mason jar, do not seal it; you just want to cover the jar). Place the container in a naturally warm (but not hot) spot. Ideally, the temperature should be around 80°F. Also, you may want to use bottled water to create a starter, because the chemicals in tap water can inhibit its development in the early stages.

DAY 2— MORNING

Take ⅓ cup (75 g) of your starter from Day 1 and discard the rest. Combine the starter with ⅓ cup (75 g) lukewarm water and ⅝ cup (75 g) all-purpose flour. Scrape the walls of the container to keep them clean. Place the container back in its naturally warm spot.

DAY 2— EVENING

Take ⅓ cup (75 g) of your starter from Day 1 and discard the rest. Combine the starter with ⅓ cup (75 g) lukewarm water and ⅝ cup (75 g) all-purpose flour. Scrape the walls of the container to keep them clean. Place the container back in its naturally warm spot. At this point, you should start seeing some sign of life, some activity, which will manifest as bubbles in the starter.

DAYS 3, 4, AND 5

Continue to repeat the process done on Day 2 until your starter can double itself within 12 hours, is very bubbly, and smells good (not too acidic). Make sure that the color stays within the yellow-brown shades, and does not take on any orange or blueish tone.

DAY 6 (OR 7)

You may have successfully created a sourdough starter. Does it double in 12 hours? Does it smell sweet? Is it full of bubbles? If the answer to any of these is no, then continue as in the previous days. Hopefully, your sourdough culture will soon come to life, but if it does not, discard the mixture and start over.

HOW TO MAINTAIN A SOURDOUGH STARTER

Learning to keep your starter healthy is the secret to making good sourdough bread. You have two main options for how to maintain your sourdough starter: either refrigerating it or keeping it at room temperature. If you just started a sourdough culture, it is recommended that you do not shift to refrigerated maintenance for a few weeks, as during those first few weeks strains of yeast and bacteria that are optimal for bread baking will be selected if it is stored at room temperature. Once the culture is stable, periods of refrigeration will not disrupt its main composition—assuming that you are good about feeding the starter at the right time.

When keeping the starter at room temperature, it is ideal to feed it once every 12 hours: twice a day. In the beginning, use the same amount of starter, water, and flour, in a 1:1:1 ratio for each feeding. This means that every 12 hours you will take some of your starter and combine it with equal amounts of water and flour (always in terms of weight, not volume). The excess starter can either be discarded or used in another preparation. After several days at room temperature, your starter should become very active and you will need to change the ratios. The amounts for your feedings could then become, for instance, 1:2:2. This means that you will use half the amount of starter, and keeping the same amounts of water and flour you used during the first few days. What matters is that the hydration (the proportion of water to flour) remains constant. The amount of starter taken can change depending on how active the starter is from day to day, how warm your room is, and how capable you are of doing two feedings in a day. If you want to feed your starter only once a day, you can add a small amount of starter to the mixture of water and flour.

You can also make life even easier by alternating between leaving the starter unfed in the refrigerator, and then bringing it to room temperature and feeding it when you want to make bread. Ideally, you want to leave the starter unfed in the fridge for no more than five days, and then feed it at room temperature at least three times before putting the starter, just fed, back into the refrigerator.

Always choose the least cold spot of your fridge to keep your starter, and make sure the overall temperature of the fridge does not go below 36°F.

Although not optimal, if it does happen that you leave your starter unfed in the fridge for a prolonged amount of time, do not worry. It takes a very long time to kill a stable sourdough culture. If this occurs, let your sourdough starter stay at room temperature longer, with repeated feedings, to regenerate all of the yeast cells and good bacteria.

FERMENTATION WITH OLD DOUGH

Finally, there is what the French call pâte fermentée and the Italians call pasta di riporto, which is simply using a piece of old dough from a previous batch made with yeast or sourdough to ferment a new dough. In the United States, this practice is also called Gold Rush starter or cowboy starter, because those hunting gold in California during the nineteenth century used it. Using old dough is the simplest way to keep a starter and, in fact, it was the preferred method used by old-time home bakers. Nowadays, the method is widely used by professional bakers, but is often ignored by home bakers. This is probably due to the fact that old dough needs to be used within a week, and most contemporary home bakers do not bake that often.

If you want to revive the tradition of the Gold Rush starter, save a piece of dough when you make your next bread. It can be cut out before or after adding salt, but know that when it contains salt it will rise slower, giving you more time to make use of it.

Keep the piece of dough in a covered container in the refrigerator, making sure to leave the lid slightly open. To make new bread, simply add the old dough to the new one.

If you notice that the old dough looks overripe, i.e., the fermentation has gone too far and the dough has a very soft consistency, just feed it as you would a stiff starter and wait for it to double in size before adding it to your final dough.

MAKING A BREAD DOUGH

MISE EN PLACE

Before you start mixing a dough, it is important to make sure that you have all of the ingredients at hand and ready. Ready means two things: weighed/measured and at the right temperature. Additionally, there could be ingredients that need to be prepared ahead, like cooked and drained vegetables or grains, crushed spices, and so on. All of this, including the weighing/measuring and bringing the ingredients to the right temperature, requires extra time. You do not want that extra time to impact your fermentation schedule. When the leavening agent is added to flour and water, you want to be able devote your full attention to dough development. So do make sure to have everything ready before the fermentation starts, and your chances of success will increase considerably.

MIXING

The way you combine ingredients does impact dough development—in fact, many professional bakers would say that the mixing stage has the biggest impact on how a batch of dough turns out. You can combine the ingredients by hand or using a mixer, which in a home kitchen will most likely be a stand mixer.

The traditional way is to combine the ingredients on a wooden board, making a well in the center of the flour and adding the wet ingredients gradually. There is nothing wrong with this method, but it is even simpler to start by combining the ingredients in a large bowl and then transferring the dough to a clean surface in order to work it further. When mixing in a bowl, by hand or machine, it is easier to start with the main wet ingredients and then add the flour(s). This will ensure that no flour remains on the bottom of the bowl. On the other hand, when using this method, it is advisable to never add all of the wet ingredients at once, but always reserve a portion of them to be added after the main dry ingredients have been incorporated in the mix. This is done because if the dough is having trouble coming together, it is better to avoid changing the amount of flour in a bread recipe, because that would alter the proportions required for the other ingredients, including the salt and leavening agent. What instead is easily done, and will not alter all the other proportions, is adding more liquids, i.e., changing the hydration of the dough.

After the full amount of flour has been added to, it is easy to see how the dough is coming up together and decide whether to add more liquids, and how much of them. No recipe will ever be able to tell you how much liquid your specific flour will be able to absorb in the unique conditions in your kitchen at each moment. This is the art of mixing: understanding the optimal hydration for each specific recipe. As with every skill, it will develop with time. Use the recipe as your basic script, remember to reserve some of the liquid indicated for later, and be ready to add more liquid, or refrain from adding what you've reserved, depending on how your dough will feel and look.

KNEADING

Although it is possible to make good bread without kneading, a dough benefits from being worked in some way or another. The mechanical action of working a dough helps the gluten net develop, helps distribute the gasses, and oxygenates the mixture.

When using a mixer, start by combining ingredients at the lowest speed available. This will give time for the dough to come together without stressing or overheating it. It is also advisable to let the mixture rest after the ingredients have just been combined to allow the gluten net to form spontaneously (autolysis). In later stages of the mixing process, when the gluten net is close to being well developed, the speed can be

increased. This will be mostly necessary for sweet doughs and high-hydration doughs.

The old-fashioned but always valid way of working a dough consists of transferring the combined ingredients to a flour-dusted work surface and then pressing on the dough in a rhythmic way, using mostly the heels of your hands. The dough should be worked in an even way. Therefore, it does help to rotate the dough and repeat the kneading process from different points of the dough. As with mixer-based working of the dough, it will save you effort to take breaks while kneading and allow the dough to benefit from the spontaneous processes involved in autolysis.

Another method of working the dough is the slap and fold technique. This is a modern technique of French origin, and it highly simplifies the work of kneading. Slap and fold is particularly good for sticky doughs with high hydration. It consists of pulling the dough up toward you, stretching it sideways and vertically, and then folding it back on itself and away from you (to get a better understanding of this method, watch a few of the many available online tutorials). The dough is rotated and the process is repeated. A series of slap and folds are alternated with periods of rest until the dough has been properly developed—it feels smooth and elastic when pulled and stretched.

A similar technique commonly used in contemporary baking is the stretch and fold method. This method consists of pulling the dough from one side and stretching it vertically, then folding the stretched strand over the rest of the dough. The routine is repeated from each side of the dough. One can do this without taking the dough out of its resting bowl/container or alternatively by transferring the dough to a clean surface first. Some also flip the dough upside down after the first set of stretch and folds and then repeat the series from all sides, then flip the dough back over again and let it proof in its container.

This method can be used alone, in which case several series of stretch and folds needs to be performed in the early stages of the fermentation, or it can be used to complement hand- or mixer-based kneading. In this case, a few series of stretch and folds are given at regular intervals while the dough is undergoing its first fermentation.

After the mixing stage, the dough needs to be left alone so that it can rise. It is always important to cover the dough at this stage, to ensure that the humidity within is preserved. This first fermentation, or bulk fermentation, really starts from the moment the starter or yeast is added to the dough, so do calculate your overall fermentation time accordingly and know that the longer you will be kneading/working the dough, the shorter this stage of proofing will be.

Understanding when to stop the first fermentation and proceed to shaping is a true art, and it will develop with time, as you work with specific loaves over and over again. Remember that practice does make perfect. However, also be aware that perfection in bread baking is never fully achieved, because the dough will surprise you from time to time. This unpredictability is the true beauty of bread making, so while you want to keep an eye on fermentation, try not to be overly pedantic about it.

When the dough has undergone bulk fermentation, it is time to shape it. Always make sure to pay attention to mise en place before you actually start shaping: prepare the shaping surface, and have proofing baskets, scale, bench scrapers, the baking implement, and so on at the ready. You do this because shaping needs to be done fast so that the dough does not dry out.

Some recipes require a special shaping, but most breads are generally shaped either like a round (boule in French) or like a short log (bâtard in French, filone in Italian).

To shape a bâtard, you want to roughly preshape your dough into a ball and let it rest for 10 to 15 minutes, covered. Flatten the round into a rectangle, pull the far end of the dough over two-thirds of the dough, and then fold the closer end over the top of the dough. This is similar to folding a letter into thirds so that it can fit into an envelope. Turn the dough so that a shorter end is facing you. Grab the top of the dough and pull it to the center of the dough. Tuck the top part of the dough and then roll it. Repeat these tucks and rolls until you end up with a short log. Seal the ends of the log and then gently roll it to the desired length.

To shape a boule, repeat the steps to shape a bâtard. Flip it over so that the seam is facing up. Roll the bâtard over itself, starting from the end closest to you.

Turn the dough 90°, place your hands at the far end of the dough, and drag it toward you, creating tension. Repeat the turning and dragging twice until you have a nice, even round.

Once your loaves are shaped, all you have to do is place them in a proofing basket or on a baking sheet and let them rest some more.

It is important to make sure that the loaves do not dry out at this point, so you want to cover the proofing basket or baking sheet with a flour-dusted kitchen towel or plastic wrap coated with olive oil. You can also just place the proofing basket in a large resealable plastic bag. The recipe you are following will give you indications on the length of time needed for this second fermentation, but your eyes will come in handy, too.

As a rule of thumb, do not wait for the loaves to double their size, as sometimes suggested by recipes. If you see a visible rise, about 1½ times the initial volume, that is sufficient.

You can also try to gently push the dough with your finger. If it leaves an indent that springs back relatively fast, the loaf is proofed.

As discussed on page 34, it is common to make one or several cuts on the top of bread loaves before baking them. Scoring is an art, and mastery comes with repetition and multiple tries, as with any other skill. It helps to see how other bakers score their loaves, so it is OK to initially imitate other people's scorings and then later on develop your own signature style.

Be aware that scoring is not always necessary—in most traditional Italian loaves, for instance, bread is unscored and the irregular way in which every loaf breaks open (or doesn't open at all) during baking is part of its charm.

Once the oven is ready (see page 31 for several methods of obtaining a perfect oven temperature), put the bread inside. Regarding knowing when your bread is ready, color will help in giving you an indication of how cooked a loaf is, but there are also other cues that can help. A traditional way of knowing if a loaf of bread is ready is lifting it and knocking on its bottom. If it sounds hollow, the loaf is ready. This method is useless, however, with sweet breads that are not supposed to develop a crust. In such cases, a dough thermometer will do wonders, as you can check when your bread reaches the temperature that indicates that the bread is properly cooked, not only on the outside but also inside. Most breads are ready when the internal temperature reaches 200°F.

Upon removing the bread from the oven, you want to let the bread to cool down before cutting into it, as the cooking continues until the loaf is at room temperature.

ENCYCLOPEDIA OF GRAINS & PULSES

What we commonly know as grains are more precisely defined as cereals. Cereal designates a variety of herbaceous plants that produce the seeds or "berries" from which we mill flour. The term *cereal* derives from Latin, meaning "what belongs to the goddess Ceres," the Roman goddess of the harvest.

Most grains are members of the grass family, Poaceae. Given that grasses are the most widely found plant on Earth, it is not surprising that humans and animals alike have grown to thrive on them. Cereals such as wheat, emmer, einkorn, barley, rye, oats, rice, maize, millet, sorghum, and teff are all members of the grass family, whereas buckwheat, amaranth, and quinoa are entirely different plants, called pseudocereals. In addition to cereals and pseudocereals, flour can also be milled from a number of other plants. For instance, most pulses can be dried and ground into flour, as can root vegetables, nuts, seeds, and even coffee plants.

These days, heritage grain varieties are gaining increasing popularity. Here you will find listed the most commonly known old varieties—be aware, though, that these are just *some* of the countless varieties of grains that are cultivated or stored in seed banks across the globe. In our encyclopedia we have included all the main sources of flour used to make different breads, crusts, and other grain-based products. This knowledge will help you to move around with confidence in the vast world of grains and flours.

WHEAT

People have grown wheat for thousands of years, dating back to the very dawn of farming. Through intensive, continuous cultivation, many different varieties of wheat have developed, due to adaptation, evolution, and the work of farmers and agronomists. Starting in the 1700s, farming methods began to advance rapidly, and there are now thousands of wheat varieties worldwide, with new ones every year. The twentieth century ushered in the Green Revolution, a set of studies and initiatives led by Norman Borlaug, which gave rise to a radical increase in agricultural productivity around the world, aided by mechanization, irrigation, chemical fertilizers, genetic modification, and pesticides. The Green Revolution is believed to have saved over a billion people from starvation, a feat for which Borlaug deservedly received the Nobel Peace Prize. However, it also resulted it many ancient varieties of wheat and heritage landraces falling out of use. Fortunately, these have recently seen a resurgence alongside the growing market for organic food.

Einkorn Wheat

Einkorn wheat was one of the earliest types of wheat to be domesticated. It initially grew only in the northern part of the Fertile Crescent and later spread to the Caucasus and Central Europe. This type of wheat prefers colder climates and, while largely replaced by common wheat, has continued to grow sporadically in Northern France and elsewhere. Although einkorn produces low yields and can be a challenge to farm, it has become increasingly popular due to its digestibility compared to common wheat and other cereals.

Emmer

Like einkorn, emmer was among the first wheats to be domesticated. Though more widely farmed than einkorn, it was likewise supplanted by common wheat. Nevertheless, its cultivation is growing once more, particularly in Italy. Much like einkorn wheat, the renewed popularity of emmer is largely due to its digestibility. Emmer is also prized for the unique flavor it lends to both bread and pasta. In Tuscany, whole grains of emmer are often used in soups.

Black Winter Emmer

An old variety of emmer that dates back 5,000 years, this wheat is prized for its dark purple and black husks. It can grow in quite extreme weather, tolerating both heavy rain and drought. There is currently a scarcity of this variety of emmer, though limited amounts of seed are available. It is difficult to thresh and mostly used for ornamental purposes.

Ethiopian Blue Tinge

This dark purple Ethiopian variety of emmer is easy to thresh and gives a high yield, making it much more popular than the similar-looking Black Winter Emmer. Ethiopian Blue Tinge is widely believed to have additional health benefits because of the high concentration of polyphenol antioxidants it contains. Interestingly, this wheat is said to taste like tea.

Durum Wheat

Durum wheat is a modified type of emmer, developed through hybridization about 9,000 years ago. "Durum" means hard—it is in fact the hardest of all wheat species. However, it is not to be confused with hard wheat, a variety of common wheat that is genetically very different from durum. The hardness of this wheat makes it difficult to mill it into very fine flour, and its gluten is also different than that found in common wheat. This is why durum is mostly used for pasta, semolina, and couscous as opposed to bread baking. After common wheat, durum wheat is the most cultivated, growing much better in hot and arid climates. Like common wheat, durum has been cultivated intensively for thousands of years and undergone extensive genetic manipulation. However, old varieties are once more enjoying a renewal in popularity.

Bulgur

To become bulgur, durum wheat is boiled, then dried, and subsequently cracked into pieces. The pieces are then sieved to divide the pieces by size. This method was a common way to preserve wheat in ancient Babylon, which then spread to the Middle East, where it is still a staple in local cuisine.

Freekeh

Freekeh is made of "green" durum wheat, which is harvested before the ripening process is complete. The wheat is then immediately toasted and cracked. In Lebanon, where freekeh is particularly common, wheat is piled and left to dry in the sun for 24 hours before being set alight. Though the straw and chaff burn away, the seeds remain intact because of their moisture content. Served much like rice, it is part of many traditional North African and Mediterranean dishes.

OLD VARIETIES OF DURUM WHEAT

Hourani

This variety of durum wheat was cultivated for millennia in the Houran plateau of Northern Jordan and Southern Syria. According to food anthropologist Eli Rogosa, this ancient variety was discovered in the 1960s during the excavation of the Masada Fortress, where it had been stored for 2,000 years. Almost extinct today, it was eaten by the ancient people of what is now Israel.

Senatore Cappelli

Named after Italian nobleman Raffaele Cappelli, it was developed from a Tunisian hard wheat (Jenah Rhetifah) 100 years ago by wheat geneticist Nazareno Strampelli. This variety produces very tall plants, with ears of wheat characterized by beautiful dark awns. It has a high protein content and makes superior bread and pasta. This variety was abandoned after the 1960s in favor of lower-quality varieties, but it is now widely grown again in Southern Italy.

Sicilian Durum Wheat

In Sicily several old varieties of local wheat are being cultivated once more, thanks to the ongoing efforts of Stazione Consorziale Sperimentale di Granicoltura per la Sicilia. This local center for the preservation of regional cereals has studied and stored wheat seeds since the 1930s. The most common types of old Sicilian durum wheat are Timilia, Perciasacchi, and Russello. These varieties have been used for centuries (some say millennia) to make both pasta and bread.

Khorasan Wheat

This is an ancient variety of durum wheat. It is named after the historical Khorasan region of Central Asia, where it is still grown today. Khorasan wheat is now grown in numerous countries for its digestibility and nutritional value. Like other durum wheat, it tolerates drought well.

Saragolla

An Italian variety of Khorasan, introduced to the Abruzzi region in the fifth century AD. Its longtime cultivation is evidenced by several historical documents praising its qualities. Saragolla wheat was eventually succeeded by Senatore Cappelli, and later still by dwarf varieties of durum wheat. Its cultivation, however, continued in parts of central Italy and it is now expanding once more.

Kamut

Kamut is a patented variety of Khorasan created by two farmers from Montana, Mack and Bob Quinn, who started to cultivate it in the 1970s and registered it in 1990. Khorasan wheat actually owes much of its popularity to the Kamut brand, which has also financed scientific studies to prove the health claims of this grain.

COMMON WHEAT

Common Wheat

Common wheat was developed between 2,000 and 3,000 years ago through the selection and hybridization of ancient wheat varieties. Dating is uncertain, as precursors of our common bread wheat were surely available at an earlier time, but we know that this type of wheat became widely available in the Western world right around the first century AD. The intent of ancient wheat breeders was likely to increase their yields and create better bread—in fact, common wheat is often referred to as bread wheat. The gluten in common wheat is indeed ideal for baking, which is why it has been favored for so long. Of course, there are many other varieties of wheat, both old and new.

Hard Red Winter Wheat

This is a group of modern North American wheat grasses modified from locally adapted Eurasian varieties. It has a high yield and is resistant to pests and disease grown and is extensively across the Great Plains between Texas and Montana. Kansas is the biggest cultivator of hard red winter wheat. "Winter" refers to the fact that the seeds are planted in the fall. It has a strong gluten content that makes it ideal for breads and Asian-style noodles.

Hard Red Spring Wheat

Called "the aristocrat of wheat for baking bread," this group of modern North American wheat grasses thrives better when planted in spring and harvested in early fall. It is grown mostly in North Dakota, Montana, South Dakota, and Minnesota. Like hard red winter wheat, this family of wheat also produces a high yield and is resistant to diseases and pests.

Soft White Wheat

Soft white wheat is a group of modern North American varieties grown in Ohio, Kentucky, Indiana, Washington, Oregon, Idaho, Michigan, and New York. It has a much lower protein content and gluten quality than hard red spring wheat and is therefore mostly used for pastries, cookies, cakes, pancakes, waffles, and crackers. Soft white wheat is the base for pastry flour, and is combined with hardier wheats to make all-purpose flour.

Hard White Wheat

A commonly grown wheat variety in Australia. However, it is relatively new to North American agriculture, and has only become widely grown over the last 20 years. Like hard red wheat, it has a high protein and gluten content, but its bran is lighter in color and it is less bitter in taste.

Ivory Wheat Flour

Ivory wheat flour is made from North American hard white wheat. It is a whole wheat flour, containing every part of the ground wheat berry. Its name comes from the bran of hard white wheat, which is genetically selected to be free of color pigments; this means that whole wheat flour milled from it actually looks white. With its mild taste and good protein content, it is good for making both breads and pastries.

OLD VARIETIES OF COMMON WHEAT

Banatka Winter Wheat

This wheat variety was recently created by food anthropologist Eli Rogosa by cross-breeding two Eastern European heritage wheat landraces: Bankuti, loved for its intense flavor, and Ukrainka, a wheat variety valued for its high productivity, adaptability, and excellent baking qualities. Banatka can tolerate rain and humidity, and has thus far shown high productivity and good disease resistance. It performs best when planted in early fall.

Sonora Wheat

This variety of soft wheat was introduced to North America by Spanish missionaries in the early 1700s. It has been used for centuries to make flour tortillas and was a staple crop in the West up until the Civil War. It performs best in milder climates, and should be planted in the spring.

Turkey Red

Introduced to the United States by German Russian Mennonites in 1874, Turkey Red is the ancestor of all modern varieties of hard red winter wheat. Although its cultivation languished for many years, its popularity is on the rise, as it is easy to digest, and its good baking properties make it perfect for bread making.

Red Fife

The story tells that back in the 1800s, Scottish-born farmer David Fife was looking for a wheat variety that could grow well in Canada. A friend from his homeland sent him some hard wheat seeds thought to have come from what is now Ukraine, and from these first seeds David Fife eventually developed his sturdy Red Fife wheat. It grew so well across Canada and the United States that for a time it was one of the most popular varieties. Largely abandoned after 1900, it is now gaining new interest.

Carosella

This old variety of "soft" common wheat is traditionally cultivated in the region of Cilento, Southern Italy, and known to have been cultivated in ancient Rome. Although it does not have a very high protein content, Carosella wheat is used to make traditional pasta, and has been appreciated for millennia for its good baking properties. Its production is still limited but interest in this ancient grain is on the rise.

Gentil Rosso

Traditionally grown in Tuscany and Emilia Romagna, this is an old variety of "soft" common wheat. Although its origins are unclear, it began to be widely cultivated from the 1800s onward. By the beginning of the twentieth century it was the most grown variety of common wheat in Italy, but quickly fell out of favor due to the introduction of modern wheat varieties. Happily, after nearly a century of neglect, it is now grown again. It has good baking properties and works well in both pastries and bread.

Rouge de Bordeaux

Like Gentil Rosso, this is an older variety of "soft" common wheat, developed in the 1800s and grown in Bordeaux, France. The ears of the wheat are a little reddish at maturity and a little bit bearded like barley. It is renowned for its baking properties. It is one of several wheat varieties of French wheat becoming popular outside of France.

Marquis

This Canadian variety of common wheat is a cross of Hard Red Calcutta and Red Fife. Dr. Charles Saunders developed it in 1904, and it soon became incredibly popular, replacing all other hard wheat being cultivated in Canada at that time. Marquis is shorter than Red Fife and matures 7–10 days earlier. It has a very high yield, as well as a high protein and gluten content.

Spelt

Closely related to common wheat and considered a subspecies by some, spelt has been continuously cultivated since around 5000 BC. It is particularly suited to northern climates, and while its cultivation in North America peaked in 1900, it has continued to be farmed in Germany, Switzerland, and across Scandinavia. Although it gives inconsistent yields, it has become popular in recent years as a supposedly healthier alternative to modern varieties of common wheat. Acreage devoted to spelt is increasing also in North America as in many other regions of the world. The baking properties of spelt flour are similar to that of flour milled from common wheat.

Triticale

Triticale is a hybrid of rye and wheat. Created at the end of the nineteenth century, it has only recently been cultivated on a large scale. It has the advantages of rye, is resistant to cold, and has all the baking properties of wheat. It is a good alternative in soils and climates suitable to rye. Though largely used as grass feed, it is increasingly being used in baking.

OATS

Oats are a widely cultivated cereal, and are used in a great variety of foods. Only domesticated roughly 3,000 years ago, they are believed to be the product of the spontaneous cross-breeding of cultivated wheat and barley with nearby weeds. Oat is more tolerant of rain than any other cereal, making it extraordinarily popular in places like the United Kingdom, Scotland, Scandinavia, and Russia. Although oat flour is often used in baked goods, it cannot leaven bread. When rolled or flaked, oats can be used in porridge or granola. It is a very nutritious cereal, and can even be consumed by some people with celiac disease. However, it should be noted that oats *do* contain a protein similar to gluten that *can* be toxic for the gluten sensitive, so even so-called gluten-free oats grown in isolation should be eaten with caution by people who react to gluten.

Naked Oats

This variety of oat is originally from China, where it was grown for thousands of years. Its kernels are loose and easy to free from the chaff during threshing. Naked oats are more nutritious than common oats, and are easy to flake or process into flour.

Groats

Groats are simply hulled oats. They retain both the germ and bran of the grain and cannot be eaten raw. They can be used whole (in which case they are typically soaked in water), sprouted, or sliced into steel cut oats.

Steel Cut Oats

These are oat groats that have been chopped by large steel blades into pieces. They can be used to make porridge, though the process is, of course, longer than that required when using instant, rolled, or Scottish oats. They have a nuttier flavor and are chewier than other types of oats.

Scottish Oats

These are oats that have been coarsely ground with a stone mill into a meal, and are the typical base for oatmeal porridge. They cook quickly, and continue to be a staple in Scotland, the United Kingdom, and North America.

Rolled Oats

Rolled oats are groats that have been dehusked and either steamed or lightly baked and then rolled or pressed into flakes. They are widely used in porridge, muesli, and granola. They can also be ground and made into flour.

RYE

One of the younger domesticated cereals, the origins of rye are unclear. Like oats, it came from the spontaneous cross-breeding of weeds with cultivated wheat and barley. Since Roman times, rye has been grown extensively, and became increasingly popular in Northern and Central Europe after the Middle Ages because of its ability to adapt to poor soils, where other grains would not easily grow. Rye is also extremely tolerant of cold and can keep alive under a carpet of snow. It is, however, susceptible to ergot, a fungus that can be poisonous to both humans and animals. Fortunately, modern farming has given rise to efficient methods to prevent and control the growth of ergot. The gluten found in rye is different from that found in wheat, but can be used to make bread rise. Rye bread is popular in many countries, including the United States, Germany, and Russia.

Winter Rye

This is a rye that is planted in the fall and harvested during summer. Most rye is used as a winter crop because it is an excellent winter cover. Due to its deep roots, rye prevents soil erosion, protecting cultivated land during even the harshest winters.

Abruzzi Rye

Abruzzi is an old variety of rye that was cultivated by early North American colonists. This variety of rye produces plants capable of growing two feet taller than a standard rye plant. Abruzzi rye flour was traditionally used in thirded bread, a dense loaf made by the colonists before white wheat became widely available.

Rye Berries

Rye berries are the whole wheat kernels of threshed and harvested rye, with all the germ and bran included. They are often used in baking (though only after a proper soaking). Traditional Nordic breads, like Danish rye bread, include whole rye berries, which are sometimes boiled before being added to the dough.

Rye Chops

Similar to steel cut oats and cracked wheat, rye chops are just that—roughly chopped rye berries. Rye chops are quicker to cook and can be used in porridges as well as baking.

Rye Flakes

Rye flakes are processed similarly to rolled oats. They are first steamed, before being flaked through a rolling system, and then dried. They are a useful addition to several different types of bakes and can also be used in porridge and granola.

BARLEY

Barley cultivation predates all but that of the most ancient varieties of wheat. This cereal adapts well to different climates, and tolerates both cold and drought. It was the most commonly cultivated grain in ancient India and Greece and, along with emmer, was also a staple in Egypt. Even after wheat became the preferred grain for bread making, barley continued to be grown for the brewing of beer and distillation of whiskey. Since its farming required less care than that of other cereals, barley was historically more affordable to those of lesser means. As such, it developed a long-standing reputation as a "humble" grain. Because the particular type of gluten found in barley does not retain the gasses needed for fermentation, it is rarely used in leavened bread. Instead, it has historically been used to make flatbreads, porridge, and soups. While barley is currently the fourth-most cultivated cereal in the world, it is mostly used for its malt and as animal feed. This cereal is, however, extremely rich in nutrients, and can be a healthy addition to one's diet. The biggest producer of barley is Russia.

Flaked Barley

This is barley that has been dehulled, pearled, cooked, dried, and rolled into flakes. It can then be used in granola or porridge, as well as in baking, cooking, and brewing, where it is said to impart a rich and grainy flavor to beer.

Hulled Barley

Hulled barley is the closest thing to "whole grain" barley sold commercially. It has only the outer part of the hull removed, through a process aimed to leave part of the bran attached to the grain. It has a lengthy cooking time and needs to be soaked or boiled before it can be used in baking.

Pearl Barley

Pearl barley grains have had both their tough bran and inedible hull removed, and are then carefully polished. Unfortunately, this polishing process also removes many of the grain's nutrients. Fine barley flour is milled from pearl barley.

Pot Barley

Pot barley is a processed form of barley that is milled three times, after which the husk is partly removed and only some of the bran is left. Cooking pot barley takes about an hour. It is typically used in soups, as suggested by the name.

Quick-Cooking Barley

Quick-cooking barley is the most processed barley available today. It has been dehulled, polished, and then steamed, so it is precooked, making it much faster to prepare.

Bere Barley

This ancient variety of six-row barley looks very different from its relatives. It was once a staple in Scotland, where it was used in a number of local foods, like the traditional bere bannock loaf. Today, its cultivation is largely confined to the Orkney islands.

Arizona Barley

A wild variety of barley, it originates from a region spanning northern Mexico and the southwestern United States. It is an annual grass and grows in salt-rich habitats, like irrigation ditches, canals, and ponds. Although it is considered to be at risk of extinction in the wild, farmers have been known to use it to enhance cultivated barley.

Meadow Barley

This cool-season perennial grass is native to the western United States and can be found from California to Alaska. It is often used as a quick cover for soil stabilization on wet, dry, and salt-rich land. Although its seeds are edible, it is not typically grown for sustenance, and is usually only consumed by wild animals.

Low Barley or Dwarf Barley

This wild variety of barley is also found in the western United States, growing from Idaho to California. An annual grass, dwarf barley prefers moist habitats. Like other kinds of wild barley, it is used to enhance cultivated varieties through crossing.

Purple Barley

This heirloom variety of domesticated barley is notable for both its striking purple hue and for being "hulless." This means that even though the seed does indeed have a hull, it is loosely attached and easy to remove without the need to "pearlize" the barley. First brought to North America in the early 1920s, its origins go back to Tibet and the Middle East. For many years, purple barley was stored in the USDA Seed Repository, and it has only recently started to be grown in North America as a gourmet variety.

Black Nile Barley

This variety was developed from a domesticated North African barley, and was introduced to North America fairly recently. Like Purple Barley, Black Nile Barley is a hulless barley, and does not require pearlizing.

GLUTEN-FREE GRAINS

RICE

Almost as old as wheat, rice was domesticated in China between 10,000 and 12,000 years ago. Consumed by more people than any other cereal, rice is the third-highest-produced agricultural commodity on the planet. It is mostly eaten in grain form, but can also be ground into flour or pressed into milk. Since rice does not contain gluten, it cannot serve to leaven bread but can be used in combination with wheat, or combined with ingredients that mimic natural leavening to make gluten-free breads. Rice is very nutritious and highly digestible but, unfortunately, easily absorbs chemicals from the soil in which it is grown, including arsenic. While arsenic can occur naturally in soil, widespread use of chemical fertilizers has increased its concentration significantly. It is therefore important to know where your rice comes from. Rice is grown extensively around the globe, and China is its biggest producer.

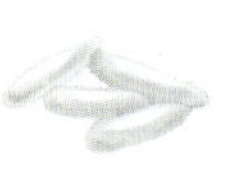

White Rice

White rice are grains that have had their husk, bran, and germ removed. The practice of polishing rice dates back to ancient China, as the process prolonged its shelf life, enhanced its flavor, and made it easier to digest. Like other processed grains, white rice has had part of its nutrients stripped, but it can be part of a healthy diet.

Brown Rice

Like white rice, brown rice grains have had their husks removed. However, their bran is left intact. Brown rice flour makes an ideal coating for artisanal loaves, as it has a more subtle color than that of white rice flour. As a whole grain, brown rice has long been considered a healthier alternative to white rice. However, recent studies have shown that it is actually the bran and the husk of the rice that retain the most chemicals and minerals from the soil, including trace amounts of arsenic. We recommend checking the area of origin (rice from California, India, and Pakistan are good options), taking the time to rinse the rice before cooking it, cooking it with plenty of water, and then draining it afterward.

Arborio

Selected by the Italian agronomist Domenico Marchetti in 1946, this variety of Northern Italian rice is derived from the older *Vialone Nano*. It has large grains that absorb lots of water during cooking and can increase in weight up to five times, making it the ideal rice for risotto.

Parboiled Rice

Parboiled rice is rice that has been partly precooked. This process originated in India and West Africa as a way of dehusking rice by steaming it, and it was later adapted commercially to reduce cooking time.

Basmati

A long and slender variety of rice native to India, it was later introduced to the Middle East by merchants. Although basmati plants and grains have been cultivated in the United States, the Indian government has argued that these strains are but imitations of true basmati, which only grows in certain parts of India and Pakistan. Basmati rice has a lower glycemic index score than most other rice varieties.

Black Rice

Different varieties of black rice, characterized by their dark color, can be found across Asia. Some of these are glutinous varieties, have a similar texture to sticky rice, and are commonly used in sweet desserts.

Jasmine Rice

Mostly grown in Southeast Asia, this popular long-grain rice is named for its floral scent. It has the ideal consistency for high-heat cooking, and is often used in stir-fried dishes. It has a higher glycemic index score than basmati.

Rosematta Rice

This Indian rice originates from the Palakkad region of Kerala. It has a rich and unique flavor and is considered an excellent accompaniment to meat dishes. The rice is parboiled in its red husks, giving grains a yellow-pink color.

Red Cargo Rice

A long whole-grain rice with a red bran, its name comes from the fact that it used to arrive in the United States in bulk, transported via ships (unlike white rice, which was imported prepackaged).

Valencia Rice

Named for its native Valencia, Spain, this variety of rice has short, rounded grains that expand considerably when cooked without becoming sticky. It is used in numerous traditional Spanish dishes, most notably paella. Valencia rice is in fact so highly valued that its cultivation and native wetlands are protected by the Spanish Department of Agriculture.

Bhutanese Red Rice

Grown in the eastern Himalayas at an elevation of 8,000 feet, Bhutanese rice comes in both short- and long-grain varieties. The short type cooks relatively quickly, at a similar speed to white rice. When processed, the red bran is left intact, making this rice a whole grain. It is slightly sticky and very flavorful.

Akamuro Rice

This Japanese rice variety comes from Hokkaido and is a translucent reddish brown color. Akamuro matures fast and grows well on lowlands. Unlike most rice, it can tolerate a cold climate. It has a delicate flavor and has recently been cultivated in North America on a small scale.

Duborskian Rice

A Russian rice variety that grows well on uplands and does not require the soil to be flooded to grow. Like Akamuro rice, it does well in cold climates and has also started to be farmed in North America on a small scale.

WILD RICE

There are four species of wild rice, most of which are native to North America. These grasses are from the *Zizania* genus, which is only indirectly related to most rice of Asian origin. There are four species of this aquatic cereal, all of which prefer shallow waters, ponds, and slow-flowing rivers.

It often serves as sustenance for nearby wildlife (ducks, for instance), and in recent times has been planted with the intention of helping local fauna. It was a staple cereal for both the Native American and ancient Chinese peoples. It is now mostly cultivated in Minnesota, California, Canada, Hungary, and Australia. Since the 1970s wild rice has become increasingly popular as a gourmet food. Although wild rice flour is not particularly common, it is sometimes used in bread and baked goods, giving them a nutty flavor.

Northern and Southern Wild Rice

These two closely related types of wild rice were the staple cereals of Native Americans, who considered wild rice sacred. Native Americans threshed the mature seeds directly from canoes, making sure to allow some seeds to fall into the water, so that they would generate the next harvest. Both varieties still grow wild in different regions of North America, as their names suggest, and continue to be cultivated today.

Manchurian Wild Rice

This plant is a close relative of North American wild rice and was used as a staple grain in ancient China. Nowadays it has almost entirely disappeared in the wild and is usually grown for its stems, which are eaten as vegetables.

Texas Wild Rice

This variety of rice grows wild in Texas and is considered an endangered grass species. Farmers do not cultivate Texas wild rice as a crop.

CORN

Corn is the second-most cultivated cereal in the world, and is used for a massive range of products, from cattle feed and ethanol to cornstarch and syrup. It was domesticated in Mexico around 8000 BC. Like rice, corn does not contain gluten and cannot leaven bread. However, many varieties of flatbread are made with maize flour. Stone-ground cornmeal or hominy can also be used to make thick savory porridges like grits, polenta, or the Brazilian dish angu. Sweet corn is often eaten whole, boiled or roasted, and the boiled grains are a popular addition to stews and salads. Corn is a good source of carbohydrates but is nutritionally less valuable than other grains. It lacks vitamin B_3, which is why Europeans who once used it as a staple cereal ended up with a sickness called pellagra. In a rich and varied diet, maize certainly has its place, but there is some concern regarding the massive industrialization of much of its cultivation. The United States is the world's largest producer of corn.

Dent Corn

The great majority of farmed corn is dent corn, also called field corn and yellow corn. Harvested when the kernels are tough, it must be processed into flour and then cooked to become edible. Most crops have been genetically modified to increase their yield. Commonly grown for cattle feed and practically ubiquitous in processed foods, it is found in cornflakes, cornstarch, gluten-free pasta and bread, cornmeal, tortillas, high-fructose corn syrup, and much more.

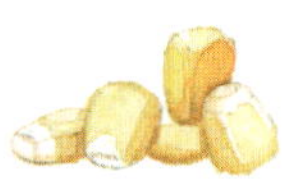

Sweet Corn

Sweet corn is typically consumed as a vegetable, often

served as corn on the cob or as whole kernels rather than being processed like a grain. It is harvested when the kernels are still soft and is either eaten when fresh or preserved through canning or freezing. While hugely popular, it actually only accounts for a minimal part of North American corn cultivation. GMO varieties are widely sold, although heritage varieties are still grown.

Flint Corn

Historically cultivated by Native Americans, flint corn has a hard outer layer and is similar to dent corn, but is often used for ornamental purposes because of its multicolored kernels. It is used to make hominy, a food made of corn that has been treated with lye or slaked lime to soften it. It can then be added to stews and beverages, or used to make grits or masa.

Blue Corn

Blue corn is grown in Mexico and the southwestern United States. The varieties of blue corn found in the United States were originally developed by the people of the Hopi tribe, who used it to make *piki*, a traditional Hopi bread. In Mexican cuisine it is used to make *tlacoyo* and tortillas. It has a higher antioxidant and protein content than yellow corn.

Waxy Corn

The starch in waxy corn contains only amylopectin and no amylose, a mutation that makes it far more digestible than dent corn. When used as feed, it also encourages more efficient weight gain and growth in animals than dent. This rare variety has unclear origins and has been subject to much research; in the early twentieth century it was found growing in China, Burma, and the Philippines. It is now widely thought that it traveled to China from the Americas in or around the 1500s, and that the mutation occurred sometime afterward.

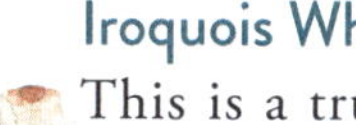

Iroquois White Corn

This is a true heritage variety of corn similar to common sweet corn. The Iroquois tribe cultivated this white corn before their farmlands were destroyed by European settlers. Fortunately, some seeds survived and continued to be cultivated, and Iroquois white corn is now commercially available in the form of dried seeds and flour. The flour is a good gluten-free alternative in breads and cookies, and is also used in tortillas and other maize breads.

BUCKWHEAT

The most common type of buckwheat, *Fagopyrum esculentum*, is not a grass, but actually more closely related to the rhubarb plant. It originated in East Asia about 10,000 years ago and from there it spread to the rest of the continent and Europe. Historically, buckwheat was a popular cereal and key component in many regional cuisines, where it was the base for pancakes, bread, pasta, and noodles. Buckwheat is also used to make beer. With the advent of modern agriculture, buckwheat production declined, as it responds poorly to fertilizer. However, demand is on the rise once more, due to the fact that buckwheat is nutrient rich as well as gluten free. The biggest producer of buckwheat is Russia.

Buckwheat Groats

These are crushed buckwheat seeds that have had their hulls removed. They can be cooked like rice, made into porridge, or ground into flour. Sometimes buckwheat is milled without removing the hulls to make wholemeal buckwheat flour. The buckwheat hulls can also be used as a natural filling for pillows. Buckwheat flour can be used for many delicious foods, from the Breton galette to Russian blini.

Kasha

This is a Slavic term that in English use is often applied to toasted buckwheat groats, but traditionally refers to buckwheat porridge, or porridge in general. Kasha is one of the oldest and most loved staples of Russian cuisine, and an important dish in Ashkenazi Jewish cuisine. There are a number of sweet and savory variations, nearly all of which include plenty of butter.

Old Varieties of Common Buckwheat

Common buckwheat has been a staple in many European regions. It tolerates cooler climates well, and thrives in acidic and low-fertility soils. It was once widely grown in Bretagne and Russia, and in the Alps. Farmers and researchers in Valtellina, Italy, have preserved two heritage Alpine varieties, and in doing so saved them from extinction: Curunìn from Baruffini and Nustràn from Teglio. Both varieties are milled into flour and used locally to make fresh pasta and bread.

Tartary Buckwheat

A close relative of common buckwheat, Tartary buckwheat grows mostly in Asia, and is particularly abundant in the Himalayas. However, it is not uncommon in Europe. This bitter variety can be used to make flour as well as porridge. Recently, researchers observed that Tartary buckwheat had a higher concentration of rutin (a bioflavonoid with several health benefits) than common buckwheat.

QUINOA

This is a leafy cereal from the same plant family as amaranth and kaniwa (see page 62). It was one of the staple foods of the Peruvian Incas and has become an increasingly popular alternative to rice and pasta. It originated in the Andes mountains around 3000 BC, in an area spanning what is now Peru and Bolivia. South America remains the world's biggest producer of quinoa but cultivation has also expanded to other areas, including China and the United States. Quinoa is often used as a substitute for rice, but can also be ground into flour and used to make bread. In terms of nutrition, quinoa is rich in proteins and several minerals and vitamins. Unfortunately, it is also rich in saponins, which can trigger symptoms for those with IBS (irritable bowel syndrome). Consequently, while quinoa can be a great gluten-free alternative to many grains, it may not be the best choice for people affected by digestive issues.

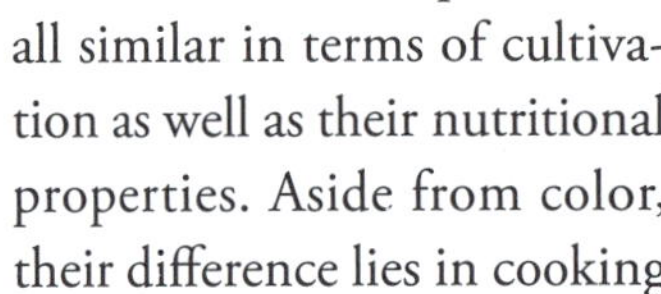

Red, White, and Black Quinoa

These varieties of quinoa are all similar in terms of cultivation as well as their nutritional properties. Aside from color, their difference lies in cooking time and texture: red and black quinoa take longer to cook than white quinoa, which has a softer, fluffier texture. In contrast, red and black quinoa are chewier and lend themselves well to salads.

MILLET

Millet is a family of grasses that produce small grains. Some varieties of millet have been grown in East Asia since at least 6000 BC. Millet spread from Asia to Europe, where it was popular throughout the Middle Ages. It remains one of the most common cereals grown in hot, arid parts of the globe, including Africa and India, which is the world's leading producer. Millet is a valuable animal feed and makes good grazing grass. This cereal is a key component in many traditional cuisines and is used in flatbreads, soups, and porridges, as well as several alcoholic beverages. Millet contains no gluten and cannot be used to leaven bread, but it is safe for gluten-sensitive people. Its nutritional profile is similar to that of wheat and rice, which makes millet a good staple cereal.

Pearl Millet

This is the most common type of millet and the most widely cultivated. It originated in West Africa around 4,500 years ago and from there it spread to India. It is still a staple cereal in some parts of Africa, like Nigeria and Namibia, because of its high tolerance to both drought and flooding.

Foxtail Millet

The oldest domesticated millet, foxtail millet has been farmed in China for over 8,000 years. It is still widely cultivated in the more arid regions of India and China. In warm climates, foxtail millet has proven to be extremely versatile, and can be grown in any season of the year.

Little Millet

Found in Central India, where it has been cultivated since 2500 BC and continues to be common today. It is generally used like rice but can also be ground into flour, and used to make bread and other foods. It is often sold unpolished, with the bran intact.

Kodo Millet

Originally from West Africa, this is grown in India and East Asia. It grows well in tropical regions, with high temperatures and plenty of rain. It can be an asset in waterlogged and coastal areas where other cereals cannot grow, but spreads like an invasive weed when introduced to cultivated land.

Finger Millet

This variety originates from the highlands of Uganda and Ethiopia. It thrives in semiarid climates and can grow at very high altitudes. It is also grown in the Himalayas as well as other regions of India. Finger millet has very small seeds, which makes it difficult to separate the bran from the endosperm, and therefore it is mostly used as whole-grain flour. Its flour is widely used in regional cuisine, including cakes, breads, puddings, porridge, and beverages.

Proso Millet

Proso millet may have first been domesticated independently in both China and the Caucasus in 5000 BC. It became the dominant millet variety in the Near East and Europe, but never reached Africa. In North and South America it is grown for animal feed, though it has recently been considered as a source for biofuel production. It thrives in arid regions and has been promoted as a gluten-free alternative, both as a grain and flour.

Kaniwa

This crop is part of the same plant family as amaranth and quinoa. Kaniwa is grown for its seeds, which can be boiled or milled into flour. It has been cultivated on the highlands of Bolivia and Peru for thousands of years. There are 200 varieties of kaniwa, but only 20 are still cultivated. Kaniwa is similar to quinoa but has a better nutritional profile. In particular, kaniwa has much lower concentrations of toxic saponins compared with quinoa.

Teff

Teff is a grass indigenous to Ethiopia and Eritrea, where it was domesticated sometime between 4000 BC and 1000 BC. Unlike wheat and many other grasses, it does not contain gluten. It is used in soups, stews, and porridges, and is also a key ingredient in injera, a fermented traditional bread. This fermentation process is not intended to leaven the bread, but to release the grain's rich proteins and minerals. Teff grows best in warm, sunny climates at a high altitude. Its cultivation is still limited to a few regions of the globe, but demand is rising because of its nutritional profile and lack of gluten. There are dark and light varieties of teff, both of which are used in similar ways. Due to the small size of the seeds, teff is always ground whole, as it is impossible to isolate the bran from the starchy section.

Sorghum

Like wheat, sorghum is part of the grass family. While there are many species of this grass, *Sorghum bicolor* is by far the most widely cultivated. This variety is native to Africa and has been farmed for thousands of years. Africa remains this nutritious gluten-free cereal's biggest producer. Sorghum is a resilient plant, and can tolerate poor soil, as well as extreme heat and drought. It is used in a number of traditional flatbreads throughout Asia and Africa, as well as a wide variety of other foods. These include sweet sorghum syrup, spirits, beer, and baked goods. It is also used as a source of biofuel and feed for livestock, although it can be difficult for animals to digest.

Amaranth

Unlike wheat, amaranth is not a grass but a leafy summer vegetable closely related to spinach, chard, and beets. Its domestication dates back to the Mayans, and it has been cultivated for over 8,000 years. The diet of the Aztec people was overwhelmingly amaranth based, and it was a key component in many religious rituals and festivities. Tragically, after the arrival of Spanish conquistadores in the 1500s, the farming of amaranth was forbidden and nearly all cultivated fields were burned. Luckily, the plant was not completely destroyed and cultivation began to spread once more in the 1970s. Much of the renewed interest in amaranth is due to its nutrient-rich profile and the fact that it does not contain gluten. Amaranth can be used to make flour and baked goods, and can also to be eaten whole in soups, stews, and other dishes. The Aztec people also "popped" it, much like popcorn. Introduction of amaranth to cultivated land can be difficult, since this plant will spread like an invasive weed. Consequently, most commercially produced amaranth has undergone genetic manipulation allowing it to tolerate chemical treatment to contain is growth. As such, it may be advisable to buy organic whenever possible. The current leading producer is China.

Adlay Millet

This grass is native to Southeast Asia, and has been domesticated throughout the Americas. The gluten-free seeds of the plant can be dried and milled into flour for bread and other baked goods. This cereal has long been used in traditional Chinese medicine, and is believed to have many beneficial properties. Recent research has suggested that Adlay millet could help manage cholesterol levels and menstrual symptoms, and even be used in the treatment and prevention of cancer.

FRUITS

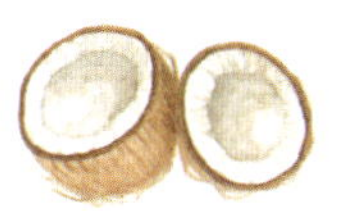

Coconut

The exact origin of the coconut has been subject to extensive debate. It is generally thought to be native to Indonesia, from where it gradually self-distributed. Protected by their sturdy shell, fruit from coastal coconut trees floated across the seas, spreading to the rest of the world. The flesh of the coconut can be used to make coconut milk and oil, from which the leftover pulp is often dried and ground into flour.

Banana

This genus of large fruit-bearing plants has been cultivated since 5000 BC, and is native to Southeast Asia. It has since spread to both Africa and the Caribbean. Banana flour is typically made from green bananas or plantains, but researchers in Chile have recently developed a way to make flour from overripe bananas and their peels.

Plantain

In Europe and the Americas, "plantain" refers to sturdier, starchier, less sweet varieties of banana that are generally cooked as part of a meal rather than eaten as a fruit, and are used and sold at varying stages of ripeness. They can be dried and milled into flour, which is rich in resistant starches and therefore low in calories. It is worth noting that in other regions of the world, especially Asia and the islands of the Pacific, there is no distinction made between plantains and bananas.

SEEDS

Chia

A flowering herb once farmed by the Aztecs, chia is now widely cultivated for its seeds in Mexico, the southwestern United States, and parts of South America. Chia seeds can be added to a number of different foods or ground into a gel for use in desserts and as a vegan egg substitute. They can be ground into flour and used in bread and other baked goods. Although chia seeds are often promoted as a health food and are rich in omega-3 fatty acid, claims of their purported health benefits have yet to be fully proven.

Grape Seed

Grape seed flour is made from the seed and skin residue left over from wine making. It is rich in antioxidants, and much research has gone into its nutritional properties. Many bakers and chefs have experimented with using it in bread and baked goods, and it can be an excellent way to add flavor, color, and nutritional value. However, it is widely agreed that adding more than a small amount can negatively impact the bread's flavor and texture.

Pumpkin Seed

Native to North America, pumpkins produce seeds that are ideal for making gluten-free flour. Pumpkin seed flour, milled from whole seeds, is suitable for people with nut allergies and can work as a substitute for almond meal. Pumpkin seed flour is rich in proteins, fats, and essential minerals.

Sunflower Seed

Sunflowers, a plant indigenous to the Americas, produce hearty seeds that are rich in omega-3 and unsaturated fatty acids and minerals. Once they have been soaked and dehydrated, these seeds can be milled into flour. Like pumpkin seed flour, this is a good nut-free substitute for almond meal.

Hemp

One of the first plants to be domesticated, hemp is a variety of *Cannabis sativa* once used as a fiber crop. Today its uses span from the production of oil and paper to plastics and biofuel. Hemp flour is milled from the "cake" left over after hemp seeds are pressed for oil. This gluten-free flour works best when blended with other flours, especially when making bread, as it will otherwise result in a very flat, dense loaf.

Flax

Flax has been farmed since antiquity for its oil, fibers, and seeds. Flaxseed meal is made from milled whole flax seeds. It is very high in fats and therefore it cannot be used as a substitute for flour, but it can be an interesting addition to bread and baked goods.

NUTS

Almond

Almonds are the seeds of the widely cultivated tree of the same name, which is native to the Middle East. Ground and whole almonds are widely used in both baking and pastry making, and are also the main ingredient of marzipan paste. Very fine almond flour, or meal, has become popular as a gluten-free substitute for wheat flour. The flour keeps all the rich nutrients of the whole almonds.

Acorn

Acorns are the nuts of the oak tree. Throughout much of the world, acorns were considered inedible and only eaten in times of great need. However, one notable exception is that of the Indigenous peoples of North America, particularly those in the area that is now California. A staple food for many, acorns were harvested and sun-dried to prevent mold and germination, and could be stored for long periods of time. They were often later crushed and ground into flour, and then leached in water to rid the flour of tannic acid. This processing method has been "rediscovered" in recent years, and acorn flour is increasingly available. It is extremely rich in antioxidants and gluten free.

Chestnut

Chestnuts are the nuts of the chestnut tree, found in temperate climates. Different varieties of chestnut can be found in Europe, East Asia, and North America. Chestnuts, and flour milled from them, have been a source of food for millennia, and chestnut cultivation is thought to date back to 2000 BC. Chestnut flour is made from ground dried chestnuts, and can be used alone or in combination with regular flour to make cakes, cookies, and bread. Chestnut flour is rich in minerals and vitamins, and low in fats.

Peanut

Peanuts are, in fact, not nuts, but the seeds of the peanut legume. Although peanuts are native to Central and South America, Asia has become the world's largest producer. Crushed peanuts left over from the manufacture of peanut oil can be milled into peanut flour. This flour, unlike almond flour, is low in fat but still high in protein. It is generally used as a thickening agent in food, but can also be used in baking.

Cashew

Cashews are the edible seeds of the tropical cashew tree, native to Brazil. Africa and Asia are the world's biggest producers of cashews. Much like almond flour, cashews are dried and milled to make flour. As a result, cashew flour is very high in fat, but also retains all of its nutrients.

Pecan

Pecans are the nuts of the tree of the same name, which is native to both Mexico and North America, both of which remain the world's biggest producers. Used in a variety of foods, pecans can also be dried and ground into flour. Pecan flour is rich in fats, proteins, minerals, and vitamins and can be used as a substitute for almond flour.

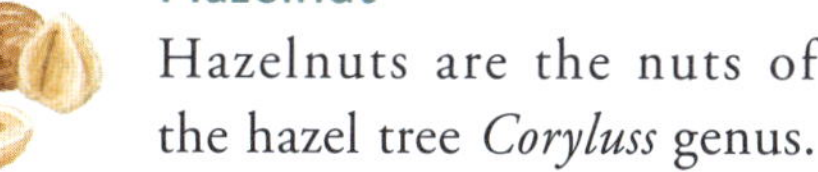

Hazelnut

Hazelnuts are the nuts of the hazel tree *Coryluss* genus. Early traces of their processing were discovered in Scotland and dated to 6000 BC. Nowadays, the largest producer is Turkey. Hazelnuts have been used since antiquity in numerous foods, including baked goods. Hazelnut flour is similar to most other nut flours, and is made from ground dried hazelnuts, retaining their fat and nutrients.

Pistachio

Pistachios are the nuts of the pistachio tree. Native to Asia and the Middle East, they have become naturalized throughout the Mediterranean. Widely eaten since antiquity, pistachios are used in a variety of foods. However, finely milled pistachio flour is a relatively recent development. This flour has a distinctive flavor and is full of the same rich nutrients found in whole pistachios.

Macadamia

Macadamia are a group of tree species native to Australia, all of which bear the macadamia nut. South Africa is currently the largest producer, followed by Australia and the United States. Macadamia nuts, like other nuts, can be dried (and sometimes roasted) and then ground into flour. The flour contains all the fats and nutrients of the macadamia nuts and can be used as one would almond flour.

TUBERS

Potato

The fourth-most cultivated crop in the world, potatoes are the tubers of herbaceous plants native to the Andes. Potatoes can be peeled, dried, and milled into potato flour, which can be used in baking in combination with regular flour or as a flour substitute in gluten-free baking. Potato starch is also widely used in both cooking and baking. This is extracted from pulverized potatoes and then dried into powder.

Sweet Potato

Sweet potatoes are the tubers of a flowering plant native to either Central or South America. They date back to at least 8000 BC and spread to the Pacific Islands as early as 1000 AD. A popular food in many cultures, this healthy and nutritious tuber can be dried and milled into flour. Sweet potato flour is low in fat and rich in nutrients.

Tapioca

This starch is derived from the cassava root, which is indigenous to Brazil. As an extracted starch, it essentially contains only carbohydrates, with no proteins and nearly no fats, significant minerals, or vitamins. It is added to various food products as a thickener or jellifying agent, and is also used in baked goods, puddings, snacks, and drinks.

Tigernut

This common tuber grows wild throughout much of the world, its cultivation dating back to 4000 BC in Egypt and 7000 BC in North America. Cultivation is currently concentrated in Spain and Egypt. Tubers can be eaten raw and are used in a number of dishes and beverages. They can also be toasted and then milled into flour. This flour is rich in starch as well as several nutrients, including proteins, fats, minerals, and vitamins, making it a healthy gluten-free alternative.

Yam

Although the terms *yam* and *sweet potato* are used interchangeably in parts of North America and Polynesia, true yams are the tubers of vine plants native to Africa and Asia. They are widely cultivated in Africa, which is the major producer. Rich in starch but low in other nutrients (particularly in protein), yams are traditionally sun-dried and milled into flour, which can be used in cooking and baking.

Cassava

Cassava is the root of a shrub native to South America but now more widely cultivated in Africa and Asia. Cassava is a staple in sub-Saharan African countries, as it thrives in arid climates and can do well in poor soils. However, raw cassava is toxic and can cause cyanide poisoning. It must be boiled or otherwise processed to remove these toxins, after which it can be consumed or dried and milled into flour. Nutritionally speaking, processed cassava contains little more than carbohydrates.

Water Chestnut

The tubers of a grass native to East Asia, water chestnuts can also be found in Australia, the Pacific Islands, and parts of Africa. They are particularly common in Chinese cuisine. Water chestnuts can be ground into a starch-rich flour that can be used in baking and frying, and as a thickener.

BEANS AND LEGUMES

Soybean

The soybean is a legume native to East Asia. It is extremely rich in proteins and suitable for extensive farming, which is why it is widely cultivated in both North and South America. The United States, Argentina, and Brazil are the world's leading producers. In the United States, soybeans are harvested and processed for their oil and flour on an industrial scale. Soy flour is usually milled from the dry bean residue left over after the soybeans have had their oil extracted, but can also be made from whole heat-processed soybeans.

White Bean

This variety of common bean is native to North America, and went on to become a widespread crop throughout the rest of the world. White bean flour is made from pulverized white beans and is packed with proteins and other important nutrients.

Black Bean

Like white beans, black beans are a variety of common beans. Native to the Americas, they are staples of Mexican, Latin American, and Dominican cuisine. Black bean flour is made from pulverized dried beans and contains the same nutrients found in whole black beans.

Black Gram or Urad Bean

This Indian legume has been grown since ancient times and is a major part of Indian cuisine. Extremely nutritious, it is rich in high-quality proteins, essential minerals, and vitamins. The dried beans can be ground into flour used in traditional foods such as chapati and dosa.

Mung Bean

An Asian legume first domesticated in the Fertile Crescent, it has been farmed in India and nearby regions for millennia. The dry beans are often ground into a dry paste used in several traditional Indian dishes. Starch can also be extracted from the flour and used to make noodles.

Green Pea

A legume of Mediterranean origin, peas are have been widely cultivated for thousands of years, dating back to at least 4400 BC in Egypt and 3600 BC in India. Nowadays, green peas are usually eaten fresh, but in antiquity they were grown for their dry seeds. These seeds can be milled to make a pale green flour. It has a very mild flavor, and is easy to use in many baking recipes. Green pea flour is a good way to boost the nutritional value of bread and other baked goods.

Fava Bean

This legume is native to North Africa as well as South and Southwest Asia. Often eaten fresh, fava beans are also popular dried. Dried fava beans can be milled into an earthy flour that lends itself well to savory baked goods, but may not work as well in sweeter or more delicately flavored bakes. Like other legumes, fava beans and their flour are low in fat but rich in proteins, minerals, and vitamins.

Chickpea

Chickpeas are one of the earliest cultivated legumes, and were first domesticated in the Fertile Crescent in 5000 BC. They are grown for their dry seeds, which have become a staple in Mediterranean, Indian, Middle Eastern, and other regional cuisines. Chickpea flour, ground from the dry seeds, is the main ingredient of numerous flatbreads and other foods. Chickpeas are some of the most nutrient-rich legumes and are particularly high in vegetable proteins.

Lentils

Like chickpeas, lentils were one of the earliest legumes to be domesticated, in the ancient Near East. They are cultivated for their dried seeds, which are generally boiled and used in many regional foods. Dry lentils can be milled into a versatile flour, which has a mild flavor and rich nutritional profile.

Coffee

Remarkably, a process has recently been developed to extract flour from the very same plant from which we harvest coffee beans. This patented process repurposes the waste from coffee production, making a flour that can be used in baking. However, it should be noted that it may affect the dough's flavor and texture if added in large quantities.

GENERAL NOTES ABOUT THE RECIPES

MEASUREMENTS

As already stated numerous times, using weight measurements instead of volumetric measurements is overwhelmingly beneficial in bread making. That said, there are a large number of people who refuse to leave their measuring cups and spoons behind when baking, and so the recipes provide both a volume measurement and a weight measurement for each ingredient involved in the dough (additions such as fruits and nuts which will not affect the proper development of the dough just have a volume measurement). The weight measurement is in grams, as that allows for far more precision than the imperial ounce.

FLOUR

Most recipes call for all-purpose or bread flour. But feel free to make substitutions using different types of flours, like spelt, emmer, einkorn, rye, heritage wheat, and whole wheat. A recipe will be negatively affected only if the change is over 40 percent of the total flour amount, and only for flours that have worse baking properties than regular white flour. Just be aware that each flour behaves slightly differently and absorbs a different amount of water, so when making substitutions, watch the dough closely and regulate the hydration accordingly.

SOURDOUGH STARTER

Unless otherwise specified, when sourdough starter is listed as an ingredient, we refer to a 100 percent hydration flour starter (see page 40). Feel free to change the type of flour used to feed the starter, but if changing the hydration (the water/flour ratio) of the starter, the amount of water in the recipe will need to be altered accordingly.

PRE-FERMENTS

Whenever a recipe calls for a sourdough starter, know that this can be substituted by an equal amount of pre-ferment. See pages 37–38 for suggestions on some options.

KNEADING

There is never only one right way of kneading/working a dough. For each recipe, feel free to use your favorite way, just make sure that the end result meets the recipe's needs in terms of dough development and gluten strength. Check pages 42–44 for tips on kneading and mixing.

FERMENTATION

Times for the first and second fermentation are always just a general guide; they can never be precise, because fermentation times depend on several variables that only you know, such as ambient temperature, the initial temperature of the ingredients, the strength of your leavening agent, and so on. Learn to read the dough, and make sure your eyes are on it more than on the timer.

LOAVES

When you think of bread, chances are that the recipes in this chapter are what immediately come to mind. Capable of rounding out the table morning, noon, and night, these loaves are the focus of the skilled bread maker's practice, requiring considerable skill and knowledge, and rewarding these qualities with awe-inspiring results that bring smiles to the faces of all who encounter them.

Featuring enough recipes to keep even the most devoted bakers busy for the rest of their lives and a number of shaping techniques that will help novices and artisans develop and sharpen their skills, this chapter is a master class in the art of bread making.

PANIS FARREUS

YIELD: 1 LOAF / **ACTIVE TIME:** 50 MINUTES / **TOTAL TIME:** 6 HOURS

This bread is inspired by the ancient Roman bread of the same name, which was made of emmer (farro), but possibly also with einkorn in early times. It was linked to a very special occasion, the confarreatio (meaning "with farro"), the traditional Roman wedding ceremony.

INGREDIENTS:

1¾ CUPS (400 G) SOURDOUGH STARTER (SEE PAGE 40)

6⅔ CUPS (800 G) EINKORN FLOUR, PLUS MORE AS NEEDED

1¾ CUPS PLUS 2 TABLESPOONS (427 G) WATER

2 TEASPOONS (12 G) FINE SEA SALT

1. Place all of the ingredients, except for the salt and 2 tablespoons of the water, in a large bowl and knead for about 10 minutes. Dissolve the salt in 2 tablespoons of the water and add the mixture to the dough. Knead for another 5 minutes.

2. Cover the bowl with a kitchen towel, place the dough in a naturally warm spot, and let it rest for 2½ hours.

3. Place the dough on a flour-dusted work surface and gently shape it into a round.

4. Cover a banneton or a medium bowl with kitchen towels and heavily dust them with flour. Use the floured linen to create a little hill in the middle of the basket.

5. Make a hole in the middle of the round and carefully enlarge the hole, flattening the round a bit to look like a big doughnut.

6. Place the round in the basket, making sure that the central part of the linen sticks out of the hole, which will help the dough keep its shape. Let it rest, covered with kitchen towels, for 2 to 3 hours at room temperature.

7. Preheat the oven to 480°F and place a baking stone or steel in the oven as it warms.

8. Invert the dough onto a parchment-lined peel. Transfer the dough to the heated implement in the oven and bake with steam, using one of the methods described on page 32, for 10 minutes.

9. Open the oven to remove the steam. Reduce the temperature to 390°F and bake for 1 hour.

10. Remove the bread from the oven, place it on a wire rack, and let it cool completely before slicing and serving.

PANE AQUILANO

YIELD: 1 LOAF / **ACTIVE TIME:** 1 HOUR / **TOTAL TIME:** 15 HOURS

Not many are aware of this fact, even in Italy, but bread from the Abruzzi region is outstanding. This traditional sourdough loaf is a clear example of the mastery residing in that baking heritage.

INGREDIENTS:

- 11.6 OZ. (329 G) BREAD FLOUR, PLUS MORE AS NEEDED
- 3½ OZ. (99 G) FINELY GROUND WHOLE WHEAT FLOUR
- 10.9 OZ. (309 G) WATER
- 3½ OZ. (99 G) STIFF SOURDOUGH STARTER (SEE PAGE 40)
- 1 SMALL POTATO, BOILED, PEELED, AND PRESSED THROUGH A POTATO RICER
- 2 TEASPOONS (11 G) FINE SEA SALT
- SEMOLINA FLOUR, AS NEEDED

1. Place the bread flour, whole wheat flour, and two-thirds of the water in the work bowl of a stand mixer fitted with the dough hook and work the mixture on low. Gradually add the starter and work the mixture until it comes together as a shaggy dough.

2. Add the potato and continue to work the dough until it is smooth.

3. Gradually add the salt and remaining water and work the dough until they have been incorporated. Shape the dough into a ball, place it in a clean bowl, and cover it with plastic wrap. Let the dough rise at room temperature for 1 hour, fold it, and let it rest for another hour. Fold the dough again and let it rest for 6 hours.

4. Place the dough on a flour-dusted work surface and fold it over itself. Cover the dough with a kitchen towel and let it rest for 30 minutes.

5. Using your hands, spread the dough into a rectangle. Fold a long side toward the center of the dough and then fold the other long side over it.

6. Place the dough, seam side down, on a semolina-dusted kitchen towel that is large enough to also cover the top of the dough. Let it rest for 1 hour.

7. Preheat the oven to 390°F and place a baking stone or steel on the middle rack of the oven as it warms.

8. Place the dough on a semolina-dusted peel and slide it onto the heated baking implement. Bake until the bread is dark brown, feels lighter when lifted, and makes a hollow sound when tapped, about 50 minutes.

9. Remove the bread from the oven, place it on a wire rack, and let it cool for at least 4 hours before serving.

PITTA CALABRESE

YIELD: 3 LOAVES / **ACTIVE TIME:** 1 HOUR / **TOTAL TIME:** 14 HOURS

A Calabrian sandwich bread, pitta Calabrese has most certainly Greek origins, as the name clearly suggests. Generally ring shaped and quite flat, pitta is great when filled with meat, and in Catanzaro it forms the foundation of two popular sandwiches: u'suffritt, with pork and offal, and u'morzeddhu, with entrails and tripe.

INGREDIENTS:

- 1 PACKET (7 G) OF ACTIVE DRY YEAST OR 6.3 OZ. (179 G) STIFF SOURDOUGH STARTER (SEE PAGE 40)
- 16.9 OZ. (479 G) WATER
- 2 TEASPOONS (14 G) HONEY (OPTIONAL)
- 12.3 OZ. (349 G) BREAD FLOUR
- 12.3 OZ. (349 G) STONE-GROUND ALL-PURPOSE FLOUR, PLUS MORE AS NEEDED
- 1 TEASPOON (5.5 G) FINE SEA SALT
- EXTRA-VIRGIN OLIVE OIL, AS NEEDED

1. If using active dry yeast, warm the water until it is about 105°F, place it in the work bowl of a stand mixer fitted with the dough hook, and add the yeast and, if desired, honey. Gently stir to combine and let the mixture sit until it starts to foam, about 10 minutes.

2. Add the flours and work the mixture on low until combined. If using a starter, add it gradually and work the mixture until it comes together as a dough.

3. Raise the speed and work the dough until it is smooth and elastic. Add the salt and work the dough for another 10 minutes.

4. Coat a clean bowl with olive oil, place the dough in it, and cover the bowl with plastic wrap. Place the dough in a naturally warm spot and let it rest for 3 hours.

5. Place the dough on a flour-dusted work surface, divide it into three pieces, and shape them into rounds. Cover the dough with a kitchen towel and let it rest for another 3 hours.

6. Preheat the oven to 410°F and place a baking stone or steel on the middle rack of the oven as it warms.

7. Roll out each round into a disk and make a hole in the center with a glass or ring cutter. Use a parchment-lined peel to slide the dough onto the heated baking implement and bake for 15 minutes.

8. Reduce the temperature to 355°F and bake until the bread is golden brown, feels lighter when lifted, and makes a hollow sound when tapped, about 15 minutes.

9. Remove the bread from the oven, place it on a wire rack, and let it cool for 2 hours before serving.

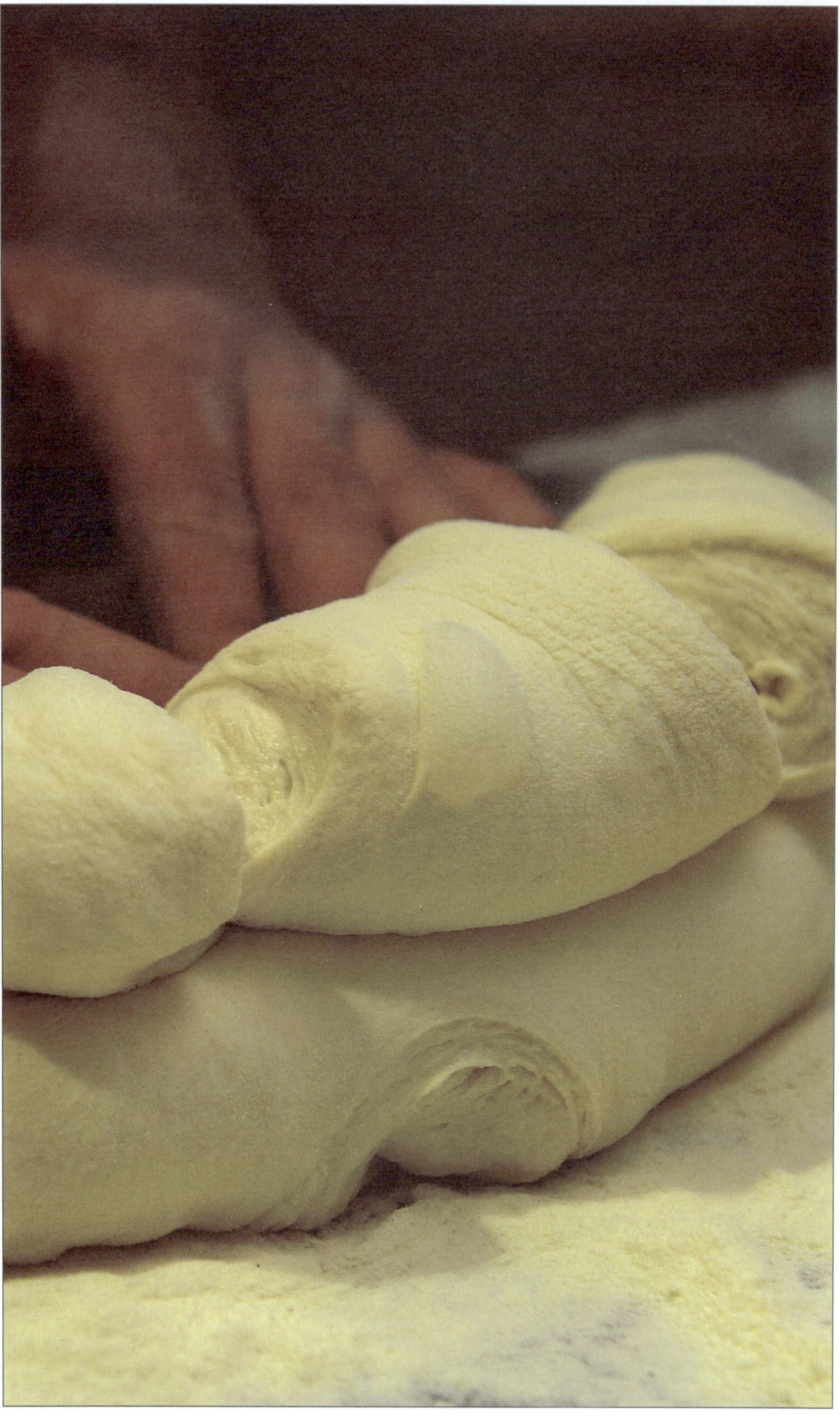

PANE DI MATERA

YIELD: 2 LOAVES / **ACTIVE TIME:** 2 HOURS / **TOTAL TIME:** 24 HOURS

The real pane di Matera can only be made around Matera, with local ingredients and using a very specific method involving fresh wild yeast derived from fermented fruit. It is possible to get close to it in your home, however, and this recipe helps you do just that.

INGREDIENTS:

- 2.2 LBS. (997 G) FINELY GROUND DURUM WHEAT FLOUR (SEMOLA RIMACINATA), PLUS MORE AS NEEDED
- 24.3 OZ. (689 G) WATER
- 6.3 OZ. (179 G) STIFF SOURDOUGH STARTER (SEE PAGE 40), FED TWICE WITH FINELY GROUND DURUM WHEAT FLOUR
- 1 (HEAPING) TABLESPOON (17.5 G) FINE SEA SALT

1. Place the flour and 21.1 oz. of the water in the work bowl of a stand mixer fitted with the dough hook and work the mixture until it just comes together and there are no lumps. Cover the bowl and let the dough rest for 1 hour.

2. Add the starter and remaining water and work the dough until it is smooth and elastic. Add the salt and work the dough until it has been incorporated.

3. Transfer the dough to a large bowl, cover it with plastic wrap, and let it rest for 30 minutes.

4. Stretch and fold the dough over itself a few times. Cover the dough, let it rest for 30 minutes, and stretch and fold the dough over itself a few times. Rest for another 30 minutes, repeat the stretches and folds, and place the dough back in the bowl. Cover the bowl and store the dough in the refrigerator overnight.

5. Remove the dough from the refrigerator and let it rest at room temperature for 3 hours.

6. Place the dough on a flour-dusted work surface and divide it in half.

7. Preheat the oven to 480°F and place a baking stone or steel on the middle rack of the oven as it warms.

8. Slightly flatten each piece of the dough and shape the pieces into ovals. Fold the edges of both sides of the ovals underneath the dough, roll the edges up tightly, and shape the pieces of dough into logs. Bend the logs into half-moons and score three perpendicular cuts on the curved sides of the half-moons, where the two halves meet. Squeeze a bit of the loaves from the side opposite to the cuts so that they open.

9. Use a parchment-lined peel to slide the loaves onto the heated baking implement and bake with steam, using one of the methods described on page 32.

10. Reduce the temperature to 390°F and bake for 30 minutes. Reduce the temperature to 350°F, remove the skillet, and leave the oven door open a crack. Bake until the bread is golden brown, feels lighter when lifted, and makes a hollow sound when tapped, about 15 minutes.

11. Remove the bread from the oven, place it on a wire rack, and let it cool for 2 hours before serving.

FRISELLE

YIELD: 6 LOAVES / **ACTIVE TIME:** 1 HOUR / **TOTAL TIME:** 5 HOURS

These crunchy bread "wheels" from Apulia are relatively easy to make at home and can last a few weeks if stored properly. Eaten as the base for an open-faced sandwich, they are best if slightly wet with water before proceeding to add the typical toppings of olive oil, tomatoes, oregano, and anchovies.

INGREDIENTS:

- 9 OZ. (255 G) WARM WATER (105°F)
- 3½ TEASPOONS (10.5 G) ACTIVE DRY YEAST
- 17.6 OZ. (499 G) BREAD FLOUR
- 17.6 OZ. (499 G) FINELY GROUND DURUM WHEAT FLOUR (SEMOLA RIMACINATA), PLUS MORE AS NEEDED
- 2 TEASPOONS (11 G) FINE SEA SALT

1. Place the water and yeast in the work bowl of a stand mixer fitted with the dough hook, gently stir to combine, and let the mixture sit until it starts to foam, about 10 minutes.

2. Add the remaining ingredients and work the mixture until it comes together as a smooth, elastic dough. Shape the dough into a ball, cover the work bowl with plastic wrap, and let the dough rest for 2 hours.

3. Line two baking sheets with parchment paper. Place the dough on a flour-dusted work surface, divide it into six pieces, and shape them into 14-inch-long logs.

4. Shape the logs into circles and pinch the ends of the circles to join them together. Place them on the baking sheets, cover them with kitchen towels, and let them rest for 1 hour.

5. Preheat the oven to 430°F. Place the friselle in the oven and bake them for 20 minutes.

6. Remove the friselle from the oven and let them cool.

7. Cut them in half at their equators and place them back on the baking sheets, cut side up.

8. Reduce the temperature to 340°F. Place the friselle back in the oven and bake them until they are golden brown, about 1 hour.

9. Remove the friselle from the oven, place them on wire racks, and let them cool before serving.

CUDDURA C'A CIUCIULENA

YIELD: 1 LOAF / **ACTIVE TIME:** 1 HOUR / **TOTAL TIME:** 6 HOURS

This traditional Calabrian bread is characteristic of the province of Reggio, where it is enjoyed during holidays and seen as an omen of good fortune and prosperity.

1. Line a baking sheet with parchment paper. Place the water, yeast, and sugar in the work bowl of a stand mixer fitted with the dough hook, gently stir to combine, and let the mixture sit until it starts to foam, about 10 minutes.

2. Add the flour and olive oil and work the mixture until it comes together as a smooth and elastic dough, incorporating the salt toward the end.

3. Place the dough on a flour-dusted work surface and divide it into two pieces, keeping one piece half the size of the other. Roll the pieces into logs that are the same length.

4. Place the larger piece of dough on the baking sheet and shape it into a circle. Shape the smaller piece of dough into a circle and place it on top of the larger piece of dough. Cover the dough with a kitchen towel, place it in a naturally warm spot, and let it rest for 3 hours.

5. Preheat the oven to 350°F and set it on convection mode, if available. Moisten the dough with a bit of water and sprinkle the sesame seeds over it. Using scissors, make incisions that resemble ears of wheat all over the top circle.

6. Place the bread in the oven and bake with steam, using one of the methods described on page 32. Bake until the bread is golden brown, feels lighter when lifted, and makes a hollow sound when tapped, about 30 minutes.

7. Remove the bread from the oven, place it on a wire rack, and let it cool for 2 hours before serving.

INGREDIENTS:

- 10.6 OZ. (300 G) WARM WATER (105°F), PLUS MORE AS NEEDED
- 1 PACKET (7 G) OF ACTIVE DRY YEAST
- 1 TEASPOON (4 G) SUGAR
- 21.1 OZ. (598 G) FINELY GROUND DURUM WHEAT FLOUR (SEMOLA RIMACINATA), PLUS MORE AS NEEDED
- 3½ OZ. (99 G) EXTRA-VIRGIN OLIVE OIL
- 2 TEASPOONS (12 G) FINE SEA SALT
- ⅓ CUP SESAME SEEDS, FOR TOPPING

PANE DI ALTAMURA

YIELD: 2 LOAVES / **ACTIVE TIME:** 2 HOURS / **TOTAL TIME:** 24 HOURS

Like pane di Matera, Altamura's famed bread can only be made there. Here's a recipe for those who can't wait to try it, but can't get to Italy anytime soon.

INGREDIENTS:

- 28.2 OZ. (799 G) FINELY GROUND DURUM WHEAT FLOUR (SEMOLA RIMACINATA), PLUS MORE AS NEEDED
- 7.7 OZ. (218 G) BREAD FLOUR
- 24.3 OZ. (689 G) WATER
- 6.3 OZ. (179 G) STIFF SOURDOUGH STARTER (SEE PAGE 40), FED TWICE WITH FINELY GROUND DURUM WHEAT FLOUR
- 1 (HEAPING) TABLESPOON (17.5 G) FINE SEA SALT

1. Place the flours and 21.1 oz. of the water in the work bowl of a stand mixer fitted with the dough hook and work the mixture until it just comes together and there are no lumps. Cover the bowl and let the dough rest for 1 hour.

2. Add the starter and remaining water and work the dough until it is smooth and elastic. Add the salt and work the dough until it has been incorporated.

3. Transfer the dough to a large bowl, cover it with plastic wrap, and let it rest for 30 minutes.

4. Stretch and fold the dough over itself a few times. Cover the dough, let it rest for 30 minutes, and stretch and fold the dough over itself a few times. Rest for another 30 minutes, repeat the stretches and folds, and place the dough back in the bowl. Cover the bowl and store the dough in the refrigerator overnight.

5. Remove the dough from the refrigerator and let it rest at room temperature for 30 minutes.

6. Place the dough on a flour-dusted work surface, divide it in half, and shape the pieces into rounds. Cover the rounds with a kitchen towel and let them rest for 2½ hours.

7. Preheat the oven to 480°F and place a baking stone or steel on the middle rack of the oven as it warms.

8. Using a lame or sharp knife, make two cuts in the shape of a cross on the top of each round.

9. Use a parchment-lined peel to slide the loaves onto the heated baking implement, and bake with steam, using one of the methods described on page 32.

10. Bake for 10 minutes, reduce the temperature to 390°F, and bake for 30 minutes.

11. Reduce the temperature to 350°F and open the oven door a crack. Leave it open and bake until the bread is golden brown, feels lighter when lifted, and makes a hollow sound when tapped, 15 to 20 minutes.

12. Remove the bread from the oven, place it on a wire rack, and let it cool for 2 hours before serving.

Pane di Altamura, see page 85

PANE COCCOI

YIELD: 2 LOAVES / **ACTIVE TIME:** 1 HOUR / **TOTAL TIME:** 7 HOURS

This is an ancient Sardinian bread which was traditionally prepared for special occasions like weddings and Easter but is now an everyday item. Coccoi is generally made with a piece of dough saved from a previous bake, which we replace with stiff sourdough starter here.

INGREDIENTS:

- 1 CUP (227 G) WATER
- 2 TEASPOONS (12 G) FINE SEA SALT
- 17.6 OZ. (499 G) FINELY GROUND DURUM WHEAT FLOUR (SEMOLA RIMACINATA), PLUS MORE AS NEEDED
- 3½ OZ. (99 G) STIFF SOURDOUGH STARTER (SEE PAGE 40), FED 8 TO 12 HOURS EARLIER WITH FINELY GROUND DURUM WHEAT FLOUR

1. Place the water and salt in the work bowl of a stand mixer fitted with the dough hook and stir to combine.

2. Add the flour and work the mixture until it just comes together as a dough. Add the starter and work the dough until it is smooth and elastic. Shape the dough into a ball, place it in a clean bowl, and cover the bowl with plastic wrap. Let the dough rest for 1 hour.

3. Place the dough on a flour-dusted work surface, divide it in half, and shape the pieces into logs.

4. Flatten the logs, dust them with flour, and use your hands to create a depression in the center of each log. The depressions should run the entire length of the logs.

5. Fold each log over itself, like a long pocket, and make incisions along the edges.

6. You can shape the log into a crown or just curve it a bit, making the cuts open up slightly.

7. Line two baking sheets with parchment paper, place the loaves on them, cover them with kitchen towels, and let them rest until they have doubled in size, about 1½ hours.

8. Preheat the oven to 450°F. If the cuts became less visible during the rise, redo them.

9. Place the loaves in the oven and bake until they are golden brown, feel lighter when lifted, and make a hollow sound when tapped, about 35 minutes.

10. Remove the loaves from the oven, place them on a wire rack, and let them cool for 2 hours before serving.

TORTA DI PASQUA

YIELD: 1 TORTA / **ACTIVE TIME:** 30 MINUTES / **TOTAL TIME:** 4 HOURS AND 30 MINUTES

The most beloved Easter treat in Central Italy is not a cake but this savory bread. Torta di Pasqua has a long tradition behind it, dating to the Middle Ages, when it was supposedly created by the nuns in the Ancona monastery known as Santa Maria Maddalena di Serra de' Conti. Here is a simplified version, though it still requires a cake pan that is substantially deeper than normal.

INGREDIENTS:

- ⅓ CUP (76 G) LUKEWARM WHOLE MILK (90°F)
- 1 PACKET (7 G) OF ACTIVE DRY YEAST
- 5 EGGS
- ½ CUP (100 G) EXTRA-VIRGIN OLIVE OIL, PLUS MORE AS NEEDED
- 2 CUPS (200 G) GRATED PARMESAN CHEESE
- ½ CUP (50 G) GRATED PECORINO CHEESE
- 17.6 OZ. (499 G) BREAD FLOUR
- 1½ TEASPOONS (8.2 G) FINE SEA SALT
- BLACK PEPPER, TO TASTE
- 3½ OZ. EMMENTAL CHEESE, CUBED

1. Place the milk and yeast in a bowl, gently stir to combine, and let the mixture sit until it starts to foam, about 10 minutes.

2. Place the eggs, oil, Parmesan, pecorino, and yeast mixture in the work bowl of a stand mixer fitted with the dough hook. Work the mixture until it comes together as a dough.

3. Add the flour, salt, and a generous pinch of black pepper and knead the dough until it is smooth and elastic.

4. Coat a deep, round 9-inch cake pan with olive oil, place the dough in it, and distribute the Emmental over it, pushing the cubes deep into the dough. Cover the pan with plastic wrap and let the dough rise until it has reached the edge of the pan, 2 to 3 hours.

5. Preheat the oven to 350°F.

6. Place the bread in the oven and bake until it is just dark brown, about 1 hour. If the bread is darkening too much, cover it with aluminum foil toward the end of baking. Remove the bread from the oven and let it cool completely before removing it from the pan, slicing, and serving.

PANE TOSCANO

YIELD: 1 LOAF / **ACTIVE TIME:** 1 HOUR / **TOTAL TIME:** 30 HOURS

Pane Toscano is also called pane sciapo or pane sciocco, which both refer to the peculiar absence of salt. One popular story for this unique characteristic is tied to the rivalry between Pisa and Florence, and to the Pisan block of the salt supply, which caused Florentines to learn to make bread without salt, rather than stomach the shame of surrender. Another tale holds that Florentines simply did not want to pay the tax on salt. Either way, pane Toscano has become central to Tuscan cuisine and is the absolute king of many iconic recipes, from ribollita and panzanella alla Toscana to cacciucco.

INGREDIENTS:

FOR THE BIGA

- ⅓ CUP (76 G) LUKEWARM WATER (90°F)
- ⅓ TEASPOON (1 G) ACTIVE DRY YEAST
- 1 CUP (120 G) BREAD FLOUR

FOR THE DOUGH

- 8½ OZ. (241 G) WATER
- ½ TEASPOON (1.5 G) ACTIVE DRY YEAST
- 14 OZ. (397 G) BREAD FLOUR, PLUS MORE AS NEEDED

1. To prepare the biga, place the water and yeast in a bowl, gently stir to combine, and let the mixture sit until it starts to foam, about 10 minutes. Add the flour and stir until it has been incorporated. Cover the bowl and let the biga chill in the refrigerator for 1 day.
2. To begin preparations for the dough, warm one-third of the water to 90°F. Add the yeast, gently stir to combine, and let the mixture sit until it starts to foam, about 10 minutes.
3. Place the flour, yeast mixture, and remaining water in the work bowl of a stand mixer fitted with the dough hook and work the mixture until combined.
4. Add the biga and work the mixture until it comes together as a smooth, elastic dough.
5. Shape the dough into a round and place it in a large, clean bowl. Cover the bowl with plastic wrap and let the dough rest until it has almost doubled in size, about 3 hours.
6. Place the dough on a flour-dusted work surface and flatten it into a rectangle. Working from the short sides, fold the dough over itself like a letter and shape it into a log.
7. Place the dough on a flour-dusted kitchen towel, fold the towel over the loaf, and let it rest, seam side up, for 2 hours. Preheat the oven to 480°F and place a baking stone or steel on the middle rack of the oven as it warms.
8. Invert the dough onto a parchment-lined peel and make two diagonal cuts in it with a razor. Slide the bread onto the heated baking implement and bake with steam, using one of the methods described on page 32.
9. Bake for 15 minutes, reduce the temperature to 420°F, and bake until a pale crust has formed and the bread feels lighter, 20 to 25 minutes. Keep in mind that this bread won't take on much color because there is no salt.
10. Remove the bread from the oven, place it on a wire rack, and let it cool completely before slicing and serving.

PANE DI GENZANO

YIELD: 2 LOAVES / **ACTIVE TIME:** 1 HOUR / **TOTAL TIME:** 32 HOURS

This is one of the most celebrated Italian breads, and its true recipe is a trade secret of the bakers from Genzano, a beautiful town in the hills overlooking Rome. Here's a cheat version to try at home.

INGREDIENTS:

FOR THE BIGA

2.6 OZ. (74 G) SOURDOUGH STARTER (SEE PAGE 40)

2.6 OZ. (74 G) WATER

5.3 OZ. (150 G) BREAD FLOUR

FOR THE DOUGH

31 OZ. (879 G) BREAD FLOUR, PLUS MORE AS NEEDED

22.9 OZ. (649 G) WATER

1 TABLESPOON (17 G) FINE SEA SALT

WHEAT BRAN, AS NEEDED

1. To prepare the biga, place all of the ingredients in a bowl and stir until combined. Cover the bowl and let the biga chill in the refrigerator for 1 day.

2. To begin preparations for the dough, place the flour and four-fifths of the water in the work bowl of a stand mixer fitted with the dough hook and work the mixture until combined. Let the mixture rest for 1 hour.

3. Add the biga and work the mixture until it has been incorporated. Add the salt and remaining water and work the mixture until it comes together as a smooth, elastic dough.

4. Shape the dough into a round and place it in a large, clean bowl. Cover the bowl with plastic wrap and let the dough rise until it has almost doubled in size, about 4 hours.

5. Place the dough on a flour-dusted work surface and divide it in half. Flatten the pieces into rectangles. Working from the short sides, fold the rectangles over themselves like a letter and shape them into loaves.

6. Dust two kitchen towels with wheat bran. Place the loaves on the towels, fold the towels over them, and let them rest, seam side down, for 2 to 3 hours.

7. Preheat the oven to the maximum temperature and place a place a baking stone or steel on the middle rack of the oven as it warms.

8. Invert the loaves onto a parchment-lined peel. Slide them onto the heated baking implement and bake with steam, using one of the methods described on page 32.

9. Bake for 15 minutes, reduce the temperature to 420°F, and bake until the bread has a dark crust, feels lighter when lifted, and makes a hollow sound when tapped, 30 to 35 minutes.

10. Remove the loaves from the oven, place them on a wire rack, and let them cool completely before slicing and serving.

PANE DI LARIANO

YIELD: 2 LOAVES / **ACTIVE TIME:** 1 HOUR / **TOTAL TIME:** 32 HOURS

Pane di Lariano is similar to Pane di Genzano, but made with a finely ground and partly sifted whole wheat flour known as tipo 2. The recipe below is an adaptation with regular flours and is of course not the real thing, which only the bakers from Lariano know how to make.

INGREDIENTS:

FOR THE BIGA

- 2.6 OZ. (74 G) SOURDOUGH STARTER (SEE PAGE 40)
- 2.6 OZ. (74 G) WATER
- 5.3 OZ. (150 G) BREAD FLOUR

FOR THE DOUGH

- 23.2 OZ. (658 G) BREAD FLOUR, PLUS MORE AS NEEDED
- 8.1 OZ. (230 G) FINELY GROUND WHOLE WHEAT FLOUR
- 22.9 OZ. (649 G) WATER
- 1 TABLESPOON (17 G) FINE SEA SALT
- WHEAT BRAN, AS NEEDED

1. To prepare the biga, place all of the ingredients in a bowl and stir until combined. Cover the bowl and let the biga chill in the refrigerator for 1 day.

2. To begin preparations for the dough, place the flours and four-fifths of the water in the work bowl of a stand mixer fitted with the dough hook and work the mixture until combined. Let the mixture rest for 1 hour.

3. Add the biga and work the mixture until it has been incorporated. Add the salt and remaining water and work the mixture until it comes together as a smooth, elastic dough.

4. Shape the dough into a round and place it in a large, clean bowl. Cover the bowl with plastic wrap and let the dough rest until it has almost doubled in size, about 4 hours.

5. Place the dough on a flour-dusted work surface and divide it in half. Flatten the pieces into rectangles. Working from the short sides, fold the rectangles over themselves like a letter and shape them into logs.

6. Dust two kitchen towels with wheat bran. Place the loaves on the towels, fold the towels over the loaves, and let them rest, seam side down, for 2 to 3 hours.

7. Preheat the oven to 480°F and place a baking stone or steel on the middle rack of the oven as it warms.

8. Invert the loaves onto a parchment-lined peel. Slide them onto the heated baking implement and bake with steam, using one of the methods described on page 32.

9. Bake for 15 minutes, reduce the temperature to 420°F, and bake until the bread has a dark crust, feels lighter when lifted, and makes a hollow sound when tapped, 30 to 35 minutes.

10. Remove the loaves from the oven, place them on a wire rack, and let them cool completely before slicing and serving.

PANE BIOVE

YIELD: 2 LOAVES / **ACTIVE TIME:** 40 MINUTES / **TOTAL TIME:** 2 HOURS AND 30 MINUTES

While the most popular bread in Lombardy is michette, a roll with a hollow inside that is almost impossible to get right at home, in Piedmont the daily bread is la biova, or pane biove, which is a rather simple bread that can easily be produced by home bakers.

INGREDIENTS:

- 9.9 OZ. (281 G) LUKEWARM WATER (90°F)
- 1 PACKET (7 G) OF ACTIVE DRY YEAST
- 17.6 OZ. (499 G) BREAD FLOUR
- 1 TABLESPOON (7 G) BARLEY MALT
- 1½ TEASPOONS (8.2 G) FINE SEA SALT
- 1 OZ. (28 G) LARD, PLUS MORE AS NEEDED
- SEMOLINA FLOUR, AS NEEDED

1. Line a baking sheet with parchment paper. Place the water and yeast in the work bowl of a stand mixer fitted with the dough hook, gently stir to combine, and let the mixture sit until it starts to foam, about 10 minutes.

2. Add the flour and work the mixture on low until incorporated. Add the malt, salt, and lard and work the mixture until it comes together as a firm dough.

3. Raise the speed to high and work the dough until it is smooth and elastic, about 10 minutes. Shape the dough into a ball and place it on the baking sheet. Cover it with a kitchen towel and let it rest for 30 minutes.

4. Place the dough on a semolina-dusted work surface, divide it in half, and shape each piece into a round. Stretch each round into a log.

5. Use a rolling pin to flatten each log into a 2⅓-inch-thick rectangle. Starting from a long side, roll each rectangle up tightly.

6. Roll each piece of dough into a long, 2-inch-wide strip. Roll each strip up and place the dough, seam side down, on the work surface. Cover the dough with kitchen towels and use some object to prevent the dough from expanding horizontally. Let the dough rest for 30 minutes.

7. Preheat the oven to 390°F and line a baking sheet with parchment paper. Place the loaves on the baking sheet and make a deep cut in each one.

8. Place the loaves in the oven and bake until they are golden brown, feel lighter when lifted, and make a hollow sound when tapped, about 30 minutes.

9. Remove the bread from the oven, place it on a wire rack, and let it cool completely before slicing and serving.

PANE PUGLIESE

YIELD: 1 LOAF / **ACTIVE TIME:** 30 MINUTES / **TOTAL TIME:** 6 HOURS

In Apulia, bread made with durum wheat is synonymous with big, rustic, and crusty loaves. The most famous one is pane di Altamura (see page 85), which is a cherished local food. Here is a version of one such bread for the home baker, based around sourdough.

INGREDIENTS:

- ⅔ CUP (100 G) SOURDOUGH STARTER (SEE PAGE 40)
- 1⅔ CUPS (317 G) WATER
- 2½ CUPS (400 G) FINE SEMOLINA FLOUR (SEMOLA RIMACINATA), PLUS MORE AS NEEDED
- ¾ CUP PLUS 1 (SCANT) TABLESPOON (100 G) BREAD FLOUR
- 2 TEASPOONS (12 G) FINE SEA SALT

1. In the work bowl of a stand mixer fitted with the dough hook, combine the starter and water. Add the flours and work the mixture on low for 8 minutes.

2. Add the salt and work the dough until it is incorporated. Knead at low speed for 5 minutes, raise the speed to medium, and work the dough until it is smooth, 2 to 3 minutes.

3. Place the dough in a clean bowl, cover it with plastic wrap, and let it rest until it has increased to 1½ times its original size, 2 to 2½ hours. Make a series of folds during the first 1½ hours.

4. Place the dough on a flour-dusted work surface and shape it into a tight round. Place the shaped round, seam side up, in a banneton or a bowl lined with a floured kitchen towel. Cover it with a kitchen towel and let the dough rest at room temperature for 1½ to 2 hours.

5. Preheat the oven to 480°F and place a baking stone or steel on the middle rack of the oven as it warms.

6. Invert the dough onto a parchment-lined peel or flat baking sheet and score a cross on the top. Slide it onto the heated baking implement and bake for 10 minutes, then gradually reduce the temperature to 360°F and bake until the bread is golden brown, feels lighter when lifted, and makes a hollow sound when tapped, 30 to 40 minutes.

7. Remove the bread from the oven, place it on a wire rack, and let it cool completely before slicing and serving.

MAROCCA DI CASOLA

YIELD: 2 LOAVES / **ACTIVE TIME:** 30 MINUTES / **TOTAL TIME:** 20 HOURS

This is an ancient bread from Casola in Lunigiana, a town in Northern Italy. It is made almost entirely of chestnut flour, which is what was locally available in the past, when wheat flour was too expensive. It makes a very interesting bread with unique aromas.

INGREDIENTS:

- 1 MEDIUM POTATO, PEELED AND CHOPPED
- ⅔ CUP (100 G) STIFF SOURDOUGH STARTER (SEE PAGE 40)
- 3¾ CUPS (337 G) CHESTNUT FLOUR, PLUS MORE AS NEEDED
- 1 CUP (120 G) ALL-PURPOSE FLOUR, PLUS MORE AS NEEDED
- 1 CUP (227 G) WATER
- 1 TEASPOON (6 G) FINE SEA SALT
- 1½ TABLESPOONS (20 G) EXTRA-VIRGIN OLIVE OIL

1. Place the potato in a saucepan, cover it with water, and bring it to a boil. Cook until the potato is fork-tender, about 15 minutes. Drain and let the potato cool completely.

2. In the work bowl of a stand mixer fitted with the dough hook, combine the starter, flours, and water and work the mixture on low until it comes together as a dough.

3. Shape the dough into a round, place it in a clean mixing bowl, and cover it with plastic wrap. Let the dough rest at room temperature for 2 to 3 hours.

4. Knead the salt, oil, and potato into the dough. Divide the dough into two rounds and place them in small bannetons that have been dusted with a combination of chestnut flour and all-purpose flour. Let the rounds rest at room temperature for 3 to 4 hours, until they look proofed: they will not rise much, but cracks on the surface indicate that the loaves are proofed.

5. Preheat the oven to 390°F.

6. Invert the rounds onto a parchment-lined baking sheet and score each one with a slash in the center. Place the loaves in the oven and bake until they are golden brown, feel lighter when lifted, and make a hollow sound when tapped, 35 to 40 minutes.

7. Remove the loaves from the oven, place them on a wire rack, and let them cool completely before slicing and serving.

PANE SICILIANO

YIELD: 2 LOAVES / **ACTIVE TIME:** 30 MINUTES / **TOTAL TIME:** 3 HOURS AND 50 MINUTES

Sicilian bread comes in many shapes, but it is easily recognizable because of its typical topping of sesame seeds and its soft, compact crumb. Traditionally this bread is made with old dough from a previous bake, but it can also be made with yeast (or sourdough).

INGREDIENTS:

- 1⅓ CUPS (302 G) WATER
- 1 PACKET (7 G) OF ACTIVE DRY YEAST
- 1 TEASPOON (5 G) HONEY
- 2½ CUPS (400 G) FINE SEMOLINA FLOUR (SEMOLA RIMACINATA), PLUS MORE AS NEEDED
- 1¼ CUPS (150 G) BREAD FLOUR
- 2 TEASPOONS (9 G) EXTRA-VIRGIN OLIVE OIL
- 2 TEASPOONS (12 G) FINE SEA SALT
- SESAME SEEDS, FOR TOPPING

1. Warm 3½ tablespoons of the water until it is about 105°F. Add the yeast and water to the work bowl of a stand mixer fitted with the dough hook and gently stir to combine. Let the mixture sit until it starts to foam, about 10 minutes.

2. Add the honey, flours, olive oil, and remaining water and work the mixture on low until it comes together as a dough. Add the salt and work the dough until it is incorporated. Knead at low speed for 5 minutes, raise the speed to medium, and work the dough until it is smooth, 2 to 3 minutes.

3. Shape the dough into a ball and place it in a clean mixing bowl. Cover the bowl with plastic wrap and let the dough rest until it has doubled in size, about 1½ hours.

4. Sprinkle the sesame seeds over a baking sheet and set them aside.

5. Place the dough on a flour-dusted work surface and divide it in half. Flatten each piece and then shape them into rectangles. Flatten each piece once again, fold the top side down, and fold the bottom side up. Pull both sides together and press down on the seam to seal. Place the loaves on the baking sheet with the sesame seeds, seam side up. Cover the loaves with a floured kitchen towel and let them rest at room temperature for 1 hour.

6. Preheat the oven to 430°F and place a baking stone or steel on the middle rack of the oven as it warms.

7. Invert the loaves onto a parchment-lined peel and score each one, making one shallow lengthwise cut and two shallow crosswise cuts. Slide the loaves onto the heated baking implement and bake for 15 minutes.

8. Reduce the temperature to 375°F and bake until the loaves are golden brown, feel lighter when lifted, and make a hollow sound when tapped, 25 to 30 minutes.

9. Remove the loaves from the oven, place them on a wire rack, and let them cool completely before slicing and serving.

PANE CAFONE

YIELD: 2 LOAVES / **ACTIVE TIME:** 30 MINUTES / **TOTAL TIME:** 8 HOURS

This is a traditional bread from Campania, the region surrounding Naples. In Neapolitan, the term ca' fun means "peasants," as this bread was brought to bustling Naples by people who emigrated from the countryside.

INGREDIENTS:

- ⅔ CUP (100 G) STIFF SOURDOUGH STARTER (SEE PAGE 40)
- 1 TEASPOON (5 G) HONEY
- 1⅘ CUPS (440 G) WATER
- 5 CUPS (600 G) BREAD FLOUR, PLUS MORE AS NEEDED
- 2½ TEASPOONS (15 G) FINE SEA SALT
- SEMOLINA FLOUR, AS NEEDED

1. In the work bowl of a stand mixer fitted with the dough hook, combine the starter, honey, and water. Add the bread flour and work the mixture on low until it just comes together. Add the salt and work the dough until it is incorporated. Knead at low speed for 3 minutes, raise the speed to medium, and work the dough until it is smooth, 2 to 3 minutes.

2. Cover the work bowl with plastic wrap and let the dough rest at room temperature until it has doubled in size, about 4 hours.

3. Place the dough on a flour-dusted work surface and divide it in half. Flatten each piece and then shape them into rectangles. Flatten the dough once again, fold the top side down, and fold the bottom side up. Pull both sides together and press down on the seam to seal the pieces of dough. Place the loaves on a generously flour-dusted baking sheet, seam side up. Cover the loaves with a floured kitchen towel and let them rest at room temperature for 3 hours, until they can be poked with a finger without bouncing back, as it is OK to slightly overproof this type of bread.

4. Preheat the oven to the maximum temperature and place a baking stone or steel on the middle rack of the oven as it warms.

5. Invert the loaves onto a semolina-dusted peel and score them on the sides. Slide them onto the heated baking implement.

6. Reduce the temperature to 480°F and bake for 20 minutes, then reduce the temperature to 430°F and bake until the bread is golden brown, feels lighter when lifted, and makes a hollow sound when tapped, 20 to 30 minutes.

7. Remove the loaves from the oven, place them on a wire rack, and let them cool completely before slicing and serving.

COPPIA FERRARESE

YIELD: 3 LOAVES / **ACTIVE TIME:** 50 MINUTES / **TOTAL TIME:** 5 HOURS

In Northern Italy, bread doughs are drier compared to those from Central and Southern Italy. Coppia Ferrarese, from the city of Ferrara, is a classic example of this tendency. Its special shape and the addition of olive oil make the bread crunchy on the outside and at the ends, and soft at the junction of the two arms.

INGREDIENTS:

- 6.2 OZ. (176 G) WATER
- ⅔ PACKET (4.5 G) OF ACTIVE DRY YEAST
- 17½ OZ. (496 G) ALL-PURPOSE FLOUR, PLUS MORE AS NEEDED
- 1¾ OZ. (50 G) EXTRA-VIRGIN OLIVE OIL
- 2 TEASPOONS (12 G) FINE SEA SALT

1. Place the water and yeast in the work bowl of a stand mixer fitted with the dough hook, gently stir to combine, and let the mixture sit until it starts to foam, about 10 minutes.

2. Add the flour and work the mixture on low until incorporated. Add the olive oil and work the mixture, gradually increasing the speed with the intent to reach medium speed after 10 to 15 minutes.

3. Add the salt and work the dough until it is smooth and elastic, about 5 minutes. Shape the dough into a ball and place it in a mixing bowl. Cover it with plastic wrap and let the dough rest until it has doubled in size, 2 to 2½ hours.

4. Preheat the oven to 430°F and line a baking sheet with parchment paper.

5. Remove a small piece from the dough (smaller than a golf ball), cover it, and set aside. Shape the remaining dough into a ball, place it on a flour-dusted work surface, and roll it out into a large, ⅛-inch-thick disk. Using a pizza cutter or another sharp implement, cut the disk into six triangles.

6. Roll each triangle up into a log, starting from the base. Take two rolled-up logs and place them next to each other, lengthwise, on the baking sheet. Use a small piece of the dough you put aside to join the rolled-up logs at their centers, leaving most of each log uncovered. Turn the free ends of each log so that they form an arch facing away from the center. Repeat with the remaining rolled-up logs.

7. Cover the coppia with a kitchen towel and let them rest for 20 minutes.

8. Place the coppia in the oven and bake until they are golden brown, about 20 minutes.

9. Remove the coppia from the oven, transfer them to wire racks, and let them cool completely before enjoying.

PARROZZO MOLISANO

YIELD: 1 LOAF / **ACTIVE TIME:** 1 HOUR / **TOTAL TIME:** 10 HOURS

In Molise, a region traditionally poor of resources, corn from the Americas became a staple. This local bread called parrozzo (from pane rozzo, "coarse bread") is an example of using both corn and potatoes to replace a portion of the wheat flour in a bread, and the result is a loaf with a very interesting consistency and flavor.

INGREDIENTS:

- 5.3 OZ. (150 G) BREAD FLOUR, PLUS MORE AS NEEDED
- 3½ OZ. (99 G) WHOLE WHEAT FLOUR
- 11.6 OZ. (329 G) WATER
- 5.3 OZ. (150 G) STIFF SOURDOUGH STARTER (SEE PAGE 40)
- 5.3 OZ. (150 G) POLENTA, COOKED AND COOLED
- 5.3 OZ. (150 G) MASHED POTATOES, COOLED
- 1½ TEASPOONS (9 G) FINE SEA SALT
- SEMOLINA FLOUR, AS NEEDED

1. Place the bread flour, whole wheat flour, and two-thirds of the water in the work bowl of a stand mixer fitted with the dough hook and work the mixture on low. Gradually add the starter and work the mixture until it comes together as a shaggy dough.

2. Add the polenta and potatoes and continue to work the dough until it is smooth.

3. Gradually add the salt and remaining water and work the dough until they have been incorporated. Shape the dough into a ball, place it in a clean bowl, and cover it with plastic wrap. Let the dough rest at room temperature for 30 minutes, fold it, and let it rest for another 30 minutes. Fold the dough again and let it rest for another hour.

4. Place the dough on a flour-dusted work surface and fold it over itself. Cover the dough with a kitchen towel and let it rest for 30 minutes.

5. Spread the dough into a rectangle with your hands. Fold a long side toward the center of the dough and then fold the other long side over it.

6. Place the dough, seam side down, on a semolina-dusted kitchen towel that is large enough to also cover the top of the dough. Let it rest for 4 hours.

7. Preheat the oven to the maximum temperature and place a baking stone or steel on the middle rack of the oven as it warms.

8. Place the dough on a semolina-dusted peel and slide it onto the heated baking implement. Bake for 15 minutes and reduce the temperature to 390°F. Bake until the bread is dark brown, feels lighter when lifted, and makes a hollow sound when tapped, about 30 minutes.

9. Remove the bread from the oven, place it on a wire rack, and let it cool for 2 hours before serving.

PAIN DE PROVENCE

YIELD: 2 LOAVES / **ACTIVE TIME:** 30 MINUTES / **TOTAL TIME:** 4 HOURS AND 30 MINUTES

This is a simple, rustic white bread typical of Provence, France, flavored with the mixture of herbs the beautiful region is famed for.

INGREDIENTS:

1½ CUPS (360 G) WATER

2½ TEASPOONS (7 G) ACTIVE DRY YEAST

1 TABLESPOON PLUS 2 TEASPOONS (20 G) SUGAR

4⅙ CUPS (500 G) ALL-PURPOSE FLOUR, PLUS MORE AS NEEDED

3 TABLESPOONS (10 G) HERBES DE PROVENCE

2 TABLESPOONS (26 G) EXTRA-VIRGIN OLIVE OIL

2 TEASPOONS (12 G) FINE SEA SALT

SEMOLINA FLOUR, AS NEEDED

1. Warm 3½ tablespoons of the water until it is about 105°F. Add the yeast, sugar, and water to the work bowl of a stand mixer fitted with the dough hook and gently stir to combine. Let the mixture sit until it starts to foam, about 10 minutes.

2. In a separate bowl, combine the all-purpose flour and herbes de Provence.

3. Add the flour mixture to the yeast mixture and work the dough on low for 10 minutes.

4. Add the olive oil and salt and work the dough on low until it is smooth, about 10 minutes.

5. Cover the work bowl with plastic wrap and let the dough rest at room temperature until it has doubled in size, about 2 hours.

6. Press down on the dough to deflate it and divide it in half. Shape each piece of dough into a round and transfer them to flour-dusted bannetons. Cover the loaves with floured kitchen towels and let them rest until they have increased to 1½ times their original size, about 1½ hours.

7. Preheat the oven to 480°F and place a baking stone or steel on the middle rack of the oven as it warms.

8. Invert the rounds onto a semolina-dusted peel and score them. Place them on the heated baking implement and bake with steam, using one of the methods described on page 32.

9. Reduce the temperature to 430°F and bake for 20 minutes.

10. Open the oven door to remove the steam, reduce the temperature to 390°F, and bake until the bread is golden brown, feels lighter when lifted, and makes a hollow sound when tapped, 25 to 30 minutes.

11. Remove the loaves from the oven, place them on a wire rack, and let them cool completely before slicing and serving.

PAIN DE CAMPAGNE

YIELD: 2 LOAVES / **ACTIVE TIME:** 30 MINUTES / **TOTAL TIME:** 5 HOURS AND 30 MINUTES

This is the traditional French country bread that many modern bakers have taken inspiration from. There is no definitive recipe for it, as it comes in infinite variations. What is quite constant is the use of natural fermentation and using whole wheat or rye flour as part of the cereal component.

INGREDIENTS:

- ⅔ CUP (150 G) SOURDOUGH STARTER (SEE PAGE 40)
- 1½ CUPS (340 G) WATER
- 1⅔ CUPS (200 G) BREAD FLOUR
- 1⅔ CUPS (200 G) ALL-PURPOSE FLOUR, PLUS MORE AS NEEDED
- 1 CUP (100 G) RYE FLOUR
- 2 TEASPOONS (12 G) FINE SEA SALT
- SEMOLINA FLOUR, AS NEEDED

1. In the work bowl of a stand mixer fitted with the dough hook, combine the starter and water. Add all of the flours, except for the semolina, and work the mixture on low until it just comes together. Let the dough rest for 40 minutes.

2. Add the salt and work the dough until it is incorporated. Knead at low speed for 5 minutes, raise the speed to medium, and work the dough until it is smooth and elastic, about 5 minutes. Cover the work bowl with plastic wrap and let the dough rest at room temperature for 2 hours.

3. Place the dough on a semolina-dusted work surface, divide it in half, and shape it into two rounds. Place the shaped rounds in bannetons lined with floured kitchen towels and let them rest at room temperature for 2 to 3 hours.

4. Preheat the oven to the maximum temperature and place a baking stone or steel on the middle rack of the oven as it warms.

5. Invert the rounds onto a semolina-dusted peel and score each one with four intersecting cuts. Slide them onto the heated baking implement and bake with steam, using one of the methods described on page 32.

6. Reduce the temperature to 480°F and bake for 25 minutes.

7. Open the oven door to release the steam, reduce the temperature to 440°F, and bake until the loaves are golden brown, feel lighter when lifted, and make a hollow sound when tapped, 20 to 30 minutes.

8. Remove the loaves from the oven, place them on a wire rack, and let them cool completely before slicing and serving.

PAIN DE MIE

YIELD: 1 LOAF / **ACTIVE TIME:** 50 MINUTES / **TOTAL TIME:** 4 HOURS

This bread traditionally requires a special tin with a lid, which gives it a more regular shape and crumb, but it can also be baked in a regular loaf pan.

INGREDIENTS:

- ½ CUP (100 G) WATER, PLUS MORE AS NEEDED
- 2½ TEASPOONS (7 G) ACTIVE DRY YEAST
- 1 TABLESPOON PLUS 1 TEASPOON (20 G) SUGAR
- 1 CUP (200 G) WARM MILK (105°F), PLUS MORE AS NEEDED
- 4⅙ CUPS (500 G) ALL-PURPOSE FLOUR, PLUS MORE AS NEEDED
- 4 TABLESPOONS (57 G) UNSALTED BUTTER
- 1½ TEASPOONS (9 G) FINE SEA SALT

1. Warm 3½ tablespoons of the water until it is about 105°F. Add the yeast, sugar, and water to the work bowl of a stand mixer fitted with the dough hook and gently stir to combine. Let the mixture sit until it starts to foam, about 10 minutes.

2. Add the milk, flour, and remaining water and work the mixture on low until it comes together as a dough. Add the butter and salt and work the dough until it is incorporated. Knead at low speed for 7 minutes, raise the speed to medium, and work the dough until it is smooth and elastic, 2 to 3 minutes.

3. Shape the dough into a ball and place it in a clean mixing bowl. Place the bowl in a naturally warm spot, cover it with plastic wrap, and let the dough rest until it has doubled in size, about 1½ hours.

4. Preheat the oven to 430°F. Coat a 2 lb. loaf pan with nonstick cooking spray.

5. Press down to deflate the dough, shape it into a log, and place it in the pan. Cover it with plastic wrap and let it rest until it fills three-quarters of the pan.

6. Brush the dough with milk and water and place it in the oven. Reduce the temperature to 360°F and bake until the bread is golden brown and feels lighter when lifted, 40 to 45 minutes.

7. Remove the bread from the oven and let it cool in the pan for 10 minutes. Invert the loaf onto a wire rack and let it cool completely before slicing and serving.

EASY WHITE LOAF

YIELD: 1 LOAF / **ACTIVE TIME:** 15 MINUTES / **TOTAL TIME:** 2 HOURS AND 40 MINUTES

This is one of the easiest white loaves one could possibly make. It contains only yeast, water, flour, and salt. Thanks to a rather fast process, this crunchy, rustic-looking, delicious loaf of bread can be on your table in less than three hours.

INGREDIENTS:

- 1 CUP PLUS 1½ TABLESPOONS (249 G) WATER
- 1 PACKET (7 G) OF ACTIVE DRY YEAST
- 3¼ CUPS (390 G) BREAD FLOUR, PLUS MORE AS NEEDED
- 1½ TEASPOONS (9 G) FINE SEA SALT

1. Warm 3½ tablespoons of the water until it is about 105°F. Add the yeast and water to the work bowl of a stand mixer fitted with the dough hook and gently stir to combine. Let the mixture sit until it starts to foam, about 10 minutes.

2. Add the flour and remaining water and work the mixture on low until it comes together as a dough. Add the salt and work the dough until it is incorporated. Knead at low speed for 5 minutes, raise the speed to medium, and work the dough until it is smooth, 2 to 3 minutes.

3. Shape the dough into a ball, place it in a clean mixing bowl, and cover it with plastic wrap. Let the dough rest for 1 hour.

4. Place the dough on a flour-dusted work surface and shape it into a round.

5. Place the shaped round in a bowl lined with a floured kitchen towel, cover the bowl with plastic wrap or a kitchen towel, and let it rest until it has doubled in size, about 1 hour.

6. Preheat the oven to 520°F and place a baking stone or steel on the middle rack of the oven as it warms.

7. Invert the loaf onto a parchment-lined peel. Score the loaf with a sharp knife or scissors, slide it onto the heated baking implement, and bake with steam, using one of the methods described on page 32.

8. Reduce the temperature to 460°F and bake for 10 minutes, then reduce the temperature to 430°F and bake until the bread is golden brown, feels lighter when lifted, and makes a hollow sound when tapped, 15 to 20 minutes.

9. Remove the bread from the oven, place it on a wire rack, and let it cool completely before slicing and serving.

WHITE SANDWICH LOAF

YIELD: 1 LOAF / **ACTIVE TIME:** 20 MINUTES / **TOTAL TIME:** 3 HOURS AND 25 MINUTES

What a luxury to be able to make your own soft and fluffy sandwich bread. This delicious loaf will take toast to a whole new level, effortlessly.

INGREDIENTS:

- ¾ CUP PLUS 1½ TABLESPOONS (192 G) WATER
- 1 PACKET (7 G) OF ACTIVE DRY YEAST
- 3¼ CUPS (390 G) BREAD FLOUR, PLUS MORE AS NEEDED
- ⅓ CUP (76 G) MILK
- 1½ TABLESPOONS (18 G) SUGAR
- 1½ TEASPOONS (9 G) FINE SEA SALT
- 1.8 OZ. (50 G) UNSALTED BUTTER, SOFTENED

1. Warm 3½ tablespoons of the water until it is about 105°F. Add the yeast and water to the work bowl of a stand mixer fitted with the dough hook and gently stir to combine. Let the mixture sit until it starts to foam, about 10 minutes.

2. Add the flour, milk, sugar, and remaining water and work the mixture on low until it comes together as a dough. Add the salt and butter and work the dough until they are incorporated. Knead at low speed for 5 minutes, raise the speed to medium, and work the dough until it is smooth, 2 to 3 minutes.

3. Shape the dough into a ball, place it in a clean mixing bowl, and cover it with plastic wrap. Let it rest until it has doubled in size, 1½ to 2 hours.

4. Coat a 2 lb. loaf pan with nonstick cooking spray. Place the dough on a flour-dusted work surface and gently roll it out into a rectangle, making sure that the shorter side of the rectangle fits the length of the loaf pan. Roll up the dough from a short side and place it in the prepared loaf pan, seam side down.

5. Cover the dough with plastic wrap or a kitchen towel and let it rest until it has doubled in size, about 1 hour.

6. Position a rack in the lowest part of the oven and preheat the oven to 390°F.

7. Place the loaf pan directly on the lower rack. Reduce the temperature to 360°F and bake until the bread is golden brown, 35 to 40 minutes, reducing the temperature further if the top starts browning too quickly.

8. Remove the bread from the oven, place it on a wire rack, and let it cool completely before slicing and serving.

EASY OVERNIGHT LOAF

YIELD: 1 LOAF / **ACTIVE TIME:** 15 MINUTES / **TOTAL TIME:** 24 HOURS

This is a perfect weekend loaf. Started the previous evening, it is ready to be baked first thing in the morning, as you sip that first cup of coffee.

1. Warm 3½ tablespoons of the water until it is about 105°F. Add the yeast and water to the work bowl of a stand mixer fitted with the dough hook and gently stir to combine. Let the mixture sit until it starts to foam, about 10 minutes.

2. Add the flour and remaining water and work the mixture on low until it comes together as a dough. Add the salt and work the dough until it is incorporated. Knead at low speed for 5 minutes, raise the speed to medium, and work the dough until it is smooth, 2 to 3 minutes.

3. Shape the dough into a ball, place it in a clean mixing bowl, and cover it with plastic wrap. Let the dough rest for 1½ hours.

4. Place the dough on a flour-dusted work surface and shape it into a round.

5. Place the shaped round in a bowl lined with a floured kitchen towel and cover the bowl with plastic wrap.

6. Let the dough rest in the refrigerator (on a middle or lower shelf is best) overnight.

7. Preheat the oven to 480°F and place a baking stone or steel on the middle rack of the oven as it warms.

8. Remove the loaf from the refrigerator and let it rest at room temperature until it has doubled in size, about 1 hour.

9. Invert the loaf onto a parchment-lined peel. Score the loaf with a long cut down the middle, slide it onto the heated baking implement, and bake with steam, using one of the methods described on page 32.

10. Reduce the temperature to 460°F and bake for 10 minutes, then reduce the temperature to 430°F and bake until the bread is golden brown, feels lighter when lifted, and makes a hollow sound when tapped, 15 to 20 minutes.

11. Remove the bread from the oven, place it on a wire rack, and let it cool completely before slicing and serving.

INGREDIENTS:

- 1 CUP PLUS 1½ TABLESPOONS (249 G) WATER
- ½ PACKET (3.5 G) OF ACTIVE DRY YEAST
- 3¼ CUPS (390 G) BREAD FLOUR, PLUS MORE AS NEEDED
- 1½ TEASPOONS (9 G) FINE SEA SALT

SESAME LOAF

YIELD: 1 LOAF / **ACTIVE TIME:** 20 MINUTES / **TOTAL TIME:** 3 HOURS AND 50 MINUTES

Sesame seeds and whole wheat confer that irresistible nutty taste that goes so well with ham, cheese, and egg in the morning.

1. Warm 3½ tablespoons of the water until it is about 105°F. Add the yeast and water to the work bowl of a stand mixer fitted with the dough hook and gently stir to combine. Let the mixture sit until it starts to foam, about 10 minutes.

2. Add the flours, olive oil, and remaining water and work the mixture on low until it comes together as a dough. Add the salt and work the dough until it is incorporated. Knead at low speed for 5 minutes, raise the speed to medium, and work the dough until it is smooth, 2 to 3 minutes.

3. Cover the bowl with plastic wrap and let the dough rest until it has doubled in size, about 1½ hours.

4. Spread the sesame seeds on the bottom of a loaf pan or oblong banneton and spray them with water. Invert the dough onto a flour-dusted work surface and shape it into a round. Gently fold the round to form an oval. Place the loaf, seam side up, on the moistened seeds.

5. Cover the loaf with a kitchen towel and let it rest until it has almost doubled in size, 1 to 1½ hours.

6. Preheat the oven to 480°F and place a baking stone or steel on the middle rack of the oven as it warms.

7. Invert the loaf onto a parchment-lined peel. Score it with a sharp knife or scissors, slide it onto the heated baking implement, and bake with steam, using one of the methods described on page 32.

8. Reduce the temperature to 430°F and bake for 15 minutes, then reduce the temperature to 390°F and bake until the bread is golden brown, feels lighter when lifted, and makes a hollow sound when tapped, 15 to 20 minutes.

9. Remove the bread from the oven, place it on a wire rack, and let it cool completely before slicing and serving.

INGREDIENTS:

- 1⅙ CUPS (265 G) WATER
- ⅔ PACKET (4.5 G) OF ACTIVE DRY YEAST
- 2⅘ CUPS (336 G) BREAD FLOUR, PLUS MORE AS NEEDED
- ½ CUP (60 G) WHOLE WHEAT FLOUR
- 1½ TABLESPOONS (22.5 G) EXTRA-VIRGIN OLIVE OIL
- 1½ TEASPOONS (7 G) FINE SEA SALT
- ¼ CUP SESAME SEEDS, FOR TOPPING

OLIVE OIL & BLACK PEPPER LOAF

YIELD: 1 LOAF / **ACTIVE TIME:** 15 MINUTES / **TOTAL TIME:** 3 HOURS

Who doesn't like to dip crusty bread in black pepper–infused olive oil? Here you have the spice already in the bread!

INGREDIENTS:

1 CUP (227 G) WATER

1 PACKET (7 G) OF ACTIVE DRY YEAST

3¼ CUPS (390 G) BREAD FLOUR, PLUS MORE AS NEEDED

2 TABLESPOONS (26 G) EXTRA-VIRGIN OLIVE OIL

1½ TEASPOONS (3.5 G) FRESHLY GROUND BLACK PEPPER

1½ TEASPOONS (9 G) FINE SEA SALT

1. Warm 3½ tablespoons of the water until it is about 105°F. Add the yeast and water to the work bowl of a stand mixer fitted with the dough hook and gently stir to combine. Let the mixture sit until it starts to foam, about 10 minutes.

2. Add the flour, olive oil, pepper, and remaining water and work the mixture on low until it comes together as a dough. Add the salt and work the dough until it is incorporated. Knead at low speed for 5 minutes, raise the speed to medium, and work the dough until it is smooth, 2 to 3 minutes.

3. Shape the dough into a ball, place it in a clean mixing bowl, and cover it with plastic wrap. Let the dough rest at room temperature until it has doubled in size, 1 to 1½ hours.

4. Place the dough on a flour-dusted work surface and shape it into a round.

5. Place the shaped round in a bowl lined with a floured kitchen towel and cover the bowl with plastic wrap. Let it rest until it has doubled in size, about 1 hour.

6. Preheat the oven to 480°F and place a baking stone or steel on the middle rack of the oven as it warms.

7. Invert the loaf onto a parchment-lined peel. Score three diagonal slashes on the top of the loaf with a sharp knife or scissors, slide it onto the heated baking implement, and bake with steam, using one of the methods described on page 32.

8. Reduce the temperature to 445°F and bake for 15 minutes, then reduce the temperature to 410°F and bake until the bread is golden brown, feels lighter when lifted, and makes a hollow sound when tapped, 10 to 15 minutes.

9. Remove the bread from the oven, place it on a wire rack, and let it cool completely before slicing and serving.

PUMPERNICKEL LOAF

YIELD: 1 LOAF / **ACTIVE TIME:** 30 MINUTES / **TOTAL TIME:** 24 HOURS

Pumpernickel is a traditional dark rye bread from the northwestern German region of Westphalia. Making it properly means using a rye-based starter and whole rye berries, so the process needs to be started the evening before the day you are planning to bake.

1. In a large bowl, combine all of the ingredients with a spoon, adding the salt last.

2. Coat a ½-gallon loaf pan, preferably one with a lid, with nonstick cooking spray and pour the dough into the pan. Let the dough rest, covered, for 3½ hours.

3. Preheat the oven to 320°F.

4. Place the bread in the oven and bake for 2½ hours.

5. Remove the bread from the oven, place it on a wire rack, and let it cool completely before slicing and serving.

INGREDIENTS:

- 4 CUPS (420 G) DARK RYE FLOUR
- 1½ CUPS (340 G) RYE SOUR (SEE PAGE 660)
- ¾ CUP (90 G) RYE BERRIES, SOAKED IN WATER OVERNIGHT, BOILED FOR 30 MINUTES, AND DRAINED
- ⅗ CUP (136 G) WATER
- ⅙ CUP (56 G) MOLASSES
- 2 TEASPOONS (12 G) FINE SEA SALT

POTATO BREAD

YIELD: 1 LOAF / **ACTIVE TIME:** 20 MINUTES / **TOTAL TIME:** 4 HOURS

If you are one of those who passes the time dreaming of the elaborate Dagwood sandwiches you could construct, this is the bread to help you realize those visions.

INGREDIENTS:

- ¾ CUP (170 G) WARM WATER (105°F)
- 2 TEASPOONS (6 G) ACTIVE DRY YEAST
- 3⅛ CUPS (375 G) ALL-PURPOSE FLOUR, PLUS MORE AS NEEDED
- 1¼ TEASPOONS (7 G) FINE SEA SALT
- 3½ TABLESPOONS (43 G) SUGAR
- 6 TABLESPOONS (85 G) UNSALTED BUTTER, SOFTENED
- 1 LARGE EGG
- ½ CUP (105 G) PLAIN MASHED POTATOES, COOLED TO ROOM TEMPERATURE

1. Place all of the ingredients in the work bowl of a stand mixer fitted with the dough hook and mix on low until the mixture comes together as a dough. Raise the speed to high and work the dough until it is smooth and elastic, 3 to 4 minutes.

2. Coat a mixing bowl with nonstick cooking spray. Form the dough into a ball, place it in the bowl, and cover the bowl with plastic wrap. Let the dough rest in a naturally warm spot until it has doubled in size, about 1 hour.

3. Place the dough on a flour-dusted work surface and press it into a rough square. Fold the bottom third of the dough to the center, then fold the top third to the center, overlapping it over the bottom third. Turn the dough and repeat the folds so that the dough will fit in a 9 x 5–inch loaf pan.

4. Coat a 9 x 5–inch loaf pan with nonstick cooking spray, place the dough in it, and let it rest until it has tripled in size, about 1 hour.

5. Preheat the oven to 350°F.

6. Place the bread in the oven and bake until it is golden brown and feels lighter when lifted, 35 to 45 minutes.

7. Remove the bread from the oven, remove it from the pan, and place it on a wire rack. Let the bread cool completely before slicing and serving.

GARLIC & ROSEMARY POTATO BREAD

YIELD: 1 LOAF / **ACTIVE TIME:** 1 HOUR / **TOTAL TIME:** 5 HOURS

For tips on roasting garlic, check out the first step of the recipe on page 151.

INGREDIENTS:

FOR THE BIGA

- 4 OZ. (113 G) BREAD FLOUR
- ¼ TEASPOON (¾ G) ACTIVE DRY YEAST
- ⅓ CUP (76 G) LUKEWARM WATER (90°F)

FOR THE DOUGH

- 4 CUPS (908 G) WATER
- 2 TABLESPOONS PLUS 1 TEASPOON (38 G) FINE SEA SALT
- 1 LARGE RUSSET POTATO, PEELED AND DICED
- 5 OZ. (142 G) BIGA
- 1 TEASPOON (3 G) ACTIVE DRY YEAST
- 2 TEASPOONS (8 G) INFUSED OIL FROM ROASTED GARLIC, PLUS MORE AS NEEDED
- 9½ OZ. (269 G) BREAD FLOUR, PLUS MORE AS NEEDED
- ⅛ TEASPOON (0.2 G) WHITE PEPPER
- 12 GARLIC CLOVES, ROASTED
- 1 TABLESPOON (2 G) FINELY CHOPPED FRESH ROSEMARY

1. To prepare the biga, place all of the ingredients in a mixing bowl and whisk to combine. Cover the bowl with plastic wrap and let the biga rest for 2 hours.

2. To begin preparations for the dough, place the water and 2 tablespoons of the salt in a saucepan and bring to a boil. Add the potato and cook until it is very tender, 20 to 25 minutes. Reserve ½ cup of the cooking liquid and then drain the potato.

3. Place the potato in a small bowl and mash until it is smooth.

4. Let the reserved liquid and potato cool to 90°F.

5. Place the reserved liquid, biga, and yeast in the work bowl of a stand mixer fitted with the dough hook, gently stir to combine, and let the mixture sit until it starts to foam, about 10 minutes.

6. Add the infused oil, flour, white pepper, roasted garlic, rosemary, and the remaining salt and knead the mixture on low for 1 minute. Raise the speed to medium and knead until it comes together as a smooth dough.

7. Place the dough in a flour-dusted bowl and cover it with plastic wrap. Let the dough rest at room temperature until it has doubled in size, about 1½ hours.

8. Coat an 8 x 4–inch loaf pan with nonstick cooking spray. Place the dough on a flour-dusted work surface and punch it down to deflate it. Shape the dough into a tight ball and place it in the prepared loaf pan, seam side down. Cover it with plastic wrap and let the dough rise until it has doubled in size.

9. Preheat the oven to 350°F.

10. Place the bread in the oven and bake until it is golden brown and feels lighter when lifted, 45 to 50 minutes.

11. Remove the bread from the oven, remove it from the pan, and transfer it to a wire rack. Brush it with some more reserved oil and let it cool completely before slicing and serving.

SCALI BREAD

YIELD: 1 LOAF / **ACTIVE TIME:** 45 MINUTES / **TOTAL TIME:** 4 HOURS

This crusty loaf with a soft interior is a staple in Italian American homes in the Northeast.

INGREDIENTS:

- ½ CUP PLUS 1 TABLESPOON (130 G) LUKEWARM WATER (90°F)
- 1½ TEASPOONS (4.5 G) ACTIVE DRY YEAST
- 8 OZ. (227 G) BREAD FLOUR, PLUS MORE AS NEEDED
- 2 TEASPOONS (8 G) SUGAR
- 1½ TEASPOONS (9 G) FINE SEA SALT
- 1 TABLESPOON (14 G) UNSALTED BUTTER, SOFTENED
- 1 EGG, BEATEN
- SESAME SEEDS, FOR TOPPING

1. Place the water and yeast in the work bowl of a stand mixer fitted with the dough hook, gently stir to combine, and let the mixture sit until it starts to foam, about 10 minutes.

2. Add the flour, sugar, and salt and work the mixture on low until it just starts to come together as a dough, about 1 minute.

3. Add the butter, raise the speed to medium, and work the dough until it is elastic and pulls away clean from the side of the work bowl.

4. Coat a mixing bowl with nonstick cooking spray. Place the dough on a flour-dusted work surface and knead it until it is extensible. Shape the dough into a ball, place it in the bowl, and cover the bowl with a kitchen towel. Place the dough in a naturally warm spot and let it rest until it has doubled in size, 1 to 2 hours.

5. Preheat the oven to 350°F. Line an 18 x 13–inch baking sheet with parchment paper.

6. Place the dough on a flour-dusted work surface and flatten it into a rough rectangle that is about 6 inches across. Starting from a near end, roll the dough up while tucking in the sides, so that the dough becomes shaped like a football. Pinch the seam to seal and place the dough on the pan, seam side down. Cover the dough with plastic wrap, place it in a naturally warm spot, and let it rest until it has doubled in size.

7. Brush the dough with the beaten egg and sprinkle sesame seeds over the top. Using a very sharp knife, cut a seam on the top of the bread at a 45-degree angle. Place the dough in the oven and bake with steam, using one of the methods described on page 32.

8. Bake until the bread is golden brown, feels lighter when lifted, and makes a hollow sound when tapped, about 20 minutes.

9. Remove the bread from the oven, place it on a wire rack, and let it cool before slicing and serving.

FALL HARVEST LOAF

YIELD: 1 LOAF / **ACTIVE TIME:** 45 MINUTES / **TOTAL TIME:** 4 HOURS

If you can't get enough of the smell of freshly baked bread, this loaf resides at a whole new olfactory level.

INGREDIENTS:

- 6 OZ. (170 G) LUKEWARM WATER (90°F)
- 1 TABLESPOON (9 G) ACTIVE DRY YEAST
- 2 EGGS, 1 BEATEN
- 1 EGG YOLK
- 2 TABLESPOONS (28 G) EXTRA-VIRGIN OLIVE OIL
- 1 OZ. (28 G) SUGAR
- 15 OZ. (425 G) BREAD FLOUR, PLUS MORE AS NEEDED
- 1 TEASPOON (2 G) GROUND CLOVES
- 1 TABLESPOON (10 G) CINNAMON
- 1 CUP DRIED CRANBERRIES
- ½ CUP PUMPKIN SEEDS, TOASTED
- 2 TEASPOONS (12 G) FINE SEA SALT

1. Place the water and yeast in the work bowl of a stand mixer fitted with the dough hook, gently stir to combine, and let the mixture sit until it starts to foam, about 10 minutes.

2. Add the unbeaten egg, egg yolk, olive oil, and sugar. Then add the flour, cloves, cinnamon, cranberries, pumpkin seeds, and salt. Work the mixture on low until it just starts to come together as a dough, about 1 minute.

3. Raise the speed to medium and work the dough until it is elastic and pulls away from the side of the bowl, about 6 minutes.

4. Coat a mixing bowl with nonstick cooking spray. Place the dough on a flour-dusted work surface and knead it until it is extensible. Shape the dough into a ball, place it in the bowl, and cover the bowl with a kitchen towel. Place the dough in a naturally warm spot and let it rest until it has doubled in size, 1 to 2 hours.

5. Preheat the oven to 350°F. Coat an 8 x 4–inch loaf pan with nonstick cooking spray.

6. Place the dough on a flour-dusted work surface and roll it into a tight round. Pinch the ends together and place the dough in the loaf pan, seam side down. Cover the dough with plastic wrap, place it in a naturally warm spot, and let it rest until it has doubled in size.

7. Brush the dough with the beaten egg. Using a very sharp knife, cut a seam on the top of the bread for its entire length. Place the dough in the oven and bake until it is golden brown, feels lighter when lifted, and makes a hollow sound when tapped, 35 to 45 minutes.

8. Remove the bread from the oven, place it on a wire rack, and let it cool before slicing and serving.

WINTER HARVEST LOAF

YIELD: 1 LOAF / **ACTIVE TIME:** 45 MINUTES / **TOTAL TIME:** 4 HOURS

A loaf for those times when the cold and bleak world outside starts to wear you down.

1. Place the water and yeast in the work bowl of a stand mixer fitted with the dough hook, gently whisk to combine, and let the mixture sit until it starts to foam, about 10 minutes.

2. Add the unbeaten egg, egg yolk, olive oil, sugar, and molasses. Then add the flour, cocoa powder, oats, millet, caraway, and salt. Work the mixture on low until it just starts to come together as a dough, about 1 minute.

3. Raise the speed to medium and work the dough until it is elastic and pulls away from the side of the bowl, about 6 minutes.

4. Coat a mixing bowl with nonstick cooking spray. Place the dough on a flour-dusted work surface and knead it until it is extensible. Shape the dough into a ball, place it in the bowl, and cover the bowl with a kitchen towel. Place the dough in a naturally warm spot and let it rest until it has doubled in size, 1 to 2 hours.

5. Preheat the oven to 350°F. Coat an 8 x 4–inch loaf pan with nonstick cooking spray.

6. Place the dough on a flour-dusted work surface and roll it into a tight round. Pinch the ends together and place the dough in the loaf pan, seam side down. Cover the dough with plastic wrap, place it in a naturally warm spot, and let it rest until it has doubled in size.

7. Brush the dough with the beaten egg and sprinkle some oats over the top. Using a very sharp knife, cut a seam on the top of the bread for its entire length. Place the dough in the oven and bake until it is golden brown, feels lighter when lifted, and makes a hollow sound when tapped, 35 to 45 minutes.

8. Remove the bread from the oven, place it on a wire rack, and let it cool before slicing and serving.

INGREDIENTS:

- 6 OZ. (170 G) LUKEWARM WATER (90°F)
- 1 TABLESPOON (9 G) ACTIVE DRY YEAST
- 2 EGGS, 1 BEATEN
- 1 EGG YOLK
- 2 TABLESPOONS (28 G) EXTRA-VIRGIN OLIVE OIL
- 1 OZ. (28 G) SUGAR
- 1 TABLESPOON (21.2 G) MOLASSES
- 15 OZ. (425 G) BREAD FLOUR, PLUS MORE AS NEEDED
- 4 TEASPOONS (10 G) COCOA POWDER
- ¼ CUP ROLLED OATS, PLUS MORE FOR TOPPING
- ½ CUP MILLET
- 2 TABLESPOONS CARAWAY SEEDS, TOASTED
- 1 TABLESPOON FENNEL SEEDS, TOASTED
- 2 TEASPOONS (12 G) FINE SEA SALT

FARMHOUSE FOUGASSE

YIELD: 1 LOAF / **ACTIVE TIME:** 30 MINUTES / **TOTAL TIME:** 3 HOURS

Enriching a fougasse with vegetables somehow makes this loaf even more fun and delicious.

1. Place the water and yeast in the work bowl of a stand mixer fitted with the dough hook, gently stir to combine, and let the mixture sit until it starts to foam, about 10 minutes.

2. Add the olive oil, flour, herbs, garlic, and salt and work the mixture on low for 1 minute. Raise the speed to medium and work the mixture until it comes together as a smooth dough, about 5 minutes.

3. Remove the dough from the work bowl, place it on a flour-dusted work surface, and knead it until it is elastic. Shape the dough into a ball, return it to the work bowl, and cover it with plastic wrap. Place the dough in a naturally warm spot and let it rest until it has doubled in size.

4. Turn the dough out onto a flour-dusted work surface. Lightly sprinkle flour over the top of the dough. Using a rolling pin, roll the dough outward by starting in the middle of the dough and rolling toward you until it is an approximately 10 x 6–inch oval.

5. Preheat the oven to 350°F. Coat an 18 x 13–inch baking sheet with olive oil. Carefully place the dough in the center of the prepared pan.

6. Using a pizza cutter, cut a lengthwise line in the center of the oval, leaving an inch uncut at each end so that the dough remains in one piece. Make three small, angled slices to the left of the center cut. Do the same to the right of the center cut.

7. The bread should resemble a leaf. Distribute the cauliflower, squash, and bell pepper over the dough, brush the vegetables and dough with olive oil, cover the pan with plastic wrap, and let it rest until it has doubled in size.

8. Preheat the oven to 350°F.

9. Sprinkle the Parmesan over the bread, place it in the oven, and bake until it is golden brown and feels lighter when lifted, 20 to 30 minutes.

10. Remove the fougasse from the oven and brush it with more olive oil. Transfer it to a wire rack and let it cool before enjoying.

INGREDIENTS:

- 9 OZ. (255 G) LUKEWARM WATER (90°F)
- 2½ TEASPOONS (7.5 G) ACTIVE DRY YEAST
- 3 TABLESPOONS (40 G) EXTRA-VIRGIN OLIVE OIL, PLUS MORE AS NEEDED
- 15 OZ. (425 G) BREAD FLOUR, PLUS MORE AS NEEDED
- 1 TABLESPOON FINELY CHOPPED FRESH MINT
- 1 TABLESPOON FINELY CHOPPED FRESH PARSLEY
- 1 TABLESPOON FINELY CHOPPED FRESH DILL
- 2 GARLIC CLOVES, MINCED
- 1 TABLESPOON (16 G) FINE SEA SALT, PLUS MORE TO TASTE
- ½ CUP CHOPPED PURPLE CAULIFLOWER
- 1 SUMMER SQUASH, SLICED
- ½ BELL PEPPER, SLICED THIN
- ¼ CUP FRESHLY SHAVED PARMESAN CHEESE, FOR TOPPING

FOUGASSE

YIELD: 1 LOAF / **ACTIVE TIME:** 30 MINUTES / **TOTAL TIME:** 3 HOURS

This classic, leaf-shaped bread hails from the region of Provence, France.

INGREDIENTS:

- 9 OZ. (255 G) LUKEWARM WATER (90°F)
- 2½ TEASPOONS (7.5 G) ACTIVE DRY YEAST
- 3 TABLESPOONS (40 G) EXTRA-VIRGIN OLIVE OIL, PLUS MORE AS NEEDED
- 15 OZ. (425 G) BREAD FLOUR, PLUS MORE AS NEEDED
- 1 TABLESPOON PLUS 1 TEASPOON (1.7 G) DRIED BASIL
- 2 GARLIC CLOVES, MINCED
- 1 TABLESPOON (16 G) FINE SEA SALT
- ¼ CUP FRESHLY SHAVED PARMESAN CHEESE, FOR TOPPING

1. Place the water and yeast in the work bowl of a stand mixer fitted with the dough hook, gently stir to combine, and let the mixture sit until it starts to foam, about 10 minutes.

2. Add the olive oil, flour, basil, garlic, and salt and work the mixture on low for 1 minute. Raise the speed to medium and work the mixture until it comes together as a smooth dough, about 5 minutes.

3. Remove the dough from the work bowl, place it on a flour-dusted work surface, and knead it until it is elastic. Shape the dough into a ball, return it to the work bowl, and cover it with plastic wrap. Place the dough in a naturally warm spot and let it rest until it has doubled in size.

4. Turn the dough out onto a flour-dusted work surface. Lightly sprinkle flour over the top of the dough. Using a rolling pin, roll the dough outward by starting in the middle of the dough and rolling toward you until it is an approximately 10 x 6–inch oval.

5. Preheat the oven to 350°F. Coat an 18 x 13–inch baking sheet with olive oil. Carefully place the dough in the center of the prepared pan.

6. Using a pizza cutter, cut a lengthwise line in the center of the oval, leaving an inch uncut at each end so that the dough remains in one piece. Make three small, angled slices to the left of the center cut. Do the same to the right of the center cut.

7. The bread should resemble a leaf. Lightly brush the dough with olive oil, cover the pan with plastic wrap, and let it rest until it has doubled in size.

8. Preheat the oven to 350°F.

9. Sprinkle the Parmesan over the bread, place it in the oven, and bake until it is golden brown and feels lighter when lifted, 20 to 30 minutes.

10. Remove the fougasse from the oven and brush it with more olive oil. Transfer it to a wire rack and let it cool before enjoying.

Fougasse, *see page 135*

IRISH SODA BREAD

YIELD: 1 LOAF / **ACTIVE TIME:** 30 MINUTES / **TOTAL TIME:** 1 HOUR AND 30 MINUTES

Irish soda bread is an older style of bread that is not made with yeast. It is well-balanced, with a light sweetness and a bit of earthiness coming from the caraway.

INGREDIENTS:

- 7 OZ. (198 G) ALL-PURPOSE FLOUR, PLUS MORE AS NEEDED
- 1 OZ. (28 G) SUGAR
- ½ TEASPOON (2 G) BAKING POWDER
- ¼ TEASPOON PLUS ⅛ TEASPOON (2.2 G) BAKING SODA
- ¼ TEASPOON (1.5 G) FINE SEA SALT
- 5 OZ. RAISINS
- 1 TEASPOON CARAWAY SEEDS
- 1 EGG
- ⅓ CUP (76 G) BUTTERMILK
- ⅓ CUP (76 G) SOUR CREAM

1. Preheat the oven to 350°F. Coat a round 6-inch cake pan with nonstick cooking spray.

2. Place the flour, sugar, baking powder, baking soda, salt, raisins, and caraway seeds in the work bowl of a stand mixer fitted with the paddle attachment and beat until combined.

3. In a mixing bowl, combine the egg, buttermilk, and sour cream. With the mixer running on low, gradually pour in the buttermilk mixture and beat until the resulting mixture comes together as a smooth dough.

4. Transfer the dough to the prepared cake pan and spread it into an even layer. Using a flour-dusted paring knife, cut a cross in the center of the dough.

5. Place the bread in the oven and bake until it is golden brown and a cake tester inserted into the center of the loaf comes out clean, 35 to 45 minutes.

6. Remove the bread from the oven and let it cool completely before slicing and serving.

1/3 cup
80 ml

BROWN IRISH SODA BREAD

YIELD: 2 LOAVES / **ACTIVE TIME:** 45 MINUTES / **TOTAL TIME:** 1 HOUR AND 30 MINUTES

Serve this traditional-leaning soda bread recipe with smoked salmon or raspberry preserves.

INGREDIENTS:

- 4 CUPS (480 G) WHOLE WHEAT FLOUR
- 1 CUP (120 G) ALL-PURPOSE FLOUR, PLUS MORE AS NEEDED
- ⅓ CUP ROLLED OATS
- 1 TEASPOON (5 G) BAKING SODA
- 1½ TEASPOONS (9 G) FINE SEA SALT
- 2 TABLESPOONS (24 G) BROWN SUGAR
- ¼ CUP (57 G) UNSALTED BUTTER, SOFTENED
- 1 LARGE EGG, AT ROOM TEMPERATURE
- 2¾ CUPS (625 G) BUTTERMILK, AT ROOM TEMPERATURE

1. For conventional ovens, preheat the oven to 425°F 20 minutes prior to baking. For convection ovens, preheat the oven to 400°F 20 minutes prior to baking.

2. In a mixing bowl, add the flours, oats, baking soda, salt, and brown sugar and stir the mixture with a fork until combined.

3. Add the butter to the dry mixture. Using your hands, work the butter into the mixture until well combined. Create a well in the center of the mixture and set it aside.

4. In another bowl, combine the egg and buttermilk and mix with a fork until well blended.

5. Pour the egg mixture into the well in the dry mixture and use a fork to combine the two mixtures.

6. In the bowl, fold and knead the dough eight times. Mix until there is no dry flour remaining in the bowl and the dough is evenly moistened.

7. Scrape the dough out of the bowl and place it on a lightly flour-dusted work surface. Sprinkle the top of the dough with flour. Divide the dough in half. Working quickly, shape each piece into a round. Sprinkle flour on top as needed to make sure the dough isn't sticky, but do not knead the flour into the dough. Line a baking sheet with parchment paper, place the rounds on it, and use a bench scraper to score a deep X into the top of each loaf.

8. Place the loaves in the oven and bake until the loaves are a deep golden brown and feel lighter when lifted, 35 to 45 minutes.

9. Remove the loaves from the oven, place them on a wire rack, and let them cool completely before slicing and serving.

CHOCOLATE SODA BREAD

YIELD: 1 LOAF / **ACTIVE TIME:** 10 MINUTES / **TOTAL TIME:** 1 HOUR

The addition of chocolate chips and a little sugar to a classic soda bread makes for a quick and delicious treat, while keeping some of the rustic charm of traditional versions of this bread.

1. Preheat the oven to 430°F. In a large bowl, combine all of the ingredients, except for the chocolate chips.

2. Place the dough on a clean work surface and knead for 2 minutes, then quickly incorporate the chocolate chips, making sure that they do not melt in your hands.

3. Shape the dough into a ball. Line a baking dish with parchment paper and transfer the dough into it.

4. Flatten the ball into a thick disk and slash a deep cross on the top of the loaf.

5. Place the bread in the oven and bake for 20 minutes. Reduce the temperature to 340°F and bake until it is a deep golden brown and feels lighter when lifted, 20 to 25 minutes.

6. Remove the bread from the oven, place it on a wire rack, and let it cool completely before slicing and serving.

INGREDIENTS:

- 4⅙ CUPS (500 G) ALL-PURPOSE FLOUR
- 2 CUPS (454 G) BUTTERMILK
- 1 TEASPOON (5 G) BAKING SODA
- 3 TABLESPOONS (36 G) SUGAR
- 1 TEASPOON (6 G) FINE SEA SALT
- ⅔ CUP CHOCOLATE CHIPS

COTTAGE LOAF

YIELD: 1 LOAF / **ACTIVE TIME:** 25 MINUTES / **TOTAL TIME:** 3 HOURS AND 20 MINUTES

Arguably the most traditional British loaf, cottage bread is rarely found in bakeries nowadays, which is a pity, considering that it is very easy to make, lovely to look at, and wonderful to serve, thanks to its mild taste, soft texture, and appealing shape.

INGREDIENTS:

1¼ CUPS (284 G) LUKEWARM WATER (90°F)

1 PACKET (7 G) OF ACTIVE DRY YEAST

3⅔ CUPS (400 G) BREAD FLOUR, PLUS MORE AS NEEDED

1 TABLESPOON (21 G) HONEY

1 TEASPOON (6 G) FINE SEA SALT

1.4 OZ. (40 G) UNSALTED BUTTER, SOFTENED

1. Warm 3½ tablespoons of the water until it is about 105°F. Add the yeast and water to the work bowl of a stand mixer fitted with the dough hook and gently stir to combine. Let the mixture sit until it starts to foam, about 10 minutes.

2. Add the flour and remaining water and work the mixture on low until it comes together as a dough. Add the salt and work the dough until it is incorporated. Knead at low speed for 5 minutes, raise the speed to medium, and work the dough until it is smooth, 2 to 3 minutes.

3. Shape the dough into a ball, place it in a clean mixing bowl, and cover it with plastic wrap. Place the dough in a naturally warm spot and let it rest until it has doubled in size, 1 to 1½ hours.

4. Place the dough on a flour-dusted work surface and deflate it by folding it over itself a few times, as you would fold a letter. Divide the dough into two pieces, one that is bigger (about two-thirds of the dough) and one that is smaller (about one-third of the dough), and shape them into rounds.

5. Place the bigger round on a parchment-lined peel and set the smaller round over the bigger one. Seal the rounds together by placing a finger in the middle of the smaller round and pressing it against the bigger round. Cover the dough with a floured kitchen towel and let it rest until it has almost doubled in size, about 1 hour.

6. Preheat the oven to 415°F and place a baking stone or steel on the middle rack of the oven as it warms.

7. Score the top round, making shallow cuts on the sides. Slide the loaf onto the heated baking implement and bake with steam, using one of the methods described on page 32.

8. Bake for 15 minutes, reduce the temperature to 375°F, and bake until the bread is golden brown, feels lighter when lifted, and makes a hollow sound when tapped, 20 to 25 minutes.

9. Remove the bread from the oven, place it on a wire rack, and let it cool completely before slicing and serving.

CHOCOLATE & CINNAMON BREAD

YIELD: 1 LOAF / **ACTIVE TIME:** 20 MINUTES / **TOTAL TIME:** 3 HOURS AND 50 MINUTES

This bread is surprisingly tasty with cheese, and heavenly with good butter.

INGREDIENTS:

- 1 CUP PLUS 2 TABLESPOONS (260 G) WATER
- ⅔ PACKET (4.5 G) OF ACTIVE DRY YEAST
- 2⅔ CUPS (320 G) BREAD FLOUR, PLUS MORE AS NEEDED
- ½ CUP (60 G) WHOLE WHEAT FLOUR
- 1 TABLESPOON (15 G) COCOA POWDER
- 1 TEASPOON (2.5 G) CINNAMON
- 1½ TEASPOONS (9 G) FINE SEA SALT
- 1¾ OZ. BITTERSWEET CHOCOLATE CHIPS

1. Warm 3½ tablespoons of the water until it is about 105°F. Add the yeast and water to the work bowl of a stand mixer fitted with the dough hook and gently stir to combine. Let the mixture sit until it starts to foam, about 10 minutes.

2. Add the flours, cocoa powder, cinnamon, and remaining water and work the mixture on low until it comes together as a dough. Add the salt and work the dough until it is incorporated. Knead at low speed for 5 minutes, raise the speed to medium, and work the dough until it is smooth, 2 to 3 minutes. Add the chocolate chips and fold until they are evenly distributed.

3. Shape the dough into a ball, place it in a clean mixing bowl, and cover it with plastic wrap. Let the dough rest until it has doubled in size, about 1½ hours.

4. Place the dough on a flour-dusted work surface and shape it into a round. Place the shaped round, seam side up, in a bowl or banneton lined with a floured kitchen towel and cover it with another kitchen towel. Let the dough rest at room temperature until it has almost doubled in size, 1 to 1½ hours.

5. Preheat the oven to 480°F and place a baking stone or steel on the middle rack of the oven as it warms.

6. Invert the dough onto a parchment-lined peel and score it. Slide it onto the heated baking implement and bake with steam, using one of the methods described on page 32.

7. Reduce the temperature to 445°F and bake for 15 minutes, then reduce the temperature to 390°F and bake until the bread is golden brown, feels lighter when lifted, and makes a hollow sound when tapped, 20 to 30 minutes.

8. Remove the bread from the oven, place it on a wire rack, and let it cool completely before slicing and serving.

MOLASSES WHEAT BREAD

YIELD: 1 LOAF / **ACTIVE TIME:** 45 MINUTES / **TOTAL TIME:** 4 HOURS

A hearty bread with a wonderful balance of sweet and earthy flavors.

1. Place the water and yeast in the work bowl of a stand mixer fitted with the dough hook, gently stir to combine, and let the mixture sit until it starts to foam, about 10 minutes.

2. Add the sugar, honey, molasses, flours, oats, cocoa powder, and salt and knead the mixture on low for 1 minute.

3. Add the butter a little at a time with the mixer running. When all of the butter has been added, raise the speed to medium and knead the dough until it begins to pull away from the side of the work bowl, about 6 minutes.

4. Coat a mixing bowl with nonstick cooking spray. Remove the dough from the work bowl, place it on a flour-dusted work surface, and shape it into a ball. Place the dough in the bowl, cover it with plastic wrap, place it in a naturally warm spot, and let it rest until it has doubled in size, 1 to 2 hours.

5. Coat an 8 x 4–inch loaf pan with nonstick cooking spray.

6. Place the dough on a flour-dusted work surface and shape it into a tight round. Tuck in the sides to form the dough into a loaf shape and place it in the prepared loaf pan, seam side down.

7. Cover the pan with plastic wrap and let the dough rise until it has doubled in size.

8. Preheat the oven to 350°F.

9. Brush the dough with the beaten egg and sprinkle oats over the top. Using a sharp knife, cut a slit that runs the length of the entire loaf down the center.

10. Place the bread in the oven and bake until it is golden brown and feels lighter when lifted, 35 to 45 minutes.

11. Remove the bread from the oven, place the pan on a wire rack, and let it cool before slicing and serving.

INGREDIENTS:

- 5 OZ. (142 G) LUKEWARM WATER (90°F)
- 2 TEASPOONS (6 G) ACTIVE DRY YEAST
- ¾ TEASPOON (3 G) SUGAR
- 1 OZ. (28 G) HONEY
- 1 OZ. (28 G) MOLASSES
- 5 OZ. (142 G) ALL-PURPOSE FLOUR, PLUS MORE AS NEEDED
- 3½ OZ. (99 G) WHOLE WHEAT FLOUR
- 1 OZ. (28 G) ROLLED OATS, PLUS MORE FOR TOPPING
- 1 TEASPOON (2.5 G) COCOA POWDER
- 1 TEASPOON (6 G) FINE SEA SALT
- ½ OZ. (14 G) UNSALTED BUTTER, SOFTENED
- 1 EGG, BEATEN

HONEY OAT BREAD

YIELD: 3 LOAVES / **ACTIVE TIME:** 20 MINUTES / **TOTAL TIME:** 3 HOURS AND 50 MINUTES

Even the biggest fans of rustic, extra-crusty bread sometimes enjoy a soft and sweet loaf. The oats provide extra flavor and give this lovely bread a whole-grain feel.

INGREDIENTS:

- 3¾ CUPS (338 G) ROLLED OATS
- 3½ CUPS (800 G) WATER
- 3½ TEASPOONS (10 G) ACTIVE DRY YEAST
- 6½ CUPS (780 G) BREAD FLOUR, PLUS MORE AS NEEDED
- ½ CUP (60 G) WHOLE WHEAT FLOUR
- ½ CUP (170 G) HONEY
- 1½ TABLESPOONS (27 G) FINE SEA SALT

1. In a large bowl, soak the oats in ½ cup of the water for 30 minutes. Drain the oats and set aside.

2. Warm 3½ tablespoons of the water until it is about 105°F. Add the yeast and water to the work bowl of a stand mixer fitted with the dough hook and gently stir to combine. Let the mixture sit until it starts to foam, about 10 minutes.

3. Add the flours, honey, and remaining water and work the mixture on low until it comes together as a dough. Add the salt and work the dough until it is incorporated. Knead at low speed for 5 minutes, raise the speed to medium, and work the dough until it is smooth, 2 to 3 minutes, incorporating the oats near the end of the kneading process.

4. Shape the dough into a ball and place it in a clean mixing bowl. Cover the bowl with plastic wrap, place the dough in a naturally warm spot, and let it rest for 1 hour.

5. Place the dough on a flour-dusted work surface and divide it into three pieces. Lightly shape them into rough ovals. Cover the dough with a kitchen towel and let it rest for 20 minutes.

6. Coat three 1-pound loaf pans with nonstick cooking spray. Shape the pieces of dough into loaves and place them in the loaf pans. Let the dough rest until it rises above the edges of the pans, about 1 hour.

7. Preheat the oven to 350°F. Place the bread in the oven and bake until the loaves are golden brown, feel lighter when lifted, and make a hollow sound when tapped, 30 to 35 minutes.

8. Remove the loaves from the oven, place them on a wire rack, and let them cool completely before slicing and serving.

CINNAMON RAISIN BREAD

YIELD: 2 LOAVES / **ACTIVE TIME:** 45 MINUTES / **TOTAL TIME:** 4 HOURS

A recipe for the bread that provided everyone's favorite childhood toast.

1. To begin preparations for the dough, combine the water, milk, melted butter, yeast, and unbeaten egg in the work bowl of a stand mixer fitted with the dough hook. Add the flour, sugar, salt, cinnamon, and raisins and work the mixture on low for 1 minute. Raise the speed to medium and knead until the mixture comes together as a dough and pulls away from the side of the bowl.

2. Transfer the dough to a clean bowl, cover it with plastic wrap, and let it rest until it has doubled in size.

3. Wipe out the work bowl of the stand mixer and prepare the filling. Add all of the ingredients, fit the mixer with the paddle attachment, and beat the mixture until it is a crumbly meal, about 5 minutes. Set the filling aside.

4. Turn the dough out onto a flour-dusted work surface and divide it in half. Use a rolling pin to roll each piece into a rectangle that is about 8 x 6 inches.

5. Spread 1 cup of the filling evenly across each piece of dough, leaving an inch of dough uncovered on the wide side closest to yourself.

6. Working from the wide side farthest away from you, roll the pieces of dough up tightly. Pinch the seams and ends to seal the dough.

7. Coat two 8 x 4–inch loaf pans with nonstick cooking spray and place a piece of dough in each one.

8. Cover the loaves with plastic wrap and let them rest until they crest above the edges of the pans.

9. Preheat the oven to 350°F.

10. Brush both loaves with the beaten egg. Place them in the oven and bake until they are golden brown and feel lighter when lifted, 40 to 45 minutes.

11. Remove the loaves from the oven, place the pans on a wire rack, and let the loaves cool completely before slicing and serving.

INGREDIENTS:

FOR THE DOUGH

- 3 OZ. (85 G) WATER
- 3 OZ. (85 G) MILK
- 4 OZ. (113 G) UNSALTED BUTTER, MELTED
- 5 TEASPOONS (15 G) ACTIVE DRY YEAST
- 2 EGGS, 1 BEATEN
- 15 OZ. (425 G) BREAD FLOUR, PLUS MORE AS NEEDED
- 2 OZ. (57 G) SUGAR
- 1 TABLESPOON (16 G) FINE SEA SALT
- 1½ TEASPOONS (5 G) CINNAMON
- 5 OZ. (142 G) RAISINS

FOR THE FILLING

- 4 OZ. LIGHT BROWN SUGAR
- 5 OZ. ALL-PURPOSE FLOUR
- 1½ TEASPOONS CINNAMON
- 3 OZ. UNSALTED BUTTER, SOFTENED
- ¼ TEASPOON KOSHER SALT
- ¾ TEASPOON COCOA POWDER

ROASTED GARLIC BREAD

YIELD: 1 LOAF / **ACTIVE TIME:** 15 MINUTES / **TOTAL TIME:** 3 HOURS AND 50 MINUTES

Garlic is a staple of Mediterranean cuisine, and, when roasted, it discloses all of its complex aromas. This loaf will make for a very special garlic bread, perfect to dip in extra-virgin olive oil of the highest quality.

INGREDIENTS:

- 1 HEAD OF GARLIC
- 2 TABLESPOONS (26 G) EXTRA-VIRGIN OLIVE OIL
- 1 CUP PLUS 1 TABLESPOON (242 G) WATER
- ⅔ PACKET (4.5 G) OF ACTIVE DRY YEAST
- 3¼ CUPS (390 G) BREAD FLOUR, PLUS MORE AS NEEDED
- 1⅓ TEASPOONS (8 G) FINE SEA SALT

1. Preheat the oven to 380°F. Cut the top ½ inch off the head of garlic, place the head of garlic in a square of aluminum foil, and drizzle the olive oil over the top. Form the foil into a pouch, close it, and place it in the oven. Roast the garlic until it is well browned and very soft, 30 to 40 minutes. Remove it from the oven and transfer the garlic cloves and the infused oil to a small bowl. Let the garlic and infused oil cool completely.

2. Warm 3½ tablespoons of the water until it is about 105°F. Add the yeast and water to the work bowl of a stand mixer fitted with the dough hook and gently stir to combine. Let the mixture sit until it starts to foam, about 10 minutes.

3. Add the flour and remaining water and work on low until it comes together as a dough. Add the salt and work the dough until it is incorporated. Knead at low speed for 5 minutes, raise the speed to medium, and work until it is smooth, 2 to 3 minutes.

4. Add the garlic and infused oil and stretch and fold the dough to incorporate them. Shape the dough into a ball, place it in a clean mixing bowl, and cover it with plastic wrap. Let rest for 1½ hours.

5. Place the dough on a flour-dusted work surface and shape it into a round. Place the shaped round in a bowl or banneton basket lined with a floured kitchen towel and cover the bowl with plastic wrap. Let the dough rest at room temperature until it has doubled in size, about 1½ hours.

6. Preheat the oven to 520°F and place a baking stone or steel on the middle rack of the oven as it warms.

7. Invert the dough onto a parchment-lined peel and score it with a deep cut in the middle. Slide it onto the heated baking implement and bake with steam, using one of the methods described on page 32.

8. Reduce the temperature to 460°F and bake for 10 minutes, then reduce the temperature to 430°F and bake until the bread is golden brown, feels lighter when lifted, and makes a hollow sound when tapped, 15 to 20 minutes.

9. Remove the bread from the oven, place it on a wire rack, and let it cool completely before slicing and serving.

Cinnamon Raisin Bread, *see page 150*

COUNTRY WHOLE WHEAT BREAD

YIELD: 1 LOAF / **ACTIVE TIME:** 45 MINUTES / **TOTAL TIME:** 4 HOURS

This bread is great for sandwiches, or toasted with a bit of homemade jam.

INGREDIENTS:

- 8 OZ. (227 G) LUKEWARM WATER (90°F)
- 2 TEASPOONS (6 G) ACTIVE DRY YEAST
- 10 OZ. (283 G) BREAD FLOUR, PLUS MORE AS NEEDED
- 2 OZ. (57 G) WHOLE WHEAT FLOUR
- 1 TABLESPOON PLUS 1 TEASPOON (16 G) SUGAR
- 1½ TEASPOONS (9 G) FINE SEA SALT
- 1½ OZ. (43 G) UNSALTED BUTTER, SOFTENED

1. Place the water and yeast in the work bowl of a stand mixer fitted with the dough hook, gently stir to combine, and let the mixture sit until it starts to foam, about 10 minutes.

2. Add the flours, sugar, and salt and work the mixture on low until it just starts to come together as a dough, about 1 minute.

3. Add the butter, raise the speed to medium, and work the dough until it is elastic and pulls away clean from the side of the work bowl.

4. Coat a mixing bowl with nonstick cooking spray. Place the dough on a flour-dusted work surface and knead it until it is extensible. Shape the dough into a ball, place it in the bowl, and cover the bowl with a kitchen towel. Place the dough in a naturally warm spot and let it rest until it has doubled in size, 1 to 2 hours.

5. Coat an 8 x 4–inch loaf pan with nonstick cooking spray.

6. Place the dough on a flour-dusted work surface and shape it into a tight round. Place it in the prepared loaf pan, seam side down, cover it with plastic wrap, and place it in a naturally warm spot. Let the dough rise until it has doubled in size.

7. Preheat the oven to 350°F.

8. Place the bread in the oven and bake until it is golden brown and feels lighter when lifted, 35 to 45 minutes.

9. Remove the bread from the oven, place it on a wire rack, and let it cool before enjoying.

BREAD WITH PÂTÉ FERMENTÉE

YIELD: 1 LOAF / **ACTIVE TIME:** 15 MINUTES / **TOTAL TIME:** 24 HOURS

Pre-fermenting some of the flour the night before will result in bread with a more complex aroma and taste, resembling that of sourdough bread. Learning this simple pre-ferment of French origin will also help when adapting any recipe calling for sourdough, as pâté fermentée makes for a perfect substitute. This pre-ferment also has the advantage of tasting milder than both sourdough and other pre-ferments because it contains salt, which slows down fermentation.

INGREDIENTS:

FOR THE PÂTÉ FERMENTÉE

⅔ CUP (80 G) BREAD FLOUR

3⅓ TABLESPOONS (50 G) WATER, AT ROOM TEMPERATURE

½ TEASPOON (1.7 G) INSTANT YEAST

⅓ TEASPOON (2 G) FINE SEA SALT

FOR THE DOUGH

1½ CUPS (340 G) WATER

½ PACKET (3.5 G) OF ACTIVE DRY YEAST OR ⅓ PACKET (2.5 G) OF INSTANT YEAST

4¼ CUPS (510 G) BREAD FLOUR, PLUS MORE AS NEEDED

1½ TEASPOONS (9 G) FINE SEA SALT

1. To prepare the pâté fermentée, combine all of the ingredients in a mixing bowl and let it rest at room temperature overnight.

2. The next day, begin preparations for the dough. If using active dry yeast, warm 3½ tablespoons of the water until it is about 105°F. Add the yeast and water to the work bowl of a stand mixer fitted with the dough hook and gently stir to combine. Let the mixture sit until it starts to foam, about 10 minutes.

3. Add the flour and remaining water and work the mixture on low until it comes together as a dough. Add the salt and work the dough until it is incorporated. Knead at low speed for 5 minutes, raise the speed to medium, and work the dough until it is smooth, 2 to 3 minutes.

4. Shape the dough into a ball, place it in a clean mixing bowl, and cover it with plastic wrap. Let the dough rest for 2 hours.

5. Place the dough on a flour-dusted work surface and shape it into two rounds.

6. Place the shaped rounds in two bowls that are at least three times their size and lined with floured kitchen towels. Cover the dough with plastic wrap or a kitchen towel and let it rest until it has almost doubled in size, about 1½ hours.

7. Preheat the oven to 500°F and place a baking stone or steel on the middle rack of the oven as it warms.

8. Invert the loaves onto a parchment-lined peel. Score the loaves with a long cut down the middle, slide them onto the heated baking implement, and bake with steam, using one of the methods described on page 32.

9. Reduce the temperature to 445°F and bake for 10 minutes, then reduce the temperature to 410°F and bake until the bread is golden brown, feels lighter when lifted, and makes a hollow sound when tapped, 15 to 20 minutes.

10. Remove the bread from the oven, place it on a wire rack, and let it cool completely before slicing and serving.

CIABATTA

YIELD: 2 LOAVES / **ACTIVE TIME:** 2 HOURS AND 30 MINUTES / **TOTAL TIME:** 24 HOURS

It wouldn't be a stretch to say that the United States has had a love affair with ciabatta over the last few years, so much so that one couldn't be blamed for getting a little sick of the stuff. Consider this recipe the antidote to your ciabatta exhaustion. Spongy yet sturdy, it will have you falling in love all over again.

INGREDIENTS:

FOR THE LEVAIN

- ¼ CUP (30 G) ALL-PURPOSE FLOUR
- 1/10 CUP (24 G) WATER
- 1/5 CUP (12 G) SOURDOUGH STARTER (SEE PAGE 40)

FOR THE DOUGH

- 9½ CUPS (1 KG) FRESHLY MILLED WHOLE WHEAT FLOUR
- ¼ CUP (35 G) LEVAIN
- 4 CUPS (908 G) WATER
- 2⅓ TABLESPOONS (34 G) FINE SEA SALT
- 1 TEASPOON (2 G) INSTANT YEAST
- 3 TABLESPOONS (40 G) EXTRA-VIRGIN OLIVE OIL, PLUS MORE AS NEEDED
- ¼ CUP (28 G) TOASTED WHEAT GERM

1. To prepare the levain, place all of the ingredients in a mixing bowl and stir to combine. Let the levain rest in a naturally warm spot for 4 hours before using.

2. To begin preparations for the dough, place the flour, levain, and 90 percent of the water in the work bowl of a stand mixer fitted with the dough hook and work the mixture on low until it comes together as a shaggy mass. Sprinkle the salt, yeast, olive oil, wheat germ, and remaining water on top and mix by hand. Once combined, the ingredients should have a temperature of 78°F. If the dough's temperature is different, cover the bowl and place the dough in a drafty or warmer area of the kitchen to adjust its overall temperature. Let the dough rest for 1½ hours.

3. Fold the dough five to seven times, waiting 12 minutes between each fold, until the dough is smooth and elastic.

4. Coat a large container with olive oil, place the dough in it, and store it in the refrigerator overnight.

5. Remove the dough from the refrigerator and divide it in half. Let the dough rest at room temperature for 30 minutes.

6. Preheat the oven to 500°F and place a baking stone or steel on the middle rack of the oven as it warms. Invert the loaves onto a parchment-lined peel and slide them onto the heated baking implement. Reduce the temperature to 450°F and cook until they are golden brown and feel lighter when lifted, about 25 minutes.

7. Remove the ciabattas from the oven, place them on a wire rack, and let them cool completely before slicing and serving.

CIABATTA WITH POOLISH

YIELD: 6 TO 8 LOAVES / **ACTIVE TIME:** 30 MINUTES / **TOTAL TIME:** 24 HOURS

Ciabatta is a bread with a high ratio of water to flour, and it is meant to be filled. Copyrighted in 1982 by Arnaldo Cavallari and Francesco Favaron, who initially called it ciabatta polesana, this bread echoes the name and shape of an analogous bread with a much older history, paposcia del Gargano, from Apulia. Paposcia means "slipper" in the local Apulian dialect, which, incidentally, is the meaning of the word "ciabatta."

INGREDIENTS:

FOR THE POOLISH

- 1/6 TEASPOON (½ G) ACTIVE DRY YEAST
- ⅓ CUP (76 G) WATER
- ⅚ CUP (100 G) ALL-PURPOSE FLOUR

FOR THE DOUGH

- 4 CUPS PLUS 1¾ TABLESPOONS (496 G) ALL-PURPOSE FLOUR
- 1½ CUPS PLUS 3⅓ TABLESPOONS (390 G) WATER
- 2 TEASPOONS (12 G) FINE SEA SALT

1. The night before you plan to bake, prepare the poolish by combining the yeast, water, and flour in an airtight container. Cover the container and let the poolish rest at room temperature overnight.

2. The next morning, to begin preparations for the dough, place the poolish, flour, and 1½ cups of the water in the work bowl of a stand mixer fitted with the dough hook and work the mixture until it comes together as a dough. Cover the bowl with plastic wrap and let the dough rest at room temperature for 30 minutes.

3. Add the salt and remaining water to the dough and knead until they are incorporated. Let the dough rest for an hour, performing three sets of stretches and folds every 20 minutes.

4. Cover the dough with a kitchen towel and let it rest at room temperature for 30 minutes.

5. On a flour-dusted work surface, divide the dough in half and shape each piece into a log, making sure not to press down too hard on the dough and deflate it. Cut each log into either four pieces for smaller ciabattas or three pieces for larger ciabattas.

6. Transfer the pieces to a heavily flour-dusted baking sheet and sprinkle flour over the top. Let the ciabattas rest for 1½ hours.

7. Preheat the oven to 480°F and place a baking stone or steel on the middle rack of the oven as it warms.

8. Stretch the ciabattas until they resemble slippers and place them on a parchment-lined peel. Slide the dough onto the heated baking implement and bake with steam, using one of the methods described on page 32.

9. Bake for 10 minutes, briefly open the oven to release steam, and then reduce the temperature to 410°F. Bake for an additional 10 to 20 minutes, which will depend on the size of your ciabattas and the color you prefer.

10. Remove the ciabattas from the oven, place them on a wire rack, and let them cool completely before slicing and serving.

CIABATTA WITH BIGA

YIELD: 2 LOAVES / **ACTIVE TIME:** 40 MINUTES / **TOTAL TIME:** 24 HOURS

The Italian answer to the French baguette, ciabatta has staked its claim as one of the most popular breads in the world. As this recipe uses a high-hydration dough, we use the double-hydration method—adding the water in two parts so the dough gets a chance to build some gluten and form a structure before it receives the remaining water.

INGREDIENTS:

FOR THE BIGA

- 1 CUP PLUS 2 TABLESPOONS (257 G) WATER
- 1/8 TEASPOON (1/2 G) FRESH YEAST
- 3 1/3 CUPS (400 G) BREAD FLOUR

FOR THE DOUGH

- 2 2/3 CUPS (605 G) PLUS 1/2 CUP (115 G) WATER, KEPT SEPARATE
- 2 1/2 TEASPOONS (6 G) FRESH YEAST
- 6 1/2 CUPS (780 G) BREAD FLOUR, PLUS MORE AS NEEDED
- 3 CUPS (340 G) BIGA
- 1 TABLESPOON (18 G) FINE SEA SALT
- EXTRA-VIRGIN OLIVE OIL, AS NEEDED

1. The day before you plan to bake, make the biga. Place all of the ingredients in a bowl, mix by hand until combined, and cover the bowl with plastic wrap. Let the biga rest at room temperature for 16 to 18 hours.

2. The next day, begin preparations for the dough. Place all of the dough ingredients, except for ½ cup of the water and the olive oil, in the work bowl of a stand mixer fitted with the dough hook and work the mixture on low until the dough comes together.

3. Gradually add the remaining water and knead the dough on low until it is smooth and developed.

4. Coat a large container with olive oil and place the dough in it. Let the dough let it rest for 45 minutes.

5. Fold the dough and let it rest for an additional 45 minutes. Repeat this process three more times for a total of four folds, each followed by a 45-minute period of rest.

6. Turn the dough out onto a generously flour-dusted work surface, making sure not to press down too hard on the dough and deflate it.

7. Sprinkle flour on top of the dough. Divide the dough in half, using two flour-dusted bench scrapers. Dust a baking sheet with flour and place the dough on it.

8. Preheat the oven to 470°F and place a baking stone or steel on the middle rack of the oven as it warms. Place the dough in a naturally warm spot and let it rest for 30 minutes.

9. Transfer the dough to a peel and slide it onto the heated baking implement.

10. Bake the ciabattas until they are golden brown, about 25 minutes.

11. Remove the ciabattas from the oven, place them on a wire rack, and let them cool completely before slicing and serving.

CIABATTA WITH OLIVE OIL

YIELD: 2 LOAVES / **ACTIVE TIME:** 30 MINUTES / **TOTAL TIME:** 4 HOURS AND 30 MINUTES

Ciabatta, with its large holes, delightfully chewy texture, and crisp crust, is Italian country bread at its finest.

INGREDIENTS:

- 4¼ CUPS (510 G) UNBLEACHED ALL-PURPOSE FLOUR, PLUS MORE AS NEEDED
- 1 TEASPOON (3 G) INSTANT YEAST
- 1½ CUPS (340 G) WATER, AT ROOM TEMPERATURE
- 2 TABLESPOONS (26 G) EXTRA-VIRGIN OLIVE OIL
- 2 TEASPOONS (11 G) FINE SEA SALT

1. Place all of the ingredients, except the salt, in the work bowl of a stand mixer fitted with the dough hook and work the mixture on low until it comes together as a dough. Add the salt and work the dough until it is incorporated. Knead at low speed for 5 minutes, raise the speed to medium, and work the dough until it is smooth, 2 to 3 minutes.

2. Place the dough in a clean bowl, cover the bowl with plastic wrap, and let the dough rest at room temperature for 3 hours, folding the edges of the dough into the center every 30 minutes.

3. Turn the dough out onto a generously flour-dusted work surface. Cut the dough in half and gently stretch the pieces into rough rectangles, each about 4 x 10 inches. Place the pieces of dough on a large piece of parchment paper and sprinkle a bit of flour over the top. Cover the loaves loosely with plastic wrap and let them rest until they are light and airy, about 1 hour.

4. Preheat the oven to 500°F and place a baking stone or steel on the middle rack of the oven as it warms.

5. Use a peel to transfer the loaves onto the heated baking implement and bake with steam, using one of the methods described on page 32.

6. Bake for 5 minutes and reduce the temperature to 450°F. Continue baking the ciabattas until they're a deep golden brown and feel firm and very light, about 25 minutes.

7. Remove the ciabattas from the oven, place them on a wire rack, and let them cool completely before slicing and serving.

Ciabatta with Olive Oil, *see page 163*

SOURDOUGH CIABATTA

YIELD: 6 TO 8 LOAVES / **ACTIVE TIME:** 40 MINUTES / **TOTAL TIME:** 7 HOURS

Modern ciabatta is made with yeast, but the bread that inspired it, paposcia del Gargano, was made with the scraps of overproofed dough that remained in the kneading trough used to make the weekly large country loaves. As such, this sourdough version is in line with that tradition.

INGREDIENTS:

- ½ (HEAPING) CUP (125 G) SOURDOUGH STARTER (SEE PAGE 40)
- 1⅖ CUPS PLUS 2 TABLESPOONS (347 G) WATER
- 2½ CUPS (300 G) BREAD FLOUR
- ⅚ CUP (100 G) ALL-PURPOSE FLOUR, PLUS MORE AS NEEDED
- 1½ TEASPOONS (9 G) FINE SEA SALT
- 1 TEASPOON (5 G) HONEY

1. In the work bowl of a stand mixer fitted with the dough hook, combine the starter with 1⅖ cups of the water. Add the flours, mix until the dough comes together, and then work the dough on low for 5 minutes.

2. Cover the bowl with a kitchen towel and let the dough rest for 30 minutes.

3. Incorporate the salt and honey. Add the remaining water, if the dough can absorb it. This dough is supposed to be well hydrated, but not liquid.

4. Knead the dough until smooth and elastic, about 10 minutes.

5. Cover the bowl with plastic wrap and let rest for 3½ hours.

6. Place the dough on a flour-dusted work surface, divide it in half, and shape each piece into a log, making sure not to press down too hard on the dough and deflate it. Cut each log into three or four pieces.

7. Transfer the pieces to a heavily flour-dusted baking sheet and generously sprinkle flour over them. Let the dough rest for 2 hours.

8. Preheat the oven to 480°F and place a baking stone or steel on the middle rack of the oven as it warms.

9. Stretch the pieces of dough until they are long and resemble slippers. Place the pieces of dough on a parchment-lined peel, slide them onto the heated baking implement, and bake with steam, using one of the methods described on page 32.

10. Bake for 10 minutes, open the oven door, and let the steam out. Reduce the temperature to 410°F and bake for another 10 to 20 minutes, depending on the size of the ciabattas and what color you prefer them to be.

11. Remove the ciabattas from the oven, place them on a wire rack, and let them cool completely before slicing and serving.

LIGHT WHOLE WHEAT SOURDOUGH BREAD

YIELD: 2 LARGE LOAVES / **ACTIVE TIME:** 30 MINUTES / **TOTAL TIME:** 24 HOURS

Here's a mild sourdough bread that is fermented for many hours with a small amount of sourdough. It's a great way to practice with different flours, as a small amount will not affect the behavior of the loaf during fermentation too much.

INGREDIENTS:

FOR THE LEVAIN

- ½ CUP (60 G) WHOLE WHEAT FLOUR (STONE-GROUND PREFERRED)
- ⅓ CUP (40 G) BREAD FLOUR
- ¼ CUP (57 G) WATER
- 2 TEASPOONS (10 G) SOURDOUGH STARTER (SEE PAGE 40)

FOR THE DOUGH

- 7½ CUPS (900 G) BREAD FLOUR, PLUS MORE AS NEEDED
- ¾ CUP (90 G) WHOLE WHEAT FLOUR
- 3 CUPS (681 G) WATER
- 3⅖ TEASPOONS (20 G) FINE SEA SALT

1. The night before you are planning to bake, prepare the levain. Place all of the ingredients in a mixing bowl and stir until combined. Cover the bowl with plastic wrap and let the levain rest at room temperature for 12 to 16 hours.

2. The next day, begin preparations for the dough. Place the flours and water in the work bowl of a stand mixer and work the mixture on low until it comes together as a dough. Let the dough rest for 30 minutes.

3. Add the levain and work the dough until the levain has been thoroughly incorporated. Add the salt and work the dough until it is smooth and well developed.

4. Place the dough in a clean bowl, cover it with a kitchen towel, and place it in a naturally warm spot. Let it rest for 3 hours. During this rising period, give the dough three folds, stretching the dough and folding it upon itself several times.

5. Place the dough on a flour-dusted work surface and divide it into two pieces. Give the pieces a light shaping and let them rest for 30 minutes.

6. Shape the dough into loaves, place them in bannetons or bowls, and cover them with floured kitchen towels.

7. Let the dough rest until it is proofed, 3 to 5 hours, depending on the temperature and humidity in the kitchen.

8. When the dough is just about proofed, preheat the oven to the maximum temperature and place a cast-iron Dutch oven with its lid on in the oven as it warms.

9. Remove the Dutch oven from the oven. Score one piece of dough, gently insert it into the Dutch oven, put the lid back on the pot, and place the Dutch oven in the oven. Bake for 30 minutes, remove the lid, and then finish baking until the bread is the desired color, feels lighter when lifted, and makes a hollow sound when tapped.

10. Remove the loaf from the oven, place it on a wire rack, and let it cool completely before slicing and serving. Repeat Steps 9 and 10 with the remaining piece of dough.

24-HOUR SOURDOUGH BREAD

YIELD: 1 LOAF / **ACTIVE TIME:** 20 MINUTES / **TOTAL TIME:** 24 HOURS

When time at home is scarce, even baking a basic sourdough loaf can become trying. No worries. You can let the wild yeasts and lactic acid work for you while you attend to your daily routine.

INGREDIENTS:

- ½ CUP PLUS 1 TABLESPOON (120 G) SOURDOUGH STARTER (SEE PAGE 40)
- 1 CUP (227 G) WATER
- 3¼ CUPS (390 G) BREAD FLOUR, PLUS MORE AS NEEDED
- 1½ TEASPOONS (9 G) FINE SEA SALT

1. The night before you are planning to bake, combine the starter and water in the work bowl of a stand mixer fitted with the dough hook. In another mixing bowl, combine the flour and salt and then add this mixture to the wet mixture. Work the mixture on low until it comes together as a dough, 5 to 6 minutes. Transfer the dough to a plastic, ceramic, or glass container, cover it with plastic wrap, and let the dough rest for 2½ hours, folding it at the 30-minute and 1-hour marks.

2. Shape the dough into a large round and place it in a generously flour-dusted banneton. Place the basket in a large resealable plastic bag, seal the bag, and place it in the refrigerator until the following evening.

3. Around 6 PM on the evening of the second day, remove the dough from the refrigerator and let it rest at room temperature for 2 to 3 hours, still sealed in the plastic bag. Preheat the oven to 520°F and place a baking stone or steel on the middle rack of the oven as it warms.

4. Invert the dough onto a parchment-lined peel and score it. Place it on the heated baking implement and bake with steam, using one of the methods described on page 32.

5. Reduce the temperature to 460°F and bake for 10 minutes, then reduce the temperature to 430°F and bake until the bread is golden brown, feels lighter when lifted, and makes a hollow sound when tapped, 15 to 20 minutes.

6. Remove the bread from the oven, place it on a wire rack, and let it cool completely before slicing and serving.

NO-KNEAD SOURDOUGH BREAD

YIELD: 1 LOAF / **ACTIVE TIME:** 15 MINUTES / **TOTAL TIME:** 24 HOURS

This is a very simple and rustic country sourdough that does not require kneading or even a proofing basket—just a good starter, an oven, and your attention. The result is the quintessential crusty sourdough, which pairs wonderfully with Italian cold cuts or roasted vegetables. It also works wonderfully as a base for bruschetta.

INGREDIENTS:

- ¾ CUP (170 G) SOURDOUGH STARTER (SEE PAGE 40)
- 1 CUP PLUS 2 TABLESPOONS (257 G) WATER
- 2¼ CUPS (270 G) BREAD FLOUR
- 1 CUP (120 G) ALL-PURPOSE FLOUR
- 2 TEASPOONS (12 G) FINE SEA SALT
- SEMOLINA FLOUR, AS NEEDED

1. The evening before baking, mix the starter and water in a large bowl. Add the flours and salt and work the dough as little as possible, just enough to combine it. Do not use a stand mixer; mix first with a spoon and then gently with your hands.

2. Cover the bowl tightly with plastic wrap. Let the dough rest at room temperature for 2 hours, then place the dough in the refrigerator overnight.

3. Remove the dough from the refrigerator. If it has almost doubled in size, let it rest at room temperature for 30 minutes. If the dough has not doubled in size, let it rest at room temperature for 2 hours.

4. Dust a work surface and a kitchen towel with semolina flour, place the dough on it, and fold the corners of the dough toward the center, making it a rough rectangle.

5. Flip the dough over onto the semolina-dusted kitchen towel, seam side down. Gently close the kitchen towel, leaving enough space for the loaf to rise, and generously sprinkle it with semolina flour.

6. Let the dough rest at room temperature until it has almost doubled in size, 1½ to 3 hours. It's ready when you poke the dough with a finger and it springs back slowly.

7. Preheat the oven to 520°F and place a baking stone or steel on the middle rack of the oven as it warms.

8. Invert the loaf onto a parchment-lined peel. Score the loaf with a sharp knife or scissors, slide it onto the heated baking implement, and bake with steam, using one of the methods described on page 32.

9. Reduce the temperature to 460°F and bake for 10 to 15 minutes, then reduce the temperature to 430°F and bake until the bread is golden brown, feels lighter when lifted, and makes a hollow sound when tapped, 20 to 25 minutes.

10. Remove the bread from the oven, place it on a wire rack, and let it cool completely before slicing and serving.

48-HOUR SOURDOUGH BREAD

YIELD: 1 LOAF / **ACTIVE TIME:** 20 MINUTES / **TOTAL TIME:** 48 HOURS

Who said that bread can be baked only on weekends or vacations? Following the suggested time schedule, it is possible to bake a spectacular sourdough loaf even during a busy workweek. Feel free to modify this basic recipe by playing with different flours.

INGREDIENTS:

- ½ CUP PLUS 1 TABLESPOON (120 G) SOURDOUGH STARTER (SEE PAGE 40)
- 1 CUP (227 G) WATER
- 3¼ CUPS (390 G) BREAD FLOUR, PLUS MORE AS NEEDED
- 1½ TEASPOONS (9 G) FINE SEA SALT

1. Around 6 PM on the evening of the first day, combine the starter and water in the work bowl of a stand mixer fitted with the dough hook. In another mixing bowl, combine the flour and salt and then add this mixture to the wet mixture. Work the resulting mixture on low until it comes together as a dough, 5 to 6 minutes. Transfer the dough to a clean bowl, cover it with plastic wrap, and refrigerate the dough overnight.

2. Around 6 PM on the evening of the second day, remove the dough from the refrigerator. If it has almost doubled in size, let it rest at room temperature for 30 minutes. If the dough has not doubled in size, let it rest at room temperature for 2 hours.

3. Shape the dough into a large round and place it in a generously flour-dusted banneton. Place the banneton in a large resealable plastic bag, seal the bag, and place it in the refrigerator until the following evening.

4. Around 6 PM on the evening of the third day, remove the dough from the refrigerator and let it rest at room temperature for 2 to 3 hours, still sealed in the plastic bag. Preheat the oven to 520°F and place a baking stone or steel on the middle rack of the oven as it warms.

5. Invert the dough onto a parchment-lined peel and score it. Place it on the heated baking implement and bake with steam, using one of the methods described on page 32.

6. Reduce the temperature to 460°F and bake for 10 minutes, then reduce the temperature to 430°F and bake until the bread is golden brown, feels lighter when lifted, and makes a hollow sound when tapped, 15 to 20 minutes.

7. Remove the bread from the oven, place it on a wire rack, and let it cool completely before slicing and serving.

ALMOND SOURDOUGH BREAD

YIELD: 1 LOAF / **ACTIVE TIME:** 30 MINUTES / **TOTAL TIME:** 5 HOURS AND 30 MINUTES

Almonds make a wonderful addition to bread—especially sourdough bread. Their mild vanilla flavor and sweet nuttiness beautifully complement the delicate tang of a sourdough loaf.

INGREDIENTS:

- 1 CUP BLANCHED ALMONDS
- 1 CUP (227 G) WATER
- ½ CUP PLUS 1 TABLESPOON (120 G) SOURDOUGH STARTER (SEE PAGE 40)
- 3¼ CUPS (390 G) BREAD FLOUR, PLUS MORE AS NEEDED
- 1½ TEASPOONS (9 G) FINE SEA SALT

1. Preheat the oven to 390°F. Place the almonds on a baking sheet, place them in the oven, and roast until they are lightly browned and fragrant, about 10 minutes. Remove the almonds from the oven and let them cool completely.

2. In the work bowl of a stand mixer fitted with the dough hook, combine the water and starter. Add the flour and work the mixture on low for 5 minutes until it comes together as a dough. Let the dough rest for 20 minutes.

3. Add the salt and work the dough until it is smooth and elastic, about 5 minutes. Add the almonds and work the dough until they are evenly distributed.

4. Place the dough in a clean bowl, cover it with plastic wrap, and let it rest until it has increased to 1½ times its original size, 2 to 2½ hours. Make a series of folds during the first hour.

5. Place the dough on a flour-dusted work surface and shape it into a round. Place the shaped round in a banneton or a bowl lined with a floured kitchen towel. Cover the dough with a kitchen towel and let the dough rest at room temperature for 1½ to 2 hours.

6. Preheat the oven to 520°F and place a baking stone or steel on the middle rack of the oven as it warms.

7. Invert the dough onto a parchment-lined peel and score it. Place it on the heated baking implement and bake with steam, using one of the methods described on page 32.

8. Reduce the temperature to 460°F and bake for 10 minutes, then reduce the temperature to 430°F and bake until the bread is golden brown, feels lighter when lifted, and makes a hollow sound when tapped, 20 to 25 minutes.

9. Remove the bread from the oven, place it on a wire rack, and let it cool completely before slicing and serving.

BLUEBERRY SOURDOUGH BREAD

YIELD: 1 LOAF / **ACTIVE TIME:** 30 MINUTES / **TOTAL TIME:** 6 HOURS

Blueberries give a tangy bite to a rustic sourdough, making it an incredible match with good cheese and honey or jam.

INGREDIENTS:

- ⅔ CUP (150 G) SOURDOUGH STARTER (SEE PAGE 40)
- 1 CUP (227 G) WATER, AT ROOM TEMPERATURE
- 3⅓ TABLESPOONS (65 G) SWEETENED CONDENSED MILK
- 3¼ CUPS (390 G) BREAD FLOUR, PLUS MORE AS NEEDED
- 1 CUP (120 G) WHOLE WHEAT FLOUR
- 1½ TEASPOONS (9 G) FINE SEA SALT
- 1 CUP FRESH BLUEBERRIES

1. In the work bowl of a stand mixer fitted with the dough hook, combine the starter, water, and condensed milk. Add the flours and work the mixture on low until it comes together as a dough. Add the salt and work the dough until it is incorporated. Knead at low speed for 5 minutes, raise the speed to medium, and work the dough until it is smooth, 2 to 3 minutes.

2. Place the dough in a clean bowl, cover it with plastic wrap, and let it rest until it has increased to 1½ times its original size, 2 to 2½ hours. Make a series of folds during the first 1½ hours.

3. Place the dough on a flour-dusted work surface and shape it into a round. Place the shaped round in a proofing basket or a bowl lined with a floured kitchen towel. Cover it with a kitchen towel and let the dough rest at room temperature for 1½ to 2 hours.

4. Preheat the oven to 520°F and place a baking stone or steel on the middle rack of the oven as it warms.

5. Invert the dough onto a parchment-lined peel and score it. Place it on the heated baking implement and bake with steam, using one of the methods described on page 32.

6. Reduce the temperature to 460°F and bake for 10 minutes, then reduce the temperature to 430°F and bake until the bread is golden brown, feels lighter when lifted, and makes a hollow sound when tapped, 20 to 25 minutes.

7. Remove the bread from the oven, place it on a wire rack, and let it cool completely before slicing and serving.

CHOCOLATE & HAZELNUT SOURDOUGH BREAD

YIELD: 1 LOAF / **ACTIVE TIME:** 30 MINUTES / **TOTAL TIME:** 5 HOURS AND 30 MINUTES

Unsweetened cocoa lends this bread a wonderful dark hue, and the nuttiness of hazelnuts makes this loaf a real treat with sweet spreads as well as, surprisingly perhaps, cheese.

INGREDIENTS:

- ⅔ CUP BLANCHED HAZELNUTS
- 1 CUP PLUS 1 TABLESPOON (242 G) WATER, AT ROOM TEMPERATURE
- ½ CUP PLUS 1 TABLESPOON (120 G) SOURDOUGH STARTER (SEE PAGE 40)
- 3¼ CUPS (390 G) BREAD FLOUR, PLUS MORE AS NEEDED
- 1½ TEASPOONS (9 G) FINE SEA SALT
- 3 TABLESPOONS (16 G) UNSWEETENED COCOA POWDER

1. Preheat the oven to 390°F. Place the hazelnuts on a baking sheet, place them in the oven, and roast until they are lightly browned and fragrant, about 10 minutes. Remove the hazelnuts from the oven and let them cool completely.

2. In the work bowl of a stand mixer fitted with the dough hook, combine the water and starter. Add the flour and work on low until it just comes together. Let the dough rest for 20 minutes.

3. Add the salt and cocoa powder and work the dough until they are incorporated. Knead at low speed for 5 minutes, raise the speed to medium, and work the dough until it is smooth, 2 to 3 minutes, incorporating the hazelnuts toward the end of the kneading process.

4. Place the dough in a clean bowl, cover it with plastic wrap, and let it rest until it has increased to 1½ times its original size, 2 to 2½ hours. Make a series of folds during the first hour.

5. Place the dough on a flour-dusted work surface and shape it into a round. Place the shaped round in a banneton or a bowl lined with a floured kitchen towel. Cover it with a kitchen towel and let the dough rest at room temperature for 1½ to 2 hours.

6. Preheat the oven to 520°F and place a baking stone or steel on the middle rack of the oven as it warms.

7. Invert the dough onto a parchment-lined peel and score it. Place it on the heated baking implement and bake with steam, using one of the methods described on page 32.

8. Reduce the temperature to 460°F and bake for 10 minutes, then reduce the temperature to 430°F and bake until the bread is golden brown, feels lighter when lifted, and makes a hollow sound when tapped, 20 to 25 minutes.

9. Remove the bread from the oven, place it on a wire rack, and let it cool completely before slicing and serving.

COFFEE SOURDOUGH BREAD

YIELD: 1 LOAF / **ACTIVE TIME:** 30 MINUTES / **TOTAL TIME:** 5 HOURS

The addition of espresso to sourdough gives the bread a lovely dark crust and adds a hint of the very best part of the day—that first cup of coffee—to the flavor. It's a bread that screams for butter and jam.

INGREDIENTS:

- ¾ CUP PLUS 3 TABLESPOONS (215 G) WATER, AT ROOM TEMPERATURE
- ⅔ CUP PLUS 1 TABLESPOON (165 G) SOURDOUGH STARTER (SEE PAGE 40)
- 4 CUPS (480 G) BREAD FLOUR, PLUS MORE AS NEEDED
- ½ CUP (60 G) WHOLE WHEAT FLOUR
- ⅖ CUP (112 G) FINELY GROUND ESPRESSO
- 2 TEASPOONS (14 G) HONEY
- 2 TEASPOONS (12 G) FINE SEA SALT

1. In the work bowl of a stand mixer fitted with the dough hook, combine the water and starter. Add the flours and work on low until it just comes together. Let the dough rest for 20 minutes.

2. Add the espresso, honey, and salt and work the dough until they are incorporated. Knead at low speed for 5 minutes, raise the speed to medium, and work the dough until it is smooth, 2 to 3 minutes.

3. Place the dough in a clean bowl, cover it with plastic wrap, and let it rest until it has increased to 1½ times its original size, 2 to 2½ hours. Make a series of folds during the first 1½ hours.

4. Place the dough on a flour-dusted work surface and shape it into a round. Place the shaped round in a banneton or a bowl lined with a floured kitchen towel. Cover it with a kitchen towel and let the dough rest at room temperature for 1½ to 2 hours.

5. Preheat the oven to 520°F and place a baking stone or steel on the middle rack of the oven as it warms.

6. Invert the dough onto a parchment-lined peel and score it. Place it on the heated baking implement and bake with steam, using one of the methods described on page 32.

7. Reduce the temperature to 460°F and bake for 10 minutes, then reduce the temperature to 430°F and bake until the bread is golden brown, feels lighter when lifted, and makes a hollow sound when tapped, 20 to 25 minutes.

8. Remove the bread from the oven, place it on a wire rack, and let it cool completely before slicing and serving.

WALNUT & RAISIN SOURDOUGH BREAD

YIELD: 1 LOAF / **ACTIVE TIME:** 30 MINUTES / **TOTAL TIME:** 5 HOURS AND 30 MINUTES

Raisins and walnuts are truly a match made in heaven, resulting in a sourdough that is impossible not to love.

INGREDIENTS:

- 1 CUP (227 G) WATER, AT ROOM TEMPERATURE
- ½ CUP PLUS 1 TABLESPOON (120 G) SOURDOUGH STARTER (SEE PAGE 40)
- 3¼ CUPS (390 G) BREAD FLOUR, PLUS MORE AS NEEDED
- 1½ TEASPOONS (9 G) FINE SEA SALT
- ¼ CUP RAISINS, SOAKED IN WARM WATER, DRAINED, AND SQUEEZED TO REMOVE EXCESS WATER
- ⅓ CUP WALNUTS

1. In the work bowl of a stand mixer fitted with the dough hook, combine the water and starter. Add the flour and work on low until it just comes together. Let the dough rest for 20 minutes.

2. Add the salt and work the dough until it is incorporated. Knead at low speed for 5 minutes, raise the speed to medium, and work the dough until it is smooth, 2 to 3 minutes, incorporating the raisins and walnuts toward the end of the kneading process.

3. Place the dough in a clean bowl, cover it with plastic wrap, and let it rest until it has increased to 1½ times its original size, 2 to 2½ hours. Make a series of folds during the first hour.

4. Place the dough on a flour-dusted work surface and shape it into a round. Place the shaped round in a banneton or a bowl lined with a floured kitchen towel. Cover it with a kitchen towel and let the dough rest at room temperature for 1½ to 2 hours.

5. Preheat the oven to 520°F and place a baking stone or steel on the middle rack of the oven as it warms.

6. Invert the dough onto a parchment-lined peel and score it. Place it on the heated baking implement and bake with steam, using one of the methods described on page 32.

7. Reduce the temperature to 460°F and bake for 10 minutes, then reduce the temperature to 430°F and bake until the bread is golden brown, feels lighter when lifted, and makes a hollow sound when tapped, 20 to 25 minutes.

8. Remove the bread from the oven, place it on a wire rack, and let it cool completely before slicing and serving.

OLIVE SOURDOUGH BREAD

YIELD: 1 LARGE LOAF / **ACTIVE TIME:** 30 MINUTES / **TOTAL TIME:** 5 HOURS AND 30 MINUTES

Olives are a wonderful addition to a basic sourdough, enhancing its rustic character and enriching the bread with earthy Mediterranean flavors.

INGREDIENTS:

- 1⅓ CUPS (302 G) WATER
- ⅔ CUP (150 G) SOURDOUGH STARTER (SEE PAGE 40)
- 3¼ CUPS (390 G) BREAD FLOUR, PLUS MORE AS NEEDED
- ¾ CUP (90 G) WHOLE WHEAT FLOUR
- 1½ TEASPOONS (9 G) FINE SEA SALT
- 1 CUP OLIVES, DRAINED AND PITTED

1. In the work bowl of a stand mixer fitted with the dough hook, combine the water and starter. Add the flours and work on low until it just comes together. Let the dough rest for 20 minutes.

2. Add the salt and work the dough until it is incorporated. Knead at low speed for 5 minutes, raise the speed to medium, and work the dough until it is smooth, 2 to 3 minutes, incorporating the olives toward the end of the kneading process.

3. Place the dough in a clean bowl, cover it with plastic wrap, and let it rest until it has increased to 1½ times its original size, 2 to 2½ hours. Make a series of folds during the first 1½ hours.

4. Place the dough on a flour-dusted work surface and shape it into a round. Place the shaped round in a banneton or a bowl lined with a floured kitchen towel. Cover it with a kitchen towel and let the dough rest at room temperature for 1½ to 2 hours.

5. Preheat the oven to 520°F and place a baking stone or steel on the middle rack of the oven as it warms.

6. Invert the dough onto a parchment-lined peel and score it. Place it on the heated baking implement and bake with steam, using one of the methods described on page 32.

7. Reduce the temperature to 460°F and bake for 15 minutes, then reduce the temperature to 430°F and bake until the bread is golden brown, feels lighter when lifted, and makes a hollow sound when tapped, 20 to 25 minutes.

8. Remove the bread from the oven, place it on a wire rack, and let it cool completely before slicing and serving.

Walnut & Raisin Sourdough Bread, *see page 184*

CHICKPEA SOURDOUGH BREAD

YIELD: 1 LOAF / **ACTIVE TIME:** 30 MINUTES / **TOTAL TIME:** 5 HOURS AND 30 MINUTES

If you want to increase the protein content in your bread, chickpea flour is a great option. This loaf is great with earthy spreads like pâté or tapenade.

INGREDIENTS:

- 1⅖ CUPS (317 G) WATER, AT ROOM TEMPERATURE
- ⅔ CUP (150 G) SOURDOUGH STARTER (SEE PAGE 40)
- 3 CUPS (360 G) BREAD FLOUR, PLUS MORE AS NEEDED
- ⅔ CUP (57 G) CHICKPEA FLOUR
- 2 TEASPOONS (12 G) FINE SEA SALT

1. In the work bowl of a stand mixer fitted with the dough hook, combine the water and starter. Add the flours and work on low until it just comes together. Let the dough rest for 20 minutes.

2. Add the salt and work the dough until it is incorporated. Knead at low speed for 5 minutes, raise the speed to medium, and work the dough until it is smooth, 2 to 3 minutes.

3. Place the dough in a clean bowl, cover it with plastic wrap, and let it rest until it has increased to 1½ times its original size, 2 to 2½ hours. Make a series of folds during the first 1½ hours.

4. Place the dough on a flour-dusted work surface and shape it into a round. Place the shaped round in a banneton or a bowl lined with a floured kitchen towel. Cover it with a kitchen towel and let the dough rest at room temperature for 1½ to 2 hours.

5. Preheat the oven to 520°F and place a baking stone or steel on the middle rack of the oven as it warms.

6. Invert the dough onto a parchment-lined peel and score it. Place it on the heated baking implement and bake with steam, using one of the methods described on page 32.

7. Reduce the temperature to 460°F and bake for 15 minutes, then reduce the temperature to 430°F and bake until the bread is golden brown, feels lighter when lifted, and makes a hollow sound when tapped, 20 to 25 minutes.

8. Remove the bread from the oven, place it on a wire rack, and let it cool completely before slicing and serving.

TURMERIC & LENTIL SOURDOUGH BREAD

YIELD: 1 LOAF / **ACTIVE TIME:** 40 MINUTES / **TOTAL TIME:** 6 HOURS

This loaf is as delicious as it is nutritious, enriched with proteins from the lentils and powerful antioxidants from the turmeric and garlic. Incidentally, this bread also has a vibrant, aesthetically pleasing color.

INGREDIENTS:

FOR THE LENTILS

- ½ CUP DRIED RED LENTILS
- ⅔ CUP WATER
- 2 GARLIC CLOVES
- 1 BAY LEAF
- PINCH OF FINE SEA SALT

FOR THE DOUGH

- 1 CUP PLUS 1 TABLESPOON (242 G) WATER
- ½ CUP PLUS 1 TABLESPOON (120 G) SOURDOUGH STARTER (SEE PAGE 40)
- 3¼ CUPS (390 G) BREAD FLOUR, PLUS MORE AS NEEDED
- ½ TEASPOON (1.5 G) TURMERIC
- 1½ TEASPOONS (9 G) FINE SEA SALT

1. To prepare the lentils, place all of the ingredients in a saucepan, bring them to a simmer, and cook until the lentils are starting to fall apart. Remove the bay leaf, discard it, and mash the lentils and garlic until they are smooth. Let the lentils cool completely.

2. To begin preparations for the dough, place the water and starter in the work bowl of a stand mixer fitted with the dough hook. Add the flour and work the mixture on low until it just comes together. Let the dough rest for 20 minutes.

3. Add the lentils, turmeric, and salt and work the dough until it is incorporated. Knead at low speed for 5 minutes, raise the speed to medium, and work the dough until it is smooth, 2 to 3 minutes.

4. Place the dough in a clean bowl, fold it over itself, cover it with plastic wrap, and let it rest for 2 hours. Fold the dough after the first hour.

5. Place the dough on a flour-dusted work surface and shape it into a round. Place the shaped round in a banneton or a bowl lined with a floured kitchen towel. Cover it with a kitchen towel and let the dough rest at room temperature for 2½ to 3 hours.

6. Preheat the oven to 475°F and place a baking stone or steel on the middle rack of the oven as it warms.

7. Invert the dough onto a parchment-lined peel and score it. Place it on the heated baking implement and bake with steam, using one of the methods described on page 32.

8. Bake for 15 minutes, then reduce the temperature to 410°F and bake until the bread is golden brown, feels lighter when lifted, and makes a hollow sound when tapped, 20 to 25 minutes.

9. Remove the bread from the oven, place it on a wire rack, and let it cool completely before slicing and serving.

SEMOLINA SOURDOUGH BREAD

YIELD: 2 LOAVES / **ACTIVE TIME:** 30 MINUTES / **TOTAL TIME:** 5 HOURS AND 30 MINUTES

Whole wheat semolina flour (or durum flour) supplies a golden touch to your crumb and an extra crunch to your crust. It is also a healthy choice, because it is rich in fiber and highly digestible. It makes a perfect accompaniment to Italian cold cuts and aged cheeses.

INGREDIENTS:

- 2⁄3 CUP PLUS 1 TABLESPOON (165 G) SOURDOUGH STARTER (SEE PAGE 40)
- 1 1⁄3 CUPS (302 G) WATER
- 3 1⁄4 CUPS (390 G) BREAD FLOUR, PLUS MORE AS NEEDED
- 1 CUP (160 G) SEMOLINA FLOUR
- 2 TEASPOONS (12 G) FINE SEA SALT

1. In the work bowl of a stand mixer fitted with the dough hook, combine the starter and water. Add the flours and work on low until it just comes together. Let the dough rest for 20 minutes.

2. Add the salt and work the dough until it is incorporated. Knead at low speed for 5 minutes, raise the speed to medium, and work the dough until it is smooth, 2 to 3 minutes.

3. Place the dough in a clean bowl, cover it with plastic wrap, and let it rest until it has increased to 1½ times its original size, 2 to 2½ hours.

4. Place the dough on a clean work surface and shape it into two logs. Place the loaves in two bannetons or loaf pans lined with floured kitchen towels. Cover the dough with kitchen towels and let it rest at room temperature for 1½ to 2 hours.

5. Preheat the oven to 520°F and place a baking stone or steel on the middle rack of the oven as it warms.

6. Invert the loaves onto a parchment-lined peel and score them. Slide them onto the heated baking implement and bake with steam, using one of the methods described on page 32.

7. Reduce the temperature to 460°F and bake for 15 minutes, then reduce the temperature to 430°F and bake until the bread is golden brown, feels lighter when lifted, and makes a hollow sound when tapped, 20 to 25 minutes.

8. Remove the loaves from the oven, place them on a wire rack, and let them cool completely before slicing and serving.

BARLEY SOURDOUGH BREAD

YIELD: 1 LOAF / **ACTIVE TIME:** 30 MINUTES / **TOTAL TIME:** 5 HOURS AND 30 MINUTES

Barley is a fantastic cereal, rich in nutrients and enzymes that will give your crust a beautiful deep-brown color. The gluten contained in barley is not ideal for bread baking, but when combined with wheat it can result in a gorgeous bread.

INGREDIENTS:

- 1 CUP PLUS 2 TABLESPOONS (257 G) WATER
- 1 CUP PLUS 1 TABLESPOON (242 G) SOURDOUGH STARTER (SEE PAGE 40)
- 3 CUPS (360 G) BREAD FLOUR, PLUS MORE AS NEEDED
- 1 CUP (85 G) BARLEY FLOUR
- 1½ TEASPOONS (9 G) FINE SEA SALT

1. In the work bowl of a stand mixer fitted with the dough hook, combine the water and starter. Add the flours and work on low until it just comes together. Let the dough rest for 20 minutes.

2. Add the salt and work the dough until it is incorporated. Knead at low speed for 5 minutes, raise the speed to medium, and work the dough until it is smooth, 2 to 3 minutes.

3. Place the dough in a clean bowl, cover it with plastic wrap, and let it rest until it has increased to 1½ times its original size, 2 to 2½ hours. Make a series of folds during the first hour.

4. Place the dough on a flour-dusted work surface and shape it into a round. Place the shaped round in a banneton or a bowl lined with a floured kitchen towel. Cover it with a kitchen towel and let the dough rest at room temperature for 1½ to 2 hours.

5. Preheat the oven to 520°F and place a baking stone or steel on the middle rack of the oven as it warms.

6. Invert the dough onto a parchment-lined peel and score it. Place it on the heated baking implement and bake with steam, using one of the methods described on page 32.

7. Reduce the temperature to 460°F and bake for 15 minutes, then reduce the temperature to 430°F and bake until the bread is golden brown, feels lighter when lifted, and makes a hollow sound when tapped, 20 to 25 minutes.

8. Remove the bread from the oven, place it on a wire rack, and let it cool completely before slicing and serving.

EXTREME COUNTRY SOURDOUGH BREAD

YIELD: 1 LOAF / **ACTIVE TIME:** 30 MINUTES / **TOTAL TIME:** 24 HOURS

For a beginner, this is a rather easy way to approach a highly hydrated country sourdough, displaying the open and irregular crumb that is so popular nowadays. Make sure you work your dough until you see that it becomes very elastic and do not add more water if the dough will not absorb it. Every flour is different, so add as much water as the one you are using can take.

INGREDIENTS:

FOR THE LEVAIN

- 1½ TEASPOONS (8 G) SOURDOUGH STARTER (SEE PAGE 40)
- ⅓ CUP (75 G) WATER
- ⅗ CUP (70 G) BREAD FLOUR

FOR THE DOUGH

- ¼ CUP PLUS 5 TABLESPOONS (128 G) WATER, PLUS MORE AS NEEDED
- 3¼ CUPS (390 G) STRONG BREAD FLOUR, PLUS MORE AS NEEDED
- 2 TEASPOONS (12 G) FINE SEA SALT

1. To prepare the levain, place all of the ingredients in a mixing bowl, cover the bowl with plastic wrap, and let the levain rest at room temperature for 12 to 18 hours.

2. To begin preparations for the dough, place four-fifths of the water, the levain, and flour in the work bowl of a stand mixer fitted with the dough hook and work the mixture on low until the dough comes together. Cover the work bowl with a kitchen towel and let the dough rest for 40 minutes.

3. In another bowl, combine the salt and remaining water and stir until the salt has dissolved. Add the salt water to the dough and knead to incorporate. Knead the dough on low until it is smooth and elastic, about 5 minutes.

4. Place the dough in a clean bowl, cover it with plastic wrap, and let it rest for 2½ hours. Fold the dough after 40 minutes and again after 1 hour and 20 minutes. With each fold, incorporate about 1½ tablespoons of water, unless the dough already seems too hydrated and loose.

5. Place the dough on a flour-dusted work surface and shape it into a round. Place the shaped round in a banneton or a bowl lined with a floured kitchen towel. Cover it with a kitchen towel and let the dough rest at room temperature for 2 to 3 hours.

6. Preheat the oven to 520°F and place a baking stone or steel on the middle rack of the oven as it warms.

7. Invert the dough onto a parchment-lined peel and score it. Place it on the heated baking implement and bake with steam, using one of the methods described on page 32.

8. Reduce the temperature to 460°F and bake for 10 to 15 minutes. Reduce the temperature to 430°F and bake until the bread is golden brown, feels lighter when lifted, and makes a hollow sound when tapped, 20 to 25 minutes.

9. Remove the bread from the oven, place it on a wire rack, and let it cool completely before slicing and serving.

ROMAN COUNTRY SOURDOUGH BREAD

YIELD: 1 LOAF / **ACTIVE TIME:** 15 MINUTES / **TOTAL TIME:** 6 HOURS

Rome is surrounded by lovely countryside with beautiful hills and volcanic lakes, an area that locals call Castelli Romani. The traditional country sourdoughs of this region have a chewy and pitted interior, and a thick and dark crust.

INGREDIENTS:

- ⅔ CUP (150 G) SOURDOUGH STARTER (SEE PAGE 40)
- 1½ CUPS (340 G) WATER
- 3 CUPS (360 G) BREAD FLOUR
- 3 CUPS (360 G) ALL-PURPOSE FLOUR
- ½ CUP (60 G) WHOLE WHEAT FLOUR
- 2 TEASPOONS (12 G) FINE SEA SALT
- SEMOLINA FLOUR, AS NEEDED

1. In the work bowl of a stand mixer fitted with the dough hook, combine the starter and water. Add all of the flours, except for the semolina, and work the mixture on low until it just comes together. Let the dough rest for 20 minutes.

2. Add the salt and work the dough until it is incorporated. Knead at low speed for 5 minutes, raise the speed to medium, and work the dough until it is smooth, 2 to 3 minutes.

3. Place the dough in a clean bowl, cover it with plastic wrap, and let it rest for 2½ hours.

4. Preheat the oven to the maximum temperature and place a baking stone or steel on the middle rack of the oven as it warms.

5. Dust a work surface with semolina flour, place the dough on it, and fold the corners into the center to shape it into a rectangle. Flip the dough over onto a semolina-dusted kitchen towel and heavily sprinkle the loaf with semolina. Carefully close the kitchen towel, leaving enough space for the loaf to rise.

6. Let the dough rest at room temperature until it has almost doubled in size, 2 to 3 hours. It's ready when you poke the dough with a finger and it springs back slowly.

7. Invert the loaf onto a parchment-lined peel, slide it onto the heated baking implement, and bake with a little bit of steam, using one of the methods described on page 32.

8. Bake for 15 minutes, reduce the temperature to 460°F, and open the oven door to let the steam out.

9. Bake for 20 minutes, then lower the temperature to 390°F and bake until the bread is dark brown, feels lighter when lifted, and makes a hollow sound when tapped.

10. Remove the bread from the oven, place it on a wire rack, and let it cool completely before slicing and serving.

EASY SOURDOUGH BREAD

YIELD: 1 LOAF / **ACTIVE TIME:** 30 MINUTES / **TOTAL TIME:** 24 HOURS

A foundational recipe that has the tangy taste and crispy crust everyone wants in a sourdough.

INGREDIENTS:

- 1 CUP (227 G) WATER
- 3⅓ CUPS (400 G) BREAD FLOUR, PLUS MORE AS NEEDED
- ⅓ CUP (38 G) WHOLE WHEAT FLOUR
- 1 CUP (227 G) SOURDOUGH STARTER (SEE PAGE 40)
- 2 TEASPOONS (12 G) FINE SEA SALT

1. Place the water and flours in the work bowl of a stand mixer fitted with the dough hook and work the mixture on low for 6 minutes. Cover the work bowl with plastic wrap and let the dough rest at room temperature for 1 hour.

2. Place the work bowl back on the mixer and add the starter and salt. Knead the mixture at low speed until the dough starts to come together, about 2 minutes. Raise the speed to medium and knead until the dough is elastic and pulls away from the side of the bowl, about 3 minutes.

3. Shape the dough into a ball, spray the seam side with water, and place it in a flour-dusted banneton, seam side down. Cover the dough with plastic wrap and let it rest at room temperature for 2 hours.

4. Place the dough in the refrigerator overnight.

5. Preheat the oven to 450°F and place a baking stone or steel on the middle rack of the oven as it warms.

6. Invert the dough onto a parchment-lined peel and score it. Slide the dough onto the heated baking implement and bake with steam, using one of the methods described on page 32.

7. Bake for 20 minutes, open the oven door to release the steam, and bake until the bread is golden brown, feels lighter when lifted, and makes a hollow sound when tapped, about 20 minutes.

8. Remove the bread from the oven, place it on a wire rack, and let it cool completely before slicing and serving.

HARVEST SOURDOUGH BREAD

YIELD: 1 LOAF / **ACTIVE TIME:** 30 MINUTES / **TOTAL TIME:** 24 HOURS

This bread is great in just about any situation, but becomes sublime when used as the base of a sandwich filled with Thanksgiving leftovers.

INGREDIENTS:

- 1 CUP (227 G) WATER
- 3⅓ CUPS (400 G) BREAD FLOUR, PLUS MORE AS NEEDED
- ⅓ CUP (38 G) WHOLE WHEAT FLOUR
- ¼ CUP DRIED CRANBERRIES
- 2 TABLESPOONS PUMPKIN SEEDS, PLUS MORE FOR TOPPING
- 2 TABLESPOONS SUNFLOWER SEEDS, PLUS MORE FOR TOPPING
- 2 TABLESPOONS POPPY SEEDS, PLUS MORE FOR TOPPING
- 2 TABLESPOONS CHIA SEEDS, PLUS MORE FOR TOPPING
- 1 CUP (227 G) SOURDOUGH STARTER (SEE PAGE 40)
- 2 TEASPOONS (12 G) FINE SEA SALT

1. Place the water and flours in the work bowl of a stand mixer fitted with the dough hook and work the mixture on low for 6 minutes. Cover the work bowl with plastic wrap and let the dough rest at room temperature for 1 hour.

2. Place the work bowl back on the mixer and add the cranberries, seeds, starter, and salt. Knead the mixture at low speed until the dough starts to come together, about 2 minutes. Raise the speed to medium and knead until the dough is elastic and pulls away from the side of the bowl, about 3 minutes.

3. Shape the dough into a ball. Combine the seeds for topping on a plate. Shape the dough into a ball and spray the seam side with water. Roll the top of the dough in the mixture until coated.

4. Place the dough in a flour-dusted banneton, seam side down. Cover it with plastic wrap and let it rest at room temperature for 2 hours.

5. Place the dough in the refrigerator overnight.

6. Preheat the oven to 450°F and place a baking stone or steel on the middle rack of the oven as it warms.

7. Transfer the dough onto a parchment-lined peel and score it. Slide the dough onto the heated baking implement and bake with steam, using one of the methods described on page 32.

8. Bake for 20 minutes, open the oven door to release the steam, and bake until the bread is golden brown, feels lighter when lifted, and makes a hollow sound when tapped, about 20 minutes.

9. Remove the bread from the oven, place it on a wire rack, and let it cool completely before slicing and serving.

MULTIGRAIN SOURDOUGH BREAD

YIELD: 1 LOAF / **ACTIVE TIME:** 30 MINUTES / **TOTAL TIME:** 24 HOURS

The texture provided by the oats and seeds is the drawing card here.

1. Place the water and flours in the work bowl of a stand mixer fitted with the dough hook and work the mixture on low for 6 minutes. Cover the work bowl with plastic wrap and let the dough rest at room temperature for 1 hour.

2. Place the work bowl back on the mixer and add the oats, seeds, millet, starter, and salt. Knead the mixture at low speed until the dough starts to come together, about 2 minutes. Raise the speed to medium and knead until the dough is elastic and pulls away from the side of the bowl, about 3 minutes.

3. Shape the dough into a ball. Place some oats for topping on a plate. Shape the dough into a ball and spray the seam side with water. Roll the top of the dough in the oats until coated.

4. Place the dough in a flour-dusted banneton, seam side down. Cover it with plastic wrap and let it rest at room temperature for 2 hours.

5. Place the dough in the refrigerator overnight.

6. Preheat the oven to 450°F and place a baking stone or steel on the middle rack of the oven as it warms.

7. Invert the dough onto a parchment-lined peel and score it. Slide the dough onto the heated baking implement and bake with steam, using one of the methods described on page 32.

8. Bake for 20 minutes, open the oven door to release the steam, and bake until the bread is golden brown, feels lighter when lifted, and makes a hollow sound when tapped, about 20 minutes.

9. Remove the bread from the oven, place it on a wire rack, and let it cool completely before slicing and serving.

INGREDIENTS:

- 1 CUP (227 G) WATER
- 3⅓ CUPS (400 G) BREAD FLOUR, PLUS MORE AS NEEDED
- ⅓ CUP (38 G) WHOLE WHEAT FLOUR
- 1 CUP ROLLED OATS, PLUS MORE FOR TOPPING
- ¼ CUP SUNFLOWER SEEDS
- ¼ CUP MILLET
- 1 CUP (227 G) SOURDOUGH STARTER (SEE PAGE 40)
- 2 TEASPOONS (12 G) FINE SEA SALT

STOUT SOURDOUGH BREAD

YIELD: 1 LOAF / **ACTIVE TIME:** 30 MINUTES / **TOTAL TIME:** 24 HOURS

The stout adds still another layer of fermented flavor to the bread, plus a bit of sweetness.

INGREDIENTS:

- ½ CUP (119 G) DARK STOUT
- ½ CUP (114 G) WATER, AT ROOM TEMPERATURE
- 3⅓ CUPS (400 G) BREAD FLOUR, PLUS MORE AS NEEDED
- ⅓ CUP (38 G) WHOLE WHEAT FLOUR
- 1 CUP (227 G) SOURDOUGH STARTER (SEE PAGE 40)
- 2 TEASPOONS (12 G) FINE SEA SALT

1. Place the stout, water, and flours in the work bowl of a stand mixer fitted with the dough hook and work the mixture on low for 6 minutes. Cover the work bowl with plastic wrap and let the dough rest at room temperature for 1 hour.

2. Place the work bowl back on the mixer and add the starter and salt. Knead the mixture at low speed until the dough starts to come together, about 2 minutes. Raise the speed to medium and knead until the dough is elastic and pulls away from the side of the bowl, about 3 minutes.

3. Shape the dough into a ball, spray the seam side with water, and place it in a flour-dusted banneton, seam side down. Cover the dough with plastic wrap and let it rest at room temperature for 2 hours.

4. Place the dough in the refrigerator overnight.

5. Preheat the oven to 450°F and place a baking stone or steel on the middle rack of the oven as it warms.

6. Invert the dough onto a parchment-lined peel and score it. Slide the dough onto the heated baking implement and bake with steam, using one of the methods described on page 32.

7. Bake for 20 minutes, open the oven door to release the steam, and bake until the bread is golden brown, feels lighter when lifted, and makes a hollow sound when tapped, about 20 minutes.

8. Remove the bread from the oven, place it on a wire rack, and let it cool completely before slicing and serving.

CARAMELIZED ONION SOURDOUGH BREAD

YIELD: 1 LOAF / **ACTIVE TIME:** 30 MINUTES / **TOTAL TIME:** 24 HOURS

The sweetness of caramelized onions cuts beautifully against sourdough's celebrated tang.

INGREDIENTS:

- 1 TEASPOON (4 G) EXTRA-VIRGIN OLIVE OIL
- 1 WHITE ONION, SLICED THIN
- 1 TABLESPOON (13 G) SUGAR
- 1 CUP (227 G) WATER
- 3⅓ CUPS (400 G) BREAD FLOUR, PLUS MORE AS NEEDED
- ⅓ CUP (38 G) WHOLE WHEAT FLOUR
- 1 CUP (227 G) SOURDOUGH STARTER (SEE PAGE 40)
- 2 TEASPOONS (12 G) FINE SEA SALT
- 1 CUP WHITE SESAME SEEDS, FOR TOPPING

1. Place the olive oil in a large skillet and warm it over medium heat. Add the onion and sugar, reduce the heat to medium-low, and cook the onion, stirring frequently, until it starts to caramelize, about 30 minutes. Remove the pan from heat and let the onion cool.

2. Place the water and flours in the work bowl of a stand mixer fitted with the dough hook and work the mixture on low for 6 minutes. Cover the work bowl with plastic wrap and let the dough rest at room temperature for 1 hour.

3. Place the work bowl back on the mixer and add the caramelized onion, starter, and salt. Knead the mixture at low speed until the dough starts to come together, about 2 minutes. Raise the speed to medium and knead until the dough is elastic and pulls away from the side of the bowl, about 3 minutes.

4. Place the sesame seeds on a plate. Shape the dough into a ball and spray the seam side with water. Roll the top of the dough in the sesame seeds until coated.

5. Place the dough in a flour-dusted banneton, seam side down, cover it with plastic wrap, and let it rest at room temperature for 2 hours.

6. Place the dough in the refrigerator overnight.

7. Preheat the oven to 450°F and place a baking stone or steel on the middle rack of the oven as it warms.

8. Invert the dough onto a parchment-lined peel and score it. Slide the dough onto the heated baking implement and bake with steam, using one of the methods described on page 32.

9. Bake for 20 minutes, open the oven door to release the steam, and bake until the bread is golden brown, feels lighter when lifted, and makes a hollow sound when tapped, about 20 minutes.

10. Remove the bread from the oven, place it on a wire rack, and let it cool completely before slicing and serving.

Caramelized Onion Sourdough Bread, see page 205

BLACK SESAME SOURDOUGH BREAD

YIELD: 1 BOULE / **ACTIVE TIME:** 30 MINUTES / **TOTAL TIME:** 24 HOURS

Black tahini lends this bread plenty of earthiness, plus an eye-catching smoky look.

INGREDIENTS:

- 1 CUP (227 G) WATER
- 3⅓ CUPS (400 G) BREAD FLOUR, PLUS MORE AS NEEDED
- ⅓ CUP (38 G) WHOLE WHEAT FLOUR
- ½ CUP (128 G) BLACK TAHINI PASTE
- 1 CUP (227 G) SOURDOUGH STARTER (SEE PAGE 40)
- 2 TEASPOONS (12 G) FINE SEA SALT
- 1 CUP BLACK SESAME SEEDS, FOR TOPPING

1. Place the water and flours in the work bowl of a stand mixer fitted with the dough hook and work the mixture on low for 6 minutes. Cover the work bowl with plastic wrap and let the dough rest at room temperature for 1 hour.

2. Place the work bowl back on the mixer and add the tahini paste, starter, and salt. Knead the mixture at low speed until the dough starts to come together, about 2 minutes. Raise the speed to medium and knead until the dough is elastic and pulls away from the side of the bowl, about 3 minutes.

3. Place the sesame seeds on a plate. Shape the dough into a ball and spray the seam side with water. Roll the top of the dough in the sesame seeds until coated.

4. Place the dough in a flour-dusted banneton, seam side down, cover it with plastic wrap, and let it rest at room temperature for 2 hours.

5. Place the dough in the refrigerator overnight.

6. Preheat the oven to 450°F and place a baking stone or steel on the middle rack of the oven as it warms.

7. Invert the dough onto a parchment-lined peel and score it. Slide the dough onto the heated baking implement and bake with steam, using one of the methods described on page 32.

8. Bake for 20 minutes, open the oven door to release the steam, and bake until the bread is golden brown, feels lighter when lifted, and makes a hollow sound when tapped, about 20 minutes.

9. Remove the bread from the oven, place it on a wire rack, and let it cool completely before slicing and serving.

RYE COUNTRY LOAF

YIELD: 3 LOAVES / **ACTIVE TIME:** 1 HOUR / **TOTAL TIME:** 24 HOURS

Inspired by traditional French country breads, these loaves carry an extremely complex flavor.

INGREDIENTS:

FOR THE RYE STARTER

- 1 TEASPOON (7 G) SOURDOUGH STARTER (SEE PAGE 40)
- ¾ CUP (80 G) WHOLE RYE FLOUR
- ¼ CUP (60 G) WATER

FOR THE LEVAIN

- 1 TEASPOON (7 G) SOURDOUGH STARTER
- ¼ CUP (30 G) STONE-GROUND WHEAT FLOUR
- ¼ CUP (30 G) ALL-PURPOSE FLOUR
- 2 TABLESPOONS (30 G) WATER

FOR THE DOUGH

- 4⅛ CUPS (495 G) ALL-PURPOSE FLOUR, PLUS MORE AS NEEDED
- 3½ CUPS (420 G) STONE-GROUND WHOLE WHEAT FLOUR
- 3 CUPS (681 G) WATER
- 1⅓ TABLESPOONS (24 G) FINE SEA SALT

1. To prepare the rye starter, place all of the ingredients in a large bowl and stir until combined. To prepare the levain, place all of the ingredients in another large bowl and stir until combined. Cover the bowls and let the rye starter and levain rest at room temperature for 12 to 16 hours.

2. To begin preparations for the dough, in the work bowl of a stand mixer fitted with the dough hook, combine the flours and water and work the mixture on low until it just comes together. Let the dough rest for 30 minutes.

3. Add the rye starter, levain, and salt and work the dough until it is incorporated. Knead at low speed for 5 minutes.

4. Place the dough in a clean bowl, cover it with plastic wrap, and let it rest for 3 to 5 hours, making three folds. At the end of this rest, the dough will feel stronger and more elastic.

5. Place the dough on a flour-dusted work surface, divide it into three pieces, and lightly shape them. Cover the shaped loaves with flour-dusted kitchen towels and let them rest for 30 minutes.

6. Shape the loaves into their final shapes, place them in bannetons or bowls lined with floured kitchen towels, and cover them with kitchen towels. Let the dough rest at room temperature for 3 to 5 hours.

7. Preheat the oven to the maximum temperature and place a cast-iron Dutch oven with its lid on in the oven as it warms.

8. Remove the Dutch oven from the oven. Score the dough, gently place it in the Dutch oven, put the lid back on the pot, and place the Dutch oven in the oven. Bake for 30 minutes, remove the lid, and then finish baking until the bread is the desired color, feels lighter when lifted, and makes a hollow sound when tapped.

9. Remove the loaf from the oven, place it on a wire rack, and let it cool completely before slicing and serving. Repeat Steps 8 and 9 with the remaining pieces of dough.

BLUE PEA FLOWER SOURDOUGH BREAD

YIELD: 1 LOAF / **ACTIVE TIME:** 30 MINUTES / **TOTAL TIME:** 24 HOURS

Due to the high acidity of sourdough, the blue pea flower powder will actually produce a loaf that is closer to purple. It's a unique bread—both in terms of looks and taste.

INGREDIENTS:

- 1 CUP (227 G) WATER
- 3⅓ CUPS (400 G) BREAD FLOUR, PLUS MORE AS NEEDED
- ⅓ CUP (38 G) WHOLE WHEAT FLOUR
- ¼ CUP (24 G) BLUE PEA FLOWER POWDER
- 1 CUP (227 G) SOURDOUGH STARTER (SEE PAGE 40)
- 2 TEASPOONS (12 G) FINE SEA SALT

1. Place the water, flours, and blue pea flower powder in the work bowl of a stand mixer fitted with the dough hook and work the mixture on low for 6 minutes. Cover the work bowl with plastic wrap and let the dough rest at room temperature for 1 hour.

2. Place the work bowl back on the mixer and add the starter and salt. Knead the mixture at low speed until the dough starts to come together, about 2 minutes. Raise the speed to medium and knead until the dough is elastic and pulls away from the side of the bowl, about 3 minutes.

3. Shape the dough into a ball, spray the seam side with water, and place it in a flour-dusted banneton, seam side down. Cover the dough with plastic wrap and let it rest at room temperature for 2 hours.

4. Place the dough in the refrigerator overnight.

5. Preheat the oven to 450°F and place a baking stone or steel on the middle rack of the oven as it warms.

6. Invert the dough onto a parchment-lined peel and score it. Slide the dough onto the heated baking implement and bake with steam, using one of the methods described on page 32.

7. Bake for 20 minutes, open the oven door to release the steam, and bake until the bread is golden brown, feels lighter when lifted, and makes a hollow sound when tapped, about 20 minutes.

8. Remove the bread from the oven, place it on a wire rack, and let it cool completely before slicing and serving.

Blue Pea Flower Sourdough Bread, *see page 211*

RYE SOURDOUGH BREAD

YIELD: 1 LOAF / **ACTIVE TIME:** 30 MINUTES / **TOTAL TIME:** 24 HOURS

The rye flour brings a little spice and a little fruitiness to the proceedings.

INGREDIENTS:

- 2 TABLESPOONS CARAWAY SEEDS
- 1 CUP (227 G) WATER
- 3⅓ CUPS (400 G) BREAD FLOUR
- ⅓ CUP (35 G) DARK RYE FLOUR, PLUS MORE AS NEEDED
- 1 CUP (227 G) SOURDOUGH STARTER (SEE PAGE 40)
- 2 TEASPOONS (12 G) FINE SEA SALT

1. Place the caraway seeds in a dry skillet and toast over medium heat until they are fragrant, shaking the pan frequently. Remove the pan from heat and let the seeds cool.

2. Place the water and flours in the work bowl of a stand mixer fitted with the dough hook and work the mixture on low for 6 minutes. Cover the work bowl with plastic wrap and let the dough rest at room temperature for 1 hour.

3. Place the work bowl back on the mixer and add the toasted caraway seeds, starter, and salt. Knead the mixture at low speed until the dough starts to come together, about 2 minutes. Raise the speed to medium and knead until the dough is elastic and pulls away from the side of the bowl, about 3 minutes.

4. Shape the dough into a ball, spray the seam side with water, and place it in a flour-dusted banneton, seam side down. Cover the dough with plastic wrap and let it rest at room temperature for 2 hours.

5. Place the dough in the refrigerator overnight.

6. Preheat the oven to 450°F and place a baking stone or steel on the middle rack of the oven as it warms.

7. Invert the dough onto a parchment-lined peel and score it. Slide the dough onto the heated baking implement and bake with steam, using one of the methods described on page 32.

8. Bake for 20 minutes, open the oven door to release the steam, and bake until the bread is golden brown, feels lighter when lifted, and makes a hollow sound when tapped, about 20 minutes.

9. Remove the bread from the oven, place it on a wire rack, and let it cool completely before slicing and serving.

BLACK GARLIC SOURDOUGH BREAD

YIELD: 1 LOAF / **ACTIVE TIME:** 30 MINUTES / **TOTAL TIME:** 24 HOURS

Adding the beguiling flavor of black garlic to sourdough's unique tang will cause all who encounter this bread to savor it in complete silence.

INGREDIENTS:

- 1 CUP (227 G) WATER
- 3⅓ CUPS (400 G) BREAD FLOUR, PLUS MORE AS NEEDED
- ⅓ CUP (38 G) WHOLE WHEAT FLOUR
- CLOVES FROM 1 BULB OF BLACK GARLIC
- 2 GARLIC CLOVES, MINCED
- 1 CUP (227 G) SOURDOUGH STARTER (SEE PAGE 40)
- 2 TEASPOONS (12 G) FINE SEA SALT

1. Place the water and flours in the work bowl of a stand mixer fitted with the dough hook and work the mixture on low for 6 minutes. Cover the work bowl with plastic wrap and let the dough rest at room temperature for 1 hour.

2. Place the work bowl back on the mixer and add the black garlic, garlic, starter, and salt. Knead the mixture at low speed until the dough starts to come together, about 2 minutes. Raise the speed to medium and knead until the dough is elastic and pulls away from the side of the bowl, about 3 minutes.

3. Shape the dough into a ball, spray the seam side with water, and place it in a flour-dusted banneton, seam side down. Cover the dough with plastic wrap and let it rest at room temperature for 2 hours.

4. Place the dough in the refrigerator overnight.

5. Preheat the oven to 450°F and place a baking stone or steel on the middle rack of the oven as it warms.

6. Invert the dough onto a parchment-lined peel and score it. Slide the dough onto the heated baking implement and bake with steam, using one of the methods described on page 32.

7. Bake for 20 minutes, open the oven door to release the steam, and bake until the bread is golden brown, feels lighter when lifted, and makes a hollow sound when tapped, about 20 minutes.

8. Remove the bread from the oven, place it on a wire rack, and let it cool completely before slicing and serving.

ALL THE SEEDS SOURDOUGH BREAD

YIELD: 1 LOAF / **ACTIVE TIME:** 30 MINUTES / **TOTAL TIME:** 24 HOURS

A strong collection of seeds lends this bread texture, nuttiness, and complex flavor.

INGREDIENTS:

- 1 CUP (227 G) WATER
- 3⅓ CUPS (400 G) BREAD FLOUR, PLUS MORE AS NEEDED
- ⅓ CUP (38 G) WHOLE WHEAT FLOUR
- 2 TABLESPOONS SUNFLOWER SEEDS
- 2 TABLESPOONS BLACK SESAME SEEDS
- 2 TABLESPOONS WHITE SESAME SEEDS, PLUS MORE FOR TOPPING
- 2 TABLESPOONS CHIA SEEDS
- 2 TABLESPOONS MILLET
- 2 TABLESPOONS PUMPKIN SEEDS
- 2 TABLESPOONS POPPY SEEDS, PLUS MORE FOR TOPPING
- 1 CUP (227 G) SOURDOUGH STARTER (SEE PAGE 40)
- 2 TEASPOONS (12 G) FINE SEA SALT

1. Place the water and flours in the work bowl of a stand mixer fitted with the dough hook and work the mixture on low for 6 minutes. Cover the work bowl with plastic wrap and let the dough rest at room temperature for 1 hour.

2. Place the work bowl back on the mixer and add the seeds, starter, and salt. Knead the mixture at low speed until the dough starts to come together, about 2 minutes. Raise the speed to medium and knead until the dough is elastic and pulls away from the side of the bowl, about 3 minutes.

3. Combine the seeds designated for topping on a plate. Shape the dough into a ball and spray the seam side with water. Roll the top of the dough in the mixture until coated.

4. Place the dough in a flour-dusted banneton, seam side down. Cover it with plastic wrap and let it rest at room temperature for 2 hours.

5. Place the dough in the refrigerator overnight.

6. Preheat the oven to 450°F and place a baking stone or steel on the middle rack of the oven as it warms.

7. Invert the dough onto a parchment-lined peel and score it. Slide the dough onto the heated baking implement and bake with steam, using one of the methods described on page 32.

8. Bake for 20 minutes, open the oven door to release the steam, and bake until the bread is golden brown, feels lighter when lifted, and makes a hollow sound when tapped, about 20 minutes.

9. Remove the bread from the oven, place it on a wire rack, and let it cool completely before slicing and serving.

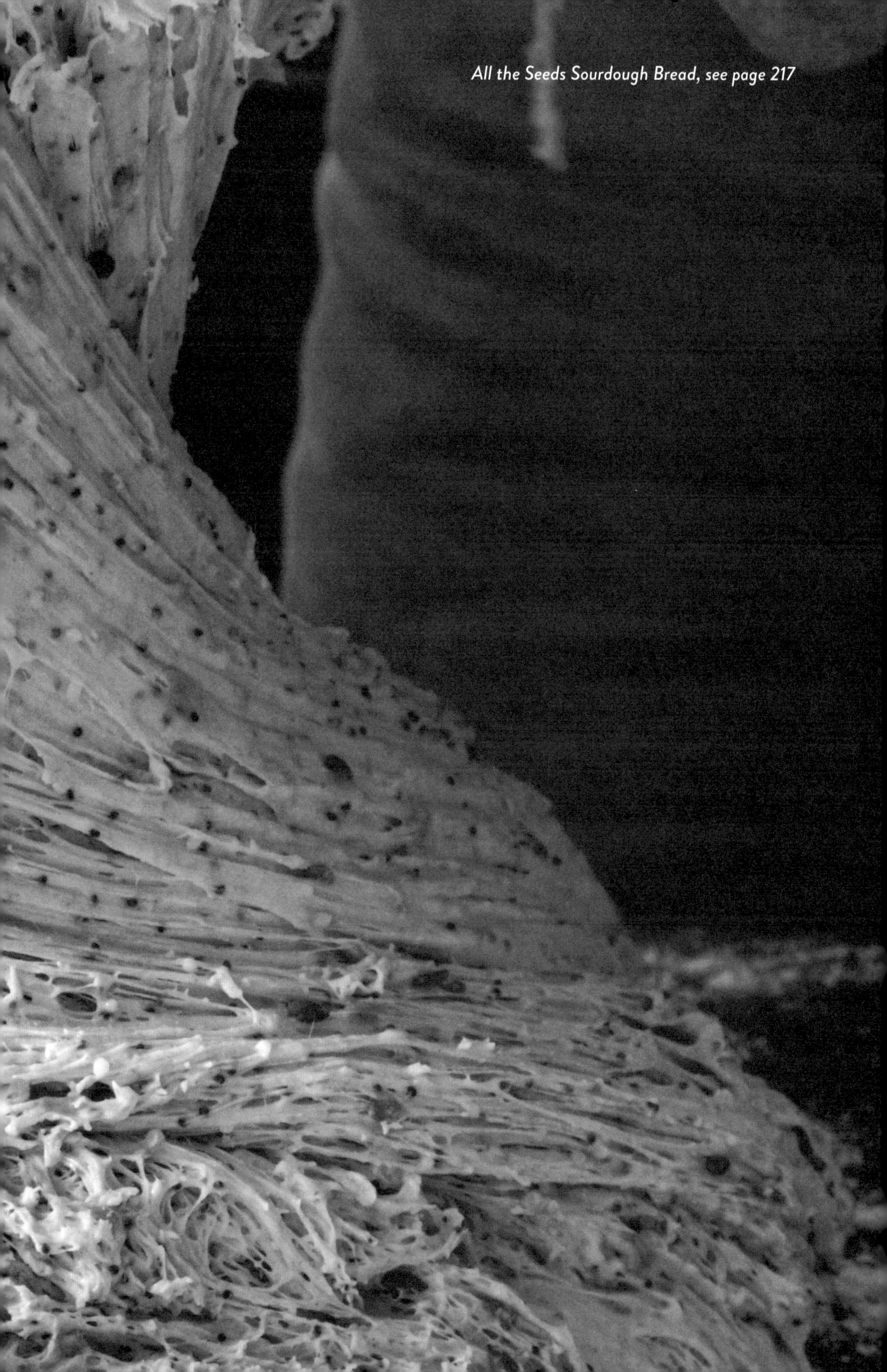

All the Seeds Sourdough Bread, *see page 217*

SUMMER BERRY SOURDOUGH

YIELD: 1 LOAF / **ACTIVE TIME:** 30 MINUTES / **TOTAL TIME:** 24 HOURS

Once your freezer is filled up, this is a wonderful spot for some of your berry-picking haul.

INGREDIENTS:

- 1 CUP (227 G) WATER
- 3⅓ CUPS (400 G) BREAD FLOUR, PLUS MORE AS NEEDED
- ⅓ CUP (38 G) WHOLE WHEAT FLOUR
- 2 TABLESPOONS LAVENDER BUDS
- ¼ CUP FROZEN BLUEBERRIES
- ¼ CUP FROZEN RASPBERRIES
- ¼ CUP FROZEN BLACKBERRIES
- 1 CUP (227 G) SOURDOUGH STARTER (SEE PAGE 40)
- 2 TEASPOONS (12 G) FINE SEA SALT

1. Place the water, flours, and lavender in the work bowl of a stand mixer fitted with the dough hook and work the mixture on low for 6 minutes. Cover the work bowl with plastic wrap and let the dough rest at room temperature for 1 hour.

2. Place the work bowl back on the mixer and add the berries, starter, and salt. Knead the mixture at low speed until the dough starts to come together, about 2 minutes. Raise the speed to medium and knead until the dough is elastic and pulls away from the side of the bowl, about 3 minutes.

3. Shape the dough into a ball and spray the seam side with water. Place the dough in a flour-dusted banneton, seam side down. Cover it with plastic wrap and let it rest at room temperature for 2 hours.

4. Place the dough in the refrigerator overnight.

5. Preheat the oven to 450°F and place a baking stone or steel on the middle rack of the oven as it warms.

6. Invert the dough onto a parchment-lined peel and score it. Slide the dough onto the heated baking implement and bake with steam, using one of the methods described on page 32.

7. Bake for 20 minutes, open the oven door to release the steam, and bake until the bread is golden brown, feels lighter when lifted, and makes a hollow sound when tapped, about 20 minutes.

8. Remove the bread from the oven, place it on a wire rack, and let it cool completely before slicing and serving.

SPINACH & HERB SOURDOUGH BREAD

YIELD: 1 LOAF / **ACTIVE TIME:** 30 MINUTES / **TOTAL TIME:** 24 HOURS

A beautiful and fresh-tasting sourdough that will lift any sandwich.

INGREDIENTS:

- 1 CUP BABY SPINACH
- 1 CUP (227 G) WATER
- 3⅓ CUPS (400 G) BREAD FLOUR, PLUS MORE AS NEEDED
- ⅓ CUP (38 G) WHOLE WHEAT FLOUR
- 1 TABLESPOON FRESH THYME LEAVES
- 1 TABLESPOON FINELY CHOPPED FRESH SAGE
- 1 TABLESPOON FINELY CHOPPED FRESH ROSEMARY
- 1 TABLESPOON FINELY CHOPPED FRESH BASIL
- 1 CUP (227 G) SOURDOUGH STARTER (SEE PAGE 40)
- 2 TEASPOONS (12 G) FINE SEA SALT

1. Prepare an ice bath and bring water to a boil in a small saucepan. Place the spinach in the pan and cook it for 30 seconds. Transfer the spinach to the ice bath to shock it. When cool, drain the spinach and squeeze it to remove as much water as possible.

2. Place the spinach and water in a blender and puree until smooth.

3. Place the puree and flours in the work bowl of a stand mixer fitted with the dough hook and work the mixture on low for 6 minutes. Cover the work bowl with plastic wrap and let the dough rest at room temperature for 1 hour.

4. Place the work bowl back on the mixer and add the herbs, starter, and salt. Knead the mixture at low speed until the dough starts to come together, about 2 minutes. Raise the speed to medium and knead until the dough is elastic and pulls away from the side of the bowl, about 3 minutes.

5. Shape the dough into a ball and spray the seam side with water. Place the dough in a flour-dusted banneton, seam side down. Cover it with plastic wrap and let it rest at room temperature for 2 hours.

6. Place the dough in the refrigerator overnight.

7. Preheat the oven to 450°F and place a baking stone or steel on the middle rack of the oven as it warms.

8. Invert the dough onto a parchment-lined peel and score it. Slide the dough onto the heated baking implement and bake with steam, using one of the methods described on page 32.

9. Bake for 20 minutes, open the oven door to release the steam, and bake until the bread is golden brown, feels lighter when lifted, and makes a hollow sound when tapped, about 20 minutes.

10. Remove the bread from the oven, place it on a wire rack, and let it cool completely before slicing and serving.

SOURDOUGH BAGUETTES

YIELD: 2 BAGUETTES / **ACTIVE TIME:** 1 HOUR AND 30 MINUTES / **TOTAL TIME:** 24 HOURS

These are a bit more involved than a standard baguette, but the additional effort will be well worth it.

INGREDIENTS:

- 5 OZ. (142 G) WATER
- 11½ OZ. (326 G) BREAD FLOUR, PLUS MORE AS NEEDED
- ½ OZ. (14 G) WHOLE WHEAT FLOUR
- 1 TEASPOON (4 G) SUGAR
- 1 CUP (227 G) SOURDOUGH STARTER (SEE PAGE 40)
- 1 TABLESPOON (16 G) FINE SEA SALT

1. Place the water and flours in the work bowl of a stand mixer fitted with the dough hook and work the mixture on low for 6 minutes. Cover the work bowl with plastic wrap and let the dough rest at room temperature for 1 hour.

2. Place the work bowl back on the mixer and add the sugar, starter, and salt. Knead at low speed until the dough starts to come together, about 2 minutes. Raise the speed to medium and knead until it is elastic and pulls away from the side of the bowl, about 3 minutes.

3. Shape the dough into a ball and spray the seam side with water. Place the dough in a flour-dusted banneton, seam side down. Cover it with plastic wrap and let it rest at room temperature for 2 hours.

4. Place the dough on a flour-dusted work surface, divide it in half, and shape each piece into a ball. Cover the dough with a damp kitchen towel and let it rest on the counter for 15 minutes.

5. Punch down the balls of dough and lightly shape them into ovals. Working with one piece at a time, take the side of the dough closest to you and roll it away. Starting halfway up the dough, fold in the corners and roll the dough into a rough baguette shape.

6. Place both hands over one piece of dough. Gently roll the dough while moving your hands back and forth over it and lightly pressing down until it is about 16 inches long.

7. Place the baguettes on a baguette pan, cover them with plastic wrap, and place them in the refrigerator overnight.

8. Remove the dough from the refrigerator, place it in a naturally warm spot, and let it rest for 2 hours.

9. Preheat the oven to 450°F.

10. Using a very sharp knife, cut four slits at a 45-degree angle along the length of each baguette.

11. Place the baguettes in the oven and bake with steam, using one of the methods described on page 32. Bake until the baguettes are a deep golden brown, feel lighter when lifted, and make a hollow sound when tapped, 20 to 30 minutes.

12. Remove the baguettes from the oven, place them on a wire rack, and let them cool slightly before slicing and serving.

BAGUETTES WITH LEVAIN DE PÂTE

YIELD: 4 LOAVES / **ACTIVE TIME:** 40 MINUTES / **TOTAL TIME:** 20 HOURS

First of all, congratulations on even trying a baguette recipe at home. It's one of the hardest "simple" breads to produce, because it is quite unforgiving—at every stage of production. Anyway, if they don't come out perfect the first time, don't panic—next time will be better, and eventually you'll nail it.

INGREDIENTS:

FOR THE LEVAIN

- ⅓ CUP (40 G) BREAD FLOUR
- 3 TABLESPOONS (45 G) WATER
- 1 TABLESPOON (10 G) STIFF SOURDOUGH STARTER (SEE PAGE 659)

FOR THE DOUGH

- 6⅓ CUPS (760 G) BREAD FLOUR, PLUS MORE AS NEEDED
- ⅓ CUP (40 G) WHEAT GERM
- 2¼ CUPS (530 G) WATER
- 1 TABLESPOON (18 G) FINE SEA SALT
- 1 TEASPOON (3 G) INSTANT YEAST
- RICE FLOUR, AS NEEDED

1. To prepare the levain, combine all of the ingredients in a mixing bowl, cover it with plastic wrap, and let the mixture rest at room temperature for 6 hours.

2. To begin preparations for the dough, place the flour, wheat germ, levain, and water in the work bowl of a stand mixer fitted with the dough hook and work the mixture on low until it comes together as a dough and no traces of flour are visible, about 5 minutes. Let the dough rest for 15 to 30 minutes.

3. Add the salt and yeast and mix on high, working the dough until it is smooth and elastic, about 6 minutes. Transfer the dough to a large container with a lid, fold the dough neatly, and cover the container. Place it on the lowest shelf of the refrigerator and refrigerate for 12 hours.

4. Remove the dough from the refrigerator and place it on a flour-dusted work surface. Divide the dough into four pieces and lightly shape them into rectangles. Cover the dough with kitchen towels and let it rest for 30 minutes.

5. Shape the dough into baguettes and put them in a baguette baking pan lined with floured kitchen towels, seam side up. Let them rest at room temperature for 1 hour.

6. Preheat the oven to 455°F and place a baking stone or steel on the middle rack of the oven as it warms.

7. Dust the tops of the baguettes with rice flour, roll them onto a peel, and score them with five to seven slashes.

8. Slide the baguettes onto the heated baking implement and bake with steam, using one of the methods described on page 32.

9. Bake until the baguettes are golden brown and their internal temperature is 203°F, about 28 minutes.

10. Remove the baguettes from the oven, place them on a wire rack, and let them cool completely before slicing and serving.

PAN CUBANO

YIELD: 3 LOAVES / ACTIVE TIME: 1 HOUR / TOTAL TIME: 5 HOURS

A recipe for a traditional Cuban bread that is in the style of a French baguette, but crispier and more flavorful, thanks to the use of lard in the dough.

INGREDIENTS:

- 8 OZ. (227 G) LUKEWARM WATER (90°F)
- 1 TABLESPOON (9 G) ACTIVE DRY YEAST
- 2 TEASPOONS (8 G) SUGAR
- 2 OZ. (57 G) LARD, MELTED AND COOLED SLIGHTLY
- ½ OZ. (14 G) EXTRA-VIRGIN OLIVE OIL
- 6 OZ. (170 G) ALL-PURPOSE FLOUR
- 6 OZ. (170 G) BREAD FLOUR, PLUS MORE AS NEEDED
- 1 TABLESPOON (16 G) FINE SEA SALT

1. Place the water and yeast in the work bowl of a stand mixer fitted with the dough hook, gently stir to combine, and let the mixture sit until it starts to foam, about 10 minutes.

2. Add the remaining ingredients and knead on low until the mixture comes together as a dough. Raise the speed to medium and knead the dough until it is smooth, about 8 minutes.

3. Place the dough on a flour-dusted work surface and knead it into a ball. Return it to the work bowl, cover it with plastic wrap, and let it rest at room temperature until it has doubled in size.

4. Divide the dough into three 12 oz. portions and shape them into balls. Coat an 18 x 13–inch baking sheet with nonstick cooking spray. Place the balls on the pan and cover them with plastic wrap. Let the dough rest at room temperature until it has doubled in size.

5. Place one ball of dough on a flour-dusted work surface and punch it down until it is a rough oval. Take the side of the dough closest to you and roll it away. Starting halfway up the dough, fold in the corners and roll the dough into a rough baguette shape.

6. Place both hands over the dough. Gently roll the dough while moving your hands back and forth over it and lightly pressing down until it is the length of the wall in a baguette pan (about 16 inches).

7. Place the bread on the baking sheet and repeat the shaping process with the remaining pieces of dough. When all of the dough has been shaped, cover it with plastic wrap, and let it rest until it has doubled in size.

8. Preheat the oven to 450°F. Coat a baguette pan with nonstick cooking spray.

9. Using a very sharp knife, cut four slits at a 45-degree angle along the length of each loaf.

10. Place the loaves in the oven and bake with steam, using one of the methods described on page 32. Bake until the bread is a deep golden brown and feels lighter when lifted, 20 to 30 minutes.

11. Remove the loaves from the oven, place them on a wire rack, and let them cool slightly before slicing and serving.

HOLIDAY BRIOCHE

YIELD: 1 LOAF / **ACTIVE TIME:** 45 MINUTES / **TOTAL TIME:** 4 HOURS

Break this one out during the holiday season, and watch people's eyes light up the second they see its beautiful shape on the table.

1. To prepare the sponge, place all of the ingredients in the work bowl of a stand mixer fitted with the dough hook. Cover the bowl with plastic wrap and let the mixture sit until it starts to bubble, about 30 minutes.

2. To begin preparations for the dough, add the 4 unbeaten eggs to the sponge and whisk to incorporate.

3. Add the sugar, flour, and salt and work the mixture at low speed for 5 minutes.

4. Over the course of 2 minutes, add the butter a little at a time with the mixer running. When all of the butter has been added, knead the mixture for 5 minutes.

5. Raise the speed to medium and work the dough until it begins to pull away from the side of the work bowl, about 6 minutes.

6. Cover the work bowl with a kitchen towel, place the dough in a naturally warm spot, and let it rest until it has doubled in size, about 1 hour.

7. Preheat the oven to 350°F. Coat a baking sheet with nonstick cooking spray. Divide the dough into four equal pieces and roll each one into a large, thin circle. Stack the pieces of dough on top of one another and place the stack on top of a piece of parchment paper.

8. Place a 3-inch circular object in the center of the stack and cut the dough into 16 equal pieces. Working around the dough, take two strands and twist them away from one another two times. Pinch the ends to join the two strands together. Once the brioche has been shaped, remove the circular object.

9. Use the parchment paper to lift up the brioche and place it on the baking sheet. Cover the pan with plastic wrap and let it rest for 30 minutes.

10. Brush the brioche with the beaten egg, place it in the oven, and bake until it is golden brown and the internal temperature is at least 200°F, 35 to 45 minutes.

11. Remove the brioche from the oven, place it on a wire rack, and let it cool completely. If desired, dust the brioche with confectioners' sugar before serving.

INGREDIENTS:

FOR THE SPONGE

- ½ CUP (113 G) WHOLE MILK, WARMED
- 4½ TEASPOONS (15 G) ACTIVE DRY YEAST
- 2 TABLESPOONS (42 G) HONEY
- 1 CUP (120 G) BREAD FLOUR

FOR THE DOUGH

- 5 EGGS, 1 BEATEN
- ⅓ (SCANT) CUP (60 G) SUGAR
- 3¾ CUPS (450 G) BREAD FLOUR, PLUS MORE AS NEEDED
- 2 TEASPOONS (12 G) FINE SEA SALT
- ½ CUP (113 G) UNSALTED BUTTER, SOFTENED

CONFECTIONERS' SUGAR, FOR TOPPING (OPTIONAL)

Holiday Brioche, see page 227

BRIOCHE

YIELD: 2 LOAVES / **ACTIVE TIME:** 45 MINUTES / **TOTAL TIME:** 4 HOURS

Generous amounts of eggs and butter create the rich and soft crumb in this classic French bread.

INGREDIENTS:

FOR THE SPONGE

- ½ CUP (114 G) MILK, WARMED TO 105°F
- 4½ TEASPOONS (13.5 G) ACTIVE DRY YEAST
- 2 TABLESPOONS (42 G) HONEY
- 4 OZ. (113 G) BREAD FLOUR

FOR THE DOUGH

- 5 EGGS, 1 BEATEN
- 2 OZ. (57 G) SUGAR
- 1 LB. (454 G) BREAD FLOUR
- 2 TEASPOONS (12 G) FINE SEA SALT
- 4 OZ. (113 G) UNSALTED BUTTER, SOFTENED

1. To prepare the sponge, place all of the ingredients in the work bowl of a stand mixer. Cover it with plastic wrap and let the mixture rest until it starts to bubble, about 30 minutes.

2. To begin preparations for the dough, add the four unbeaten eggs to the sponge and whisk until incorporated.

3. Add the sugar, flour, and salt, fit the mixer with the dough hook, and knead the mixture on low for 5 minutes.

4. Over the course of 2 minutes, add the butter a little at a time with the mixer running. When all of the butter has been added, knead the mixture on low for 5 minutes.

5. Raise the speed to medium and knead the dough until it begins to pull away from the side of the work bowl, about 6 minutes. Cover the bowl with a kitchen towel, place the dough in a naturally warm spot, and let it rest until it has doubled in size, about 1 hour.

6. Preheat the oven to 350°F. Coat two 8 x 4–inch loaf pans with nonstick cooking spray.

7. Divide the dough into two equal pieces and flatten each one into a rectangle that is the width of a loaf pan. Tuck in the sides to shape the dough into loaves and place them in the loaf pans, seam side down.

8. Cover the pans with plastic wrap and let the dough rest until it has crested over the top of the pans.

9. Brush the loaves with the beaten egg, place them in the oven, and bake until they are golden brown, feel lighter when lifted, and make a hollow sound when tapped, 35 to 45 minutes.

10. Remove the loaves from the oven, place the pans on a wire rack, and let the brioche cool before slicing and serving.

SEEDED BRIOCHE

YIELD: 2 LOAVES / **ACTIVE TIME:** 45 MINUTES / **TOTAL TIME:** 4 HOURS

Here's a delicious twist on the French classic, adding a bit of crunch to the famed softness.

INGREDIENTS:

FOR THE SPONGE

- ½ CUP (114 G) MILK, WARMED TO 105°F
- 4½ TEASPOONS (13.5 G) ACTIVE DRY YEAST
- 2 TABLESPOONS (42 G) HONEY
- 4 OZ. (113 G) BREAD FLOUR

FOR THE DOUGH

- 5 EGGS, 1 BEATEN
- 2 OZ. (57 G) SUGAR
- 1 LB. (454 G) BREAD FLOUR
- 2 TEASPOONS (12 G) FINE SEA SALT
- ¼ CUP SUNFLOWER SEEDS
- ¼ CUP MILLET
- ¼ CUP POPPY SEEDS
- ¼ CUP WHITE SESAME SEEDS
- 4 OZ. (113 G) UNSALTED BUTTER, SOFTENED

1. To prepare the sponge, place all of the ingredients in the work bowl of a stand mixer. Cover it with plastic wrap and let the mixture rest until it starts to bubble, about 30 minutes.

2. To begin preparations for the dough, add the four unbeaten eggs to the sponge and whisk until incorporated.

3. Add the sugar, flour, salt, and seeds, fit the mixer with the dough hook, and knead the mixture on low for 5 minutes.

4. Over the course of 2 minutes, add the butter a little at a time with the mixer running. When all of the butter has been added, knead the mixture on low for 5 minutes.

5. Raise the speed to medium and knead the dough until it begins to pull away from the side of the work bowl, about 6 minutes. Cover the bowl with a kitchen towel, place the dough in a naturally warm spot, and let it rest until it has doubled in size, about 1 hour.

6. Preheat the oven to 350°F. Coat two 8 x 4–inch loaf pans with nonstick cooking spray.

7. Divide the dough into two equal pieces and flatten each one into a rectangle that is the width of a loaf pan. Tuck in the sides to shape the dough into loaves and place them in the loaf pans, seam side down.

8. Cover the pans with plastic wrap and let the dough rest until it has crested over the top of the pans.

9. Brush the loaves with the beaten egg, place them in the oven, and bake until they are golden brown, feel lighter when lifted, and make a hollow sound when tapped, 35 to 45 minutes.

10. Remove the loaves from the oven, place the pans on a wire rack, and let the brioche cool before slicing and serving.

GLUTEN-FREE BRIOCHE

YIELD: 1 LOAF / **ACTIVE TIME:** 30 MINUTES / **TOTAL TIME:** 2 HOURS AND 30 MINUTES

This is guaranteed to be one of the best gluten-free breads you've ever had. Make sure you check your chosen gluten-free flour mix before adding the xanthan gum, as some will already include it.

1. Place the water and yeast in the work bowl of a stand mixer fitted with the whisk attachment, gently stir to combine, and let the mixture sit until it starts to foam, about 10 minutes.

2. Add the sugar, eggs, butter, flour, xanthan gum, and salt and whip the mixture on medium for 10 minutes until it is a smooth batter.

3. Coat an 8 x 4–inch loaf pan with nonstick cooking spray. Pour the batter into the prepared loaf pan and bang the pan on the countertop to remove any air bubbles. Cover the pan tightly with plastic wrap, place it in a naturally warm spot, and let it rest until it reaches the lip of the pan, about 1 hour.

4. Preheat the oven to 350°F.

5. Place the pan in the oven and bake until the bread is golden brown and feels lighter when lifted, 35 to 45 minutes. Make sure you do not open the oven at any point while the bread is baking, as this will cause the bread to collapse.

6. Remove the bread from the oven, place the pan on a wire rack, and let the bread cool completely before slicing and serving.

INGREDIENTS:

- 3 OZ. (85 G) LUKEWARM WATER (90°F)
- 4½ TEASPOONS (13.5 G) ACTIVE DRY YEAST
- 3½ OZ. (99 G) SUGAR
- 6 EGGS
- 4 OZ. (113 G) UNSALTED BUTTER, MELTED
- 9 OZ. (255 G) GLUTEN-FREE ALL-PURPOSE FLOUR MIX
- 1 TABLESPOON (9 G) XANTHAN GUM
- 1½ TEASPOONS (9 G) FINE SEA SALT

JAPANESE MILK BREAD

YIELD: 1 LOAF / **ACTIVE TIME:** 45 MINUTES / **TOTAL TIME:** 4 HOURS

This springy loaf is made with a unique technique known as tangzhong, which uses a paste of water and flour.

INGREDIENTS:

FOR THE TANGZHONG

- 2½ OZ. (71 G) WATER
- 2 TABLESPOONS (15 G) BREAD FLOUR

FOR THE DOUGH

- 3 OZ. (85 G) MILK
- 1 EGG
- 1 EGG YOLK
- 3 TABLESPOONS (38 G) SUGAR
- 1 TABLESPOON (9 G) ACTIVE DRY YEAST
- 10 OZ. (283 G) BREAD FLOUR, PLUS MORE AS NEEDED
- 1½ TEASPOONS (9 G) FINE SEA SALT
- 1½ OZ. (45 G) UNSALTED BUTTER, SOFTENED

1. To prepare the tangzhong, place the water and flour in a small saucepan and whisk to combine. Cook over medium-low heat until the mixture thickens and starts to bubble, about 2 minutes. Pour the mixture into a small bowl and let it cool completely. If done correctly, the mixture will thicken significantly as it cools.

2. To begin preparations for the dough, place the tangzhong, milk, egg, egg yolk, sugar, and yeast in the work bowl of a stand mixer fitted with the dough hook and stir to combine. Add the flour, salt, and butter and knead on low for 1 minute. Raise the speed to medium and knead the mixture until it comes together as a smooth dough and begins to pull away from the side of the work bowl, 6 to 8 minutes.

3. Coat a mixing bowl with nonstick cooking spray. Remove the dough from the work bowl, place it on a flour-dusted work surface, and shape it into a ball. Place the dough in the bowl, cover it with plastic wrap, place it in a naturally warm spot, and let it rest until it has doubled in size.

4. Coat an 8 x 4–inch loaf pan with nonstick cooking spray. Place the dough on a flour-dusted work surface and roll it into a tight ball. Place the dough in the prepared loaf pan, seam side down, cover it with plastic wrap, and place it in a naturally warm spot. Let the dough rest until it has doubled in size.

5. Preheat the oven to 350°F.

6. Place the pan in the oven and bake until the bread is golden brown and feels lighter when lifted, 35 to 45 minutes.

7. Remove the bread from the oven, remove the loaf from the pan, and place it on a wire rack. Let it cool completely before slicing serving.

CHALLAH

YIELD: 1 LOAF / **ACTIVE TIME:** 1 HOUR / **TOTAL TIME:** 5 HOURS

A bread with a taste and texture that matches the elegance of its looks.

INGREDIENTS:

- 1½ CUPS (340 G) LUKEWARM WATER (90°F)
- 1 TABLESPOON PLUS 2 TEASPOONS (15 G) ACTIVE DRY YEAST
- 4 EGGS, 1 BEATEN
- ¼ CUP (50 G) EXTRA-VIRGIN OLIVE OIL
- 7 CUPS (840 G) BREAD FLOUR, PLUS MORE AS NEEDED
- ¼ CUP (50 G) SUGAR
- 1⅓ TABLESPOONS (24 G) FINE SEA SALT

1. Place the water and yeast in the work bowl of a stand mixer fitted with the dough hook, stir to combine, and let the mixture rest until it starts to foam, about 10 minutes.

2. Add the 3 unbeaten eggs, olive oil, flour, sugar, and salt to the work bowl, and work the mixture on low until it comes together as a dough. Raise the speed to medium and knead until the dough becomes elastic and begins to pull away from the side of the work bowl, about 6 minutes.

3. Cover the work bowl with a kitchen towel, place it in a naturally warm spot, and let the dough rise until it has doubled in size, about 2 hours.

4. Place the dough on a flour-dusted work surface and punch it down to deflate it. Divide the dough into four pieces that are each about 12.7 oz. Shape each piece into an oval, cover them with kitchen towels, and let them rest for 15 to 30 minutes.

5. Line a baking sheet with parchment paper.

6. Using the palms of your hands, gently roll the pieces of dough into strands that are about 2 feet long.

7. Take the strands and fan them out so that one end of each of them is touching. Press down on the ends where they are touching. Take the rightmost strand (Strand 1) and cross it over to the left so that it is horizontal. Take the leftmost strand (Strand 2) and cross it over to the right so that it is horizontal.

8. Move Strand 1 between the two strands that have yet to move. Move the strand to the right of Strand 1 to the left so that it is horizontal. This will be known as Strand 3.

9. Move Strand 2 between Strand 1 and Strand 4. Move Strand 4 to the right so that it is horizontal.

10. Repeat moving the horizontal strands to the middle and replacing them with the opposite, outer strands until the entire loaf is braided. Pinch the ends of the loaf together and tuck them under the bread.

11. Preheat the oven to 350°F.

12. Brush the dough with the beaten egg. If you want to top the bread with poppy seeds, sesame seeds, or herbs, now is the time to sprinkle them over the top.

13. Place the bread in the oven and bake until it is golden brown, feels lighter when lifted, and makes a hollow sound when tapped, about 30 minutes.

14. Remove the challah from the oven, place it on a wire rack, and let it cool completely.

Challah, see page 238

MARBLED CHALLAH

YIELD: 1 LOAF / **ACTIVE TIME:** 1 HOUR / **TOTAL TIME:** 5 HOURS

The contrasting colors and flavors of the doughs are sure to set off a swirl of emotions.

1. Place the water and yeast in the work bowl of a stand mixer fitted with the dough hook, stir to combine, and let the mixture sit until it starts to foam, about 10 minutes.

2. Add the 3 unbeaten eggs, olive oil, flour, sugar, and salt to the work bowl and work the mixture on low until it comes together as a dough, about 2 minutes.

3. Raise the speed to medium and knead until the dough becomes elastic and begins to pull away from the side of the work bowl, about 6 minutes.

4. Remove half of the dough, place it in a mixing bowl, and set it aside. Add the cocoa powder, caraway seeds, and molasses to the dough in the work bowl and knead until incorporated, about 5 minutes.

5. Cover the bowls with kitchen towels, place them in a naturally warm spot, and let the dough rest until it has doubled in size, about 2 hours.

6. Place the pieces of dough on a flour-dusted work surface and punch them down to deflate them. Divide each piece of dough in half so that you have four pieces that are each about 12.7 oz. Shape each piece into an oval, cover the dough with kitchen towels, and let it rest for 15 to 30 minutes.

7. Line a baking sheet with parchment paper.

8. Using the palms of your hands, gently roll the pieces of dough into strands that are about 2 feet long.

9. Take the strands and fan them out, alternating light and dark strands, so that one end of each of them is touching. Press down on the ends where they are touching. Take the rightmost strand (Strand 1) and cross it over to the left so that it is horizontal. Take the leftmost strand (Strand 2) and cross it over to the right so that it is horizontal.

10. Move Strand 1 between the two strands that have yet to move. Move the strand to the right of Strand 1 to the left so that it is horizontal. This will be known as Strand 3.

INGREDIENTS:

- 1½ CUPS (340 G) LUKEWARM WATER (90°F)
- 1 TABLESPOON PLUS 2 TEASPOONS (15 G) ACTIVE DRY YEAST
- 4 EGGS, 1 BEATEN
- ¼ CUP (50 G) EXTRA-VIRGIN OLIVE OIL
- 2 LBS. (907 G) BREAD FLOUR, PLUS MORE AS NEEDED
- ¼ CUP (50 G) SUGAR
- 1⅓ TABLESPOONS (24 G) FINE SEA SALT
- 2 TEASPOONS (5 G) COCOA POWDER
- 1 TEASPOON (3 G) CARAWAY SEEDS
- 2 TABLESPOONS (42.5 G) MOLASSES

11. Move Strand 2 between Strand 1 and Strand 4. Move Strand 4 to the right so that it is horizontal.

12. Repeat moving the horizontal strands to the middle and replacing them with the opposite, outer strands until the entire loaf is braided. Pinch the ends of the loaf together and tuck them under the bread.

13. Place the dough on the baking sheet, cover it with plastic wrap, place it in a naturally warm spot, and let it rest until it has doubled in size.

14. Preheat the oven to 350°F.

15. Brush the dough with the beaten egg.

16. Place the bread in the oven and bake until it is golden brown, feels lighter when lifted, and makes a hollow sound when tapped, about 30 minutes.

17. Remove the challah from the oven, place it on a wire rack, and let it cool completely.

WHOLE WHEAT CHALLAH

YIELD: 1 LOAF / **ACTIVE TIME:** 1 HOUR AND 30 MINUTES / **TOTAL TIME:** 4 HOURS

Simple, pillowy, and delicious, this whole wheat loaf gives the classic bread a whole new dimension.

INGREDIENTS:

- 1 PACKET (7 G) OF ACTIVE DRY YEAST
- ¾ CUP (170 G) WARM WATER (105°F)
- 1 TEASPOON (4 G) SUGAR
- 3 LARGE EGGS, 1 BEATEN
- ¼ CUP (50 G) CANOLA OIL
- 3¼ CUPS (390 G) WHOLE WHEAT FLOUR, PLUS MORE AS NEEDED
- ¼ CUP (84 G) HONEY
- 1 TEASPOON (5 G) KOSHER SALT, PLUS MORE FOR TOPPING

1. Place the yeast and water in the work bowl of a stand mixer fitted with the dough hook, stir to combine, and let the mixture sit until it starts to foam, about 10 minutes.

2. Add the 2 unbeaten eggs, canola oil, flour, honey, and salt to the work bowl and work the mixture on low until it comes together as a dough, about 2 minutes.

3. Raise the speed to medium and knead until the dough becomes elastic and begins to pull away from the side of the work bowl, about 6 minutes.

4. Cover the bowl with a kitchen towel, place it in a naturally warm spot, and let the dough rest until it has doubled in size, about 2 hours.

5. Place the dough on a flour-dusted work surface and punch it down to deflate it. Divide the dough into four pieces that are each about 12.7 oz. Shape each piece into an oval, cover the dough with kitchen towels, and let it rest for 15 to 30 minutes.

6. Line a baking sheet with parchment paper.

7. Using the palms of your hands, gently roll the pieces of dough into strands that are about 2 feet long.

8. Take the strands and fan them out so that one end of each of them is touching. Press down on the ends where they are touching. Take the rightmost strand (Strand 1) and cross it over to the left so that it is horizontal. Take the leftmost strand (Strand 2) and cross it over to the right so that it is horizontal.

9. Move Strand 1 between the two strands that have yet to move. Move the strand to the right of Strand 1 to the left so that it is horizontal. This will be known as Strand 3.

10. Move Strand 2 between Strand 1 and Strand 4. Move Strand 4 to the right so that it is horizontal.

11. Repeat moving the horizontal strands to the middle and replacing them with the opposite, outer strands until the entire loaf is braided. Pinch the ends of the loaf together and tuck them under the bread.

12. Place the dough on the baking sheet, cover it with plastic wrap, place it in a naturally warm spot, and let it rest until it has doubled in size.

13. Preheat the oven to 350°F.

14. Brush the dough with the beaten egg and sprinkle some salt over the top.

15. Place the bread in the oven and bake until it is golden brown, feels lighter when lifted, and makes a hollow sound when tapped, about 30 minutes.

16. Remove the challah from the oven, place it on a wire rack, and let it cool completely.

CHALLAH WITH RAISINS

YIELD: 1 LOAF / **ACTIVE TIME:** 50 MINUTES / **TOTAL TIME:** 4 HOURS

Raisins are the most common addition to challah, and they turn this bread into a real treat.

INGREDIENTS:

- 1 CUP (227 G) WARM WATER (105°F)
- 2½ TEASPOONS (8 G) ACTIVE DRY YEAST
- 4⅙ CUPS (500 G) ALL-PURPOSE FLOUR, PLUS MORE AS NEEDED
- ⅓ CUP (65 G) SUGAR
- 3 EGGS, 1 UNBEATEN
- 2 TABLESPOONS (30 G) HONEY
- ⅓ CUP (70 G) CANOLA OIL
- 1¾ TEASPOONS (10 G) FINE SEA SALT
- ¾ CUP (120 G) RAISINS

1. Place the water and yeast in the work bowl of stand mixer fitted with the dough hook and gently stir to combine. Let the mixture sit until it starts to foam, about 10 minutes.

2. Add half of the flour and the sugar and work the mixture on low until it just comes together as a dough. Add the beaten eggs one at a time and work the mixture until well combined. Add the honey and remaining flour and work the dough on low for 5 minutes.

3. Gradually add the canola oil with the mixer running and continue to work the dough on low. Add the salt and raisins and work the dough until incorporated. Work the dough until it is smooth, about 10 minutes.

4. Cover the bowl with a kitchen towel, place it in a naturally warm spot, and let the dough rest until it has doubled in size, about 1 hour.

5. Place the dough on a flour-dusted work surface and punch it down to deflate it. Divide the dough into four pieces that are each about 12.7 oz. Shape each piece into an oval, cover the dough with kitchen towels, and let it rest for 15 to 30 minutes.

6. Line a baking sheet with parchment paper.

7. Using the palms of your hands, gently roll the pieces of dough into strands that are about 2 feet long.

8. Take the strands and fan them out so that one end of each of them is touching. Press down on the ends where they are touching. Take the rightmost strand (Strand 1) and cross it over to the left so that it is horizontal. Take the leftmost strand (Strand 2) and cross it over to the right so that it is horizontal.

9. Move Strand 1 between the two strands that have yet to move. Move the strand to the right of Strand 1 to the left so that it is horizontal. This will be known as Strand 3.

10. Move Strand 2 between Strand 1 and Strand 4. Move Strand 4 to the right so that it is horizontal.

11. Repeat moving the horizontal strands to the middle and replacing them with the opposite, outer strands until the entire loaf is braided. Pinch the ends of the loaf together and tuck them under the bread.

12. Place the dough on the baking sheet, cover it with plastic wrap, place it in a naturally warm spot, and let it rest until it has doubled in size.

13. Preheat the oven to 350°F.

14. Brush the dough with the beaten egg.

15. Place the bread in the oven and bake until it is golden brown, feels lighter when lifted, and makes a hollow sound when tapped, 30 to 35 minutes.

16. Remove the challah from the oven, place it on a wire rack, and let it cool completely.

ZINGERMAN'S RYE BREAD

YIELD: 2 LOAVES / **ACTIVE TIME:** 1 HOUR / **TOTAL TIME:** 4 HOURS AND 30 MINUTES

This rye comes from one of the best bakeries in the US, Zingerman's Bakehouse in Ann Arbor, Michigan. So, what makes this a great rye bread? The use of two unique elements—the Rye Sour and day-old rye bread.

INGREDIENTS:

- ¼ CUP (50 G) DAY-OLD RYE BREAD, TORN INTO SMALL PIECES
- ¾ CUP (170 G) WATER
- 2¼ CUPS (338 G) RYE SOUR (SEE PAGE 660)
- 1½ TEASPOONS (3 G) INSTANT YEAST
- ½ TEASPOON (3 G) GROUND CARAWAY SEEDS
- 3½ CUPS PLUS 1 TABLESPOON (426 G) ALL-PURPOSE FLOUR, PLUS MORE AS NEEDED
- 1 TABLESPOON (18 G) FINE SEA SALT
- CORNMEAL, AS NEEDED

1. Place the bread pieces and ½ cup of water in a large bowl and let the bread soak for 15 minutes.

2. Place the bread-and-water mixture, remaining water, Rye Sour, yeast, and caraway seeds in a large, wide mixing bowl and stir the mixture with a wooden spoon until it is well combined. Add half of the flour and stir until the mixture looks like thick pancake batter. Add the salt and remaining flour and stir until the mixture comes together as a shaggy mass.

3. Scrape the dough out of the bowl onto a clean work surface and knead until it is smooth, 6 to 8 minutes. If the dough begins to stick, use a plastic scraper to clean the surface. As rye has a different chemical makeup than wheat flour, it tends to be sticky. Still, do not add more flour. Just keep gently kneading and the dough will come together.

4. Coat a large bowl with nonstick cooking spray and place the dough in it. Cover the bowl with plastic wrap and let it rest until it has increased in size by 50 percent, about 1 hour.

5. Uncover the dough and turn it out onto a lightly flour-dusted work surface. Divide the dough in half. Lightly shape the pieces of dough into rounds, cover them with plastic wrap, and let them rest for 30 minutes.

6. Form the rounds into loaves, place them on a cornmeal-dusted cutting board, and cover them with plastic wrap. Let them rest for 40 minutes to 1 hour.

7. Preheat the oven to 450°F and place a baking stone or steel on the middle rack of the oven as it warms.

8. Uncover the loaves and spray them with water. Place the loaves on a cornmeal-dusted peel and score them with five uniform cuts that are perpendicular to the length of the loaves.

9. Slide the loaves onto the heated baking implement and bake with steam, using one of the methods described on page 32.

10. Bake for 8 minutes and open the door to release the steam. Bake the loaves until they have the desired color, 32 to 35 minutes.

11. Remove the loaves from the oven, place them on a wire rack, and spray them generously with water. Let the loaves cool completely before slicing and serving.

RYE BREAD WITH CARAWAY & MUSTARD SEEDS

YIELD: 3 LOAVES / **ACTIVE TIME:** 1 HOUR / **TOTAL TIME:** 5 HOURS

This is a wonderfully chewy, tangy, and very flavorful loaf that goes well with cured or smoked meats, poultry, or fish. This bread has a tight crumb because it is made with a high proportion of rye flour, which is low in gluten, and so doesn't rise high in the oven.

INGREDIENTS:

- ¼ CUP (60 G) VERY WARM WATER (115°F)
- 1½ TEASPOONS (3 G) ACTIVE DRY YEAST
- 2½ CUPS (275 G) RYE FLOUR, PLUS MORE AS NEEDED
- 1 CUP (120 G) BREAD FLOUR
- 1 TABLESPOON PLUS 2 TEASPOONS CARAWAY SEEDS
- 2 TABLESPOONS MUSTARD SEEDS
- ½ CUP COOKED RYE BERRIES
- 1 TABLESPOON PLUS 1 TEASPOON (20 G) KOSHER SALT
- 1¾ CUPS (397 G) ROOM-TEMPERATURE WATER, PLUS MORE AS NEEDED
- 1¼ CUPS (200 G) STIFF SOURDOUGH STARTER (SEE PAGE 659), AT ROOM TEMPERATURE
- EXTRA-VIRGIN OLIVE OIL, AS NEEDED
- CORNMEAL, AS NEEDED

1. Place the warm water and yeast in a small bowl and gently stir to combine. Let the mixture sit for 3 minutes.

2. In a large bowl, combine the flours, caraway seeds, mustard seeds, rye berries, and salt. Add the room-temperature water and the yeast mixture and work the mixture with your hands until it comes together as a shaggy mass. Knead until it comes together as a smooth, sticky dough, adding tablespoons of room-temperature water if the dough seems too stiff.

3. Place the dough on a flour-dusted work surface and flatten it into a rectangle. Place the starter on top of the rye dough, stretching it to cover it. Fold the whole mass up like a letter, folding the top third of the rectangle down and the bottom third up over it, and then gently knead to combine the doughs together. Continue to knead until the dough becomes smooth and supple, about 4 minutes. Cover the dough with a kitchen towel or plastic wrap and let it rest for 20 minutes.

4. Loosen the dough from the work surface with a bench scraper, lift it up, and lightly dust the work surface with flour. Knead the dough for 2 to 3 minutes, until it feels gluey, supple, and just slightly firm.

5. Coat a large bowl with olive oil. Shape the dough into a loose ball, place it in the bowl, turn the dough to coat it with oil. Cover the bowl tightly with plastic wrap and let the dough rest at room temperature until it has doubled in size, 1½ to 2 hours.

6. Generously dust a peel with cornmeal. Place the dough on a lightly flour-dusted work surface and divide it into three pieces. Shape each piece of dough into a round and place them, seam side down, on the peel, leaving 2 to 3 inches between them. Coat a piece of plastic wrap with olive oil and cover the loaves with it. Let the loaves rest at room temperature until they have doubled in size, 1½ to 2 hours. If the loaves start to split, they have become too acidic and are overproofed, and should be baked right away. Don't worry: they'll still taste good, just with a tangier flavor.

7. About 30 minutes before baking, preheat the oven to 430°F and place a baking stone or steel on the middle rack of the oven as it warms.

8. Sprinkle a little rye flour on top of each loaf and score the top of each loaf. Slide the loaves onto the heated baking implement and bake with steam, using one of the methods described on page 32.

9. Bake for 20 minutes, then reduce the temperature to 390°F and bake until the loaves are a rich reddish brown and sound hollow when tapped on the bottom, 15 to 20 minutes.

10. Remove the loaves from the oven, place them on a wire rack, and let them cool completely before slicing and serving.

SWEDISH LIGHT RYE BREAD

YIELD: 2 LOAVES / **ACTIVE TIME:** 30 MINUTES / **TOTAL TIME:** 4 HOURS

The most common and traditional Swedish loaf is soft and slightly sweet. It is generally made with commercial yeast, and it makes a good and versatile sandwich bread.

1. Warm 3 tablespoons of the water until it is about 105°F. Add the yeast and water to the work bowl of a stand mixer fitted with the dough hook and gently stir to combine. Let the mixture sit until it starts to foam, about 10 minutes.

2. Add the flours, milk, maple syrup, butter, and remaining water and work the mixture on low until it comes together as a dough. Add the salt and work the dough until it is incorporated. Knead at low speed for 5 minutes, raise the speed to medium, and work the dough until it is smooth, 2 to 3 minutes.

3. Shape the dough into a ball, place it in a clean mixing bowl, and cover it with plastic wrap. Let the dough rest for 1 to 1½ hours.

4. Divide the dough in half, place the pieces of dough on a flour-dusted work surface, and shape them into rounds.

5. Place the shaped rounds in loaf pans or bannetons lined with floured kitchen towels and cover them with plastic wrap. Let the dough rest until it has doubled in size, 1 to 1½ hours.

6. Preheat the oven to 430°F and place a baking stone or steel on the middle rack of the oven as it warms.

7. Invert the loaves onto a parchment-lined peel and score them. Place them on the heated baking implement and bake with steam, using one of the methods described on page 32.

8. Bake for 25 minutes, then reduce the temperature to 375°F and bake until the loaves are dark brown and sound hollow when tapped, 20 to 25 minutes.

9. Remove the loaves from the oven, place them on a wire rack, and let them cool completely before slicing and serving.

INGREDIENTS:

- ⅔ CUP (150 G) WATER
- 1 PACKET (7 G) OF ACTIVE DRY YEAST
- 1¼ CUPS (130 G) LIGHT RYE FLOUR
- 3 (SCANT) CUPS (350 G) BREAD FLOUR, PLUS MORE AS NEEDED
- ⅔ CUP (150 G) LUKEWARM MILK (90°F)
- 2 TABLESPOONS (30 G) LIGHT MAPLE SYRUP OR BARLEY MALT
- 1 TABLESPOON (15 G) UNSALTED BUTTER
- 2 TEASPOONS (12 G) FINE SEA SALT

POLISH LIGHT RYE BREAD

YIELD: 2 LOAVES / **ACTIVE TIME:** 30 MINUTES / **TOTAL TIME:** 4 HOURS

Poland has a rich bread-baking tradition, and its light rye breads are particularly delicious. They are typically flavored with caraway seeds and fermented with sourdough, but here is a quicker version that will still make an amazing loaf that will pair wonderfully with deli meats and, of course, with butter.

INGREDIENTS:

- 1⅓ CUPS (302 G) WATER
- 1 PACKET (7 G) OF ACTIVE DRY YEAST
- 1 TABLESPOON CARAWAY SEEDS
- 1 TEASPOON (4 G) SUGAR
- 1¼ CUPS (130 G) MEDIUM RYE FLOUR
- 3 (SCANT) CUPS (350 G) BREAD FLOUR, PLUS MORE AS NEEDED
- 1 TABLESPOON (15 G) UNSALTED BUTTER
- 2 TEASPOONS (12 G) FINE SEA SALT

1. Warm 3 tablespoons of the water until it is about 105°F. Add the yeast and water to the work bowl of a stand mixer fitted with the dough hook and gently stir to combine. Let the mixture sit until it starts to foam, about 10 minutes.

2. Add the caraway seeds, sugar, flours, butter, and remaining water and work the mixture on low until it comes together as a dough. Add the salt and work the dough until it is incorporated. Knead at low speed for 5 minutes, raise the speed to medium, and work the dough until it is smooth, 2 to 3 minutes.

3. Shape the dough into a ball, place it in a clean mixing bowl, and cover it with plastic wrap. Let the dough rest for 1 to 1½ hours.

4. Divide the dough in half, place the pieces of dough on a flour-dusted work surface, and shape them into rounds.

5. Place the shaped rounds in loaf pans or bannetons lined with floured kitchen towels and cover them with plastic wrap. Let the dough rest until it has doubled in size, 1 to 1½ hours.

6. Preheat the oven to 520°F and place a baking stone or steel on the middle rack of the oven as it warms.

7. Invert the loaves onto a parchment-lined peel and score them. Place them on the heated baking implement and bake with steam, using one of the methods described on page 32.

8. Reduce the temperature to 440°F and bake for 20 minutes, then reduce the temperature to 375°F and bake until the loaves are dark brown and sound hollow when tapped, 15 to 20 minutes.

9. Remove the loaves from the oven, place them on a wire rack, and let them cool completely before slicing and serving.

LIMPPU

YIELD: 1 LOAF / **ACTIVE TIME:** 30 MINUTES / **TOTAL TIME:** 20 HOURS

Traditional Finnish dark rye bread is made lighter by a proportion of wheat flour. As with other dark rye breads, its preparation needs to start the night before baking day. This bread is easier to make in a loaf pan.

INGREDIENTS:

- 1¾ CUPS (ABOUT 400 G) WATER
- 3¼ CUPS (300 G) DARK RYE FLOUR
- 2½ CUPS (250 G) ALL-PURPOSE FLOUR
- ¼ CUP (60 G) RYE SOUR (SEE PAGE 660)
- 2 TABLESPOONS (43 G) MOLASSES
- 1 TEASPOON (6 G) FINE SEA SALT

1. In the work bowl of a stand mixer fitted with the dough hook, combine the water with half of the flours and the rye sour. Cover the work bowl and let the mixture rest at room temperature for 12 hours.

2. Add the remaining flours and the molasses and work the mixture on low until it comes together as a dough. Add the salt and work the dough until it is incorporated. Knead at low speed for 5 minutes, raise the speed to medium, and work the dough until it is smooth, 2 to 3 minutes.

3. Coat a 9 x 5–inch loaf pan with nonstick cooking spray, place the dough in it, and cover it with a kitchen towel. Let the dough rest until it has almost doubled in size, about 3 hours.

4. Preheat the oven to 350°F, place the loaf pan in the oven, and bake until the bread is dark brown, about 1 hour and 20 minutes.

5. Remove the bread from the oven, place it on a wire rack, and let it cool completely before slicing and serving.

RUGBRØD

YIELD: 2 LOAVES / **ACTIVE TIME:** 30 MINUTES / **TOTAL TIME:** 2 DAYS

Soft and substantial, this quintessential Danish loaf can be used to make the traditional Danish sandwich smørrebrød, which has recently become fashionable outside of Denmark. Smørrebrød is an open sandwich that is spread with butter and topped with various options, such as liver pâté and pickles, eggs and caviar, or cold cuts and spreads, among others.

INGREDIENTS:

- 6 CUPS (640 G) DARK RYE FLOUR
- ¾ CUP (90 G) RYE CHOPS, SOAKED IN WATER OVERNIGHT, BOILED FOR 15 MINUTES, DRAINED, AND COOLED
- 1⅓ CUPS (300 G) RYE SOUR (SEE PAGE 660)
- 1⅔ CUPS (377 G) LUKEWARM WATER (90°F)
- 1¼ CUPS (ABOUT 280 G) DARK BEER
- 2 TABLESPOONS (43 G) MOLASSES
- 1½ TEASPOONS (9 G) FINE SEA SALT

1. Place all of the ingredients, except for the salt, in a large bowl and stir with a wooden spoon until the mixture just comes together. Cover the bowl with a kitchen towel and let it rest for 15 minutes.

2. Add the salt and stir until it is incorporated.

3. Coat two 9 x 5–inch loaf pans with nonstick cooking spray. Divide the wet dough between the pans and place them in two resealable plastic bags. Let the dough rest at room temperature until it has almost doubled in size, about 4 hours.

4. Preheat the oven to 320°F, place the loaf pans in the oven, and bake until the breads are dark brown and feel lighter, about 2½ hours.

5. Remove the loaves from the oven, place them on a wire rack, and let them cool for a whole day before slicing and serving.

Rugbrød, see page 257

RUISLEIPÄ

YIELD: 4 LOAVES / **ACTIVE TIME:** 30 MINUTES / **TOTAL TIME:** 27 HOURS

This is the definitive Finnish rye bread, extremely sour and wonderful with butter. Traditionally, it is made with a hole in the center, so as to be stored for months on a stick hanging from the ceiling.

INGREDIENTS:

- ½ (SCANT) CUP (100 G) RYE SOUR (SEE PAGE 660)
- 10 CUPS (1 KG) DARK RYE FLOUR, PLUS MORE AS NEEDED
- 3 CUPS (681 G) LUKEWARM WATER (90°F), PLUS MORE AS NEEDED
- 3½ TEASPOONS (21 G) FINE SEA SALT

1. The day before you are going to bake, place the Rye Sour, half of the flour, and the water in the work bowl of a stand mixer fitted with the dough hook and work the mixture until it just comes together. Cover the work bowl with plastic wrap and let the mixture rest at room temperature for 20 hours.

2. Add the remaining flour and the salt and work the dough on low until it is smooth, 10 to 15 minutes, adding more water if the dough is too stiff.

3. Shape the dough into a ball, place it in a clean mixing bowl, and cover it with plastic wrap. Let the dough rest at room temperature for 1½ hours.

4. Line a baking sheet with parchment paper. Place the dough on a flour-dusted work surface and cut it into four pieces. Shape each piece into a round, moisten one hand, and flatten the rounds with your palm. Use a glass or a pastry cutter to make a hole in the center of each piece of dough, place them on the baking sheet, and cover them with a damp kitchen towel. Place the loaves in a naturally warm spot and let them rest for 2 hours.

5. Preheat the oven to 480°F and place a baking stone or steel on the middle rack of the oven as it warms.

6. Invert the loaves onto a parchment-lined peel and slide them onto the heated baking implement.

7. Bake for 10 to 15 minutes, reduce the temperature to 390°F, and bake for 15 minutes. Reduce the temperature to 360°F and bake until the loaves make a hollow sound when tapped, 40 to 50 minutes.

8. Remove the loaves from the oven, place them on a wire rack, and let them cool completely before slicing and serving.

BORODINSKY BREAD

YIELD: 2 LOAVES / **ACTIVE TIME:** 30 MINUTES / **TOTAL TIME:** 14 HOURS AND 30 MINUTES

This popular Russian dark rye bread is flavored with coriander seeds. Its origin is mysterious, but its charm is certain. It needs to be started the night before baking; however, it is easy in this recipe to substitute the traditional rye sourdough starter with commercial yeast.

1. In a small saucepan, bring 1¼ cups of the water close to a boil.

2. In the work bowl of a stand mixer, add the hot water and 2 cups of the rye flour. Add the coriander, stir to combine, and let the mixture cool to 85°F.

3. Add the Rye Sour and stir to incorporate. Cover the work bowl with plastic wrap and let the mixture rest at room temperature for 12 hours.

4. Add the remaining rye flour and the whole wheat flour, molasses, and salt and work the mixture on low until combined. Add the remaining water 1 tablespoon at a time, stopping when the dough becomes easy to knead and not too sticky. Knead at low speed for 5 minutes, raise the speed to medium, and work the dough until it is smooth, 2 to 3 minutes.

5. Place the dough on a generously flour-dusted work surface and roll it out. Fold the dough like a letter a few times, rolling it out after each fold, and then divide the dough in half.

6. Divide the dough in half. Shape the pieces into tight rounds. Transfer the rounds to generously flour-dusted bannetons, cover them with floured kitchen towels, and let them rest for 2 hours.

7. Preheat the oven to 320°F. Place the loaves on a parchment-lined baking sheet, place them in the oven, and bake until they are well browned and feel lighter when lifted, about 1½ hours.

8. Remove the loaves from the oven, place them on a wire rack, and let them cool completely before slicing and serving.

INGREDIENTS:

- 1¼ CUPS PLUS ⅖ TO ⅗ CUP (360 G TO 400 G) WATER
- 6 CUPS (630 G) DARK RYE FLOUR, PLUS MORE AS NEEDED
- 2 TEASPOONS (3 G) GROUND CORIANDER
- ¼ CUP (57 G) RYE SOUR (SEE PAGE 660)
- ¾ CUP (90 G) WHOLE WHEAT FLOUR
- 2 TABLESPOONS (43 G) MOLASSES
- 1 TEASPOON (ABOUT 6 G) FINE SEA SALT

WALNUT & SPELT LOAF

YIELD: 2 LOAVES / **ACTIVE TIME:** 30 MINUTES / **TOTAL TIME:** 24 HOURS

Moist, chewy, and with a delectably earthy sense of terroir, this bread can be served to discerning guests with fine cheese or dressed down for your morning toast.

INGREDIENTS:

FOR THE SOAKER

- ½ CUP (75 G) CRACKED RYE BERRIES
- ¼ CUP (42 G) BROWN FLAXSEEDS
- 1 CUP (227 G) WATER

FOR THE DOUGH

- ⅔ CUP (150 G) SOURDOUGH STARTER (SEE PAGE 40)
- 2 CUPS (454 G) WATER
- 4⅓ CUPS (495 G) LIGHT SPELT FLOUR, PLUS MORE AS NEEDED
- ½ CUP (58 G) WHOLE SPELT FLOUR
- ½ CUP (60 G) KAMUT FLOUR
- 1 TABLESPOON (18 G) FINE SEA SALT
- 1⅓ CUPS WALNUTS

1. To prepare the soaker, place all of the ingredients in a large bowl and lightly stir to combine. Let the mixture soak for at least 2 hours and not more than 5 hours ahead of mixing the dough. If you are pressed for time, use hot tap water and cool the mixture in the refrigerator for 15 minutes.

2. To begin preparations for the dough, combine the soaker, starter, and water in the work bowl of a stand mixer fitted with the dough hook. Add the flours and work on low until it just comes together as a loose dough. Let the dough rest for 30 minutes.

3. Add the salt and work the dough until it is incorporated. Knead at low speed for 5 minutes, raise the speed to medium, and work the dough until it is smooth, 2 to 3 minutes, incorporating the walnuts toward the end of the kneading process.

4. Shape the dough into a ball, place it in a clean mixing bowl, and cover it with plastic wrap. Let the dough rest until it is has increased to 1½ times its original size, 4 to 6 hours, folding it every hour.

5. Coat two 2 lb. loaf pans with nonstick cooking spray. Place the dough on a flour-dusted work surface, divide it in half, and lightly shape the pieces into logs. Place them in the loaf pans, seam side down, cover the pans with plastic wrap, and place them in the refrigerator overnight.

6. Preheat the oven to 500°F. Place the bread in the oven and bake with steam, using one of the methods described on page 32. Bake until the bread is a deep golden brown and feels lighter when lifted, about 35 minutes.

7. Remove the loaves from the oven and let them cool in the pans for 10 minutes. Turn them out onto a wire rack and let them cool completely before using or storing.

SPROUTED SPELT LOAF

YIELD: 1 LOAF / **ACTIVE TIME:** 2 HOURS / **TOTAL TIME:** 4 DAYS

This technique was developed and refined by Raymond Calvel, author of the seminal *Le Goût du Pain (The Taste of Bread)* and bread guru to Julia Child. These steps require strict timing—though the specific times can change, try to keep the time intervals as close to the suggested times as possible.

INGREDIENTS:

FOR THE SOAKER

- 1 CUP (180 G) SPELT BERRIES
- WATER, AS NEEDED

FOR THE LEVAIN

- ½ CUP (60 G) WHEAT FLOUR
- ½ CUP (58 G) SPELT FLOUR
- ¼ CUP (60 G) WATER
- 2 TABLESPOONS (30 G) SOURDOUGH STARTER (SEE PAGE 40)

FOR THE DOUGH

- 3 CUPS (681 G) WATER
- 1 CUP (150 G) LEVAIN
- 3¾ CUPS (425 G) SPELT FLOUR, PLUS MORE AS NEEDED
- 2¼ CUPS (270 G) WHEAT FLOUR
- 1 TABLESPOON PLUS ½ TEASPOON (21 G) FINE SEA SALT

1. Prepare the soaker three full days before you are going to bake the bread. At 10 AM, place the spelt berries in a large bowl and cover them completely with cold water. Check on the berries occasionally to ensure they remain completely covered. At 3 PM, drain the berries. Rinse them, toss, and place the berries in a large fine-mesh sieve. Cover them with a kitchen towel and let them rest at room temperature overnight.

2. On the second day at 4 AM, rinse the berries and toss them. Cover them with a kitchen towel and let them rest at room temperature. At 3 PM, rinse the berries and toss them. Cover them with a kitchen towel and let them rest at room temperature overnight.

3. On the third day at 4 AM, rinse the berries and toss them. Cover them with a kitchen towel and let them rest at room temperature. At 3 PM, rinse the berries and toss them. Cover them with a kitchen towel and let them rest at room temperature overnight.

4. During the third day, prepare the levain. Place all of the ingredients in a large bowl and work the mixture by hand until combined. Cover the bowl with plastic wrap and let the levain rest overnight.

5. On the fourth day, the berries should have sprouted. To begin preparations for the dough, place the water, levain, and flours in the work bowl of a stand mixer fitted with the dough hook and work the mixture on low until it just comes together as a dough. Let the dough rest for 30 minutes.

6. Add the salt and mix for 3 minutes on low. Raise the speed to medium and knead the dough for 2 minutes. Reduce the speed to low, add the sprouted berries, and work the mixture until they are incoporated.

7. Shape the dough into a ball, place it in a clean mixing bowl, and cover it with plastic wrap. Let the dough rest until it has doubled in size, about 3 hours, folding it after the first hour and again after the second hour.

8. Place the dough on a flour-dusted work surface and lightly shape it into a ball. Cover the dough with a flour-dusted kitchen towel and let it rest for 20 minutes.

9. Shape the dough into a ball and place it, seam side up, in a banneton or a bowl lined with a floured kitchen towel. Place the dough in a naturally warm spot, cover it with a kitchen towel, and let it rest for 1 hour.

10. Preheat the oven to 475°F and place a baking stone or steel on the middle rack of the oven as it warms.

11. Invert the dough onto a parchment-lined peel and score it. Slide it onto the heated baking implement and bake with steam, using one of the methods described on page 32.

12. Bake the bread until it is a deep golden brown, feels lighter when lifted, and makes a hollow sound when tapped, about 35 minutes.

13. Remove the bread from the oven, place it on a wire rack, and let it cool completely before slicing and serving.

GRITS BREAD

YIELD: 1 LOAF / **ACTIVE TIME:** 4 HOURS / **TOTAL TIME:** 20 HOURS

This brilliant spin on cornbread produces a delicious, moist, and eye-catching loaf.

1. About 12 hours before you plan to start mixing, begin preparations for the dough. Place the grits and water in a medium saucepan and let the mixture sit at room temperature.

2. About 8 hours prior to mixing, prepare the soaker. Combine the ingredients in a mixing bowl, cover the bowl with a kitchen towel, and let the mixture sit at room temperature.

3. Prepare the levain right after preparing the soaker. Combine the ingredients in a mixing bowl, cover the bowl with plastic wrap, and let the levain sit at room temperature.

4. About 2 hours prior to mixing, bring the grits and water to a boil. Reduce the heat so that the grits simmer and cook, gently stirring occasionally, until the grits are tender. Stir in the butter, season the grits with salt to taste, remove the pan from heat, and let the grits cool.

5. Place 1¾ cups of the cooked grits, the soaker, levain, salt, buttermilk, salt, and flours in the work bowl of a stand mixer fitted with the dough hook and work the mixture on low until it comes together as a rough, shaggy dough.

6. Cover the mixing bowl with plastic wrap and place it in a naturally warm location. Let the dough rest for 4 hours, folding all of the corners of the dough to the center every 45 minutes.

7. Coat a 2 lb. loaf pan with nonstick cooking spray and transfer the dough into it. Cover the dough with a kitchen towel and let it rest in a naturally warm spot until it is about ½ inch from the lip of the pan.

8. Preheat the oven to 450°F.

9. Place the bread in the oven and bake with steam, using one of the methods described on page 32. Bake until the bread is a deep golden brown and feels lighter when lifted, about 1 hour.

10. Remove the bread from the oven, place the pan on a wire rack, and let it cool completely before enjoying.

INGREDIENTS:

FOR THE DOUGH

- ⅔ CUP (84 G) GRITS, RINSED WELL
- 2⅛ CUPS (270 G) WATER
- ½ CUP (113 G) UNSALTED BUTTER
- 1½ TEASPOONS (9 G) FINE SEA SALT, PLUS MORE TO TASTE
- 2½ CUPS (570 G) BUTTERMILK
- 3⅔ CUPS (440 G) BREAD FLOUR
- ¾ (HEAPING) CUP (95 G) WHOLE WHEAT FLOUR

FOR THE SOAKER

- 2¾ CUPS (425 G) CORNMEAL
- 1¾ CUPS (400 G) BUTTERMILK

FOR THE LEVAIN

- ½ CUP (113 G) COLD WATER
- 1 CUP (113 G) WHOLE WHEAT FLOUR

PIZZA, FOCACCIA & FLATBREADS

As we all know, pizza has become universally beloved, and this uncommon affection has significantly raised the esteem that this humble flatbread enjoys in the world of bread makers. Though even poorly produced versions of it can be enjoyable, in the hands of the artisan pizza has the potential to become transcendent, as the pies turned out by Chris Bianco, Mark Iacono, and other top pizzaiolos show.

While the recipes and techniques shared in this chapter will not immediately put you on the level of those masters, there is plenty to get you started on the road toward pizza perfection. And, once you get there, you'll find dozens of other dazzling flatbreads that you can utilize your skills upon.

BUILDING THE PERFECT PIZZA

When talking about pizza, people often sound as if they are referring to one specific type of flatbread. But, as the recipes in this book make clear, pizza is not one, but many. From deep dish to Detroit, from pepperoni pies to pizza alla pala, there are myriad variations on everyone's favorite flatbread.

The many possibilities are exciting, but they can also be daunting. That's why it's important to first familiarize yourself with the fundamentals of pizza making and the tools needed to create the essential doughs in your own kitchen.

INGREDIENTS

Different pizza doughs will require different ingredients. But there are basic ingredients that most pizzas share, such as flour, water, salt, fat, and yeast.

Flour

As discussed earlier in the book, not all flours are the same—not even all wheat flour is the same—and this must be kept in mind when setting out to make pizza. One important aspect to consider is how extensible and elastic the dough needs to be for a particular style of pizza. A weaker flour may provide plenty of stretchiness, but it is generally lacking in terms of its potential to create elasticity, meaning that the resulting dough will not spring back once it is spread out. Another factor that is important is the amount of time the dough is supposed to ferment. Stronger flours can accommodate long fermentation times, while doughs made with weaker flours will lose their structure in the process.

Based on these considerations—stretchiness vs. elasticity and fermentation time—we can choose the strength we want in our flour for each type of pizza.

Generally speaking, a flour with a protein content of lower than 10.5 percent is weak, 10.5 to 11 percent is medium, above 11 to 12.5 percent is medium-strong, and over 12.5 is strong.

Gluten is formed by two proteins contained in flour, glutenin and gliadin, and therefore protein content is a good proxy of how much gluten will be developed when combining a specific flour with water. We have to be aware, however, that this is just an approximation. More precise measures exist but are not readily available to the home baker.

As a rule of thumb, most pan pizzas require a moderately strong flour, one that can produce a dough that has the strength to bear the weight of the toppings without releasing the carbon dioxide created during fermentation, while also being extensible enough not to spring back too energetically once it has been stretched. In other words, we need a flour with a protein content between 10.5 and 11 percent. A good all-purpose flour could do the job, but if the protein content is too low, it's best to blend it with a stronger flour, such as a bread flour.

For Neapolitan pizza, there is a growing consensus that a very fine soft wheat flour, such as the Italian "00" flour, is ideal. However, the term "00" tells us nothing about the strength of the flour, which can be anything from 7 to 14 percent. If looking into popular Italian "00" flours, the protein content tends to be higher than an all-purpose flour, between 11.5 and 12.5 percent—the same level commonly found in bread flour. Such proportions of protein should enable the dough to be stretchable but also elastic, since a Neapolitan pizza dough does need to spring back quite energetically when it is stretched. You can buy the specialty pizza flours, but be aware that you can achieve acceptable results with bread flour.

The trademark of Roman pizzas such as pizza bianca, pizza al taglio, and pizza alla pala is the dough's long fermentation times. All of these require a dough that has fermented for a minimum of several hours, and often days. This extended fermentation is what gives Roman pizza its lightness and digestibility, both of which are further bolstered by the longer baking times compared to Neapolitan pizza. Considering the lengthy fermentation time and extended period in the oven, a strong flour is best, one with a protein content between 12.5 and 14 percent. This type of flour will allow the gluten net formed during mixing to retain its structure during the fermentation. Again, an ordinary bread flour can do the job, but if you can find a particularly strong bread flour or, even better, a flour intended for long fermentation, you may achieve even better results.

There is no general rule of thumb when it comes to the optimal flour to use for American-style pizza pies, as they differ quite a bit from one another. American pizzas, however, do share the common characteristic of not requiring an extremely long fermentation. Thus, a very strong flour is completely unnecessary. Any medium-strength flour should yield good results for most regional American pizzas, with the exception of Detroit-style pizza. For that one, a medium-strong flour, with a protein content of between 11 and 12.5 percent, may be best.

With its emphasis on quality, wholesome ingredients, and continual glances toward Neapolitan pizza for inspiration, a medium-strong flour is advisable for gourmet pizzas. Today, however, many gourmet pizzas are inspired by the long-fermented doughs that feature in Roman pizza, in which case a strong flour is recommended. Furthermore, although buying organic flour is always advisable, this is even more relevant for gourmet pizza. Recently, stone-ground and artisan whole wheat flours have become part of this line of pizza baking, with interesting results. Consider experimenting with each of these if gourmet pizza is where your pizza making journey has settled.

Water

In the two capitals of the pizza world, Naples and New York City, there is much discussion about how the unique properties of the local water affects the pizza dough produced. Although this is more myth than reality, there are characteristics in water that will wield influence over any dough, anywhere. In particular, it is worth checking the amount of minerals in the water you are using, a measure classified as the "hardness" of water, and the pH level of your water. Medium-hard water that has a pH around 7 is ideal for pizza dough. If you live in an area with soft water, add more salt to the dough. If you have hard water, reduce the amount of salt. In terms of pH, add more salt if your water has a pH closer to 6, and less if it is closer to 8. If your water has too much chlorine, that is also not ideal for making pizza; if your tap water is highly chlorinated, use purified water.

Another characteristic relevant to pizza making is the temperature of the water. Use nearly ice-cold water when making dough during hot weather, and also when you are making a dough with high hydration content.

Salt

In baking, salt is not only used for taste; it serves several functions that influence the chemistry within a dough, and the development of that dough. For pizza, salt is generally used in higher percentages as compared to other baking preparations. This is done to increase the tenacity of the dough, which, especially in Neapolitan pizza, needs enough elasticity to spring back once it has been stretched out. It is important to avoid adding the salt at the same time as the yeast, because salt can inhibit the activity of the yeast. The proper time to add salt depends on how tenacious and elastic we want the dough to be. For a round pizza, like a Neapolitan-style one, the salt is added quite close to the beginning of mixing the dough.

For pan pizza, it is better to add the salt toward the end of the kneading process, because this type of dough needs to be more extensible than elastic. Regarding the type of salt, any type works, as the differences in results between table, kosher, and the other varieties of salt are truly minimal—please feel comfortable using whichever of these you have.

Yeast

There are several types of yeasts available, and they will all do the job in pizza making. Active dry yeast is by far most accessible, available at most grocery stores. Instant yeast can be tougher to find at a supermarket, but it does have the advantage of not having to be activated like active dry yeast.

If you prefer to use instant yeast, a slight adjustment will need to be made to the following recipes, as 1 teaspoon of instant yeast is equivalent to 1¼ teaspoons of active dry yeast in terms of leavening power.

OLD DOUGH & PRE-FERMENTS

A pre-ferment simply means a mixture of flour and water that a leavening agent has been added to and left to ferment, from a few hours to a few days, and then added to new dough. In pizza making, it is common to use pre-ferments both with yeast and on their own.

The easiest pre-ferment you can use is a piece of dough from a previous bake. Old dough, known as pasta di riporto in Italy, can keep in the refrigerator for up to five days, and it simply needs to be taken out and added to your dough, lending complexity to the flavor of your crusts. For the occasional home baker, it will be difficult to have old dough on hand, so a pre-ferment will have to be created for the occasion. This is achieved by combining a small amount of yeast with water and flour and letting the mixture rest at room temperature for several hours.

Sourdough

Traditionally, sourdough was rarely used for pizza. Contrary to the commonly held belief, brewer's yeast was widely available long before the later part of the 1800s, and even before then, using brewer's yeast in baking was so popular in France that its wholesomeness was at the center of a lively official debate during much of the 1700s. As history tends to repeat itself, yeast's health benefits have again been questioned during the last two decades. As a result, many home bakers, and a limited number of professional bakers, have embraced sourdough for pizza. And good results can be obtained when utilizing a wild yeast, particularly when making gourmet pizza.

Fats

The fat of election for almost every pizza is olive oil. For pizza making, it is advisable to use extra-virgin olive oil.

Sauces

Tomatoes are not native to Europe and only became popular in Italy in the 1800s. One can

therefore find a large number of traditional pizza recipes that do not include tomato sauce. For all of the recipes that do include tomato sauce, like the famed Neapolitan pizza, it is important to know that the best sauce for pizza is uncooked. When putting an already-cooked tomato sauce on pizza dough, the result will be a sauce that is overdone, if not burned, and does no justice to the original taste of the tomatoes.

The best tomatoes for sauce are peeled, whole canned tomatoes, ideally the San Marzano variety.

The practice of using precooked tomato sauce over pizza is likely a result of the poor-quality canned tomatoes available in the past in the US. This led to people altering their taste with vinegar, sugar, and seasonings. When using high-quality canned tomatoes, however, little adulteration is required. The sauce should leave the tomato as untouched as possible in an effort to preserve the original flavor. To make a perfect sauce, simply crush the peeled tomatoes, add salt and olive oil, a little dried oregano if one desires, and, voilà, the sauce is ready. The sauce will be cooked to perfection in the oven. If using fresh tomatoes, peeling will be required, as will a brief sautéing. In any case, make sure you do not use hot tomato sauce over the uncooked pizza dough. A cold tomato sauce will also be detrimental to the optimal rise in the oven. The best option is to always have your sauce at room temperature before applying it to pizza dough.

FUNDAMENTALS

There are three main methods to making a pizza dough. You may feel more comfortable with a specific one or alternate between them based on your mood, the amount of time and energy available, or a specific outcome you have in mind.

HAND MIXING

When mixing by hand, it is important to start by combining the flour and water, followed by any other ingredients; depending on the recipe, the additional ingredients can be incorporated later in a large bowl. The use of a mixing bowl will minimize the mess that is inevitably created when mixing by hand. Once the flour is combined with the water to form a dough, it can be transferred to a flour-dusted work surface and kneaded. One exception are doughs with high levels of hydration, which can be kneaded in the same bowl they were mixed in.

In terms of kneading the dough, there is not one way, but many. The best method is whichever gives you the best feel for the dough and the confidence to work it energetically. Don't be nervous, just follow your instincts—I bet you'll be surprised.

The first approach to kneading pizza dough is the traditional method: after combining the

flour, water, and yeast in a bowl, one turns the dough out onto a flour-dusted work surface and works it with the palms of their hands until the mass comes together. Add the salt and any other ingredients and keep working the dough with your palms until they are thoroughly incorporated. At this point, you can start stretching the dough—pulling it toward you with one hand, pushing it away with the other, and then folding it over itself. Continue to stretch and fold the dough until the dough is well developed, smooth, and extensible (you are able to stretch it without tearing it).

When the water-to-flour ratio is high (over 70 percent hydration with a flour of average strength), it is possible to knead the dough directly in the bowl you used to combine the flour, water, and yeast in. After combining them, let the dough rest for a minimum of 15 minutes and a maximum of 30 minutes (the optimal amount of time will depend on the amount of yeast included in the recipe). The salt is then worked into the dough until thoroughly incorporated. Over the next hour, stretch and fold the dough, pulling up one side with both hands, folding it back on itself, and letting it rest for 15 to 20 minutes before repeating the stretch-and-fold two more times. When the dough is well developed, it is then left to rest to complete bulk fermentation.

Another effective kneading method is known as the slap and fold technique. This method works best with highly hydrated doughs, and involves turning your mixed dough out on a countertop, picking it up with one hand on each side, slapping the dough down on the work surface, and folding the upper part of the dough over the bottom. The dough is then turned 90 degrees and the movement is repeated until the dough appears smooth and well developed.

While there are various kneading techniques, one thing that will aid any approach is working the dough for only a few minutes at a time before covering it with a damp kitchen towel and letting it rest for a bit before kneading

for another few minutes, repeating the process until the dough feels smooth and springs back when pulled from one corner.

Keep in mind that kneading by hand is an intuitive process. It is best to let your hands inform your brain as to when the dough is ready, a feel that will be developed with practice.

To check whether a dough has been worked enough, it is common to perform the "windowpane" test. This simply means taking a piece of dough and stretching it between your fingers: if it can be stretched to where you can almost see through it and it does not tear, the dough is ready.

MACHINE MIXING

When using a stand mixer to mix pizza dough, it is necessary to start at low speed in order to give the dough time to take shape and properly develop the gluten net. It is also useful to let the dough rest between intervals, which keeps it from getting too warm and aids in the formation of gluten through autolysis, a series of biochemical reactions that occur when mixing a dough.

Mixing times are dependent on the flour that is being used. A weak flour requires less energetic mixing for a shorter period of time, while a strong flour will require more work to achieve optimal development. Depending on the flour, one may need to conclude the mixing at high speed.

If mixing very small batches of dough with a mixer, it is best to add the water first, then the flour and yeast. If mixing larger batches of dough, proceed as usual, adding the flour first, then the water and yeast. It is generally best to add the salt and any fats at a later stage, allowing the water to hydrate the flour and start changing its structure without any interference. Generally, an interval of 15 to 20 minutes before adding salt and fats is sufficient.

Overall, machine mixing should not last more than 15 active minutes, combined with a minimum of 15 minutes of rest in between intervals of active mixing.

The first interval of active mixing is done at low speed, with the aim of incorporating the water into the flour. This stage should not last more than 5 minutes. The dough is then left to rest, covered, for about 10 to 15 minutes. After this rest, salt and fats can be added and the dough is worked at low speed for another 5 minutes. If additional water is required, this stage is a good time to incorporate it. Let the dough rest for another 15 minutes before commencing the final stage, which should be done at a higher speed to achieve ideal gluten development. When the dough is well developed, it should adhere to the dough hook attachment and should not break when pulled from one side.

NO-KNEAD MIXING

This technique involves mixing ingredients by hand or machine just enough to combine them—which generally takes only a few minutes—and then letting the dough rest in a covered bowl for an extended amount of time. This technique is particularly effective with wet doughs featuring high hydration. These doughs can be helped by simply stretching the mass and folding it on itself a few times during the first hours of fermentation. The dough is developed mostly through autolysis, where time allows the dough to catalyze its own transformation.

FERMENTATION

Pizza comes from living doughs, meaning doughs that ferment through the interaction of the myriad microorganisms living in them. It is therefore useful to understand fermentation techniques, which will help considerably in your attempt to master these recipes.

When starting to discuss fermentation, it is valuable to distinguish between doughs fermented directly, by simply adding yeast to the mix, and doughs that are instead fermented indirectly with a starter, also known as a pre-ferment.

The fermentation process begins the moment the leavening agent, either yeast or a pre-ferment, is added to the dough. Every dough requires a period of rest after mixing, which allows the fermentation to proceed undisturbed and the carbon dioxide generated by the yeast—and lactic acid in sourdough—to foment, a process that makes the dough grow visibly.

After the first fermentation, when the dough has expanded to 1½ to 2 times its original size, it needs to be shaped according to the specific recipe. The period of rest generally given to a dough after the shaping stage is called the second fermentation, or proofing. During this stage, the dough continues to expand while the microorganisms in it keep "eating" the sugars present in the flour. It is important to end the second fermentation before all of the sugars have been consumed, so that there is room for a final expansion. When a proofing stage

has exceeded optimal fermentation and all of the sugars have been exhausted, the dough is defined as "overproofed." This will generally result in harder and flatter crusts, owing to the loss of the gluten network that traps the carbon dioxide inside the dough, allowing it to become soft and voluminous.

Although it is important to avoid overproofing, pizza doughs do benefit from extended fermentation times. While there are "cheat" recipes with short leavening times, in most cases it's better not to expedite the process by overloading the dough with excessive amounts of yeast. Besides producing clearly inferior taste and structure, a fermentation of less than four hours will result in products that are less digestible.

Conversely, pizza dough that has been fermented for an extended amount of time, sometimes even days, results in an extremely light crust that will melt in your mouth and also agrees with your stomach. The good news about long fermentation is that it does not require much effort, just a bit of planning ahead. Time is, in fact, the most important ingredient in a tasty and digestible crust.

FORMING DOUGH INTO A TIGHT BALL

Part of the process of properly making most pizza doughs is forming the rested dough into a tight ball before it is shaped and slid into the oven. Doing so means that the dough will better retain the gasses created from fermentation even when it is being shaped.

There are two ways to create a tight ball of dough. One way is to pull all of the sides of a piece of dough toward the bottom and pinch them together. Alternatively, the piece of dough can be slightly flattened and folded in on itself from different angles a few times until it looks like a ball.

Whichever of these is employed, the final step is rolling the resulting ball over an unfloured work surface, cupping your hand over the ball and moving it in circular motion until the surface is tight and smooth.

SHAPING PIZZA

There are numerous ways to shape a pizza and, with time, you will develop your own style. As a rule of thumb, pizza does not require the use of a rolling pin. Exceptions are specific regional varieties (like St. Louis–style pizza) that require a crust that departs from the classical Neapolitan style.

One method relies on gravity. The trick is to slightly flatten the ball of pizza dough, then grab the top edge with both hands and lift it, allowing the bottom edge of the dough to come in contact with the work surface underneath. The hands need to keep shifting around the dough in a clockwise fashion, allowing the dough to slowly stretch on all sides. If done properly, this technique will provide a perfectly shaped round of dough that will be thinner in the center and thicker on the edges.

An alternative method involves placing the dough on a work surface that has been dusted with semolina or cornmeal and gently stretching the dough by pressing in opposite directions with each hand. The dough is rotated on the surface while being stretched until the desired shape is achieved.

Whatever approach is used, the most important thing when shaping pizza dough is making sure the dough is thicker around the edge.

Lastly, when getting acquainted with pizza making it is essential to learn how to master the loading of the pizza on the peel and into the oven without altering the pizza's shape or losing the toppings. One way is to heavily dust a peel (or a flat baking sheet) with semolina flour or cornmeal and place the dough on the peel before distributing the toppings. Another method consists of stretching the dough directly on a piece of semolina-dusted parchment paper before loading it onto the peel. This final method will ensure that the transfer to the heated baking implement in the oven is uneventful.

EQUIPMENT

Pizza is most often baked directly on a hot surface. Exceptions are Chicago deep dish, Detroit-style pizza, and Rome's pizza al taglio. In these cases, a rimmed sheet pan or baking dish will suffice. Below follows a description of the essential tools needed for classic pizza crusts.

Baking Stone/Steel: A baking stone or a baking steel is essential when making pizza in a home oven.

These surfaces are so important because of their ability to retain heat. A baking steel will actually cook pizza about 30 percent faster than a baking stone, which results in a crispier crust. A baking steel is also more or less indestructible; a stone will crack over time, or if dropped. Both steel and stone need to be pre-seasoned before using and both should only be cleaned with warm water. (Because stone is porous, you never want to use soap when cleaning it.) If you are planning on cooking multiple pizzas, one after another, it is worth investing in both a baking stone and steel and using them in tandem, placing the steel on

top of the stone. In doing this, the stone becomes a heat sink, allowing the steel to hold heat better between removing a cooked pizza and firing an uncooked one. Since these tools can be used for more than pizza, it is wise to purchase rectangular ones, as that shape will accommodate the widest range of preparations. No matter the material you choose, preheating a baking stone and/or steel for as long as possible before baking will improve the end result.

Baking Peel: It is very difficult to load a pizza and all its toppings on a baking stone or steel without a baking peel. Make sure to find one that is suitable for the size of your oven.

Home Oven: With a regular oven, the crust will never be exactly the same as what a good pizzeria can produce. But it can still be very good, especially if you employ a few tricks. To start, you want to place your baking stone or baking steel on the highest rack in your oven and then set your broiler to high so the stone becomes extremely hot. Once you have preheated the stone with the broiler, shut the broiler off and preheat the oven to the highest temperature it can achieve. When it reaches that temperature, the oven is ready to produce a quality pizza.

Grill: An outdoor grill can be a surprisingly great ally in making a perfect pizza crust. With

the right materials, you can even achieve that wood-fired touch that is so in demand today. What you'll need are a grill lid and a baking stone or baking steel. The lid will retain the steam from the cooking pizza and will also help to keep the temperature high. The stone/steel will allow the temperature of the grill to be maximized and not dispersed. If you are thinking of using the grill to make pizza, be sure to buy a stone/steel that will fit on your grill.

Electric Pizza Ovens: There are several electric pizza ovens made for home use that promise to reach high temperatures and are often relatively affordable. Be sure to research this option thoroughly before purchasing, as the technology hasn't necessarily followed through on the promise.

Outdoor Gas and Wood-Fired Ovens: For the committed pizza baker with plenty of room and resources, an outdoor pizza oven is probably the safest bet if pizzeria-quality pizza is the goal. There are several models to choose from, and most are reliable in terms of performance. Cooking times are massively reduced with wood-fired ovens, although the heat is not always evenly distributed in them, so you will likely need some practice before achieving optimal results.

Pizza Cutter: The best option is a "rocker" pizza cutter, which features a long, rounded blade and appears as though it would be equally good for doing battle in the Middle Ages. But if you don't have space to store a rocker cutter, a traditional pizza wheel cutter will be just fine.

Scale: No matter what type of pizza you are baking, a scale will make life a whole lot easier. There are plenty of inexpensive scales on the market, and learning to measure ingredients when making a dough is the only way to really master the craft. By weighing ingredients, it also becomes easier to calculate percentages and scale ingredients for batches of various sizes. As most of the ingredients in this book are listed by weight, a scale will come in very handy.

Stand Mixer: A stand mixer makes the preparation of pizza dough a much less messy concern, as ingredients are just mixed in a bowl rather than flying all over the kitchen while you knead them by hand. Mixing with a machine not only saves you energy and time, it also ensures more consistent results when it comes to dough development and strength.

Bench Scraper: This inexpensive tool can be used to divide dough and remove it from a work surface without deflating it.

PIZZA DOUGHS

There are a number of doughs one can use as the foundation of the perfect pizza.

The doughs featured on the next few pages will help you craft a variety of pizzas, employing some of the most widely used techniques available to home and commercial bakers alike. Always keep in mind that a recipe is just a canovaccio, a thread around which to build your own method, and this is even more true when it comes to leavened goods. Every recipe needs to be adapted to your own skills, tools, ingredients, baking conditions, and taste and texture preferences. Also, remember that doughs behave differently according to the initial temperature of the ingredients, and the final temperature of the dough, whether it be room or refrigerator temperature, etc. The times provided should be used as estimates. The best tip is to learn to recognize when your doughs are ready to be used, which will come with practice and a little bit of passion.

The following recipes feature various water-to-flour ratios and fermentation approaches, each of which will give you a slightly different result. One thing that is important to remember when working with pizza dough, after 48 hours, the gluten in the dough will start to deteriorate, and the quality of the pizza with it, so it is optimal to use the dough at some point within that window.

QUICK PIZZA DOUGH

YIELD: 4 BALLS OF DOUGH / **ACTIVE TIME:** 20 MINUTES / **TOTAL TIME:** 2 HOURS

A simple and relatively quick pizza dough recipe that can accommodate any topping of your choice.

1. Warm 3½ tablespoons of the water until it is 105°F. Add the water and the yeast to a bowl and gently stir. Let it sit until it starts to foam, about 10 minutes.

2. In a large bowl, combine the flour, yeast mixture, and remaining water and work the mixture until it just holds together. If kneading by hand, transfer the dough to a flour-dusted work surface. Work the dough until it is smooth and elastic.

3. Add the salt and knead until the dough is developed, elastic, and extensible, about 5 minutes. Coat a container that allows the dough to get at least three times bigger with olive oil. Form the dough into a ball and place it in the container. Let it rest in a naturally warm spot until it has doubled in size, about 1 hour.

4. Transfer the dough to a flour-dusted work surface, divide it into four pieces, and shape them into tight balls. Coat a baking dish with high sides with olive oil and place the balls in it, leaving enough space between them so that they won't touch when fully risen. Coat plastic wrap with olive oil, cover the baking dish with it, and let the dough rest for 40 minutes to 1 hour before using it to make pizza.

INGREDIENTS:

15½ OZ. (439 G) WATER

3⅓ TEASPOONS (10 G) ACTIVE DRY YEAST

23.2 OZ. (657 G) BREAD FLOUR OR "00" FLOUR, PLUS MORE AS NEEDED

1 TABLESPOON (17 G) FINE SEA SALT

EXTRA-VIRGIN OLIVE OIL, AS NEEDED

NEAPOLITAN PIZZA DOUGH

YIELD: 4 BALLS OF DOUGH / **ACTIVE TIME:** 30 MINUTES / **TOTAL TIME:** 8 TO 12 HOURS

This dough is inspired by the classic Neapolitan pizza dough as described by the collective trademark Verace Pizza Napoletana. The original Neapolitan pizza includes neither fats nor sugar and uses only a pinch of yeast, letting time do all the work. The fundamentals are a good flour and proper technique when working the dough. This dough can be started in the morning and baked the evening of the same day.

INGREDIENTS:

14.8 OZ. (419.5 G) WATER

⅛ TEASPOON PLUS 1 PINCH (0.2 G) ACTIVE DRY YEAST

23.9 OZ. (677.5 G) BREAD FLOUR OR "00" FLOUR, PLUS MORE AS NEEDED

1 TABLESPOON (17 G) FINE SEA SALT

EXTRA-VIRGIN OLIVE OIL, AS NEEDED

1. Warm 3½ tablespoons of the water until it is 105°F. Add the water and the yeast to a bowl and gently stir. Let it sit until it starts to foam, about 10 minutes.

2. In a large bowl, combine the flour, yeast mixture, and remaining water and work the mixture until it just holds together. If kneading by hand, transfer the dough to a flour-dusted work surface. Work the dough until it is smooth and elastic.

3. Add the salt and knead until the dough is very developed, elastic, and extensible. A Neapolitan-style pizza dough needs to be very well developed, which means the gluten in the dough should be at maximum strength. The resulting dough needs to be both extensible and elastic, meaning it needs to be easy to spread out thin but it also needs to spring back quite energetically, in order not to lose its shape.

4. Coat an airtight container that allows the dough to get at least three times bigger with olive oil. Form the dough into a ball, place it in the container, and cover the container. Let it rest in a naturally warm spot until it has doubled in size, about 1 hour. For a classic Neapolitan dough, the room temperature should be 73°F. If your kitchen is colder, let the dough rest for longer before shaping it into balls.

5. Transfer the dough to a flour-dusted work surface, divide it into four pieces, and shape them into very tight balls. Coat a baking dish with high sides with olive oil and place the balls in it, leaving enough space between them so that they won't touch when fully risen. Coat plastic wrap with olive oil, cover the baking dish with it, and let the dough rest for 6 to 8 hours before using it to make pizza.

62 PERCENT HYDRATION PIZZA DOUGH

YIELD: 4 BALLS OF DOUGH / **ACTIVE TIME:** 30 MINUTES / **TOTAL TIME:** 27 HOURS

This recipe represents a twist on the classic Neapolitan pizza dough. By performing only the first stage of fermentation at room temperature and the rest in the refrigerator, it is easy to make the dough in the evening and have the pizza balls ready for dinner the following night. Like a classic Neapolitan pizza, this dough is relatively dry, so it can withstand a more energetic stretch when shaping it and can also be stretched thinner compared to doughs with higher hydration.

INGREDIENTS:

- 14.8 OZ. (419.5 G) WATER
- 1¼ TEASPOONS (3.7 G) ACTIVE DRY YEAST
- 23.9 OZ. (677.5 G) BREAD FLOUR OR "00" FLOUR, PLUS MORE AS NEEDED
- 1 TABLESPOON (17 G) FINE SEA SALT
- EXTRA-VIRGIN OLIVE OIL, AS NEEDED

1. Warm 3½ tablespoons of the water until it is 105°F. Add the water and the yeast to a bowl and gently stir. Let it sit until it starts to foam, about 10 minutes.

2. In a large bowl, combine the flour, yeast mixture, and remaining water and work the mixture until it just holds together. If kneading by hand, transfer the dough to a flour-dusted work surface. Work the dough until it is smooth and elastic.

3. Add the salt and knead until the dough is developed, elastic, and extensible, about 5 minutes. Coat an airtight container that allows the dough to get at least three times bigger with olive oil. Form the dough into a ball, place it in the container, and cover the container. Let it rest in a naturally warm spot until it has doubled in size, 3 to 4 hours.

4. Transfer the dough to a flour-dusted work surface, divide it into four pieces, and shape them into tight balls. Coat a baking dish with high sides with olive oil and place the balls in it, leaving enough space between them so that they won't touch when fully risen. Coat plastic wrap with olive oil, cover the baking dish with it, and chill the dough in the refrigerator for a minimum of 20 hours.

5. After this period of cold fermentation, remove the dough from the refrigerator and let it sit at room temperature for 1 to 2 hours before using it to make pizza.

67 PERCENT HYDRATION PIZZA DOUGH

YIELD: 4 BALLS OF DOUGH / **ACTIVE TIME:** 30 MINUTES / **TOTAL TIME:** 27 HOURS

With 67 percent hydration, this dough will be soft but not overly sticky, and it will be easy to handle. This level of hydration works with most styles of pizza.

INGREDIENTS:

- 15½ OZ. (439.4) WATER
- 1¼ TEASPOONS (3.7 G) ACTIVE DRY YEAST
- 23.3 OZ. (660.5 G) BREAD FLOUR OR "00" FLOUR, PLUS MORE AS NEEDED
- 1 TABLESPOON (17 G) FINE SEA SALT
- EXTRA-VIRGIN OLIVE OIL, AS NEEDED

1. Warm 3½ tablespoons of the water until it is 105°F. Add the water and the yeast to a bowl and gently stir. Let it sit until it starts to foam, about 10 minutes.

2. In a large bowl, combine the flour, yeast mixture, and remaining water and work the mixture until it just holds together. If kneading by hand, transfer the dough to a flour-dusted work surface. Work the dough until it is smooth and elastic.

3. Add the salt and knead until the dough is developed, elastic, and extensible, about 5 minutes. Coat an airtight container that allows the dough to get at least three times bigger with olive oil. Form the dough into a ball, place it in the container, and cover the container. Let it rest in a naturally warm spot until it has doubled in size, 3 to 4 hours.

4. Transfer the dough to a flour-dusted work surface, divide it into four pieces, and shape them into tight balls. Coat a baking dish with high sides with olive oil and place the balls in it, leaving enough space between them so that they won't touch when fully risen. Coat plastic wrap with olive oil, cover the baking dish with it, and chill the dough in the refrigerator for a minimum of 20 hours.

5. After this period of cold fermentation, remove the dough from the refrigerator and let it sit at room temperature for 1 to 2 hours before using it to make pizza.

72 PERCENT HYDRATION PIZZA DOUGH

YIELD: 4 BALLS OF DOUGH / **ACTIVE TIME:** 30 MINUTES / **TOTAL TIME:** 27 HOURS

This dough has the highest water-to-flour ratio of the pizza dough recipes in this book. The mass will be slightly sticky in the initial stages, but not as difficult to work with as the extremely hydrated doughs that feature in other baking recipes (those doughs are not recommended for pizza). A dough with this level of hydration is good for a thick-crust pizza.

INGREDIENTS:

16.2 OZ. (459 G) WATER

1¼ TEASPOONS (3.7 G) ACTIVE DRY YEAST

22.6 OZ. (640 G) BREAD FLOUR OR "00" FLOUR, PLUS MORE AS NEEDED

1 TABLESPOON (17 G) FINE SEA SALT

EXTRA-VIRGIN OLIVE OIL, AS NEEDED

1. Warm 3½ tablespoons of the water until it is 105°F. Add the water and the yeast to a bowl and gently stir. Let it sit until it starts to foam, about 10 minutes.

2. In a large bowl, combine the flour, yeast mixture, and remaining water and work the mixture until it just holds together. If kneading by hand, transfer the dough to a flour-dusted work surface. Work the dough until it is smooth and elastic.

3. Add the salt and knead until the dough is developed, elastic, and extensible, about 5 minutes. Coat an airtight container that allows the dough to get at least three times bigger with olive oil. Form the dough into a ball, place it in the container, and cover the container. Let it rest in a naturally warm spot until it has doubled in size, 3 to 4 hours.

4. Transfer the dough to a flour-dusted work surface, divide it into four pieces, and shape them into tight balls. Coat a baking dish with high sides with olive oil and place the balls in it, leaving enough space between them so that they won't touch when fully risen. Coat plastic wrap with olive oil, cover the baking dish with it, and chill in the refrigerator for a minimum of 20 hours.

5. After this period of cold fermentation, remove the dough from the refrigerator and let it sit at room temperature for 1 to 2 hours before using it to make pizza.

72 Percent Hydration Pizza Dough, see page 293

NO-KNEAD PIZZA DOUGH

YIELD: 4 BALLS OF DOUGH / **ACTIVE TIME:** 10 MINUTES / **TOTAL TIME:** 10 HOURS

The easiest pizza dough to make is one that does not require kneading. Kneading is fundamental in a proper Neapolitan-style pizza, but if you're short on time and just shooting for a "good enough" crust, a no-knead approach will surely get you there.

INGREDIENTS:

- 16.2 OZ. (459 G) WATER
- ⅛ TEASPOON PLUS 1 PINCH (0.2 G) ACTIVE DRY YEAST
- 22.6 OZ. (640 G) BREAD FLOUR OR "00" FLOUR, PLUS MORE AS NEEDED
- 1 TABLESPOON (17 G) FINE SEA SALT
- EXTRA-VIRGIN OLIVE OIL, AS NEEDED

1. Warm 3½ tablespoons of the water until it is 105°F. Add the water and the yeast to a bowl and gently stir. Let it sit until it starts to foam, about 10 minutes.

2. In a large bowl, combine the flour, yeast mixture, and remaining water and work the mixture until there are no more lumps. Cover the bowl with plastic wrap and let it rest until it has doubled in size, 8 to 12 hours.

3. Transfer the dough to a flour-dusted work surface, divide it into four pieces, and shape them into tight balls. Coat a baking dish with high sides with olive oil and place the balls in it, leaving enough space between them so that they won't touch when fully risen. Coat plastic wrap with olive oil, cover the baking dish with it, and let the dough rest for 1 hour before using it to make pizza.

PIZZA DOUGH WITH BIGA

YIELD: 4 BALLS OF DOUGH / **ACTIVE TIME:** 40 MINUTES / **TOTAL TIME:** 24 HOURS

Bakers in Italy turn to their biga day after day. If you're lucky enough to have enjoyed the results of their devotion, you have a good idea of how delicious this pizza dough will be.

INGREDIENTS:

FOR THE BIGA

- 3½ OZ. (100 G) BREAD FLOUR
- 1¾ OZ. (50 G) WATER
- ⅛ TEASPOON PLUS 1 PINCH (0.2 G) ACTIVE DRY YEAST
- EXTRA-VIRGIN OLIVE OIL, AS NEEDED

FOR THE DOUGH

- 13.4 OZ. (380 G) WATER
- ¼ TEASPOON PLUS 1 PINCH (0.4 G) ACTIVE DRY YEAST
- 20.1 OZ. (569.7 G) BREAD FLOUR OR "00" FLOUR, PLUS MORE AS NEEDED
- 5.3 OZ. (150 G) BIGA
- 3½ TEASPOONS (18 G) FINE SEA SALT

1. To prepare the biga, place all of the ingredients in a mixing bowl and work the mixture until comes together as a sticky dough. Coat a bowl large enough to allow the dough to get at least three times bigger with olive oil, place the biga in it, and cover the bowl with plastic wrap. Place the biga in a naturally cool spot and let it rest until it has tripled in size, about 18 hours. Use immediately or store in the refrigerator for up to 5 days.

2. To begin preparations for the dough, warm 3½ tablespoons of the water until it is 105°F. Add the water and the yeast to a bowl and gently stir. Let it sit until it starts to foam, about 10 minutes.

3. In a large bowl, combine the flour, yeast mixture, remaining water, and biga and work the mixture until it just holds together. If kneading by hand, transfer the dough to a flour-dusted work surface. Work the dough until it is smooth and elastic.

4. Add the salt and knead until the dough is developed, elastic, and extensible, about 5 minutes. Coat an airtight container that allows the dough to get at least three times bigger with olive oil. Form the dough into a ball, place it in the container, and cover the container. Let it rest in a naturally warm spot until it has doubled in size, 2 to 3 hours.

5. Transfer the dough to a flour-dusted work surface, divide it into four pieces, and shape them into tight balls. Coat a baking dish with high sides with olive oil and place the balls in it, leaving enough space between them so that they won't touch when fully risen. Coat plastic wrap with olive oil, cover the baking dish with it, and chill in the refrigerator for a minimum of 20 hours.

6. After this period of cold fermentation, remove the dough from the refrigerator and let it sit at room temperature for 1 to 2 hours before using it to make pizza.

Pizza Dough with Biga, see page 297

SOURDOUGH PIZZA DOUGH

YIELD: 4 BALLS OF DOUGH / **ACTIVE TIME:** 40 MINUTES / **TOTAL TIME:** 24 HOURS

For all the sourdough fans, here is a simple method. When using sourdough to make pizza, it is important to have a very lively starter and levain. If these are part of the equation, a sourdough crust can equal and even surpass a yeast-based one in terms of texture and flavor.

INGREDIENTS:

FOR THE LEVAIN

- 1¾ OZ. (50 G) SOURDOUGH STARTER (SEE PAGE 40)
- 1¾ OZ. (50 G) WATER
- 2.6 OZ. (75 G) BREAD FLOUR OR "00" FLOUR

FOR THE DOUGH

- 5.3 OZ. (150 G) LEVAIN
- 20.1 OZ. (569.7 G) BREAD FLOUR OR "00" FLOUR, PLUS MORE AS NEEDED
- 13.4 OZ. (380 G) WATER
- 1 TABLESPOON (17 G) FINE SEA SALT

1. To prepare the levain, place all of the ingredients in a mixing bowl and stir to combine. Cover the bowl with plastic wrap and let the levain rest in a naturally warm spot until it has doubled in size, about 2 hours.

2. To begin preparations for the dough, combine the levain, flour, and water in a mixing bowl and work the mixture until it just holds together. Transfer the dough to a flour-dusted work surface and knead until it is compact, smooth, and elastic.

3. Add the salt and knead until the dough is developed, elastic, and extensible, about 5 minutes. Coat an airtight container that allows the dough to get at least three times bigger with olive oil. Form the dough into a ball, place it in the container, and cover the container. Let it rest in a naturally warm spot until it has doubled in size, about 2 hours.

4. Transfer the dough to a flour-dusted work surface, divide it into four pieces, and shape them into tight balls. Coat a baking dish with high sides with olive oil and place the balls in it, leaving enough space between them so that they won't touch when fully risen. Coat plastic wrap with olive oil, cover the baking dish with it, and chill in the refrigerator for a minimum of 20 hours.

5. After this period of cold fermentation, remove the dough from the refrigerator and let it sit at room temperature for 1 to 2 hours before using it to make pizza.

bambum

PIZZA DOUGH WITH OLD DOUGH

YIELD: 4 BALLS OF DOUGH / **ACTIVE TIME:** 40 MINUTES / **TOTAL TIME:** 24 HOURS

If you don't have a biga ready to go, but happen to have some already fermented pizza dough from a previous bake on hand, this method will come in handy. If refrigerated, old dough—or pasta di riporto in Italian—can be used for up to one week after it first has been made, and it is good to go straight out of the fridge.

1. Warm 3½ tablespoons of the water until it is 105°F. Add the water and yeast to a bowl and gently stir. Let it sit until it starts to foam, about 10 minutes.

2. In a large bowl, combine the old dough, flour, yeast mixture, and remaining water and work the mixture until it just holds together. If kneading by hand, transfer the dough to a flour-dusted work surface. Work the dough until it is smooth and elastic.

3. Add the salt and knead until the dough is developed, elastic, and extensible, about 5 minutes. Coat an airtight container that allows the dough to get at least three times bigger with olive oil. Form the dough into a ball, place it in the container, and cover the container. Let it rest in a naturally warm spot until it has doubled in size, 2 to 3 hours.

4. Transfer the dough to a flour-dusted work surface, divide it into four pieces, and shape them into tight balls. Coat a baking dish with high sides with olive oil and place the balls in it, leaving enough space between them so that they won't touch when fully risen. Coat plastic wrap with olive oil, cover the baking dish with it, and chill in the refrigerator for a minimum of 20 hours.

5. After this period of cold fermentation, remove the dough from the refrigerator and let it sit at room temperature for 1 to 2 hours before using it to make pizza.

INGREDIENTS:

13.4 OZ. (380 G) WATER

¼ TEASPOON PLUS 1 PINCH (0.4 G) ACTIVE DRY YEAST

5.3 OZ. (150 G) OLD DOUGH

20.1 OZ. (569.7 G) BREAD FLOUR OR "00" FLOUR, PLUS MORE AS NEEDED

1 TABLESPOON (17 G) FINE SEA SALT

EXTRA-VIRGIN OLIVE OIL, AS NEEDED

PIZZA AL TAGLIO DOUGH

YIELD: DOUGH FOR 1 LARGE PAN PIZZA / **ACTIVE TIME:** 30 MINUTES / **TOTAL TIME:** 5 HOURS

This dough will give you a soft pizza al taglio with a nice, complex texture. It takes several hours to make, but keep in mind that most of it is rising time, during which you can attend to other activities.

INGREDIENTS:

- 17.3 OZ. (490 G) WATER
- 1¼ TEASPOONS (3.7 G) ACTIVE DRY YEAST
- 15.9 OZ. (450 G) BREAD FLOUR OR STRONG "00" FLOUR
- 8.8 OZ. (250 G) ALL-PURPOSE FLOUR, PLUS MORE AS NEEDED
- 1 TABLESPOON (13 G) EXTRA-VIRGIN OLIVE OIL, PLUS MORE AS NEEDED
- 1 TABLESPOON (17 G) FINE SEA SALT

1. Warm 3½ tablespoons of the water until it is 105°F. Add the water and the yeast to a bowl and gently stir. Let it sit until it starts to foam, about 10 minutes.

2. In a large bowl, combine the flours, yeast mixture, and remaining water and work the mixture until it just holds together. If kneading by hand, transfer the dough to a flour-dusted work surface. Work the dough until it is smooth and elastic.

3. Add the olive oil and salt and knead until the dough is developed, elastic, and extensible, about 5 minutes. Coat an airtight container that allows the dough to get at least three times bigger with olive oil. Form the dough into a ball, place it in the container, and cover the container. Let it rest in a naturally warm spot until it has doubled in size, 3 to 4 hours.

PIZZA ALLA PALA DOUGH

YIELD: 2 BALLS OF DOUGH / **ACTIVE TIME:** 30 MINUTES / **TOTAL TIME:** 7 HOURS

Compared to other types of pizza, this is likely the one with the most alveolated crust, due to the long fermentation time, the strong flour used, and the relatively high water content.

1. Warm 3½ tablespoons of the water until it is 105°F. Add the water and the yeast to a bowl and gently stir. Let it sit until it starts to foam, about 10 minutes.

2. In a large bowl, combine the flour and three-quarters of the remaining water and work the mixture until combined. Add the yeast mixture, malt, and sugar and work the mixture until it just holds together. If kneading by hand, transfer the dough to a flour-dusted work surface. Work the dough until it is smooth and elastic, about 10 minutes.

3. Add the salt and remaining water and knead until the dough is developed, elastic, and extensible, about 5 minutes. Coat an airtight container that allows the dough to get at least three times bigger with olive oil. Form the dough into a ball, place it in the container, and cover the container. Let it rest in a naturally warm spot until doubled in size and is full of bubbles, about 5 hours.

4. Line two baking sheets with parchment paper and dust the parchment paper with flour. Place the dough onto a flour-dusted work surface and divide it into two pieces. Place a piece of dough on each baking sheet, shape them into ovals, and let them rest in a naturally warm spot for 2 to 3 hours, stretching the dough lengthwise every 30 minutes and taking care not to deflate them.

5. After the last stretch, generously drizzle olive oil and sprinkle sea salt over the pieces of dough. Let them rest for another 15 minutes before using them to make pizza.

INGREDIENTS:

- 18½ OZ. (524 G) WATER
- 1¼ TEASPOONS (3.7 G) ACTIVE DRY YEAST
- 24.7 OZ. (700 G) BREAD FLOUR OR STRONG "00" FLOUR, PLUS MORE AS NEEDED
- 2 TEASPOONS (6 G) DIASTATIC MALT
- 1¾ TEASPOONS (7 G) SUGAR
- 1 TABLESPOON (17 G) FINE SEA SALT, PLUS MORE TO TASTE
- EXTRA-VIRGIN OLIVE OIL, AS NEEDED

PIZZA MARINARA

YIELD: 1 PIZZA / **ACTIVE TIME:** 15 MINUTES / **TOTAL TIME:** 45 MINUTES

According to the European Union, there are only two authentic Neapolitan pizzas that deserve the TSG (Traditional Speciality Guaranteed) appellation: this and pizza Margherita. Pizza marinara is possibly the oldest variety of Neapolitan pizza still popular today, and it is surprising in its simplicity. The key to making a good version of this pizza at home is to use top-notch ingredients, as that is the only way to do justice to this simple topping.

INGREDIENTS:

- SEMOLINA FLOUR, AS NEEDED
- 1 BALL OF PIZZA DOUGH
- ⅓ CUP PIZZA SAUCE (SEE PAGE 661)
- 1 GARLIC CLOVE, SLICED THIN
- SALT, TO TASTE
- DRIED OREGANO, TO TASTE
- EXTRA-VIRGIN OLIVE OIL, TO TASTE

1. Place a baking stone or steel on the middle rack of the oven and preheat the oven to the maximum temperature.

2. Dust a work surface with semolina flour, place the dough on the work surface, and gently stretch it into a round. Cover the dough with the sauce and top it with the garlic. Season the pizza with salt and dried oregano and drizzle olive oil over the top.

3. Using a peel or a flat baking sheet, transfer the pizza to the heated baking implement in the oven. Bake for about 15 minutes, until the crust is golden brown and starting to char. Remove the pizza from the oven and let it cool slightly before slicing and serving.

Pizza Marinara, see page 305

PIZZA MARGHERITA

YIELD: 1 PIZZA / **ACTIVE TIME:** 15 MINUTES / **TOTAL TIME:** 45 MINUTES

For most, both in Italy and abroad, this is the true original Neapolitan pizza: gooey mozzarella and a tomato sauce base. Buon appetito.

INGREDIENTS:

- SEMOLINA FLOUR, AS NEEDED
- 1 BALL OF PIZZA DOUGH
- ⅓ CUP PIZZA SAUCE (SEE PAGE 661)
- 4 OZ. FRESH MOZZARELLA CHEESE, DRAINED AND CUT INTO SHORT STRIPS
- FRESH BASIL LEAVES, TO TASTE
- SALT, TO TASTE
- EXTRA-VIRGIN OLIVE OIL, TO TASTE

1. Place a baking stone or steel on the middle rack of the oven and preheat the oven to the maximum temperature.

2. Dust a work surface with semolina flour, place the dough on the work surface, and gently stretch it into a round. Cover the dough with the sauce and top it with the mozzarella and basil. Season with salt and drizzle olive oil over the pizza.

3. Using a peel or a flat baking sheet, transfer the pizza to the heated baking implement in the oven. Bake for about 15 minutes, until the crust is golden brown and starting to char. Remove the pizza from the oven and let it cool slightly before slicing and serving.

PIZZA ROMANA

YIELD: 1 PIZZA / **ACTIVE TIME:** 15 MINUTES / **TOTAL TIME:** 45 MINUTES

There are two different versions of this pizza: with or without mozzarella. It also has two names: it is Romana to the Neapolitans, who created the topping, and Napoli for everyone else. What never changes in this pizza is the presence of tomato sauce, anchovies, capers, and oregano.

INGREDIENTS:

- SEMOLINA FLOUR, AS NEEDED
- 1 BALL OF PIZZA DOUGH
- ⅓ CUP PIZZA SAUCE (SEE PAGE 661)
- 2½ OZ. FRESH MOZZARELLA CHEESE, DRAINED AND CUT INTO SHORT STRIPS
- 4 ANCHOVIES IN OLIVE OIL, DRAINED AND CHOPPED
- 1 TABLESPOON CAPERS, DRAINED
- SALT, TO TASTE
- DRIED OREGANO, TO TASTE
- EXTRA-VIRGIN OLIVE OIL, TO TASTE

1. Place a baking stone or steel on the middle rack of the oven and preheat the oven to the maximum temperature.

2. Dust a work surface with semolina flour, place the dough on the work surface, and gently stretch it into a round. Cover the dough with the sauce and top it with the mozzarella, anchovies, and capers. Season with salt and oregano and drizzle olive oil over the pizza.

3. Using a peel or a flat baking sheet, transfer the pizza to the heated baking implement in the oven. Bake for about 15 minutes, until the crust is golden brown and starting to char. Remove the pizza from the oven and let it cool slightly before slicing and serving.

PIZZA CAPRICCIOSA

YIELD: 1 PIZZA / **ACTIVE TIME:** 15 MINUTES / **TOTAL TIME:** 45 MINUTES

Capricciosa means "capricious" in Italian, and in Neapolitan pizza jargon this means a topping that, as it cannot make a simple decision, gladly indulges.

1. Place a baking stone or steel on the middle rack of the oven and preheat the oven to the maximum temperature.

2. Dust a work surface with semolina flour, place the dough on the work surface, and gently stretch it into a round. Cover the dough with the sauce and top it with the artichokes and mushrooms. Season with salt and drizzle olive oil over the pizza.

3. Using a peel or a flat baking sheet, transfer the pizza to the heated baking implement in the oven. Bake for about 5 minutes, until the crust starts to brown. Remove the pizza, distribute the mozzarella, prosciutto, and olives over the top, and return the pizza to the oven. Bake for about 10 minutes, until the crust is golden brown and starting to char. Remove the pizza from the oven and let it cool slightly before slicing and serving.

INGREDIENTS:

- SEMOLINA FLOUR, AS NEEDED
- 1 BALL OF PIZZA DOUGH
- ⅓ CUP PIZZA SAUCE (SEE PAGE 661)
- 2 ARTICHOKE HEARTS, CHOPPED
- ¼ CUP SLICED MUSHROOMS
- SALT, TO TASTE
- EXTRA-VIRGIN OLIVE OIL, TO TASTE
- 3 OZ. FRESH MOZZARELLA CHEESE, DRAINED AND CUT INTO SHORT STRIPS
- 2 SLICES OF PROSCIUTTO, TORN
- 1 SMALL HANDFUL OF PITTED BLACK OLIVES, SLICED OR LEFT WHOLE
- FRESH BASIL LEAVES, TO TASTE

PIZZA BOSCAIOLA

YIELD: 1 PIZZA / **ACTIVE TIME:** 25 MINUTES / **TOTAL TIME:** 55 MINUTES

Boscaiola means "from the woods" in Italian, referring to mushrooms and game. Here, the game component is just humble sausage, but the pizza retains its earthy and substantial promise.

INGREDIENTS:

- EXTRA-VIRGIN OLIVE OIL, AS NEEDED
- 1 LINK OF ITALIAN SAUSAGE, CASING REMOVED AND CRUMBLED
- SEMOLINA FLOUR, AS NEEDED
- 1 BALL OF PIZZA DOUGH
- ⅓ CUP PIZZA SAUCE (SEE PAGE 661)
- ½ CUP SLICED MUSHROOMS
- SALT, TO TASTE
- 3 OZ. FRESH MOZZARELLA CHEESE, DRAINED AND CUT INTO SHORT STRIPS

1. Place a baking stone or steel on the middle rack of the oven and preheat the oven to the maximum temperature.

2. Coat the bottom of a skillet with olive oil and warm it over medium-high heat. Add the sausage and cook until it starts to brown, about 6 minutes, stirring occasionally. Remove the pan from heat and set the sausage aside.

3. Dust a work surface with semolina flour, place the dough on the work surface, and gently stretch it into a round. Cover the dough with the sauce and top it with the mushrooms and sausage. Season with salt and drizzle olive oil over the pizza.

4. Using a peel or a flat baking sheet, transfer the pizza to the heated baking implement in the oven. Bake for about 5 minutes, until the crust starts to brown. Remove the pizza, distribute the mozzarella over the top, and return the pizza to the oven. Bake for about 10 minutes, until the crust is golden brown and starting to char. Remove the pizza from the oven and let it cool slightly before slicing and serving.

PIZZA DIAVOLA

YIELD: 1 PIZZA / **ACTIVE TIME:** 15 MINUTES / **TOTAL TIME:** 50 MINUTES

This pizza's "from hell" moniker refers to its hot and spicy bite. This is the topping that inspired the pepperoni pizza that became an American classic.

INGREDIENTS:

- 2 TABLESPOONS EXTRA-VIRGIN OLIVE OIL, PLUS MORE TO TASTE
- RED PEPPER FLAKES, TO TASTE
- SEMOLINA FLOUR, AS NEEDED
- 1 BALL OF PIZZA DOUGH
- ⅓ CUP PIZZA SAUCE (SEE PAGE 661)
- 2½ OZ. CACIOCAVALLO OR PROVOLA CHEESE, CUBED
- 5 SLICES OF SPICY SALAMI
- SALT, TO TASTE
- DRIED OREGANO, TO TASTE

1. Place a baking stone or steel on the middle rack of the oven and preheat the oven to the maximum temperature. Combine the olive oil and red pepper flakes in a small bowl and set the mixture aside.

2. Dust a work surface with semolina flour, place the dough on the work surface, and gently stretch it into a round. Cover the dough with the sauce and top it with the cheese and salami. Season with salt and oregano and drizzle the spicy olive oil over the pizza.

3. Using a peel or a flat baking sheet, transfer the pizza to the heated baking implement in the oven. Bake for about 15 minutes, until the crust is golden brown and starting to char. Remove the pizza from the oven and let it cool slightly before slicing and serving.

PIZZA STAGIONI

YIELD: 1 PIZZA / **ACTIVE TIME:** 15 MINUTES / **TOTAL TIME:** 50 MINUTES

Meaning "four seasons" in Italian, the name here refers to the toppings being divided into four sections, each one featuring a different seasonal ingredient. Swapping in mushrooms for the artichokes and prosciutto for the pepperoni are popular choices.

INGREDIENTS:

- EXTRA-VIRGIN OLIVE OIL, TO TASTE
- 4 OZ. SEAFOOD (SHRIMP, CALAMARI, MUSSELS, CRAB, AND/OR TUNA RECOMMENDED)
- SALT, TO TASTE
- SEMOLINA FLOUR, AS NEEDED
- 1 BALL OF PIZZA DOUGH
- ⅓ CUP PIZZA SAUCE (SEE PAGE 661)
- 3 OZ. FRESH MOZZARELLA CHEESE, DRAINED AND CUT INTO SHORT STRIPS
- 2 ARTICHOKE HEARTS IN OLIVE OIL, DRAINED AND CUT INTO WEDGES
- 8 SLICES OF PEPPERONI
- 1 TOMATO, SLICED

1. Place a baking stone or steel on the middle rack of the oven and preheat the oven to the maximum temperature.

2. Coat the bottom of a skillet with olive oil and warm it over medium-high heat. Add the seafood, season with salt, and cook until the seafood is just cooked through, about 4 minutes. Remove the pan from heat and set the seafood aside. If using mussels, discard any mussels that did not open and remove the meat from those that did open.

3. Dust a work surface with semolina flour, place the dough on the work surface, and gently stretch it into a round. Cover the dough with the sauce and top it with the mozzarella. Place the artichokes, pepperoni, seafood, and tomato on their own section of the pizza. Season with salt and drizzle olive oil over the pizza.

4. Using a peel or a flat baking sheet, transfer the pizza to the heated baking implement in the oven. Bake for about 15 minutes, until the crust is golden brown and starting to char. Remove and let cool slightly before slicing and serving.

PIZZA ORTOLANA

YIELD: 1 PIZZA / **ACTIVE TIME:** 30 MINUTES / **TOTAL TIME:** 1 HOUR AND 15 MINUTES

As you may expect of a pizza that trumpets being "from the garden," the topping features no cheese—just tomato sauce and fresh vegetables.

INGREDIENTS:

- ¼ CUP MUSHROOMS, CHOPPED
- SALT AND PEPPER, TO TASTE
- EXTRA-VIRGIN OLIVE OIL, TO TASTE
- ½ BELL PEPPER, SLICED
- ½ SMALL EGGPLANT, SLICED
- SEMOLINA FLOUR, AS NEEDED
- 1 BALL OF PIZZA DOUGH
- ⅓ CUP PIZZA SAUCE (SEE PAGE 661)
- ¼ ONION, SLICED
- FRESH BASIL LEAVES, TO TASTE
- DRIED OREGANO, TO TASTE

1. Place a baking stone or steel on the middle rack of the oven and preheat the oven to the maximum temperature. Place the mushrooms in a bowl, season with salt and pepper, and generously drizzle olive oil over them. Stir to combine and let the mixture sit for 10 minutes. Drain the mushrooms and set them aside.

2. Place the bell pepper and eggplant on an aluminum foil–lined baking sheet, season with salt and pepper, drizzle olive oil over the vegetables, and place them in the oven. Roast until they are tender and browned, about 25 minutes. Remove the vegetables from the oven and let them cool.

3. Dust a work surface with semolina flour, place the dough on the work surface, and gently stretch it into a round. Cover the dough with the sauce and top it with the mushrooms, eggplant, peppers, onion, and basil. Season with salt and oregano and drizzle olive oil over the pizza.

4. Using a peel or a flat baking sheet, transfer the pizza to the heated baking implement in the oven. Bake for about 15 minutes, until the crust is golden brown and starting to char. Remove the pizza from the oven and let it cool slightly before slicing and serving.

Pizza Ortolana, see page 317

PIZZA QUATTRO FORMAGGI

YIELD: 1 PIZZA / **ACTIVE TIME:** 15 MINUTES / **TOTAL TIME:** 45 MINUTES

That's right: "four cheeses." As you might expect, this is the gooiest traditional Italian pizza, and a must-have for cheese lovers.

INGREDIENTS:

- SEMOLINA FLOUR, AS NEEDED
- 1 BALL OF PIZZA DOUGH
- ⅓ CUP PIZZA SAUCE (OPTIONAL; SEE PAGE 661)
- 2 OZ. FRESH MOZZARELLA CHEESE, DRAINED AND CUT INTO SHORT STRIPS
- 2 OZ. FONTINA OR PROVOLONE CHEESE, SHREDDED
- 2 OZ. GORGONZOLA CHEESE, CRUMBLED
- 2 OZ. PECORINO OR PARMESAN CHEESE, GRATED
- SALT AND PEPPER, TO TASTE
- EXTRA-VIRGIN OLIVE OIL, TO TASTE

1. Place a baking stone or steel on the middle rack of the oven and preheat the oven to the maximum temperature.

2. Dust a work surface with semolina flour, place the dough on the work surface, and gently stretch it into a round. If using, top the dough with the sauce. Top the pizza with the cheeses, season with salt and pepper, and drizzle olive oil over the pizza.

3. Using a peel or a flat baking sheet, transfer the pizza to the heated baking implement in the oven. Bake for about 15 minutes, until the crust is golden brown and starting to char. Remove the pizza from the oven and let it cool slightly before slicing and serving.

PIZZA PESCATORA

YIELD: 1 PIZZA / **ACTIVE TIME:** 25 MINUTES / **TOTAL TIME:** 1 HOUR

You can take the easy road and use a frozen and/or precooked mix of seafood or go the slightly more arduous—and much more delicious—route of using fresh seafood.

INGREDIENTS:

- EXTRA-VIRGIN OLIVE OIL, AS NEEDED
- 5 LARGE SHRIMP, SHELLED AND DEVEINED
- HANDFUL OF CALAMARI RINGS
- 6 MUSSELS, DEBEARDED AND RINSED WELL
- HANDFUL OF BABY OCTOPUS
- ½ GARLIC CLOVE, MINCED
- SALT AND BLACK PEPPER, TO TASTE
- RED PEPPER FLAKES, TO TASTE
- SEMOLINA FLOUR, AS NEEDED
- 1 BALL OF PIZZA DOUGH
- ¼ CUP PIZZA SAUCE (SEE PAGE 661)
- DRIED OREGANO, TO TASTE
- FRESH BASIL LEAVES, TO TASTE

1. Place a baking stone or steel on the middle rack of the oven and preheat the oven to the maximum temperature.

2. Coat the bottom of a skillet with olive oil and warm it over medium-high heat. Add all of the seafood and garlic, season with salt and red pepper flakes, and cook until most of the mussels have opened and the rest of the seafood is just cooked through, about 4 minutes. Remove from heat, discard any mussels that did not open, and remove the meat from those that did open.

3. Dust a work surface with semolina flour, place the dough on the work surface, and gently stretch it into a round. Cover the dough with the sauce and season with oregano and pepper.

4. Using a peel or a flat baking sheet, transfer the pizza to the heated baking implement in the oven. Bake for about 5 minutes, until the crust starts to brown. Remove the pizza, distribute the seafood over it, drizzle olive oil and sprinkle basil on top, and return the pizza to the oven. Bake for about 10 minutes, until the crust is golden brown and starting to char. Remove the pizza from the oven and let it cool slightly before slicing and serving.

PIZZA CARRETTIERA

YIELD: 1 PIZZA / **ACTIVE TIME:** 25 MINUTES / **TOTAL TIME:** 1 HOUR

The name refers to a sandwich filling popular with the Neapolitan carrettieri, who spent the day pushing around goods in a wooden trolleys. Substantial and extremely tasty, this is a must, assuming one can get hold of broccoli rabe.

1. Place a baking stone or steel on the middle rack of the oven and preheat the oven to the maximum temperature.

2. Coat the bottom of a skillet with olive oil and warm it over medium-high heat. Add the garlic and broccoli rabe and cook, stirring frequently, until the broccoli rabe has softened, about 8 minutes. Season with salt and pepper, add the sausage, and cook until the sausage is browned, about 6 minutes, stirring as necessary. Remove the pan from heat and let the mixture cool.

3. Dust a work surface with semolina flour, place the dough on the work surface, and gently stretch it into a round. Distribute the broccoli rabe and sausage over the dough, top it with the mozzarella, and drizzle olive oil over the pizza.

4. Using a peel or a flat baking sheet, transfer the pizza to the heated baking implement in the oven. Bake for about 15 minutes, until the crust is golden brown and starting to char. Remove the pizza from the oven and let it cool slightly before slicing and serving.

INGREDIENTS:

- EXTRA-VIRGIN OLIVE OIL, AS NEEDED
- ½ GARLIC CLOVE, MINCED
- 5 OZ. BROCCOLI RABE, TRIMMED
- SALT AND PEPPER, TO TASTE
- 1 LINK OF ITALIAN SAUSAGE, CASING REMOVED AND CRUMBLED
- SEMOLINA FLOUR, AS NEEDED
- 1 BALL OF PIZZA DOUGH
- 3 OZ. FRESH MOZZARELLA CHEESE, DRAINED AND CUT INTO SHORT STRIPS

Pizza Carrettiera, *see page 323*

PIZZA CAPRESE

YIELD: 1 PIZZA / **ACTIVE TIME:** 15 MINUTES / **TOTAL TIME:** 45 MINUTES

A slight variation on the Margherita that is inspired by the classic caprese salad. Perfect for a hot summer night.

INGREDIENTS:

- SEMOLINA FLOUR, AS NEEDED
- 1 BALL OF PIZZA DOUGH
- ⅓ CUP PIZZA SAUCE (SEE PAGE 661)
- 4½ OZ. FRESH MOZZARELLA CHEESE, DRAINED AND SLICED
- 1 TOMATO, SLICED
- SALT AND PEPPER, TO TASTE
- DRIED OREGANO, TO TASTE
- EXTRA-VIRGIN OLIVE OIL, TO TASTE
- FRESH BASIL LEAVES, FOR GARNISH

1. Place a baking stone or steel on the middle rack of the oven and preheat the oven to the maximum temperature.

2. Dust a work surface with semolina flour, place the dough on the work surface, and gently stretch it into a round. Cover the dough with the sauce and top it with the mozzarella and tomato. Season with salt, pepper, and oregano and drizzle olive oil over the pizza.

3. Using a peel or a flat baking sheet, transfer the pizza to the heated baking implement in the oven. Bake for about 15 minutes, until the crust is golden brown and starting to char. Remove the pizza from the oven and let it cool slightly before slicing and serving.

PIZZA AL TAGLIO WITH WILD MUSHROOMS & TWO CHEESES

YIELD: 1 LARGE PAN PIZZA / **ACTIVE TIME:** 1 HOUR / **TOTAL TIME:** 3 HOURS AND 30 MINUTES

This preparation suggests sautéing the mushrooms, but don't hesitate to roast them in the oven before adding them to this pizza on the go.

1. Once the dough has finished its initial rise, place it on a flour-dusted work surface and form it into a loose ball, making sure not to compress the core of the dough. Coat an 18 × 13–inch baking pan with olive oil, place the dough in the center, and gently stretch it into an oval. Brush the dough with olive oil, cover it with plastic wrap, and let rest at room temperature for 1 hour. Preheat the oven to 445°F.

2. Use your hands to flatten the dough and stretch it toward the edges of the pan.

3. Drizzle olive oil over the dough and let it rest at room temperature for another 30 minutes.

4. Season the pizza with salt, place it in the oven, and bake it for about 20 to 25 minutes, until the edges are slightly crispy.

5. While the pizza is in the oven, coat the bottom of a skillet with olive oil and warm it over medium-high heat. Add the mushrooms, season with salt, and cook, stirring occasionally, until they start to brown, about 10 minutes. Remove the pan from heat and let the mushrooms cool.

6. Remove the pizza from the oven and let it cool slightly. Top with the caciocavallo, mozzarella, parsley, red pepper flakes, and sautéed mushrooms, slice, and serve.

INGREDIENTS:

PIZZA AL TAGLIO DOUGH (SEE PAGE 303)

ALL-PURPOSE FLOUR, AS NEEDED

EXTRA-VIRGIN OLIVE OIL, AS NEEDED

SALT, TO TASTE

14 OZ. MUSHROOMS, SLICED

7 OZ. CACIOCAVALLO CHEESE, SLICED

13.2 OZ. BUFFALO MOZZARELLA CHEESE, DRAINED AND TORN

¼ CUP FRESH PARSLEY, CHOPPED

RED PEPPER FLAKES, TO TASTE

Pizza Caprese, *see page 326*

PIZZA AL TAGLIO WITH KALE & BACON

YIELD: 1 LARGE PAN PIZZA / **ACTIVE TIME:** 1 HOUR / **TOTAL TIME:** 3 HOURS AND 30 MINUTES

Kale is a good match for bacon, as it is substantial for a vegetable and packs a strong flavor.

INGREDIENTS:

- PIZZA AL TAGLIO DOUGH (SEE PAGE 303)
- ALL-PURPOSE FLOUR, AS NEEDED
- EXTRA-VIRGIN OLIVE OIL, AS NEEDED
- SALT, TO TASTE
- 6 OZ. BACON, CHOPPED
- 3 OZ. KALE, STEMMED AND CHOPPED
- 1 CUP PIZZA SAUCE (SEE PAGE 661)
- 1 LB. FRESH MOZZARELLA CHEESE, DRAINED AND TORN

1. Once the dough has finished its initial rise, place it on a flour-dusted work surface and form it into a loose ball, making sure not to compress the core of the dough. Coat an 18 × 13–inch baking pan with olive oil, place the dough in the center, and gently stretch it into an oval. Brush the dough with olive oil, cover it with plastic wrap, and let rest at room temperature for 1 hour. Preheat the oven to 445°F.

2. Use your hands to flatten the dough and stretch it toward the edges of the pan.

3. Drizzle olive oil over the dough and let it rest at room temperature for another 30 minutes.

4. While the dough is resting, place the bacon in a skillet and cook it over medium heat, stirring occasionally, until it is browned all over, about 8 minutes. Remove the bacon from the pan with a slotted spoon, transfer it to a paper towel–lined plate, and let it drain.

5. Add the kale to the pan and cook it in the bacon fat until it just starts to wilt, 2 to 3 minutes. Remove the pan from heat and let the kale cool.

6. Cover the dough with the sauce, season with salt, and place it in the oven. Bake for about 15 minutes, until the edges are starting to brown.

7. Remove the pizza from the oven and top it with the mozzarella, bacon, and kale. Return the pizza to the oven and bake until the edges are crispy and the cheese has melted, 10 to 12 minutes.

8. Remove the pizza from the oven and let it cool briefly before slicing and serving.

PIZZA AL TAGLIO WITH BUFALA, EGGPLANT & GARLIC

YIELD: 1 LARGE PAN PIZZA / **ACTIVE TIME:** 1 HOUR / **TOTAL TIME:** 3 HOURS AND 30 MINUTES

For pizza al taglio, you can bake the toppings with the dough, as in most pizzas, or bake the dough before adding the toppings, which is becoming increasingly popular. One advantage to baking the dough before adding the toppings: the pizza can support a larger amount of accompaniments.

INGREDIENTS:

PIZZA AL TAGLIO DOUGH (SEE PAGE 303)

ALL-PURPOSE FLOUR, AS NEEDED

EXTRA-VIRGIN OLIVE OIL, AS NEEDED

14 OZ. EGGPLANT, SLICED

SALT, TO TASTE

6 GARLIC CLOVES, MINCED

RED PEPPER FLAKES, TO TASTE

13.2 OZ. BUFFALO MOZZARELLA CHEESE, DRAINED AND TORN

¼ CUP FRESH PARSLEY, CHOPPED

1. Once the dough has finished its initial rise, place it on a flour-dusted work surface and form it into a loose ball, making sure not to compress the core of the dough. Coat an 18 × 13–inch baking pan with olive oil, place the dough in the center, and gently stretch it into an oval. Brush the dough with olive oil, cover it with plastic wrap, and let rest at room temperature for 1 hour. Preheat the oven to 445°F.

2. Prepare a gas or charcoal grill for medium heat. Place the eggplant in a mixing bowl, drizzle olive oil over it, and season with salt. Toss to combine and then place the eggplant on the grill. Cook until it is tender and charred all over, about 8 minutes, turning it occasionally. Remove the eggplant from the grill and let it cool. When the eggplant is cool enough to handle, chop it and set it aside.

3. Use your hands to flatten the dough and stretch it toward the edges of the pan.

4. Drizzle olive oil over the dough and let it rest at room temperature for another 30 minutes.

5. Season the pizza with salt, place it in the oven, and bake it for about 20 to 25 minutes, until the edges are slightly crispy.

6. While the pizza is in the oven, coat the bottom of a skillet with olive oil and warm it over medium-high heat. Add the garlic, season with salt and red pepper flakes, and cook, stirring occasionally, until the garlic starts to brown, about 2 minutes. Remove the pan from heat and set the garlic aside.

7. Remove the pizza from the oven and let it cool slightly. Top it with the mozzarella, parsley, eggplant, and garlic, drizzle olive oil over the pizza, slice, and serve.

PEPPER, PINE NUT & RAISIN PIZZA AL TAGLIO

YIELD: 1 LARGE PAN PIZZA / **ACTIVE TIME:** 1 HOUR / **TOTAL TIME:** 3 HOURS AND 30 MINUTES

Sweet raisins were made to complement roasted peppers and the buttery texture of pine nuts.

INGREDIENTS:

- PIZZA AL TAGLIO DOUGH (SEE PAGE 303)
- ALL-PURPOSE FLOUR, AS NEEDED
- EXTRA-VIRGIN OLIVE OIL, AS NEEDED
- 3½ OZ. RAISINS
- SALT, TO TASTE
- 17.6 OZ. ROASTED BELL PEPPERS, SLICED
- 3½ OZ. PINE NUTS

1. Once the dough has finished its initial rise, place it on a flour-dusted work surface and form it into a loose ball, making sure not to compress the core of the dough. Coat an 18 × 13–inch baking pan with olive oil, place the dough in the center, and gently stretch it into an oval. Brush the dough with olive oil, cover it with plastic wrap, and let rest at room temperature for 1 hour. Preheat the oven to 445°F.

2. Use your hands to flatten the dough and stretch it toward the edges of the pan.

3. Drizzle olive oil over the dough and let it rest at room temperature for another 30 minutes.

4. Place the raisins in a bowl, cover them with warm water, and let them soak for 30 minutes. Drain, pat the raisins dry, and set them aside.

5. Season the pizza with salt, place it in the oven, and bake it for about 20 to 25 minutes, until the edges are slightly crispy.

6. Remove the pizza from the oven and let it cool slightly. Top it with the roasted peppers, pine nuts, and raisins, and drizzle olive oil over the pizza. Season with salt, slice the pizza, and serve.

PIZZA AL TAGLIO WITH ROMAINE, SALAMI & PARMESAN

YIELD: 1 LARGE PAN PIZZA / **ACTIVE TIME:** 1 HOUR / **TOTAL TIME:** 3 HOURS AND 30 MINUTES

The famously fresh taste of romaine lettuce takes just enough of the edge off the bold flavors of salami and Parmesan.

1. Once the dough has finished its initial rise, place it on a flour-dusted work surface and form it into a loose ball, making sure not to compress the core of the dough. Coat an 18 × 13–inch baking pan with olive oil, place the dough in the center, and gently stretch it into an oval. Brush the dough with olive oil, cover it with plastic wrap, and let rest at room temperature for 1 hour. Preheat the oven to 445°F.

2. Use your hands to flatten the dough and stretch it toward the edges of the pan.

3. Drizzle olive oil over the dough and let it rest at room temperature for another 30 minutes.

4. Season the pizza with salt, place it in the oven, and bake it for about 20 to 25 minutes, until the edges are slightly crispy.

5. Remove the pizza from the oven and let it cool slightly. Top it with the lettuce, salami, and Parmesan, drizzle olive oil over the top, slice, and serve.

INGREDIENTS:

- PIZZA AL TAGLIO DOUGH (SEE PAGE 303)
- ALL-PURPOSE FLOUR, AS NEEDED
- EXTRA-VIRGIN OLIVE OIL, AS NEEDED
- 1¾ CUPS PIZZA SAUCE (SEE PAGE 661)
- SALT, TO TASTE
- 5.3 OZ. ROMAINE LETTUCE, CHOPPED
- 11.3 OZ. ITALIAN SALAMI, SLICED
- 3½ OZ. PARMESAN CHEESE, GRATED

PIZZA AL TAGLIO WITH PROSCIUTTO & BOCCONCINI

YIELD: 1 LARGE PAN PIZZA / **ACTIVE TIME:** 1 HOUR / **TOTAL TIME:** 3 HOURS AND 30 MINUTES

A classic Roman pizza topping that is always in fashion.

INGREDIENTS:

- PIZZA AL TAGLIO DOUGH (SEE PAGE 303)
- ALL-PURPOSE FLOUR, AS NEEDED
- EXTRA-VIRGIN OLIVE OIL, AS NEEDED
- SALT AND PEPPER, TO TASTE
- 11.3 OZ. PROSCIUTTO, SLICED THIN
- 8.8 OZ. FRESH BOCCONCINI, HALVED
- FRESH BASIL LEAVES, FOR GARNISH

1. Once the dough has finished its initial rise, place it on a flour-dusted work surface and form it into a loose ball, making sure not to compress the core of the dough. Coat an 18 × 13–inch baking pan with olive oil, place the dough in the center, and gently stretch it into an oval. Brush the dough with olive oil, cover it with plastic wrap, and let rest at room temperature for 1 hour. Preheat the oven to 445°F.

2. Use your hands to flatten the dough and stretch it toward the edges of the pan.

3. Drizzle olive oil over the dough and let it rest at room temperature for another 30 minutes.

4. Season the pizza with salt, place it in the oven, and bake it for about 20 to 25 minutes, until the edges are slightly crispy.

5. Remove the pizza from the oven and let it cool slightly. Top it with the prosciutto and bocconcini, drizzle olive oil over the top, and season with pepper. Garnish the pizza with basil, slice, and serve.

PIZZA ALLA PALA WITH ARTICHOKES, BROCCOLINI & SHIITAKES

YIELD: 1 PIZZA ALLA PALA / **ACTIVE TIME:** 25 MINUTES / **TOTAL TIME:** 3 HOURS

A plant-forward pizza alla pala that will transport you to the streets of Rome.

1. Preheat the oven to 480°F and place a baking stone or steel in the oven as it warms.

2. Bring water to a boil in a large saucepan and prepare an ice bath. Add salt, let the water return to a full boil, and add the broccolini. Cook for 3 minutes, drain the broccolini, and plunge it into the ice bath. Drain the broccolini again and let it dry on paper towels.

3. Coat a large skillet with olive oil and warm it over medium heat. Add the mushrooms, season them with salt, and cook until they start to brown, stirring once or twice.

4. Add the artichokes and broccolini and cook, stirring occasionally, for 2 minutes. Remove the pan from heat and set it aside.

5. Generously drizzle olive oil over the dough and season it with salt.

6. Using a peel or a flat baking sheet, transfer the pizza to the heated baking implement in the oven. Bake for 10 to 15 minutes, until the crust is golden brown and starting to char. Remove the pizza from the oven and brush it with olive oil. Distribute the vegetable mixture over the pizza, top it with the mozzarella and red onion, slice, and serve.

INGREDIENTS:

- SALT, TO TASTE
- 2 OZ. BROCCOLINI, TRIMMED
- EXTRA-VIRGIN OLIVE OIL, AS NEEDED
- 2 OZ. SHIITAKE MUSHROOMS, SLICED
- 2 OZ. ARTICHOKE HEARTS, DRAINED AND CHOPPED
- 1 BALL OF PIZZA ALLA PALA DOUGH (SEE PAGE 304)
- 9 OZ. FRESH MOZZARELLA CHEESE, DRAINED AND TORN
- ¼ CUP CHOPPED RED ONION

POTATO & LEEK PIZZA ALLA PALA

YIELD: 1 PIZZA ALLA PALA / **ACTIVE TIME:** 25 MINUTES / **TOTAL TIME:** 3 HOURS

Potato and leeks are fast friends, working in everything from soup to this beautiful take on pizza alla pala.

INGREDIENTS:

- SALT, TO TASTE
- ½ LB. POTATOES, PEELED AND SLICED THIN
- EXTRA-VIRGIN OLIVE OIL, AS NEEDED
- ½ LB. LEEKS, TRIMMED, RINSED WELL, SLICED THIN
- 1 BALL OF PIZZA ALLA PALA DOUGH (SEE PAGE 304)
- 4 OZ. PARMESAN CHEESE, GRATED

1. Preheat the oven to 480°F and place a baking stone or steel in the oven as it warms.

2. Bring water to a boil in a large saucepan. Add salt, let the water return to a full boil, and add the potatoes. Cook until they are fork-tender, 15 to 20 minutes. Drain the potatoes and set them aside.

3. Coat a large skillet with olive oil and warm it over medium heat. Add the leeks, season them with salt, and cook until they start to brown, about 8 minutes, stirring occasionally. Remove the pan from heat and set the leeks aside.

4. Generously drizzle olive oil over the dough and season it with salt.

5. Using a peel or a flat baking sheet, transfer the pizza to the heated baking implement in the oven. Bake for 10 to 15 minutes, until the crust is golden brown and starting to char. Remove the pizza from the oven and brush it with olive oil. Distribute the potatoes and leeks over the pizza, top it with the Parmesan, slice, and serve.

PIZZA ALLA PALA WITH PROSCIUTTO & ENDIVE

YIELD: 1 PIZZA ALLA PALA / **ACTIVE TIME:** 25 MINUTES / **TOTAL TIME:** 3 HOURS

The smoky bitterness of the grilled endive is perfectly balanced by the faint sweetness of the prosciutto and the mild tang of the buffalo mozzarella.

1. Preheat the oven to 480°F and place a baking stone or steel in the oven as it warms.

2. Prepare a gas or charcoal grill for medium-high heat. Place the endive in a mixing bowl, drizzle olive oil over it, and season with salt and pepper. Toss to combine and place the endive on the grill. Cook until it is charred all over, about 5 minutes, turning it as necessary. Remove the endive from the grill, let it cool slightly, and chop it. Set the endive aside.

3. Generously drizzle olive oil over the dough and season it with salt.

4. Using a peel or a flat baking sheet, transfer the pizza to the heated baking implement in the oven. Bake for 10 to 15 minutes, until the crust is golden brown and starting to char. Remove the pizza from the oven and distribute the endive over it. Drizzle olive oil over the endive, top it with the mozzarella and prosciutto, slice, and serve.

INGREDIENTS:

- ½ LB. ENDIVE
- EXTRA-VIRGIN OLIVE OIL, AS NEEDED
- SALT AND PEPPER, TO TASTE
- 1 BALL OF PIZZA ALLA PALA DOUGH (SEE PAGE 304)
- 9 OZ. BUFFALO MOZZARELLA CHEESE, DRAINED AND TORN
- 7 OZ. PROSCIUTTO, SLICED

PIZZA ALLA PALA WITH ZUCCHINI BLOSSOMS, ANCHOVIES & BURRATA

YIELD: 1 PIZZA ALLA PALA / **ACTIVE TIME:** 25 MINUTES / **TOTAL TIME:** 3 HOURS

Don't wrinkle your nose up at the inclusion of anchovies. When matched with zucchini blossoms and burrata, the flavors are out of this world delicious.

INGREDIENTS:

- 1 BALL OF PIZZA ALLA PALA DOUGH (SEE PAGE 304)
- EXTRA-VIRGIN OLIVE OIL, AS NEEDED
- 7 OZ. ZUCCHINI BLOSSOMS, STAMENS REMOVED
- SALT, TO TASTE
- 3 OZ. ANCHOVIES, HALVED
- 9 OZ. BURRATA CHEESE, TORN

1. Preheat the oven to 480°F and place a baking stone or steel in the oven as it warms.

2. Coat a large skillet with olive oil and warm it over medium heat. Add the zucchini blossoms, season them with salt, and cook, stirring occasionally, until they start to wilt, 2 to 3 minutes. Remove the pan from heat and set the zucchini blossoms aside.

3. Generously drizzle olive oil over the dough and season it with salt.

4. Using a peel or a flat baking sheet, transfer the pizza to the heated baking implement in the oven. Bake for 10 to 15 minutes, until the crust is golden brown and starting to char. Remove the pizza from the oven, distribute the zucchini blossoms and anchovies over the pizza, and top it with the burrata. Drizzle olive oil over the pizza, slice, and serve.

NEW YORK THIN-CRUST PIZZA

YIELD: 1 PIZZA / **ACTIVE TIME:** 15 MINUTES / **TOTAL TIME:** 30 MINUTES

The prototypical American pizza is this simple, pliable, thin-crust pie from New York City, which features a very simple topping of marinara sauce and mozzarella. For best results, shred the mozzarella yourself rather than buying it already shredded—it will melt better.

INGREDIENTS:

- SEMOLINA FLOUR, AS NEEDED
- 1 BALL OF 62 PERCENT HYDRATION PIZZA DOUGH (SEE PAGE 291)
- ⅓ CUP PIZZA SAUCE (SEE PAGE 661)
- 5 OZ. LOW-MOISTURE MOZZARELLA CHEESE, SHREDDED
- DRIED OREGANO, TO TASTE
- EXTRA-VIRGIN OLIVE OIL, TO TASTE

1. Place a baking stone or steel on the middle rack of the oven and preheat the oven to the maximum temperature.

2. Dust a work surface with semolina flour, place the dough on the work surface, and gently stretch it into a round. Cover the dough with the sauce and top it with the mozzarella. Season with oregano and drizzle olive oil over the pizza.

3. Using a peel or a flat baking sheet, transfer the pizza to the heated baking implement in the oven. Bake for about 15 minutes, until the crust is golden brown and starting to char. Remove the pizza from the oven and let it cool slightly before slicing and serving.

New York Thin-Crust Pizza, see page 341

CALIFORNIA-STYLE PIZZA

YIELD: 1 PIZZA / **ACTIVE TIME:** 25 MINUTES / **TOTAL TIME:** 40 MINUTES

In the 1970s and 1980s, California's kitchens forever changed the "face" of pizza, creating the gourmet pizza that quickly influenced the rest of the world. The main concept behind Californian pizza is creativity. According to Ed LaDou, one of the main chefs behind this movement, toppings are akin to the artist's color palette: every combination is allowed, so long as it tastes good. The typical Californian pizza is white and features fresh, local produce. Here's a simple version with nettles and aged ricotta. If nettles aren't available, simply substitute baby spinach.

1. Place a baking stone or steel on the middle rack of the oven and preheat the oven to the maximum temperature.

2. Dust a work surface with semolina flour, place the dough on the work surface, and gently stretch it into the desired shape. Drizzle olive oil over the dough, cover it with the mozzarella (if using), and top with the nettles. Season with salt and pepper and drizzle more olive oil over the pizza.

3. Using a peel or a flat baking sheet, transfer the pizza to the heated baking implement in the oven. Bake for about 10 minutes, until the crust is golden brown and starting to char. Remove, sprinkle the ricotta salata over the pizza, and let cool slightly before slicing and serving.

INGREDIENTS:

- SEMOLINA FLOUR, AS NEEDED
- 1 BALL OF NEAPOLITAN PIZZA DOUGH (SEE PAGE 288)
- EXTRA-VIRGIN OLIVE OIL, TO TASTE
- 1 OZ. LOW-MOISTURE MOZZARELLA CHEESE, SHREDDED (OPTIONAL)
- 4 OZ. WILD NETTLES, BOILED, DRAINED, AND PATTED DRY
- SALT AND PEPPER, TO TASTE
- 2 OZ. RICOTTA SALATA CHEESE, GRATED

NEW HAVEN TOMATO PIE

YIELD: 1 PIZZA / **ACTIVE TIME:** 15 MINUTES / **TOTAL TIME:** 30 MINUTES

In New Haven, pizza generally does not include a layer of melted mozzarella on top, allowing the tomato sauce to shine, completed by a good sprinkle of grated pecorino cheese and a generous drizzle of quality olive oil. When the mozzarella is present, it comes in smaller amounts than most American pies, functioning as a topping itself rather than a base for other toppings.

INGREDIENTS:

- SEMOLINA FLOUR, AS NEEDED
- 1 BALL OF 72 PERCENT HYDRATION PIZZA DOUGH (SEE PAGE 293)
- 5 OZ. PIZZA SAUCE (SEE PAGE 661)
- 1 OZ. PECORINO CHEESE, GRATED
- EXTRA-VIRGIN OLIVE OIL, TO TASTE
- 2 OZ. FRESH MOZZARELLA CHEESE, DRAINED AND CUT INTO SHORT STRIPS (OPTIONAL)
- FRESH BASIL LEAVES, TO TASTE (OPTIONAL)

1. Place a baking stone or steel on the middle rack of the oven and preheat the oven to the maximum temperature.

2. Dust a work surface with semolina flour, place the dough on the work surface, and gently stretch it into a round. Cover the dough with the sauce and top with the pecorino. Drizzle olive oil over the pizza. If desired, top it with the mozzarella and basil.

3. Using a peel or a flat baking sheet, transfer the pizza to the heated baking implement in the oven. Bake for about 10 minutes, until the crust is golden brown and starting to char. Remove the pizza from the oven and let it cool slightly before slicing and serving.

New Haven Tomato Pie, see page 345

CHICAGO DEEP DISH PIZZA

YIELD: 1 PIZZA / **ACTIVE TIME:** 45 MINUTES / **TOTAL TIME:** 3 HOURS

The classic pizza from Chicago is something between pizza and pie. It has the depth and flaky crust of a pie and is overflowing with cheese and tomato sauce. A delicious, decadent treat.

1. Place the yeast and water in a bowl and gently stir. Let the mixture sit until it starts to foam, 5 to 10 minutes.

2. In a large bowl, combine the flour, cornmeal, sugar, salt, melted butter, and yeast mixture. Work the mixture until it just holds together. If kneading by hand, transfer it to a flour-dusted work surface and work it until it is compact, smooth, and elastic. Form the dough into a ball and place it in an airtight container that has been coated with olive oil. Let the dough rest in a warm spot until it has doubled in size, about 1 hour.

3. Place the dough on a flour-dusted work surface and roll it out to an approximately ¼-inch-thick rectangle. Spread the softened butter over the rectangle and roll the dough up into a tight cylinder. Roll out the dough into a ¼-inch-thick rectangle and then fold it in thirds, as you would a letter you were going to put into an envelope. Bring the edges toward the center and pinch to form a ball. Place the dough in a bowl coated with olive oil, cover the bowl with a damp kitchen towel, and let it rest at room temperature until it has doubled in size, about 45 minutes.

4. Preheat the oven to 425°F. Place the dough on a flour-dusted work surface and roll it out into an approximately ¼-inch-thick disk that is a bit larger than the dish you will use to bake it. Coat the dish with olive oil and carefully place the dough in it. A good technique to transfer the dough is to roll it loosely around the rolling pin and then unroll it and fit it into the pan.

5. Cover the dough with the mozzarella and top it with the sauce, Parmesan, and pepper (if using). Place the pizza in the oven and bake for 25 to 30 minutes, until the crust is golden brown and the cheese has melted. Remove the pizza from the oven and let it cool for 10 minutes before slicing and serving.

INGREDIENTS:

- 1⅓ TEASPOONS (4 G) ACTIVE DRY YEAST
- 5 OZ. WARM WATER (105°F)
- 7 OZ. (198 G) ALL-PURPOSE FLOUR, PLUS MORE AS NEEDED
- 3 OZ. (85 G) YELLOW CORNMEAL
- 1 TEASPOON (4 G) SUGAR
- ¾ TEASPOON (4.5 G) FINE SEA SALT
- 2 OZ. (56 G) UNSALTED BUTTER, ½ MELTED; ½ AT ROOM TEMPERATURE
- EXTRA-VIRGIN OLIVE OIL, AS NEEDED
- 9 OZ. LOW-MOISTURE MOZZARELLA CHEESE, SHREDDED
- 2 CUPS PIZZA SAUCE (SEE PAGE 661)
- 1 OZ. PARMESAN CHEESE, GRATED
- ⅓ RED BELL PEPPER, SLICED (OPTIONAL)

DETROIT-STYLE PIZZA

YIELD: 1 PIZZA / **ACTIVE TIME:** 25 MINUTES / **TOTAL TIME:** 1 HOUR AND 15 MINUTES

In Detroit, pizza is not round but square, very much like traditional Italian focaccia, and, in the American tradition, it is loaded with gooey cheese.

INGREDIENTS:

- EXTRA-VIRGIN OLIVE OIL, AS NEEDED
- 3/5 BATCH OF 72 PERCENT HYDRATION PIZZA DOUGH (SEE PAGE 293)
- 12 OZ. BRICK CHEESE, CUBED
- 1¾ CUPS PIZZA SAUCE (SEE PAGE 661)
- 6 OZ. PEPPERONI, SLICED (OPTIONAL)

1. Preheat the oven to the maximum temperature. Coat a 14 × 11–inch baking pan with olive oil, place the dough in it, and gently stretch it until it covers the pan, taking care to deflate the dough as little as possible. If time allows, stretch the dough in steps, letting it rest for 10 to 15 minutes before stretching it again.

2. Drizzle olive oil over the dough and cover it with the cheese. Spoon the sauce on top, making sure to leave some cheese-only spots. If desired, top the pizza with the pepperoni.

3. Place the pizza on the lowest rack of the oven and bake for about 15 minutes, until the edges are crunchy and nearly charred. Remove the pizza from the oven and let it cool briefly before slicing and serving.

Chicago Deep Dish Pizza, see page 348

ST. LOUIS–STYLE PIZZA

YIELD: 1 PIZZA / **ACTIVE TIME:** 25 MINUTES / **TOTAL TIME:** 1 HOUR AND 15 MINUTES

There are two distinctive features of St. Louis pizza: the cracker-thin crust, which is not leavened and therefore quick to prepare, and the cheese, a regional blend called Provel, which can be approximated at home by blending cheddar, Swiss, and provolone.

1. In a large bowl, combine the flour, baking powder, salt, olive oil, corn syrup, and water. Work the mixture until it is a very stiff dough. Form the dough into a ball, cover with a damp kitchen towel, and let it rest at room temperature for 30 minutes.

2. Place a baking stone or steel on the middle rack of the oven and preheat it to 450°F. Dust a work surface with semolina flour, place the dough on it, and roll it into a paper-thin disk, letting it rest at regular intervals.

3. Dust a peel or a flat baking sheet with semolina flour, transfer the dough onto it, and cover the dough with the sauce. Combine the cheeses in a bowl and top the pizza with the mixture. Distribute the sausage and pepperoni (if desired) over the pizza, transfer it to the heated baking implement in the oven, and bake for about 10 minutes, until the crust is crispy and golden brown.

4. Remove the pizza from the oven and let it cool slightly before slicing and serving.

INGREDIENTS:

- 5 OZ. (141 G) ALL-PURPOSE FLOUR
- ½ TEASPOON (2 G) BAKING POWDER
- ½ TEASPOON (0.5 G) FINE SEA SALT
- 1½ TEASPOONS (7 G) EXTRA-VIRGIN OLIVE OIL
- 1½ TEASPOONS (9.7 G) DARK CORN SYRUP
- 3 OZ. (42 G) WATER
- SEMOLINA FLOUR, AS NEEDED
- 7 OZ. PIZZA SAUCE (SEE PAGE 661)
- 2 OZ. SHARP WHITE CHEDDAR CHEESE, SHREDDED
- 2 OZ. SWISS CHEESE, SHREDDED
- 2 OZ. SMOKED PROVOLONE CHEESE, SHREDDED
- 2 OZ. ITALIAN SAUSAGE, CASING REMOVED, CHOPPED (OPTIONAL)
- 2 OZ. PEPPERONI, SLICED (OPTIONAL)

HAWAIIAN PIZZA

YIELD: 1 PIZZA / **ACTIVE TIME:** 15 MINUTES / **TOTAL TIME:** 35 MINUTES

Whether you love it or hate it, you can't ignore it. Hawaiian pizza, which actually originated in Canada during the 1960s, has become one of the most popular, and divisive, pizzas out there.

INGREDIENTS:

- SEMOLINA FLOUR, AS NEEDED
- 1 BALL OF PIZZA DOUGH
- ⅓ CUP PIZZA SAUCE (SEE PAGE 661)
- 5 OZ. LOW-MOISTURE MOZZARELLA CHEESE, SHREDDED
- 3 SLICES OF THICK-CUT HAM OR CANADIAN BACON, CHOPPED
- 5 SLICES OF CANNED PINEAPPLE, DRAINED AND PATTED DRY
- SALT AND PEPPER, TO TASTE
- EXTRA-VIRGIN OLIVE OIL, TO TASTE

1. Place a baking stone or steel on the middle rack of the oven and preheat the oven to the maximum temperature.

2. Dust a work surface with semolina flour, place the dough on the work surface, and gently stretch it into a round. Cover the dough with the sauce and top with the mozzarella, ham, and pineapple. Season with salt and pepper and drizzle olive oil over the pizza.

3. Using a peel or a flat baking sheet, transfer the pizza to the heated baking implement in the oven. Bake for about 15 minutes, until the crust is golden brown and starting to char. Remove the pizza from the oven and let it cool slightly before slicing and serving.

CLASSIC PEPPERONI PIZZA

YIELD: 1 PIZZA / **ACTIVE TIME:** 15 MINUTES / **TOTAL TIME:** 35 MINUTES

An American treasure. Born in New York at the beginning of the 1900s, it is based on a locally produced salami made from beef and pork and seasoned with chile pepper and paprika.

1. Place a baking stone or steel on the middle rack of the oven and preheat the oven to the maximum temperature.

2. Dust a work surface with semolina flour, place the dough on the work surface, and gently stretch it into the desired shape. Cover the dough with the sauce, season with pepper, and top it with one-third of the pepperoni. Distribute the mozzarella over the pizza, top it with the remaining pepperoni, and drizzle olive oil over the pizza.

3. Using a peel or a flat baking sheet, transfer the pizza to the heated baking implement in the oven. Bake for about 15 minutes, until the crust is golden brown and starting to char. Remove and let cool slightly before slicing and serving.

INGREDIENTS:

- SEMOLINA FLOUR, AS NEEDED
- 1 BALL OF PIZZA DOUGH
- ⅓ CUP PIZZA SAUCE (SEE PAGE 661)
- BLACK PEPPER, TO TASTE
- 12–15 SLICES OF PEPPERONI
- 5 OZ. LOW-MOISTURE MOZZARELLA CHEESE, SHREDDED
- EXTRA-VIRGIN OLIVE OIL, TO TASTE

TERIYAKI CHICKEN PIZZA

YIELD: 1 PIZZA / **ACTIVE TIME:** 20 MINUTES / **TOTAL TIME:** 1 HOUR

After first being introduced in the 1950s, pizza in Japan has undergone really interesting developments, and some say the pizzaiolos there can stand shoulder to shoulder with anyone in the world. Here is a typical contemporary topping in the country.

INGREDIENTS:

- 3 OZ. COOKED TERIYAKI CHICKEN, CHOPPED
- ¼ CUP RED ONION, SLICED THIN
- 1 TABLESPOON SESAME OIL, PLUS MORE TO TASTE
- SALT AND SHICHIMI PEPPER, TO TASTE
- SEMOLINA FLOUR, AS NEEDED
- 1 BALL OF PIZZA DOUGH
- ¼ CUP PINEAPPLE CHUNKS, DRAINED
- TERIYAKI SAUCE, TO TASTE
- 4 OZ. FRESH MOZZARELLA CHEESE, DRAINED AND TORN
- 2 TABLESPOONS KEWPIE MAYONNAISE, FOR GARNISH
- FRESH CILANTRO, FOR GARNISH

1. Place a baking stone or steel on the middle rack of the oven and preheat the oven to the maximum temperature.

2. Place the chicken and onion in a bowl, generously drizzle sesame oil over the mixture, season with salt and shichimi pepper, and let the mixture marinate for 10 minutes. Drain the mixture and set it aside.

3. Dust a work surface with semolina flour, place the dough on the work surface, and gently stretch it into the desired shape. Cover the dough with the chicken mixture and pineapple. Drizzle teriyaki sauce and the sesame oil over the pizza.

4. Using a peel or a flat baking sheet, transfer the pizza to the heated baking implement in the oven. Bake for about 5 minutes, until the crust starts to brown. Remove the pizza, distribute the mozzarella over the top, and return the pizza to the oven. Bake for about 10 minutes, until the crust is golden brown and starting to char.

5. Remove the pizza from the oven and let it cool slightly before garnishing with the mayonnaise and cilantro, slicing, and serving.

NATTO & BACON PIZZA

YIELD: 1 PIZZA / **ACTIVE TIME:** 25 MINUTES / **TOTAL TIME:** 1 HOUR

Natto are fermented soybeans, one of those super-nutritious Japanese ingredients that you can find in specialty stores. Using it on pizza is a recent trend in Japan, and it's a great way to transform this superfood into something yummy.

INGREDIENTS:

- EXTRA-VIRGIN OLIVE OIL, AS NEEDED
- 5 OZ. NATTO
- 2 OZ. BACON, CHOPPED
- SALT AND SHICHIMI PEPPER, TO TASTE
- SEMOLINA FLOUR, AS NEEDED
- 1 BALL OF PIZZA DOUGH
- 4 OZ. LOW-MOISTURE MOZZARELLA CHEESE, SHREDDED
- SCALLIONS, CHOPPED, FOR GARNISH

1. Place a baking stone or steel on the middle rack of the oven and preheat the oven to the maximum temperature.

2. Coat the bottom of a skillet with olive oil and warm it over medium-high heat. Add the natto and bacon and cook, stirring occasionally, until the bacon starts to get crispy, about 6 minutes. Remove the pan from heat, season with salt and shichimi pepper, and let the mixture cool.

3. Dust a work surface with semolina flour, place the dough on the surface, and gently stretch it into the desired shape. Distribute the natto mixture over the dough and top it with the mozzarella.

4. Using a peel or a flat baking sheet, transfer the pizza to the heated baking implement in the oven. Bake for about 15 minutes, until the crust is golden brown and starting to char.

5. Remove the pizza from the oven and let it cool slightly before garnishing with scallions, slicing, and serving.

TOM YUM PIZZA WITH SHRIMP

YIELD: 1 PIZZA / **ACTIVE TIME:** 15 MINUTES / **TOTAL TIME:** 45 MINUTES

Inspired by the ingredients of the famously delicious soup, this is truly a slice of Thailand.

1. Place a baking stone or steel on the middle rack of the oven and preheat the oven to the maximum temperature. Combine the Tom Yum Paste and sauce in a small bowl and set it aside.

2. Dust a work surface with semolina flour, place the dough on the work surface, and gently stretch it into the desired shape. Cover the dough with the sauce mixture and top it with the mushrooms and shrimp. Season with salt and drizzle canola oil over the pizza.

3. Using a peel or a flat baking sheet, transfer the pizza to the heated baking implement in the oven. Bake for about 7 minutes, until the crust has started to brown. Remove the pizza from the oven, distribute the mozzarella over the top, and return the pizza to the oven. Bake for about 8 minutes, until the cheese has melted and the crust is golden brown and starting to char. Remove the pizza from the oven and let it cool slightly before garnishing with cilantro, slicing, and serving.

INGREDIENTS:

- 2 TABLESPOONS TOM YUM PASTE (SEE PAGE 661)
- 2 TABLESPOONS PIZZA SAUCE (SEE PAGE 661)
- SEMOLINA FLOUR, AS NEEDED
- 1 BALL OF PIZZA DOUGH
- ½ CUP OYSTER MUSHROOMS, SLICED THIN
- 6 LARGE SHRIMP, SHELLS REMOVED, DEVEINED
- SALT, TO TASTE
- CANOLA OIL, TO TASTE
- 4 OZ. FRESH MOZZARELLA CHEESE, DRAINED AND SLICED
- FRESH CILANTRO, FOR GARNISH

PIZZA WITH PEKING DUCK

YIELD: 1 PIZZA / **ACTIVE TIME:** 15 MINUTES / **TOTAL TIME:** 45 MINUTES

Pizza in China is often stuffed, but in the US, several scrumptious Chinese-inspired toppings are regularly used.

1. Place a baking stone or steel on the middle rack of the oven and preheat the oven to the maximum temperature.

2. Dust a work surface with semolina flour, place the dough on the work surface, and gently stretch it into the desired shape. Drizzle sesame oil over the dough, cover it with half of the mozzarella, and top it with the duck, mushrooms, and scallion. Drizzle hoisin sauce over the pizza and sprinkle the remaining mozzarella on top.

3. Using a peel or a flat baking sheet, transfer the pizza to the heated baking implement in the oven. Bake for about 15 minutes, until the crust is golden brown and starting to char.

4. Remove the pizza from the oven and let it cool slightly before garnishing with the sesame seeds, slicing, and serving.

INGREDIENTS:

- SEMOLINA FLOUR, AS NEEDED
- 1 BALL OF PIZZA DOUGH
- SESAME OIL, AS NEEDED
- 3 OZ. LOW-MOISTURE MOZZARELLA CHEESE, SHREDDED
- 4 OZ. DUCK CONFIT (SEE PAGE 662), SHREDDED
- ½ CUP THINLY SLICED SHIITAKE MUSHROOMS
- 1 SCALLION, TRIMMED AND SLICED THIN
- HOISIN SAUCE (SEE PAGE 662), TO TASTE
- SESAME SEEDS, FOR GARNISH

CHICKEN SATAY & MANGO PIZZA

YIELD: 1 PIZZA / **ACTIVE TIME:** 20 MINUTES / **TOTAL TIME:** 1 HOUR

Australia has a very dynamic food scene, and pizza does not receive short shrift—here is one of the country's most popular toppings.

INGREDIENTS:

- 3 OZ. COOKED CHICKEN BREAST, SLICED
- ½ TEASPOON CURRY POWDER
- SALT, TO TASTE
- EXTRA-VIRGIN OLIVE OIL, AS NEEDED
- 1 TABLESPOON CRUNCHY PEANUT BUTTER
- 2 TABLESPOONS COCONUT CREAM
- PINCH OF RED PEPPER FLAKES
- SEMOLINA FLOUR, AS NEEDED
- 1 BALL OF PIZZA DOUGH
- ½ RED BELL PEPPER, SLICED
- FLESH OF ½ SMALL MANGO, SLICED THIN

1. Place a baking stone or steel on the middle rack of the oven and preheat the oven to the maximum temperature.

2. Place the chicken, curry powder, salt, and a generous amount of olive oil in a bowl and stir to combine. Place the peanut butter, coconut cream, and red pepper flakes in a separate bowl and stir to combine. Set the mixtures aside.

3. Dust a work surface with semolina flour, place the dough on the work surface, and gently stretch it into the desired shape. Cover the dough with the peanut sauce and top it with the chicken mixture, pepper, and mango. Season with salt and drizzle olive oil over the pizza.

4. Using a peel or a flat baking sheet, transfer the pizza to the heated baking implement in the oven. Bake for about 15 minutes, until the crust is golden brown and starting to char.

5. Remove the pizza from the oven and let it cool slightly before slicing and serving.

MINCEMEAT & VEGETABLE PIZZA

YIELD: 1 PIZZA / **ACTIVE TIME:** 25 MINUTES / **TOTAL TIME:** 1 HOUR

Pizza has become a popular street food in Iran, and this pie showcases just one of several interesting toppings popular in the country. As one would expect, Iranians' favorites have been influenced by the flavors of the local cuisine.

1. Place a baking stone or steel on the middle rack of the oven and preheat the oven to the maximum temperature.

2. Coat the bottom of a skillet with olive oil and warm it over medium-high heat. Add the ground beef and pepper, season with the advieh and salt, and cook, breaking up the meat with a wooden spoon, until it is browned and the pepper is tender, about 8 minutes. Remove the pan from heat and let the mixture cool.

3. Dust a work surface with semolina flour, place the dough on the work surface, and gently stretch it into the desired shape. Cover the dough with half of the mozzarella and top it with the ground beef mixture, tomatoes, corn, and onion. Sprinkle the remaining mozzarella over the pizza.

4. Using a peel or a flat baking sheet, transfer the pizza to the heated baking implement in the oven. Bake for about 15 minutes, until the crust is golden brown and starting to char. Remove the pizza from the oven and let the pizza cool slightly before slicing and serving.

INGREDIENTS:

- EXTRA-VIRGIN OLIVE OIL, AS NEEDED
- 4 OZ. GROUND BEEF
- ½ SMALL YELLOW BELL PEPPER, CHOPPED
- 1 TEASPOON ADVIEH
- SALT, TO TASTE
- SEMOLINA FLOUR, AS NEEDED
- 1 BALL OF PIZZA DOUGH
- 4 OZ. LOW-MOISTURE MOZZARELLA CHEESE, SHREDDED
- ½ CUP CHERRY TOMATOES, SLICED
- 2 TABLESPOONS CANNED CORN, DRAINED
- ½ SMALL RED ONION, SLICED THIN

LAHMACUN

YIELD: 1 PIZZA / **ACTIVE TIME:** 10 MINUTES / **TOTAL TIME:** 40 MINUTES

In Turkey, pizza is not really pizza—instead, it is a local flatbread called lahmacun. Lahmacun means "dough with meat," and the bread consists of a thin layer of flattened dough covered by a spicy paste containing raw meat. This is then baked together. With this one, it is important to bake the "pizza" at a lower temperature than usual, as this will allow the meat to get fully cooked.

INGREDIENTS:

- 1 BALL OF 62 PERCENT HYDRATION PIZZA DOUGH (SEE PAGE 291)
- ¼ CUP LAHMACUN SPREAD (SEE PAGE 663)
- JUICE OF 1 LEMON WEDGE
- SUMAC POWDER, TO TASTE
- ¼ SMALL RED ONION, SLICED
- ⅓ TOMATO, SLICED
- 2 TABLESPOONS MINCED CUCUMBER
- 2 TABLESPOONS CRUMBLED FETA CHEESE
- EXTRA-VIRGIN OLIVE OIL, TO TASTE
- FRESH HERBS, FOR GARNISH

1. Place a baking stone or steel on the middle rack of the oven and preheat the oven to 410°F.

2. Place the dough on a piece of parchment paper and gently stretch it into a very thin round. Cover the dough with the Lahmacun Spread.

3. Using a peel or a flat baking sheet, transfer the pizza to the heated baking implement in the oven. Bake for about 12 minutes, until the crust is golden brown and starting to char. Remove the pizza from the oven and top it with the lemon juice, sumac powder, onion, tomato, cucumber, and feta. Drizzle olive oil over the pizza, garnish with fresh herbs, slice, and serve.

PIZZA À LA PORTUGUESA

YIELD: 1 PIZZA / **ACTIVE TIME:** 15 MINUTES / **TOTAL TIME:** 45 MINUTES

If you happen to hear about a "Portuguese" pizza, chances are good that it is Brazilian and has little to do with how pizza is made in Portugal. There are many variations on the toppings; this combination is one of the most typical.

INGREDIENTS:

- SEMOLINA FLOUR, AS NEEDED
- 1 BALL OF PIZZA DOUGH
- ⅓ CUP PIZZA SAUCE (SEE PAGE 661)
- 4 OZ. LOW-MOISTURE MOZZARELLA CHEESE, SHREDDED
- ¼ SMALL ONION, SLICED THIN
- 2 SLICES OF THICK-CUT HAM, CHOPPED
- HANDFUL OF OLIVES, PITTED
- 2 HARD-BOILED EGGS, SLICED
- DRIED OREGANO, TO TASTE
- EXTRA-VIRGIN OLIVE OIL, TO TASTE

1. Place a baking stone or steel on the middle rack of the oven and preheat the oven to the maximum temperature.

2. Dust a work surface with semolina flour, place the dough on the work surface, and gently stretch it into the desired shape. Cover the dough with the sauce and top it with the mozzarella, onion, ham, and olives.

3. Using a peel or a flat baking sheet, transfer the pizza to the heated baking implement in the oven. Bake for about 15 minutes, until the crust is golden brown and starting to char.

4. Remove the pizza from the oven, top it with the eggs, and season with oregano. Drizzle olive oil over the pizza and let it cool slightly before slicing and serving.

ARGENTINIAN-STYLE THICK-CRUST PIZZA

YIELD: 1 PIZZA / **ACTIVE TIME:** 20 MINUTES / **TOTAL TIME:** 1 HOUR

In Argentina, this pizza is known as fugazza, a name tied to the Ligurians who emigrated to the country. This pie is as thick as a focaccia, but topped with mozzarella like a pizza.

INGREDIENTS:

- EXTRA-VIRGIN OLIVE OIL, AS NEEDED
- ½ YELLOW ONION, SLICED
- ½ RED ONION, SLICED
- SALT, TO TASTE
- 1 BALL OF PIZZA ALLA PALA DOUGH (SEE PAGE 304)
- 9 OZ. FRESH MOZZARELLA CHEESE, DRAINED AND SLICED
- DRIED OREGANO, TO TASTE

1. Place a baking stone or steel on the middle rack of the oven and preheat the oven to 480°F.

2. Coat the bottom of a skillet with olive oil and warm it over medium-high heat. Add the onions and cook, stirring occasionally, until they start to brown, about 10 minutes. Remove the pan from heat, season the onions with salt, and let them cool completely.

3. Coat a square baking dish with olive oil, place the dough in it, and gently spread it until it is approximately ½ inch thick. Place the dish in the oven and bake for about 10 minutes, until the crust starts to brown.

4. Remove the pizza from the oven, distribute the mozzarella and onions over the top, and return the pizza to the oven. Bake for about 10 minutes, until the crust is golden brown and starting to char and the cheese has melted.

5. Remove the pizza from the oven and let it cool slightly before seasoning with dried oregano, slicing, and serving.

CHORIZO & JALAPEÑO PIZZA

YIELD: 1 PIZZA / **ACTIVE TIME:** 15 MINUTES / **TOTAL TIME:** 45 MINUTES

Mexico is one of the world's biggest consumers of pizza, second only to the US. This pizza, which features spicy and earthy flavors that are a perfect match for an Italian flatbread, sheds light on that surprising stat.

1. Place a baking stone or steel on the middle rack of the oven and preheat the oven to the maximum temperature.

2. Coat the bottom of a skillet with olive oil and warm it over medium-high heat. Add the chorizo and cook, stirring occasionally, until it is browned, about 8 minutes. Remove the pan from heat and let the chorizo cool.

3. Dust a work surface with semolina flour, place the dough on the work surface, and gently stretch it into the desired shape. Cover the pizza with the mozzarella and top it with the onion, chorizo, and pickled jalapeños. Season with salt and drizzle olive oil over the pizza.

4. Using a peel or a flat baking sheet, transfer the pizza to the heated baking implement in the oven. Bake for about 15 minutes, until the crust is golden brown and starting to char.

5. Remove the pizza from the oven and let it cool slightly before slicing and serving.

INGREDIENTS:

- EXTRA-VIRGIN OLIVE OIL, AS NEEDED
- 1 LINK OF CHORIZO, CASING REMOVED, CHOPPED
- SEMOLINA FLOUR, AS NEEDED
- 1 BALL OF PIZZA DOUGH
- 3 OZ. LOW-MOISTURE MOZZARELLA CHEESE, SHREDDED
- ½ WHITE OR RED ONION, SLICED THIN
- 3 TABLESPOONS PICKLED JALAPEÑO PEPPERS
- SALT, TO TASTE

GARLIC FINGERS

YIELD: 1 PIZZA / **ACTIVE TIME:** 15 MINUTES / **TOTAL TIME:** 45 MINUTES

In Canada, one can find a pizza that is a bit like garlic bread smothered in mozzarella cheese and dipped in a local sauce called donair. For the sticklers out there, this is probably more of a flatbread than a pizza, but no one will care about such superficialities after the first bite.

1. Place a baking stone or steel on the middle rack of the oven and preheat the oven to the maximum temperature.

2. Dust a work surface with semolina flour, place the dough on the work surface, and gently stretch it into the desired shape. Cover the dough with the Garlic Butter and top it with the mozzarella.

3. Using a peel or a flat baking sheet, transfer the pizza to the heated baking implement in the oven. Bake for about 15 minutes, until the crust is golden brown and starting to char. Remove the pizza from the oven and let it cool slightly before slicing it into thin strips and serving with Donair Sauce.

IINGREDIENTS:

SEMOLINA FLOUR, AS NEEDED

1 BALL OF PIZZA DOUGH

1 TABLESPOON GARLIC BUTTER (SEE PAGE 664), SOFTENED

5 OZ. LOW-MOISTURE MOZZARELLA CHEESE, SHREDDED

DONAIR SAUCE (SEE PAGE 663), FOR SERVING

SQUASH BLOSSOM & RICOTTA PIZZA

YIELD: 1 PIZZA / **ACTIVE TIME:** 15 MINUTES / **TOTAL TIME:** 45 MINUTES

This pizza is as beautiful, fresh, and simple as great cooking gets.

1. Place a baking stone or steel on the middle rack of the oven and preheat the oven to the maximum temperature.

2. Dust a work surface with semolina flour, place the dough on the work surface, and gently stretch it into the desired shape.

3. Drizzle olive oil over the dough, cover it with the shredded mozzarella, and distribute the squash blossoms over the cheese. Open the squash blossoms up so that they cover as much of the pizza as possible. Distribute dollops of the ricotta over the pizza, season with salt and pepper, and drizzle more olive oil over the top.

4. Dust a peel or a flat baking sheet with semolina and use it to transfer the pizza to the heated baking implement in the oven. Bake for 15 minutes, until the crust is golden brown and starting to char. Remove, sprinkle the lemon zest over the pizza, and let it cool slightly before serving.

INGREDIENTS:

- SEMOLINA FLOUR, AS NEEDED
- 1 BALL OF PIZZA DOUGH
- EXTRA-VIRGIN OLIVE OIL, TO TASTE
- 4 OZ. LOW-MOISTURE MOZZARELLA CHEESE, SHREDDED
- 3 SQUASH BLOSSOMS, STAMENS REMOVED, SLICED LENGTHWISE
- 3 OZ. RICOTTA CHEESE
- SALT AND PEPPER, TO TASTE
- ZEST OF 1 LEMON

PIZZA WITH PROSCIUTTO, ARUGULA & PARMESAN

YIELD: 1 PIZZA / **ACTIVE TIME:** 15 MINUTES / **TOTAL TIME:** 45 MINUTES

For all the lovers of prosciutto, here it is paired with its perfect partners, arugula and Parmesan.

INGREDIENTS:

- SEMOLINA FLOUR, AS NEEDED
- 1 BALL OF PIZZA DOUGH
- ⅓ CUP PIZZA SAUCE (SEE PAGE 661)
- SALT AND PEPPER, TO TASTE
- EXTRA-VIRGIN OLIVE OIL, TO TASTE
- 4 OZ. FRESH MOZZARELLA CHEESE, DRAINED AND TORN
- 3 OZ. PROSCIUTTO, SLICED THIN
- HANDFUL OF ARUGULA
- 2 OZ. PARMESAN CHEESE, SHAVED

1. Place a baking stone or steel on the middle rack of the oven and preheat the oven to the maximum temperature.

2. Dust a work surface with semolina flour, place the dough on the work surface, and gently stretch it into the desired shape. Cover the dough with the sauce, season with salt and pepper, and drizzle olive oil over the top.

3. Using a peel or a flat baking sheet, transfer the pizza to the heated baking implement in the oven. Bake for about 7 minutes, until the crust has started to brown. Remove the pizza from the oven, distribute the mozzarella over the top, and return the pizza to the oven. Bake for about 5 minutes, until the crust is golden brown and starting to char and the cheese has melted.

4. Remove the pizza from the oven and top it with the prosciutto, arugula, and Parmesan. Season with salt and pepper, drizzle olive oil over the pizza, and serve.

Pizza with Prosciutto, Arugula & Parmesan, see page 379

MASHED POTATO, BACON & SCALLION PIZZA

YIELD: 4 SERVINGS / **ACTIVE TIME:** 25 MINUTES / **TOTAL TIME:** 45 MINUTES

Combining pizza and a dressed baked potato may seem odd at first, but this mashup is guaranteed to become a staple of your Pizza Nights.

INGREDIENTS:

- SEMOLINA FLOUR, AS NEEDED
- 1 BALL OF PIZZA DOUGH
- 2 TABLESPOONS EXTRA-VIRGIN OLIVE OIL
- SALT AND PEPPER, TO TASTE
- 2 TABLESPOONS GRATED ASIAGO CHEESE
- ¾ CUP MASHED POTATOES
- 1½ CUPS GRATED MOZZARELLA CHEESE
- HEAVY CREAM, TO TASTE
- 4 STRIPS OF BACON, COOKED AND CHOPPED
- ½ CUP CHOPPED SCALLIONS
- 1 TEASPOON FINELY CHOPPED FRESH PARSLEY
- 1 TEASPOON FINELY CHOPPED FRESH ROSEMARY
- 1 TEASPOON FINELY CHOPPED FRESH THYME

1. Place a baking stone or steel on the middle rack of the oven and preheat the oven to the maximum temperature.

2. Dust a work surface with semolina flour, place the dough on the work surface, and gently stretch it into the desired shape. Brush the dough with the olive oil, season with pepper, and sprinkle the Asiago over the top. Spread the mashed potatoes over the dough and then top it with the mozzarella. Generously drizzle cream over the pizza, top it with the bacon, scallions, and minced herbs, and season with salt.

3. Using a peel or a flat baking sheet, transfer the pizza to the heated baking implement in the oven. Bake for about 15 minutes, until the crust is golden brown and starting to char. Remove the pizza from the oven and let it cool slightly before slicing and serving.

PIZZA WITH ASPARAGUS, PINE NUTS & BUFALA

YIELD: 1 PIZZA / **ACTIVE TIME:** 20 MINUTES / **TOTAL TIME:** 1 HOUR

A delicate combination that makes good use of fresh and delicious Mediterranean-inclined ingredients.

1. Place a baking stone or steel on the middle rack of the oven and preheat the oven to the maximum temperature.

2. Bring a pot of salted water to a boil and prepare an ice bath. Add the asparagus to the boiling water and cook for 2 minutes. Drain, transfer the asparagus to the ice bath, and let it cool completely. Drain the asparagus again, pat it dry, and halve each spear lengthwise.

3. Dust a work surface with semolina flour, place the dough on the work surface, and gently stretch it into the desired shape. Drizzle olive oil over the dough, cover it with the shredded mozzarella, and distribute the asparagus and pine nuts over the top. Season with salt and pepper and drizzle olive oil over the pizza.

4. Using a peel or a flat baking sheet, transfer the pizza to the heated baking implement in the oven. Bake for about 15 minutes, until the crust is golden brown and starting to char. Remove the pizza from the oven and top it with the buffalo mozzarella. Sprinkle the lemon zest and drizzle olive oil over the pizza and let it cool slightly before slicing and serving.

INGREDIENTS:

- SALT AND PEPPER, TO TASTE
- 3–4 ASPARAGUS STALKS, TRIMMED
- SEMOLINA FLOUR, AS NEEDED
- 1 BALL OF PIZZA DOUGH
- EXTRA-VIRGIN OLIVE OIL, TO TASTE
- 2 OZ. LOW-MOISTURE MOZZARELLA CHEESE, SHREDDED
- HANDFUL OF PINE NUTS
- 2 OZ. BUFFALO MOZZARELLA CHEESE, DRAINED AND TORN
- ZEST OF ½ LEMON

POTATO & PESTO PIZZA

YIELD: 1 PIZZA / **ACTIVE TIME:** 20 MINUTES / **TOTAL TIME:** 1 HOUR

A hard-and-fast rule: potatoes make a great pizza topping. The Basil Pesto is there to add color and flavor to this simple, elegant topping.

INGREDIENTS:

- SALT AND PEPPER, TO TASTE
- 1 SMALL POTATO, SLICED
- SEMOLINA FLOUR, AS NEEDED
- 1 BALL OF PIZZA DOUGH
- 2 OZ. CACIOCAVALLO CHEESE, SLICED
- ¼ CUP BASIL PESTO (SEE PAGE 664)
- EXTRA-VIRGIN OLIVE OIL, AS NEEDED

1. Place a baking stone or steel on the middle rack of the oven and preheat the oven to the maximum temperature.

2. Bring a pot of salted water to a boil and prepare an ice bath. Add the potato to the boiling water, cook for 1 minute, drain, and place it in the ice bath. Let it sit for 2 minutes, drain, and pat the potato dry with paper towels.

3. Dust a work surface with semolina flour, place the dough on the work surface, and gently stretch it into the desired shape. Distribute the caciocavallo, pesto, and potato over the dough, season with salt and pepper, and drizzle olive oil over the pizza.

4. Using a peel or a flat baking sheet, transfer the pizza to the heated baking implement in the oven. Bake for about 15 minutes, until the crust is golden brown and starting to char. Remove the pizza from the oven and let it cool slightly before slicing and serving.

PIZZA WITH SWORDFISH, PINE NUTS & CHERRY TOMATOES

YIELD: 1 PIZZA / **ACTIVE TIME:** 15 MINUTES / **TOTAL TIME:** 45 MINUTES

A topping that will transport you to sunny Sicily, where small, fresh swordfish is often the catch of the day.

1. Place a baking stone or steel on the middle rack of the oven and preheat the oven to the maximum temperature.

2. Dust a work surface with semolina flour, place the dough on the work surface, and gently stretch it into the desired shape.

3. Drizzle olive oil over the dough and top it with the mozzarella. Season with salt and drizzle olive oil over the pizza.

4. Using a peel or a flat baking sheet, transfer the pizza to the heated baking implement in the oven. Bake for about 15 minutes, until the crust is golden brown and starting to char.

5. Remove the pizza from the oven and top it with the arugula, Swordfish Carpaccio, pine nuts, and cherry tomatoes. Season with salt and pepper, drizzle olive oil and balsamic vinegar over the pizza, and let it cool slightly before slicing and serving.

INGREDIENTS:

SEMOLINA FLOUR, AS NEEDED

1 BALL OF PIZZA DOUGH

EXTRA-VIRGIN OLIVE OIL, TO TASTE

1 OZ. LOW-MOISTURE MOZZARELLA CHEESE, SHREDDED

SALT AND PEPPER, TO TASTE

HANDFUL OF ARUGULA

2 OZ. SWORDFISH CARPACCIO (SEE PAGE 665)

1 TABLESPOON PINE NUTS

HANDFUL OF CHERRY TOMATOES, QUARTERED

BALSAMIC VINEGAR, FOR GARNISH

BBQ CHICKEN PIZZA

YIELD: 1 PIZZA / **ACTIVE TIME:** 15 MINUTES / **TOTAL TIME:** 45 MINUTES

Topping pizza with this savory staple has become hugely popular in the last few years, and once you find the ideal BBQ sauce for it, you'll see why.

INGREDIENTS:

- SEMOLINA FLOUR, AS NEEDED
- 1 BALL OF PIZZA DOUGH
- 6 TABLESPOONS SPICY BBQ SAUCE
- 4 OZ. COOKED CHICKEN BREAST, CHOPPED
- ¼ CUP PEPPERONCINI, SLICED
- ½ SMALL RED ONION, SLICED THIN
- RED PEPPER FLAKES, TO TASTE
- SALT, TO TASTE
- EXTRA-VIRGIN OLIVE OIL, TO TASTE
- 4 OZ. GOUDA OR MONTEREY JACK CHEESE, SHREDDED
- FRESH CILANTRO, CHOPPED, FOR GARNISH

1. Place a baking stone or steel on the middle rack of the oven and preheat the oven to the maximum temperature.

2. Dust a work surface with semolina flour, place the dough on the work surface, and gently stretch it into the desired shape. Spread the sauce over the dough and top it with the chicken, pepperoncini, and onion. Season with red pepper flakes and salt, drizzle olive oil over the top, and then sprinkle the cheese over the pizza.

3. Using a peel or a flat baking sheet, transfer the pizza to the heated baking implement in the oven. Bake for about 15 minutes, until the crust is golden brown and starting to char. Remove the pizza from the oven and let it cool slightly before garnishing it with cilantro, slicing, and serving.

GRILLED ZUCCHINI & EGGPLANT PIZZA

YIELD: 1 PIZZA / **ACTIVE TIME:** 20 MINUTES / **TOTAL TIME:** 55 MINUTES

No meat, no problem. The meaty taste and texture of eggplant add some heft to this all-veggie pie.

1. Prepare a gas or charcoal grill for medium heat (400°F). Place a baking stone or steel on the middle rack of the oven and preheat the oven to the maximum temperature.

2. Place the vegetables in a bowl, season with salt and pepper, and drizzle olive oil over them. Place them on the grill and cook until they are charred all over and have softened slightly, about 5 minutes. Remove the vegetables from the grill and let them cool.

3. Dust a work surface with semolina flour, place the dough on the work surface, and gently stretch it into the desired shape. Cover the dough with the sauce and top it with the mozzarella and grilled vegetables. Season with salt and pepper and drizzle olive oil over the pizza.

4. Using a peel or a flat baking sheet, transfer the pizza to the heated baking implement in the oven. Bake for about 15 minutes, until the crust is golden brown and starting to char. Remove the pizza from the oven, sprinkle Parmesan and drizzle olive oil over it, and let the pizza cool slightly before slicing and serving.

INGREDIENTS:

- ⅓ SMALL EGGPLANT, SLICED LENGTHWISE
- ⅓ ZUCCHINI, SLICED LENGTHWISE
- ¼ BELL PEPPER, SLICED
- SALT AND PEPPER, TO TASTE
- EXTRA-VIRGIN OLIVE OIL, AS NEEDED
- SEMOLINA FLOUR, AS NEEDED
- 1 BALL OF PIZZA DOUGH
- ⅓ CUP PIZZA SAUCE (SEE PAGE 661)
- 3 OZ. LOW-MOISTURE MOZZARELLA CHEESE, SHREDDED
- PARMESAN CHEESE, GRATED, FOR GARNISH

QUICK FOCACCIA DOUGH

YIELD: DOUGH FOR 1 LARGE FOCACCIA / **ACTIVE TIME:** 15 MINUTES / **TOTAL TIME:** 1 HOUR AND 30 MINUTES

The simplest and quickest focaccia dough, providing a wonderfully soft dough in just a couple of hours.

1. Place the water and yeast in a bowl, gently stir to combine, and let the mixture sit until it starts to foam, about 10 minutes.

2. In a large bowl, combine the flours, sugar, and yeast mixture and work the mixture until it just holds together. Place the dough on a flour-dusted work surface and knead the dough until it is compact, smooth, and elastic.

3. Add the olive oil and salt and knead until the dough is developed, elastic, and extensible, about 5 minutes. Coat a large, clean bowl with olive oil, shape the dough into a ball, and place it in the bowl. Cover the bowl with plastic wrap, place the dough in a naturally warm spot, and let it rest until it has doubled in size, about 1 hour.

4. After 1 hour, the dough can be stretched and flavored as desired. It will need another 30 minutes to 1 hour for the second rise before baking.

INGREDIENTS:

- 2 CUPS (454 G) WARM WATER (105°F)
- 3½ TEASPOONS (10.5 G) ACTIVE DRY YEAST
- 17.6 OZ. (500 G) BREAD FLOUR
- 7 OZ. (198 G) ALL-PURPOSE FLOUR, PLUS MORE AS NEEDED
- 2 TEASPOONS (8 G) SUGAR
- 5 TABLESPOONS (65 G) EXTRA-VIRGIN OLIVE OIL, PLUS MORE AS NEEDED
- 2½ TEASPOONS (13 G) FINE SEA SALT

CLASSIC FOCACCIA DOUGH

YIELD: DOUGH FOR 1 LARGE FOCACCIA / **ACTIVE TIME:** 30 MINUTES / **TOTAL TIME:** 5 HOURS

This dough will give you a soft focaccia with a nice, complex texture. It takes several hours to make, but keep in mind that most of it is rising time, during which you can attend to other activities.

INGREDIENTS:

- 17 OZ. (482 G) WARM WATER (105°F)
- ¾ TEASPOON (2.2 G) ACTIVE DRY YEAST
- 21 OZ. (595 G) BREAD FLOUR
- 3 OZ. (85 G) ALL-PURPOSE FLOUR, PLUS MORE AS NEEDED
- 2 TABLESPOONS (26 G) EXTRA-VIRGIN OLIVE OIL, PLUS MORE AS NEEDED
- 2 TEASPOONS (11 G) FINE SEA SALT

1. Place the water and yeast in a bowl, gently stir to combine, and let the mixture sit until it starts to foam, about 10 minutes.

2. In a large bowl, combine the flours and yeast mixture. Work the mixture until it just comes together. Place the dough on a flour-dusted work surface and knead the dough until it is compact, smooth, and elastic.

3. Add the olive oil and salt and knead the dough until it is developed, elastic, and extensible, about 5 minutes. Coat a large, clean bowl with olive oil, shape the dough into a ball, and place it in the bowl. Cover the bowl with plastic wrap, place the dough in a naturally warm spot, and let it rest until it has doubled in size, 3 to 4 hours.

4. Stretch and flavor the dough as desired. It will need another 1½ to 2 hours for the second rise before baking. The extra rising time can only benefit the dough, as the relatively low amount of yeast in this recipe means the risk of overproofing is small.

LOW-HYDRATION FOCACCIA DOUGH

YIELD: DOUGH FOR 1 LARGE FOCACCIA / **ACTIVE TIME:** 30 MINUTES / **TOTAL TIME:** 27 HOURS

This dough is quite dry for a focaccia, making it perfect for recipes that need a rather thin and substantial focaccia base.

1. Place the water and yeast in a bowl, gently stir to combine, and let the mixture sit until it starts to foam, about 10 minutes.

2. In a large bowl, combine the flours and yeast mixture. Work the mixture until it just comes together as a dough. Place the dough on a flour-dusted work surface and knead until it is compact, smooth, and elastic.

3. Add the salt and knead until the dough is developed, elastic, and extensible, about 5 minutes. Add the olive oil and knead until it has been incorporated. Coat a large, clean bowl with olive oil, shape the dough into a ball, and place it in the bowl. Cover the bowl with plastic wrap and let it rest in the refrigerator for 24 hours.

4. Remove the dough from the refrigerator and let it warm to room temperature before making focaccia.

INGREDIENTS:

- 13 OZ. (368.5 G) WARM WATER (105°F)
- 1 (HEAPING) TEASPOON (3.2 G) ACTIVE DRY YEAST
- 10.6 OZ. (300 G) BREAD FLOUR
- 10.6 OZ. (300 G) ALL-PURPOSE FLOUR, PLUS MORE AS NEEDED
- 2⅔ TEASPOONS (14⅔ G) FINE SEA SALT
- 2 TABLESPOONS (26 G) EXTRA-VIRGIN OLIVE OIL

HIGH-HYDRATION FOCACCIA DOUGH

YIELD: DOUGH FOR 1 LARGE FOCACCIA / **ACTIVE TIME:** 30 MINUTES / **TOTAL TIME:** 27 HOURS

This dough is rather wet, but not "liquid" like the more hydrated doughs in this book. It is perfect for a Focaccia Genovese (see page 466) and for focaccia that need to be thick without being overly pillowy.

INGREDIENTS:

17.3 OZ. (490 G) WARM WATER (105°F)

1⅔ TEASPOONS (5 G) ACTIVE DRY YEAST

17.6 OZ. (500 G) BREAD FLOUR OR "00" FLOUR

7 OZ. (198 G) ALL-PURPOSE FLOUR, PLUS MORE AS NEEDED

1 TABLESPOON (17 G) FINE SEA SALT

2 TABLESPOONS (26 G) EXTRA-VIRGIN OLIVE OIL

1. Place the water and yeast in a bowl, gently stir to combine, and let the mixture sit until it starts to foam, about 10 minutes.

2. In a large bowl, combine the flours and yeast mixture. Work the mixture until it just comes together as a dough. Place the dough on a flour-dusted work surface and knead until it is compact, smooth, and elastic.

3. Add the salt and knead until the dough is developed, elastic, and extensible, about 5 minutes. Add the olive oil and knead until it has been incorporated. Coat a large, clean bowl with olive oil, shape the dough into a ball, and place it in the bowl. Cover the bowl with plastic wrap and let it rest in the refrigerator for 24 hours.

4. Remove the dough from the refrigerator and let it warm to room temperature before making focaccia.

PIZZA DI GRANTURCO

YIELD: 8 SMALL FOCACCIA / **ACTIVE TIME:** 10 MINUTES / **TOTAL TIME:** 45 MINUTES

Pizza di granturco was traditionally made from cornmeal and cooked among the embers of a fireplace or a wood-fired stove. Serve with sautéed vegetables, such as broccoli rabe.

1. Preheat the oven to 430°F and place a baking stone or steel on the middle rack of the oven as it warms.

2. In a large bowl, combine the cornmeal and salt. Using a wooden spoon, gradually incorporate the boiling water and work the mixture until it just comes together as a dough. Place the dough on a cornmeal-dusted work surface and knead until it is smooth. Divide the dough into eight pieces, shape them into rounds, and flatten them into rather thick disks.

3. Place the disks directly on the heated baking implement and bake for about 25 minutes, until the tops are crispy. Remove the focaccia from the oven and let them cool slightly before serving.

INGREDIENTS:

- 17.6 OZ. (500 G) CORNMEAL, PLUS MORE AS NEEDED
- 1 TEASPOON (5.5 G) FINE SEA SALT
- 31¾ OZ. (900 G) BOILING WATER

PIZZ'ONTA

YIELD: 12 SMALL FOCACCIA / **ACTIVE TIME:** 30 MINUTES / **TOTAL TIME:** 4 HOURS

In Abruzzi, it is very common to eat a fried crunchy focaccia called pizz'onta, or "greasy pizza." This focaccia is very easy to make at home, and it is out-of-this-world scrumptious, perfect with cheese and cold cuts or grilled steak tips.

INGREDIENTS:

- 8½ OZ. (241 G) WATER
- 1¼ TEASPOONS (3.7 G) ACTIVE DRY YEAST
- 14 OZ. (397 G) BREAD FLOUR, PLUS MORE AS NEEDED
- 2 TEASPOONS (8 G) SUGAR
- 1 TEASPOON (6 G) FINE SEA SALT, PLUS MORE TO TASTE
- 2 TABLESPOONS (26 G) EXTRA-VIRGIN OLIVE OIL, PLUS MORE AS NEEDED

1. Warm 3½ tablespoons of the water until it is 105°F. Add the yeast and water to a bowl and gently stir to combine. Let the mixture sit until it starts to foam, about 10 minutes.

2. In a large bowl, combine the flour, yeast mixture, remaining water, and the sugar. Work the mixture until it just comes together as a dough. If kneading by hand, place the dough on a flour-dusted work surface. Work the dough until it is compact, smooth, and elastic.

3. Add the salt and olive oil and work the dough until it is developed, elastic, and extensible, about 5 minutes. Coat a large, clean bowl with olive oil, shape the dough into a ball, and place it in the bowl. Cover the bowl with plastic wrap, place it in a naturally warm spot, and let it rest until it has doubled in size, about 2 hours.

4. Place the dough on a flour-dusted work surface, divide it into 12 pieces, and shape them into rounds, taking care not to overwork the dough. Cover the dough with a kitchen towel and let it rest for 30 minutes.

5. Add olive oil to a Dutch oven until it is approximately 2 inches deep and warm it to 350°F. Flatten the rounds and, working in batches, fry them until they are golden brown on both sides, about 4 minutes.

6. Transfer the fried focaccia to a paper towel–lined plate to drain and season them with salt before serving.

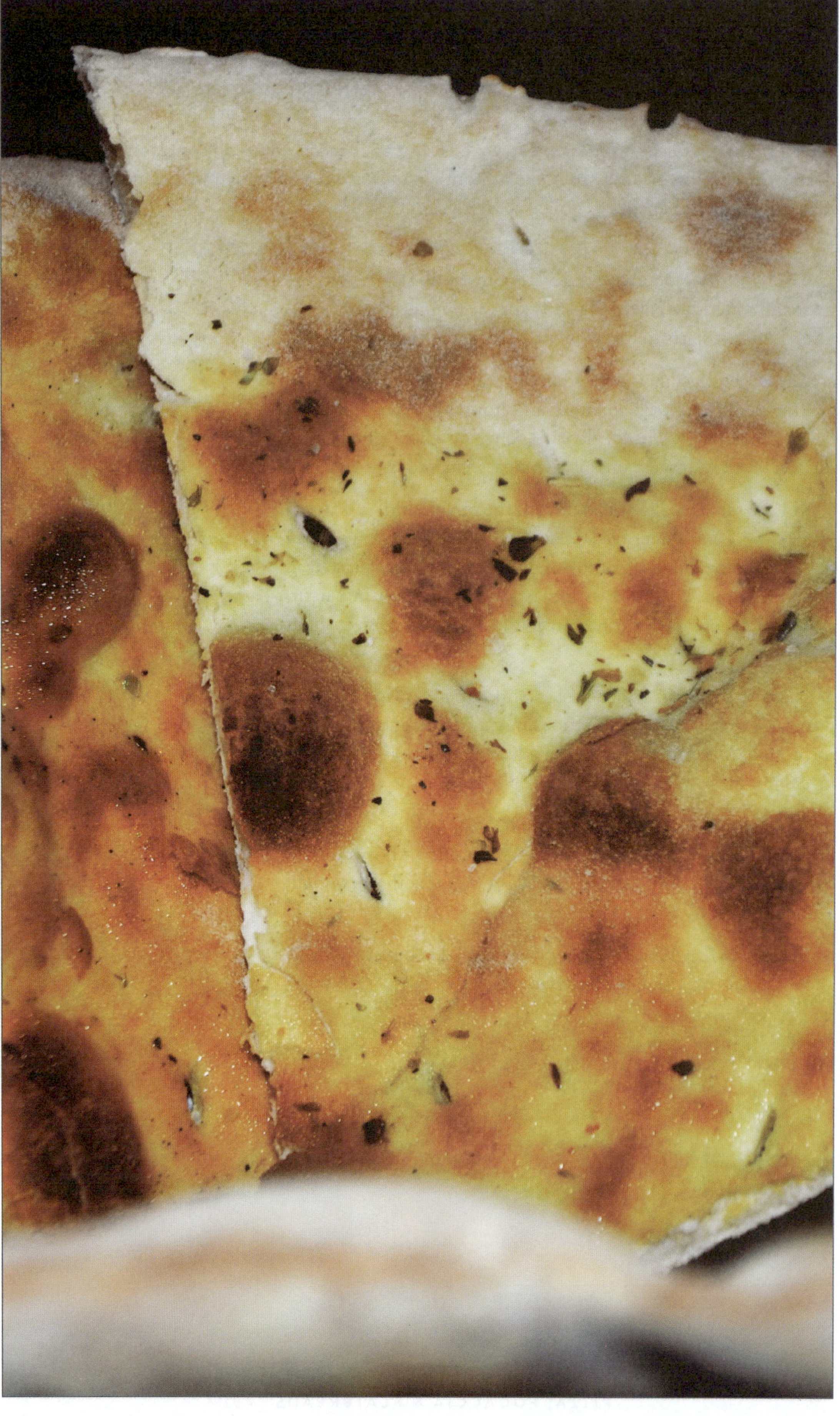

PIZZA ASSETTATA

YIELD: 1 LARGE FOCACCIA / **ACTIVE TIME:** 25 MINUTES / **TOTAL TIME:** 1 HOUR AND 15 MINUTES

As this focaccia is unleavened, it is among the quickest and easiest focaccia to make.

INGREDIENTS:

- 12.3 OZ. (349 G) BREAD FLOUR, PLUS MORE AS NEEDED
- 12.3 OZ. (349 G) FINELY GROUND DURUM WHEAT FLOUR (SEMOLA RIMACINATA)
- 2 TEASPOONS (11 G) FINE SEA SALT
- 16.6 OZ. (471 G) WARM WATER (105°F)
- 1¾ OZ. (50 G) EXTRA-VIRGIN OLIVE OIL, PLUS MORE AS NEEDED
- 1 TABLESPOON FENNEL SEEDS
- 1 TEASPOON RED PEPPER FLAKES
- COARSE SEA SALT, FOR TOPPING

1. In a large bowl, combine the flours and fine sea salt. Gradually incorporate the water and work the mixture with your hands until it just comes together as a dough. Add the olive oil, fennel seeds, and red pepper flakes and work the dough until they have been incorporated.

2. If kneading by hand, place the dough on a flour-dusted work surface. Work it until it is smooth, compact, and elastic, about 10 minutes. Shape the dough into a ball, cover it with plastic wrap, and let it rest at room temperature for 30 minutes.

3. Preheat the oven to 430°F. Coat an 18 × 13–inch baking pan with olive oil. Place the dough on a flour-dusted work surface and roll it out into a rectangle that will fit in the pan. Place the dough in the pan, drizzle olive oil over the dough, and sprinkle coarse salt on top.

4. Place the focaccia in the oven and bake for 20 to 25 minutes, until it is a light golden brown. Remove the focaccia from the oven and let it cool slightly before serving.

PANUOZZO

YIELD: 6 SMALL FOCACCIA / **ACTIVE TIME:** 20 MINUTES / **TOTAL TIME:** 3 HOURS AND 30 MINUTES

A focaccia traditionally made with pizza dough, panuozzo is truly special because it is baked twice: first to cook the bread, and then to incorporate the fillings. The most typical fillings are thin slices of pancetta or bacon with mozzarella, but the options are endless for this scrumptious flatbread.

1. Place the dough on a flour-dusted work surface and cut it into six pieces. Stretch the pieces of dough into 8- to 10-inch-long ovals, place them on pieces of flour-dusted parchment paper, and cover them with kitchen towels or plastic wrap coated with olive oil. Let the dough rest in a naturally warm spot for 2 to 3 hours.

2. Preheat the oven to 410°F and place a baking stone or steel on the middle rack of the oven as it warms.

3. Using a peel or a flat baking sheet, slide the focaccia onto the heated baking implement and bake for 15 to 20 minutes, until the crust is set. Remove the focaccia from the oven and let them cool before cutting a slit along the equator of each focaccia.

4. Fill each focaccia with an equal amount of the pancetta, mozzarella, tomatoes, and lettuce. Sprinkle red pepper flakes and salt over the filling and drizzle olive oil over it.

5. Return the focaccia to the oven and bake for about 10 minutes, until the pancetta looks cooked through and the mozzarella has melted. Remove the focaccia from the oven and let them cool briefly before serving.

INGREDIENTS:

HIGH-HYDRATION FOCACCIA DOUGH (SEE PAGE 399)

ALL-PURPOSE FLOUR, AS NEEDED

EXTRA-VIRGIN OLIVE OIL, TO TASTE

12.7 OZ. PANCETTA OR BACON, SLICED THIN

26.4 OZ. FRESH MOZZARELLA CHEESE, DRAINED AND SLICED

2 TOMATOES, SLICED

12 LETTUCE LEAVES

RED PEPPER FLAKES, TO TASTE

SALT, TO TASTE

PARIGINA

YIELD: 1 LARGE FOCACCIA / **ACTIVE TIME:** 20 MINUTES / **TOTAL TIME:** 3 HOURS AND 30 MINUTES

If you are walking the streets of Naples during the day, you will probably stumble upon this beloved street food. Decadent and delicious, parigina typically features multiple layers of toppings, such as tomato sauce, ham, cheese, puff pastry, and heavy cream.

INGREDIENTS:

- EXTRA-VIRGIN OLIVE OIL, AS NEEDED
- LOW-HYDRATION FOCACCIA DOUGH (SEE PAGE 398)
- 23 OZ. CANNED WHOLE PEELED TOMATOES, DRAINED AND CRUSHED BY HAND
- SALT, TO TASTE
- 7 OZ. HAM, SLICED
- 14 OZ. CACIOCAVALLO CHEESE OR LOW-MOISTURE MOZZARELLA CHEESE, SLICED THIN
- 1 SHEET OF FROZEN PUFF PASTRY, THAWED
- 2 EGG YOLKS
- ¼ CUP HEAVY CREAM

1. Coat an 18 x 13–inch baking sheet with olive oil, place the dough on it, and stretch the dough toward the edges of the pan, taking care not to tear it. Cover the dough with olive oil–coated plastic wrap and let it rest at room temperature for 2 hours. As the dough rests, stretch it toward the edges of the pan every 20 minutes until it covers the entire pan.

2. Preheat the oven to 390°F. Spread the tomatoes over the dough, making sure to leave a 1-inch border of dough at the edges. Season the tomatoes with salt. Cover the tomatoes with a layer of ham and top this with a layer of cheese. Cover the focaccia with the puff pastry, beat the egg yolks and cream together until combined, and brush the puff pastry with the egg wash.

3. Place the focaccia in the oven and bake until it is golden brown, 30 to 35 minutes.

4. Remove the focaccia from the oven and let it cool slightly before cutting it into squares and serving.

MONTANARE

YIELD: 20 MINIATURE FOCACCIA / **ACTIVE TIME:** 45 MINUTES / **TOTAL TIME:** 2 HOURS AND 45 MINUTES

A recipe that dates back to a time when people living in cities didn't have a kitchen large enough to accommodate an oven, and so focaccia was fried rather than baked. These miniature focaccia are a real treat, and particularly beloved by children.

INGREDIENTS:

- ½ BATCH OF NEAPOLITAN PIZZA DOUGH (SEE PAGE 288)
- ALL-PURPOSE FLOUR, AS NEEDED
- EXTRA-VIRGIN OLIVE OIL, AS NEEDED
- 26.4 OZ. (748 G) CLASSIC TOMATO SAUCE (SEE PAGE 665), WARMED, FOR TOPPING
- PECORINO CHEESE, GRATED, FOR TOPPING
- FRESH BASIL, FOR TOPPING
- MOZZARELLA CHEESE, SLICED, FOR TOPPING (OPTIONAL)

1. Place the dough on a flour-dusted work surface, divide it into 20 pieces, and shape each piece into a ball. Coat a piece of plastic wrap with olive oil, place it over the balls of dough, and let them rest at room temperature until they have doubled in size, about 2 hours.

2. Add olive oil to a deep skillet until it is about 1 inch deep and warm it to 350°F. Flatten the balls of dough. Working in batches of three, gently slip them into the hot oil and cook until they are golden brown, turning them frequently, about 5 minutes. Place the cooked focaccia on paper towel–lined plates to drain.

3. When all of the focaccia have been cooked, top them with the sauce, pecorino, basil, and, if desired, mozzarella. Drizzle olive oil over the focaccia and serve.

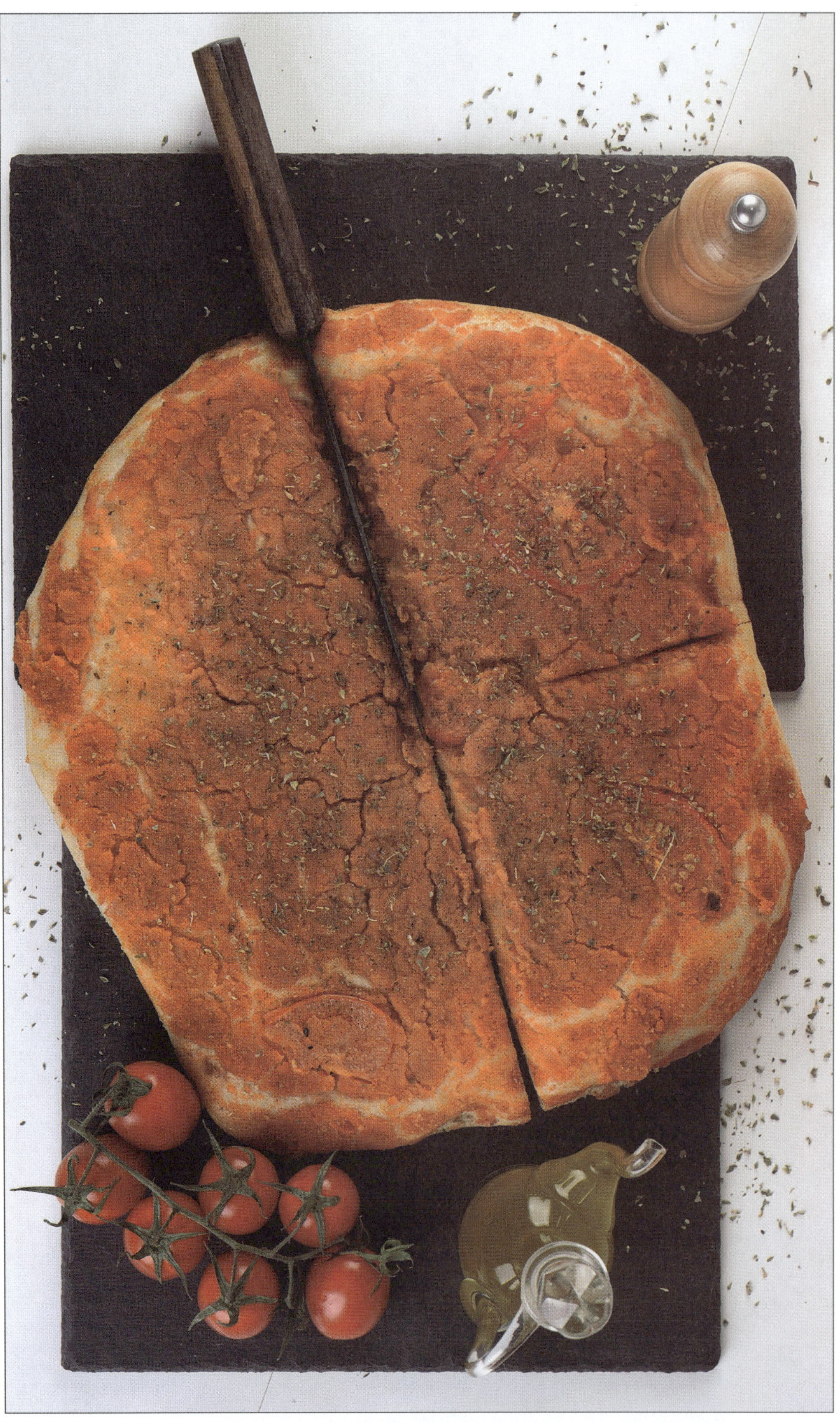

GRUPARIATA

YIELD: 1 FOCACCIA / **ACTIVE TIME:** 30 MINUTES / **TOTAL TIME:** 3 HOURS AND 30 MINUTES

Hailing from Calabria, this is a very tall and fluffy focaccia with a pleasantly red crumb that is due to the presence of tomatoes and chili powder in the dough.

INGREDIENTS:

- 1.2 OZ. (34 G) EXTRA-VIRGIN OLIVE OIL, PLUS MORE AS NEEDED
- 14 OZ. (397 G) WARM WATER (105°F)
- 2½ TEASPOONS (7.5 G) ACTIVE DRY YEAST
- 17.6 OZ. (500 G) BREAD FLOUR
- 10.6 OZ. (300 G) "00" FLOUR
- 1 LB. (454 G) CANNED WHOLE PEELED TOMATOES, DRAINED AND CHOPPED
- 2 TABLESPOONS (16 G) CHILI POWDER
- 2½ TEASPOONS (13 G) FINE SEA SALT, PLUS MORE TO TASTE
- 2 GARLIC CLOVES, MINCED
- FRESH OREGANO, FINELY CHOPPED, TO TASTE
- ANCHOVIES IN OLIVE OIL, DRAINED AND TORN, TO TASTE
- 1 FRESH TOMATO, SLICED
- FRESH ROSEMARY, TO TASTE

1. Line a deep, round 13-inch cake pan with parchment paper and coat it with olive oil. Place the water and yeast in a bowl, gently stir to combine, and let the mixture sit until it starts to foam, about 10 minutes.

2. In a large bowl, combine the flours, peeled tomatoes, chili powder, olive oil, salt, and yeast mixture and work the mixture until it comes together as a smooth, developed dough.

3. Incorporate the garlic and a few pinches of oregano into the dough and transfer it into the cake pan. Cover the pan with a kitchen towel and let the dough rest at room temperature until it has doubled in size, about 2½ hours.

4. Preheat the oven to 390°F. Cover the focaccia with anchovies and the fresh tomato slices, pressing down on them so that they are embedded deep within the dough. Sprinkle rosemary, additional oregano, and salt over the dough and drizzle some olive oil over the top.

5. Place the focaccia in the oven and bake for 30 to 35 minutes, until it is golden brown. Remove the focaccia from the oven and let it cool slightly before serving.

LESTOPITTA

YIELD: 8 SMALL FOCACCIA / **ACTIVE TIME:** 45 MINUTES / **TOTAL TIME:** 2 HOURS AND 45 MINUTES

This fried focaccia is crunchy when hot, but softens as it cools. It is usually wrapped around a savory filling when eaten in its softer, cooler state.

1. Combine the flour, water, and olive oil in a mixing bowl and work the mixture until it is smooth and elastic. Cover the bowl with plastic wrap and let the dough rest at room temperature for 1 hour.

2. Divide the dough into eight pieces and shape them into balls. Coat a piece of plastic wrap with olive oil, place it over the balls of dough, and let them rest at room temperature until they have doubled in size, about 1 hour.

3. Add olive oil to a deep skillet until it is about 1 inch deep and warm it to 350°F. Flatten the balls of dough. Working in batches of three, gently slip the focaccia into the hot oil and cook until they are golden brown, turning them frequently. Place the cooked focaccia on paper towel–lined plates to drain. Serve the focaccia warm, or wait until they have cooled and fill them with anything you desire.

INGREDIENTS:

- 14 OZ. (397 G) FINELY GROUND DURUM WHEAT FLOUR (SEMOLA RIMACINATA)
- 7 OZ. (198 G) WATER
- 2 TABLESPOONS (26 G) EXTRA-VIRGIN OLIVE OIL, PLUS MORE AS NEEDED

FOCACCIA BARESE

YIELD: 2 SMALL FOCACCIA / **ACTIVE TIME:** 30 MINUTES / **TOTAL TIME:** 4 HOURS

Bari is the birthplace of one of the most prototypical Italian focaccia, the Barese. This is the most popular version—round and topped with fresh tomatoes and olives—but many variations can be found.

INGREDIENTS:

- 14 OZ. (397 G) WATER
- 2 TEASPOONS (6 G) ACTIVE DRY YEAST
- 14 OZ. (397 G) BREAD FLOUR, PLUS MORE AS NEEDED
- 7 OZ. (198 G) FINELY GROUND DURUM WHEAT FLOUR (SEMOLA RIMACINATA)
- 1 POTATO, BOILED, PEELED, AND MASHED
- 2½ TEASPOONS (15 G) FINE SEA SALT, PLUS MORE TO TASTE
- EXTRA-VIRGIN OLIVE OIL, AS NEEDED
- 2 VERY RIPE TOMATOES, CHOPPED
- GREEN OLIVES, PITTED AND CHOPPED, TO TASTE
- FRESH OREGANO, CHOPPED, TO TASTE

1. Warm 3½ tablespoons of the water until it is 105°F. Add the yeast and water to a bowl and gently stir to combine. Let the mixture sit until it starts to foam, about 10 minutes.

2. In a large bowl, combine the flours, potato, yeast mixture, and remaining water. Work the mixture until it comes together as a dough. If kneading by hand, place the dough on a flour-dusted work surface. Work it until it is compact, smooth, and elastic.

3. Add the salt and work the dough until it is developed, elastic, and extensible, about 5 minutes. Coat a large, clean bowl with olive oil, shape the dough into a ball, and place it in the bowl. Cover the bowl with plastic wrap, place it in a naturally warm spot, and let it rest until it has doubled in size, about 2 hours.

4. Generously coat two 10-inch cast-iron skillets or round cake pans with olive oil. Place the dough on a flour-dusted work surface and divide it in half. Place a piece of dough in each pan and spread it to the edge, making sure not to press down too hard on the dough and deflate it. Let the dough rest in a naturally warm spot for 1 hour.

5. Preheat the oven to the maximum temperature. Top the focaccia with the tomatoes, olives, and oregano, season it with salt, and drizzle olive oil over the top. Place the pans directly on the bottom of the oven and bake for 10 minutes.

6. Transfer the pans to the middle rack and bake until the edges of the focaccia look brown and crunchy, 5 to 7 more minutes.

7. Remove the focaccia from the oven and let them cool slightly before serving.

PIZZA SCIMA

YIELD: 1 LARGE FOCACCIA / **ACTIVE TIME:** 25 MINUTES / **TOTAL TIME:** 1 HOUR AND 15 MINUTES

Notwithstanding the name, which implies that it is "dull," this focaccia carries a distinctive flavor and crunchiness, both of which are provided by the high amount of olive oil in the dough. The "dull," then, refers to it being unleavened, as was typical in the Jewish communities that traditionally inhabited parts of Abruzzi.

1. In a large bowl, combine the flours, baking soda, and salt. Incorporate the olive oil, wine, and water gradually and work the mixture until it just holds together. Place the dough on a flour-dusted work surface and knead until it is compact, smooth, and elastic. Shape the dough into a ball, cover it with plastic wrap, and let it rest at room temperature for 30 minutes.

2. Preheat the oven to 430°F and place a baking stone or steel on the middle rack of the oven as it warms.

3. Place the dough on a flour-dusted work surface. Using a rolling pin, roll the dough out until it is approximately ¾ inch thick. Place the dough on a piece of parchment paper and make deep cuts in it, working in a crosshatch pattern and taking care not to cut all the way through.

4. Using a peel or flat baking sheet, transfer the dough onto the heated baking implement and bake for about 20 to 30 minutes, until it is golden brown. Remove the focaccia from the oven and let it cool slightly before serving.

INGREDIENTS:

- 17.6 OZ. (500 G) BREAD FLOUR
- 7 OZ. (198 G) ALL-PURPOSE FLOUR, PLUS MORE AS NEEDED
- ¼ TEASPOON (1.5 G) BAKING SODA
- 2 TEASPOONS (11 G) FINE SEA SALT
- 2.8 OZ. (79 G) EXTRA-VIRGIN OLIVE OIL
- 2.8 OZ. (79 G) WHITE WINE
- 6.3 OZ. (179 G) WATER

FOCACCIA DI ALTAMURA

YIELD: 2 SMALL FOCACCIA / **ACTIVE TIME:** 30 MINUTES / **TOTAL TIME:** 4 HOURS

In Altamura, focaccia is made from 100 percent durum wheat flour and features a topping of onions and fresh tomatoes.

1. Place the water and yeast in a bowl, gently stir to combine, and let the mixture sit until it starts to foam, about 10 minutes.

2. In a large bowl, combine the flour and yeast mixture and work the mixture until it just holds together. If kneading by hand, place the dough on a flour-dusted work surface. Work it until it is compact, smooth, and elastic.

3. Add the salt and work the dough until it is developed, elastic, and extensible, about 5 minutes. Coat a large, clean bowl with olive oil, shape the dough into a ball, and place it in the bowl. Cover the bowl with plastic wrap, place it in a naturally warm spot, and let it rest until it has doubled in size, about 2 hours.

4. Generously coat two 10-inch cast-iron skillets or round cake pans with olive oil. Place the dough on a flour-dusted work surface and divide it in half. Place a piece of dough in each pan and spread it to the edge, making sure not to press down too hard on the dough and deflate the focaccia. Let the dough rest at room temperature for 1 hour.

5. Preheat the oven to the maximum temperature. Top the focaccia with the onion, press the tomatoes into the dough, season with salt and oregano, and drizzle olive oil over the focaccia. Place the pans directly on the bottom of the oven and bake for 10 minutes.

6. Transfer the pans to the middle rack and bake until the edges look brown and crunchy, 5 to 7 more minutes.

7. Remove the focaccia from the oven and let them cool slightly before serving.

INGREDIENTS:

- 14 OZ. (397 G) WARM WATER (105°F)
- 2 TEASPOONS (6 G) ACTIVE DRY YEAST
- 21.1 OZ. (598 G) FINELY GROUND DURUM WHEAT FLOUR (SEMOLA RIMACINATA), PLUS MORE AS NEEDED
- 2½ TEASPOONS (13.7 G) FINE SEA SALT, PLUS MORE TO TASTE
- EXTRA-VIRGIN OLIVE OIL, AS NEEDED
- 1 LARGE ONION, SLICED
- 2 VERY RIPE TOMATOES, SLICED
- FRESH OREGANO, FINELY CHOPPED, TO TASTE

PUDDICA SALENTINA

YIELD: 2 SMALL FOCACCIA / **ACTIVE TIME:** 30 MINUTES / **TOTAL TIME:** 4 HOURS

In Salento, particularly in the city of Brindisi, Apulian focaccia is made without durum flour and with capers in place of olives as a topping.

INGREDIENTS:

- 14 OZ. (397 G) WATER
- 2 TEASPOONS (6 G) ACTIVE DRY YEAST
- 14 OZ. (397 G) BREAD FLOUR
- 7 OZ. (198 G) ALL-PURPOSE FLOUR, PLUS MORE AS NEEDED
- 2½ TEASPOONS (15 G) FINE SEA SALT, PLUS MORE TO TASTE
- EXTRA-VIRGIN OLIVE OIL, AS NEEDED
- CAPERS, DRAINED AND RINSED, TO TASTE
- 2 VERY RIPE TOMATOES, CHOPPED
- FRESH OREGANO, CHOPPED, TO TASTE

1. Warm 3½ tablespoons of the water until it is 105°F. Add the yeast and water to a bowl and gently stir to combine. Let the mixture sit until it starts to foam, about 10 minutes.

2. In a large bowl, combine the flours, yeast mixture, and remaining water and work the mixture until it comes together as a dough. If kneading by hand, place the dough on a flour-dusted work surface. Work it until it is compact, smooth, and elastic.

3. Add the salt and work the dough until it is developed, elastic, and extensible, about 5 minutes. Coat a large, clean bowl with olive oil, shape the dough into a ball, and place it in the bowl. Cover the bowl with plastic wrap, place it in a naturally warm spot, and let it rest until it has doubled in size, about 2 hours.

4. Generously coat two 10-inch cast-iron skillets or round cake pans with olive oil. Place the dough on a flour-dusted work surface and divide it in half. Place a piece of dough in each pan and spread it to the edge, making sure not to press down too hard on the dough and deflate it. Let the dough rest at room temperature for 1 hour.

5. Preheat the oven to the maximum temperature. Top the focaccia with capers, press the tomatoes into the dough, season with salt and oregano, and drizzle olive oil over the focaccia. Place the pans directly on the bottom of the oven and bake for 10 minutes.

6. Transfer the pans to the middle rack and bake until the edges look brown and crunchy, 5 to 7 more minutes.

7. Remove the focaccia from the oven and let them cool slightly before serving.

PAPOSCIA DEL GARGANO

YIELD: 5 MEDIUM FOCACCIA / **ACTIVE TIME:** 30 MINUTES / **TOTAL TIME:** 9 HOURS AND 30 MINUTES

From the beautiful Gargano region of Apulia, this focaccia is possibly the original version of ciabatta. Traditionally made with scraps of leftover dough and baked in wood-fired ovens, it can be made at home—with some adjustments—and is surely worth trying, as it also makes a delicious bread for sandwiches.

1. Place the water and yeast in a bowl, gently stir to combine, and let the mixture sit until it starts to foam, about 10 minutes.

2. In a large bowl, combine the bread flour and yeast mixture and work the mixture until it just comes together as a dough. Place the dough on a flour-dusted work surface and knead until it is compact, smooth, and elastic.

3. Add the salt and knead until the dough is smooth, elastic, and extensible. Coat a large, clean bowl with olive oil, divide the dough into five pieces, and shape them into balls. Place them in the bowl, cover it with plastic wrap, and let the dough rest at room temperature for at least 8 hours.

4. Preheat the oven to the maximum temperature and place a baking stone or steel on the middle rack of the oven as it warms.

5. Dust a peel or flat baking sheet with semolina flour. Place three focaccia on it at a time and stretch them into long ovals. Use the peel or flat baking sheet to transfer the focaccia to the heated baking implement and bake for about 10 minutes, until the focaccia are golden brown and crispy.

6. Remove the focaccia from the oven and let them cool slightly before serving.

INGREDIENTS:

- 14.8 OZ. (420 G) WARM WATER (105°F)
- 1 (SCANT) TEASPOON (2.7 G) ACTIVE DRY YEAST
- 22.9 OZ. (650 G) BREAD FLOUR, PLUS MORE AS NEEDED
- 2½ TEASPOONS (13.7 G) FINE SEA SALT
- EXTRA-VIRGIN OLIVE OIL, AS NEEDED
- SEMOLINA FLOUR, AS NEEDED

Paposcia del Gargano, see page 419

CAVICIONE

YIELD: 1 MEDIUM FOCACCIA / **ACTIVE TIME:** 45 MINUTES / **TOTAL TIME:** 5 HOURS

In Ischitella, the typical Apulian calzone is filled with sautéed spring onions, which give it a very special flavor.

INGREDIENTS:

- 8.8 OZ. (249 G) WARM WATER (105°F), PLUS MORE AS NEEDED
- 2 TEASPOONS (6 G) ACTIVE DRY YEAST
- 17.6 OZ. (500 G) ALL-PURPOSE FLOUR, PLUS MORE AS NEEDED
- 1½ TEASPOONS (8.2 G) FINE SEA SALT, PLUS MORE TO TASTE
- EXTRA-VIRGIN OLIVE OIL, AS NEEDED
- 1 LB. SPRING ONIONS, CHOPPED
- 5 OZ. PITTED BLACK OLIVES
- 4 OZ. ANCHOVIES IN OLIVE OIL, DRAINED

1. Place the water and yeast in a bowl, gently stir to combine, and let the mixture sit until it starts to foam, about 10 minutes.

2. In a large bowl, combine the flour and yeast mixture and work the mixture until it just holds together. Place the dough on a flour-dusted work surface and knead until it is compact, smooth, and elastic.

3. Add the salt and knead until the dough is smooth, elastic, and extensible. Coat a large, clean bowl with olive oil, shape the dough into a ball, and place it in the bowl. Cover the bowl with plastic wrap, place it in a naturally warm spot, and let it rest until it has doubled in size, about 2 hours.

4. Coat the bottom of a skillet with olive oil and warm it over medium-high heat. Add the onions and cook, stirring occasionally, until they are tender and starting to brown, about 10 minutes. Remove the pan from heat and let the onions cool completely.

5. Coat a 10-inch cast-iron skillet or round cake pan with olive oil. Place the dough on a flour-dusted work surface and divide it into two pieces, making sure one piece is slightly bigger than the other. Roll out that piece into a disk that is slightly larger than the pan. Place the disk in the pan and top it with the onions, olives, and anchovies.

6. Roll out the second piece of dough so that it will fit within the pan, place it over the filling, and crimp the edge to seal the focaccia. Brush the top of the focaccia with olive oil and use a fork to poke holes in it. Coat a piece of plastic wrap with olive oil, place it over the pan, and let the focaccia rest for 1 hour.

7. Preheat the oven to 430°F. Place the focaccia in the oven and bake for 20 minutes. Reduce the temperature to 350°F and bake for another 20 to 25 minutes, until the focaccia is golden brown on the top and bottom.

8. Remove the focaccia from the oven and let it cool slightly before serving.

SCEBLASTI & PIZZO LECCESE

YIELD: 1 LARGE FOCACCIA / **ACTIVE TIME:** 45 MINUTES / **TOTAL TIME:** 3 HOURS

Deep in the Apulian inland, one can still find a focaccia that dates back to Greek times. It is rich with healthy, yummy vegetables and makes a great way to present them to your family. There are two main variations: in Zollino this focaccia is called sceblasti, a Greek word that means "without shape," because the dough is more like a batter. It includes a blend of different vegetables and is richer than the version that we find in Lecce, which is known as pizzo Leccese. Here is a method for both versions.

INGREDIENTS:

- 14.8 OZ. (420 G) WARM WATER (105°F)
- 2 TEASPOONS (6 G) ACTIVE DRY YEAST
- 21.1 OZ. (600 G) ALL-PURPOSE FLOUR, PLUS MORE AS NEEDED
- 2½ TEASPOONS (13.7 G) FINE SEA SALT, PLUS MORE TO TASTE
- 2.8 OZ. (79 G) EXTRA-VIRGIN OLIVE OIL, PLUS MORE AS NEEDED
- 2 MEDIUM ONIONS, SLICED
- 7 OZ. CHERRY TOMATOES
- 1 ZUCCHINI (OMIT IF MAKING PIZZO LECCESE)
- 7 OZ. COOKED FRESH PUMPKIN (OMIT IF MAKING PIZZO LECCESE)
- 7 OZ. PITTED BLACK OLIVES
- ½ CUP PIZZA SAUCE (SEE PAGE 661)
- FRESH OREGANO, FINELY CHOPPED, TO TASTE
- RED PEPPER FLAKES, TO TASTE (OPTIONAL)

1. Place the water and yeast in a bowl, gently stir to combine, and let the mixture sit until it starts to foam, about 10 minutes.

2. In a large bowl, combine the flour and yeast mixture and work the mixture until it just comes together as a dough. Place the dough on a flour-dusted work surface and knead until it is compact, smooth, and elastic.

3. Add the salt and knead until the dough is smooth, elastic, and extensible. Coat a large, clean bowl with olive oil, shape the dough into a ball, and place it in the bowl. Cover the bowl with plastic wrap, place it in a naturally warm spot, and let it rest until it has doubled in size, about 2 hours.

4. Preheat the oven to the maximum temperature and place a baking stone or steel on the middle rack of the oven as it warms. While the dough is rising, mince all of the vegetables and combine them with the sauce, olive oil, and salt, oregano, and, if desired, red pepper flakes.

5. Flatten the dough and spread the vegetables over it, folding the dough over the vegetables and working with your hands to incorporate them into the dough. Using a peel or flat baking sheet, transfer the focaccia onto the heated baking implement. Bake the focaccia until it is golden brown, about 20 minutes.

6. Remove the focaccia from the oven and let it cool briefly before serving.

CALZONE PUGLIESE

YIELD: 1 MEDIUM FOCACCIA / **ACTIVE TIME:** 45 MINUTES / **TOTAL TIME:** 4 HOURS

Although the name "calzone" evokes the popular Neapolitan pizza pockets, in Apulia it refers to a round pie made from two layers of focaccia dough.

INGREDIENTS:

- 8.8 OZ. (249 G) WARM WATER (105°F)
- 2 TEASPOONS (6 G) ACTIVE DRY YEAST
- 17.6 OZ. (500 G) ALL-PURPOSE FLOUR, PLUS MORE AS NEEDED
- 1½ TEASPOONS (8.2 G) FINE SEA SALT, PLUS MORE TO TASTE
- EXTRA-VIRGIN OLIVE OIL, AS NEEDED
- 3 ONIONS, SLICED
- 5 OZ. CHERRY TOMATOES
- 5 OZ. PITTED BLACK OLIVES
- 2–3 ANCHOVIES, DRAINED
- 2 TABLESPOONS CAPERS IN BRINE, DRAINED AND RINSED

1. Place the water and yeast in a bowl, gently stir to combine, and let the mixture sit until it starts to foam, about 10 minutes.

2. In a large bowl, combine the flour and yeast mixture and work the mixture until it just holds together. Place the dough on a flour-dusted work surface and knead until it is compact, smooth, and elastic.

3. Add the salt and knead until the dough is smooth, elastic, and extensible. Coat a large, clean bowl with olive oil, shape the dough into a ball, and place it in the bowl. Cover the bowl with plastic wrap, place it in a naturally warm spot, and let it rest until it has doubled in size, about 2 hours.

4. Coat the bottom of a skillet with olive oil and warm it over medium-high heat. Add the onions and cook, stirring occasionally, until they are translucent, about 3 minutes. Add the cherry tomatoes and cook until they start to collapse, about 10 minutes. Remove the pan from heat and let the mixture cool completely.

5. Coat a 10-inch cast-iron skillet or round cake pan with olive oil. Place the dough on a flour-dusted work surface and divide it into two pieces, making sure one piece is slightly larger than the other. Roll out that piece into a disk that is slightly larger than the pan. Place the disk in the pan, top it with the onion-and-tomato mixture, and distribute the olives, anchovies, and capers over the top.

6. Roll out the second piece of dough so that it will fit within the pan, place it over the filling, and crimp the edge to seal the focaccia. Brush the top of the focaccia with olive oil and use a fork to poke holes in it. Coat a piece of plastic wrap with olive oil, place it over the pan, and let the focaccia rest for 1 hour.

7. Preheat the oven to 430°F. Place the focaccia in the oven and bake for 20 minutes. Reduce the temperature to 350°F and bake for another 20 to 25 minutes, until the focaccia is golden brown on the top and bottom.

8. Remove the focaccia from the oven and let it cool slightly before serving.

VASTEDDA CON SAMBUCO

YIELD: 1 MEDIUM FOCACCIA / **ACTIVE TIME:** 30 MINUTES / **TOTAL TIME:** 4 HOURS

A delicious, inventive focaccia that is enriched with eggs, flavored with elderflowers, and filled with salami and cheese.

INGREDIENTS:

- 12.3 OZ. (350 G) WARM WATER (105°F)
- 2½ TEASPOONS (7.5 G) ACTIVE DRY YEAST
- 21.1 OZ. (600 G) ALL-PURPOSE FLOUR, PLUS MORE AS NEEDED
- 3½ OZ. (100 G) LARD OR BUTTER
- ELDERFLOWERS, FRESH OR DRIED, TO TASTE
- 1½ TEASPOONS (8.2 G) FINE SEA SALT
- 5 EGGS
- EXTRA-VIRGIN OLIVE OIL, AS NEEDED
- 1 LB. SALAMI, SLICED
- 1 LB. CACIOCAVALLO OR TUMA CHEESE, DICED

1. Place the water and yeast in a bowl, gently stir to combine, and let the mixture sit until it starts to foam, about 10 minutes.

2. In a large bowl, combine the flour, lard or butter, a handful of elderflowers, and the yeast mixture and work the mixture until it just comes together as a dough. Place the dough on a flour-dusted work surface and knead until it is compact, smooth, and elastic.

3. Add the salt and eggs and knead until the dough is smooth, elastic, and extensible. Coat a large, clean bowl with olive oil, shape the dough into a ball, and place it in the bowl. Cover the bowl with plastic wrap, place it in a naturally warm spot, and let it rest until it has doubled in size, about 2 hours.

4. Coat a 10-inch cast-iron skillet or round cake pan with olive oil. Place the dough on a flour-dusted work surface and divide it into two pieces, making sure one piece is slightly larger than the other. Roll out that piece into a round that is slightly larger than the pan. Place the round in the pan and layer the salami and caciocavallo or tuma on top.

5. Roll out the second piece of dough so that it will fit within the pan, place it over the filling, and crimp the edge to seal the focaccia. Brush the top of the focaccia with olive oil and use a fork to poke holes in it. Coat a piece of plastic wrap with olive oil, place it over the pan, and let the focaccia rest for 1 hour.

6. Preheat the oven to 390°F. Sprinkle elderflowers over the focaccia and drizzle olive oil over the top. Place the focaccia in the oven and bake for 30 to 35 minutes, until it is golden brown and crispy.

7. Remove the focaccia from the oven and let it cool slightly before serving.

FOCACCIA DI CARNEVALE SALENTINA

YIELD: 1 SMALL FOCACCIA / **ACTIVE TIME:** 45 MINUTES / **TOTAL TIME:** 4 HOURS

This rich and delicious Apulian calzone is typical of the region of Salento, where it is presented during the Carnival.

1. Warm 3½ tablespoons of the water until it is 105°F. Add the yeast and water to a bowl and gently stir to combine. Let the mixture sit until it starts to foam, about 10 minutes.

2. In a large bowl, combine the flour, yeast mixture, and remaining water and work the mixture until it comes together as a dough. If kneading by hand, place the dough on a flour-dusted work surface. Work it until it is compact, smooth, and elastic.

3. Add the salt and work the dough until it is developed, elastic, and extensible, about 5 minutes. Coat a large, clean bowl with olive oil, shape the dough into a ball, and place it in the bowl. Cover the bowl with plastic wrap, place it in a naturally warm spot, and let it rest until it has doubled in size, about 2 hours.

4. Coat the bottom of a skillet with olive oil and warm it over medium-high heat. Add the onion and sausage, season with salt and pepper, and cook, stirring frequently, until the sausage is browned and the onion is tender, about 10 minutes. Remove the pan from heat and let the mixture cool.

5. Coat a 10-inch cast-iron skillet or a round cake pan with olive oil. Place the dough on a flour-dusted work surface and divide it into two pieces, making sure one piece is slightly bigger than the other. Roll out that piece into a disk that is slightly larger than the pan. Place it in the pan, top it with the onion-and-sausage mixture, and distribute the tomatoes, pecorino, and mozzarella over the mixture.

6. Roll out the second piece of dough so it will fit within the pan, place it over the filling, and crimp the edge to seal the focaccia. Brush the top of the focaccia with olive oil and use a fork to poke holes in it. Coat a piece of plastic wrap with olive oil, place it over the pan, and let the focaccia rest for 1 hour.

7. Preheat the oven to 430°F. Place the focaccia in the oven and bake for 20 minutes. Reduce the temperature to 350°F and bake for another 20 to 25 minutes, until the focaccia is golden brown on the top and bottom.

8. Remove the focaccia from the oven and let it cool slightly before serving.

INGREDIENTS:

- 8.8 OZ. (250 G) WATER
- 2 TEASPOONS (6 G) ACTIVE DRY YEAST
- 17½ OZ. (496 G) ALL-PURPOSE FLOUR, PLUS MORE AS NEEDED
- 1½ TEASPOONS (9 G) FINE SEA SALT, PLUS MORE TO TASTE
- EXTRA-VIRGIN OLIVE OIL, AS NEEDED
- 1 ONION, SLICED
- 14 OZ. ITALIAN SAUSAGE, CHOPPED
- BLACK PEPPER, TO TASTE
- 3 SMALL TOMATOES, PEELED, SEEDED, AND SLICED
- 2½ OZ. PECORINO CHEESE, GRATED
- 10 OZ. FRESH MOZZARELLA CHEESE, DRAINED AND TORN

Focaccia di Carnevale Salentina, *see page 427*

SFINCIONE PALERMITANO

YIELD: 1 LARGE FOCACCIA / **ACTIVE TIME:** 1 HOUR / **TOTAL TIME:** 4 HOURS AND 30 MINUTES

The soft and spongy consistency of this Sicilian focaccia's crumb makes this one of the greatest treats the Mediterranean region has to offer.

INGREDIENTS:

- 22½ OZ. (638 G) WATER
- 2½ TEASPOONS (7.5 G) ACTIVE DRY YEAST
- 19¾ OZ. (560 G) BREAD FLOUR, PLUS MORE AS NEEDED
- 8.4 OZ. (238 G) FINE SEMOLINA FLOUR
- 1 TABLESPOON (18 G) FINE SEA SALT, PLUS MORE TO TASTE
- EXTRA-VIRGIN OLIVE OIL, AS NEEDED
- 2 ONIONS, SLICED
- 23 OZ. CRUSHED TOMATOES
- 11–14 ANCHOVIES IN OLIVE OIL, DRAINED AND TORN
- BLACK PEPPER, TO TASTE
- 1 LB. CACIOCAVALLO CHEESE, TWO-THIRDS CUBED, ONE-THIRD GRATED
- FRESH OREGANO, CHOPPED, TO TASTE
- BREAD CRUMBS, TO TASTE

1. Warm 3½ tablespoons of the water until it is 105°F. Add the yeast and water to a bowl and gently stir to combine. Let the mixture sit until it starts to foam, about 10 minutes.

2. In a large bowl, combine the flours, yeast mixture, and remaining water until the mixture comes together as a dough. If kneading by hand, place the dough on a flour-dusted work surface. Work the dough until it is compact, smooth, and elastic.

3. Add the salt and work the dough until it is developed, elastic, and extensible, about 5 minutes. Coat a large, clean bowl with olive oil, shape the dough into a ball, and place it in the bowl. Cover the bowl with plastic wrap, place it in a naturally warm spot, and let it rest until it has doubled in size, about 2 hours.

4. Coat the bottom of a skillet with olive oil and warm it over medium-low heat. Add the onions and cook, stirring frequently, until they are starting to brown, about 12 minutes. Add the tomatoes and three anchovies, cover the skillet, reduce the heat, and simmer until the flavor is to your liking, 20 to 30 minutes.

5. Season with salt and pepper, remove the pan from heat, and let the mixture cool completely.

6. Coat an 18 x 13–inch baking pan with olive oil, place the dough in the pan, and gently stretch it until it covers the entire pan. Cover the dough with plastic wrap and let it rest for 1 hour.

7. Preheat the oven to 430°F. Top the focaccia with the cubed caciocavallo and remaining anchovies and press down on them until they are embedded in the dough. Cover them with the tomato sauce, generously sprinkle oregano over the sauce, and drizzle olive oil over everything. Sprinkle the grated caciocavallo and a generous handful of bread crumbs over the focaccia.

8. Place the focaccia in the oven and bake for 20 minutes. Reduce the temperature to 350°F and bake for another 15 to 20 minutes, until the focaccia is golden brown on the edges and on the bottom.

9. Remove the focaccia from the oven and let it cool slightly before serving.

FACCIA DI VECCHIA

YIELD: 6 MEDIUM FOCACCIA / **ACTIVE TIME:** 1 HOUR / **TOTAL TIME:** 5 HOURS

The toppings here are the same as the ones used in sfincione, but the smaller focaccia are baked directly on the stone, as a Neapolitan pizza would be. Some versions omit both the cheese and the anchovies from the toppings, so if that sounds more to your taste, don't hesitate to go that route.

1. Place the water and yeast in a bowl, gently stir to combine, and let the mixture sit until it starts to foam, 5 to 10 minutes.

2. In a large bowl, combine the flours and yeast mixture and work the mixture until it just comes together as a dough. Place the dough on a flour-dusted work surface and knead until it is compact, smooth, and elastic.

3. Add the salt and knead until the dough is smooth, elastic, and extensible. Coat a large, clean bowl with olive oil, shape the dough into a ball, and place it in the bowl. Cover the bowl with plastic wrap, place it in a naturally warm spot, and let it rest until it has doubled in size, about 2 hours.

4. Coat the bottom of a skillet with olive oil and warm it over medium-low heat. Add the onions and cook, stirring occasionally, until they are tender, about 10 minutes. Add the tomatoes and three of the anchovies, cover the skillet, reduce the heat to low, and cook until the flavor of the mixture is to your liking, 20 to 30 minutes. Remove the pan from heat, season with salt and pepper, and let the mixture cool completely.

5. Place the dough on a flour-dusted work surface and divide it into six pieces. Shape the pieces into balls, coat a piece of plastic wrap with olive oil, and place it over the balls of dough. Let them rest for 1 hour.

6. Preheat the oven to the maximum temperature and place a baking stone or steel on the middle rack of the oven as it warms.

7. Gently flatten the balls of dough and cover them with the tomato sauce. Top them with the tuma, the remaining anchovies, the caciocavallo, and a generous amount of oregano, bread crumbs, and olive oil.

8. Using a peel or flat baking sheet, transfer the focaccia onto the heated baking implement and bake for about 30 minutes, until the edges are golden brown.

9. Remove the focaccia from the oven and let them cool slightly before serving.

INGREDIENTS:

19.4 OZ. (550 G) WARM WATER (105°F)

2½ TEASPOONS (7.5 G) ACTIVE DRY YEAST

19¾ OZ. (560 G) BREAD FLOUR, PLUS MORE AS NEEDED

8.4 OZ. (238 G) FINELY GROUND DURUM WHEAT FLOUR (SEMOLA RIMACINATA)

1 TABLESPOON (17 G) FINE SEA SALT, PLUS MORE TO TASTE

EXTRA-VIRGIN OLIVE OIL, AS NEEDED

2 ONIONS, SLICED

23 OZ. CANNED WHOLE PEELED TOMATOES, WITH THEIR LIQUID, GENTLY CRUSHED BY HAND

11-14 ANCHOVIES IN OLIVE OIL, DRAINED AND TORN

BLACK PEPPER, TO TASTE

10½ OZ. TUMA CHEESE, CUBED

7 OZ. CACIOCAVALLO CHEESE, GRATED

FRESH OREGANO, FINELY CHOPPED, TO TASTE

BREAD CRUMBS, TO TASTE

MUSTAZZEDDU

YIELD: 1 LARGE FOCACCIA / **ACTIVE TIME:** 40 MINUTES / **TOTAL TIME:** 4 HOURS AND 30 MINUTES

Traditionally, this was the sustenance food of the Sardinian women who baked for their community; they used to make this focaccia to feed themselves during the daylong process of making large batches of bread.

INGREDIENTS:

- 28 OZ. CHERRY TOMATOES, CHOPPED
- 2 GARLIC CLOVES, CHOPPED
- 4 FRESH BASIL LEAVES
- 1 TABLESPOON (12.5 G) EXTRA-VIRGIN OLIVE OIL, PLUS MORE AS NEEDED
- 1½ TEASPOONS (9 G) FINE SEA SALT, PLUS MORE TO TASTE
- 11.6 OZ. (329 G) WATER
- 2 TEASPOONS (6 G) ACTIVE DRY YEAST
- 12.3 OZ. (349 G) FINELY GROUND DURUM WHEAT FLOUR (SEMOLA RIMACINATA)
- 5.3 OZ. (150 G) BREAD FLOUR, PLUS MORE AS NEEDED
- BLACK PEPPER, TO TASTE

1. Place the tomatoes, garlic, basil leaves, and a generous amount of olive oil in a bowl, season the mixture with salt, and stir to combine. Let the mixture sit for 2 hours, drain it in a colander, and let it drain further for 1 hour.

2. Warm 3½ tablespoons of the water until it is about 105°F. Add the yeast and water to a bowl and gently stir to combine. Let the mixture sit until it starts to foam, about 10 minutes.

3. In a large bowl, combine the flours, olive oil, yeast mixture, and remaining water until the dough holds together. Add the salt and work the dough until it is compact, smooth, and elastic. Cover the bowl with a damp kitchen towel and let it rest at room temperature until it has doubled in size, about 2 hours.

4. Place the dough on a flour-dusted work surface and roll it out until it is an approximately ¾-inch-thick disk. Line a baking sheet with parchment paper, place the dough on it, cover it with the kitchen towel, and let it rest for another hour.

5. Position a rack in the middle of the oven and preheat the oven to 430°F. Place the tomato mixture on the focaccia, making sure to leave some dough uncovered at the edges. Season the focaccia with salt and pepper and fold the dough over the filling. You can leave the filling exposed or cover it completely; both are traditional in Sardinia.

6. Brush the dough with olive oil, place the pan directly on the bottom of the oven, and bake for 10 minutes. Reduce the temperature to 390°F, transfer the focaccia to the center rack, and bake for 30 to 40 minutes, until it is golden brown on the edges and on the bottom. Remove the focaccia from the oven and let it cool slightly before serving.

FOCACCIA MESSINESE

YIELD: 1 LARGE FOCACCIA / **ACTIVE TIME:** 40 MINUTES / **TOTAL TIME:** 4 HOURS AND 30 MINUTES

This delicious focaccia reigns in Messina, where escarole is queen. If you're searching for some way to make salad look and taste amazing, look no further.

INGREDIENTS:

- 14.8 OZ. (420 G) WARM WATER (105°F)
- 2½ TEASPOONS (7.5 G) ACTIVE DRY YEAST
- 1 LB. (454 G) BREAD FLOUR, PLUS MORE AS NEEDED
- 8.8 OZ. (249 G) FINELY GROUND DURUM WHEAT FLOUR (SEMOLA RIMACINATA)
- 0.7 OZ. (20 G) EXTRA-VIRGIN OLIVE OIL, PLUS MORE AS NEEDED
- 1 TABLESPOON (17 G) FINE SEA SALT, PLUS MORE TO TASTE
- 12 ANCHOVIES IN OLIVE OIL, DRAINED AND TORN
- 21.1 OZ. (598 G) CACIOCAVALLO CHEESE, CUBED
- 14 OZ. (397 G) ESCAROLE, CHOPPED
- 3 TOMATOES, CHOPPED
- FRESH OREGANO, FINELY CHOPPED, TO TASTE
- BLACK PEPPER, TO TASTE

1. Place the water and yeast in a bowl, gently stir to combine, and let the mixture sit until it starts to foam, about 10 minutes.

2. In a large bowl, combine the flours, olive oil, and yeast mixture and work the mixture until it just comes together as a dough. Place the dough on a flour-dusted work surface and knead until it is compact, smooth, and elastic.

3. Add the salt and knead until the dough is smooth, elastic, and extensible. Coat a large, clean bowl with olive oil, shape the dough into a ball, and place it in the bowl. Cover the bowl with plastic wrap, place it in a naturally warm spot, and let it rest until it has doubled in size, about 2 hours.

4. Coat an 18 × 13–inch baking pan with olive oil, place the dough on it, and brush the dough with more olive oil. Cover the pan with a kitchen towel and let the dough rest for 30 minutes.

5. Gently stretch the dough until it covers the entire pan. Let it rest for another hour.

6. Preheat the oven to 390°F. Press the anchovies and caciocavallo into the dough and top it with the escarole and tomatoes. Season the focaccia with oregano, salt, and pepper and drizzle olive oil over the top.

7. Place the focaccia in the oven and bake for 20 to 30 minutes, until it is golden brown and crispy on the edges and on the bottom.

8. Remove the focaccia from the oven and let it cool slightly before slicing and serving.

Focaccia Messinese, see page 435

RIANATA

YIELD: 1 LARGE FOCACCIA / **ACTIVE TIME:** 40 MINUTES / **TOTAL TIME:** 4 HOURS AND 45 MINUTES

A simple and scrumptious focaccia loaded with tomatoes and oregano. Don't hesitate to be extravagant with the latter, as rianata means "with oregano."

INGREDIENTS:

- 14.8 OZ. (420 G) WATER
- 2½ TEASPOONS (7.5 G) ACTIVE DRY YEAST
- 1 LB. (454 G) BREAD FLOUR, PLUS MORE AS NEEDED
- 8.8 OZ. (250 G) FINE SEMOLINA FLOUR
- 1 TABLESPOON PLUS 1 TEASPOON (17 G) EXTRA-VIRGIN OLIVE OIL, PLUS MORE AS NEEDED
- 1 TABLESPOON (18 G) FINE SEA SALT, PLUS MORE TO TASTE
- 7-8 ANCHOVIES IN OLIVE OIL, DRAINED
- 30 CHERRY TOMATOES, HALVED
- ½ LB. PECORINO CHEESE, GRATED
- FRESH OREGANO, CHOPPED, TO TASTE

1. Warm 3½ tablespoons of the water until it is 105°F. Add the yeast and water to a bowl and gently stir to combine. Let the mixture sit until it starts to foam, about 10 minutes.

2. In a large bowl, combine the flours, olive oil, yeast mixture, and remaining water until the mixture comes together as a dough. Place the dough on a flour-dusted work surface and knead the dough until it is compact, smooth, and elastic.

3. Add the salt and knead until the dough is developed, elastic, and extensible, about 5 minutes. Coat a large, clean bowl with olive oil, shape the dough into a ball, and place it in the bowl. Cover the bowl with plastic wrap, place it in a naturally warm spot, and let it rest until it has doubled in size, about 2 hours.

4. Coat an 18 x 13–inch baking sheet with olive oil, place the dough on it, and brush the dough with more olive oil. Cover the dough with a kitchen towel and let the dough rest for 30 minutes.

5. Gently stretch the dough until it covers the entire pan. Let it rest for another hour.

6. Preheat the oven to 430°F. Press the anchovies and tomatoes into the dough, sprinkle the pecorino over the top, season with salt and oregano, and drizzle olive oil over the focaccia.

7. Place the focaccia in the oven and bake for 20 to 30 minutes, until the focaccia is golden brown and crispy on the edges and on the bottom.

8. Remove the focaccia from the oven and let it cool slightly before serving.

SCACCIA RAGUSANA

YIELD: 3 MEDIUM FOCACCIA / **ACTIVE TIME:** 1 HOUR AND 15 MINUTES / **TOTAL TIME:** 3 HOURS AND 20 MINUTES

This layered focaccia from Ragusa and Modica is a beloved street food and comes in many variations. Popular fillings are eggplant with tomato sauce, broccoli with Italian sausage, and this one, with tomato sauce, onions, and caciocavallo cheese.

INGREDIENTS:

- 11.8 OZ. (335 G) WARM WATER (105°F)
- 2 TEASPOONS (6 G) ACTIVE DRY YEAST
- 21.1 OZ. (598 G) FINELY GROUND DURUM WHEAT FLOUR (SEMOLA RIMACINATA), PLUS MORE AS NEEDED
- 1½ TEASPOONS (8.2 G) FINE SEA SALT, PLUS MORE TO TASTE
- EXTRA-VIRGIN OLIVE OIL, AS NEEDED
- 21 OZ. ONIONS, SLICED THIN
- 21 OZ. CANNED WHOLE PEELED TOMATOES, DRAINED AND CRUSHED BY HAND
- 10½ OZ. CACIOCAVALLO CHEESE, GRATED

1. Place the water and yeast in a bowl, gently stir to combine, and let the mixture sit until it starts to foam, about 10 minutes.

2. In a large bowl, combine the flour and yeast mixture and work the mixture until it just holds together. Place the dough on a flour-dusted work surface and knead until it is compact, smooth, and elastic.

3. Coat a large, clean bowl with olive oil, shape the dough into a ball, and place it in the bowl. Cover the bowl with plastic wrap, place it in a naturally warm spot, and let it rest until it has doubled in size, about 2 hours.

4. Coat the bottom of a skillet with olive oil and warm it over medium-low heat. Add the onions and cook, stirring occasionally, until they are tender, about 10 minutes. Add the tomatoes, cover the skillet, reduce the heat to low, and cook until the flavor of the mixture is to your liking, 20 to 30 minutes. Remove the pan from heat, season the mixture with salt, and let it cool completely.

5. Preheat the oven to 430°F and line a baking sheet with parchment paper. Place the dough on a flour-dusted work surface, divide it into three pieces, and shape them into balls. Roll each ball into a thin rectangle. Cover each focaccia with some of the tomato sauce and a generous sprinkle of the caciocavallo, leaving a 1-inch border around the edges. Fold the short ends of the focaccia toward the center. Cover the focaccia with more tomato sauce and caciocavallo, leaving a border near the edges again. Fold the short ends of the focaccia toward the center. Cover the focaccia with more sauce and caciocavallo and fold the focaccia in half.

6. Place the focaccia on the baking sheet, brush them with olive oil, and poke holes in them with a fork. Place the focaccia in the oven and bake for 25 to 30 minutes, until they are golden brown and crispy.

7. Remove the focaccia from the oven and let them cool slightly before serving.

FOCACCETTE DI AULLA

YIELD: 16 SMALL FOCACCIA / **ACTIVE TIME:** 30 MINUTES / **TOTAL TIME:** 4 HOURS

These miniature focaccia are really fragrant due to the presence of cornmeal. Focaccette di Aulla are traditionally baked in special pans called testi, which are placed directly over an open fire. Here you find a recipe developed for the standard kitchen oven. And a tip: focaccette are delicious when cut open while still warm and filled with fresh cheese and cold cuts.

INGREDIENTS:

- 10.6 OZ. (300 G) LUKEWARM WATER (90°F)
- 1¾ TEASPOONS (5.2 G) ACTIVE DRY YEAST
- 8.8 OZ. (250 G) ALL-PURPOSE FLOUR, PLUS MORE AS NEEDED
- 8.8 OZ. (950 G) FINELY GROUND CORNMEAL
- 1¾ TEASPOONS (9.5 G) FINE SEA SALT
- EXTRA-VIRGIN OLIVE OIL, AS NEEDED

1. Place the water and yeast in a bowl, gently stir to combine, and let the mixture sit until it starts to foam, about 10 minutes.

2. In a large bowl, combine the flour and cornmeal and then incorporate the yeast mixture. Work the mixture until it just comes together as a dough. If kneading by hand, place the dough on a flour-dusted work surface. Work it until it is compact, smooth, and elastic.

3. Add the salt and knead until the dough is developed, elastic, and extensible, about 5 minutes. Coat a large, clean bowl with olive oil, shape the dough into a ball, and place it in the bowl. Cover the bowl with plastic wrap, place it in a naturally warm spot, and let it rest until it has doubled in size, about 2 hours.

4. Divide the dough into 16 pieces and shape each piece into a ball. Cover the balls with plastic wrap and let them rest for 1 hour.

5. Preheat the oven to 390°F and place a baking stone or steel on the middle rack of the oven as it warms. Flatten the balls of dough until they are approximately ½ inch thick.

6. Using a peel or flat baking sheet, transfer the focaccia onto the heated baking implement and bake until they are golden brown, 15 to 20 minutes.

7. Remove the focaccia from the oven and let them cool slightly before serving.

FOCACCIA PORTOSCUSESE

YIELD: 4 MEDIUM FOCACCIA / **ACTIVE TIME:** 40 MINUTES / **TOTAL TIME:** 3 HOURS AND 45 MINUTES

Here's a traditional Sardinian focaccia that looks like a Neapolitan pizza but has a special dough that contains more potato than flour. A must try!

INGREDIENTS:

- 5.3 OZ. (150 G) MILK
- 2 TEASPOONS (6 G) ACTIVE DRY YEAST
- 10.6 OZ. (300 G) BREAD FLOUR, PLUS MORE AS NEEDED
- 28.2 OZ. (800 G) POTATOES, BOILED, PEELED, AND MASHED
- 1½ TEASPOONS (8.2 G) FINE SEA SALT, PLUS MORE TO TASTE
- EXTRA-VIRGIN OLIVE OIL, AS NEEDED
- 14 OZ. ONIONS, SLICED THIN
- 14 OZ. CANNED WHOLE PEELED TOMATOES, DRAINED AND GENTLY CRUSHED BY HAND
- 7 OZ. PECORINO CHEESE, GRATED

1. Warm 3½ tablespoons of the milk until it is 105°F. Add the milk and yeast to a bowl and gently stir to combine. Let the mixture sit until it starts to foam, about 10 minutes.

2. In a large bowl, combine the flour, potatoes, and yeast mixture until a soft and not-too-sticky dough forms. If needed, gradually add the remaining milk; how much you need depends on how watery the potatoes are.

3. Work the salt into the dough, place the dough on a flour-dusted work surface, and work the dough until it is smooth. Coat a large, clean bowl with olive oil, shape the dough into a ball, and place it in the bowl. Cover the bowl with plastic wrap, place it in a naturally warm spot, and let it rest until it has doubled in size, about 2 hours.

4. Coat the bottom of a skillet with olive oil and warm it over medium-low heat. Add the onions and cook, stirring occasionally, until they are tender, about 10 minutes. Add the tomatoes, cover the skillet, reduce the heat to low, and cook until the flavor of the mixture is to your liking, 20 to 30 minutes. Remove the pan from heat, season the mixture with salt, and let it cool completely.

5. Place the dough on a flour-dusted work surface and divide it into four pieces. Shape the pieces into balls, coat a piece of plastic wrap with olive oil, and place it over the dough. Let the dough rest for 1 hour.

6. Preheat the oven to 390°F and place a baking stone or steel on the middle rack of the oven as it warms. Gently flatten the balls of dough and cover them with the tomato sauce. Sprinkle the pecorino over the focaccia and drizzle olive oil on top. Use a peel to transfer the focaccia onto the heated baking implement and bake for 20 to 25 minutes, until the edges and bottom are golden brown.

7. Remove the focaccia from the oven and let them cool slightly before serving.

SCHIACCIA TOSCANA

YIELD: 1 LARGE FOCACCIA / **ACTIVE TIME:** 30 MINUTES / **TOTAL TIME:** 4 HOURS AND 30 MINUTES

This focaccia is rather thin and crunchy, making it the perfect flatbread to pair with an early evening aperitif.

INGREDIENTS:

- 7 OZ. (198 G) WARM WATER (105°F)
- 1¾ TEASPOONS (5.2 G) ACTIVE DRY YEAST
- 17.6 OZ. (500 G) ALL-PURPOSE FLOUR, PLUS MORE AS NEEDED
- 1¾ OZ. (50 G) WHITE WINE
- 1¾ OZ. (50 G) MILK
- 1 TABLESPOON (13 G) SUGAR
- 1 TEASPOON (5.5 G) FINE SEA SALT, PLUS MORE TO TASTE
- EXTRA-VIRGIN OLIVE OIL, AS NEEDED

1. Place the water and yeast in a bowl, gently stir to combine, and let the mixture sit until it starts to foam, about 10 minutes.

2. In a large bowl, combine the flour, wine, milk, sugar, and yeast mixture. Work the mixture until it just comes together as a dough. If kneading by hand, place the dough on a flour-dusted work surface. Knead the dough until it is compact, smooth, and elastic.

3. Add the salt and work the dough until it is developed, elastic, and extensible, about 5 minutes. Coat a large, clean bowl with olive oil, shape the dough into a ball, and place it in the bowl. Cover the bowl with plastic wrap, place it in a naturally warm spot, and let it rest until it has doubled in size, about 2 hours.

4. Generously coat an 18 × 13–inch baking pan with olive oil, place the dough in the center of the pan, and gently flatten it into an oval. Brush the dough with olive oil, cover it with plastic wrap, and let it rest for 30 minutes.

5. Use your hands to flatten the dough and spread it toward the edges of the baking pan. If the dough does not want to extend to the edges of the pan right away, let it rest for 15 to 20 minutes before trying again.

6. Brush the focaccia with more olive oil and use your fingers to make indentations in the dough. Cover the focaccia with plastic wrap and let it rest for another 30 minutes.

7. Preheat the oven to 480°F.

8. Brush the dough with more olive oil and season it with salt. Place the focaccia in the oven and bake for 15 minutes, until the valleys between the bubbles are a deep golden brown. As this focaccia is supposed to be slightly crunchy, you want the bottom to be golden brown as well.

9. Remove the focaccia from the oven and let it cool slightly before serving.

SCHIACCIA ALL'UVA

YIELD: 1 LARGE FOCACCIA / **ACTIVE TIME:** 40 MINUTES / **TOTAL TIME:** 3 HOURS

Popular in Tuscany since the days of the Etruscans, this grape-enriched focaccia was linked to the rituals of the vendemmia, the local wine grape harvest, and made with the unsalted bread dough that is traditional in the region.

INGREDIENTS:

18.3 OZ. (519 G) WATER

1 TABLESPOON (9 G) ACTIVE DRY YEAST

31¾ OZ. (900 G) ALL-PURPOSE FLOUR, PLUS MORE AS NEEDED

2 TEASPOONS (14 G) HONEY

2.8 OZ. (79 G) EXTRA-VIRGIN OLIVE OIL, PLUS MORE AS NEEDED

4 OZ. (113 G) SUGAR

2.8 LBS. PURPLE GRAPES

CASTER SUGAR, FOR TOPPING

1. Place the water and yeast in a bowl, gently stir to combine, and let the mixture sit until it starts to foam, about 10 minutes.

2. In a large bowl, combine the flour, honey, and yeast mixture. Work the mixture until it just holds together. If kneading by hand, place the dough on a flour-dusted work surface. Work it until it is compact, smooth, and elastic. Coat a large, clean bowl with olive oil, shape the dough into a ball, and place it in the bowl. Cover the bowl with plastic wrap, place it in a naturally warm spot, and let it rest until it has doubled in size, about 2 hours.

3. Preheat the oven to 360°F. Working the dough with your hands, incorporate the sugar and olive oil. Divide the dough in half and roll each piece into a rectangle that is approximately the size of an 18 × 13–inch baking sheet.

4. Coat the baking sheet with olive oil and place one piece of dough on it. Place half of the grapes on top of the dough and gently press down on them. Sprinkle caster sugar and drizzle olive oil over the grapes.

5. Cover the grapes with the remaining piece of dough and crimp the edges to seal the focaccia. Place the remaining grapes on top of the focaccia and gently press down on them. Sprinkle caster sugar and drizzle olive oil over the grapes.

6. Place the focaccia in the oven and bake for 40 minutes, until it is golden brown. Remove the focaccia from the oven and let it cool briefly before serving.

SCHIACCIATA CON CIPOLLA E SALVIA

YIELD: 1 LARGE FOCACCIA / **ACTIVE TIME:** 40 MINUTES / **TOTAL TIME:** 4 HOURS AND 30 MINUTES

In Umbria, it is very typical to eat a thin focaccia flavored with golden onions and sage, a delicious combination that can provide ample warmth on a cold winter day.

INGREDIENTS:

- 10.6 OZ. (300 G) WARM WATER (105°F)
- 1¾ TEASPOONS (5.2 G) ACTIVE DRY YEAST
- 17.6 OZ. (500 G) ALL-PURPOSE FLOUR, PLUS MORE AS NEEDED
- 2½ TEASPOONS (10 G) SUGAR
- 1 TEASPOON (5.5 G) FINE SEA SALT, PLUS MORE TO TASTE
- 30 FRESH SAGE LEAVES, FINELY CHOPPED
- EXTRA-VIRGIN OLIVE OIL, AS NEEDED
- 4 LARGE YELLOW ONIONS, SLICED THIN

1. Place the water and yeast in a bowl, gently stir to combine, and let the mixture sit until it starts to foam, about 10 minutes.

2. In a large bowl, combine the flour, sugar, and yeast mixture. Work the mixture until it just comes together as a dough. If kneading by hand, place the dough on a flour-dusted work surface. Work it until it is compact, smooth, and elastic.

3. Add the salt and half of the sage and knead until they have been incorporated and the dough appears smooth and elastic again. Coat a large, clean bowl with olive oil, shape the dough into a ball, and place it in the bowl. Cover the bowl with plastic wrap, place it in a naturally warm spot, and let it rest until it has doubled in size, about 2 hours.

4. Place the onions on a piece of parchment paper, sprinkle salt over them, and let them dry out.

5. Generously coat an 18 × 13–inch baking pan with olive oil, place the dough in the center of the pan, and gently flatten it into an oval. Brush the dough generously with olive oil, cover it with a kitchen towel, and let it rest for 30 minutes.

6. Use your hands to flatten the dough and stretch it toward the edges of the baking pan. If the dough does not want to extend to the edges of the pan right away, let it rest for 15 to 20 minutes before trying again.

7. Brush the focaccia with more olive oil and use your fingers to make indentations in the dough. Cover it with plastic wrap and let it rest for another 30 minutes. Preheat the oven to 390°F.

8. Distribute the onions and remaining sage over the focaccia. Drizzle olive oil over the top and season with just a bit of salt, keeping in mind that the onions have been salted.

9. Place the focaccia in the oven and bake for 30 to 35 minutes, until the edges are golden brown.

10. Remove the focaccia from the oven and let it cool slightly before serving.

TORTA AL TESTO

YIELD: 2 SMALL FOCACCIA / **ACTIVE TIME:** 25 MINUTES / **TOTAL TIME:** 1 HOUR

One of the many unleavened focaccia from Central Italy that have survived the test of time. Popular in Etruscan times (approximately 2,500 years ago), torta al testo is faster to make than a regular focaccia. It is traditionally cooked in a specific pan called a testo, but it still tastes delicious if cooked in a cast-iron or nonstick skillet.

1. In a large bowl, combine the flour, salt, and baking soda. Incorporate the water gradually and work the mixture until it comes together. If kneading by hand, place the dough on a flour-dusted work surface. Work it until it is compact, smooth, and elastic. Divide the dough in half and shape each piece into a ball. Cover the balls with plastic wrap and let them rest at room temperature for 30 minutes.

2. Warm a 10-inch cast-iron skillet over medium heat. Using a rolling pin, flatten each ball until it is a disk that is approximately ¼ inch thick. Use a fork to poke holes in the disks.

3. Working with one disk at a time, place it in the pan and cook until it is golden brown all over, about 6 minutes per side.

4. Cut the cooked focaccia into wedges. These can be enjoyed as is, or filled with cold cuts, cheese, or sautéed vegetables.

INGREDIENTS:

17.6 OZ. (500 G) ALL-PURPOSE FLOUR, PLUS MORE AS NEEDED

1 TEASPOON (5.5 G) FINE SEA SALT

1 TEASPOON (6 G) BAKING SODA

8.8 OZ. (250 G) WATER

TORTA AL TESTO CON I CICCIOLI

YIELD: 2 SMALL FOCACCIA / **ACTIVE TIME:** 25 MINUTES / **TOTAL TIME:** 1 HOUR AND 15 MINUTES

This classic version of torta al testo includes small bites of a rustic cured pork known as ciccioli. In the absence of ciccioli, cubed pancetta or bacon will do.

INGREDIENTS:

- 5 OZ. CICCIOLI, DICED
- 17.6 OZ. (500 G) ALL-PURPOSE FLOUR, PLUS MORE AS NEEDED
- 1 TEASPOON (5.5 G) FINE SEA SALT
- 1 TEASPOON (6 G) BAKING SODA
- 8.8 OZ. (250 G) WATER

1. Place the ciccioli in a large skillet and cook over medium heat until the fat has rendered and it starts to turn crispy, about 6 minutes. Transfer the ciccioli to a plate and let it cool.

2. In a large bowl, combine the flour, salt, and baking soda. Incorporate the water gradually and work the mixture until it comes together as a dough. Add the ciccioli. If kneading by hand, place the dough on a flour-dusted work surface. Work it until it is compact, smooth, and elastic. Divide the dough in half and shape each piece into a ball. Cover the balls with plastic wrap and let them rest at room temperature for 30 minutes.

3. Warm a 10-inch cast-iron skillet over medium heat. Using a rolling pin, flatten each ball until it is a disk that is approximately ¼ inch thick. Use a fork to poke holes in the disks.

4. Working with one disk at a time, place it in the pan and cook until it is golden brown all over, about 6 minutes per side.

5. Cut the cooked focaccia into wedges. These can be enjoyed as is, or filled with cold cuts, cheese, or sautéed vegetables.

TORTA AL TESTO CON FARINA DI MAIS

YIELD: 2 SMALL FOCACCIA / **ACTIVE TIME:** 25 MINUTES / **TOTAL TIME:** 1 HOUR

This popular version of the Umbrian torta al testo uses cornmeal. It's an easy recipe made for the modern home.

INGREDIENTS:

- 8.8 OZ. (250 G) ALL-PURPOSE FLOUR, PLUS MORE AS NEEDED
- 8.8 OZ. (250 G) CORNMEAL
- 1 TEASPOON (5.5 G) FINE SEA SALT
- 1 TEASPOON (6 G) BAKING SODA
- 8.8 OZ. (250 G) WATER

1. In a large bowl, combine the flour, cornmeal, salt, and baking soda. Incorporate the water gradually and work the mixture until it comes together as a dough. If kneading by hand, place the dough on a flour-dusted work surface. Work it until it is compact, smooth, and elastic. Divide the dough in half and shape each piece into a ball. Cover the balls with plastic wrap and let them rest at room temperature for 30 minutes.

2. Warm a 10-inch cast-iron skillet over medium heat. Using a rolling pin, flatten each ball until it is a disk that is approximately ⅓ inch thick. Use a fork to poke holes in the disks.

3. Working with one disk at a time, place the focaccia in the pan and cook until it is golden brown all over, about 6 minutes per side.

4. Cut the cooked focaccia into wedges. These can be enjoyed as is, or filled with cold cuts, cheese, or sautéed vegetables.

Torta al Testo con Farina di Mais, see page 451

CRESCIA SFOGLIATA

YIELD: 6 SMALL FOCACCIA / **ACTIVE TIME:** 45 MINUTES / **TOTAL TIME:** 4 HOURS

As one would expect from the stylish city of Urbino in the Marche region, this focaccia is a luxurious take on the piadina. Crescia sfogliata is rumored to have been born during the Renaissance, specifically in the kitchen of the duke of Urbino. It is wonderful on its own but is at its best if accompanied by Italian soft cheeses, like crescenza or stracchino, and vegetables or cold cuts.

INGREDIENTS:

- 17.6 OZ. (500 G) ALL-PURPOSE FLOUR, PLUS MORE AS NEEDED
- 7 OZ. (198 G) WATER
- 3½ OZ. (100 G) LARD, PLUS MORE AS NEEDED
- 2 EGGS
- 1¾ TEASPOONS (10.5 G) TABLE SALT
- 2 PINCHES OF BLACK PEPPER

1. In a large bowl, combine the flour, water, lard, eggs, salt, and pepper and work the mixture until it just comes together as a dough. If kneading by hand, place the dough on a flour-dusted work surface. Work it until it is compact, smooth, and elastic.

2. Shape the dough into a ball, cover it with plastic wrap, and let it rest at room temperature for 30 minutes.

3. Divide the dough into six pieces and shape them into balls. Flatten each ball into a disk, brush them with lard, and roll them up as tightly as possible. Twist the rolls into spirals. Line a baking sheet with parchment paper, place the spirals on it, and cover them with plastic wrap. Refrigerate for 30 minutes to 1 hour.

4. Remove the spirals from the refrigerator and flatten them into disks that are approximately ⅛ inch thick.

5. Warm a 10-inch skillet over medium heat. Working with one disk at a time, cook the focaccia until dark spots appear all over them, about 5 minutes per side.

6. Let the cooked focaccia cool briefly before enjoying.

PIZZA BIANCA ROMANA

YIELD: 2 SMALL FOCACCIA / **ACTIVE TIME:** 30 MINUTES / **TOTAL TIME:** 8 HOURS

In Rome, focaccia is referred to as pizza bianca, which can be found in virtually every bakery. Compared to other regional focaccias, this is probably the most alveolated one, due to the long fermentation time, strong flour used, and relatively high water content. It is scrumptious when filled with cold cuts—ideally mortadella or Parma ham—and fresh figs, but there are countless possible fillings.

INGREDIENTS:

18½ OZ. (524 G) WARM WATER (105°F)

1¼ TEASPOONS (3.7 G) ACTIVE DRY YEAST

24.7 OZ. (700 G) BREAD FLOUR OR "00" PIZZA FLOUR, PLUS MORE AS NEEDED

2 TEASPOONS (6 G) DIASTATIC MALT

1¾ TEASPOONS (44 G) SUGAR

1.4 OZ. (40 G) EXTRA-VIRGIN OLIVE OIL, PLUS MORE AS NEEDED

1 TABLESPOON (17 G) FINE SEA SALT, PLUS MORE TO TASTE

1. Place the water and yeast in a bowl, gently stir to combine, and let the mixture sit until it starts to foam, about 10 minutes.

2. In a large bowl, combine the flour, yeast mixture, malt, sugar, and olive oil and work the mixture until it just holds together. Using your hands or a stand mixer, work the dough until it is smooth and elastic, 10 to 15 minutes.

3. Add the salt and knead the dough until it is extremely elastic. Coat a large, clean bowl with olive oil, shape the dough into a ball, and place it in the bowl. Cover the bowl with plastic wrap, place it in a naturally warm spot, and let it rest until it has doubled in size and is full of bubbles, about 5 hours.

4. Line two baking sheets with parchment paper. Invert the dough onto a flour-dusted work surface and divide it in half. Place each piece of dough on a baking sheet and flatten it into an oval. Let it rest for 2 to 3 hours in a naturally warm spot, stretching the dough lengthwise every 30 minutes and being careful not to press down on it too much. After the last stretch, generously drizzle olive oil and sprinkle salt over the pieces of dough.

5. Preheat the oven to 480°F and place a baking stone or steel in the oven as it warms.

6. Using a peel or flat baking sheet, transfer one of the focaccia and its parchment paper onto the heated baking implement. Bake for 10 to 15 minutes, until it is golden brown. Remove the focaccia from the oven and brush it with olive oil. Repeat with the remaining focaccia.

CACCIANNANZE

YIELD: 1 LARGE FOCACCIA / **ACTIVE TIME:** 30 MINUTES / **TOTAL TIME:** 3 HOURS

A very simple and easy focaccia from the rural portion of the Marche region, cacciannanze is great as an appetizer but can also work as a side for dinner.

INGREDIENTS:

- CLASSIC FOCACCIA DOUGH (SEE PAGE 396)
- ALL-PURPOSE FLOUR, AS NEEDED
- EXTRA-VIRGIN OLIVE OIL, AS NEEDED
- 2 TABLESPOONS FRESH ROSEMARY
- 3 GARLIC CLOVES, SLICED THIN
- SALT, TO TASTE
- LARD, AS NEEDED (OPTIONAL)

1. Place the dough on a flour-dusted work surface and shape it into a loose ball, making sure not to press down on the dough and deflate it. Coat an 18 × 13–inch baking sheet with olive oil, place the dough in the center, and gently flatten it into an oval. Brush the dough with olive oil, cover it with plastic wrap, and let it rest at room temperature for 1 hour.

2. Place the rosemary, garlic, and a few pinches of salt in a mixing bowl and stir to combine. Use your hands to flatten the dough and stretch it toward the edges of the baking sheet. If the dough does not want to extend to the edges of the pan right away, let it rest for 15 to 20 minutes before trying again.

3. Brush the dough with olive oil, sprinkle the rosemary-and-garlic mixture over the top, and let the focaccia rest at room temperature for another 30 minutes. If desired, you can also sprinkle chunks of lard over the focaccia. Preheat the oven to 390°F.

4. Place the focaccia in the oven and bake for 15 to 20 minutes, until it is golden brown and slightly crispy on the edges. Remove the focaccia from the oven and let it cool slightly before serving.

SMACAFAM

YIELD: 1 MEDIUM FOCACCIA / **ACTIVE TIME:** 10 MINUTES / **TOTAL TIME:** 1 HOUR

The name of this dish from Trentino-Alto Adige means "keep away the hunger." Residing somewhere between a focaccia and a quiche, smacafam is typically served in bite-size pieces.

INGREDIENTS:

- BUTTER, AS NEEDED
- 14 OZ. (397 G) ALL-PURPOSE FLOUR, PLUS MORE AS NEEDED
- 2½ CUPS (569 G) WHOLE MILK
- 2 EGGS
- ½ LB. SWEET ITALIAN SAUSAGE, CHOPPED
- 2 TEASPOONS (12 G) FINE SEA SALT
- 2 PINCHES OF BLACK PEPPER

1. Preheat the oven to 360°F and coat a 13 x 9–inch baking pan with butter. Place all of the ingredients, except for about 3 oz. of the sausage, in a mixing bowl and stir until the batter looks smooth. Pour the batter into the pan and sprinkle the remaining sausage over the top.

2. Place the focaccia in the oven and bake for 30 to 40 minutes, until the edges are golden brown. Remove the focaccia from the oven and let it cool briefly before serving.

PINZA ONTA POLESANA

YIELD: 1 LARGE FOCACCIA / **ACTIVE TIME:** 40 MINUTES / **TOTAL TIME:** 4 HOURS

Most versions of this recipe include ciccioli, a type of processed pork that pancetta or bacon can be substituted for; the meat can also be removed altogether. This focaccia is traditionally made with lard, but feel free to use butter or margarine if you prefer.

INGREDIENTS:

- 7 OZ. PANCETTA, DICED
- 4.6 OZ. (130 G) LUKEWARM WATER (90°F)
- 2 TEASPOONS (6 G) ACTIVE DRY YEAST
- 21.1 OZ. (600 G) ALL-PURPOSE FLOUR, PLUS MORE AS NEEDED
- 7 OZ. (198 G) WHOLE MILK
- 4.2 OZ. (119 G) LARD, AT ROOM TEMPERATURE AND CHOPPED, PLUS MORE AS NEEDED
- 2 TEASPOONS (11 G) FINE SEA SALT
- 2 PINCHES OF BLACK PEPPER
- EXTRA-VIRGIN OLIVE OIL, AS NEEDED
- BREAD CRUMBS, AS NEEDED
- COARSE SEA SALT, TO TASTE

1. Place half of the pancetta in a skillet and cook over medium heat until the fat has rendered, about 4 minutes. Transfer the pancetta to a paper towel–lined plate to cool.

2. Place the water and yeast in a bowl, gently stir to combine, and let the mixture sit until it starts to foam, about 10 minutes.

3. In a large bowl, combine the flour, milk, half of the lard, and the yeast mixture and work the mixture until it just holds together. If kneading by hand, place the dough on a flour-dusted work surface. Work the dough until it is compact, smooth, and elastic.

4. Add the fine sea salt, pepper, and the cooled pancetta and work the dough until it is developed, elastic, and extensible, about 5 minutes. Coat a large, clean bowl with olive oil, shape the dough into a ball, and place it in the bowl. Cover the bowl with plastic wrap, place it in a naturally warm spot, and let it rest until it has doubled in size, about 2 hours.

5. Coat an 18 × 13–inch baking pan with lard and sprinkle a light coating of bread crumbs over the pan. Place the dough in the pan and stretch it into a thick rectangle, making sure not to stretch it all the way to the edges of the pan. Cover the pan with plastic wrap and let the dough rest at room temperature for 1 hour.

6. Gently stretch the dough until it covers the entire pan. Let it rest for another 30 minutes. Preheat the oven to 410°F.

7. Sprinkle coarse sea salt over the focaccia and top it with the remaining lard. Place the focaccia in the oven and bake until it is golden brown and crispy, 30 to 35 minutes.

8. Remove the focaccia from the oven and let it cool briefly before slicing and serving.

TIROT

YIELD: 1 LARGE FOCACCIA / **ACTIVE TIME:** 40 MINUTES / **TOTAL TIME:** 4 HOURS AND 45 MINUTES

Typical of Lombardy, the region surrounding Milan, this focaccia is enriched with yellow onions, which confer a sweet note and provide a contrast to the crunchy crust.

INGREDIENTS:

- 13 OZ. (368.5 G) LUKEWARM WATER (90°F)
- 2 TEASPOONS (6 G) ACTIVE DRY YEAST
- 21.1 OZ. (600 G) ALL-PURPOSE FLOUR, PLUS MORE AS NEEDED
- 5.3 OZ. (150 G) LARD, AT ROOM TEMPERATURE AND CHOPPED, PLUS MORE AS NEEDED
- 1 LB. YELLOW ONIONS, SLICED THIN
- 2 TEASPOONS (11 G) FINE SEA SALT, PLUS MORE TO TASTE
- EXTRA-VIRGIN OLIVE OIL, AS NEEDED
- BREAD CRUMBS, AS NEEDED

1. Place the water and yeast in a bowl, gently stir to combine, and let the mixture sit until it starts to foam, about 10 minutes.

2. In a large bowl, combine the flour, two-thirds of the lard, and the yeast mixture and work the mixture until it just holds together. If kneading by hand, place the dough on a flour-dusted work surface. Work the dough until it is compact, smooth, and elastic.

3. Add the onions and salt and work the dough until the onions are well incorporated. Coat a large, clean bowl with olive oil, shape the dough into a ball, and place it in the bowl. Cover the bowl with plastic wrap, place it in a naturally warm spot, and let it rest until it has doubled in size, about 2 hours.

4. Coat an 18 × 13–inch baking pan with lard and sprinkle a light coating of bread crumbs on top to prevent the focaccia from sticking to the pan. Place the dough on a flour-dusted work surface and press it out into a thick rectangle that is smaller than the pan. Place the dough in the pan, brush the surface with olive oil, and cover the dough with a kitchen towel. Let it rest for 30 minutes.

5. Gently stretch the dough until it covers the whole pan. Let it rest for another hour.

6. Preheat the oven to 390°F.

7. Season the focaccia with salt and top it with the remaining lard. Place it in the oven and bake until the focaccia is golden brown and crispy, 30 to 35 minutes.

8. Remove the focaccia from the oven and let it cool briefly before serving.

PIZZA AL PADELLINO

YIELD: 1 SMALL FOCACCIA / **ACTIVE TIME:** 15 MINUTES / **TOTAL TIME:** 4 HOURS AND 30 MINUTES

This delicious focaccia is also called pizza al tegamino, and it is a popular street food in Turin. Although nowadays it is considered a local delicacy, pizza al padellino does not have a centuries-old tradition like most local focaccia. Instead, it is a relative newcomer on the scene.

INGREDIENTS:

- 1 BALL OF NEAPOLITAN PIZZA DOUGH (SEE PAGE 288)
- 1 TABLESPOON EXTRA-VIRGIN OLIVE OIL, PLUS MORE TO TASTE
- 1 CUP CRUSHED TOMATOES
- ½ (SCANT) TEASPOON FINE SEA SALT, PLUS MORE TO TASTE
- 2 PINCHES OF DRIED OREGANO
- 7 OZ. FRESH MOZZARELLA CHEESE, DRAINED AND SLICED

1. Place the ball of dough on a piece of parchment paper, cover it with a kitchen towel, and let it rest at room temperature until it looks soft and fully risen, 2 to 3 hours.

2. Place the dough in a 10-inch cast-iron skillet and gently spread it to the edge of the pan, making sure not to press down too hard on the dough and deflate it. Brush the dough with olive oil, cover the skillet with plastic wrap, and let the dough rest at room temperature for 30 minutes.

3. Preheat the oven to 480°F.

4. Place the tomatoes, salt, oregano, and olive oil in a mixing bowl and stir to combine. Spread the sauce over the focaccia, season it with salt, and generously drizzle olive oil over the top.

5. Place the focaccia in the oven and bake for about 10 minutes, until it is a light golden brown. Remove the focaccia, top it with the mozzarella, and return it to the oven. Bake until the mozzarella has melted and the edges of the focaccia are golden brown, about 10 minutes.

6. Remove the focaccia from the oven and let it cool briefly before serving.

FOCACCIA GENOVESE

YIELD: 1 LARGE FOCACCIA / **ACTIVE TIME:** 30 MINUTES / **TOTAL TIME:** 2 HOURS

The quintessential focaccia hails, without a doubt, from Genoa. This focaccia is generally of medium height, salty, and soft. Producing a high-quality version of this at home can be challenging, but it is achievable after a few attempts.

INGREDIENTS:

- CLASSIC FOCACCIA DOUGH (SEE PAGE 396)
- ALL-PURPOSE FLOUR, AS NEEDED
- 3 TABLESPOONS EXTRA-VIRGIN OLIVE OIL, PLUS MORE AS NEEDED
- ⅔ CUP WATER
- 1 TEASPOON FINE SEA SALT
- COARSE SEA SALT, TO TASTE

1. Place the dough on a flour-dusted work surface and shape it into a loose ball, making sure not to compress the core of the dough and deflate it. Coat an 18 × 13-inch baking pan with olive oil, place the dough on the pan, and gently flatten the dough into an oval. Cover the dough with a kitchen towel and let it rest at room temperature for 30 minutes to 1 hour.

2. Stretch the dough toward the edges of the baking pan. If the dough does not want to extend to the edges of the pan right away, let it rest for 15 to 20 minutes before trying again. Cover the dough with the kitchen towel and let it rest for another 30 minutes to 1 hour.

3. Place the olive oil, water, and fine sea salt in a mixing bowl and stir to combine. Set the mixture aside. Lightly dust the focaccia with flour and press down on the dough with two fingers to make deep indentations in it. Cover the focaccia with half of the olive oil mixture and let it rest for another 30 minutes.

4. Preheat the oven to 445°F. Cover the focaccia with the remaining olive oil mixture and sprinkle coarse sea salt over the top. Place the focaccia in the oven and bake for 15 to 20 minutes, until the focaccia is a light golden brown. As this focaccia is supposed to be soft, it's far better to remove it too early as opposed to too late. Remove the focaccia from the oven and let it cool briefly before serving.

FOCACCIA CON LE OLIVE

YIELD: 1 LARGE FOCACCIA / **ACTIVE TIME:** 20 MINUTES / **TOTAL TIME:** 3 HOURS AND 30 MINUTES

This is a typical Ligurian focaccia, but similar versions exist in other regions. You can use any type of olive, but Taggiasca olives are a great choice.

INGREDIENTS:

- CLASSIC FOCACCIA DOUGH (SEE PAGE 396)
- ALL-PURPOSE FLOUR, AS NEEDED
- 3½ TABLESPOONS EXTRA-VIRGIN OLIVE OIL, PLUS MORE AS NEEDED
- 5⅓ OZ. WATER
- 1 TEASPOON FINE SEA SALT
- 10 OZ. GREEN OLIVES, PITTED

1. Place the dough on a flour-dusted work surface and shape it into a loose ball, making sure not to compress the core of the dough and deflate it. Coat an 18 x 13-inch baking sheet with olive oil, place the dough on the pan, and gently flatten the dough into an oval. Cover the dough with a kitchen towel and let it rest at room temperature for 1 hour.

2. Stretch the dough toward the edges of the baking sheet. If the dough does not want to extend to the edges of the pan right away, let it rest for 15 to 20 minutes before trying again. Cover the dough with the kitchen towel and let it rest for another 30 minutes.

3. Place the olive oil, water, and salt in a mixing bowl and stir to combine. Cover the focaccia with half of the mixture and let it rest for another hour.

4. Preheat the oven to 445°F. Distribute the olives over the focaccia, pressing them into the dough until it doesn't bounce back. Brush the focaccia with the remaining olive oil mixture.

5. Place the focaccia in the oven and bake until it is golden brown, about 15 minutes. Remove the focaccia from the oven and let it cool briefly before serving.

PISSALANDREA

YIELD: 1 SMALL FOCACCIA / **ACTIVE TIME:** 45 MINUTES / **TOTAL TIME:** 3 HOURS AND 30 MINUTES

Often referred to as the Ligurian take on Neapolitan pizza, this actually dates back to long before the famous pie became popular in Naples. While it does have tomato sauce, its spongy crust, olives, and anchovies put pissalandrea in a world all its own.

INGREDIENTS:

- 3 OZ. EXTRA-VIRGIN OLIVE OIL, PLUS MORE AS NEEDED
- ½ BATCH OF CLASSIC FOCACCIA DOUGH (SEE PAGE 396)
- 1 ONION, SLICED THIN
- 21.1 OZ. CANNED WHOLE PEELED TOMATOES, CRUSHED BY HAND
- ¾ TEASPOON FINE SEA SALT, PLUS MORE TO TASTE
- 2 PINCHES OF DRIED OREGANO
- 4 ANCHOVIES IN OLIVE OIL, DRAINED AND CHOPPED
- ½ LB. BLACK OLIVES, PITTED
- 9 GARLIC CLOVES, UNPEELED (OPTIONAL)
- 1 TABLESPOON CAPERS IN BRINE, DRAINED AND RINSED (OPTIONAL)

1. Coat a medium cast-iron skillet or a round 10-inch cake pan with olive oil, place the dough in the pan, and flatten it slightly. Cover the dough with a kitchen towel and let it rest at room temperature for 1 hour.

2. Place the onion and olive oil in a saucepan and cook, stirring occasionally, over medium-high heat until the onion starts to soften, about 5 minutes. Add the tomatoes, salt, and oregano and simmer until the flavor is to your liking, about 30 minutes. Remove the pan from heat and let the sauce cool completely.

3. Gently stretch the dough toward the edge of the pan. If the dough does not want to extend to the edge of the pan right away, let it rest for 15 to 20 minutes before trying again. When the dough is covering the pan, brush it with olive oil, cover it with the kitchen towel, and let it rest until it looks completely risen, about 45 minutes.

4. Preheat the oven to 430°F.

5. Spread the sauce over the focaccia, making sure not to press down too hard on the dough and deflate it. Top the focaccia with the anchovies, olives, and, if desired, the garlic and capers. Season with salt and drizzle olive oil over the focaccia.

6. Place the focaccia in the oven and bake until it is golden brown, 20 to 30 minutes.

7. Remove the focaccia from the oven and let it cool briefly before serving.

500g ℮

FARINATA

YIELD: 1 LARGE FOCACCIA / **ACTIVE TIME:** 20 MINUTES / **TOTAL TIME:** 3 HOURS

Born during a time when wheat was scarce, farinata is a true poor man's focaccia. Though, believe me, it does not want for flavor.

1. In a large bowl, combine the chickpea flour and salt. While whisking constantly, gradually add the water. If possible, use a handheld mixer, as you do not want lumps to form in the dough. When all of the water has been incorporated, cover the batter with a kitchen towel and let it rest at room temperature for 2 to 3 hours.

2. Preheat the oven to 480°F.

3. Remove the foam that has gathered on the surface of the batter. Discard the foam. Stir the olive oil and, if desired, the rosemary into the batter.

4. Coat an 18 x 13–inch baking sheet with olive oil, pour the batter into the pan, and use a rubber spatula to even the surface. Generously drizzle olive oil over the focaccia.

5. Place the focaccia on the upper rack of the oven and bake until it is set and lightly brown, 10 to 15 minutes.

6. Remove the focaccia from the oven and let it cool briefly before seasoning it with pepper and cutting it into squares.

INGREDIENTS:

- 14 OZ. (397 G) CHICKPEA FLOUR
- 2 TEASPOONS (11 G) FINE SEA SALT
- 5 CUPS (1135 G) WATER
- 3½ OZ. (100 G) EXTRA-VIRGIN OLIVE OIL, PLUS MORE AS NEEDED
- 1 TABLESPOON FRESH ROSEMARY (OPTIONAL)
- BLACK PEPPER, TO TASTE

CHISOLA PIACENTINA

YIELD: 1 SMALL FOCACCIA / **ACTIVE TIME:** 40 MINUTES / **TOTAL TIME:** 4 HOURS

In Piacenza, like in other parts of the Emilia-Romagna region, focaccia is enriched with different types of cured pork and lard. This is a tremendous treat every once in a while—any more frequent than that, and it becomes dangerously decadent.

INGREDIENTS:

- 7 OZ. PANCETTA, DICED
- 1¾ OZ. LARD, PLUS MORE AS NEEDED
- 5.3 OZ. (150 G) LUKEWARM WATER (90°F)
- 1¾ TEASPOONS (5.2 G) ACTIVE DRY YEAST
- 10.6 OZ. (300 G) BREAD FLOUR
- 10.6 OZ. (300 G) ALL-PURPOSE FLOUR, PLUS MORE AS NEEDED
- 3½ OZ. (100 G) WHITE WINE
- 1½ TEASPOONS (8.2 G) FINE SEA SALT
- EXTRA-VIRGIN OLIVE OIL, AS NEEDED

1. Place the pancetta and lard in a skillet and cook over medium heat, stirring occasionally, until the pancetta is browned, about 6 to 8 minutes. Transfer the pancetta to a bowl, making sure to reserve the rendered fat as well.

2. Place the water and yeast in a bowl, gently stir to combine, and let the mixture sit until it starts to foam, about 10 minutes.

3. In a large bowl, combine the flours, wine, and yeast mixture and work the mixture until it just comes together. If kneading by hand, place the dough on a flour-dusted work surface. Work it until it is compact, smooth, and elastic.

4. Add the salt, pancetta, and its rendered fat and work the dough until they have been incorporated and the dough is developed, elastic, and extensible, about 5 minutes. Coat a large, clean bowl with olive oil, shape the dough into a ball, and place it in the bowl. Cover the bowl with plastic wrap, place it in a naturally warm spot, and let it rest until it has doubled in size, about 2 hours.

5. Place the dough on a flour-dusted work surface and roll it out until it is an approximately ⅓-inch-thick disk. Coat a medium cast-iron skillet or a round 10-inch cake pan with lard and place the focaccia in the pan. Brush the focaccia with lard, cover it with a kitchen towel, and let it rest for 1 hour.

6. Preheat the oven to 390°F.

7. Top the focaccia with more lard, place it in the oven, and bake until it is golden brown, about 30 minutes.

8. Remove the focaccia from the oven and let it cool briefly before serving.

PIADINA

YIELD: 4 PIADINA / **ACTIVE TIME:** 30 MINUTES / **TOTAL TIME:** 1 HOUR AND 30 MINUTES

This small, round, flat focaccia from the Romagna side of the Emilia-Romagna region is more reminiscent of pita bread than its Italian relatives. Unleavened and cooked on the stove, piadina used to be made with cereals that were not optimal for bread baking. It is delicious when filled with creamy cheese and ham, but innumerable other fillings can be used.

INGREDIENTS:

- 2 TEASPOONS (11 G) FINE SEA SALT
- 4.8 OZ. (136 G) LUKEWARM WATER (90°F)
- 18 OZ. (510 G) ALL-PURPOSE FLOUR, PLUS MORE AS NEEDED
- 1½ TEASPOONS (9 G) BAKING SODA
- 3½ OZ. (100 G) LARD, PLUS MORE AS NEEDED

1. Combine the salt and water in a bowl and stir until the salt has dissolved. In a large bowl, combine the flour and baking soda. Add the lard and salted water and work the mixture until it just comes together. Place the dough on a flour-dusted work surface and knead the dough until it is compact, smooth, and elastic. Coat an airtight container with lard, shape the dough into a ball, place it in the container, and let the dough rest at room temperature for 30 minutes.

2. Place the dough on a flour-dusted work surface and divide it into four pieces. Shape the pieces into balls and roll each one until it is an approximately ⅛-inch-thick disk.

3. Warm a dry skillet over medium-high heat. When the skillet is hot, cook one piadina at a time. Cook until dark brown spots appear on both sides, about 5 minutes per side. Pop any big bubbles with a fork as the piadina cooks.

4. Serve once all of the piadina have been cooked.

CRESCENTA BOLOGNESE

YIELD: 1 LARGE FOCACCIA / **ACTIVE TIME:** 45 MINUTES / **TOTAL TIME:** 5 HOURS

Hailing from the city of Bologna, crescenta is a tall and fluffy focaccia enriched with prosciutto and pancetta. It was once the breakfast of the city's bakers, who made this focaccia using leftover dough from their morning preparations and scraps of cured meat from nearby butchers.

INGREDIENTS:

- 11 OZ. (312 G) LUKEWARM WATER (90°F)
- ⅔ TEASPOON (2 G) ACTIVE DRY YEAST
- ½ LB. PROSCIUTTO
- ½ LB. PANCETTA
- 24¾ OZ. (700 G) BREAD FLOUR, PLUS MORE AS NEEDED
- 2½ OZ. (71 G) LARD, PLUS MORE AS NEEDED
- ½ LB. (227 G) BIGA (SEE PAGE 659)
- 1 TABLESPOON (13 G) SUGAR
- 2⅔ TEASPOONS (14.5 G) FINE SEA SALT
- EXTRA-VIRGIN OLIVE OIL, AS NEEDED

1. Place the water and yeast in a bowl, gently stir to combine, and let the mixture sit until it starts to foam, about 10 minutes.

2. Place the prosciutto and pancetta in a food processor and blitz until very finely chopped. Set the mixture aside.

3. In a large bowl, combine the flour, lard, biga, sugar, and yeast mixture and work the mixture until it just comes together. Place the dough on a flour-dusted work surface and knead the dough until it is compact, smooth, and elastic.

4. Add the salt and cured meat mixture and knead the dough until it is developed, elastic, and extensible, about 5 minutes. Coat a large, clean bowl with olive oil, shape the dough into a ball, and place it in the bowl. Cover the bowl with plastic wrap, place it in a naturally warm spot, and let it rest until it has doubled in size, about 2 hours.

5. Place the dough on a flour-dusted work surface and shape it into a ball. Coat an 18 x 13–inch baking sheet with lard and place the dough in the center. Brush the surface of the dough with lard and gently press it into an oval. Cover the dough with a kitchen towel and let it rest for 1 hour.

6. Stretch the dough toward the edges of the baking sheet. If the dough does not want to extend to the edges of the pan right away, let it rest for 15 to 20 minutes before trying again. Once it has been stretched to the edges of the pan, cover it with a kitchen towel and let it rest until fully risen, about 1 hour. You may need to stretch the dough again halfway through this final rise to get the desired result.

7. Position a rack in the middle of the oven and preheat the oven to 430°F. Brush the focaccia with lard, place it in the oven, and bake until it is golden brown, 25 to 30 minutes.

8. Remove the focaccia from the oven and let it cool slightly before serving.

VIKING UNLEAVENED BARLEY BREAD

YIELD: 16 FLATBREADS / **ACTIVE TIME:** 1 HOUR / **TOTAL TIME:** 2 DAYS

This recipe is inspired by the authentic remains of a Viking bread found in a grave in Birka, Sweden, that was dated back to the ninth or tenth century.

1. In a large bowl, combine the flours and flaxseeds with ¾ cup of the water. The dough should be sticky, but not too wet. If the dough absorbs the first portion of the water, add the remaining water.

2. Add the lard and salt. Knead just enough to combine all of the ingredients.

3. Cover the bowl with plastic wrap and place the dough in the refrigerator for 2 days.

4. Preheat the oven to 375°F. Line two baking sheets with parchment paper.

5. Place the dough on a heavily flour-dusted work surface, divide it into four pieces, and then divide each piece into four smaller pieces.

6. Shape the 16 pieces of dough into balls and flatten the balls into rounds.

7. Make four big incisions in each round so it looks like a clover leaf, and then make a few small incisions with a fork. Place the rounds on the baking sheets.

8. Place the flatbreads in the oven and bake until they are golden brown, 10 to 20 minutes.

9. Remove the flatbreads from the oven, place the pans on a wire rack, and let them cool completely before serving.

INGREDIENTS:

- 3½ CUPS (300 G) BARLEY FLOUR, PLUS MORE AS NEEDED
- 1 CUP (100 G) GRAHAM FLOUR
- 2 TABLESPOONS (30 G) CRUSHED FLAXSEEDS
- 1¼ CUPS (284 G) WATER
- 2 TABLESPOONS (26 G) LARD
- 1 TEASPOON (6 G) FINE SEA SALT

NAAN

YIELD: 8 PIECES / **ACTIVE TIME:** 1 HOUR / **TOTAL TIME:** 3 TO 4 HOURS

Naan is the most common type of leavened bread in both Central and Southern Asia. It is generally baked in a tandoor, but it can also be cooked in a frying pan, like in the version below.

1. Place the yeast, sugar, and ½ cup of water in a large bowl, gently stir to combine, and let the mixture sit until it starts to foam, about 10 minutes.

2. Add the flour, salt, baking powder, and remaining water and stir to combine. Add the yogurt and 2 tablespoons of the butter and work the mixture until it comes together as a soft dough.

3. Transfer the dough to a flour-dusted work surface and knead until it is springy and elastic, about 10 minutes.

4. Coat the inside of a clean mixing bowl with nonstick cooking spray. Place the ball of dough in the bowl, cover it loosely with plastic wrap, put it in a naturally warm spot, and let the dough rest until it has doubled in size, 1 to 2 hours.

5. Punch down the dough, place it on a flour-dusted work surface, and roll it into a circle. Cut the circle into eight triangles, as you would a pizza.

6. Warm a large cast-iron skillet over high heat for 5 minutes. Working with one piece of dough at a time, roll it out to soften the edges and give it a teardrop shape. Brush both sides with some of the olive oil and place it in the skillet.

7. Cook for 1 minute, turn the naan over, and cover the pan. Cook for another minute, transfer the cooked naan to a plate, and brush it with some of the remaining butter. Cover it with a kitchen towel while you cook the remaining naan.

INGREDIENTS:

- 1½ TEASPOONS (4.5 G) ACTIVE DRY YEAST
- 1½ TEASPOONS (6 G) SUGAR
- 1 CUP (227 G) WARM WATER (105°F)
- 3 CUPS (360 G) ALL-PURPOSE FLOUR, PLUS MORE AS NEEDED
- ¼ TEASPOON (1.5 G) FINE SEA SALT
- 1 TEASPOON (4 G) BAKING POWDER
- ½ CUP (113 G) PLAIN YOGURT
- ¼ CUP (56 G) UNSALTED BUTTER, MELTED, PLUS MORE AS NEEDED
- ¼ CUP EXTRA-VIRGIN OLIVE OIL

LEFSE

YIELD: 2 LEFSE / **ACTIVE TIME:** 1 HOUR / **TOTAL TIME:** 2 HOURS

This potato-based flatbread has been made popular in the United States by Norwegian immigrants in the Midwest, and it is now easy to find all the specific tools to make it like a real Norwegian grandma. The recipe below is adapted to require no specific tools.

INGREDIENTS:

- 1 LB. (450 G) STARCHY POTATOES, PEELED AND DICED
- 2.6 OZ. (75 G) UNSALTED BUTTER
- 1½ CUPS (180 G) ALL-PURPOSE FLOUR, PLUS MORE AS NEEDED
- ½ TEASPOON (3 G) FINE SEA SALT

1. Bring water to a boil in a large saucepan. Add the potatoes and cook until they are fork-tender, 15 to 20 minutes. Drain the potatoes, place them in a bowl, and add the butter. Mash until the potatoes are smooth.

2. Add half of the flour to the mashed potatoes and work the mixture until it just comes together.

3. Place the dough on a flour-dusted work surface, add the salt, and knead to incorporate. Incorporate the remaining flour a little bit at a time, stopping when you reach a consistency that allows you to roll the dough.

4. Shape the dough into a ball and divide it in half. Roll each piece into a round and flatten each round into a thin disk.

5. Warm a large cast-iron skillet over medium-high heat.

6. Roll one disk at a time around a floured rolling pin and transfer it to the heated skillet.

7. Cook until the lefse is browned on both sides, 4 to 6 minutes, turning it over once.

8. Transfer the cooked lefse to a plate and cook the remaining lefse.

ROTI

YIELD: 15 ROTI / **ACTIVE TIME:** 30 MINUTES / **TOTAL TIME:** 2 HOURS

Roti, also known as chapati, is one of the most traditional breads of the whole Indian subcontinent, a staple food eaten with classic local dishes. One thing to keep in mind: it is crucial to find the right whole wheat flour for this recipe.

INGREDIENTS:

- 2½ CUPS (282 G) FINELY GROUND WHOLE WHEAT FLOUR, PLUS MORE AS NEEDED
- 4 TEASPOONS (16 G) CANOLA OIL
- 1 TEASPOON (6 G) FINE SEA SALT
- 1 CUP (227 G) WATER
- EXTRA-VIRGIN OLIVE OIL, AS NEEDED

1. Place all of the ingredients, except ¼ cup of the water, in the work bowl of a stand mixer fitted with the dough hook. Knead the mixture, checking it regularly, until it comes together as a soft, but not sticky, dough. If the dough is not coming together, add the rest of the water, if needed, a little at a time. Coat a large, clean bowl with olive oil, shape the dough into a ball, and place it in the bowl. Cover the bowl with plastic wrap and let the dough rest for 1 hour.

2. Transfer the dough to a flour-dusted work surface, divide it into 15 pieces, and shape them into rounds.

3. Warm a cast-iron skillet over medium-high heat. Coat the skillet with nonstick cooking spray, flatten one of the rounds into a thin disk, and place it in the pan. Cook until it is browned and bubbly on both sides, gently pressing down on the surface as it cooks, about 30 seconds per side.

4. Remove the cooked roti from the pan, transfer it to a plate, and cover it loosely with aluminum foil. Repeat with the remaining roti.

POORI

YIELD: 18 POORI / **ACTIVE TIME:** 30 MINUTES / **TOTAL TIME:** 50 MINUTES

A delicious, crunchy, unleavened flatbread from India, poori is often eaten at breakfast, but it can also accompany just about any Indian dish.

INGREDIENTS:

- 1½ CUPS (180 G) ULTRA-FINE WHOLE WHEAT FLOUR
- 4 TEASPOONS (16 G) CANOLA OIL, PLUS MORE AS NEEDED
- ⅓ CUP (75 G) WATER, PLUS MORE AS NEEDED
- ⅓ TEASPOON (2 G) FINE SEA SALT

1. Place all of the ingredients in a mixing bowl and work the mixture until it just comes together as a stiff dough. Be careful to not overwork the mixture, and add extra water only if the dough is really struggling to come together.

2. Shape the dough into a ball, cover the bowl with plastic wrap, and let it rest at room temperature for 15 minutes.

3. Divide the dough into 18 pieces and shape them into rounds. Place them on a parchment-lined baking sheet.

4. Add canola oil to a Dutch oven until it is about 2 inches deep and warm it to 350°F.

5. Roll two of the rounds into disks that are about ⅓ inch thick. Gently slip them into the hot oil and fry until they are puffy and golden brown, 4 to 5 minutes.

6. Transfer the cooked poori to a baking sheet lined with paper towels. Repeat with the remaining disks and serve the poori warm.

Roti, see page 484

TUNNBRÖD

YIELD: 12 TUNNBRÖD / **ACTIVE TIME:** 30 MINUTES / **TOTAL TIME:** 2 HOURS AND 30 MINUTES

This soft flatbread from northern Sweden is traditionally made with a combination of wheat, rye, and barley, and is often used as a wrap, encasing mashed potatoes and sausage, herring, or other popular foods in Scandinavia.

INGREDIENTS:

- 1½ CUPS (340 G) MILK
- 2½ TEASPOONS (7 G) ACTIVE DRY YEAST
- 2¼ CUPS (270 G) ALL-PURPOSE FLOUR, PLUS MORE AS NEEDED
- 1 CUP (100 G) GRAHAM FLOUR
- ¾ CUP (80 G) RYE FLOUR
- 2⅓ TABLESPOONS (50 G) LIGHT MOLASSES
- 1 TEASPOON (6 G) FENNEL SEEDS, CRUSHED
- 4 TABLESPOONS (57 G) UNSALTED BUTTER
- 1 TEASPOON (6 G) FINE SEA SALT

1. Warm the milk to 105°F, place it in the work bowl of a stand mixer fitted with the dough hook, and add the yeast. Gently stir to combine and let it sit until it starts to foam, about 10 minutes.

2. Add the flours, molasses, and fennel seeds and work the mixture on low for 5 minutes. Gradually add the butter and knead until it has been incorporated. Add the salt and knead the dough until it is smooth, about 3 minutes. Coat a large, clean bowl with nonstick cooking spray, shape the dough into a ball, and place it in the bowl. Cover the bowl with plastic wrap, place it in a naturally warm spot, and let it rest until it has doubled in size, about 1 to 1½ hours.

3. Divide the dough into 12 pieces, place them on a piece of parchment paper, and roll them into disks. Cover them with a kitchen towel and let them rest for 1 hour.

4. Working with one disk at a time, place them on a flour-dusted work surface and roll them out until they are ⅕ inch thick. Use a fork to poke some shallow holes on the top of each disk.

5. Warm a cast-iron skillet over medium-high heat and lightly coat it with nonstick cooking spray. Working with one tunnbröd at a time, add them to the pan and cook until they are browned on both sides, 4 to 6 minutes, turning them over once.

6. Stack the cooked tunnbröd on a plate, separating each one with a piece of parchment paper.

AREPAS

YIELD: 6 AREPAS / **ACTIVE TIME:** 20 MINUTES / **TOTAL TIME:** 50 MINUTES

This traditional bread is commonly eaten in Venezuela and Colombia, as well as other Central and South American areas. It can be eaten with a dip or split and filled like a sandwich.

INGREDIENTS:

- 4 CUPS (600 G) AREPA FLOUR (PRECOOKED CORNMEAL)
- 1⅔ CUPS (380 G) WARM WATER (105°F)
- 1 TEASPOON (6 G) FINE SEA SALT
- CANOLA OIL, AS NEEDED

1. In a large bowl, combine all of the ingredients, except for the canola oil, and work the mixture until it comes together.

2. Cover the bowl with a kitchen towel and let the dough rest for 30 minutes.

3. Place the dough on a piece of parchment paper and roll it out until it is ⅘ inch thick. Use a glass or a pastry cutter to cut six disks out of it, trimming the edges of the disks to make them as perfectly circular as possible.

4. Coat the bottom of a cast-iron grill pan with canola oil and warm it over medium-high heat.

5. Working in batches to avoid crowding the pan, add the arepas to the pan and cook until browned on both sides, 6 to 8 minutes, turning them over once. If the centers of the arepas are too soft for your liking, you can finish them by placing them on a baking sheet and baking for 10 minutes at 400°F.

Arepas, see page 489

PARATHA

YIELD: 8 SERVINGS / **ACTIVE TIME:** 25 MINUTES / **TOTAL TIME:** 30 MINUTES

If you cannot find ghee easily, substitute the same amount of clarified butter.

INGREDIENTS:

- 2 CUPS (240 G) PASTRY FLOUR, PLUS MORE AS NEEDED
- 1 CUP (113 G) WHOLE WHEAT FLOUR
- ¼ TEASPOON (1.5 G) FINE SEA SALT
- 1 CUP (227 G) WARM WATER (105°F)
- 5 TABLESPOONS (65 G) CANOLA OIL, PLUS MORE AS NEEDED
- 5 TABLESPOONS GHEE

1. Place the flours and salt in the work bowl of a stand mixer fitted with a dough hook. Turn the mixer on low and slowly add the warm water. Mix until incorporated and then slowly add the canola oil. When the canola oil has been incorporated, place the dough on a flour-dusted work surface and knead until it is smooth, about 8 minutes.

2. Divide the dough into eight small balls and dust them with pastry flour.

3. Use your hands to roll each ball into a long rope. Spiral each rope into a large disk.

4. Use a rolling pin to flatten the disks until they are no more than ¼ inch thick. Lightly brush each disk with a small amount of canola oil.

5. Warm a large cast-iron skillet over high heat for 4 minutes. Brush the surface with some of the ghee and place a disk of the dough on the surface. Cook until it is blistered and brown, about 1 minute. Turn the paratha over and cook the other side. Transfer the cooked paratha to a plate and repeat with the remaining disks.

6. Serve warm or at room temperature.

CORN TORTILLAS

YIELD: 32 TORTILLAS / **ACTIVE TIME:** 30 MINUTES / **TOTAL TIME:** 1 HOUR AND 15 MINUTES

With this recipe and a tortilla press, you're well on your way to taking taco night to the next level.

INGREDIENTS:

- 1 LB. (454 G) MASA HARINA
- 1½ TABLESPOONS (27 G) FINE SEA SALT
- 3 CUPS (681 G) WARM WATER (105°F), PLUS MORE AS NEEDED

1. In the work bowl of a stand mixer fitted with the paddle attachment, combine the masa harina and salt. With the mixer on low speed, slowly begin to add the water. The mixture should come together as a soft, smooth dough. You want the masa to be moist enough so that when a small ball of it is pressed flat in your hands, the edges do not crack. Also, it should not stick to your hands when you peel it off your palm.

2. Let the masa rest for 10 minutes and check the hydration again. You may need to add more water, depending on environmental conditions.

3. Warm a large cast-iron skillet over high heat. Portion the masa into 1 oz. balls and cover them with a damp kitchen towel.

4. Line a tortilla press with two 8-inch circles of plastic. You can use a grocery store bag, a resealable bag, or even a standard kitchen trash bag as a source for the plastic. Place a masa ball in the center of one circle and gently push down on it with the palm of one hand to flatten. Place the other plastic circle on top and then close the tortilla press, applying firm, even pressure to flatten the masa into a round tortilla.

5. Open the tortilla press and remove the top layer of plastic. Carefully pick up the tortilla and remove the bottom piece of plastic.

6. Gently lay the tortilla flat in the pan, taking care to not wrinkle it. Cook for 15 to 30 seconds, until the edge begins to lift up slightly. Turn the tortilla over and let it cook for 30 to 45 seconds before turning it over one last time. If the hydration of the masa was correct and the heat is high enough, the tortilla should puff up and inflate. Remove the tortilla from the pan and store in a tortilla warmer lined with a kitchen towel. Repeat until all of the prepared masa has been made into tortillas.

Corn Tortillas, see page 493

FLOUR TORTILLAS

YIELD: 18 TORTILLAS / **ACTIVE TIME:** 45 MINUTES / **TOTAL TIME:** 1 HOUR AND 30 MINUTES

These will have a bit more heft, and a bit more chew than corn tortillas, making them perfect for burritos and other hefty wraps.

INGREDIENTS:

- 1 LB. (454 G) ALL-PURPOSE FLOUR, PLUS MORE AS NEEDED
- 1 TABLESPOON (17 G) FINE SEA SALT
- 1 TABLESPOON (12 G) BAKING POWDER
- 2½ OZ. (70 G) LARD OR UNSALTED BUTTER, MELTED
- 8-10 OZ. (227 TO 280 G) WARM WATER (105°F)

1. In the work bowl of a stand mixer fitted with the paddle attachment, combine the flour, salt, and baking powder and beat on low speed for 30 seconds.

2. Gradually add the lard and beat until the mixture is a coarse meal.

3. Fit the mixer with the dough hook and set it to low speed. Add the water in a slow stream until the dough begins to come together, 2 to 3 minutes. The dough should begin to pull away from the side of the mixing bowl, leaving no residue behind. Increase the speed to medium and continue mixing until the dough becomes very soft, shiny, and elastic. Please note that more or less of the water may be required due to environmental conditions and/or variations in the flour.

4. Remove the dough from the work bowl and place it in a mixing bowl. Cover with plastic wrap or a damp kitchen towel and let it rest at room temperature for 30 to 45 minutes.

5. Portion the dough into rounds the size of golf balls, approximately 1½ oz. each. Using the palms of your hands, roll the rounds in a circular motion until they are seamless balls. Place them on a parchment-lined baking sheet and cover with plastic wrap. Let them rest at room temperature for 20 minutes.

6. Working on a very smooth and flour-dusted work surface, roll out the balls of dough until they are between ⅛ and ¼ inch thick and about 8 inches in diameter. Stack the tortillas, separating each one with pieces of parchment paper that have been cut to size.

7. Warm a cast-iron skillet over medium-high heat. Gently place a tortilla in the pan. It should immediately sizzle and start to puff up. Do not puncture it. Cook, turning frequently, for 20 to 30 seconds per side, until the tortilla is lightly golden brown in spots. Place in a kitchen towel, a tortilla warmer, or a plastic resealable bag so it continues to steam and repeat with the remaining tortillas.

PITA BREAD

YIELD: 8 SERVINGS / **ACTIVE TIME:** 1 HOUR / **TOTAL TIME:** 3 HOURS

A foundational preparation in Mediterranean cuisine. If you get in the habit of making this at home, a satisfying dinner is never far away.

1. In a large mixing bowl, add the water, yeast, and sugar and gently stir to combine. Let the mixture sit until it starts to foam, about 10 minutes.

2. Add the flours and salt to the mixing bowl and work the mixture until it comes together as a smooth dough. Cover the bowl with a kitchen towel and let it rest for about 15 minutes.

3. Preheat the oven to 500°F and place a baking stone or steel on the floor of the oven as it warms.

4. Divide the dough into eight pieces and form them into balls. Place the balls on a flour-dusted work surface and roll them out until they are about ¼ inch thick.

5. Working with one pita at a time, place the pita on the baking stone and bake until it is puffy and brown, 6 to 8 minutes.

6. Remove the cooked pita from the oven and serve warm or at room temperature. Repeat with the remaining pitas.

INGREDIENTS:

- 1 CUP (227 G) LUKEWARM WATER (90°F)
- 1 TABLESPOON (9 G) ACTIVE DRY YEAST
- 1 TABLESPOON (12 G) SUGAR
- 1¾ CUPS (210 G) ALL-PURPOSE FLOUR, PLUS MORE AS NEEDED
- 1 CUP (113 G) WHOLE WHEAT FLOUR
- 1 TABLESPOON (17 G) FINE SEA SALT

INJERA

YIELD: 1 INJERA / **ACTIVE TIME:** 1 HOUR / **TOTAL TIME:** 3 DAYS

If you've ever eaten at an Ethiopian restaurant, you know that the centerpiece of the meal is a thick, spongy bread that's placed in the middle of the table. The dishes go around it, and you eat by ripping apart the bread and scooping up the other foods. While the ingredients are minimal, you have to plan pretty far ahead of time when making injera, as the "flour" needs to sit for several days to break down the grain.

INGREDIENTS:

- ½ TEASPOON (1.5 G) ACTIVE DRY YEAST
- 2 CUPS (454 G) WARM WATER (105°F)
- 1½ CUPS (202 G) GROUND TEFF
- SALT, TO TASTE
- CANOLA OIL, AS NEEDED

1. Preheat the oven to 450°F. Place the yeast and water in a large bowl, gently stir to combine, and let the mixture sit until it starts to foam, about 10 minutes.

2. Place the teff in a large bowl and add the yeast mixture. Stir until the mixture comes together as a stiff dough. Cover the bowl with a kitchen towel and place it in a naturally warm spot. Let the dough sit for 2 to 3 days. During this time, it will bubble, turn brown, and develop a pleasant sour smell.

3. When you're ready to make the injera, add salt to the mixture until some of the sourness has dissipated. The mixture should now resemble pancake batter.

4. Place a large cast-iron skillet over medium heat and brush it with canola oil. Pour enough batter into the skillet to coat the bottom. You want it to be thinner than a pancake, but thicker than a crepe. Tilt the skillet to spread the batter evenly over the bottom. Cook until holes form in the injera and the edges crisp up and lift away from the pan. As you do not flip the injera, make sure it's cooked through.

5. Once the injera is cooked, use a spatula to lift it out and place it on a plate to cool. If you cook a batch of injeras, separate them with pieces of parchment paper between each one as you stack them on top of one another.

KNÄCKEBRÖD

YIELD: 12 KNÄCKEBRÖD / **ACTIVE TIME:** 50 MINUTES / **TOTAL TIME:** 2 HOURS AND 30 MINUTES

Knäckebröd means crispy bread, or crackers, in Swedish. These crunchy and flavorful flatbreads stay fresh for a long time and, as they can accompany a variety of foods, are a traditional part of the Swedish smörgåsbord.

INGREDIENTS:

- 1⅓ CUPS (300 G) WATER
- 1¾ TEASPOONS (5 G) ACTIVE DRY YEAST
- 1 TABLESPOON (5 G) CARAWAY SEEDS
- ½ CUP (50 G) LIGHT RYE FLOUR
- 2½ CUPS (300 G) BREAD FLOUR
- ½ CUP (60 G) ALL-PURPOSE FLOUR, PLUS MORE AS NEEDED
- 1 CUP MIXED SEEDS (SESAME, SUNFLOWER, ETC.)
- 1½ TEASPOONS (9 G) FINE SEA SALT

1. Warm 3 tablespoons of the water to 105°F. Place it in the work bowl of a stand mixer fitted with dough hook, add the yeast and caraway seeds, and gently stir to combine. Let the mixture sit until it starts to foam, about 10 minutes.

2. Add the flours, yeast mixture, and seeds and work the mixture on low for 4 minutes. Add the salt and work the dough until it is smooth, about 4 minutes.

3. Coat a large, clean bowl with nonstick cooking spray, shape the dough into a ball, and place it in the bowl. Cover the bowl with plastic wrap, place it in a naturally warm spot, and let it rest until it has doubled in size, about 1½ hours.

4. Place the dough on a flour-dusted work, roll it into a long log, and cut it into 12 pieces. Shape each piece into a round, place them on a parchment-lined baking sheet, and cover them with a kitchen towel. Let the knäckebröd rest for 40 minutes.

5. Preheat the oven to the maximum temperature and place a baking stone or steel on the middle rack of the oven as it warms.

6. Place the knäckebröd on a flour-dusted work surface and roll them out as thin as possible without tearing the dough. Use a fork to poke shallow holes in the knäckebröd.

7. Using a peel or a flat baking sheet, slide a few knäckebröd onto the heated baking implement and bake until they are lightly golden brown and crispy, about 10 minutes.

8. Remove the knäckebröd from the oven and let them cool on wire racks before serving.

SCHÜTTELBROT

YIELD: 8 SCHÜTTELBROT / **ACTIVE TIME:** 40 MINUTES / **TOTAL TIME:** 2 HOURS AND 30 MINUTES

This is a crunchy flatbread common in the Trentino-Alto Adige area of Italy. Originating during the Middle Ages, it was popular among the common people, intended to last through the long winters when food was scarce.

INGREDIENTS:

- 1½ CUPS (340 G) WARM WATER (105°F)
- 2½ TEASPOONS (7 G) ACTIVE DRY YEAST
- 3½ CUPS (365 G) MEDIUM RYE FLOUR
- 1¼ CUPS (150 G) ALL-PURPOSE FLOUR, PLUS MORE AS NEEDED
- 2 TEASPOONS (6 G) MIXED SEEDS (FENNEL, CARAWAY, CORIANDER, ETC.)
- 1½ TEASPOONS (9 G) FINE SEA SALT
- 1 TEASPOON (4 G) SUGAR
- 3⅓ TABLESPOONS (50 G) BUTTERMILK

1. Place the water and yeast in the work bowl of a stand mixer fitted with the dough hook and gently stir to combine. Let the mixture sit until it starts to foam, about 10 minutes.

2. Add the remaining ingredients and work the mixture on low until it comes together as a smooth dough, about 15 minutes.

3. Knead the dough by hand or with the stand mixer for about 15 minutes.

4. Coat a large, clean bowl with nonstick cooking spray, shape the dough into a ball, and place it in the bowl. Cover the bowl with plastic wrap, place it in a naturally warm spot, and let it rest for 40 minutes.

5. Place the dough on a flour-dusted work, roll it into a long log, and cut it into eight pieces. Shape each piece into a round, place them on a parchment-lined baking sheet, and cover them with a kitchen towel. Let the schüttelbrot rest for 1 hour.

6. Place the schüttelbrot on a flour-dusted work surface and roll them out until they are ⅕ inch thick. Cover the flatbreads with a kitchen towel and let them rest for 20 minutes.

7. Preheat the oven to 410°F and place a baking stone on the middle rack of the oven as it warms.

8. Using a peel or flat baking sheet, transfer the flatbreads to the heated baking implement and bake for about 20 minutes, until they are a light golden brown.

9. Remove the schüttelbrot from the oven and let them cool on wire racks before serving.

GALLETTE DEL MARINAIO

YIELD: 8 GALLETTE / **ACTIVE TIME:** 30 MINUTES / **TOTAL TIME:** 2 HOURS AND 30 MINUTES

This flatbread was born in Liguria around the fifteenth century to sustain fishermen during their lengthy trips. Gallette del marinaio are not eaten as they are but need to be softened, often in water and vinegar, and are a popular ingredient in many Ligurian recipes.

INGREDIENTS:

- 8.8 OZ. (250 G) LUKEWARM WATER (90°F)
- ½ TEASPOON (1.5 G) ACTIVE DRY YEAST
- 17.6 OZ. (500 G) BREAD FLOUR, PLUS MORE AS NEEDED

1. Line three baking sheets with parchment paper. Place the water and yeast in the work bowl of a stand mixer fitted with the dough hook, gently stir to combine, and let the mixture sit until it starts to foam, about 10 minutes.

2. Add the flour and work the mixture on low until it comes together as a firm dough.

3. Raise the speed to high and work the dough until it is smooth and elastic, about 10 minutes.

4. Divide the dough into 3 oz. pieces and shape them into tight rounds.

5. Place the dough balls on one of the baking sheets, cover them with a kitchen towel, and let them rest for 1 hour.

6. Place the balls of dough on a flour-dusted work surface and roll them into ¼-inch-thick disks. Place the gallette on the baking sheets and cover them with kitchen towels. Let them rest for 45 minutes.

7. Preheat the oven to 430°F. Poke holes in the tops of the gallette with a fork and place them in the oven. Bake for about 10 minutes.

8. Remove the gallette from the baking sheets and place them directly on the oven's racks. Bake until they are golden brown, about 5 minutes.

9. Turn the oven off, crack open the oven door, and let the gallette cool in the oven.

PANE CARASAU

YIELD: 20 CARASAU / **ACTIVE TIME:** 1 HOUR / **TOTAL TIME:** 3 HOURS

Pane carasau is one of the most famous Sardinian specialties and can be used in innumerable ways. A very ancient bread, it is also known as carta musica ("music paper") in Italy for the noise it makes when chewed, while the name carasau derives from the method of baking the bread twice to make it crispy, a practice known as carasatura.

INGREDIENTS:

- 9.3 OZ. (264 G) WARM WATER (105°F)
- 1¾ TEASPOONS (5.2 G) ACTIVE DRY YEAST
- 1 TEASPOON (4 G) SUGAR
- 17.6 OZ. (500 G) FINELY GROUND DURUM WHEAT FLOUR (SEMOLA RIMACINATA), PLUS MORE AS NEEDED
- 1 TEASPOON (5.5 G) FINE SEA SALT
- EXTRA-VIRGIN OLIVE OIL, AS NEEDED

1. Place the water, yeast, and sugar in the work bowl of a stand mixer fitted with the dough hook, gently stir to combine, and let the mixture sit until it starts to foam, about 10 minutes.

2. Add the flour and work the mixture until it just comes together as a dough.

3. Add the salt and work the dough until it is smooth and elastic. Coat a large, clean bowl with olive oil, shape the dough into a ball, and place it in the bowl. Cover the bowl with plastic wrap, place it in a naturally warm spot, and let it rest for 1 hour.

4. Place the dough on a flour-dusted work surface, divide it into 10 pieces, and shape them into rounds. Cover the rounds with kitchen towels and let them rest for 30 minutes.

5. Preheat the oven to the maximum temperature and place a baking stone or steel in the oven as it warms. Flatten the rounds into 1/10-inch-thick disks, cover them with kitchen towels, and let them rest for another 30 minutes.

6. Using a peel or flat baking sheet, slide one round at a time onto the heated baking implement and bake until it puffs up, 3 to 5 minutes.

7. Remove the bread from the oven and let it cool slightly.

8. When all of the carasau have been baked, cut them in half at their equators and gently press down to flatten them.

9. Slide a few carasau at a time onto the baking stone and bake until they are crispy, about 30 seconds. Remove them from the oven and let the carasau cool before serving.

ROLLS, BUNS & THE BREAKFAST TABLE

Though not as complicated as turning out a perfectly developed sourdough loaf, and not as certain to wow everyone as a pizza fashioned by someone who really knows what they are doing, the recipes in this chapter are undoubtedly worthy of an aspiring bread maker's time.

This worthiness is tied to their ability to improve everyday moments, and turn what could be taken for granted into an outright occasion. Perhaps it is a holiday dinner where a basket of fluffy dinner rolls lingers in your loved ones' minds. Maybe it's a summer barbecue where taking the time to make the burger buns takes things to the next level. Or maybe it's just a typical weekend morning, except there's a platter of muffins pulled fresh from the oven that put everyone in a good mood for the rest of the day.

MAFALDE

YIELD: 10 ROLLS / **ACTIVE TIME:** 1 HOUR / **TOTAL TIME:** 3 HOURS AND 30 MINUTES

Mafalde are the quintessential Sicilian bread, made with semola and shaped to resemble either the rod of Asclepius (the symbol of medicine) or an S.

INGREDIENTS:

- 24.7 OZ. (700 G) WARM WATER (105°F)
- 1½ PACKETS (10.5 G) OF ACTIVE DRY YEAST
- 1 TEASPOON (7 G) HONEY
- 6½ CUPS (800 G) FINELY GROUND DURUM WHEAT FLOUR (SEMOLA RIMACINATA)
- 1⅔ CUPS (200 G) ALL-PURPOSE FLOUR, PLUS MORE AS NEEDED
- 6⅓ TABLESPOONS (80 G) EXTRA-VIRGIN OLIVE OIL
- 1 TABLESPOON (19 G) FINE SEA SALT
- SESAME SEEDS, FOR TOPPING

1. Place the water, yeast, and honey in the work bowl of a stand mixer fitted with the dough hook, gently stir to combine, and let the mixture sit until it starts to foam, about 10 minutes.

2. Add the flours and work the mixture until it just comes together as a dough.

3. Add the olive oil and salt and work the dough until it is smooth and elastic. Shape the dough into a ball, place it in a clean bowl, and cover the bowl with plastic wrap. Let the dough rest for 15 minutes.

4. Line two baking sheets with parchment paper. Place the dough on a flour-dusted work surface and divide it into 10 pieces. Roll each piece into a 6-inch-long log. Brush the tops of the logs with water, dip the tops in sesame seeds until coated, and place the logs on the baking sheets. Cover them with kitchen towels and let them rest for 1½ hours.

5. Preheat the oven to 410°F.

6. Place the rolls in the oven and bake for 20 minutes. Reduce the temperature to 350°F and bake until they are golden brown, about 10 minutes.

7. Remove the mafalde from the oven, place them on wire racks, and let them cool before serving.

BULKIE ROLLS

YIELD: 8 ROLLS / **ACTIVE TIME:** 45 MINUTES / **TOTAL TIME:** 4 HOURS

A New England staple for sandwiches, and not too shabby when it comes to burger buns.

1. Place the water, yeast, unbeaten egg, egg yolk, olive oil, and sugar in the work bowl of a stand mixer fitted with the dough hook and stir to combine. Add the flour and salt and knead on low for 1 minute. Raise the speed to medium and knead the mixture until it comes together as a smooth dough and begins to pull away from the side of the work bowl, 6 to 8 minutes.

2. Coat a mixing bowl with nonstick cooking spray. Remove the dough from the work bowl, place it on a flour-dusted work surface, and shape it into a ball. Place the dough in the bowl, cover it with plastic wrap, place it in a naturally warm spot, and let it rest until it has doubled in size.

3. Line an 18 x 13–inch baking sheet with parchment paper. Place the dough on a flour-dusted work surface and divide it into eight 3½ oz. portions. Roll the portions into tight balls. Place the balls on the pan, cover the pan with plastic wrap, and place it in a naturally warm spot. Let the rolls rest until it has doubled in size.

4. Preheat the oven to 350°F.

5. Brush the rolls with the beaten egg. Using a sharp knife, score an X on top of each roll.

6. Place the pan in the oven and bake until the rolls are golden brown and feel lighter when lifted, 20 to 25 minutes.

7. Remove the rolls from the oven, transfer them to a wire rack, and let them cool completely before enjoying.

INGREDIENTS:

- ¾ CUP (170 G) WATER
- 1½ TEASPOONS (4.5 G) ACTIVE DRY YEAST
- 2 EGGS, 1 BEATEN
- 1 EGG YOLK
- 2 TABLESPOONS (28 G) EXTRA-VIRGIN OLIVE OIL
- 1 OZ. (28 G) SUGAR
- 3½ CUPS (425 G) BREAD FLOUR, PLUS MORE AS NEEDED
- 1 TEASPOON (6 G) FINE SEA SALT

Bulkie Rolls, see page 513

PAN CACIATO DI SAN MARTINO

YIELD: 9 ROLLS / **ACTIVE TIME:** 1 HOUR / **TOTAL TIME:** 4 HOURS AND 30 MINUTES

Also called pan nociato ("bread with nuts"), pan caciato ("bread with cheese") is a delicious Umbrian bread that is typically made to celebrate Saint Martin's Day, November 11.

INGREDIENTS:

- ½ CUP (114 G) LUKEWARM WHOLE MILK (90°F)
- 1 PACKET (7 G) OF ACTIVE DRY YEAST
- 11.6 OZ. (330 G) ALL-PURPOSE FLOUR, PLUS MORE AS NEEDED
- 6 OZ. (170 G) BREAD FLOUR
- ¾ CUP (85 G) PARMESAN CHEESE, GRATED
- ½ CUP (113 G) WATER
- ¼ CUP (50 G) EXTRA-VIRGIN OLIVE OIL, PLUS MORE AS NEEDED
- 1 TEASPOON (5.5 G) FINE SEA SALT
- 1½ CUPS WALNUTS, COARSELY CHOPPED
- 3 OZ. PECORINO CHEESE, DICED

1. Place the milk and yeast in the work bowl of a stand mixer fitted with the paddle attachment, gently stir to combine, and let the mixture sit until it starts to foam, about 10 minutes.

2. Add the flours, Parmesan, and water and work the mixture until it comes together as a dough.

3. Add the olive oil and salt and knead the dough until it is smooth and elastic.

4. Place the dough on a flour-dusted work surface, roll it out into a rectangle, distribute the walnuts and pecorino over it, and roll the dough up. Knead it until the walnuts and pecorino are evenly distributed. Shape the dough into a ball. Coat a bowl with olive oil, place the dough in it, and cover it with plastic wrap. Let the dough rest for 1½ hours.

5. Line a baking sheet with parchment paper. Place the dough on the flour-dusted work surface and divide it into nine pieces. Shape each piece into a round, press down to flatten the rounds slightly, and arrange them on the baking sheet.

6. Cover the rolls with a kitchen towel and let them rest for 1½ hours.

7. Preheat the oven to 340°F.

8. Place the rolls in the oven and bake until they are just golden brown, 20 to 25 minutes.

9. Remove the rolls from the oven and let them cool slightly before serving.

SEMPRE FRESCHI

YIELD: 9 ROLLS / **ACTIVE TIME:** 1 HOUR / **TOTAL TIME:** 3 HOURS AND 30 MINUTES

Meaning "always fresh," these rolls are readily available in Sicilian bakeries and particularly popular in Palermo.

INGREDIENTS:

- 1 PACKET (7 G) OF ACTIVE DRY YEAST
- 1 TEASPOON (7 G) HONEY
- 2 CUPS (450 G) WARM WATER (105°F)
- 3⅓ CUPS (400 G) FINELY GROUND DURUM WHEAT FLOUR (SEMOLA RIMACINATA)
- 3⅓ CUPS (400 G) ALL-PURPOSE FLOUR, PLUS MORE AS NEEDED
- 2 TEASPOONS (8 G) SUGAR
- 2 TABLESPOONS (26 G) EXTRA-VIRGIN OLIVE OIL
- 3½ TEASPOONS (19 G) FINE SEA SALT

1. Place the yeast, honey, and water in the work bowl of a stand mixer fitted with the dough hook, gently stir to combine, and let the mixture sit until it starts to foam, about 10 minutes.

2. Add the flours and work the mixture until it just comes together as a dough.

3. Add the sugar, olive oil, and salt and work the dough until it is smooth and elastic. Shape the dough into a ball, place it in a clean bowl, and cover the bowl with plastic wrap. Let the dough rest for 40 minutes.

4. Line two baking sheets with parchment paper. Place the dough on a flour-dusted work surface and divide it into nine pieces. Use a rolling pin to each piece into a ¼-inch-thick rectangle. Roll the rectangles up, starting from a short side.

5. Place the rolls on the baking sheets, seam side down, and let them rest for 1½ hours, brushing them with water a few times so they don't get dry.

6. Preheat the oven to 430°F and set it on convection mode, if available.

7. Place the rolls in the oven and bake until they are golden brown, 12 to 15 minutes.

8. Remove the rolls from the oven, remove them from the baking sheets, wrap them in linen towels, and let them cool. Wrapping them up as they cool makes for an extremely soft crumb that is very much worth it.

POTATO ROLLS

YIELD: 12 ROLLS / **ACTIVE TIME:** 1 HOUR / **TOTAL TIME:** 5 HOURS

With just the starch of one potato, you can transform white bread into a moist, spongy marvel.

INGREDIENTS:

- 4 CUPS (908 G) WATER
- 2½ TABLESPOONS (41 G) FINE SEA SALT
- 1 LARGE RUSSET POTATO, PEELED AND DICED
- 1¾ TEASPOONS (5.2 G) ACTIVE DRY YEAST
- 3½ TABLESPOONS (44 G) SUGAR
- 1 EGG
- 2⅚ CUPS (340 G) BREAD FLOUR, PLUS MORE AS NEEDED

1. Place the water and 2 tablespoons of the salt in a saucepan and bring it to a boil. Add the potato and cook until it is very tender, 20 to 25 minutes. Reserve ½ cup of the cooking liquid and then drain the potato.

2. Place the potato in a small bowl and mash it with a fork until smooth.

3. Let the reserved liquid and potato cool to 90°F.

4. Place the reserved liquid and yeast in the work bowl of a stand mixer fitted with the dough hook, gently stir to combine, and let the mixture sit until it starts to foam, about 10 minutes.

5. Add the sugar, egg, ⅔ cup of the potato, the flour, and the remaining salt and knead the mixture on low for 1 minute. Raise the speed to medium and knead until it comes together as a smooth dough.

6. Dust a bowl with flour. Transfer the dough to the bowl and cover it with plastic wrap. Let the dough rest until it has doubled in size, about 1½ hours.

7. Place the dough on a flour-dusted work surface, divide it into 12 pieces, and shape them into small balls.

8. Line an 18 x 13–inch baking sheet with parchment paper and coat it with nonstick cooking spray. Place the rolls on the prepared pan, dust them with flour, and cover them with plastic wrap. Place the pan in a naturally warm spot and let the rolls rest until they have doubled in size.

9. Preheat the oven to 350°F.

10. Place the rolls in the oven and bake until they are golden brown and feel lighter when lifted, 20 to 25 minutes.

11. Remove the rolls from the oven and let them cool slightly before enjoying.

LIGHTER THAN A CLOUD BISCUITS

YIELD: 16 BISCUITS / **ACTIVE TIME:** 45 MINUTES / **TOTAL TIME:** 1 HOUR AND 45 MINUTES

These are amazing with butter and honey or with gravy . . . really, they're amazing with anything.

INGREDIENTS:

- 1 CUP (227 G) BUTTERMILK (105°F)
- 2¼ TEASPOONS (7 G) INSTANT YEAST
- 2½ CUPS (300 G) ALL-PURPOSE FLOUR, PLUS MORE AS NEEDED
- 2 TEASPOONS (8 G) BAKING POWDER
- ½ TEASPOON (3 G) BAKING SODA
- ½ TABLESPOON (6 G) SUGAR
- 1 TEASPOON (6 G) FINE SEA SALT
- ½ CUP (113 G) UNSALTED BUTTER, CHILLED AND CUBED, PLUS MELTED BUTTER FOR TOPPING

1. Preheat the oven to 150°F. Maintain the temperature for 10 to 15 minutes, then turn off the oven. Line two baking sheets with parchment paper.

2. In a small bowl, stir the buttermilk and yeast together until dissolved. In the work bowl of a stand mixer fitted with the paddle attachment, mix the flour, baking powder, baking soda, sugar, and salt on low until combined.

3. Add the cold butter and mix until just incorporated, about 1 minute. Slowly mix in the buttermilk mixture until the dough comes together, about 1 minute. Fit the mixer with the dough hook and mix on low until the dough is shiny and smooth, about 3 minutes.

4. On a lightly flour-dusted work surface, knead the dough briefly to form a smooth ball. Roll the dough out into a 10-inch circle, about ½ inch thick. Using a flour-dusted 2½-inch biscuit cutter, cut rounds out of the dough and place them on the baking sheets. Cover the biscuits with kitchen towels and place the baking sheets in the warm oven. Let the biscuits rest until they have doubled in size, about 30 minutes.

5. Remove the biscuits from the oven and preheat the oven to 350°F.

6. Place the biscuits in the oven and bake until they are golden brown, 12 to 14 minutes.

7. Remove the biscuits from the oven, brush the tops with melted butter, and serve warm.

SESAME COUNTRY BUNS

YIELD: 8 BUNS / **ACTIVE TIME:** 45 MINUTES / **TOTAL TIME:** 4 HOURS

A go-to preparation, whether you're looking for dinner rolls or hamburger buns.

INGREDIENTS:

- 9 OZ. (255 G) LUKEWARM WATER (90°F)
- 1 TABLESPOON (9 G) ACTIVE DRY YEAST
- 3¾ CUPS (450 G) BREAD FLOUR, PLUS MORE AS NEEDED
- 1 TEASPOON (4 G) SUGAR
- 1 TABLESPOON (16 G) FINE SEA SALT
- 2 TABLESPOONS (28 G) UNSALTED BUTTER, SOFTENED
- 1 EGG, BEATEN
- WHITE SESAME SEEDS, FOR TOPPING

1. Place the water and yeast in the work bowl of a stand mixer fitted with the dough hook, gently stir to combine, and let the mixture sit until it starts to foam, about 10 minutes.

2. Add the flour, sugar, and salt and work the mixture on low until it just starts to come together as a dough, about 1 minute.

3. Add the butter, raise the speed to medium, and work the dough until it comes away clean from the side of the work bowl and is elastic.

4. Coat a mixing bowl with nonstick cooking spray. Place the dough on a flour-dusted work surface and knead until it is extensible. Shape the dough into a ball, place it in the bowl, and cover the bowl with a kitchen towel. Place the dough in a naturally warm spot and let it rest until it has doubled in size, 1 to 2 hours.

5. Preheat the oven to 350°F. Line an 18 x 13–inch baking sheet with parchment paper.

6. Portion the dough into eight pieces that are each about 3½ oz. and shape them into rounds. Place the rounds on the pan, cover them with plastic wrap, and place them in a naturally warm spot. Let the rolls rest until they have doubled in size.

7. Gently brush the rolls with the beaten egg and sprinkle the sesame seeds over them.

8. Place the rolls in the oven and bake until they are golden brown, about 20 minutes.

9. Remove the rolls from the oven, place them on a wire rack, and let them cool before enjoying.

PORTUGUESE SWEET ROLLS

YIELD: 10 ROLLS / **ACTIVE TIME:** 45 MINUTES / **TOTAL TIME:** 4 HOURS

Serve these alongside a spicy or smoky protein.

INGREDIENTS:

- 1 CUP (227 G) WATER
- 2 TABLESPOONS (18 G) ACTIVE DRY YEAST
- 2 EGGS
- 5 OZ. (142 G) SUGAR
- 5⅓ CUPS (650 G) BREAD FLOUR, PLUS MORE AS NEEDED
- 1⅓ TABLESPOONS (22 G) FINE SEA SALT
- ½ CUP (113 G) UNSALTED BUTTER, SOFTENED; PLUS ¼ CUP MELTED BUTTER

1. Place the water, yeast, eggs, and sugar in the work bowl of a stand mixer fitted with the dough hook and whisk to combine. Add the flour, salt, and softened butter and knead on low for 1 minute. Raise the speed to medium and knead the mixture until it comes together as a smooth dough and begins to pull away from the side of the work bowl, 6 to 8 minutes.

2. Coat a mixing bowl with nonstick cooking spray. Shape the dough into a ball, place it in the bowl, and cover it with plastic wrap. Place the dough in a naturally warm spot and let it rest until it has doubled in size.

3. Line an 18 x 13–inch baking sheet with parchment paper. Place the dough on a flour-dusted work surface and divide it into ten 3½ oz. portions. Roll the portions into tight balls. Place the balls on the pan, cover them with plastic wrap, and place them in a naturally warm spot. Let them rest until they have doubled in size.

4. Preheat the oven to 350°F.

5. Place the pan in the oven and bake until the rolls are golden brown and feel lighter when lifted, 20 to 25 minutes.

6. Remove the rolls from the oven, transfer them to a wire rack, and brush them with the melted butter. Let them cool completely before enjoying.

PRETZEL BUNS

YIELD: 10 BUNS / **ACTIVE TIME:** 45 MINUTES / **TOTAL TIME:** 4 HOURS

The beautifully burnished outside and powerful flavor of these buns are a result of the alkaline solution.

INGREDIENTS:

FOR THE DOUGH

- 1½ CUPS (340 G) LUKEWARM WATER (90°F)
- 1½ TEASPOONS (4.5 G) ACTIVE DRY YEAST
- 4⅓ TABLESPOONS (57 G) DARK BROWN SUGAR
- 4¼ CUPS (510 G) BREAD FLOUR, PLUS MORE AS NEEDED
- 2 TEASPOONS (12 G) FINE SEA SALT

FOR THE ALKALINE SOLUTION

- 2 CUPS WATER
- 2 TABLESPOONS BAKING SODA

1. To begin preparations for the dough, place the water and yeast in the work bowl of a stand mixer fitted with the dough hook, gently stir to combine, and let the mixture sit until it starts to foam, about 10 minutes.

2. Add the brown sugar, flour, and salt and knead on low for 1 minute. Raise the speed to medium and knead the mixture until it comes together as a smooth dough and begins to pull away from the side of the work bowl, about 6 to 8 minutes.

3. Coat a mixing bowl with nonstick cooking spray. Remove the dough from the work bowl, place it on a flour-dusted work surface, and shape it into a ball. Place the dough in the bowl, cover it with plastic wrap, place it in a naturally warm spot, and let it rest until it has doubled in size.

4. Preheat the oven to 350°F. Line an 18 x 13–inch baking sheet with parchment paper.

5. To prepare the alkaline solution, place the water and baking soda in a small saucepan and bring it to a boil. Remove the saucepan from heat and set aside.

6. Place the dough on a flour-dusted work surface and divide it into 10 pieces. Shape each one into a ball and place the balls on the pan. Cover them with plastic wrap, place them in a naturally warm spot, and let them rest until they have doubled in size.

7. Brush the buns with the alkaline solution and score a small X on the top of each one.

8. Place the buns in the oven and bake until they are golden brown and feel lighter when lifted, 20 to 25 minutes.

9. Remove the buns from the oven, transfer them to a wire rack, and let them cool before enjoying.

ST. LUCIA BUNS

YIELD: 10 BUNS / **ACTIVE TIME:** 45 MINUTES / **TOTAL TIME:** 4 HOURS

These buns are also known in Sweden as lussekatter, a name inspired by their resemblance to a cat's tail.

1. Place the milk and yeast in the work bowl of a stand mixer fitted with the dough hook, gently whisk to combine, and let the mixture sit until it starts to foam, about 10 minutes.

2. Add the butter, unbeaten egg, saffron, sugar, flour, and salt and knead on low for 1 minute. Raise the speed to medium and knead the mixture until it comes together as a smooth dough and begins to pull away from the side of the work bowl, about 6 to 8 minutes.

3. Coat a mixing bowl with nonstick cooking spray. Shape the dough into a ball, place it in the bowl, and cover it with plastic wrap. Place the dough in a naturally warm spot and let it rest until it has doubled in size.

4. Preheat the oven to 350°F. Line an 18 x 13–inch baking sheet with parchment paper.

5. Place the dough on a flour-dusted work surface and divide it into 10 portions. Shape each one into a ball and then use your hands to roll the balls out into 14-inch-long strands. Curl the ends of the strands in opposite directions so that each strand forms an S. Place the buns on the pan, cover them with plastic wrap, place them in a naturally warm spot, and let them rest until they have doubled in size.

6. Brush the buns with the beaten egg. Drain the raisins and place one in the middle of each curl.

7. Place the buns in the oven and bake until they are golden brown and feel lighter when lifted, 15 to 20 minutes.

8. Remove the buns from the oven, place them on a wire rack, and let them cool before enjoying.

INGREDIENTS:

- ¼ CUP (57 G) MILK, WARMED (90°F)
- 1 TABLESPOON (9 G) ACTIVE DRY YEAST
- ¾ CUP (170 G) UNSALTED BUTTER, MELTED
- 2 EGGS, 1 BEATEN
- PINCH OF SAFFRON THREADS
- 6½ OZ. (184 G) SUGAR
- 7½ CUPS (905 G) BREAD FLOUR, PLUS MORE AS NEEDED
- ½ TEASPOON (3 G) FINE SEA SALT
- ½ CUP RAISINS, SOAKED IN HOT WATER

BENNE BUNS

YIELD: 12 BUNS / **ACTIVE TIME:** 45 MINUTES / **TOTAL TIME:** 4 HOURS

Benne seeds are the forebears of white sesame seeds, and they lend a nutty, honeyed flavor to these buns.

INGREDIENTS:

- 1 CUP (227 G) LUKEWARM WATER (90°F)
- 4 TEASPOONS (12 G) ACTIVE DRY YEAST
- 5 OZ. (142 G) SUGAR
- ½ CUP (113 G) UNSALTED BUTTER, MELTED
- 2 EGGS
- 4⅔ CUPS (565 G) ALL-PURPOSE FLOUR, PLUS MORE AS NEEDED
- 4 OZ. (113 G) BENNE SEED FLOUR OR SESAME SEED FLOUR
- 1 TABLESPOON (16 G) FINE SEA SALT
- 1½ OZ. (42 G) BENNE SEEDS, TOASTED

1. Place the water and yeast in the work bowl of a stand mixer fitted with the dough hook, gently stir to combine, and let the mixture sit until it starts to foam, about 10 minutes.

2. Add the sugar, butter, eggs, flours, salt, and benne seeds and knead on low for 1 minute. Raise the speed to medium and knead the mixture until it comes together as a smooth dough and begins to pull away from the side of the work bowl, about 6 to 8 minutes.

3. Coat a mixing bowl with nonstick cooking spray. Shape the dough into a ball, place it in the bowl, and cover it with plastic wrap. Place the dough in a naturally warm spot and let it rest until it has doubled in size.

4. Preheat the oven to 350°F. Line an 18 x 13–inch baking sheet with parchment paper.

5. Place the dough on a flour-dusted work surface and divide it into 12 portions. Place the buns on the pan, cover them with plastic wrap, place them in a naturally warm spot, and let them rest until they have doubled in size.

6. Place the buns in the oven and bake until they are golden brown and feel lighter when lifted, 20 to 25 minutes.

7. Remove the buns from the oven, place them on a wire rack, and let them cool before enjoying.

SOFT DINNER ROLLS

YIELD: 10 ROLLS / **ACTIVE TIME:** 25 MINUTES / **TOTAL TIME:** 3 HOURS

These pillowy rolls are wonderful for sopping up any remaining juice or sauce, and they also make for a great, and edible, centerpiece for a dinner party.

INGREDIENTS:

- 1 CUP PLUS 1 TABLESPOON (242 G) MILK
- 2 TEASPOONS (6.5 G) ACTIVE DRY YEAST
- 3⅓ CUPS (400 G) BREAD FLOUR, PLUS MORE AS NEEDED
- 2 EGGS
- 2 TABLESPOONS (25 G) SUGAR
- 2 TEASPOONS (12 G) FINE SEA SALT
- ½ CUP (113 G) UNSALTED BUTTER; PLUS MELTED BUTTER, AS NEEDED

1. Warm 3 tablespoons of the milk until it is 105°F. Add the yeast and milk to a bowl and gently stir to combine. Let the mixture sit until it starts to foam, about 10 minutes.

2. In the work bowl of a stand mixer fitted with the dough hook, combine the yeast mixture and the remaining ingredients, except for the butter, and work the mixture until it comes together as a smooth dough.

3. Add the butter in pieces and raise the speed to high. Knead the dough for 8 to 10 minutes.

4. Shape the dough into a ball, place it in a clean mixing bowl, and cover it with plastic wrap. Let the dough rest at room temperature until it has doubled in size, 1 to 1½ hours.

5. Place the dough on a flour-dusted work surface and divide it into 10 pieces. Roughly shape the pieces into rounds, cover them with a kitchen towel, and let them rest for 15 minutes.

6. Coat a baking dish with melted butter. Shape the dough into tight rounds, place them in the baking dish, and cover it with butter-coated plastic wrap. Let the rolls rest at room temperature until they have doubled in size, 1 to 1½ hours.

7. Preheat the oven to 390°F.

8. Brush the rolls with melted butter and place them in the oven. Bake until they are golden brown, 20 to 25 minutes.

9. Remove the rolls from the oven, place them on a wire rack, and let them cool slightly before serving.

CRUSTY DINNER ROLLS

YIELD: 8 ROLLS / **ACTIVE TIME:** 10 MINUTES / **TOTAL TIME:** 10 HOURS

For all who love a crunch in their rolls, here is a foolproof no-knead recipe that uses just a pinch of yeast. The flavor will remind you of sourdough, without the hassle of maintaining a starter.

INGREDIENTS:

- 1¼ CUPS (280 G) WATER
- ⅓ TEASPOON (1 G) ACTIVE DRY YEAST
- 1⅓ CUPS (160 G) BREAD FLOUR
- 1 CUP (120 G) ALL-PURPOSE FLOUR, PLUS MORE AS NEEDED
- ½ CUP (60 G) WHOLE WHEAT FLOUR
- 1½ TEASPOONS (9 G) FINE SEA SALT

1. Warm 3 tablespoons of the water until it is 105°F. Add the yeast and water to a bowl and gently stir to combine. Let the mixture sit until it starts to foam, about 10 minutes.

2. In the work bowl of a stand mixer fitted with the dough hook, combine the yeast mixture with the remaining ingredients and work the mixture until it just comes together. Cover the bowl with plastic wrap and let the dough rest at room temperature until it has doubled in size, 8 to 10 hours.

3. Place the dough on a generously flour-dusted work surface and gently fold it on itself, stretching out each one of the corners before folding it into the center. Cover the dough with a kitchen towel and let it rest for 45 minutes.

4. Preheat the oven to 480°F. Line a baking dish with parchment paper. Sprinkle flour over the dough and then use a bench scraper or a sharp knife to cut the dough in half. Cut each piece into four pieces and place them in the baking dish.

5. Place the rolls in the oven and bake for 15 minutes. Reduce the temperature to 410°F and bake until the rolls are golden brown, about 5 minutes.

6. Remove the rolls from the oven, place them on a wire rack, and let them cool slightly before serving.

PÃO DE QUEIJO

YIELD: 12 BUNS / **ACTIVE TIME:** 20 MINUTES / **TOTAL TIME:** 45 MINUTES

A delicious gluten-free bread that is revered in Brazil.

INGREDIENTS:

- 11 OZ. (312 G) TAPIOCA STARCH
- 1 CUP (227 G) MILK
- ½ CUP (113 G) UNSALTED BUTTER
- 1 TEASPOON (6 G) FINE SEA SALT
- 2 EGGS
- 1½ CUPS (150 G) GRATED PARMESAN CHEESE

1. Preheat the oven to 350°F. Line an 18 x 13–inch baking sheet with parchment paper. Place the tapioca starch in the work bowl of a stand mixer fitted with the paddle attachment.

2. Place the milk, butter, and salt in a small saucepan and warm it over medium heat until the butter has melted and the mixture is simmering.

3. Turn the mixer on low and slowly pour the milk mixture into the work bowl. Raise the speed to medium and work the mixture until it has cooled considerably.

4. Add the eggs one at a time and beat to incorporate. Add the Parmesan and beat the mixture until incorporated.

5. Scoop twelve 2 oz. portions of the dough onto the pan, making sure to leave enough space between them.

6. Place the pan in the oven and bake until the buns are puffy and light golden brown, 15 to 20 minutes.

7. Remove the buns from the oven and enjoy immediately.

Pão de Queijo, see page 535

OLIVE ROLLS

YIELD: 14 ROLLS / **ACTIVE TIME:** 25 MINUTES / **TOTAL TIME:** 3 HOURS

Olives are a perfect addition to dinner rolls, making them as fitting at a casual affair as they are at a more formal one.

INGREDIENTS:

- 1½ CUPS (340 G) WATER
- 1 TABLESPOON (8 G) ACTIVE DRY YEAST
- 5⅛ CUPS (615 G) BREAD FLOUR, PLUS MORE AS NEEDED
- ⅓ CUP PLUS 2 TABLESPOONS (90 G) EXTRA-VIRGIN OLIVE OIL
- 3 TABLESPOONS (40 G) SUGAR
- 2½ TEASPOONS (15 G) FINE SEA SALT
- ⅔ CUP PITTED OLIVES, DRAINED, PRESSED, AND CHOPPED

1. Warm 3 tablespoons of the water until it is about 105°F. Add the yeast and water to a bowl and gently stir to combine. Let the mixture sit until it starts to foam, about 10 minutes.

2. In the work bowl of a stand mixer fitted with the dough hook, combine the yeast mixture with the remaining ingredients, except for the olives, and work the mixture until it comes together as a smooth dough, about 10 minutes. Cover the bowl with plastic wrap and let the dough rest at room temperature until it has doubled in size, 8 to 10 hours.

3. Add the olives to the dough and gently fold to incorporate them. Shape the dough into a ball, place it in a clean mixing bowl, and cover it with plastic wrap. Let the dough rest at room temperature until it has doubled in size, 1 to 1½ hours.

4. Line a baking sheet with parchment paper. Place the dough on a flour-dusted work surface and divide it into 14 pieces. Shape the dough into tight rounds, place them on the baking sheet, and cover the rolls with plastic wrap. Let them rest at room temperature until they have doubled in size, 1 to 1½ hours.

5. Preheat the oven to 410°F.

6. Place the rolls in the oven and bake until they are golden brown, about 15 minutes.

7. Remove the rolls from the oven, place them on a wire rack, and let them cool slightly before serving.

FOOLPROOF SOURDOUGH ROLLS

YIELD: 10 ROLLS / **ACTIVE TIME:** 30 MINUTES / **TOTAL TIME:** 24 HOURS

This is a great recipe for using sourdough starter leftovers, and it's also a fantastic way to have freshly baked bread in the morning without having to plan ahead.

INGREDIENTS:

- ⅓ CUP (75 G) SOURDOUGH STARTER (SEE PAGE 40)
- 2¼ CUPS (510 G) WATER
- 3 CUPS (360 G) BREAD FLOUR
- 1⅔ CUPS (200 G) ALL-PURPOSE FLOUR, PLUS MORE AS NEEDED
- 1¼ CUPS (150 G) WHOLE WHEAT FLOUR
- 2½ TEASPOONS (15 G) FINE SEA SALT

1. In the evening of the first day, combine the starter with the water in a large bowl and add the flours. Let the mixture rest, covered, for 45 minutes. Then add the salt and combine well.

2. Cover the bowl with plastic wrap and let the dough rest for 30 minutes. Fold the dough three times, cover it, and let it rest for another 30 minutes. Perform three more folds, cover the dough, and let it rest at room temperature overnight.

3. Preheat the oven to 475°F and place a baking stone or steel on the middle rack of the oven as it warms. Place the dough on a flour-dusted work surface and fold it like a letter. Let it rest for 10 minutes and fold it again.

4. Carefully flip the dough over and let it rest for an hour.

5. Cut the dough into 10 pieces and use a parchment-lined peel to transfer them to the heated baking implement. Bake until they are golden brown, about 15 minutes.

6. Remove the rolls from the oven, place them on a wire rack, and let them cool slightly before serving.

HOT CROSS BUNS

YIELD: 12 TO 15 BUNS / **ACTIVE TIME:** 50 MINUTES / **TOTAL TIME:** 4 HOURS

Traditional sweet buns originated in England, probably in Saint Albans, during the Middle Ages. They were supposed to be eaten only on the Friday preceding Easter or at burials. As delicious as they are, hot cross buns are now available year-round in several places.

1. To begin preparations for the dough, warm the water until it is about 105°F. Place the water and yeast in a bowl and gently stir to combine. Let the mixture sit until it starts to foam, about 10 minutes.

2. In the work bowl of a stand mixer fitted with the dough hook, combine the yeast mixture with the milk, half of the flour, and the sugar.

3. Add one egg at a time and incorporate well. Add the rest of the flour and start working the mixture until it starts to come together.

4. Add the butter in pieces, continuing to work the dough, and incorporate the salt toward the end. Knead the dough until it feels smooth. The mixing process takes about 20 minutes from start to finish.

5. Cover the dough with a kitchen towel, place it in a naturally warm spot, and let it rest until it looks fully risen, 1 to 2 hours.

6. Place the dough on a clean work surface. Incorporate all of the other ingredients, folding them in until evenly distributed.

7. Divide the dough into 12 to 15 pieces and roll them into small rounds. Line two baking sheets with parchment paper and place the rounds on them.

8. Cover the baking sheets with plastic wrap and let the dough rest for 1 to 1½ hours.

9. Preheat the oven to 425°F.

10. To prepare the cross, combine the flour with the water and then fill a piping bag with the mixture. Decorate the top of each bun by piping a cross over it.

11. Place the buns in the oven and bake until they are golden brown and feel lighter when lifted, about 20 minutes. Remove the buns from the oven and, while still warm, glaze the buns with the apricot jam.

INGREDIENTS:

FOR THE DOUGH

- ½ CUP (115 G) WATER
- 1 TABLESPOON (8.5 G) ACTIVE DRY YEAST
- ¾ CUP (170 G) LUKEWARM MILK (90°F)
- 4⅛ CUPS (500 G) ALL-PURPOSE FLOUR
- ⅓ CUP (70 G) SUGAR
- 2 EGGS
- 3½ TABLESPOONS (50 G) UNSALTED BUTTER
- 1¾ TEASPOONS (10 G) FINE SEA SALT
- ⅔ CUP RAISINS
- 1 CUP CHOPPED CANDIED ORANGE PEELS
- 1 APPLE, PEELED, CORED, AND FINELY DICED
- ZEST OF 1 ORANGE
- 1 TEASPOON GROUND CINNAMON

FOR THE CROSS

- ¾ CUP ALL-PURPOSE FLOUR
- ⅓ CUP WATER

FOR THE GLAZE

- APRICOT JAM, AS NEEDED

Hot Cross Buns, see page 541

SPELT ROLLS WITH DATES & FIGS

YIELD: 10 TO 12 ROLLS / **ACTIVE TIME:** 40 MINUTES / **TOTAL TIME:** 24 HOURS

These rolls are wonderful for a winter breakfast or brunch, and they are a great way to use sourdough starter leftovers. The overnight fermentation allows you to save some time, and it gives a more complex flavor.

1. In a large bowl, combine all of the ingredients, except for the chia seeds, with a spoon and then by hand, without kneading.

2. Cover the bowl with plastic wrap and let the dough rest at room temperature for 1 hour, making folds every 30 minutes. Place the dough in the refrigerator and let it rest overnight.

3. Remove the dough from the refrigerator and let it rest at room temperature for 1½ hours.

4. Preheat the oven to 480°F. Place the dough on a flour-dusted work surface and divide it into 10 to 12 pieces. Form the pieces into rolls of assorted shapes—rounds, ovals, and so on—and place them on a baking sheet. Cover with a kitchen towel and let the rolls rest for 1 hour.

5. Brush the rolls with water and sprinkle chia seeds over them. Place the rolls in the oven and bake for 12 to 15 minutes. Reduce the temperature to 430°F and bake until the rolls are browned and feel lighter, 12 to 15 minutes.

6. Remove the rolls from the oven, place them on a wire rack, and let them cool slightly before serving.

INGREDIENTS:

¾ CUP (170 G) SOURDOUGH STARTER (SEE PAGE 40)

2½ CUPS (300 G) BREAD FLOUR, PLUS MORE AS NEEDED

¾ CUP PLUS 1 TABLESPOON (80 G) WHOLE SPELT FLOUR

1¼ CUPS (280 G) WATER, PLUS MORE AS NEEDED

1 TEASPOON (6 G) FINE SEA SALT

½ TEASPOON (4 G) MALT SYRUP

½ CUP DRIED FIGS, CHOPPED

½ CUP DRIED DATES, CHOPPED

WATER, AS NEEDED

CHIA SEEDS, FOR TOPPING

ROSEMARY & GARLIC ROLLS

YIELD: 8 ROLLS / **ACTIVE TIME:** 30 MINUTES / **TOTAL TIME:** 3 HOURS

These rolls are so incredibly tasty and a great accompaniment to salads and meats alike.

INGREDIENTS:

1 CUP (227 G) WARM WATER (105°F)

2½ TEASPOONS (7 G) ACTIVE DRY YEAST

1 TABLESPOON (12 G) SUGAR

1 TABLESPOON (14 G) UNSALTED BUTTER, MELTED, PLUS MORE AS NEEDED

1 TEASPOON (6 G) FINE SEA SALT

2 GARLIC CLOVES, MINCED

4 CUPS (480 G) ALL-PURPOSE FLOUR, PLUS MORE AS NEEDED

1 TEASPOON FRESH ROSEMARY

1 EGG, LIGHTLY BEATEN

FLAKY SEA SALT, FOR TOPPING

1. Place the water, yeast, and sugar in the work bowl of a stand mixer fitted with the dough hook and gently stir to combine. Let the mixture sit until it starts to foam, about 10 minutes.

2. Add the melted butter, fine sea salt, and garlic and half of the flour. Work the mixture until it comes together as a sticky dough. With the mixer running, gradually add the remaining flour and work the dough until it is soft and smooth. Add the rosemary and work the dough until it is evenly distributed. Form the dough into a ball.

3. Coat the bottom and sides of a large bowl with butter. Place the dough in the bowl, cover it loosely with plastic wrap, place it in a naturally warm spot, and let it rest until it has doubled in size, 45 minutes to 1 hour.

4. Place a cast-iron skillet in the oven and preheat the oven to 400°F.

5. Place the dough on a lightly flour-dusted work surface. Divide it into eight pieces and shape the pieces into rounds.

6. Remove the skillet from the oven and coat the bottom of it with butter. Place the rolls in the skillet, brush the tops with the beaten egg, and sprinkle flaky sea salt over the top.

7. Return the skillet to the oven and bake until the rolls are golden brown and feel lighter when lifted, 25 to 30 minutes.

8. Remove the rolls from the oven, place them on a wire rack, and let them cool slightly before serving.

SWEET POTATO ROLLS

YIELD: 18 SMALL ROLLS / **ACTIVE TIME:** 1 HOUR / **TOTAL TIME:** 3 HOURS

There's something about the color and flavor of sweet potatoes that says "goodness." These rolls won't disappoint. They're delicious served with savory dishes like roast pork or chicken, but also great for breakfast with homemade jam.

INGREDIENTS:

- 1 LARGE SWEET POTATO, PEELED AND DICED
- 1 PACKET (7 G) OF ACTIVE DRY YEAST
- ½ CUP (115 G) WARM WATER (105°F)
- 2 TABLESPOONS (24 G) LIGHT BROWN SUGAR
- 2 CUPS (240 G) ALL-PURPOSE FLOUR, PLUS MORE AS NEEDED
- ⅓ CUP (75 G) UNSALTED BUTTER, MELTED
- ¼ CUP (85 G) HONEY
- 1 EGG, LIGHTLY BEATEN
- ½ TEASPOON (3 G) FINE SEA SALT
- ½ TEASPOON (2 G) GROUND GINGER
- ¼ TEASPOON (1 G) GROUND NUTMEG
- 1½ CUPS (175 G) WHOLE WHEAT FLOUR

1. Place the sweet potato in a saucepan, cover with water, and bring to a boil. Reduce the heat and simmer the sweet potato until tender, about 20 minutes. Drain, place it in a bowl, and mash until smooth.

2. In the work bowl of a stand mixer fitted with the dough hook, combine the yeast and warm water. Add the brown sugar and ¼ cup of the all-purpose flour and gently stir. Let the mixture sit until it starts to foam, about 10 minutes.

3. Melt the butter in a cast-iron skillet and add it to the sweet potato. Add the honey, egg, salt, ginger, and nutmeg and stir to combine.

4. Add the sweet potato mixture to the yeast mixture and stir to combine. Add the remaining all-purpose flour and the whole wheat flour and work the mixture until it comes together as a smooth, elastic dough, about 10 minutes.

5. Coat a large bowl with nonstick cooking spray. Shape the dough into a ball, place it in the bowl, and cover it loosely with plastic wrap. Place the bowl in a naturally warm spot and let it rest until it has doubled in size, 1 to 2 hours.

6. Line two baking sheets with parchment paper. Punch down the dough to deflate it and place it on a flour-dusted work surface. Divide the dough into 18 pieces and shape them into balls. Place the rolls on the baking sheets, cover them with kitchen towels, and let them rest for 30 minutes.

7. Preheat the oven to 375°F.

8. Place the rolls in the oven and bake until they are golden brown, about 30 minutes.

9. Remove the rolls from the oven and serve warm.

BURGER BUNS

YIELD: 10 BUNS / **ACTIVE TIME:** 25 MINUTES / **TOTAL TIME:** 3 HOURS

If you must, you can use butter or shortening to make these buns, but the lard is suggested for a reason: it simply tastes better.

INGREDIENTS:

- 1 CUP PLUS 1 TABLESPOON (240 G) WATER
- 2 TEASPOONS (6.5 G) ACTIVE DRY YEAST
- 4⅛ CUPS (495 G) BREAD FLOUR, PLUS MORE AS NEEDED
- 3⅔ TABLESPOONS (45 G) SUGAR
- 2 TEASPOONS (12 G) FINE SEA SALT
- 3⅔ TABLESPOONS (55 G) LARD

1. Warm 3 tablespoons of the water until it is about 105°F. Add the yeast and water to a bowl and gently stir to combine. Let the mixture sit until it starts to foam, about 10 minutes.

2. In the work bowl of a stand mixer fitted with the dough hook, combine the yeast mixture and the remaining ingredients, except for the lard. Work the mixture on low until it comes together as a smooth dough, about 5 minutes.

3. Add the lard, increase the speed to high, and knead until the dough is elastic, about 8 minutes. Shape the dough into a ball, place it in a clean mixing bowl, and cover the bowl with plastic wrap. Let the dough rest at room temperature until it has doubled in size, 1 to 1½ hours.

4. Line a baking sheet with parchment paper. Place the dough on a flour-dusted work surface and divide it into 10 pieces. Roughly shape the dough into rounds, cover them with a kitchen towel, and let them rest for 15 minutes.

5. Shape the dough into tight rounds, place them on the baking sheet, and cover the buns with plastic wrap. Let them rest at room temperature until they have doubled in size, 1 to 1½ hours.

6. Preheat the oven to 360°F.

7. Place the buns in the oven and bake until they are golden brown, about 25 minutes.

8. Remove the buns from the oven, place them on a wire rack, and let them cool slightly before serving.

BRIOCHE BURGER BUNS

YIELD: 10 BUNS / **ACTIVE TIME:** 25 MINUTES / **TOTAL TIME:** 3 HOURS

The addition of eggs, butter, and sugar to this dough makes for extremely soft and slightly sweet buns that will pair wonderfully with rich and savory accompaniments.

1. Warm 3 tablespoons of the water until it is about 105°F. Add the yeast and water to a bowl and gently stir to combine. Let the mixture sit until it starts to foam, about 10 minutes.

2. In the work bowl of a stand mixer fitted with the dough hook, combine the yeast mixture and the remaining ingredients, except for the butter, 1 egg, and the sesame seeds. Work the mixture on low until it comes together as a smooth dough, about 5 minutes.

3. Add the butter gradually, increase the speed to high, and knead until the dough is elastic, about 8 minutes. Shape the dough into a ball, place it in a clean mixing bowl, and cover the bowl with plastic wrap. Let the dough rest at room temperature until it has doubled in size, 1 to 1½ hours.

4. Line a baking sheet with parchment paper. Place the dough on a flour-dusted work surface and divide it into 10 pieces. Roughly shape the dough into rounds, cover them with a kitchen towel, and let them rest for 15 minutes.

5. Shape the dough into tight rounds, place them on the baking sheet, and cover the buns with plastic wrap. Let them rest at room temperature until they have doubled in size, 1 to 1½ hours.

6. Preheat the oven to 360°F.

7. Brush the buns with the remaining egg, sprinkle the sesame seeds over them, and place them in the oven. Bake until they are golden brown, about 25 minutes.

8. Remove the buns from the oven, place them on a wire rack, and let them cool slightly before serving.

INGREDIENTS:

- 1 CUP (227 G) LUKEWARM WATER (90°F)
- 2 TEASPOONS (6.5 G) ACTIVE DRY YEAST
- 4⅛ CUPS (495 G) BREAD FLOUR, PLUS MORE AS NEEDED
- 2 TABLESPOONS (25 G) CASTER (SUPERFINE) SUGAR
- 3 TABLESPOONS (45 G) LUKEWARM MILK (90°F)
- 1 EGG YOLK, BEATEN
- 1½ TEASPOONS (9 G) FINE SEA SALT
- ⅓ CUP (75 G) UNSALTED BUTTER, SOFTENED
- 2 LARGE EGGS, BEATEN
- 2 TABLESPOONS SESAME SEEDS, FOR TOPPING

SOURDOUGH HAMBURGER BUNS

YIELD: 8 BUNS / **ACTIVE TIME:** 25 MINUTES / **TOTAL TIME:** 5 HOURS

When you have a sourdough starter at hand, the temptation to use it in every baked good is strong. Here's a recipe for light and fluffy burger buns that can help you use up the sourdough you would typically discard.

INGREDIENTS:

- ¾ CUP (170 G) SOURDOUGH STARTER (SEE PAGE 40)
- ¾ CUP (170 G) WATER
- 4⅛ CUPS (495 G) BREAD FLOUR, PLUS MORE AS NEEDED
- 2½ TABLESPOONS (30 G) SUGAR
- 2 TEASPOONS (12 G) FINE SEA SALT
- 3 TABLESPOONS (42 G) UNSALTED BUTTER
- 1 EGG, BEATEN
- 2 TABLESPOONS SESAME SEEDS

1. In the work bowl of a stand mixer fitted with the dough hook, combine all of the ingredients, except for the butter, egg, and sesame seeds. Work the mixture on low until it comes together as a smooth dough, about 5 minutes.

2. Add the butter gradually, increase the speed to high, and knead until the dough is elastic, about 8 minutes. Shape the dough into a ball, place it in a clean mixing bowl, and cover the bowl with plastic wrap. Let the dough rest at room temperature until it has doubled in size, 2 to 2½ hours.

3. Line a baking sheet with parchment paper. Place the dough on a flour-dusted work surface and divide it into eight pieces. Shape the dough into tight rounds, place them on the baking sheet, and cover the buns with plastic wrap. Let them rest at room temperature until they have doubled in size, 1½ to 2 hours.

4. Preheat the oven to 360°F.

5. Brush the buns with the egg, sprinkle the sesame seeds over them, and place them in the oven. Bake until they are golden brown, about 25 minutes.

6. Remove the buns from the oven, place them on a wire rack, and let them cool slightly before serving.

MUFFOLETTA BUNS

YIELD: 8 BUNS / **ACTIVE TIME:** 30 MINUTES / **TOTAL TIME:** 6 HOURS

If you are tired of the usual burger buns, give these a try—in Sicily, these buns are usually filled with meats and pecorino cheese, or tomatoes and anchovies, but it will also go wonderfully with your standard burger.

INGREDIENTS:

- 1 CUP PLUS 1 TABLESPOON (242 G) WATER
- 2 TEASPOONS (6 G) ACTIVE DRY YEAST
- 4½ CUPS (730 G) FINELY GROUND DURUM WHEAT FLOUR (SEMOLA RIMACINATA), PLUS MORE AS NEEDED
- 2 TABLESPOONS (26 G) EXTRA-VIRGIN OLIVE OIL
- 2 TABLESPOONS (42 G) HONEY
- 1½ TEASPOONS (9 G) FINE SEA SALT

1. Warm 3 tablespoons of the water until it is about 105°F. Add the yeast and water to a bowl and gently stir to combine. Let the mixture sit until it starts to foam, about 10 minutes.

2. In the work bowl of a stand mixer fitted with the dough hook, combine the yeast mixture and the remaining ingredients, except for the salt. Work the mixture on low until it comes together as a smooth dough, about 5 minutes.

3. Add the salt and knead until it is incorporated and the dough is elastic, about 5 minutes. Shape the dough into a ball, place it in a clean mixing bowl, and cover the bowl with plastic wrap. Let the dough rest at room temperature until it has doubled in size, about 2 hours.

4. Line a baking sheet with parchment paper. Place the dough on a flour-dusted work surface and divide it into eight pieces. Shape the dough into tight rounds, place them on the baking sheet, and cover the buns with plastic wrap. Let them rest at room temperature until they have doubled in size, about 1 hour.

5. Preheat the oven to 430°F and place a baking stone or baking sheet on the middle rack of the oven as it warms.

6. Dust your palm with flour and press down on one of the buns to flatten it. Using a flour-dusted peel, slide the bun onto the heated baking implement and bake until it is golden brown, 15 to 20 minutes.

7. Remove the bun from the oven, place it on a wire rack, and let it cool.

8. Repeat Steps 6 and 7 with the remaining buns.

KALE-FILLED BUNS

YIELD: 10 TO 12 BUNS / **ACTIVE TIME:** 30 MINUTES / **TOTAL TIME:** 2 HOURS AND 30 MINUTES

These buns build on the same concept of cinnamon buns, but instead use a savory filling. Here is one possible filling, but feel free to try different combinations.

INGREDIENTS:

FOR THE FILLING

- EXTRA-VIRGIN OLIVE OIL, AS NEEDED
- 6½ CUPS CHOPPED KALE
- SALT AND PEPPER, TO TASTE
- 1 CUP GRATED CHEDDAR CHEESE
- 1 GARLIC CLOVE, MINCED

FOR THE DOUGH

- 2½ TEASPOONS (7 G) ACTIVE DRY YEAST
- ⅔ CUP (150 G) LUKEWARM WATER (90°F)
- ½ CUP (115 G) LUKEWARM MILK (90°F)
- 2 TABLESPOONS (26 G) EXTRA-VIRGIN OLIVE OIL
- 1 TABLESPOON (21 G) HONEY
- 2 CUPS (240 G) ALL-PURPOSE FLOUR, PLUS MORE AS NEEDED
- 2 CUPS (200 G) WHITE SPELT FLOUR
- 1 TEASPOON (5 G) FINE SEA SALT

1. To prepare the filling, coat the bottom of a large skillet with olive oil and warm it over medium heat. Add the kale, season it with salt and pepper, and cook, stirring occasionally, for 5 minutes. Stir in the cheddar and garlic and cook until the kale is tender. Remove the pan from heat and let the filling cool.

2. To begin preparations for the dough, place the yeast, water, and milk in the work bowl of a stand mixer fitted with the dough hook, gently stir, and let the mixture sit until it starts to foam, about 10 minutes.

3. Add the remaining ingredients and knead on low until the mixture comes together as a smooth dough, about 8 minutes. Cover the work bowl with plastic wrap and let the dough rest at room temperature for 45 minutes.

4. Place the dough on a flour-dusted work surface and shape it into a rectangular log. Spread the filling over the dough and then roll the dough up tightly, starting from a short side.

5. Coat a muffin pan with nonstick cooking spray. Cut the dough into 10 to 12 slices that are ⅔ inch thick and place them in the muffin pan. Cover the buns with a kitchen towel and let them rest at room temperature for 45 minutes.

6. Preheat the oven to 430°F. Place the muffin pan in the oven and bake the buns until they are golden brown, 10 to 15 minutes.

7. Remove the buns from the oven, place them on a wire rack, and let them cool slightly before serving.

SESAME BAGELS, MONTREAL STYLE

YIELD: 30 BAGELS / **ACTIVE TIME:** 50 MINUTES / **TOTAL TIME:** 1 HOUR AND 30 MINUTES

Smaller, thinner, sweeter, and more dense than the New York version, Montreal-style bagels are a good choice for those who want nothing more than a bit of cream cheese atop their bagel.

INGREDIENTS:

- 16 CUPS (1920 G) ENRICHED WHITE FLOUR, PLUS MORE AS NEEDED
- 3¾ CUPS (850 G) WATER
- ⅓ CUP (28 G) MALTED BARLEY FLOUR
- 2 TABLESPOONS (26 G) CANOLA OIL
- 6 TABLESPOONS (56 G) FRESH YEAST
- 6 TABLESPOONS (80 G) SUGAR
- 2½ TABLESPOONS HONEY
- 3½ CUPS SESAME SEEDS

1. In the work bowl of a stand mixer fitted with the dough hook, add all of the ingredients, except for the honey and sesame seeds, and work the mixture until it comes together as a slightly sticky dough, about 8 minutes. Cover the bowl with a kitchen towel and let the dough rest for 20 minutes.

2. Place the dough on a flour-dusted work surface, cut it into 30 strips that are 1½ inches wide, and roll each strip out into a 9-inch-long rope. Join the ends of the ropes together.

3. Bring a large pot of water to boil. Add the honey and stir until it has liquefied.

4. Working in batches of six, add the bagels in the pot to the pot and cook until they rise to the top, about 4 minutes.

5. Remove the bagels from the pot with a strainer and let them cool for 1 minute.

6. Preheat the oven to 325°F. Line baking sheets with parchment paper.

7. Generously top the bagels with the sesame seeds and place them on the baking sheets.

8. Place the bagels in the oven and bake until they are golden brown, 16 to 18 minutes, turning them over halfway through.

9. Remove the bagels from the oven, transfer them to a wire rack, and let them cool before serving.

SEAWEED & SOURDOUGH BAGELS

YIELD: 18 BAGELS / **ACTIVE TIME:** 2 HOURS / **TOTAL TIME:** 5 TO 6 HOURS

Seaweed lends bagels a brininess that is unmatched—just try not to think of sitting seaside while enjoying one.

1. Place the water in the work bowl of a stand mixer fitted with the dough hook and add the starter, flour, and yeast. Work the mixture on low until it just comes together as a shaggy dough. Cover the bowl and let the dough rest for 20 minutes.

2. Add the salt and work the dough on low for 2 minutes. Raise the speed to medium and knead until the dough is elastic.

3. Coat a large bowl with nonstick cooking spray. Place the dough in it, cover the bowl with plastic wrap, and place it in a naturally warm spot. Let the dough rest for 2 hours, perform a stretch and fold after 1 hour.

4. Preheat the oven to 500°F and place a baking stone or steel on the middle rack of the oven as it warms.

5. Place the dough on a flour-dusted work surface and cut it into 18 pieces. Roll the pieces into tight balls, making sure the seam sides are down. Cover the balls with a kitchen towel and let them rest until they have relaxed, about 45 minutes.

6. Poke a hole in the center of each ball and stretch gently to widen it. If the bagels are difficult to stretch and the dough resists, they need more time to rest. Cover the bagels with the kitchen towel and let them rest for another 45 minutes.

7. Fill a Dutch oven with water and bring to a boil. Gently lift with a bench scraper and drop it into the boiling water. It should float—if it does not, the rest of the bagels need more resting time. Multiple bagels can be boiled at once, but make sure not to crowd the pot.

8. Cook until the edges of the bagels begin to darken, about 30 seconds, flip them over. After the second side is boiled, remove the bagels with a strainer and let them drain on a wire rack.

9. Dust a peel with cornmeal and use a spatula to place the boiled bagels on it, spacing them out so they don't stick together. Sprinkle the dulse flakes over the bagels.

10. Gently slide the bagels onto the heat baking implement and bake until they are golden brown, 10 to 15 minutes.

11. Remove the bagels from the oven, transfer them to wire racks, and let them cool before serving.

INGREDIENTS:

- 2¼ CUPS (510 G) LUKEWARM WATER (90°F)
- 1⅓ CUPS (280 G) SOURDOUGH STARTER (SEE PAGE 40)
- 9 CUPS (1080 G) ALL-PURPOSE FLOUR, PLUS MORE AS NEEDED
- 2 TEASPOONS (6 G) ACTIVE DRY YEAST
- 1 TABLESPOON PLUS ½ TEASPOON (21 G) FINE SEA SALT
- CORNMEAL, AS NEEDED
- DULSE (SEAWEED) FLAKES, TO TASTE

NEW YORK–STYLE BAGELS

YIELD: 12 BAGELS / **ACTIVE TIME:** 45 MINUTES / **TOTAL TIME:** 24 HOURS

Delicious with sweet or savory fillings (or simply on their own), these chewy bagels are as versatile as they come.

INGREDIENTS:

7 CUPS (840 G) BREAD FLOUR

¼ CUP (50 G) SUGAR

1⅓ TABLESPOONS (24 G) FINE SEA SALT

1 EGG

¼ CUP (50 G) CANOLA OIL

1½ CUPS (340 G) COLD WATER

2 TEASPOONS (6 G) ACTIVE DRY YEAST

CORNMEAL, AS NEEDED

1. Place all of the ingredients, except for the cornmeal, in the work bowl of a stand mixer fitted with the dough hook and mix on low until the mixture comes together as a smooth dough.

2. Dust a baking sheet with cornmeal. Divide the dough into 12 pieces, roll them into 9-inch-long ropes, and then join the ends together to form them into bagels.

3. Lightly sprinkle cornmeal on a baking sheet and transfer the bagels onto it. Place the pan in the refrigerator and let the bagels rest overnight.

4. When you are ready to bake, remove the bagels from the refrigerator, place them in a moist, naturally warm spot, and let them rest until they are puffy, about 2 hours.

5. Preheat the oven to 450°F and line two baking sheets with parchment paper.

6. Bring a large pot of water to a boil. Drop a few bagels at a time into the boiling water. As soon as the bagels rise to the surface, 30 to 60 seconds, remove them with a strainer and place them on the baking sheets.

7. When all of the bagels have been boiled, place the baking sheets in the oven. Bake until they are golden brown, 18 to 20 minutes.

8. Remove the bagels from the oven, transfer them to wire racks, and let them cool before serving.

New York–Style Bagels, see page 559

CINNAMON RAISIN BAGELS

YIELD: 12 BAGELS / **ACTIVE TIME:** 45 MINUTES / **TOTAL TIME:** 24 HOURS

Warm cinnamon and juicy raisins make these the perfect breakfast bagels, especially when they've come straight out of the oven.

INGREDIENTS:

- 7 CUPS (840 G) BREAD FLOUR
- ¼ CUP (50 G) SUGAR
- 1⅓ TABLESPOONS (24 G) FINE SEA SALT
- 1 EGG
- ¼ CUP (50 G) CANOLA OIL
- 1½ CUPS (340 G) COLD WATER
- 2¼ TEASPOONS (7 G) FRESH YEAST
- 1 TABLESPOON (3 G) CINNAMON
- 1 CUP RAISINS
- CORNMEAL, AS NEEDED

1. Place all of the ingredients, except for the cornmeal, in the work bowl of a stand mixer fitted with the dough hook and mix on low until the mixture comes together as a smooth dough.

2. Dust a baking sheet with cornmeal. Divide the dough into 12 pieces, roll them into 9-inch-long ropes, and then join the ends together to form them into bagels.

3. Lightly sprinkle cornmeal on a baking sheet and transfer the bagels onto it. Place the pan in the refrigerator and let the bagels rest overnight.

4. When you are ready to bake, remove the bagels from the refrigerator, place them in a moist, naturally warm spot, and let them rest until they are puffy, about 2 hours.

5. Preheat the oven to 450°F and line two baking sheets with parchment paper.

6. Bring a large pot of water to a boil. Drop a few bagels at a time into the boiling water. As soon as the bagels rise to the surface, 30 to 60 seconds, remove them with a strainer and place them on the baking sheets.

7. When all of the bagels have been boiled, place the baking sheets in the oven. Bake until they are golden brown, 18 to 20 minutes.

8. Remove the bagels from the oven, transfer them to wire racks, and let them cool before serving.

PUMPERNICKEL BAGELS

YIELD: 12 BAGELS / **ACTIVE TIME:** 45 MINUTES / **TOTAL TIME:** 24 HOURS

Caraway seeds and rye meal pack these hearty bagels with flavor.

INGREDIENTS:

- 7 CUPS (840 G) BREAD FLOUR
- ¼ CUP (50 G) SUGAR
- 1⅓ TABLESPOONS (24 G) FINE SEA SALT
- ¼ CUP (50 G) CANOLA OIL
- 1¾ CUPS (340 G) COLD WATER
- 2 TEASPOONS (6 G) FRESH YEAST
- ¼ CUP (27 G) WHOLE CARAWAY SEEDS
- ½ CUP (60 G) RYE MEAL OR CHOPS
- ⅓ CUP (100 G) CARAMEL COLOR
- CORNMEAL, AS NEEDED

1. Place all of the ingredients, except for the cornmeal, in the work bowl of a stand mixer fitted with the dough hook and mix on low until the mixture comes together as a smooth dough.

2. Dust a baking sheet with cornmeal. Divide the dough into 12 pieces, roll them into 9-inch-long ropes, and then join the ends together to form them into bagels.

3. Lightly sprinkle cornmeal on a baking sheet and transfer the bagels onto it. Place the pan in the refrigerator and let the bagels rest overnight.

4. When you are ready to bake, remove the bagels from the refrigerator, place them in a moist, naturally warm spot, and let them rest until they are puffy, about 2 hours.

5. Preheat the oven to 450°F and line two baking sheets with parchment paper.

6. Bring a large pot of water to a boil. Drop a few bagels at a time into the boiling water. As soon as the bagels rise to the surface, 30 to 60 seconds, remove them with a strainer and place them on the baking sheets.

7. When all of the bagels have been boiled, place the baking sheets in the oven. Bake until they are golden brown, 18 to 20 minutes.

8. Remove the bagels from the oven, transfer them to wire racks, and let them cool before serving.

BIALYS

YIELD: 8 BIALYS / **ACTIVE TIME:** 1 HOUR AND 30 MINUTES / **TOTAL TIME:** 3 HOURS AND 30 MINUTES

Created in Bialystok, Poland, these tasty treats are the bagel's first cousin. The ones you'll usually find in America are soft and chewy all over, but the original versions had crisp centers that cracked when torn and chewy, soft edges. They were eaten with butter in Poland, while in the United States they're often eaten with smoked fish.

INGREDIENTS:

FOR THE BIALYS

- 1½ CUPS PLUS 1 TABLESPOON (355 G) WATER, AT ROOM TEMPERATURE
- 1 TEASPOON (3 G) INSTANT YEAST
- 4 CUPS PLUS 1 TABLESPOON (485 G) BREAD FLOUR, PLUS MORE AS NEEDED
- 2 TEASPOONS (12 G) FINE SEA SALT
- ½ CUP PLUS 2 TABLESPOONS (118 G) FILLING

FOR THE FILLING

- 1¾ CUPS PLUS 3 TABLESPOONS CHOPPED ONIONS
- 2 TEASPOONS FINE SEA SALT
- 2 TABLESPOONS CANOLA OIL
- 2 TABLESPOONS PLUS 1½ TEASPOONS POPPY SEEDS

1. To begin preparations for the bialys, place the water, yeast, and half of the flour in a large bowl. Mix with a wooden spoon until the mixture looks like a thick pancake batter.

2. Add the salt and remaining flour and stir the mixture until it just comes together as a shaggy dough.

3. Place the dough on a flour-dusted work surface and knead until it is smooth, about 5 minutes.

4. Coat a clean bowl with nonstick cooking spray, place the dough in the bowl, and cover it with plastic wrap. Let the dough rest for 30 minutes.

5. Turn the dough onto a flour-dusted work surface. Divide the dough into eight pieces and shape them into rounds. Dust the rounds with flour and cover them with plastic wrap. Let them rest for 30 minutes.

6. Preheat the oven to 400°F. To prepare the filling, place the onions, salt, canola oil, and poppy seeds in a mixing bowl and then spread the mixture out on a rimmed baking sheet. Bake until the onions are just starting to brown, about 30 minutes. Remove the filling from the oven and let it cool completely before adding it to your dough.

7. Line a baking sheet with parchment paper. Take the rounds and shape them to create a thin center and raised sides. Place the bialys on a lightly flour-dusted work surface. Place 1 tablespoon of the onion filling in the center of each bialy. Place the bialys on the baking sheet, cover them with a kitchen towel, and let them rest for 1 hour.

8. Preheat the oven to 375°F.

9. Press the center of each bialy down again before baking. Place the bialys in the oven and bake until they are bialys are just starting to turn golden brown with some darker spots, 13 to 16 minutes.

10. Remove the bialys from the oven, place them on a wire rack, and either enjoy them while slightly warm or when they have cooled to room temperature.

CITRUS & CREAM SCONES

YIELD: 18 SCONES / **ACTIVE TIME:** 40 MINUTES / **TOTAL TIME:** 55 MINUTES

This is a delicious, unorthodox version of scones that substitutes heavy cream for the traditional buttermilk, and it is enriched by the lovely addition of candied orange to the classic raisins.

INGREDIENTS:

- 4 1/6 CUPS (500 G) ALL-PURPOSE FLOUR, PLUS MORE AS NEEDED
- 1/3 CUP (65 G) SUGAR, PLUS MORE AS NEEDED
- 4 TEASPOONS (16 G) BAKING POWDER
- 1 TEASPOON (6 G) FINE SEA SALT
- 1/2 CUP RAISINS OR CURRANTS
- 1/2 CUP CANDIED ORANGE PEELS
- 2 CUPS (455 G) HEAVY CREAM, PLUS MORE AS NEEDED
- 1/4 CUP (85 G) LIGHT CLOVER HONEY
- SANDING SUGAR, FOR TOPPING

1. In a large bowl, combine the flour, sugar, baking powder, salt, raisins, and candied orange peels.

2. In a separate bowl, combine the cream and honey, making sure the honey has emulsified.

3. Pour the wet mixture into the dry ingredients and mix only until the resulting mixture comes together as a slightly wet, shaggy dough.

4. Pour out the shaggy dough onto a clean work surface and knead it until it comes together.

5. Preheat the oven to 425°F. Line two baking sheets with parchment paper.

6. Divide the dough into three pieces. Pat the pieces into 8-inch rounds. Cut each round into six triangle-shaped pieces and place the scones on the baking sheets. Brush the scones with cream and sprinkle sanding sugar over the top.

7. Place the scones in the oven and bake until they are golden brown and springy to the touch, about 15 minutes.

8. Remove the scones from the oven and let them cool slightly before serving.

CLASSIC SCONES

YIELD: 12 SCONES / **ACTIVE TIME:** 20 MINUTES / **TOTAL TIME:** 25 MINUTES

Scones are the most typical accompaniment to the unmissable English tea break. They are eaten in different ways, depending on personal taste but also on regional variations. One popular version is smothered with a generous layer of clotted cream, preceded or followed by a layer of jam.

INGREDIENTS:

- 4½ CUPS (540 G) ALL-PURPOSE FLOUR, PLUS MORE AS NEEDED
- 1½ TEASPOONS (7 G) BAKING SODA
- 1 TEASPOON (4.6 G) CREAM OF TARTAR
- 1 TABLESPOON (12 G) SUGAR
- 6 TABLESPOONS (87 G) UNSALTED BUTTER
- 1¼ CUPS (285 G) BUTTERMILK, PLUS MORE AS NEEDED

1. Preheat the oven to 450°F.

2. In a large bowl, combine all of the dry ingredients. Add the butter in pieces and work the mixture with a pastry cutter until it is well combined.

3. Add the buttermilk and work the mixture until it comes together as a dough. Shape the dough into a ball, place it on a clean work surface, and roll it out into a 1½-inch-thick square.

4. Cut the dough into 12 disks with a floured cutter—fluted ones make lovely scones.

5. Line a baking dish with parchment paper and place the scones on it. Brush the scones with buttermilk, place them in the oven, and bake until they are golden brown and springy to the touch, about 15 minutes.

6. Remove the scones from the oven and let them cool slightly before serving.

GRANOLA SCONES

YIELD: 10 SCONES / **ACTIVE TIME:** 30 MINUTES / **TOTAL TIME:** 1 HOUR

Loaded with whole grains, dried fruits, and nuts, these scones are unlike any you've ever had.

1. Preheat the oven to 375°F. Line a baking sheet with parchment paper.

2. In a large bowl, combine the flour, baking powder, baking soda, salt, cinnamon, sugar, and oats and mix until well combined. Add the butter and work the mixture with a pastry cutter until it is well combined.

3. Add the raisins, dried cherries, pumpkin seeds, and roasted almonds and work the mixture until they are evenly distributed.

4. Add the cream and work the mixture until it just comes together as a dough.

5. Pour out the dough onto a clean work surface and knead it until it comes together. Roll it out until it is 1 inch thick and cut 10 scones out of it, using a flour-dusted cutter.

6. Place the scones on the baking sheet, place them in the oven, and bake until they are golden brown and springy to the touch, 25 to 30 minutes.

7. Remove the scones from the oven and let them cool slightly before serving.

INGREDIENTS:

- 1⅔ CUPS (200 G) WHOLE WHEAT FLOUR, PLUS MORE AS NEEDED
- 1⅛ TEASPOONS (5 G) BAKING POWDER
- 1⅛ TEASPOONS (7 G) BAKING SODA
- ⅓ TEASPOON (2 G) FINE SEA SALT
- 1⅛ TEASPOONS (3 G) CINNAMON
- ⅓ CUP (65 G) SUGAR
- 2 CUPS ROLLED OATS
- ½ CUP (113 G) UNSALTED BUTTER, CUBED AND CHILLED
- ½ CUP RAISINS
- 1 CUP TART DRIED CHERRIES
- ½ CUP PUMPKIN SEEDS
- ¾ CUP WHOLE, ROASTED ALMONDS
- ½ CUP (113 G) HEAVY CREAM

BACON & CHIVE SCONES

YIELD: 24 SCONES / **ACTIVE TIME:** 30 MINUTES / **TOTAL TIME:** 45 MINUTES

Few snacks are as criminally underrated as the savory scone, and there are few savory snacks that aren't improved by bacon. This is a classic combination that allows for tons of variation—start by adding your favorite cheeses.

1. Preheat the oven to 375°F. Line two baking sheets with parchment paper.

2. In a large bowl, combine the bacon, chives, flour, baking powder, baking soda, sugar, and fine sea salt. Add the butter and work the mixture with a pastry cutter until it is well combined. Add the buttermilk and work the mixture until it just comes together as a dough.

3. Pour out the dough onto a clean work surface and knead it until it comes together. Roll it out until it is 1 inch thick and cut 24 scones out of the dough, using a flour-dusted cutter. Place the scones on the baking sheets, brush them with heavy cream, and sprinkle flaky sea salt over them.

4. Place the scones in the oven and bake until they are golden brown and springy to the touch, about 15 minutes.

5. Remove the scones from the oven and let them cool slightly before serving.

INGREDIENTS:

- ½ CUP CHOPPED CRISPY BACON
- ¼ CUP CHOPPED FRESH CHIVES
- 6¾ CUPS (810 G) ALL-PURPOSE FLOUR, PLUS MORE AS NEEDED
- 1 TABLESPOON (12 G) BAKING POWDER
- ¾ TEASPOON (4 G) BAKING SODA
- 2 TABLESPOONS (25 G) SUGAR
- 1¼ TEASPOONS (7 G) FINE SEA SALT
- 1 CUP (227 G) UNSALTED BUTTER, CUT INTO ½-INCH PIECES
- 1½ CUPS (340 G) BUTTERMILK
- HEAVY CREAM, AS NEEDED
- FLAKY SEA SALT, FOR TOPPING

CREAM CHEESE, LEMON & CURRANT SCONES

YIELD: 18 SCONES / **ACTIVE TIME:** 30 MINUTES / **TOTAL TIME:** 50 MINUTES

Incorporating cream cheese into your dough will add a luscious element to all of the qualities you already love in a scone.

INGREDIENTS:

- 3½ CUPS (420 G) ALL-PURPOSE FLOUR, PLUS MORE AS NEEDED
- 1 TABLESPOON (12 G) BAKING POWDER
- ½ TEASPOON (3 G) BAKING SODA
- ¼ CUP (50 G) SUGAR
- ½ TEASPOON (3 G) FINE SEA SALT
- ½ CUP DRIED CURRANTS
- ½ CUP (113 G) UNSALTED BUTTER, CHILLED AND CUBED
- 1 CUP (225 G) CREAM CHEESE, CHILLED
- 4 LARGE EGGS, 1 BEATEN
- ¼ CUP (57 G) BUTTERMILK
- ZEST OF 1 SMALL LEMON

1. Preheat the oven to 375°F. Line two baking sheets with parchment paper.

2. In a large bowl, combine the flour, baking powder, baking soda, sugar, salt, and dried currants. Add the butter and cream cheese and work the mixture with a pastry cutter until it is well combined. Add the unbeaten eggs, buttermilk, and lemon zest and work the mixture until it just comes together as a dough.

3. Pour out the dough onto a clean work surface and knead it until it comes together. Roll it out until it is ½ inch thick and cut 18 scones out of the dough. Place the scones on the baking sheets and brush them with the beaten egg.

4. Place the scones in the oven and bake until they are golden brown and springy to the touch, about 20 minutes.

5. Remove the scones from the oven and let them cool slightly before serving.

OATMEAL RAISIN DROP SCONES

YIELD: 12 SCONES / **ACTIVE TIME:** 20 MINUTES / **TOTAL TIME:** 50 MINUTES

These crunchy, free-form scones are fun to make, and with the endless possible combinations.

INGREDIENTS:

- 1¾ CUPS PLUS 1 TABLESPOON (215 G) ALL-PURPOSE FLOUR, PLUS MORE AS NEEDED
- ⅔ CUP (70 G) WHOLE WHEAT PASTRY FLOUR
- ½ CUP (100 G) SUGAR
- 1 TABLESPOON (12 G) BAKING POWDER
- 1¼ TEASPOONS (7 G) FINE SEA SALT
- 1 TEASPOON (3 G) CINNAMON
- ¾ TEASPOON (2 G) BAKING SODA
- 1¼ CUPS (284 G) UNSALTED BUTTER, CHILLED AND CUBED
- 2⅓ CUPS ROLLED OATS
- ⅞ CUP RAISINS
- ¾ CUP TOASTED WALNUTS, COARSELY CHOPPED
- 1½ CUPS (340 G) BUTTERMILK
- 1 LARGE EGG
- TURBINADO SUGAR, FOR TOPPING

1. Preheat the oven to 400°F. Line two baking sheets with parchment paper.

2. In a large bowl, combine the flours, sugar, baking powder, salt, cinnamon, and baking soda. Add the butter and work the mixture with a pastry cutter until it is well combined. Add the oats, raisins, and walnuts and work the mixture until they are evenly distributed.

3. In a small bowl, whisk the buttermilk and egg together. Remove ⅓ cup of this mixture and set it aside. Pour the rest of the buttermilk mixture into flour mixture and work until the resulting mixture just comes together as a dough.

4. Drop six clumps of dough (they should be about ½ cup each) onto each baking sheet. Brush the scones with the reserved buttermilk mixture and sprinkle turbinado sugar over the top.

5. Place the scones in the oven and bake until they are golden brown and springy to the touch, about 15 minutes.

6. Remove the scones from the oven and let them cool slightly before serving.

BLUEBERRY SCONES

YIELD: 10 SCONES / **ACTIVE TIME:** 20 MINUTES / **TOTAL TIME:** 50 MINUTES

Every home baker should have a reliable blueberry scone recipe. Perfect for a sit-down brunch or on-the-go eaters, you'll be stocked with scones for some time

INGREDIENTS:

- 4½ CUPS (540 G) ALL-PURPOSE FLOUR
- ¾ CUP (150 G) SUGAR, PLUS MORE AS NEEDED
- 2 TABLESPOONS (25 G) BAKING POWDER
- 1 TEASPOON (6 G) FINE SEA SALT
- 1½ CUPS (339 G) UNSALTED BUTTER, CHILLED
- 1 CUP FROZEN BLUEBERRIES
- 1½ CUPS (340 G) HEAVY CREAM, CHILLED, PLUS MORE AS NEEDED

1. Preheat the oven to 375°F. Line a baking sheet with parchment paper.

2. In a large bowl, combine the flour, sugar, baking powder, and salt. Add the butter and work the mixture with a pastry cutter until it is well combined. Add the blueberries and work the mixture until they are evenly distributed.

3. Add the cream and work until the mixture just comes together as a dough.

4. Pour out the dough onto a clean work surface and knead it until it comes together. Roll it out until it is ¾ inch thick and cut 10 scones out of the dough. Place the scones on the baking sheet, brush them with cream, and sprinkle sugar over the top.

5. Place the scones in the oven and bake until they are golden brown and springy to the touch, about 15 minutes.

6. Remove the scones from the oven and let them cool slightly before serving.

CHERRY SCONES

YIELD: 18 SCONES / **ACTIVE TIME:** 20 MINUTES / **TOTAL TIME:** 2 HOURS AND 45 MINUTES

This recipe is easy, fast, and—best of all—delicious; whole wheat lovers will find themselves coming back to it time and time again.

INGREDIENTS:

- 3 CUPS (360 G) ALL-PURPOSE FLOUR, PLUS MORE AS NEEDED
- 1½ CUPS (170 G) WHOLE WHEAT FLOUR
- 1¼ CUPS PLUS 2 TABLESPOONS (250 G) SUGAR
- 1 TABLESPOON PLUS 1¼ TEASPOONS (18 G) BAKING POWDER
- 1½ TEASPOONS (4 G) BAKING SODA
- 1½ TEASPOONS (9 G) FINE SEA SALT
- 3¾ CUPS ROLLED OATS
- ZEST OF 2 ORANGES
- 2 CUPS (454 G) UNSALTED BUTTER, CHILLED AND CUT INTO SMALL CUBES
- 1½ CUPS DRIED TART CHERRIES
- 1¼ CUPS (285 G) BUTTERMILK
- 2 TABLESPOONS HEAVY CREAM

1. In a large bowl, combine the flours, 1¼ cups of sugar, the baking powder, baking soda, salt, oats, and orange zest. Add the butter and work the mixture with a pastry cutter until it is well combined. Add the dried cherries and work the mixture until they are evenly distributed.

2. Add the buttermilk and work until the mixture just comes together as a dough.

3. Pour out the dough onto a flour-dusted work surface and knead it until it comes together. Shape the dough into a ball and divide it into three pieces. Flatten them into ¾-inch-thick disks, cover them with plastic wrap, and chill the dough in the refrigerator for 2 hours.

4. Preheat the oven to 375°F. Line a baking sheet with parchment paper.

5. Cut each disk into six pieces and place the scones on the baking sheets. Brush them with the cream and sprinkle the remaining sugar over the top.

6. Place the scones in the oven and bake until they are golden brown and springy to the touch, about 25 minutes.

7. Remove the scones from the oven and let them cool slightly before serving.

LEMON & GINGER SCONES

YIELD: 10 SCONES / **ACTIVE TIME:** 15 MINUTES / **TOTAL TIME:** 1 HOUR AND 15 MINUTES

Bright and spicy, these scones are a good option for those days in early April when the brightness of the sun does not provide the warmth that it suggests.

INGREDIENTS:

- 3 EGGS
- 10 TABLESPOONS (140 G) HEAVY CREAM
- 3¾ CUPS (450 G) ALL-PURPOSE FLOUR
- 7 TABLESPOONS (85 G) SUGAR
- 1 CUP (227 G) UNSALTED BUTTER, CHILLED AND CUBED
- 1½ TABLESPOONS (18 G) BAKING POWDER
- 1½ TEASPOONS (9 G) KOSHER SALT
- ZEST OF 2 LEMONS
- 2 CUPS DICED CRYSTALLIZED GINGER
- ROYAL ICING (SEE PAGE 666), FOR TOPPING

1. Line a baking sheet with parchment paper.

2. Place the eggs and 6 tablespoons of heavy cream in a measuring cup and whisk to combine. Set the mixture aside.

3. Place the flour, sugar, butter, baking powder, salt, and lemon zest in the work bowl of a stand mixer fitted with the paddle attachment and beat the mixture until it comes together as a crumbly dough, with the butter reduced to pea-sized pieces. Take care not to overmix the dough.

4. Transfer the dough to a mixing bowl, add the egg mixture and ginger, and gently fold the mixture until it is a smooth batter.

5. Drop 4 oz. portions of the batter onto the baking sheet, making sure to leave enough space between them. Brush the top of each portion with the remaining cream.

6. Place the scones in the refrigerator and chill for 20 minutes. Preheat the oven to 375°F.

7. Place the pan in the oven and bake until they are golden brown and a cake tester inserted into the center of each scone comes out clean, 22 to 25 minutes.

8. Remove from the oven and place the pan on a wire rack. Let the scones cool slightly before topping them with icing and serving.

BRIOCHE COL TUPPO

YIELD: 8 BRIOCHE / **ACTIVE TIME:** 1 HOUR / **TOTAL TIME:** 16 HOURS

Italians have the habit of eating "dessert" for breakfast, something that often surprises people born outside of Italy. In Sicily, the quintessential breakfast is this brioche and granita.

1. To begin preparations for the lievitino, place the milk and vanilla seeds in a saucepan and warm the mixture until it is just about to come to a simmer. Remove the pan from heat and let the mixture cool until it is (90°F). Add the yeast, gently stir to combine, and let the mixture sit until it starts to foam, about 10 minutes.

2. Add the flour and clementine zest, stir to combine, and transfer the lievitino to an airtight container. Cover the container and chill the lievitino in the refrigerator for 10 to 12 hours.

3. To begin preparations for the dough, warm ½ cup of the milk to 90°F, place it in a bowl, and add the yeast and honey. Gently stir and let the mixture sit until it starts to foam, about 10 minutes.

4. Place the mixture in the work bowl of a stand mixer fitted with the dough hook, add the flours and lievitino, and work the mixture on low until combined.

5. Add 2 of the eggs and work the mixture until they have been incorporated. Add the sugar and salt and work the mixture until it comes together as a smooth, elastic dough. Add the lard, raise the speed to medium, and knead until the dough is very elastic. Cover the bowl with plastic wrap, place it in a naturally warm spot, and let the dough rest until it doubles in size, about 2½ hours.

6. Line a baking sheet with parchment paper. Place the dough on a flour-dusted work surface and divide it into five pieces. Divide four of the pieces in half, and then divide the remaining large piece into eight small pieces. Shape the pieces of dough into rounds.

7. Make a hole in the top of each of the larger rounds and gently widen the openings. Place a smaller round in each of the openings. Place the brioche on the baking sheet.

8. Place the remaining milk and egg in a bowl and whisk to combine. Brush the brioche with some of the egg wash and let them rest until they have doubled in size, about 1½ hours. Place the remaining egg wash in the refrigerator.

9. Preheat the oven to 375°F.

10. Brush the brioche again with the egg wash and place them in the oven. Bake the brioche until they are golden brown and feel lighter when lifted, about 20 minutes. Remove the brioche from the oven and let them cool slightly before serving.

INGREDIENTS:

FOR THE LIEVITINO

½ CUP (114 G) WHOLE MILK

SEEDS OF ½ VANILLA BEAN

¼ PACKET (1.7 G) OF ACTIVE DRY YEAST

1 CUP (120 G) BREAD FLOUR

ZEST OF 2 CLEMENTINES

FOR THE DOUGH

½ CUP PLUS 2 TEASPOONS (125 G) WHOLE MILK

¼ PACKET (1.7 G) OF ACTIVE DRY YEAST

2 TEASPOONS (14 G) HONEY

5.6 OZ. (160 G) STRONG BREAD FLOUR (SUCH AS MANITOBA FLOUR)

4½ OZ. (125 G) ALL-PURPOSE FLOUR, PLUS MORE AS NEEDED

3 LARGE EGGS

2.8 OZ. (80 G) SUGAR

1 TEASPOON (5½ G) FINE SEA SALT

3.8 OZ. (108 G) LARD OR UNSALTED BUTTER

Brioche Col Tuppo, see page 581

LEMON POPPY SEED MUFFINS

YIELD: 12 TO 15 MUFFINS / **ACTIVE TIME:** 20 MINUTES / **TOTAL TIME:** 40 MINUTES

Lemon is such a bright and refreshing flavor—it brightens all that it comes into contact with. This recipe uses lemon juice, but if you'd like to bump up the lemon flavor, you can add the zest of the lemons you are juicing.

INGREDIENTS:

- ½ CUP (113 G) UNSALTED BUTTER, CUBED
- ¾ CUP (150 G) SUGAR
- 2 EGGS
- 1 CUP (227 G) SOUR CREAM
- 3 TABLESPOONS (45 G) FRESH LEMON JUICE
- 1⅔ CUPS (200 G) ALL-PURPOSE FLOUR
- 1 TEASPOON (6 G) BAKING SODA
- 1 TEASPOON (6 G) FINE SEA SALT
- 2 TABLESPOONS POPPY SEEDS

1. Preheat the oven to 350°F. Line a muffin pan with paper liners.

2. In the work bowl of a stand mixer fitted with the paddle attachment, cream the butter and sugar until light and fluffy. Incorporate the eggs one at a time, scraping down the work bowl as necessary.

3. Add the sour cream and lemon juice and beat until combined. Add the remaining ingredients and beat until the mixture comes together as a smooth batter.

4. Pour the batter into the wells of the muffin pan and place the pan in the oven.

5. Bake the muffins until they are golden brown and a cake tester inserted into their centers comes out clean, 18 to 20 minutes.

6. Remove the muffins from the oven, remove them from the pan, place them on a wire rack, and let them cool completely before serving.

DOUGHNUT SHOP MUFFINS

YIELD: 12 MUFFINS / **ACTIVE TIME:** 20 MINUTES / **TOTAL TIME:** 1 HOUR

Taking the coating of a classic cinnamon doughnut and transferring it to a lighter muffin is a surefire way to get the day started off right.

1. Preheat the oven to 375°F. Coat a muffin pan with nonstick cooking spray.

2. Place the flour, baking powder, salt, and nutmeg in a mixing bowl and whisk to combine. Set the mixture aside.

3. In the work bowl of a stand mixer fitted with the paddle attachment, cream ¾ cup of butter and the sugar until light and fluffy. Incorporate the eggs one at a time, scraping down the work bowl as necessary.

4. Add the dry mixture and beat until the mixture comes together as a smooth batter. Gradually add the milk and beat until it is incorporated. Add the blueberries and beat until they are evenly distributed.

5. Pour the batter into the wells of the muffin pan. Place the pan in the oven and bake the muffins until they are golden brown and a cake tester inserted into their centers comes out clean, 18 to 20 minutes.

6. Remove the muffins from the oven, remove them from the pan, place them on a wire rack, and let the muffins cool for 10 minutes.

7. Dip the tops of the muffins in the melted butter, sprinkle cinnamon and sugar over the top, and serve.

INGREDIENTS:

3¾ CUPS (454 G) ALL-PURPOSE FLOUR

1 TABLESPOON (12 G) BAKING POWDER

½ TEASPOON (3 G) FINE SEA SALT

½ TEASPOON (1 G) FRESHLY GRATED NUTMEG

¾ CUP (170 G) UNSALTED BUTTER, SOFTENED, PLUS MELTED BUTTER FOR TOPPING

1 CUP PLUS 2 TABLESPOONS (227 G) SUGAR, PLUS MORE FOR TOPPING

2 EGGS

1 CUP (227 G) MILK

CINNAMON, FOR TOPPING

BLUEBERRY MUFFINS

YIELD: 12 MUFFINS / **ACTIVE TIME:** 20 MINUTES / **TOTAL TIME:** 1 HOUR

Soft and sweet muffins that are bursting with fresh blueberries.

INGREDIENTS:

- 4¾ CUPS (565 G) ALL-PURPOSE FLOUR
- 1 TABLESPOON (12 G) BAKING POWDER
- 1½ TEASPOONS (9 G) FINE SEA SALT
- 1 CUP (227 G) UNSALTED BUTTER, SOFTENED
- 1½ (SCANT) CUPS (282 G) SUGAR
- 6 EGGS
- ½ CUP (113 G) SOUR CREAM
- 11 OZ. (310 G) MILK
- 2 CUPS FRESH BLUEBERRIES
- STREUSEL TOPPING (SEE PAGE 666)

1. Preheat the oven to 375°F. Line a muffin pan with paper liners.

2. Place the flour, baking powder, and salt in a mixing bowl and whisk to combine. Set the mixture aside.

3. In the work bowl of a stand mixer fitted with the paddle attachment, cream the butter and sugar until light and fluffy. Incorporate the eggs one at a time, scraping down the work bowl as necessary.

4. Add the dry mixture and beat until the mixture comes together as a smooth batter. Add the sour cream and beat to incorporate. Gradually add the milk and beat until it is incorporated. Add the blueberries and beat until they are evenly distributed.

5. Pour the batter into the wells of the muffin pan and top each portion with about 2 tablespoons of the Streusel Topping.

6. Place the pan in the oven and bake the muffins until they are golden brown and a cake tester inserted into their centers comes out clean, 18 to 20 minutes.

7. Remove the muffins from the oven, remove them from the pan, place them on a wire rack, and let them cool completely before serving.

Blueberry Muffins, see page 587

CRANBERRY & ORANGE MUFFINS

YIELD: 12 MUFFINS / **ACTIVE TIME:** 20 MINUTES / **TOTAL TIME:** 1 HOUR

These wonderfully tart muffins carry eye-opening flavor.

INGREDIENTS:

- 4¾ CUPS (565 G) ALL-PURPOSE FLOUR
- 1 TABLESPOON (12 G) BAKING POWDER
- 1½ TEASPOONS (9 G) FINE SEA SALT
- 1 CUP (227 G) UNSALTED BUTTER, SOFTENED
- 1½ (SCANT) CUPS (282 G) SUGAR
- ZEST OF 2 ORANGES
- 6 EGGS
- ½ CUP (113 G) SOUR CREAM
- 11 OZ. (310 G) MILK
- 2 CUPS FRESH OR FROZEN CRANBERRIES
- SANDING SUGAR, FOR TOPPING

1. Preheat the oven to 375°F. Line a muffin pan with paper liners.

2. Place the flour, baking powder, and salt in a mixing bowl and whisk to combine. Set the mixture aside.

3. In the work bowl of a stand mixer fitted with the paddle attachment, cream the butter, sugar, and orange zest until light and fluffy. Incorporate the eggs one at a time, scraping down the work bowl as necessary.

4. Add the dry mixture and beat until the mixture comes together as a smooth batter. Add the sour cream and beat to incorporate. Gradually add the milk and beat until it is incorporated. Add the cranberries and beat until they are evenly distributed.

5. Pour the batter into the wells of the muffin pan and sprinkle sanding sugar over each muffin.

6. Place the pan in the oven and bake the muffins until they are golden brown and a cake tester inserted into their centers comes out clean, 18 to 20 minutes.

7. Remove the muffins from the oven, remove them from the pan, place them on a wire rack, and let them cool completely before serving.

MORNING GLORY MUFFINS

YIELD: 12 MUFFINS / **ACTIVE TIME:** 20 MINUTES / **TOTAL TIME:** 1 HOUR

By turning a rich carrot cake batter into muffins, you can transform a simple Sunday brunch into an event.

INGREDIENTS:

- 1⅚ CUPS (227 G) ALL-PURPOSE FLOUR
- ½ CUP PLUS 1 TABLESPOON (113 G) SUGAR
- 2½ TABLESPOONS (28 G) DARK BROWN SUGAR
- 2 TEASPOONS (12 G) BAKING SODA
- 1½ TEASPOONS (4 G) CINNAMON
- 3 EGGS
- ½ CUP (100 G) CANOLA OIL
- 1 TEASPOON (4.5 G) PURE VANILLA EXTRACT
- 7 OZ. CARROTS, SHREDDED
- 3 OZ. DARK RAISINS
- 1 HONEYCRISP APPLE, GRATED
- 2 OZ. SWEETENED SHREDDED COCONUT
- SANDING SUGAR, FOR TOPPING

1. Preheat the oven to 375°F. Line a muffin pan with paper liners.

2. Place the flour, sugar, brown sugar, baking soda, and cinnamon in a mixing bowl and whisk to combine. Set the mixture aside.

3. In the work bowl of a stand mixer fitted with the paddle attachment, beat the eggs, canola oil, vanilla, carrots, raisins, apple, and coconut until well combined, scraping down the work bowl as necessary.

4. Add the dry mixture and beat until the mixture comes together as a smooth batter.

5. Pour the batter into the wells of the muffin pan and sprinkle sanding sugar over each muffin.

6. Place the pan in the oven and bake the muffins until they are golden brown and a cake tester inserted into their centers comes out clean, 18 to 20 minutes.

7. Remove the muffins from the oven, remove them from the pan, place them on a wire rack, and let them cool completely before serving.

BANANA & CHOCOLATE CHIP MUFFINS

YIELD: 12 MUFFINS / **ACTIVE TIME:** 20 MINUTES / **TOTAL TIME:** 1 HOUR

The pronounced notes of vanilla that ripe bananas carry are an ideal complement to rich chocolate.

INGREDIENTS:

- 2 CUPS (240 G) ALL-PURPOSE FLOUR
- 1 TEASPOON (6 G) BAKING SODA
- ¼ TEASPOON (0.6 G) CINNAMON
- ¼ TEASPOON (0.5 G) FRESHLY GRATED NUTMEG
- ½ TEASPOON (3 G) FINE SEA SALT
- 3 RIPE BANANAS, PEELED
- ½ (SCANT) CUP (113 G) LIGHT BROWN SUGAR
- 14 TABLESPOONS (170 G) SUGAR
- ¼ CUP (57 G) UNSALTED BUTTER, SOFTENED
- ½ CUP (100 G) EXTRA-VIRGIN OLIVE OIL
- 2 EGGS
- 1½ TEASPOONS (7 G) PURE VANILLA EXTRACT
- 2 TABLESPOONS (26 G) SOUR CREAM
- 1 CUP SEMISWEET CHOCOLATE CHIPS

1. Preheat the oven to 350°F. Line a muffin pan with paper liners.

2. Place the flour, baking soda, cinnamon, nutmeg, and salt in a mixing bowl and whisk to combine. Set the mixture aside.

3. In the work bowl of a stand mixer fitted with the paddle attachment, beat the bananas, brown sugar, sugar, and butter until well combined, scraping down the work bowl as necessary. Add the olive oil, eggs, and vanilla and beat until well combined.

4. Add the dry mixture and beat until the mixture comes together as a smooth batter. Add the sour cream and chocolate chips and beat to incorporate.

5. Pour the batter into the wells of the muffin pan. Place the pan in the oven and bake the muffins until they are golden brown and a cake tester inserted into their centers comes out clean, 18 to 20 minutes.

6. Remove the muffins from the oven, remove them from the pan, place them on a wire rack, and let them cool completely before serving.

BLACKBERRY & CORN MUFFINS

YIELD: 12 MUFFINS / **ACTIVE TIME:** 20 MINUTES / **TOTAL TIME:** 1 HOUR

Two of the late summer's brightest stars team up in this magical preparation.

INGREDIENTS:

- 3¾ CUPS (450 G) ALL-PURPOSE FLOUR
- 1½ CUPS (234 G) CORNMEAL
- 1⅓ TABLESPOONS (16 G) BAKING POWDER
- 1 TABLESPOON (17 G) FINE SEA SALT
- 1 CUP (227 G) UNSALTED BUTTER, SOFTENED
- 1 CUP (198 G) SUGAR
- 4 EGGS
- 2 CUPS (454 G) MILK
- 1 PINT OF FRESH BLACKBERRIES, SLICED LENGTHWISE
- 1 CUP FRESH CORN KERNELS
- CORN MUFFIN TOPPING (SEE PAGE 667)

1. Preheat the oven to 375°F. Line a muffin pan with paper liners.

2. Place the flour, cornmeal, baking powder, and salt in a mixing bowl and whisk to combine. Set the mixture aside.

3. In the work bowl of a stand mixer fitted with the paddle attachment, cream the butter and sugar until light and fluffy. Incorporate the eggs one at a time, scraping down the work bowl as necessary.

4. Add the dry mixture and beat until the mixture comes together as a smooth batter. add the milk and beat until it is incorporated. Add the blackberries and corn and beat until they are evenly distributed.

5. Pour the batter into the wells of the muffin pan and top each portion with about 2 tablespoons of the topping.

6. Place the pan in the oven and bake the muffins until they are golden brown and a cake tester inserted into their centers comes out clean, 18 to 20 minutes.

7. Remove the muffins from the oven, remove them from the pan, place them on a wire rack, and let them cool completely before serving.

CINNAMON BUNS

YIELD: 12 ROLLS / **ACTIVE TIME:** 1 HOUR / **TOTAL TIME:** 4 HOURS AND 30 MINUTES

This decadent preparation is not one you can enjoy every day, but every single encounter with it will prove memorable.

1. To prepare the filling, place all of the ingredients in the work bowl of a stand mixer fitted with a paddle attachment and beat on medium until the mixture is light and fluffy. Transfer to a mixing bowl and set aside. Wipe out the work bowl.

2. To prepare the glaze, place all of the ingredients in a mixing bowl and whisk to combine. Cover it with plastic wrap and set it aside.

3. To begin preparations for the dough, place the water and yeast in the work bowl of the stand mixer, gently stir, and let the mixture sit until foamy, about 10 minutes.

4. Add the eggs, olive oil, flour, sugar, and salt, fit the mixer with the dough hook, and work the mixture on low until the dough starts to come together, about 2 minutes. Raise the speed to medium and knead until the dough is elastic and pulls away from the side of the bowl. Cover the bowl with plastic wrap, place it in a naturally warm spot, and let the dough rest until it has doubled in size.

5. Turn the dough out onto a flour-dusted work surface. Use a rolling pin to roll the dough into a rectangle that is about 24 x 12 inches.

6. Spread the filling evenly across the dough, leaving an inch of dough uncovered on the wide side closest to yourself. Sprinkle sugar lightly over the filling. This will help provide friction and allow for a tight roll.

7. Take the side farthest away and roll the dough into a tight spiral. Pinch the seam to seal the roll closed. Cut the roll into twelve 2-inch-wide pieces.

8. Spray a large, rectangular baking dish with nonstick cooking spray. Place the buns in the pan in an even layer. Cover the rolls with plastic wrap, place them in a naturally warm spot, and let them rest until they have doubled in size.

9. Preheat the oven to 350°F. Place the buns in the oven and bake until their internal temperature is 210°F, 20 to 30 minutes.

10. Remove the buns from the oven and spread the glaze over the top. Let them cool slightly before serving.

INGREDIENTS:

FOR THE FILLING

- 1 CUP UNSALTED BUTTER, SOFTENED
- 1 CUP PLUS 2 TABLESPOONS SUGAR, PLUS MORE TO TASTE
- 1 CUP PLUS 1 TABLESPOON DARK BROWN SUGAR
- 1 TEASPOON PURE VANILLA EXTRACT
- 2 TABLESPOONS CINNAMON

FOR THE GLAZE

- 4 CUPS CONFECTIONERS' SUGAR
- ½ CUP WATER
- 1 TEASPOON PURE VANILLA EXTRACT
- PINCH OF KOSHER SALT

FOR THE DOUGH

- 1½ CUPS (340 G) LUKEWARM WATER (90°F)
- 1 TABLESPOON PLUS 2 TEASPOONS (15 G) ACTIVE DRY YEAST
- 3 EGGS
- ¼ CUP (50 G) EXTRA-VIRGIN OLIVE OIL
- 7½ CUPS (900 G) BREAD FLOUR, PLUS MORE AS NEEDED
- ¼ CUP (50 G) SUGAR, PLUS MORE TO TASTE
- 1½ TEASPOONS (9 G) FINE SEA SALT

PUMPKIN STICKY BUNS

YIELD: 12 BUNS / **ACTIVE TIME:** 1 HOUR / **TOTAL TIME:** 4 HOURS AND 30 MINUTES

With their rich flavor and gorgeous golden hue, these sticky buns are guaranteed to become your new favorite when fall arrives.

1. To prepare the filling, place all of the ingredients in the work bowl of a stand mixer fitted with the paddle attachment and beat until the mixture is light and fluffy. Transfer the filling to a mixing bowl and set aside. Wipe out the work bowl.

2. To prepare the glaze, place all of the ingredients in a mixing bowl and whisk to combine. Cover it with plastic wrap and set it aside.

3. To begin preparations for the dough, place the milk and yeast in the work bowl, gently stir, and let the mixture sit until it is foamy, about 10 minutes.

4. Add the melted butter, egg, egg yolk, and pumpkin puree and whisk to combine. Fit the mixer with the dough hook, add the flour, dark brown sugar, and salt, and work the mixture on low until the dough starts to come together, about 2 minutes. Raise the speed to medium and knead until the dough is elastic and pulls away from the side of the bowl.

5. Place the dough on a flour-dusted work surface, form it into a ball, and return it to the work bowl. Cover the bowl with plastic wrap, place it in a naturally warm spot, and let the dough to rest until it has doubled in size.

6. Spread 1 cup of the filling over the bottom of a 13 x 9–inch baking pan. Turn the dough out onto a flour-dusted work surface. Use a rolling pin to roll the dough into a rectangle that is about 24 x 12 inches. Spread the remaining filling evenly over the dough, leaving an inch of dough uncovered on the wide side closest to yourself.

7. Take the dough by the wide side farthest away from you and roll it into a tight spiral. Pinch the seam to seal the roll closed.

8. Cut the roll into twelve 2-inch-wide buns.

9. Place the 12 buns in the pan in an even layer. Cover them with plastic wrap, place them in a naturally warm spot, and let them rest until they have doubled in size.

10. Preheat the oven to 350°F.

11. Place the buns in the oven and bake until they are golden brown and their internal temperature is at least 210°F, 20 to 30 minutes.

12. Remove the buns from the oven and spread the glaze over the top. Let them cool slightly before serving.

INGREDIENTS:

FOR THE FILLING

- 1 CUP UNSALTED BUTTER, SOFTENED
- 1 CUP PLUS 2 TABLESPOONS SUGAR
- 1 CUP PLUS 1 TABLESPOON DARK BROWN SUGAR
- 1 TEASPOON PURE VANILLA EXTRACT
- 2 TABLESPOONS CINNAMON
- 1 TABLESPOON FRESHLY GRATED NUTMEG
- 1 TEASPOON GROUND GINGER
- 1 TEASPOON CARDAMOM
- ½ TEASPOON GROUND CLOVES

FOR THE GLAZE

- 4 CUPS CONFECTIONERS' SUGAR
- ½ CUP WATER
- 1 TEASPOON PURE VANILLA EXTRACT
- PINCH OF KOSHER SALT

FOR THE DOUGH

- 1 CUP (227 G) MILK, WARMED TO 95°F
- 1 TABLESPOON (9 G) ACTIVE DRY YEAST
- ½ CUP (113 G) UNSALTED BUTTER, MELTED
- 1 EGG
- 1 EGG YOLK
- ¾ CUP (170 G) PUMPKIN PUREE
- 5⅔ CUPS (680 G) BREAD FLOUR, PLUS MORE AS NEEDED
- ¼ CUP (53 G) DARK BROWN SUGAR
- 1½ TEASPOONS (9 G) FINE SEA SALT

SWEET BREADS & QUICKBREADS

This chapter features a wonderful balance of preparations—sweetbreads such as stollen and panettone that serious traditions have sprung up around, and quickbreads that, while cutting back considerably on prep time when compared to the majority of the recipes in this book, still have the ability to comfort and delight the taste buds.

Best of all, these sweetbreads and quickbreads are extremely accommodating, enabling you to experiment with different ingredients and articulate exciting flavors once you get the hang of them.

GUBANA

YIELD: 1 GUBANA / **ACTIVE TIME:** 30 MINUTES / **TOTAL TIME:** 24 HOURS

Gubana is a delicious, sweet bread that is enjoyed year-round in Friuli-Venezia Giulia, and particularly around Christmas.

1. The day before you are going to prepare the dough, begin preparations for the filling. Coat a clean, heat-resistant work surface with olive oil. Place the raisins and rum in a bowl and let the raisins soak.

2. Place half of the sugar and the water and vinegar in a medium saucepan and cook over medium heat, swirling the pan occasionally, until the mixture starts to caramelize. Add half of the walnuts and cook, stirring continually, until they are coated. Pour the mixture onto the work surface and let it cool.

3. Place the butter in a large skillet and melt it over low heat. Add the pine nuts and toast, stirring occasionally, until they are browned, about 5 minutes. Remove the pan from heat and let the pine nuts cool.

4. Crush the amaretti and biscuits and place them in a bowl. Chop the caramelized walnuts and the remaining walnuts and add them to the bowl.

5. Drain the raisins and squeeze them dry. Add them to the bowl, along with butter and the toasted pine nuts, lemon zest, vanilla, cinnamon, and remaining sugar, as well as enough rum for the mixture to be spreadable. Stir to combine, cover the mixture with plastic wrap, and chill the filling in the refrigerator overnight.

6. To begin preparations for the dough, warm the milk to 90°F. Add the yeast, gently stir to combine, and let the mixture sit until it starts to foam, about 10 minutes.

7. Place two-thirds of the flour and the egg, egg yolks, and yeast mixture in the work bowl of a stand mixer fitted with the dough hook and work the mixture until it comes together as a soft, smooth dough. Cover the work bowl with a kitchen towel, place it in a naturally warm spot, and let the dough rest for 1 hour.

8. Add the remaining flour, the salt, honey, butter, and sugar to the work bowl and work the dough vigorously until it is elastic. Cover the bowl with a kitchen towel, place it in a naturally warm spot, and let it rest for 30 minutes. Remove the filling from the refrigerator and let sit at room temperature.

INGREDIENTS:

FOR THE FILLING

- EXTRA-VIRGIN OLIVE OIL, AS NEEDED
- ⅔ CUP RAISINS
- 1 CUP RUM OR MARSALA, PLUS MORE AS NEEDED
- ½ CUP SUGAR
- 3 TABLESPOONS WATER
- ½ TEASPOON WHITE VINEGAR
- 2 CUPS WALNUTS
- 2 TABLESPOONS UNSALTED BUTTER, PLUS MORE, CHOPPED, AS NEEDED
- ⅔ CUP PINE NUTS
- 7 AMARETTI
- 1½ OZ. DRY, BISCUIT-STYLE COOKIES (PETIT BEURRE OR SIMILAR)
- ZEST OF ½ LEMON
- 1 TEASPOON PURE VANILLA EXTRACT
- 2 TEASPOONS CINNAMON

FOR THE DOUGH

- 2.1 OZ. (60 G) WHOLE MILK
- ⅔ PACKET (4.5 G) OF ACTIVE DRY YEAST
- 2⅔ CUPS (330 G) STRONG BREAD FLOUR, PLUS MORE AS NEEDED
- 1 EGG
- 2 EGG YOLKS
- ⅓ TEASPOON (1.8 G) FINE SEA SALT
- 1 TABLESPOON (19 G) HONEY
- ¼ CUP (57 G) UNSALTED BUTTER, SOFTENED
- ¼ CUP (50 G) SUGAR, PLUS MORE FOR TOPPING
- 1 EGG WHITE, LIGHTLY BEATEN

9. Place the dough on a flour-dusted work surface and roll it into an 8 x 12–inch rectangle. Spread the filling over the dough and dot it with pieces of butter. Working from a long side, roll the dough up, finishing with the seam side down. Pinch the dough at both of the short sides to seal the gubana.

10. Stretch the gubana until it is about 30 inches long. Coat a round 10-inch cake pan with high edges with butter. Place the gubana in the pan in a tight spiral, making sure one end is underneath to seal it. Cover the pan with a kitchen towel and let the gubana rise until it has doubled in size, about 1½ hours.

11. Preheat the oven to 320°F. Brush the gubana with the egg white, sprinkle some sugar over the top, and place it in the oven.

12. Bake until the gubana is golden brown and a toothpick inserted into the center comes out clean, about 1 hour.

13. Remove the gubana from the oven and let it cool before slicing and serving.

HAWAIIAN SWEET BREAD

YIELD: 1 LOAF / **ACTIVE TIME:** 45 MINUTES / **TOTAL TIME:** 4 HOURS

The crushed pineapple turns this bread into a sweeter and even softer version of brioche.

1. Place the water and yeast in the work bowl of a stand mixer fitted with the dough hook, gently stir to combine, and let the mixture sit until it starts to foam, about 10 minutes.

2. Add the pineapple, brown sugar, eggs, egg yolk, and vanilla and whisk to combine. Add the flour and salt and work the mixture on low until it just starts to come together as a dough, about 2 minutes.

3. Gradually add the softened butter and continue to knead on low until all of the butter has been incorporated.

4. Raise the speed to medium and work the dough until it comes away clean from the side of the work bowl and is elastic, about 6 minutes. Cover the bowl with a kitchen towel and let the dough rest until it has doubled in size, 1 to 2 hours.

5. Preheat the oven to 350°F. Coat a round 8-inch cake pan with nonstick cooking spray.

6. Place the dough, which will be sticky, on a flour-dusted work surface and gently knead it until it is extensible. Shape it into a large round and place it in the pan, seam side down. Cover the dough with plastic wrap, place it in a naturally warm spot, and let it rest until it has doubled in size.

7. Brush the dough with melted butter. Place the dough in the oven and bake until it is golden brown and feels lighter when lifted, 35 to 45 minutes.

8. Remove the bread from the oven, brush it with more melted butter, place it on a wire rack, and let it cool before slicing and serving.

INGREDIENTS:

- 2 TABLESPOONS (30 G) LUKEWARM WATER (90°F)
- 2½ TEASPOONS (7.5 G) ACTIVE DRY YEAST
- ¾ CUP (192 G) CRUSHED PINEAPPLE
- 1½ CUPS (330 G) LIGHT BROWN SUGAR
- 2 EGGS
- 1 EGG YOLK
- 1 TABLESPOON (14 G) PURE VANILLA EXTRACT
- 4 CUPS (480 G) BREAD FLOUR, PLUS MORE AS NEEDED
- 2 TEASPOONS (12 G) FINE SEA SALT
- ¼ CUP (57 G) UNSALTED BUTTER, SOFTENED; PLUS MELTED BUTTER, AS NEEDED

CLASSIC GINGERBREAD

YIELD: 1 LOAF / **ACTIVE TIME:** 15 MINUTES / **TOTAL TIME:** 1 HOUR AND 30 MINUTES

Softer and moister than the cookie most people picture when they hear the term, this gingerbread is a serious threat to become your favorite winter tradition.

1. Preheat the oven to 350°F. Coat an 8 x 4–inch loaf pan with nonstick cooking spray.

2. Place the flour, salt, baking soda, ginger, cinnamon, nutmeg, cloves, and allspice in a mixing bowl and whisk to combine. Set aside.

3. Combine the molasses and sour cream in a measuring cup and set the mixture aside.

4. In the work bowl of a stand mixer fitted with the paddle attachment, cream the butter and brown sugar on medium until light and fluffy, about 5 minutes. Add half of the dry mixture and beat until incorporated. Add half of the molasses mixture, beat until incorporated, and then add the remaining dry mixture. Beat to incorporate, add the remaining molasses mixture, and beat until the resulting mixture comes together as a smooth batter.

5. Pour the batter into the prepared loaf pan, place it in the oven, and bake until a cake tester inserted into the center of the loaf comes out clean, 50 to 60 minutes.

6. Remove the bread from the oven, place the pan on a wire rack, and let it cool completely.

INGREDIENTS:

- 1¾ CUPS (210 G) ALL-PURPOSE FLOUR
- ½ TEASPOON (3 G) FINE SEA SALT
- ⅛ TEASPOON (¾ G) BAKING SODA
- 2½ TEASPOONS (4.3 G) GROUND GINGER
- 1½ TEASPOONS (5 G) CINNAMON
- 1 TEASPOON (3 G) FRESHLY GRATED NUTMEG
- ½ TEASPOON (1 G) GROUND CLOVES
- ½ TEASPOON (1.5 G) ALLSPICE
- ¼ CUP (85 G) MOLASSES
- ¼ CUP (57 G) SOUR CREAM
- 1 CUP (227 G) UNSALTED BUTTER, SOFTENED
- 1 CUP PLUS 1 TABLESPOON (227 G) DARK BROWN SUGAR
- 4 EGGS

Classic Gingerbread, see page 609

BROWN BREAD

YIELD: 1 LOAF / **ACTIVE TIME:** 15 MINUTES / **TOTAL TIME:** 1 HOUR AND 30 MINUTES

A dense, chewy bread with a flavor something like a souped-up loaf of pumpernickel.

INGREDIENTS:

- 11 OZ. (312 G) MILK
- ½ CUP (170 G) MOLASSES
- 2 TABLESPOONS (27 G) LIGHT BROWN SUGAR
- 5 OZ. (142 G) ALL-PURPOSE FLOUR
- 2½ OZ. (71 G) CORNMEAL
- 5 OZ. (142 G) WHOLE WHEAT FLOUR
- 2 TEASPOONS (8 G) BAKING POWDER
- ¾ TEASPOON (4.5 G) BAKING SODA
- 5 OZ. RAISINS

1. Preheat the oven to 350°F. Coat an 8 x 4–inch loaf pan with nonstick cooking spray.

2. In the work bowl of a stand mixer fitted with the paddle attachment, combine the milk and molasses. Add the remaining ingredients and beat until the mixture comes together as a smooth batter, about 2 minutes.

3. Pour the batter into the prepared loaf pan, place it in the oven, and bake until a cake tester inserted into the center of the loaf comes out clean, 45 minutes to 1 hour.

4. Remove the bread from the oven and let it cool slightly. Remove it from the pan, place it on a wire rack, and let it cool slightly before slicing and serving.

CHOCOLATE BABKA

YIELD: 2 LOAVES / **ACTIVE TIME:** 45 MINUTES / **TOTAL TIME:** 4 HOURS

A rich, moist bread with a crumb similar to challah, but enriched with a luscious dark-chocolate filling.

INGREDIENTS:

FOR THE FILLING

- 6 OZ. DARK CHOCOLATE (55 TO 65 PERCENT)
- ¾ CUP UNSALTED BUTTER
- ¾ CUP CONFECTIONERS' SUGAR
- 1⅓ CUPS COCOA POWDER

FOR THE DOUGH

- 1½ CUPS (340 G) LUKEWARM WATER (90°F)
- 1 TABLESPOON PLUS 2 TEASPOONS (15 G) ACTIVE DRY YEAST
- 3 EGGS
- ¼ CUP (50 G) EXTRA-VIRGIN OLIVE OIL
- 7½ CUPS (904 G) BREAD FLOUR, PLUS MORE AS NEEDED
- ¼ CUP (50 G) SUGAR
- 1½ TABLESPOONS (24 G) FINE SEA SALT

1. To prepare the filling, fill a small saucepan halfway with water and bring it to a gentle simmer. In a heatproof bowl, combine the dark chocolate and butter. Place the bowl over the simmering water and stir until the mixture is melted and smooth. Remove the bowl from heat, add the confectioners' sugar and cocoa powder, and whisk until thoroughly combined. Set the mixture aside.

2. To begin preparations for the dough, whisk together the water, yeast, eggs, and olive oil in the work bowl of a stand mixer fitted with the dough hook. Add the flour, sugar, and salt and work the mixture on low for 1 minute. Raise the speed to medium and knead the mixture until it comes together as a dough and pulls away from the side of the bowl.

3. Place the dough on a flour-dusted work surface, shape it into a ball, and return it to the work bowl. Cover it with plastic wrap and let it rest until it has doubled in size.

4. Turn the dough out onto a flour-dusted work surface and divide it in half. Use a rolling pin to roll each piece into a rectangle that is about 8 x 6 inches.

5. Spread ½ cup of the filling evenly across the pieces of dough, leaving an inch of dough uncovered on the wide side closest to yourself.

6. Take the side farthest away and roll the pieces of dough into tight spirals. Using a bench scraper, cut the rolls of dough in half lengthwise. Turn the rolls of dough so that the centers are facing out. Carefully twist the dough to form 3 full turns. Pinch the ends to seal.

7. Spray two 8 x 4–inch loaf pans with nonstick cooking spray and place a piece of dough in each one.

8. Cover the loaves with plastic wrap and let them rise until they crest above the edges of the pans.

9. Preheat the oven to 350°F.

10. Place the loaves in the oven and bake until they are golden brown, feel lighter when lifted, and their internal temperature is 210°F, 45 to 55 minutes.

11. Remove the loaves from the oven, transfer them to a wire rack, and let them cool completely before slicing and serving.

DOUBLE CHOCOLATE BREAD

YIELD: 1 LOAF / **ACTIVE TIME:** 45 MINUTES / **TOTAL TIME:** 4 HOURS

Less a dessert than a great way to add contrast to a charcuterie board, or to complement a bit of foie gras.

1. Place the water and yeast in the work bowl of a stand mixer fitted with the dough hook, gently stir to combine, and let the mixture sit until it starts to foam, about 10 minutes.

2. Add the sugar, flour, cocoa powder, and salt and knead the mixture on low for 1 minute.

3. With the mixer running, gradually incorporate the butter. When all of the butter has been added, raise the speed to medium and knead the dough until it begins to pull away from the side of the work bowl, about 6 minutes.

4. Add the chocolate chips and work the mixture until they are evenly distributed. Coat a mixing bowl with nonstick cooking spray. Remove the dough from the work bowl, place it on a flour-dusted work surface, and shape it into a ball. Place the dough in the bowl, cover it with plastic wrap, place it in a naturally warm spot, and let it rest until it has doubled in size, 1 to 2 hours.

5. Preheat the oven to 350°F. Coat an 8 x 4–inch loaf pan with nonstick cooking spray.

6. Place the dough on a flour-dusted work surface and shape it into a tight round. Tuck in the sides to form the dough into a loaf shape and place it in the prepared loaf pan, seam side down.

7. Cover the pan with plastic wrap and let the dough rest until it has doubled in size.

8. Place the bread in the oven and bake until it is golden brown and feels lighter when lifted, 35 to 45 minutes.

9. Remove the bread from the oven, place the pan on a wire rack, and let the bread cool before enjoying.

INGREDIENTS:

- 1 CUP (227 G) LUKEWARM WATER (90°F)
- 3½ TEASPOONS (10.5 G) ACTIVE DRY YEAST
- ⅓ CUP (67 G) SUGAR
- 2⅚ CUPS (340 G) ALL-PURPOSE FLOUR, PLUS MORE AS NEEDED
- ¼ CUP (30 G) COCOA POWDER
- 1 TEASPOON (6 G) FINE SEA SALT
- 2 TABLESPOONS (28 G) UNSALTED BUTTER, SOFTENED
- 3 OZ. CHOCOLATE CHIPS

Double Chocolate Bread, *see page 615*

BEIGLI

YIELD: 2 BEIGLI / **ACTIVE TIME:** 30 MINUTES / **TOTAL TIME:** 24 HOURS

Popular in Central Europe as well as parts of Eastern Europe, beigli can also feature a filling based around walnuts or hazelnuts. But the poppy seed–centered option is better suited for the breakfast table.

INGREDIENTS:

FOR THE DOUGH

- ⅔ CUP (150 G) LUKEWARM SOUR CREAM (90°F)
- 2 TABLESPOONS (18 G) INSTANT YEAST
- 1 TABLESPOON (7 G) CONFECTIONERS' SUGAR
- 4⅙ CUPS (500 G) ALL-PURPOSE FLOUR
- 1 CUP PLUS 2 TABLESPOONS (250 G) UNSALTED BUTTER
- PINCH OF FINE SEA SALT
- 2 EGGS, SEPARATED

FOR THE FILLING

- 1½ CUPS POPPY SEEDS
- 1¾ CUPS CONFECTIONERS' SUGAR
- 5 OZ. WATER
- ⅓ CUP RAISINS
- ZEST AND JUICE OF 1 LEMON

1. To begin preparations for the dough, place the sour cream, yeast, and confectioners' sugar in a bowl and gently stir to combine. Set the mixture aside.

2. Place the flour, butter, and salt in a mixing bowl and work the mixture with a pastry cutter until it comes together as a crumbly dough. Add the sour cream mixture and knead until the resulting mixture comes together as a smooth dough. Cover the dough with plastic wrap and chill it in the refrigerator overnight.

3. To prepare the filling, place all of the ingredients in a food processor and pulse until well combined. Set the filling aside.

4. Line a baking sheet with parchment paper. Place the dough on a flour-dusted work surface and divide it into two pieces. Roll them out into ¼-inch-thick rectangles and spread the filling over the top, leaving a 1-inch border at the side closest to you. Working from the opposite side, roll the pieces of dough up tightly and place them on the baking sheet.

5. Place the egg yolks in a bowl and beat them. Brush the beigli with the egg yolks and let them rest for 30 minutes.

6. Preheat the oven to 350°F. Brush the beigli with the egg whites and place them in the oven. Bake until the tops are golden brown, about 40 minutes.

7. Remove the beigli from the oven and let them cool before slicing and serving.

PANETTONE

YIELD: 3 PANETTONE / **ACTIVE TIME:** 3 HOURS / **TOTAL TIME:** 2 TO 3 DAYS

Considered the king of Italian sweet breads, and maybe the king of sweet breads in general, panettone is a brioche that defies gravity.

INGREDIENTS:

1 TABLESPOON (14 G) SOURDOUGH STARTER (SEE PAGE 40)

WATER, AS NEEDED

ALL-PURPOSE FLOUR, AS NEEDED

FOR THE FIRST DOUGH

3½ OZ. (100 G) EGG YOLKS

1 CUP (227 G) WATER

4 CUPS (480 G) STRONG BREAD FLOUR OR PANETTONE FLOUR

½ CUP (100 G) SUGAR

6.3 OZ. (180 G) PASTA MADRE

4.3 OZ. (121 G) UNSALTED BUTTER, CHOPPED, PLUS MORE AS NEEDED

FOR THE SECOND DOUGH

2 CUPS (240 G) STRONG BREAD FLOUR OR PANETTONE FLOUR

6.7 OZ. (190 G) EGG YOLKS

⅓ OZ. (10 G) POWDERED MILK

1 (SCANT) TEASPOON (6 G) BARLEY MALT

1 (HEAPING) TABLESPOON (25 G) HONEY

1 TEASPOON (4.5 G) ORANGE EXTRACT

SEEDS OF 2 VANILLA BEANS

2 (SCANT) TEASPOONS (11 G) FINE SEA SALT

4.9 OZ. (139 G) SUGAR

½ CUP (113 G) UNSALTED BUTTER, CHOPPED, PLUS MORE AS NEEDED

5 OZ. DICED CANDIED ORANGE PEELS

5 OZ. CHOPPED CANDIED CITRUS PEELS

10 OZ. RAISINS

1. Begin preparations for the pasta madre 2 to 3 days before you are going to start baking the panettone. Combine the starter with 1¾ oz. water and 3½ oz. flour in a large bowl. Cover the bowl with plastic wrap and let it rest for 12 hours.

2. Combine 1¾ oz. of the pasta madre with 1¾ oz.water and 3½ oz. flour.

3. Perform three feedings of the pasta madre, one every 3 to 4 hours. The fed starter should be kept in a naturally warm spot, ideally about 79°F. The schedule should look like this: first feeding (morning): 1¾ oz. of the stiff starter with 1¾ oz. water and 3½ oz. flour; second feeding (lunchtime): 3½ oz. stiff starter, 1¾ oz. water and 3½ oz. flour; final feeding (late afternoon): 3½ oz. stiff starter, 1¾ oz. water and 3½ oz. flour.

4. To begin preparations for the first dough, place the egg yolks and water in the work bowl of a stand mixer fitted with the paddle attachment and beat to combine. Fit the mixer with the dough hook, add the flour and sugar, and work the mixture on low until combined. Gradually add the pasta madre and knead to incorporate.

5. Add the butter in three increments and knead the dough for about 6 minutes on low. The first dough should be mixed for no more than 10 minutes after the flour has been added.

6. Place the dough in a large, deep bowl and let the dough rest at room temperature until it is 3 to 4 times its original size, 10 to 12 hours.

7. To begin preparations for the second dough, place the first dough and two-thirds of the flour in the work bowl of a stand mixer fitted with the dough hook and mix on low speed for 2 minutes. Add the egg yolks and the remaining flour and knead on medium speed for about 2 minutes.

8. Add the powdered milk and barley malt and mix for 1 minute. Add the honey, orange extract, vanilla seeds, and salt and mix for 1 minute. Add the sugar and mix at medium-high speed until the sugar is fully dissolved and the dough sticks to the hook, 2 to 5 minutes.

9. Gradually add the butter and work the dough at medium speed until it wraps tightly around the hook and is elastic, about 10 minutes. Add the candied peels and raisins and work the dough until they are evenly distributed.

10. Let the dough rest in the mixing bowl for 30 minutes.

11. Coat a work surface with butter and place the dough on it. Shape the dough into three tight balls that are each 30 oz. and place them in three 26 oz. panettone molds.

12. Place the panettone molds on baking sheets. Let the rounds rise in a naturally warm spot until the dough reaches the edges of the molds, 5 to 10 hours.

13. Preheat the oven to 350°F. Gently score a cross on top of each panettone and slightly pull up on the edges of each cross. Ideally you want to perform a scarpatura, detaching the edges from the dough with a razor, but if you are making your first attempt at making panettone, just place a small piece of butter in the center of each cross, on top of the panettone.

14. Place the panettone in the oven and bake until their internal temperature is around 200°F, 35 to 45 minutes. Do not open the oven until at least 35 minutes have passed.

15. Remove the panettone from the oven, put 2 skewers in the bottom part of the panettone, and flip them upside down. Hang the panettone by the skewers and let them remain upside down until cool, 2 to 3 hours.

16. Spray fitted cellophane sheets with grain alcohol and wrap the panettone with them. Stored this way, the panettone will keep for several weeks.

CINNAMON BABKA

YIELD: 2 LOAVES / **ACTIVE TIME:** 45 MINUTES / **TOTAL TIME:** 4 HOURS

Chocolate babka gets all the attention, but those who know understand that cinnamon takes backseat to no babka.

INGREDIENTS:

FOR THE FILLING

- 1 CUP LIGHT BROWN SUGAR
- 1 TABLESPOON GROUND CINNAMON
- ½ TEASPOON FINELY GRATED ORANGE ZEST
- ¼ TEASPOON FINE SEA SALT

FOR THE DOUGH

- 1½ CUPS (340 G) LUKEWARM WATER (90°F)
- 1 TABLESPOON PLUS 2 TEASPOONS (15 G) ACTIVE DRY YEAST
- 3 EGGS
- ¼ CUP (50 G) EXTRA-VIRGIN OLIVE OIL
- 7½ CUPS (904 G) BREAD FLOUR, PLUS MORE AS NEEDED
- ¼ CUP (5 G) SUGAR
- 1½ TABLESPOONS (27 G) FINE SEA SALT

1. To prepare the filling, place all of the ingredients in a mixing bowl and whisk until thoroughly combined. Set the mixture aside.

2. To begin preparations for the dough, whisk together the water, yeast, eggs, and olive oil in the work bowl of a stand mixer fitted with the dough hook. Add the flour, sugar, and salt and work the mixture on low for 1 minute. Raise the speed to medium and knead the mixture until it comes together as a dough and pulls away from the side of the bowl.

3. Place the dough on a flour-dusted work surface, form it into a ball, and return it to the work bowl. Cover it with plastic wrap and let it rest until it has doubled in size.

4. Turn the dough out onto a flour-dusted work surface and divide it in half. Use a rolling pin to roll each piece into a rectangle that is about 8 x 6 inches.

5. Spread ½ cup of the filling evenly across the pieces of dough, leaving an inch of dough uncovered on the wide side closest to yourself.

6. Take the wide side farthest away from you and roll the pieces of dough into tight spirals. Using a bench scraper, cut the rolls of dough in half lengthwise. Turn the rolls of dough so that the centers are facing out. Carefully twist the dough to form 3 full turns. Pinch the ends to seal.

7. Coat two 8 x 4–inch loaf pans with nonstick cooking spray and place a piece of dough in each one.

8. Cover the loaves with plastic wrap and let them rise until they crest above the edges of the pans. Preheat the oven to 350°F.

9. Place the loaves in the oven and bake until they are golden brown, feel lighter when lifted, and their internal temperature is at least 210°F, 45 to 55 minutes.

10. Remove from the oven and transfer the babka to a wire rack. Let them cool completely before serving.

STOLLEN

YIELD: 2 STOLLEN / **ACTIVE TIME:** 2 HOURS / **TOTAL TIME:** 4 DAYS

Stollen is the German equivalent of panettone, a sweet bread to celebrate Christmas with what were the richest ingredients available in the winter: candied fruit, nuts, eggs, and butter.

INGREDIENTS:

- ⅔ CUP RAISINS
- ⅔ CUP GOLDEN RAISINS
- ½ CUP DRIED CHERRIES
- ⅓ CUP GRAND MARNIER
- 1 CUP SLIVERED ALMONDS
- 1 PACKET (7 G) OF ACTIVE DRY YEAST
- ½ CUP (113 G) LUKEWARM MILK (90°F)
- 4 CUPS (480 G) ALL-PURPOSE FLOUR
- 1 CUP PLUS 3 TABLESPOONS (235 G) SUGAR
- 2¾ TEASPOONS (4.5 G) GROUND GINGER
- 1 TEASPOON (6 G) FINE SEA SALT
- 1 TEASPOON (2.8 G) CINNAMON
- 1 TEASPOON (1.8 G) CARDAMOM
- 1 TEASPOON (2.2 G) FRESHLY GRATED NUTMEG
- 1 TEASPOON (2 G) LEMON ZEST
- SEEDS OF ½ VANILLA BEAN, POD RESERVED
- 2 CUPS (454 G) UNSALTED BUTTER, MELTED
- 2 LARGE EGG YOLKS
- ½ CUP CHOPPED CANDIED GINGER
- ½ CUP CANDIED CITRUS PEELS
- 1½ CUPS CONFECTIONERS' SUGAR, PLUS MORE FOR DUSTING

1. Place the raisins, cherries, and Grand Marnier in a mason jar. Place the almonds and ¼ cup water in another mason jar. Seal and let the mixtures sit at room temperature overnight.

2. Place the yeast and milk in the work bowl of a stand mixer fitted with the paddle attachment and mix on low. Add 1 cup of flour and beat the mixture until it comes together as a soft, sticky dough; this is the levain. Coat a bowl with nonstick cooking spray, place the levain in it, and cover the bowl with plastic wrap. Place the bowl in a naturally warm spot and let the levain rest for 45 minutes.

3. Add the remaining flour, 3 tablespoons of sugar, ½ teaspoon of ground ginger, the salt, cinnamon, cardamom, nutmeg, lemon zest, and vanilla seeds to the work bowl and beat to combine. With the mixer running, add half of the melted butter. Beat on low for 1 minute and then add the egg yolks. Beat until incorporated.

4. With the mixer running on low, add the levain in three increments, beating until each one is thoroughly incorporated. Raise the speed to medium and beat until the dough is smooth and glossy, about 6 minutes.

5. Drain the almonds and add them to the dough along with the candied ginger and candied citrus peels. Beat on low until they are evenly distributed. Add the raisins, cherries, and Grand Marnier and mix on low until incorporated.

6. Place the dough on a flour-dusted work surface and knead it until the fruits, almonds, candied ginger, and candied citrus peels are inside the dough rather than stuck on the surface, and dough is smooth and glossy, about 5 minutes.

7. Coat a bowl with nonstick cooking spray and place the dough in it. Cover it with plastic wrap and let the dough rest in a naturally warm spot for 1 hour.

8. Place the dough on a flour-dusted work surface and knead it. Place it back in the bowl, cover it with plastic wrap, and let it rest for another hour.

9. Divide the dough into two pieces and shape each one into an oval that is about 8 inches long. Stack two rimmed baking sheets on top of each other and line the top pan with parchment paper. Place the dough on the stacked pans and cover them with plastic wrap. Let the stollen rest for 1 hour at room temperature.

10. Preheat the oven to 350°F. Remove the plastic that is covering the stollen and place them in the oven. Bake until they are dark brown, feel lighter when lifted, and their internal temperature is at least 190°F.

11. Remove the stollen from the oven and transfer the top pan to a wire rack. Brush the hot stollen with the remaining melted butter. Combine the remaining sugar and remaining ground ginger and sprinkle the mixture all over the stollen. Let them cool on the pan.

12. Cover the stollen loosely with aluminum foil and let them rest overnight.

13. Sprinkle the stollen with the confectioners' sugar, making sure they are completely coated. Cover the stollen with plastic wrap and let them sit at room temperature for 2 days.

14. Sprinkle additional confectioners' sugar over the stollen and serve.

BANANA BREAD

YIELD: 1 LOAF / **ACTIVE TIME:** 15 MINUTES / **TOTAL TIME:** 2 HOURS

This batter can also be used to make banana muffins.

INGREDIENTS:

- 2 CUPS (240 G) ALL-PURPOSE FLOUR
- 1 TEASPOON (6 G) BAKING SODA
- ¼ TEASPOON (0.8 G) CINNAMON
- ¼ TEASPOON (¾ G) FRESHLY GRATED NUTMEG
- PINCH OF GROUND GINGER
- ½ TEASPOON (3 G) FINE SEA SALT
- 3 RIPE BANANAS
- ½ (HEAPING) CUP (113 G) LIGHT BROWN SUGAR
- 6 OZ. (170 G) SUGAR
- ¼ CUP (57 G) UNSALTED BUTTER, SOFTENED
- ½ CUP (100 G) EXTRA-VIRGIN OLIVE OIL
- 2 EGGS
- 1½ TEASPOONS (7.5 G) PURE VANILLA EXTRACT
- 2 TABLESPOONS (28 G) SOUR CREAM

1. Preheat the oven to 350°F. Coat an 8 x 4–inch loaf pan with nonstick cooking spray.

2. Place the flour, baking soda, cinnamon, nutmeg, ginger, and salt in a mixing bowl and whisk to combine. Set the mixture aside.

3. In the work bowl of a stand mixer fitted with the paddle attachment, cream the bananas, brown sugar, sugar, and butter on medium for 5 minutes. Add the olive oil, eggs, and vanilla and beat until incorporated. Add the dry mixture, reduce the speed to low, and beat until the mixture comes together as a smooth batter. Add the sour cream and beat to incorporate.

4. Pour the batter into the prepared loaf pan, place it in the oven, and bake until a cake tester inserted into the center of the loaf comes out clean, 60 to 70 minutes.

5. Remove the bread from the oven, place the pan on a wire rack, and let it cool completely.

RUM & CARAMELIZED BANANA BREAD

YIELD: 1 LOAF / **ACTIVE TIME:** 30 MINUTES / **TOTAL TIME:** 2 HOURS

This is not a typical banana bread. The rum and caramelized bananas intensify the sweetness and flavor.

INGREDIENTS:

- 2 CUPS (240 G) ALL-PURPOSE FLOUR
- 1 TEASPOON (6 G) BAKING SODA
- ¼ TEASPOON (0.8 G) CINNAMON
- ¼ TEASPOON (¾ G) ALLSPICE
- ½ TEASPOON (3 G) FINE SEA SALT
- ¼ CUP (57 G) UNSALTED BUTTER, SOFTENED
- 3½ RIPE BANANAS, SLICED
- ½ (HEAPING) CUP (113 G) LIGHT BROWN SUGAR
- 2 TABLESPOONS (28 G) SPICED RUM
- 6 OZ. (170 G) SUGAR
- ½ CUP (100 G) EXTRA-VIRGIN OLIVE OIL
- 2 EGGS
- 1½ TEASPOONS (7.5 G) PURE VANILLA EXTRACT
- 2 TABLESPOONS (28 G) CRÈME FRAÎCHE

1. Preheat the oven to 350°F. Coat an 8 x 4–inch loaf pan with nonstick cooking spray.

2. Place the flour, baking soda, cinnamon, allspice, and salt in a mixing bowl and whisk to combine. Set aside.

3. Place the butter in a large skillet and melt it over medium heat. Add the bananas and brown sugar and cook, stirring occasionally, until the bananas start to brown, about 3 minutes. Remove the pan from heat, stir in the rum, and let the mixture steep for 30 minutes.

4. In the work bowl of a stand mixer fitted with the paddle attachment, cream the caramelized banana mixture, sugar, olive oil, eggs, and vanilla on medium for 5 minutes. Add the dry mixture, reduce the speed to low, and beat until the mixture comes together as a smooth batter. Add the crème fraîche and beat to incorporate.

5. Pour the batter into the prepared loaf pan, place it in the oven, and bake until a cake tester inserted into the center of the loaf comes out clean, 60 to 70 minutes.

6. Remove the bread from the oven, place the pan on a wire rack, and let the bread cool completely.

PUMPKIN BREAD

YIELD: 1 LOAF / **ACTIVE TIME:** 15 MINUTES / **TOTAL TIME:** 2 HOURS

Try enriching this batter with a splash of spiced rum or bourbon. The alcohol will cook off in the oven, but the flavor will be noticeably enhanced.

1. Preheat the oven to 350°F. Coat an 8 x 4–inch loaf pan with nonstick cooking spray.

2. Place the flour, sugar, baking soda, baking powder, cinnamon, ginger, cloves, and salt in a mixing bowl and whisk to combine. Set aside.

3. In the work bowl of a stand mixer fitted with the whisk attachment, whip the pumpkin puree, eggs, and vanilla until combined. Add the dry mixture, reduce the speed to low, and whip until the resulting mixture comes together as a smooth batter.

4. Pour the batter into the prepared loaf pan, place it in the oven, and bake until a cake tester inserted into the center of the loaf comes out clean, 65 to 75 minutes.

5. Remove the bread from the oven, place the pan on a wire rack, and let the bread cool completely.

INGREDIENTS:

- 2⅓ CUPS (283 G) ALL-PURPOSE FLOUR
- 13 OZ. (368 G) SUGAR
- 2¼ TEASPOONS (13.5 G) BAKING SODA
- ½ TEASPOON (2 G) BAKING POWDER
- 2¼ TEASPOONS (7 G) CINNAMON
- 2¼ TEASPOONS (4 G) GROUND GINGER
- ¼ TEASPOON (½ G) GROUND CLOVES
- ¼ TEASPOON (1.5 G) FINE SEA SALT
- 15 OZ. (425 G) PUMPKIN PUREE
- 3 EGGS
- 1½ TEASPOONS (7.5 G) PURE VANILLA EXTRACT

APPLE BREAD

YIELD: 1 LOAF / **ACTIVE TIME:** 15 MINUTES / **TOTAL TIME:** 1 HOUR AND 30 MINUTES

The applesauce and Honey Syrup add a sweet and moist decadence to this seemingly standard loaf.

INGREDIENTS:

- 6¼ CUPS (757 G) ALL-PURPOSE FLOUR
- 4 TEASPOONS (13 G) CINNAMON
- 1 TEASPOON (1.7 G) GROUND GINGER
- ½ TEASPOON (1 G) GROUND CLOVES
- 4 TEASPOONS (24 G) BAKING SODA
- 1 TEASPOON (6 G) FINE SEA SALT
- 1 CUP (227 G) UNSALTED BUTTER, SOFTENED
- 20 OZ. (567 G) SUGAR
- 1 (SCANT) CUP (198 G) DARK BROWN SUGAR
- ½ CUP (100 G) CANOLA OIL
- 1 TABLESPOON (14 G) PURE VANILLA EXTRACT
- 6 EGGS
- 2 OZ. (57 G) APPLESAUCE
- 1½ CUPS (342 G) MILK
- HONEY SYRUP (SEE PAGE 667)

1. Preheat the oven to 350°F. Coat an 8 x 4–inch loaf pan with nonstick cooking spray.

2. Place the flour, cinnamon, ginger, cloves, baking soda, and salt in a mixing bowl and whisk to combine. Set aside.

3. In the work bowl of a stand mixer fitted with the paddle attachment, cream the butter, sugar, brown sugar, canola oil, and vanilla on medium until light and fluffy, about 5 minutes. Add the eggs and applesauce and beat to incorporate. Add half of the dry mixture and beat until incorporated. Add half of the milk, beat to incorporate, and then add the remaining dry mixture. Beat to incorporate, add the remaining milk, and beat until the mixture comes together as a smooth batter.

4. Pour the batter into the prepared loaf pan, place it in the oven, and bake until a cake tester inserted into the center of the loaf comes out clean, 50 to 60 minutes.

5. Remove the bread from the oven, place the pan on a wire rack, and let it cool slightly.

6. Brush the bread with the syrup and let the bread cool completely before slicing and enjoying.

ZUCCHINI BREAD

YIELD: 1 LOAF / **ACTIVE TIME:** 15 MINUTES / **TOTAL TIME:** 1 HOUR AND 30 MINUTES

Perhaps the best way to use up the surfeit of zucchini that arrives every summer.

INGREDIENTS:

- 3⅓ CUPS (397 G) ALL-PURPOSE FLOUR
- 1 TEASPOON (6 G) BAKING SODA
- 1 TEASPOON (4 G) BAKING POWDER
- 1 TEASPOON (6 G) FINE SEA SALT
- 1 TABLESPOON (9.5 G) CINNAMON
- 2 ZUCCHINI, GRATED
- 1 CUP (200 G) EXTRA-VIRGIN OLIVE OIL
- 1 CUP PLUS 2 TABLESPOONS (227 G) SUGAR
- 1 CUP PLUS 1 TABLESPOON (227 G) LIGHT BROWN SUGAR
- 3 EGGS

1. Preheat the oven to 350°F. Coat an 8 x 4–inch loaf pan with nonstick cooking spray.

2. Place the flour, baking soda, baking powder, salt, and cinnamon in a mixing bowl and whisk to combine. Set aside.

3. In the work bowl of a stand mixer fitted with the whisk attachment, beat the zucchini, olive oil, sugar, brown sugar, and eggs on medium for 5 minutes. Add the dry mixture, reduce the speed to low, and beat until the resulting mixture comes together as a batter.

4. Pour the batter into the prepared loaf pan, place it in the oven, and bake until a cake tester inserted into the center of the loaf comes out clean, 45 to 55 minutes.

5. Remove the bread from the oven, place the pan on a wire rack, and let the bread cool completely.

GLUTEN-FREE COCONUT BREAD

YIELD: 1 LOAF / **ACTIVE TIME:** 20 MINUTES / **TOTAL TIME:** 1 HOUR AND 50 MINUTES

Gluten-free recipes like this one benefit from a blend of flours, so you can get the taste and texture just right.

INGREDIENTS:

- 1 CUP (60 G) SWEETENED COCONUT FLAKES, PLUS MORE FOR TOPPING
- 8.4 OZ. (238 G) WHITE RICE FLOUR
- 3.2 OZ. (91 G) SORGHUM FLOUR
- 3.2 OZ. (91 G) TAPIOCA STARCH
- ½ TEASPOON (1.5 G) XANTHAN GUM
- 1½ TEASPOONS (6 G) BAKING POWDER
- 1 TEASPOON (6 G) BAKING SODA
- ¾ TEASPOON (4.5 G) FINE SEA SALT
- 1 CUP (198 G) SUGAR
- ½ (SCANT) CUP BROWN SUGAR
- ¾ CUP (161 G) CANOLA OIL
- 1 TEASPOON (5 G) PURE VANILLA EXTRACT
- 1 TEASPOON (5 G) COCONUT EXTRACT
- 1½ CUPS (361 G) UNSWEETENED COCONUT MILK
- 4 EGGS

1. Preheat the oven to 325°F. Coat an 8 x 4–inch loaf pan with nonstick cooking spray.

2. Lightly toast the coconut flakes in a skillet for about 5 minutes. Let them cool.

3. In a large mixing bowl, combine the flours, tapioca starch, xanthan gum, baking powder, baking soda, and salt. Set the mixture aside.

4. Combine the sugars, canola oil, vanilla, coconut extract, and coconut milk in the work bowl of a stand mixer fitted with the whisk attachment. Incorporate the eggs one at a time and then add the dry mixture. Beat until the resulting mixture comes together as a smooth batter. Add the toasted coconut and fold until they are evenly distributed.

5. Fill the prepared loaf pan about three-quarters of the way with the batter. Reserve any leftover batter for another preparation, like cupcakes.

6. Top the loaf with coconut, place it in the oven, and bake until a cake tester inserted into the center comes out clean, about 1 hour and 20 minutes.

7. Remove the bread from the oven, let it cool in the pan for 10 minutes, and then turn it out onto a wire rack. Let the bread cool completely before enjoying.

STOUT GINGERBREAD

YIELD: 1 LOAF / **ACTIVE TIME:** 15 MINUTES / **TOTAL TIME:** 1 HOUR AND 30 MINUTES

If you can find one of the marshmallow stouts that some craft breweries are now turning out, that will add yet another layer of flavor to this lovely gingerbread.

INGREDIENTS:

- 2⅓ CUPS (283 G) ALL-PURPOSE FLOUR
- 1½ TEASPOONS (6 G) BAKING POWDER
- 2 TABLESPOONS (10 G) GROUND GINGER
- ½ TEASPOON (1.6 G) CINNAMON
- ½ TEASPOON (1 G) GROUND CLOVES
- ¼ TEASPOON (¾ G) FRESHLY GRATED NUTMEG
- ¼ TEASPOON (1.5 G) FINE SEA SALT
- 1 CUP (340 G) MOLASSES
- 1 CUP (238 G) STOUT
- 1½ TEASPOONS (9 G) BAKING SODA
- 3 EGGS
- 4 OZ. (113 G) SUGAR
- ½ (HEAPING) CUP (113 G) DARK BROWN SUGAR
- ¾ CUP (161 G) CANOLA OIL

1. Preheat the oven to 350°F. Coat an 8 x 4–inch loaf pan with nonstick cooking spray.

2. Place the flour, baking powder, ginger, cinnamon, cloves, nutmeg, and salt in a mixing bowl and whisk to combine. Set the mixture aside.

3. Combine the molasses and stout in a small saucepan and bring it to a simmer over medium heat. Remove the pan from heat and whisk in the baking soda. Set the mixture aside.

4. In the work bowl of a stand mixer fitted with the paddle attachment, beat the eggs, sugar, brown sugar, and canola oil on medium until light and fluffy, about 5 minutes. Add the molasses mixture, beat until incorporated, and then add the dry mixture. Reduce the speed to low and beat until the resulting mixture comes together as a smooth batter.

5. Pour the batter into the prepared loaf pan, place it in the oven, and bake until a cake tester inserted into the center of the loaf comes out clean, 50 to 60 minutes.

6. Remove the bread from the oven, place the pan on a wire rack, and let the bread cool completely.

Stout Gingerbread, see page 637

CORNBREAD

YIELD: 1 LOAF / **ACTIVE TIME:** 10 MINUTES / **TOTAL TIME:** 1 HOUR

Full of flavor thanks to the spices, and subtly but surprisingly rich thanks to the ricotta and buttermilk, you won't hear anyone complaining if you decide to show up to the family barbecue with this cornbread.

INGREDIENTS:

- ½ CUP (113 G) UNSALTED BUTTER
- 3 EGGS
- 2 TABLESPOONS (26 G) BROWN SUGAR
- 1 CUP (138 G) CORNMEAL
- 1 CUP (120 G) ALL-PURPOSE FLOUR
- 1 TABLESPOON (12 G) BAKING POWDER
- 1½ TEASPOONS (9 G) FINE SEA SALT
- ½ TEASPOON (1 G) MUSTARD POWDER
- 1 TEASPOON (2.7 G) CHILI POWDER
- ½ CUP (168 G) HONEY
- 1 CUP (227 G) BUTTERMILK
- 2 TABLESPOONS (26 G) WHOLE-MILK RICOTTA CHEESE

1. Place the butter in a large skillet and melt it over medium heat. Cook the butter until it starts to brown and give off a nutty aroma. Remove the pan from heat and let the brown butter cool completely.

2. Preheat the oven to 325°F and position a rack in the center. Coat a large cast-iron skillet with nonstick cooking spray.

3. Place the eggs and brown sugar in the work bowl of a stand mixer fitted with the whisk attachment and whisk on high until the mixture is pale and fluffy.

4. Place the cornmeal, flour, baking powder, salt, mustard powder, and chili powder in a mixing bowl, stir to combine, and set the mixture aside.

5. Add the brown butter, honey, buttermilk, and ricotta to the stand mixer's work bowl and whisk until incorporated. Add the dry mixture and whisk until the mixture comes together as a smooth batter.

6. Pour the batter into the skillet and place it in the oven. Bake until a cake tester inserted into the center of the cornbread comes out clean, about 35 minutes.

7. Remove the cornbread from the oven and invert it onto a wire rack. Let the cornbread cool slightly before slicing and serving.

BACON & CHEDDAR CORNBREAD

YIELD: 6 TO 8 SERVINGS / **ACTIVE TIME:** 20 MINUTES / **TOTAL TIME:** 1 HOUR

The smoky-salty combination of bacon and cheddar is a perfect complement to so many foods—burgers, grilled cheese sandwiches, fried eggs—and now, cornbread.

INGREDIENTS:

- 2 CUPS (320 G) FINELY GROUND YELLOW CORNMEAL
- 1 CUP (120 G) ALL-PURPOSE FLOUR
- ¼ CUP (50 G) SUGAR
- 2 TEASPOONS (8 G) BAKING POWDER
- 1 TEASPOON (6 G) BAKING SODA
- 1 TEASPOON (6 G) FINE SEA SALT
- 1½ CUPS (340 G) MILK
- ¼ CUP (57 G) UNSALTED BUTTER
- 2 EGGS
- 1 CUP CRUNCHY BACON BITS
- ½-¾ CUP GRATED SHARP CHEDDAR CHEESE

1. Preheat the oven to 400°F.

2. In a large bowl, combine the cornmeal, flour, sugar, baking powder, baking soda, and salt. Place ½ cup of the milk in a microwave-safe measuring cup. Add 2 tablespoons of the butter, cut into pieces. Put the measuring cup in the microwave and heat on high for 1 minute, so that the butter melts. Pour this mixture over the dry ingredients and begin stirring.

3. Gradually incorporate the remaining milk and then add the eggs and continue stirring until the mixture comes together as a smooth batter. Add most of the bacon and cheddar, reserving some to sprinkle on top, and fold until evenly distributed.

4. Warm a large cast-iron skillet over medium heat and melt the remaining butter in it. Add the batter and shake the pan gently to evenly distribute. Sprinkle the reserved bacon and cheddar over the top.

5. Transfer the skillet to the oven and cook until the cornbread is a light golden brown and a toothpick inserted into the center comes out clean, 25 to 35 minutes.

6. Remove the skillet from the oven and let the cornbread cool for 10 to 15 minutes before slicing and serving.

BOLO REI

YIELD: 1 CAKE / **ACTIVE TIME:** 40 MINUTES / **TOTAL TIME:** 4 HOURS

There are several versions of king cake, which is best known for being a part of New Orleans' Mardi Gras celebrations. This version is traditional to Portugal.

INGREDIENTS:

- ⅓ CUP (75 G) WHOLE MILK
- 1¾ TEASPOONS (5.5 G) ACTIVE DRY YEAST
- 3 CUPS (360 G) ALL-PURPOSE FLOUR, PLUS MORE AS NEEDED
- ⅓ CUP (37 G) CONFECTIONERS' SUGAR
- ¼ TEASPOON (½ G) FRESHLY GRATED NUTMEG
- 1 TEASPOON (2 G) LEMON ZEST
- 2 EGGS
- 1 EGG YOLK
- 1 TEASPOON (5 G) ORANGE BLOSSOM WATER
- 6 TABLESPOONS (78 G) UNSALTED BUTTER, CUT INTO SMALL PIECES
- 1 TEASPOON (6 G) FINE SEA SALT
- 1 CUP CANDIED FRUIT, ROUGHLY CHOPPED, PLUS MORE FOR TOPPING
- 5 TABLESPOONS WARM WATER (110°F)
- 3 TABLESPOONS SUGAR

1. Place the milk in a saucepan and warm it to 100°F. Add the yeast, gently stir, and let the mixture rest until it starts to foam, about 10 minutes.

2. Place the yeast mixture in a large mixing bowl. Add the flour, confectioners' sugar, nutmeg, lemon zest, one of the eggs, the egg yolk, and orange blossom water and beat until combined.

3. Transfer the dough to the work bowl of a stand mixer fitted with the dough hook. Work the mixture until it comes together as a dough and then gradually incorporate the butter. When all of the butter has been incorporated, add the salt and candied fruit work the mixture until it is very smooth. This should take about 20 minutes. Place the dough in a naturally warm spot and let it rest until it has doubled in size, about 1 to 1½ hours.

4. Transfer the dough to flour-dusted work surface and shape it into a ball. Place the ball in a 13 x 9–inch baking pan lined with parchment paper and flatten it slightly. Make a small hole in the center of the dough and use your hands to gradually enlarge the hole, creating a ring. Cover the dough with a kitchen towel and let it rest for 1 hour.

5. Preheat the oven to 320°F. Place the remaining egg and 1 tablespoon of the warm water in a measuring cup and beat to combine. Brush the cake with the egg wash. Place it in the oven and bake until the cake is golden brown and a cake tester inserted into the center comes out clean, about 30 minutes.

6. Remove the cake from the oven. Place the sugar and the remaining warm water in a mixing bowl and stir until the sugar has dissolved. Brush the hot cake with the glaze and top with additional candied fruit. Let the cake cool completely before slicing and serving.

Bolo Rei, see page 643

PORTUGUESE SWEET BREAD

YIELD: 2 LOAVES / **ACTIVE TIME:** 40 MINUTES / **TOTAL TIME:** 3 HOURS AND 30 MINUTES

This traditional Portuguese sweet bread is usually eaten during holidays, but it is also available year-round. It is common in areas with Portuguese American influences, such as Hawaii, New Jersey, Florida, California, and Toronto.

INGREDIENTS:

FOR THE DOUGH

- 2¾ TABLESPOONS (40 G) WARM WATER (105°F)
- 1 TABLESPOON (8.5 G) ACTIVE DRY YEAST
- ⅔ CUP (150 G) MILK
- 4⅙ CUPS (500 G) ALL-PURPOSE FLOUR, PLUS MORE AS NEEDED
- ½ CUP (100 G) SUGAR, PLUS MORE FOR TOPPING
- 2 EGGS
- ¼ CUP (60 G) UNSALTED BUTTER
- ¾ TEASPOON (4 G) FINE SEA SALT

FOR THE EGG WASH

- 1 EGG
- 1 TABLESPOON WATER

1. To begin preparations for the dough, place the water and yeast in a bowl and gently stir to combine. Let the mixture sit until it starts to foam, about 10 minutes.

2. Warm the milk to 100°F. In the work bowl of a stand mixer fitted with the dough hook, combine the yeast mixture with the warmed milk.

3. Add the flour and sugar and work the mixture until it just comes together. Incorporate the eggs one at a time and then gradually incorporate the butter.

4. Add the salt and knead the dough until it feels smooth. The mixing process takes about 20 minutes from start to finish.

5. Cover the bowl with plastic wrap, place it in a naturally warm spot, and let the dough rest until it looks fully risen, 1 to 1½ hours.

6. Place the dough on a flour-dusted work surface, divide it in half, and shape it into two rounds.

7. Line a baking dish with parchment paper and dust it with flour. Place the rounds on the parchment paper and flatten them slightly. Cover the dough with a kitchen towel and let the dough rest for 1 to 1½ hours.

8. Preheat the oven to 350°F.

9. To prepare the egg wash, place the egg and water in a small bowl and gently stir to combine. Brush the rounds with the egg wash and sprinkle sugar over them.

10. Place the bread in the oven and bake until it is golden brown and feels lighter when lifted, 25 to 40 minutes.

11. Remove the bread from the oven, transfer it to a wire rack, and let it cool before slicing and serving.

PANPEPATO

YIELD: 2 MEDIUM PANPEPATO / **ACTIVE TIME:** 30 MINUTES / **TOTAL TIME:** 1 HOUR AND 15 MINUTES

In the same festive vein as panettone but originating in Central rather than Northern Italy, panpepato is enriched with candied fruit, raisins, nuts, and, more recently, chocolate. It's a very easy way to have a taste of Italy for Christmas without the long preparation process of panettone.

INGREDIENTS:

- 1 CUP RAISINS
- 1 CUP BLANCHED HAZELNUTS
- 1 CUP BLANCHED ALMONDS
- 1 CUP WALNUTS
- ¾ CUP CANDIED FRUIT
- 1 TEASPOON (2 G) CINNAMON
- 1 TEASPOON (2 G) BLACK PEPPER
- 1 TEASPOON (2 G) GROUND CLOVES
- ½ TEASPOON (1 G) FRESHLY GRATED NUTMEG
- 5½ OZ. (155 G) BITTERSWEET CHOCOLATE, MELTED, PLUS MORE FOR TOPPING
- ½ CUP PLUS 2 TABLESPOONS (210 G) HONEY
- 3 CUPS (360 G) ALL-PURPOSE FLOUR

1. Place the raisins in a bowl, cover them with warm water, and let them soak for 20 minutes. Drain the raisins, gently squeeze them, and set aside.

2. Place the hazelnuts, almonds, and walnuts in a food processor and blitz until finely chopped. Place them in a bowl, add the candied fruit, cinnamon, pepper, cloves, nutmeg, chocolate, and raisins, and work the mixture, preferably with your hands, until it is well combined.

3. Place the honey in a saucepan and warm it over medium heat until it is liquefied. Add it to the mixture. Add the flour gradually and work the mixture until it comes together as a dough.

4. Divide the dough into two balls. Line a baking sheet with parchment paper and place the balls on it.

5. Preheat the oven to 340°F.

6. Place the baking sheet in the oven and bake for 20 to 25 minutes. Do not overbake to panpepato. They do not need to take on any color to be pulled from the oven and enjoyed, so keep a close eye on them around the 20-minute mark.

7. Remove the panpepato from the oven, place them on a wire rack, and let them cool before slicing and serving. If desired, drizzle additional chocolate over the panpepato before enjoying.

ZUCCHINI & LEMON BREAD

YIELD: 1 LOAF / **ACTIVE TIME:** 30 MINUTES / **TOTAL TIME:** 1 HOUR AND 15 MINUTES

This lemony, moist cake goes great with your morning coffee or afternoon tea!

1. Preheat the oven to 350°F. To begin preparations for the batter, combine the flour, baking soda, baking powder, and salt. Set the mixture aside.

2. In another bowl, combine the sugar, zucchini, sunflower oil, egg, lemon juice, and lemon zest until combined.

3. Pour the wet mixture into the dry mixture and stir until the resulting mixture just comes together as a batter, incorporating the lemon pulp halfway through. When the dough is mixed about halfway, drop in the lemon pieces and mix very carefully, only until all of the dry ingredients are wet.

4. Coat a 9 x 5–inch loaf pan with nonstick cooking spray and pour the batter into it. Place the loaf pan in the oven and bake until a cake tester inserted into the center of the bread comes out clean, 50 to 55 minutes.

5. While the bread is in the oven, prepare the glaze. Sift the confectioners' sugar into a bowl, add the lemon juice and lemon zest, and stir until the mixture is smooth.

6. Remove the loaf from the oven and turn it out onto a wire rack. Spread the glaze over the loaf after it has cooled.

INGREDIENTS:

FOR THE BATTER

1½ CUPS (180 G) ALL-PURPOSE FLOUR

½ TEASPOON (3 G) BAKING SODA

¼ TEASPOON (1 G) BAKING POWDER

¼ TEASPOON (1 G) FINE SEA SALT

¾ CUP (150 G) SUGAR

1 CUP SHREDDED ZUCCHINI

¼ CUP (50 G) SUNFLOWER OIL

1 EGG

2 TABLESPOONS (26 G) FRESH LEMON JUICE

2 TABLESPOONS (12 G) LEMON ZEST

PULP OF 1 LEMON

FOR THE GLAZE

½ CUP CONFECTIONERS' SUGAR

1 TABLESPOON FRESH LEMON JUICE

ZEST OF 1 LEMON

CHOCOLATE CHIP BANANA BREAD

YIELD: 1 LOAF / **ACTIVE TIME:** 15 MINUTES / **TOTAL TIME:** 1 HOUR

Chocolate and bananas are the best of friends. They go together like salt and pepper! This bread is a great breakfast loaf, but it works just as well with ice cream and chocolate sauce for a fast and delicious dessert.

INGREDIENTS:

- ¾ CUP (170 G) UNSALTED BUTTER, CUBED AND SOFTENED, PLUS MORE AS NEEDED
- 1 CUP (213 G) LIGHT BROWN SUGAR
- 3 EGGS
- 1 CUP (300 G) MASHED OVERRIPE BANANAS
- 2 TABLESPOONS (30 G) SOUR CREAM
- 1¾ CUPS (210 G) ALL-PURPOSE FLOUR, PLUS MORE AS NEEDED
- ¼ TEASPOON (1 G) FINE SEA SALT
- ¼ TEASPOON (1 G) BAKING POWDER
- 1 TEASPOON (6 G) BAKING SODA
- 1 CUP SEMISWEET CHOCOLATE CHIPS
- ½ CUP CHOPPED WALNUTS (OPTIONAL)

1. Preheat the oven to 350°F. Coat an 8 x 4–inch loaf pan with butter, dust it with flour, and knock out any excess.

2. In the work bowl of a stand mixer fitted with the paddle attachment, cream together the butter and brown sugar until light and fluffy.

3. Incorporate the eggs one at a time, scraping down the work bowl as necessary. Add the bananas and sour cream and beat to incorporate.

4. Sift the flour, salt, baking powder, and baking soda into another bowl. Add the dry mixture to the butter mixture and beat until the resulting mixture just comes together as a dough.

5. Add the chocolate chips and, if desired, the walnuts and fold until they are evenly distributed.

6. Pour the dough into the loaf pan, place it in the oven, and bake until a cake tester inserted into the center of the bread comes out clean, 45 to 50 minutes.

7. Remove the bread from the oven, transfer it to a wire rack, and let it cool before slicing and serving.

PUMPKIN & GINGER LOAF

YIELD: 1 LOAF / **ACTIVE TIME:** 10 MINUTES / **TOTAL TIME:** 1 HOUR AND 10 MINUTES

Chocolate chips and roasted nuts—pecans in particular—make for great additions to this spicy, festive bread.

INGREDIENTS:

- 1½ CUPS (180 G) ALL-PURPOSE FLOUR
- ¼ TEASPOON (1 G) FINE SEA SALT
- 1 TEASPOON (4 G) BAKING POWDER
- ½ TEASPOON (3 G) BAKING SODA
- 1 TABLESPOON (2 G) CANDIED GINGER, FINELY CHOPPED
- 1 TEASPOON (1 G) CINNAMON
- PINCH OF GROUND CLOVES
- ¾ CUP (150 G) PACKED DARK BROWN SUGAR
- 1 CUP (225 G) CANNED PUMPKIN PUREE
- ½ CUP (100 G) SUNFLOWER OIL
- 2 EGGS

1. Preheat the oven to 350°F. Coat an 8 x 4–inch loaf pan with nonstick cooking spray.

2. Sift the flour, salt, baking powder, baking soda, candied ginger, cinnamon, and cloves into a mixing bowl. Set the mixture aside.

3. In the work bowl of a stand mixer fitted with the paddle attachment, cream together the brown sugar, pumpkin puree, and sunflower oil until the mixture is well combined.

4. Incorporate the eggs one at a time, scraping down the work bowl as necessary. Add the dry mixture and beat until the resulting mixture comes together as a smooth dough.

5. Pour the dough into the loaf pan, place it in the oven, and bake until a cake tester inserted into the center of the bread comes out clean, 50 to 55 minutes.

6. Remove the bread from the oven, transfer it to a wire rack, and let it cool before slicing and serving.

Chocolate Chip Banana Bread, see page 650

FETA & HERB QUICKBREAD

YIELD: 1 LOAF / **ACTIVE TIME:** 10 MINUTES / **TOTAL TIME:** 1 HOUR

A light and airy quickbread that is better suited to the spring and summer months than most of its kin.

INGREDIENTS:

- ½ CUP FINELY CHOPPED FRESH BASIL
- ½ CUP FINELY CHOPPED FRESH CHIVES
- UNSALTED BUTTER, AS NEEDED
- 2 TABLESPOONS SESAME SEEDS
- 1¼ CUPS (150 G) ALL-PURPOSE FLOUR
- 1 TABLESPOON (12 G) BAKING POWDER
- 3 LARGE EGGS
- ¼ CUP (50 G) EXTRA-VIRGIN OLIVE OIL
- ½ CUP PLUS 2 TABLESPOONS (140 G) PLAIN YOGURT
- ½ TEASPOON (3 G) FINE SEA SALT
- ½ TEASPOON (2 G) BLACK PEPPER
- 1¾ CUPS (200 G) CRUMBLED FETA CHEESE

1. Preheat the oven to 350°F. Combine the basil and chives in a small bowl and set the mixture aside. Coat a 9 x 5–inch loaf pan with butter and sprinkle half of the sesame seeds onto the bottom and sides, shaking the pan to coat.

2. Combine the flour and baking powder in a mixing bowl. In a separate bowl, whisk together the eggs, olive oil, yogurt, salt, and pepper. Stir in the feta and herb mixture. Fold the flour mixture into the egg mixture until it just comes together as a slightly lumpy batter.

3. Pour the batter into the prepared pan. Level the surface with a rubber spatula and sprinkle the remaining sesame seeds on top. Place the bread in the oven and bake until it is golden brown and a cake tester inserted into the center comes out clean, 40 to 50 minutes.

4. Remove the bread from the oven and let it cool in the pan for a few minutes. Transfer it to a wire rack and let the bread cool completely before enjoying.

APPENDIX

STIFF SOURDOUGH STARTER

YIELD: 1½ CUPS / **ACTIVE TIME:** 15 MINUTES / **TOTAL TIME:** 24 HOURS

INGREDIENTS:

- 5/6 OZ. (23.6 G) SOURDOUGH STARTER (SEE PAGE 40)
- 3½ OZ. (100 G) WATER
- 7 OZ. (200 G) ALL-PURPOSE FLOUR

1. Place the starter, half of the water, and half of the flour in a mixing bowl and stir to combine. Cover the bowl with plastic wrap and let the mixture rest at room temperature for 12 hours.

2. Place 1¾ oz. of the initial mixture and the remaining water and flour in a mixing bowl and stir to combine. Cover the bowl with plastic wrap and let the mixture rest at room temperature for 4 hours before using the stiff starter.

BIGA

YIELD: 1¾ CUPS / **ACTIVE TIME:** 10 MINUTES / **TOTAL TIME:** 8 HOURS

INGREDIENTS:

- ⅓ CUP (75 G) WARM WATER (105°F)
- ⅛ TEASPOON (0.3 G) ACTIVE DRY YEAST
- 1 CUP (120 G) UNBLEACHED ALL-PURPOSE FLOUR

1. In the work bowl of a stand mixer fitted with the dough hook, add all of the ingredients and mix on medium speed for 1 to 2 minutes. Scrape the biga into a clean bowl and cover it with plastic wrap.

2. If you plan to make the dough later that same day, let the biga rest at room temperature until it has risen to the point where it just begins to collapse, 6 to 8 hours. The biga will triple in volume and small dents and folds will begin to appear in the top as it reaches its peak and then it begins to deflate. The sponge is now in perfect condition to be used in dough. It's best if you have already weighed or measured out all of the other ingredients of your dough before the biga reaches this point, so that you can use it before it collapses too much.

3. If you're not planning to make your dough until the next day or the day after, put the covered biga in the refrigerator and let it rise there for at least 14 hours before taking it out to use in a recipe. Be sure to compensate for the cold temperature of the biga by using lukewarm water (90°F) in the dough. Or let the starter sit out, covered, until it reaches room temperature.

RYE SOUR

YIELD: 4 CUPS / **ACTIVE TIME:** 20 MINUTES / **TOTAL TIME:** 24 HOURS

1. To prepare the sour, place the flour, water, and yeast in a bowl and stir until the mixture is completely smooth.

2. Place the onion and caraway seeds in a piece of cheesecloth and tie it tightly (like a homemade tea bag), then sink the sachet completely into the flour mixture.

3. Cover the bowl tightly with plastic wrap and place it in a naturally warm spot overnight.

4. The next day, you want to feed the sour. Remove the onion/caraway sachet and scrape the sour off the cheesecloth and back into the bowl. Add the water and flour and stir until the sour is smooth. Cover the bowl with plastic wrap and let the mixture ferment for 3 to 4 hours, until it is frothy.

5. The rye sour can now be used in a rye bread recipe, with plenty left over to put in the refrigerator until the next feeding. Store it in a tightly sealed container. Any subsequent feedings need to ferment at room temperature for 3 to 4 hours before using.

6. To maintain the rye sour, add the water and rye flour to the sour and stir until smooth. Cover the bowl with plastic wrap and let the mixture ferment at room temperature for 3 to 4 hours, until it is frothy and full of fermentation bubbles. Use the sour to make more rye bread, or put it back in the refrigerator, where it will be OK for another week. Feed the sour at least once per week, and you will be able to keep it indefinitely.

INGREDIENTS:

FOR THE SOUR

- 1 CUP (103 G) MEDIUM RYE FLOUR
- ¾ CUP (170 G) WATER
- ⅛ TEASPOON (½ G) INSTANT YEAST
- ½ CUP (75 G) ONION, COARSELY CHOPPED
- 1½ TEASPOONS (3 G) CARAWAY SEEDS

TO FEED THE SOUR

- ¾ CUP (170 G) WATER, AT ROOM TEMPERATURE
- 1 CUP (103 G) MEDIUM RYE FLOUR

TO MAINTAIN THE SOUR

- 1 CUP (150 G) RYE SOUR
- ¾ CUP (170 G) WATER, AT ROOM TEMPERATURE
- 1 CUP (103 G) MEDIUM RYE FLOUR

PIZZA SAUCE

YIELD: 2 CUPS / **ACTIVE TIME:** 5 MINUTES / **TOTAL TIME:** 5 MINUTES

1. Place the tomatoes and their juices in a bowl, add the olive oil, and stir until it has been thoroughly incorporated.

2. Season the sauce with salt and oregano and stir to incorporate. If using within 2 hours, leave the sauce at room temperature. If storing in the refrigerator, where the sauce will keep for up to 3 days, return to room temperature before using.

INGREDIENTS:

- 1 LB. PEELED WHOLE SAN MARZANO TOMATOES, WITH THEIR LIQUID, CRUSHED BY HAND
- 1½ TABLESPOONS EXTRA-VIRGIN OLIVE OIL
- SALT, TO TASTE
- DRIED OREGANO, TO TASTE

TOM YUM PASTE

YIELD: 1 CUP / **ACTIVE TIME:** 10 MINUTES / **TOTAL TIME:** 25 MINUTES

1. Place all of the ingredients in a food processor, blitz until smooth, and use as desired or store in the refrigerator.

INGREDIENTS:

- 1 LEMONGRASS STALK, PEELED
- 2-INCH PIECE OF FRESH GALANGAL, PEELED AND MINCED
- 3 MAKRUT LIME LEAVES, SLICED THIN
- 1 TABLESPOON THAI CHILE PASTE
- 4 RED CHILE PEPPERS, STEMMED AND SEEDED
- 2 TABLESPOONS FISH SAUCE
- JUICE OF 2 LIMES
- 2 SHALLOTS, CHOPPED
- 2 TEASPOONS SUGAR
- 3 TABLESPOONS CHOPPED FRESH CILANTRO

DUCK CONFIT

YIELD: 4 SERVINGS / **ACTIVE TIME:** 10 MINUTES / **TOTAL TIME:** 28 HOURS

1. Place the salt, sugar, juniper berries, and pepper in a bowl and stir to combine. Taste the blend to make sure that it's a nice balance of sweet and salty. Spread the mixture over the duck.

2. Place a wire rack in a rimmed baking sheet. Place the duck on the wire rack, place it in the refrigerator, and let it chill, uncovered, overnight.

3. Preheat the oven to 300°F. Rinse the duck, pat it dry, and place it in a roasting pan. Cover the duck with the duck fat, add the remaining ingredients, and cover the pan with aluminum foil.

4. Place the duck in the oven and cook until it is very tender and the meat easily pulls away from the bone.

INGREDIENTS:

- ½ CUP KOSHER SALT
- ½ CUP WHITE SUGAR
- 1 TABLESPOON CRUSHED JUNIPER BERRIES
- 1 TEASPOON CRUSHED BLACK PEPPER
- 4 SKIN-ON DUCK LEGS
- 4 SKIN-ON, BONE-IN DUCK THIGHS
- 8 CUPS RENDERED DUCK FAT
- 2 STAR ANISE PODS
- 5 SPRIGS OF FRESH THYME
- 1 HEAD OF GARLIC, HALVED AT THE EQUATOR
- JUICE OF 1 ORANGE

HOISIN SAUCE

YIELD: ½ CUP / **ACTIVE TIME:** 5 MINUTES / **TOTAL TIME:** 5 MINUTES

1. Place the canola oil in a saucepan and warm it over medium heat. Add the garlic and cook, stirring frequently, for 1 minute.

2. Stir in the soy sauce, honey, vinegar, tahini, and sriracha and cook until the sauce is smooth, about 5 minutes.

3. Remove the pan from heat and let the sauce cool before using or storing in the refrigerator.

INGREDIENTS:

- 2 TABLESPOONS CANOLA OIL
- 4 GARLIC CLOVES, MINCED
- ¼ CUP SOY SAUCE
- 3 TABLESPOONS HONEY
- 2 TABLESPOONS WHITE VINEGAR
- 2 TABLESPOONS TAHINI PASTE
- 2 TEASPOONS SRIRACHA

LAHMACUN SPREAD

YIELD: 2 CUPS / **ACTIVE TIME:** 5 MINUTES / **TOTAL TIME:** 5 MINUTES

1. Place all of the ingredients in a food processor and blitz until the mixture is a smooth paste. Use as desired or store in the refrigerator.

INGREDIENTS:

- ¾ LB. GROUND BEEF
- ½ LARGE ONION, CHOPPED
- ½ GREEN BELL PEPPER, CHOPPED
- 1 TOMATO, CHOPPED
- 1 BUNCH FRESH PARSLEY
- 1½ TEASPOONS TAHINI PASTE
- ½ OZ. TOMATO PASTE
- ¼ TEASPOON RED PEPPER FLAKES
- ¼ TEASPOON BLACK PEPPER
- ¼ TEASPOON GROUND NUTMEG
- ½ TEASPOON CINNAMON
- ½ TEASPOON GROUND ALLSPICE
- ½ TEASPOON SUMAC POWDER
- ½ TEASPOON DRIED THYME
- ½ TEASPOON KOSHER SALT
- JUICE OF 1 LEMON WEDGE

DONAIR SAUCE

YIELD: 1¼ CUPS / **ACTIVE TIME:** 5 MINUTES / **TOTAL TIME:** 5 MINUTES

1. Place all of the ingredients in a bowl and whisk to combine. Use as desired or store in the refrigerator.

INGREDIENTS:

- 7 OZ. SWEETENED CONDENSED MILK
- ¼ CUP WHITE VINEGAR
- ½ TEASPOON GARLIC POWDER

GARLIC BUTTER

YIELD: 1¼ CUPS / **ACTIVE TIME:** 5 MINUTES / **TOTAL TIME:** 5 MINUTES

INGREDIENTS:

- 1 CUP UNSALTED BUTTER, SOFTENED
- 1½ TEASPOONS FRESH LEMON JUICE
- 2 GARLIC CLOVES, MINCED
- 1 TABLESPOON CHOPPED FRESH PARSLEY
- SALT AND PEPPER, TO TASTE

1. Place the butter in the work bowl of a stand mixer fitted with the paddle attachment and beat until it is light and fluffy.

2. Add the remaining ingredients and beat to combine. Use as desired or store in the refrigerator.

BASIL PESTO

YIELD: 1 CUP / **ACTIVE TIME:** 10 MINUTES / **TOTAL TIME:** 25 MINUTES

INGREDIENTS:

- ¼ CUP PINE NUTS
- 3 GARLIC CLOVES
- SALT AND PEPPER, TO TASTE
- 2 CUPS FIRMLY PACKED FRESH BASIL LEAVES
- ½ CUP EXTRA-VIRGIN OLIVE OIL
- ¼ CUP FRESHLY GRATED PARMESAN CHEESE
- 1 TEASPOON FRESH LEMON JUICE

1. Warm a small skillet over low heat for 1 minute. Add the pine nuts and cook, shaking the pan frequently, until they begin to give off a toasty fragrance, 2 to 3 minutes. Transfer the pine nuts to a plate and let them cool completely.

2. Place the garlic, salt, and pine nuts in a food processor or blender and pulse until the mixture is a coarse meal. Add the basil and pulse it is until finely minced. Transfer the mixture to a medium bowl and, while whisking to incorporate, add the oil in a thin stream.

3. Add the cheese and stir until thoroughly incorporated. Stir in the lemon juice, taste, and adjust the seasoning as necessary. To serve, toss pasta in the pesto.

4. Note: You can also make this pesto using a mortar and pestle, which will give it more texture.

SWORDFISH CARPACCIO

YIELD: 4 SERVINGS / **ACTIVE TIME:** 10 MINUTES / **TOTAL TIME:** 24 HOURS

1. Make sure your freezer is set to the coldest possible temperature and freeze the swordfish overnight.

2. Cut the swordfish into very thin slices, drizzle olive oil over them, cover with lemon juice, and season with salt and pepper. Refrigerate the carpaccio for 15 minutes before serving.

INGREDIENTS:

- ½ LB. SWORDFISH FILET
- EXTRA-VIRGIN OLIVE OIL, TO TASTE
- FRESH LEMON JUICE, TO TASTE
- SALT AND PEPPER, TO TASTE

CLASSIC TOMATO SAUCE

YIELD: 8 CUPS / **ACTIVE TIME:** 25 MINUTES / **TOTAL TIME:** 40 MINUTES

1. Place the olive oil in a medium saucepan and warm it over medium heat. Add the garlic and cook until it starts to brown.

2. Add the tomatoes, partially cover the pan, and cook the sauce for 20 minutes, stirring occasionally. Remove the garlic, season the sauce with salt and red pepper flakes, and add the basil.

3. Cook until the taste has developed to your liking and the sauce has the desired consistency, 5 to 10 minutes. During this last phase, leave the pan uncovered if the sauce is too liquid, or reduce the heat and add a splash of water if it is too thick. To serve, ladle the sauce over pasta.

INGREDIENTS:

- ¼ CUP EXTRA-VIRGIN OLIVE OIL
- 2 GARLIC CLOVES
- 1.8 LBS. WHOLE PEELED TOMATOES, CRUSHED BY HAND
- SALT, TO TASTE
- RED PEPPER FLAKES, TO TASTE
- HANDFUL OF FRESH BASIL, TORN

ROYAL ICING

YIELD: 3 CUPS / **ACTIVE TIME:** 5 MINUTES / **TOTAL TIME:** 5 MINUTES

1. Place the egg whites, vanilla, and confectioners' sugar in a mixing bowl and whisk until the mixture is smooth.

2. If desired, add the food coloring. If using immediately, place the icing in a piping bag. If making ahead of time, store in the refrigerator, where it will keep for 5 days.

INGREDIENTS:

- 6 EGG WHITES
- 1 TEASPOON PURE VANILLA EXTRACT
- 2 LBS. CONFECTIONERS' SUGAR
- 2 DROPS OF GEL FOOD COLORING (OPTIONAL)

STREUSEL TOPPING

YIELD: 4 CUPS / **ACTIVE TIME:** 10 MINUTES / **TOTAL TIME:** 10 MINUTES

1. In the work bowl of a stand mixer fitted with the paddle attachment, beat the flour, sugar, brown sugar, oats, cinnamon, and salt on low until combined.

2. Turn off the mixer and add the butter. Raise the speed to medium and beat the mixture until the mixture is crumbly and the butter has been absorbed by the dry ingredients. Make sure not to overwork the mixture. Use immediately or store in the refrigerator.

INGREDIENTS:

- 1¾ CUPS ALL-PURPOSE FLOUR
- ¾ CUP SUGAR
- ¾ CUP LIGHT BROWN SUGAR
- 1 CUP ROLLED OATS
- 2¼ TEASPOONS CINNAMON
- ¾ TEASPOON KOSHER SALT
- 1 CUP UNSALTED BUTTER, CHILLED AND DIVIDED INTO TABLESPOONS

CORN MUFFIN TOPPING

YIELD: 4 CUPS / **ACTIVE TIME:** 10 MINUTES / **TOTAL TIME:** 10 MINUTES

1. In the work bowl of a stand mixer fitted with the paddle attachment, add the flour, cornmeal, sugar, brown sugar, oats, and salt and beat on low until combined.

2. Turn off the mixer and add the butter. Raise the speed to medium and beat until the mixture is crumbly and the butter is being absorbed by the dry mixture. Take care not to overwork the mixture—you want it to be crumbly, not creamy. Use immediately or store in the refrigerator.

INGREDIENTS:

- 1½ CUPS ALL-PURPOSE FLOUR
- ¾ CUP CORNMEAL
- ¾ CUP SUGAR
- ¾ CUP LIGHT BROWN SUGAR
- 1 CUP ROLLED OATS
- ¾ TEASPOON KOSHER SALT
- 1 CUP UNSALTED BUTTER, CHILLED AND CUBED

HONEY SYRUP

YIELD: ¾ CUP / **ACTIVE TIME:** 10 MINUTES / **TOTAL TIME:** 1 HOUR

1. Place the water and honey in a small saucepan and bring the mixture to a boil, stirring until the honey liquifies.

2. Remove the pan from heat and let the syrup cool completely before using or storing in the refrigerator.

INGREDIENTS:

- ½ CUP WATER
- ½ CUP HONEY

INDUSTRY INSIDERS

As you know from many of the splendid preparations in the preceding chapters, as a home baker it is invaluable to get the chance to sneak a peek into the methods and recipes of professionals. This chapter contains interviews and profiles with many of those folks, as well as a few others who are equally devoted to their part in the creation of quality baked goods, from the wheat farmer to the miller.

JAMES A. BROWN

BARTON SPRINGS MILL

DRIPPING SPRINGS, TEXAS

Barton Springs Mill is the fulfillment of James A. Brown's dream to make quality grains and flours accessible to his community. James has managed in no time to tie up relationships with a rich network of local farmers, inspiring them to grow heirloom grains. Local grains are freshly milled with an authentic stone mill, and then distributed to private companies, as well as chefs and bakers, who are encouraged to use heirloom whole grains in their baking and cooking.

What is your story? How did you end up cultivating and milling grains?

As a former chef and hobbyist baker, I wanted to get into baking bread from locally and regionally grown and milled grains. After doing some research, I discovered there was no place in Texas to get those items, and it occurred to me that milling might be a great fit for me as a second career. I started my research in January 2015, and on January 2, 2016, we turned on our mill for the first time.

What inspired you?

Initially my inspiration was to make a tasty loaf of bread. It seems like an extreme to go to, just to get that! The more I talked to farmers, millers, and experts in heirloom and landrace grains, the more inspired I became. It became very clear to me that I was going to have to get involved in the entire process, from sourcing the seed, to finding farmers with the requisite talent to grow these rare grains, to cleaning, processing, and storing them in a safe way, as well as milling. Glenn Roberts of Anson Mills was a particular inspiration. Every conversation with him was information packed! It often took me a couple of months to unpack everything he would tell me in just a 10-minute conversation.

What made you decide on stone milling? What are the advantages?

I'm interested in using the entire grain, and I feel the best way to do that is through stone milling. This process creates finer bran, and thoroughly expresses the germ oil throughout the endosperm. It makes for a flour that is very easy to use in a one-for-one substitution with modern white flours. We do some sifting in our facility, but I'm always trying to move bakers, chefs, and end users toward using more whole grains. Total utilization in any food system is key, and it seems a shame not to use whole grain. Even when we do sifting, we find a home for all of the other parts that become by-products in our process. Some goes to organic farmers for the feeding of livestock. Other parts go on to be used in making other food items, such as soy sauce, or compost for mushrooms.

What are the challenges of running a stone milling facility?

I think perhaps the easiest part is the milling activity. Some of the most important work starts before the grain ever falls into the mill: expectations set with farmers about planting rates, cover crops, crop rotation, methods of harvest, grain cleaning and storage, and maintaining the strength and purity of these rare seeds. All these things lead to quality of grain that shines through once milled into flour. I would say that three-quarters of the effort goes into these processes before we even begin to mill.

Are your grains organic? Do you believe in organic farming or do you trust conventional farming?

All of our grains are certified organic by the Texas Department of Agriculture. Currently, our facility is not certified organic. I'm a firm believer in organic and sustainable farming practices, although I'm not always a staunch supporter of the policies that are in place to enforce the standards.

What type of grains and wheat do you grow and mill?

For 2017, we grew Marquis, Red Fife, Sonora, Turkey Red, and TAM 105 Hard Red Winter Wheats. We also grew northern European and Danko ryes. As I write this, we are preparing to go in with Rouge de Bordeaux, Yecora Rojo, Warthog Hard Red Winter Wheats, and Wren's Abruzzi rye. We also mill Bloody Butcher Red, Oaxacan Green, and Hopi Blue corn, as well as Mancan buckwheat.

Do you make your own seeds or do you buy them from big companies?

We purchased all of our initial seed stock from small farms and producers, as these varieties are open pollinated. Starting in 2017, we now save our own seeds and work constantly to keep the purity and strength of these varieties. Prior to the planting of our 2017 Bloody Butcher Red corn crop, we held "sorting parties" to sort 350 pounds of corn seed, one seed at a time. Not only did this spread the workload among many, it afforded us the opportunity to share with chefs and consumers what it takes to preserve these rare varieties. It's a great responsibility and one that requires a fair amount of diligence and energy. Even after planting, we will walk the fields near harvesttime and rogue our crops in order to eliminate anything that is not true to variety.

What keeps you motivated?

I'm motivated and inspired by the changes I've seen in our local food scene with the addition of freshly milled heritage and landrace grains. I still make all of my own local deliveries, and I'm in the kitchens of every one of my restaurants, speaking with chefs and bakers. That constant back-and-forth not only fuels my drive, but provides constant feedback about how we can improve what we're doing, and gives me inspiration for what we should be doing in the future, whether it be new varieties of grain or new processes that will expand the utilization of these grains.

What do you do differently from other millers or farmers?

We are utilizing a relatively new technology from the Netherlands that allows for MAPing (modified atmosphere packaging) of our grain totes. This is a process where we seal 1-ton sacks inside a vacuum bag, remove all of the oxygen, and replace it with CO_2. This protects against insect invasion, allowing us to keep all of our grains at room temperature, rather than in cold storage. This radically reduces the cost of storage so we can keep more grain on hand and buy more grain from our farmers without risk of damage. This has allowed us to work at a scale that is sustainable for our farmers, and is helping to keep the price of grain and flour low, thereby making it accessible and affordable to a broader section of the population.

What are the challenges of growing wheat and grains in this changing climate? Will we still have bread on our tables 500 years from now?

Here in Texas, I see our greatest challenge to be precipitation during the time that we need to harvest. It is always been a problem here in central Texas, but it seems to be an increasing challenge now even in more arid parts of the Panhandle. Historically, there were varieties of wheat in the 19th and early 20th century that were bred specifically to mature early and avoid these harvesttime rains. We are trying to reintroduce those varieties, like Quanah and Westar, and gauge their suitability in today's climate. But we're starting with a few ounces, so it will take time. I firmly believe we will have bread on our tables 500 years from now. There are now a few wheat breeders who are working with the right set of priorities who I believe can create safe, suitable, nutritious, and delicious wheat varieties that will thrive in our future climate.

What do you think of household mills? Are you concerned that they could replace commercial mills?

I am a proponent of household mills, and even mills for small restaurants and bakeries—anything that gets more of these grains on people's plates. I'm happy to sell whole berries to anyone who wants them. I don't think that they always make as fine a flour as my mill makes, but that's not always necessary either. I think there will always be a place for both. I especially like small-scale mills for milling amendments to a recipe at the last minute. But I *am* biased about the quality of the flour that comes from our mill. It's pretty hard to replicate our flour on a stone mill that is 2 to 3 inches in diameter, when ours is 48 inches in diameter.

What can people do to support small-scale millers and farmers?

Eat more whole grains. Foster a curiosity about the lesser-known ones. Learn more about the wide diversity in the flavors of ryes, for example. Ask your local bakery or local grocery store where they get their flour. Support farmers at local farmers markets. If you have a local or regional mill that sells retail, buy directly from them. Expect to pay more for these grains, and do it cheerfully. Regard your grains the same way you regard an heirloom tomato, and the world will be a better place for it.

PHILIPPE GUICHARD

PAYSANBIO SEMENCES PAYSANNES

AQUITAINE, FRANCE

Farmer by birth and heritage wheat champ by choice, Philippe is a force for the whole heritage grains movement in France. He has developed his own collection of old landraces of wheat and grows them together, following an evolutionary approach. Such an approach allows the plants to select themselves, rather than being selected by agronomists or a laboratory. Paysanbio Semences Paysannes farm provides high-quality heritage wheat flours to several French bakeries and restaurants.

What is your story? How did you become a wheat farmer and miller?

My father was a farmer, and always cultivated wheat. My maternal grandfather was a farmer and a miller, and my paternal grandmother made bread for the entire family. So the sowing and harvesting of wheat at the family farm was the backdrop to my childhood. After I learned more and more about it, I listened to the call of the earth and decided to become a farmer.

I did not want to take over my father's family farm because at the time he had a negative opinion about organic farming, so I went out on my own a couple of decades ago. I became an organic farmer and began to work with old wheat varieties in 1991–1992. Very few people were interested in organic farming at that time, and even less were interested in heritage seeds or old varieties of wheat.

However, I soon became convinced that these old varieties of wheat were among the tools that I needed to succeed as a farmer. I have been cultivating a mix of about a hundred different heritage varieties of wheat for a long time, and I have been selling the milled flour of my unique heritage wheats mix across France.

Is wheat the only thing you farm?

No, on an organic farm, cultivating exclusively wheat does not make sense and is not sustainable. A coherent organic farm that is in accordance with the main principles of agronomy and ecology must include the cultivation of several species and varieties. For my farm, which does not have animals, I have chosen a variety of legumes, which work well in rotation and add a lot of nitrogen to the soil. This in turn makes the soil more fertile and guarantees a good wheat harvest. Depending on the year and on the condition of the crops, I grow alfalfa, fava beans, protein peas, lentils, chickpeas, and soybeans.

What keeps you motivated?

I am passionate about my work, and constantly have new things to learn, observe, and experiment with. The recognition from my customers, who rave about the products I make and transform, also keeps me motivated.

What do you think you do differently from other farmers?

I think I am much more concerned than some other [farmers or millers] about the final quality of my product. I have always been very demanding with myself as well as those who work with me, so that the product is as close to perfect as possible. This high standard has contributed to the recognition of the quality of my products, both in the world of agriculture and in that of gastronomy and baking.

Do you make your own seeds or do you buy them from another company?

I produce 90% of the seeds I grow. Once in a great while I buy seeds for the green manure I grow, but that's it.

Why are heritage wheat varieties so important?

To me the main reason to grow heritage wheat is the soil! In fact, these varieties of wheat, with their high stems, allow for a replenishment of the soil through their straws, and guarantee that enough nitrogen is present. This ensures that the soil maintains its fertility without the need of organic fertilizers. My second reason is sentimental: they are the seeds that have been cultivated by my ancestors, who were also farmers like me. The third reason is the current demand for these old varieties.

Are your methods 100% organic?

Yes, the farm has been 100% organic for over 25 years.

Do you think organic farming is more sustainable than conventional farming?

Of course! Without any doubt this is obvious. The best indicator of the sustainability of an agricultural system is its dependence on external input. On my farm, with a turnover of about €65,000 per year, the expenses for materials/supplies external to the farm represent less than €10,000 per year, energy expenses for electricity and fuel included.

Do you have much competition? What are the greatest challenges for independent wheat farmers?

Yes, there is competition, but it is not a real competition. As no legislation regulates the production of old varieties of wheat, many millers can claim to produce flours from heritage wheat varieties. Often they even have a farmer who cultivates an old wheat variety for them. They put this one single grain in their mix and then say that they are selling heritage wheat flour. They often deceive bakers and consumers without the knowledge to recognize flour made from older wheat varieties. There are also farmers who might claim to cultivate ancient wheat but deceive their buyers.

Over time, by educating consumers and showing pictures of our cultivated fields and wheat, we can help distinguish the truth from the false. But one has to spend a lot of time explaining everything.

Another challenge to the industry is businesses with lots of money that contract farmers to cultivate old wheat varieties and then resell them at a very high price, profiting from the work of others.

How do you envision the future of wheat farming in the face of climate change? Will we still have bread on our tables 500 years from now?

Yes, as long as there are still wheat and people to cultivate it! Old varieties will always be present because they possess great capabilities to adapt to changes in climate. They are much more adaptable than humans, for sure!

What can people do to support small-scale millers and farmers?

Sharing our work and its importance. We do not necessarily need to sell massive amounts of produce; we just need to sell it regularly. It is my farm (rather than my income) that suffers most because of inconsistent sales. Some months, I sell a lot of flour, to such a point that the mill runs incessantly. Other months, it barely runs. The production rhythms are often not regular enough to allow for the development of long-term projects or investments at the farm.

GIUSEPPE NINIVAGGI

AZIENDA AGRICOLA NINIVAGGI OF FERRANDINA

BASILICATA, ITALY

Giuseppe is the continuator of a family-owned farm located in the beautiful countryside outside Matera (Basilicata, Italy). Matera is world-renowned for its semolina bread, and the whole area is ideal for durum wheat cultivation, like the neighbor Apulia, with its famous Altamura bread (see Pane Pugliese on page 227). Agricola Ninivaggi in Ferrandina farm is driven according to strict organic standards but, above all, is carried forward by the deep bond that Giuseppe Ninivaggi has with his land.

What is your story? How did you become a farmer?

I did not become a farmer so much as I was born into it. I belong to a family of farmers, who have cultivated our beautiful and sometimes harsh land for generations. As a child my father would bring me with him to the farm and it is from these early experiences that I learned to love nature and to cherish the work in the fields. As a farmer in Southern Italy, I became a wheat farmer by default, because this land is ideal for wheat cultivation, which has been grown here since antiquity.

Is wheat the only thing you farm?

I grow several other cereals on my farm, including emmer, barley, oats, as well as legumes like lentils, beans, chickpeas, and more. We also grow strawberries, flax, and fodder. In organic farming it is mandatory to follow a strict routine of crop rotation.

What keeps you motivated?

I come from ten generations of farmers, which is a great motivation. I am also excited by our ongoing projects, which include our plans to construct our very own flour mill as well as an artisan pasta-making facility, so we can sell our products directly to consumers.

What do you think you do differently from other farms, especially large conventional ones?

Conventional farming and what I do are two completely different ways to approach nature and agriculture. What I do is organic farming, which does not involve the use of fertilizers and pesticides and which, above all, is done with great respect of the environment and the soil. If you look at climate change and global warming, well, conventional and intensive agriculture is one of the major contributors to this destructive change. On the contrary, organic farming is associated with the least amount of alteration of the soil and of the seeds. I see organic farming as the only way to give back to the environment, to nature, to the soil, and, above all, to our atmosphere what we have been taking away for decades. Since the so-called Green Revolution, which brought enormous profit to many farmers, our climate has changed rapidly and has reached the level of environmental catastrophe. We are paying for it today with massive environmental pollution and loss of soil fertility. If we continue at this pace, we will continue to lose soil fertility and humus, and will be forced to increase the use of fertilizers and pesticides that pollute the environment.

Do you make your own seeds or do you buy them from a big company?

This is a very important aspect of our work. Every year we select seeds and land plots devoted to grow the seeds for the next season. Unfortu-

nately, or fortunately, big seed companies focus on patents and intensive farming, and their aims are completely incompatible with my agricultural philosophy.

Why are heritage wheat varieties so important?

For a long time, I have exclusively grown ancient varieties of wheat. The benefits to me are innumerable, both for our health and that of the soil, as well as for preserving biodiversity. With regards to our health, it took thousands of years for the human digestive system to adapt to the assimilation and digestion of wheat. Changing the type of wheat we consume so abruptly is the reason why, in recent years, the number of people with sensitivity to gluten and celiac disease has skyrocketed. Ancient grains have a much weaker type of gluten that is easier to digest. The big wheat farming companies, driven by the food industry, have selected super-high-protein wheat with super-strong gluten. It is extremely difficult to digest, hence gluten sensitivity and celiac disease.

As far as soil is concerned, organic farming does not make absolutely any use of herbicides, and here the ancient grains have another great value. The plants are very tall, so they naturally suffocate weeds, unlike genetically engineered dwarf wheat.

What are the greatest challenges you have faced so far as an organic wheat farmer?

I was born at the height of the Green Revolution, so I had to completely change my approach to the land. I had to study why our soil's humus was becoming more and more poor. Over the years I had to revolutionize my way of farming. It is still a challenge today, but it is the challenge I want to keep taking up in order to leave a better world for future generations.

What are the worst "enemies" to quality wheat farmers?

International agreements and laws can have a negative impact on good farming practices.

How do you envision the future of wheat farming in the face of climate change? Will we still have bread on our tables 500 years from now?

Cereals have been grown for more than 10,000 years and I cannot see why there shouldn't be wheat farmers in 500 years. Maybe climate change will change the areas that are best suited to wheat farming, but I think the cultivation of wheat will continue.

What can people do to support small-scale farmers?

We have to remember that "la salute vien mangiando"; health comes with eating. The most powerful medicine is nourishing ourselves with the highest-quality products. These are often not produced by big food companies, because of practical reasons, since their primary focus is profit. To get the best-quality food, it is necessary to buy directly from organic farmers. Learn their stories and get an idea of how that food was produced. I know it can be challenging but if one really wants to, it is possible.

IAN TILLINGHAST

GRAIN CRAFT

CHATTANOOGA, TENNESSEE

It should come as no surprise that a major independent miller like Grain Craft is so efficient, but it's still incredible to learn about how its mills (15 facilities in total from coast to coast) operate. According to Milling Superintendent Ian Tillinghast, "Our mill in Rosedale, Kansas, is what we call a swing mill—we can mill soft wheat or we can 'swing' the mill in order to mill hard wheat. Both present their challenges because we do not shut the process down to change the variety of wheat. We have a very good crew that can operate the mill and handle most problems that might occur."

It's amazing, but it makes more sense if you learn more about Tillinghast's bona fides. "I got my formal education in milling from Kansas State University with a bachelor of science in milling science and management. I have worked full-time in three flour mills with over 10 years of experience. I learned how to become a miller on top of my education by working in the mill and learning something new every day. Numerous people have helped me along the way, whether supervisors or subordinates. They have all helped!"

That experience has led to a simple but effective company philosophy: "Learn from your mistakes." Says Tillinghast, "Milling is all about experience. Most experienced millers have made mistakes and they learn from those mistakes, which is why they are experienced." Milling flour requires patience, which is why the Rosedale mill's deliberate approach is so reliably successful.

Who—or what—first inspired you to begin milling? Who inspires you now?

My family has always played a big influence in any success that I have had. My parents always pushed me in school and work at a young age. They instilled that when you work hard and you try, you will have success. My family still inspires me to keep doing what I love to do.

What does Grain Craft represent to you?

Grain Craft is a very close-knit company that values their employees. They trust us to do our jobs. They appreciate and trust their employees, which allows employees to be successful within the company.

What is your favorite type of grain? Why? Least favorite grain? Why?

I enjoy milling hard red winter or hard red spring wheat. It presents challenges with all the different varieties that can be grown. We can utilize most of our equipment by making fine adjustments that allow us to get the most amount of flour out of a kernel of wheat. I'm a wheat miller and don't normally get to mill any other types of grains, so I'd say low-quality wheat is my least favorite grain. It presents a whole new set of challenges that are not always easy to deal with.

How did Grain Craft come to be? Why Rosedale? What are your most popular items?

Grain Craft is the product of the merging of Milner Milling, Pendleton Flour Mills, and Cereal Food Processors in 2014.The Rosedale mill originally belonged to Cereal Food Processors. We make a variety of flours but the most popular one here at the Rosedale mill is Sunny Kansas Pastry, which is used in crackers.

Where do you get your tools/materials? What nonessential items should every home baker have?

We have a wide range of milling equipment that is used in our process. Most comes from milling equipment companies. Our material, which is soft wheat or hard wheat, comes from grain elevators around the Kansas City Metro area. My wife, who loves to bake, says a cookie scoop is a nonessential item a home baker should have.

What outlets/periodicals/newspapers do you read or consult regularly, if any?

I normally read *Milling and Baking News* and *Milling Journal.*

Brag about yourself a bit. What have been your proudest moments as a miller?

I don't have any outstanding achievements as an individual, but I have worked with some great people in my career, and have helped the mills that I worked at make a great finished product while doing it in a safe manner.

JOE LINDLEY

LINDLEY MILLS

GRAHAM, NORTH CAROLINA

One would be hard-pressed to find a mill more historic than Lindley Mills, which has been around since 1755. The scene of the Revolutionary War's bloodiest battle in North Carolina—the Battle of Lindley's Mill—the mill has withstood the test of time to produce high-quality flour for centuries. Says President Joe Lindley, "Thomas Lindley, my six-times great-grandfather, built Lindley's Mill and passed it on to his children and grandchildren. While it hasn't always been in the family, the family milling heritage helped spark my interest. Today, I am inspired to make the best possible products for our customers and to continue to push the boundaries of flour milling to achieve the most flavorful and nutritious flours."

Today, Lindley Mills functions as a jack-of-all-trades, popular for everything from its Super Sprout™ Sprouted Whole Grain Wheat Flour to several specialty products like organic rye, spelt, whole wheat, and white flours and organic yellow cornmeal and grits. The mill is flexible, and that flexibility allows Joe Lindley to custom-mill whatever his client needs. The result is a North Carolina mill that has earned—and maintained—respect over the course of three centuries.

How and when did you get your start in this industry?

My family purchased Lindley's Mill in 1975 after I graduated from college, and we worked together to begin restoration. As we looked into the area's rich milling history, I learned a lot about water-powered flour mills. We refurbished the structure, built and installed the water wheel, moved and connected grinding stones, and began milling flour. I was hooked immediately. There is nothing quite like making flour. It's satisfying and challenging, taking skill, focus, science, and craftsmanship. Most flour today is milled by large, industrial flour mills which produce high volumes of three or four flours. Instead we custom-mill a wide variety of products using different types of grain.

What is your golden rule for milling?

One axiom the old-time millers shared when I was starting out was, "You can't make good flour out of bad wheat, but you can make bad flour from good wheat." So in order to provide the best possible flour, you have to start with good wheat and treat the wheat, through the milling process, with care and respect. If you succeed, your reward will be the opportunity to mill more flour. Another rule we mill by is similar to the actual golden rule: "Make flour for others that you'd like to eat yourself." Not only do we frequently taste test our own products, but we buy most of our bread from local bakers and eat at local restaurants which use our flours. This is why we have always chosen to mill certified organic flours and why we have consistently pursued the most stringent

Global Food Safety certifications. High quality and consistency is our standard, and we want our customers to have the best.

What does Lindley Mills represent to you?

Lindley Mills represents a lifetime of work and accomplishment for both me and my wife, Teresa, who has been my partner in the mill. I couldn't have made it without all of her hard work, and we are excited to be teaching the ropes to our daughter Caroline, who has just joined us full-time. The mill is a great teacher, and we have enjoyed watching it grow. It has been a challenge and an opportunity to provide food for hundreds of millions of people over the years, as well as innovate in a category with such a wide reach.

What is your favorite type of grain? Why? Least favorite grain? Why?

We mill a large variety of grains, but wheat is by far the most prevalent and provides one-fifth of the world's food calories. Its unique possession of gluten allows it to expand and be a vehicle for other nutritious inclusions, such as other grains, fruits, and nuts. Wheat has significantly contributed to the development of human society as it has always provided a renewable and reliable source of food.

How did Lindley Mills come to be? Why Graham, NC? What are your most popular items?

My ancestor Thomas Lindley established Lindley Mills in 1755. He moved here from Pennsylvania in the 1750s and built his Mill on the Cane Creek. The location was likely chosen because of the unique shape of Cane Creek and the available water to provide power to the mill. It was also located at the intersection of the Western Trading Route and the Cape Fear Road to Wilmington, which were the major thoroughfares of the day.

Our Mill has had several brushes with Revolutionary War history, including at least one instance when flour was "requisitioned" from the Mill to feed the troops of British General Lord Cornwallis when they were camped in the area.

In the foggy dawn of September 12, 1781, the Loyalist forces captured the Governor of North Carolina, Thomas Burke, in Hillsborough and were marching him to Wilmington. The next morning, on September 13, Patriot forces laid an ambush on the ridge just yards from the Mill during a conflict that would later be called the Battle of Lindley's Mill. It was the bloodiest per-capita battle of the Revolutionary War in North Carolina. Ultimately, the Patriot forces were not able to rescue the Governor and other prisoners who were being held in the Spring Friends Meeting House farther up the road, but they did wound Colonel Fanning and slow the Loyalist forces down. Interestingly, the founder of the Mill, Thomas Lindley, died on the day of the battle, although it's unlikely that he was involved in the conflict.

Today we continue to honor the traditions of our ancestors by making the highest-quality certified organic flours we can and providing them to both large bakeries and our local neighbors. Some of our most popular items include our Super Sprout™ Sprouted Whole Grain Wheat Flour and several of our specialty products like organic rye, spelt, whole wheat, and white flours, as well as stone-ground organic yellow cornmeal and grits.

Where do you get your tools/materials? What non-essential items should every home baker have?

We sample and test wheat from all across the United States in our state-of-the-art in-house lab. Then we buy the highest-quality certified organic wheat to make our flours. We also make an effort to purchase certified organic North Carolina wheat from our neighbors whenever possible.

If you have an oven, water, salt, Lindley Mills flour, and yeast, you can make an excellent loaf of bread without fancy tools or gadgets.

What outlets/periodicals/newspapers do you read or consult regularly, if any?

I enjoy skimming *Milling & Baking News*, *QA Magazine*, *Food Business News,* and *The Wall Street Journal* to see what's happening.

Brag about yourselves a bit. What is your highest achievement and/or proudest moment as a miller?

I'd have to say my highest achievement as a miller is the creation of Super Sprout™ Sprouted Whole Grain Wheat Flour. I always wanted to create a whole wheat flour that tasted better so that more people would be interested in eating whole grains. The sprouting of the wheat unlocks the live potential of the wheat seed, enhancing the digestibility, nutritional availability, and flavor. One day, I believe that all whole wheat, whole grain flour will be made this way since it's so much more nutritious and flavorful. Being able to develop something that encourages more people to eat whole grains is quite satisfying and has been a lifetime achievement.

Where did you learn to become a miller? Please tell me about your education.

My college degree was in science, but not milling science. My milling education was trial and error and fueled by my desire to meet bakers' directives. I tailored the entire process to make the specialty products requested by our customers in the historic space we had available. I have gradually made changes to update our equipment over time and keep up with changing tastes. Today we are certainly not a traditional industrial mill, but we use both modern equipment and old-world traditions to grind the best flour.

Tell me about your milling process. What makes your mill special?

Our mill is set up to do a variety of products and to custom-mill many different grains. This allows us to stay flexible and switch between different products to custom-mill our orders fresh for the customer. Furthermore, to be grinding grain into flour in the same space that our many times great-grandfathers did more than 260 years ago is really special. Knowing the Revolutionary Era history just adds another layer.

AMBER LAMBKE

MAINE GRAINS

SKOWHEGAN, MAINE

Not every local grain movement can be traced to a specific event—but then again, Skowhegan's wasn't exactly a normal grain renaissance. "Having lost jobs in the paper, shoemaking, agricultural, and woolen industries, Skowhegan was focused on its assets. Then grassroots organizers cofounded The Kneading Conference, a gathering of bakers, grain growers, millers, and wood-fired oven builders who planned to rebuild a lost grain economy. We took local expertise and convened with people from around the world to form a conference that would focus on 'local bread.' So says Amber Lambke of Maine Grains and the Maine Grain Alliance. Situated in the Somerset Grist Mill, a repurposed historic jailhouse, Maine Grains is helping to restore downtown Skowhegan's vibrant economic center.

Since the first Kneading Conference in 2007, the movement has grown significantly. Today, places like Maine Grains seek to both inspire and learn from independent mills all across the world. As Lambke puts it, "Our mill has created opportunity and hope, for farmers, bakers, brewers, and our employees. The mill connects people around a basic thing—grain, a staple food that sustains us. Maine Grains restores a sense of self-reliance and instills shared purpose in our foodshed."

It's a testament to Lambke's passion that "a small scrappy mill town in central Maine has taken center stage in the revival of regional grain farming, village bakeries, and real bread." How do they do it? Easy: "Focusing on the grains!" The mill at Maine Grains turns slowly, keeping the flour cool and preserving its inherent flavor. Moreover, it preserves many of the nutrients found in the grains prior to the milling process. Their high-quality products have made for some very happy—and very successful—bakers.

2
3
4
7
5
8

Who—or what—first inspired you to begin milling and baking? Who inspires you now?

At that first Kneading Conference in 2007, I was inspired to learn that in 1837, our county produced 239,000 bushels of wheat—enough to feed 100,000 people in a county that only has half that number now. This helped me see that it was not a question of if we could grow wheat in Maine, but how we would regain that capacity. I traveled around the Northeast, visited Kansas State University, and later went to Denmark. The millers I met there inspired me to focus on organic grain production and stone milling as a pathway to restoring good bread in my community.

What are your golden rules for milling? What about for baking?

Start with high-quality grain, mill slowly, keep the stones cool, and the flour will feel alive. As a home baker using our freshly milled grains, I approach baking as though there is no such thing as mistakes! Experimentation leads to discovery. The future of bread lies in age-old techniques that we are only just beginning to relearn.

What is your favorite thing to bake? Why? Least favorite thing to bake? Why?

I love to make piecrust with our stone-milled flour. It is the perfect vehicle to deliver the fresh fruit of the season, as well as our local eggs and garden vegetables. That said, I also love making biscuits, which are an important part of our local heritage; our gristmill is housed in an old jail building that was once home to Alley Perry, a famed inmate baker who made biscuits for the community.

What is your favorite type of grain? Why? Least favorite grain? Why?

I love heritage red fife wheat. It makes the most aromatic flour and flavorful, sweet loaves. My least favorite grain is quinoa, because it has an awkward texture and a peculiar cult status.

How did Maine Grains come to be? Why Skowhegan, ME? What are your most popular items?

Before this, I was a community organizer and speech pathologist. Maine Grains came to be when I partnered with friend and baker Michael Scholz to restore the infrastructure for processing organic locally grown grain in Maine. We launched the mill in 2012, and our most popular products are now the stone-ground whole wheat and sifted flours, and rolled oats.

Where do you get your tools/materials? What non-essential items should every home baker have?

I like to shop antique stores for old baking tools. Every home baker should have a cast-iron griddle for making English muffins, baskets for proofing loaves, and a Dutch oven or cloche for baking loaves with a shiny crisp crust.

What book goes on your required reading list for bakers?

Being a home baker, I particularly enjoy the very approachable message in Andy and Jackie King's *Baking by Hand*.

What outlets/periodicals/newspapers do you read or consult regularly?

I read *BREAD Magazine*, the *New York Times* Food Section, the *FeedFeed*, and the Bread Bakers Guild of America newsletter.

Tell me about your most memorable collaboration with another chef.

I am always inspired to watch Amy Halloran, "Flour Ambassador" and author of *The New Bread Basket*, teach workshops on baking and making pancakes. Amy boils baking down to a simple and intuitive process that can be easily accessed by all. She follows grain from the field to the griddle and uses pancakes as a means to teach about history and agriculture.

Do you follow any cooking shows or chefs? If so, which is your favorite?

I have lived without a television for the last 20 years and so have missed some of the pop culture around cooking shows and chef personalities. That said, I do enjoy the TED Talks and writings of Dan Barber, Michael Pollan, Mark Bittman, Alice Waters, and others who understand food in the context of agriculture.

Where did you learn to bake? Please tell me about your education and apprenticeships.

From my mom! I am not formally trained at all. I benefitted from baking in the home growing up, and now from the world-class talent that convenes here in my hometown each July for The Kneading Conference, two full days of baking, oven building, and grain workshops.

JIM WILLIAMS

SEVEN STARS BAKERY

PROVIDENCE, RHODE ISLAND

When Lynn and Jim Williams met in California in the late '90s, baking was already an established part of their lives. Lynn longed to return to the Northeast and open her own bakery; Jim had already worked in the now-closed Bread Garden of Berkeley, and remained an avid follower of baking and fermentation processes. Eventually, they found a space they liked on Hope Street in Providence—and their customers are glad they did.

Their enterprise grew quickly. It wasn't long before two new locations had opened, and after a visit to Dave Miller's Bakery, Miller's Bake House, Jim and Lynn purchased their first flour mill. For Jim, it was a long road from making Sunday morning waffles as a child. "I have no formal cooking or baking education, but I worked in lots of bakeries learning the craft. Baking is all about repetition. You have to put in the time and do the work."

Known for its flavorful breads and friendly service, Seven Stars does not skip steps. Their fermentation process is rigid, but worthwhile; the bakery uses four different pre-ferments, and each loaf they bake requires at least one of them. These recipes are time-tested and made entirely in-house—and it shows in the bread.

The bread alone is enough to justify Seven Stars' popularity, but the bakery is active in the community as well. Aside from participating in local charity raffles and auctions year-round, they donate 100% of their profits to a local charity every year on their anniversary, January 2. And their commitment to locally sourced grains helps area farmers as well: "When we first started buying Northeast-sourced flour, it was rough at best, but it's getting better and better. We are part of this revolution that is happening, and it's really great to be part of it. In the end, we need good-performing, great-tasting wheat, and the Northeast source has those two all-important elements in addition to supporting our emerging grain economy."

Seven Stars has entrenched itself firmly in the Providence community. And though its bread is so tasty that patrons would visit regardless, one can't help but smile at the way this local business has spread its roots.

Who inspired you to bake? Who inspires you now?

Jim: I had always been interested in cooking and baking growing up. I had a tremendous interest in bread and brewing beer. In 1993, two very inspirational books, *Bread Alone* by Daniel Leader and *The Village Baker* by Joe Ortiz, were published on European-style, long-fermented breads. I dove in headfirst, and realized that this is what I wanted to do with my life.

Lynn: I'm inspired by bakers that have been around for a while, and continue to push the limits with whole grain breads. Dave Miller and Mike Zakowski, both based in Northern California, come to mind.

What is your golden rule(s) for baking?

Time and temperature are everything. Control those two variables, and you control the final product.

What does Seven Stars Bakery represent to you?

We take pride in offering an outstanding product, while giving our employees an excellent place of employment, all the while providing excellent customer service. The three add up to what makes Seven Stars the special place that it is.

What is your favorite thing to bake? Why? Least favorite thing to bake?

My favorite thing would be freshly milled, long-fermented whole grain breads from one single variety of wheat. Wheat is no different than grapes, hops, or even cows! There are thousands of different varieties of wheat to explore—all with different flavors and fermentation profiles. I have a lot of respect for the sweet bakers of the world, but I'm not one of them!

Where do you get your tools/materials? What nonessential items should every baker have?

Large equipment, like ovens and mixers, come from equipment companies. Any smaller items, like scrapers, scoops, and buckets, can be found at any restaurant supply store.

The important nonessential item—though I would argue it *is* essential—would be a good plastic scraper! I like them made of hard, rigid plastic. Curved for some bowls and straight sided for others. Flexible scrapers just don't work as well.

What book(s) go on your required reading list for bakers?

For the home and professional baker, *Bread* by Jeffrey Hamelman. *Advanced Bread and Pastry* by Michel Suas, for the professional baker.

What outlets/periodicals/newspapers do you read or consult regularly, if any?

Instagram has a very good bread community. Also, the Bread Bakers Guild of America is an excellent organization for both home and professional bakers. They offer events throughout the year, and a quarterly newsletter that is worth the membership alone.

Tell me about your most memorable collaboration with another chef.

It's not exactly a collaboration, but my first visit to Dave Miller's bakery, Miller's Bake House, changed the way I think about bread, grains, and milling. That visit led to a new mentor, friendship, and direction, both for myself as a baker and for Seven Stars Bakery. Shortly after that visit, we purchased our first flour mill to start milling the Northeast-sourced local grains we had previously been purchasing as flour. It led to Seven Stars becoming one of the leaders

in the country in sourcing regional grains, and milling them into whole grain flour. Very soon, we will take the next step with a new farmer. We'll be able to stand in a field of wheat, and say, "All of what I see is ours."

Do you follow any cooking shows or chefs? If so, which is your favorite?

Lately, our family has been watching *The Great British Bake Off.* Quite entertaining, especially when they make bread!

Brag about yourself a bit. What are your highest achievements and/or proudest moments as a chef?

Bakers tend to be quiet types with not much to say about themselves. I'm proud of the work we do daily at Seven Stars and the work I've done with single-variety wheats. I believe that Seven Stars is a great place to work. I wish I worked in a place like ours when I was starting out!

You mill in-house. What inspired you to make that choice, and how has it benefitted the bakery?

After that first visit to Dave's, I just knew milling was the next logical step. We jumped right in headfirst, and I couldn't see us going back to dead flour in a bag. Fresh-milled flour has an aroma that you want to do everything you can to capture. We do our best to do that in our breads every day. One of the nicest side effects to milling in-house is the interest generated by our staff. Of course, some people couldn't care less, but there are those that might have thought I was crazy at first. Not anymore. I can guarantee that there are a handful of bakers on our team that wouldn't think twice about adding a mill to their own bakery if they were to ever venture out on their own. Once you do it, it becomes what you do. There are no other options.

AMY SCHERBER

AMY'S BREAD

NEW YORK, NEW YORK

It's hard to open a small business in New York City. It's even harder when that business is a bakery. Long hours, high rent, stiff competition—the life of a New York baker requires constant diligence. But Amy's Bread has persisted, even thrived, for over 25 years. And after a slice of owner Amy Scherber's rye bread, it isn't hard to see why: Amy's is as safe a bet as there is in the city for a beautiful slice or loaf. Her secret? Passion and resolve.

"[In 1992] I wanted to have a small, local bread bakery that served retail customers and wholesale customers such as local restaurants. I found a small space on Ninth Avenue in Hell's Kitchen, got loans from friends and family to start, and opened the business on a low budget without a business partner," Scherber explains. Not the easiest beginning, to say the least. But quality won out in the end. "We have seen so many ups and downs with the economy, snowstorms, power outages, hurricanes, low-carb trends, and gluten-free diets, but we have found our place within our city to survive through all of it."

In this way, Amy's is a distinctly New York bakery—there for the local who is rushing to work, or the tourist who has a few hours to kill before their next event. And as it's spread its roots across the city, its name has become synonymous with chewy, crunchy bread you can always count on. "Local bakeries in New York provide a friendly place for people to get a treat and take a moment to relax during the crazy, busy days we have. Walking down the street, riding the subway, dealing with the noise and the bustle, all become tiring after a while, but going to a bakery for an excellent coffee and delicious treat provides that respite from the stresses of daily life."

And while every bakery must be reliable, in New York, it's a zero-sum game. There is perhaps no greater compliment, then, than to simply say that Amy's has existed for 25 years for a reason. Whether looking for a sandwich, pastry, or fresh loaf for your next dinner party, you can always count on Amy's to deliver.

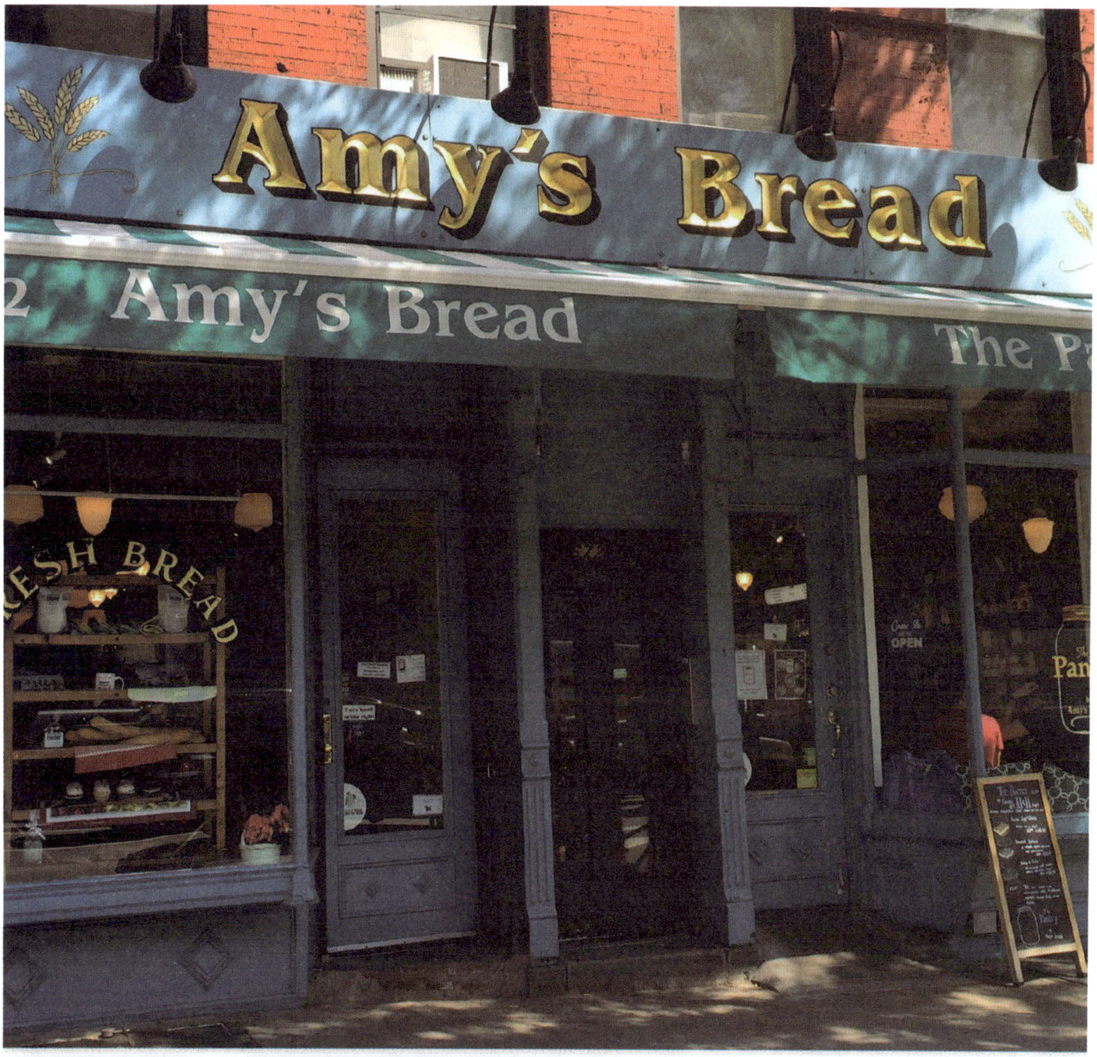

Amy's Bread
your
neighborhood baker
for 20 years

How and when did you get your start baking?

I found my passion for baking when I was in culinary school. On weekends I helped one of my chef instructors with freelance catering, and when it came to making pies and desserts for his events, I fell in love. I tried to get an externship in pastry at Bouley (in NYC) right after culinary school, but I landed on the savory side of the line. It took nearly two years to make my way back to the pastry kitchen, and I have been baking ever since.

Who inspired you to bake? Who inspires you now?

Both of my grandmothers and my mom were good bakers, and my dad worked for Pillsbury for 35 years. Pillsbury Bake-Off recipes and new products were always the topic of conversation at our house! After working in pastry at Bouley, I realized that I wanted to be a bread baker. The most inspiring bread lessons I ever had were at the boulangerie school in Aurillac, France. The classes were taught by MOFs and geared to professional bakers from the Bread Bakers Guild of America. The instructors were incredible, so skilled in all aspects of bread making. It was a joy to watch them shape loaves and work with bread dough. And their bread smelled and tasted delicious. Today I get inspired by visiting bakeries in my travels in the United States and Europe. There is always something new to try.

Amy's is a proper New York bakery. How have you tried to maintain your relationship with the local neighborhoods?

For us, being a local neighborhood bakery has always been a top priority. I have lived near my bakery in Hell's Kitchen since we opened in 1992, and I know our café is a comfortable place for many people from the neighborhood to meet with friends or work associates. In all our locations we try to take special care of our local "regulars," we make donations to our neighborhood schools and local organizations, and we take pride in being members of our communities. We also think of the Broadway community as our neighbors and are lucky to bake cakes for many casts of Broadway shows! In Chelsea Market all the businesses are a community under one roof, and that is also a unique kind of neighborhood in a busy part of the city.

What is your golden rule(s) of baking?

Make the best bread you can by taking care of the details, never cutting corners on ingredients or time. It takes time to make excellent bread and good bread cannot be rushed.

What does Amy's represent to you?

Amy's Bread is a local business that takes care of its customers and its employees, while making the best breads, pastries, and savory foods we can make. For 25 years we have cared about people and products, and that commitment to caring is what it's all about for me.

What is your favorite thing to bake? Why? Least favorite thing to bake? Why?

I love to bake crusty, grainy, free-form whole wheat loaves. The aroma and taste are so satisfying, and getting the fermentation right is a good challenge. My least favorite thing to bake is soft white bread. It reminds me of industrial bakeries that make bread without any health benefits, and what's the point of eating it?

How hard was it to get Amy's off the ground?

I started Amy's Bread in June 1992. It took hard work and time to get it off the ground, but today my husband, Troy Rohne, runs the bakery with me. He is the VP and Director of Sales. It's great to work together to make it a success. We still have many employees that have been with us anywhere from 15 to 25 years, and our long-term staff helps to keep our products consistent. They also take pride in being a part of the company for such a long time.

What are your most popular items?

Some of our most popular products are crusty white breads such as French Baguettes and

Organic Rustic Italian loaves, Chocolate Sourdough bread twists, Semolina Raisin and Fennel Bread, Oat Scones and Cherry Cream Scones, Black and White Cake, and Pecan Sticky Buns.

Where do you get your tools/materials? What non-essential items should every baker have?

We buy our ingredients from local vendors and some of our flour is grown and milled in upstate NY. We buy our tools on restaurant equipment websites and Amazon. All bakers need a good scale to measure ingredients in grams. I think a nice sturdy lame handle that can be used with a double-edged razor blade is the best way to score bread. And one must always have a good serrated knife to cut the bread after all the work is done!

What book(s) go on your required reading list for bakers?

A book I really like is *Bread: A Baker's Book of Techniques and Recipes* by Jeffrey Hamelman. You can pick it up and use any recipe without worrying about whether it will work. All the recipes and techniques are well tested and work great. For an entry-level baker I recommend *One Dough, Ten Breads: Making Great Bread by Hand* by Sarah Black. It's a step-by-step guide to making all kinds of bread, building on one technique after another. It's a great way to learn! And of course *Amy's Bread* is an excellent resource for any bread baker. It demystifies how to use starters to make your bread, and it is clear and easy to use.

What outlets/periodicals/newspapers do you read or consult regularly, if any?

King Arthur Flour has a cool magazine called *Sift* that comes out two times per year. I love the recipes and photos. I look at *Bon Appetit, Food & Wine, Martha Stewart Living* and *Edible Manhattan* to see what they are writing about, and I like *Bake* magazine, which is a professional trade magazine. I always enjoy reading the Wednesday food section of *The New York Times*. *Eater* is another good source for news about the food world.

Tell me about your most memorable collaboration(s) with another chef.

Several years ago, I worked together with Chef Ed Brown who, at that time, was the chef at Sea Grill at Rockefeller Center. He always wanted new and different breads for his bread service and over the course of a couple of years, he suggested several new breads that he would like to try. He would give me a general request such as "green olive bread" and I would work on it until I had samples for him, then he would make further suggestions until it was just right. Through that process we came up with four really good breads that have been part of our repertoire for years.

Brag about yourself a bit. What are your highest achievements and/or proudest moments as a chef?

Starting a business in NYC and staying in business for more than 25 years is something I am very proud of! The people that have worked with me over the years have all contributed to our success, and the collective energy and satisfaction from working together are also very gratifying.

Where did you learn to bake?

I spent a few months in France working in three bakeries. After watching the bakers there, I came back to New York and taught myself to bake using the bread books I had. I tested my breads on customers while I worked at Mondrian restaurant. I made all the bread and worked pastry service at night. Then I started Amy's Bread and learned even more on the fly. I continue to take courses taught by amazing bakers who are part of the Bread Bakers Guild of America. In my opinion, that is the best place to learn how to bake bread.

JESSE MERRILL

POLESTAR HEARTH

GULEPH, ONTARIO

Like many bakers, Polestar Hearth's Jesse Merrill didn't find his calling until later in life. "My education and background were in stringed instrument construction and repair, and I had a wonderful career in one of North America's premier vintage guitar shops. Eventually, I had a revelation that what I really wanted to do with my hands was work that maintained that same caliber of craftsmanship, but served my community directly, producing something so vital that it would affect the lives of folks of all demographics." At the time, Merrill had a home and family of his own, including a small brick oven he'd built himself in the backyard. So, he took a risk. He quit his job. "Soon after that teensy beginning, we bought a house with a small garage, which I was able to convert into a prep kitchen. I built a big brick oven in the backyard, and Polestar Hearth was born in earnest."

Things have changed significantly since then. While the team is still small, the output has increased exponentially. In addition to keeping his own retail hours, Merrill delivers bread to local retailers all week long. This process has helped Polestar gain some notoriety, widening its clientele to include people from all over the world. Merrill recounts a particular example in discussing his proudest moment: "Early on, an elderly European gentleman, dressed in a fine tweed suit, stopped me on delivery to tell me his story. With a hand holding my arm firmly, his eyes moist, he wanted me to know that he had spent 17 years in Canada, homesick the whole time until his wife had brought home a loaf of my bread the week before. 'Now it is OK; I can live here happily the rest of my life, thanks to you!' What more resounding accolade could I get?"

Though it is not a Polish bakery ("Polestar" refers to the North Star, not Polish culture, as often assumed), the bakery has made an impression on much of Ontario's European community—a testament to its authenticity and attention to detail. Another key factor in Polestar Hearth's popularity? The BreadShare. "This was a concept I dreamed up early on, based of course on Community Supported Agriculture. The first stumbling block in my professional baking career was learning that the local farmers market didn't have room for me. So, I called up all my friends and asked them to buy a dozen loaves of bread before I made them. I was practically giving the stuff away, trying to buy myself a business. Before I knew it, I had 13 customers, and I had to figure out how to make 13 loaves! Word got out, and in its prime the Polestar BreadShare had hundreds of subscribers. It went through different phases as we grew. First delivered door-to-door by kids with wagons—eventually we had to switch it around and have the customers come to us." The idea reinforced what Merrill had set out to do in the first place: use his hands to better the community.

Despite its changing sales policies, the constant at Polestar is its bread. Crunchy and golden brown, it is always meticulously crafted with starters that have fermented for multiple days. The result is a bread bakery that withstands any critical eye—from a first-timer to someone whose baking legacy dates back to the Old Country.

Who inspired you to bake? Who inspires you now?

That was the early days of the internet, before there were rock star bakers in North America. I pored over every word in Daniel Wing's *The Bread Builders*, eked out any little shred of information hidden between the lines of his chapter on Chad Robertson long before *Tartine Bread* was ever published. Left no stone unturned! These days some of my best inspiration comes from my bread brother Don Guerra of Barrio Bread, a giant among men, to be sure! And I have so many dear friends pushing me forward with new artistic ideas daily via social media. I'd love to name them all, but it would be hard to do. We are living in the golden age of bread, for sure!

What is your golden rule for bakers?

I'm in this to learn something from the bread, from the dough or the flour, every day. Don't ever plateau; don't get complacent. The bread can challenge you to greatness if you listen to what it has to teach you every day.

What does Polestar Hearth represent to you?

Polestar Hearth is always evolving. It's grown and changed for ten years in many unforeseen ways. What is important to me is that it is the answer to the biggest part of my creative energies—the part of me that would otherwise be drawing or sculpting or making music.

What is your favorite thing to bake? Why?

Bread! Long-fermentation sourdough bread, to be specific. I get a real kick out of using heritage grains, especially when they have a cool backstory. We get a lot of our flour from an Amish mill, and I just love knowing that that grain was grown in clean fields using only horsepower and the sweat of hardworking folks who hold some of the last living knowledge of how our civilization was born.

What is your most popular item?

Our spelt bread is a total revelation to many folks. It's completely unlike the dry, sawdust-y, pallid loaves well-intentioned folks have been choking down since the antigluten war began. Our biggest seller is a light wheat bread packed with toasted seeds that we call SuperSeed.

What nonessential items should every baker have?

A French rolling pin, slightly fatter in the middle. This is one of the secrets to making our beautiful Couronne loaves (check 'em out on Instagram). And a simple homemade lame for scoring. Mine is whittled from a disposable chopstick from a Thai restaurant. Change your blades often. If you care about beautiful scoring (and I really do), don't be afraid to throw out the razor blade whenever you start to feel the slightest resistance to your cut. It should be like painting with an artist's brush, not hacking at a tomato with a crummy kitchen knife!

Where did you learn to bake?

Right in my own backyard!

Can you talk a bit about the local grains you use? Where do you primarily get your ingredients, and why is it so important you keep things local?

We live in the heart of Ontario, in a city surrounded by farmland, some of which has grown grain for more than 200 years. Waves of immigrants came to this area starting in the late 1700s, looking for freedom and a self-sustaining livelihood. So, in one very direct way, we owe it to our ancestors to carry this self-reliance forward. To be quite honest, I don't get too hung up in historical varieties and the hype that surrounds them. We use a bit of Red Fife, but we use other wheats too, leaving varietal choices up to our Amish friends who horse farm and stone mill a good portion of the wheat and spelt we use. It's an incredibly grounding feeling to stand in a field of spelt taller than a man, and look out between the weaving stalks to watch the harnessed horses work the land, especially if you know you can take that same grain home and make a truly exceptional bread from it.

It isn't easy using local grains—some fields just don't produce well; some years are bad across the board. Yes, we do use a lot of organic wheat imported from the Canadian Prairies. It helps us keep things consistent. But to feed our belief in local economy, small farms, small business, and truly great food, we use many tonnes of local flour milled for us by three local millers. We use a custom cracked rye and purple and yellow corn, and we use hard and soft wheat flours, kamut flour, spelt flours, and malted barley and rye from our local mills. And all those grains are grown right around here, within an hour-and-a-half drive of the bakery.

AMY & ZACHARY TYSON AND BRE JAWOROSKI

BOULANGERIE, A PROPER BAKERY

KENNEBUNK, MAINE

One could be forgiven for not guessing that one of the world's tastiest croissants can be found in Kennebunk, Maine. One could even be forgiven for treating this news with a fair dose of skepticism—after all, shouldn't the finest French pastries be in France? With respect to the many wonderful patisseries across the pond, the croissant at Boulangerie, a Proper Bakery can stand up to the best of them. And the credit goes to owners Amy and Zachary Tyson, and head baker Bre Jaworowski.

The Tysons have operated Boulangerie for over ten years—ever since they purchased the big red barn they currently operate from. Amy says, "Zachary and I worked on private motor yachts. We came to Maine for work, fell in love with Kennebunk, and purchased a home. We continued to work on yachts for a number of years, but we were always looking for our next step—off boats. There was a 'bakery café' in town; when it closed, it made me realize that I really wanted a bakery in town. And, my father always said, 'If you want something done, you have to do it yourself.' So, we started planning and saving, and, five years later, we opened Boulangerie." Zachary adds, "Anywhere you go, the bakery is the happiest place in town." At Boulangerie, that's certainly true.

Theirs is a tried-and-true method: Amy is the "purist," Zachary the "engineer." She handles the spirit of the bread as he tinkers with the formulas. And Jaworowski makes everything go. Many of the recipes have come from Bre herself, tested over a period of months before she deems them acceptable to sell. "The ciabatta recipe we use today took me months to develop," says Jaworowski. "We knew we wanted a high-hydration dough but struggled to find the balance between hydration and strength." No matter where each recipe comes from, all the recipes Boulangerie uses have been tinkered with by the trio in charge to work with their bake schedule.

For many Boulangerie patrons, though, it all comes back to the croissant. Their most popular item by far, they often sell out early, to everyone's dismay. As Amy says, "Making our croissants is a four-day process, so it is difficult to whip up another batch as customers often ask us to do!" Still, baking at Boulangerie is a labor of love, even when things get a little intense. "I'm proud to give other bakers a chance to do their thing and produce beautiful, cared-for products. To be able to support some good people and give them a livelihood feels pretty amazing," says Zachary. Their proudest achievement? Amy puts it simply: "Returning customers and a line out the door!"

How and when did you get your start baking?

Amy: As a child, I watched cooking shows on PBS. Julia, Jacques, and *Great Chefs of the World.*

Zachary: "You see, there's this girl"—to impress a lady.

Bre: My love for baking actually started from television. During high school, I watched a lot of Food Network, and at that time shows like *Ace of Cakes* and *Cake Wars* were the popular shows. I remember watching those shows and thinking how amazing those works of art were and how much patience those bakers must have had. Cakes were what first got me interested in baking.

Who inspired you to bake? Who inspires you now?

Amy: I suppose the celebrity chefs of PBS inspired me to bake. I jotted down a recipe for a French loaf while watching TV, baked it (and forgot the salt), and recognized the taste 15 years later in Florence while eating Pane Toscano—which is bread made without salt. It tastes quite good with fresh olive oil drizzled on it and sea salt sprinkled over it. My loaf many years prior was quite a disappointment.

Zachary: My most beautiful wife and loving partner, Amy.

Bre: My aunt Joy is the person who ignited the fire first for my passion of baking. No one in my family baked besides her, and she seemed to have her own art form to it. She would make cookies, pies, and my ultimate favorite, Chrusciki, which is a very thin and crispy Polish fried dough. My family inspires me now to continue baking.

What is your golden rule(s) of baking?

Amy: Trust your senses. Feel, smell, touch, sound, and experience serve you better than thermometers and timers.

Zachary: Don't F it up. Everything you do matters!

Bre: Patience. Every step in bread baking requires patience and an understanding. You must not try to rush the process and you must go by feel, not time. You must respect what the dough requires.

What does Boulangerie represent to you?

Amy: My child—beautiful, difficult, expensive, and full of love.

Zachary: A culmination of a vision that functions well from the studs out. I saw it built; I trained the people in it. I know it is a place where I would be happy to spend my money with confidence that I'll be getting a quality product.

What is your favorite thing to bake? Why? Least favorite thing to bake? Why?

Amy: My favorite thing to bake is sourdough—I love the blisters and the rise. My least favorite is the Boulangerie Brownie, which is essentially a flourless chocolate cake. They smell amazing, but they are so moist that it is hard to tell when they are finished.

Zachary: My favorite is challah—the braid is challenging, and when done successfully it is quite satisfying. Least favorite: Ciabatta. Sticky.

Bre: French Baguettes are what truly drive my passion to bake. I believe a truly great baguette is hard to come by and even harder to create. There are so many aspects to a good baguette, such as crust, crumb, and scoring marks (also called "ears"), that it is easily the most judged item on a bakery's list. It has become a personal goal of mine to create one perfect French baguette in my career.

I honestly do not have a least favorite thing to bake. I do, however, have a least favorite item to finish, and that would be cakes. The patience required to beautifully decorate a cake and beautifully handcraft a loaf of bread could not be any more different from one another. I do not have the patience and skill to finish cakes that they deserve.

What are your most popular items?

Amy: Croissants. Making our croissants is a four-day process, so it is difficult to whip up another batch as customers often ask us to do.

Where do you get your tools/materials?

Amy: San Francisco Baking Institute (SFBI), King Arthur Flour (KAF), and Maine Grains.

What nonessential items should every baker have?

Good shoes and/or good floor mats (sky mat, antifatigue mat).

What book(s) go on your required reading list for bakers?

Amy: *Bread* by Hamelman. *Professional Baking* by Gisslen. *Tartine* by Chad Robertson (he makes sourdough approachable).

Zachary: *Bread Science* by Emily Buehler.

Bre: *Tartine*, Book 3. This is a beautifully photographed and well-composed book of ancient grains and unique ingredients that expose you to a whole new world of flours that go way beyond white and wheat.

What outlets/periodicals/newspapers do you read or consult regularly, if any?

Bre: For answers to questions, recipes, or advice, I turn to the Bread Bakers Guild of America. They have a wonderful database of recipes available for members, and their member list contains bakers from all walks of life from all over the world. It is a wonderful community of like-minded people coming together to help one another.

Amy: If there are any good articles in the newspapers, our customers bring them to us!

Tell me about your most memorable collaboration(s) with another chef.

Amy: We created a bread for a restaurant that no one on my team had ever tried: Cristal bread. It is a Spanish version of ciabatta, but lighter, crisper, and made with plenty of olive oil. We had to incorporate different flours to balance a high hydration, and also give it enough folds and various stages to develop the gluten. The chef was very pleased and said it was like the real thing.

Zachary: Pulled Pork Focaccia using a local food truck's (Texas Grace) pulled pork.

Do you follow any cooking shows or chefs? If so, which is your favorite?

Amy: *Iron Chef* is fun. I don't watch much TV, but *The Great British Baking Show* is a good laugh!

Zachary: Anthony Bourdain.

Where did you learn to cook? Please tell me about your education and/or apprenticeships.

Amy: I worked at Eatery in NYC in pastry, then Spago in Las Vegas, where I became the head of the Bread Department. We produced the bread for all of Wolfgang Puck's properties in Vegas—Spago, Postrio, and Chinois.

After working at Spago, I attended the Cordon Bleu in London. Zachary and I both attended specialized courses in hearth breads, sourdoughs, and croissants at both the International Culinary Center in NYC and King Arthur Flour Baking Education Center in Vermont.

Zachary: International Culinary Center, and King Arthur Flour. Trial and error. Not my mother!

Bre: I received a bachelor's degree in baking and pastry arts from Johnson & Wales University in Providence, RI. Through my schooling I interned at a high-end resort in Idaho and a small family-owned resort on St. Kitts in the Caribbean. The program at Johnson & Wales is truly wonderful, and exposes you to all aspects of baking, from bread to cakes to showpieces to plated desserts. It is thanks to Johnson & Wales and a few of my chef instructors that I got exposed to bread and discovered my life's passion.

AUGUSTO CARVALHAL DA SILVA

GARAGE BAKERY

PELOTAS, BRAZIL

Garage Bakery's story starts a decade ago, when husband-and-wife duo Augusto Carvalhal da Silva and Daniela Pierobom realized they were both dissatisfied with their respective jobs. At the time they were commuting a lot, having moved from Porto Alegre, where they both had their jobs, to their hometown of Pelotas, in order to allow their newborn baby to spend time with her grandparents.

Their work routine, though financially rewarding, involved constant traveling and left them with a very limited amount of time with their daughter, Helena. So, one day Augusto sat down with Dani and said "I don't want to do this anymore; I'd rather sell bread" and Dani was immediately on board. At that point, they had been baking at home for 10 long years, during which they had learned the basics and beyond. They resolved to call the micro-bakery Garage, echoing the niche wine producers in Bordeaux to remark that, alike them, the newborn bakery would have excellent but limited production.

Initially, both Augusto and Dani kept their day jobs; after work, Augusto would start a batch of bread and cold proof it in their fridge. The next day, before work, he'd bake it and Dani would bring the baked goods to sell at her workplace. Soon they got noticed by the local news and orders from outside the office started to appear. With these customers came restaurant owners and gourmet grocery shops, asking for a regular supply of specialty breads, such as baguettes and hamburger buns.

With sales increasing, the couple saved enough money to buy professional baking equipment by the end of the first year. The bakery moved from the apartment to the back of Augusto's father's property, a big house surrounded by a beautiful orchard. Sales kept increasing and they ventured into chocolate making, becoming excellent at it rapidly.

After a few years, it became clear they needed a place of their own to sell their products. By then, they had inherited their father's mansion and were basically living in the bakery. So, it only seemed natural to renovate the front porch and open it up to the public.

They are now planning to add a little café to their lovely store, in order to utilize more of their beautiful orchard. The key to their continuous success is Dani and Augusto's capability to innovate, adapt, and take inspiration from local ingredients and food traditions. Garage Bakery views itself as a mom-and-pop business and the owners want to keep it that way. But with high quality, limited daily production, a Callebaut excellence prize in 2021, and the admiration of their many customers and fans, they can't help transcend that humble stance.

Café 35
garage bakery

How and when did you start baking?

My first contacts were in my childhood, and were massive failures; my great-aunt would make some sweet bread dough that I'd turn into dinosaurs or whatever, only to receive a shapeless mass after baking, which was really frustrating. Later on, my mother had this book on pizza, it was one of those compilations magazines make to sell at the newsstand. I was really impressed by the delicious-looking pizzas and those over-the-top, 1970s-style recipes, and took a shot at making pizza from scratch. It came out awful, of course.

Who or what first inspired you to bake?

When I started living together with my then girlfriend, now wife, 21 years ago, she bought a book from a French baker named Olivier Anquier who lived in Brazil. It was the first time I heard about sourdough. I had relative success with the yeasted recipes in that book, so the next logical step was to make my sourdough starter. I was successful in bringing one to life, but I made awful bread with it. About a decade later or so, I gave sourdough another try after reading Peter Reinhardt's *The Bread Baker's Apprentice*. From that moment I started making edible sourdough bread.

Who or what inspires you now?

My two heroes are Raymond Calvel and Lionel Poilâne. I like Calvel's technical approach to making a product with consistent quality and reasonable production speed, without rushing things. Poilâne wrote great books on bread and coined the concept of "retro-innovation" which sounds very steampunk and I love it. His signature miche is great as well, quite unique.

What is your golden rule(s) for baking?

I don't bake anything that I don't like eating, and I don't sell anything I would not feed to my daughter. Also, first get a solid knowledge in the classic breads. Learn to make a decent yeasted bread first, then go for the sourdough. Learn how to feel the dough, learn your equipment and your environment, get to know what you are doing. Repeat processes painstakingly over and over until you can deliver exactly the same bread every time. Then, and only then, should you get "creative."

What does Garage Bakery represent to you?

Freedom to change whenever necessary. Freedom to be myself, to create. Satisfaction in feeding people and feeling their happiness. And also getting to know other bakers and other realities and getting to help people through classes and consulting.

What is your favorite thing to bake? Why?

Nowadays, it's pizza. Because I love pizza and I get to eat it! Maybe because of that old pizza booklet? I don't know, but that's something I never get tired of experimenting with. That and our baguettes, a crowd favorite here.

How did Garage Bakery come to be?

I was unhappy with my job, Dani, my wife, was unhappy with hers, we had just had a daughter, and we felt we needed an activity which allowed us to be around her more often. So I started baking bread and Dani would sell it to her coworkers; at the same time I started a Facebook page and people started to order our baked goods. In a year, we had enough money to buy actual professional equipment and renovate a space dedicated to the bakery. That was eight years ago, as of 2021. Prior to the pandemic, we were starting a small baking school with some basic courses, as well as product development and consulting. These things are halted for now, but we will resume them in the future.

What are your favorite, most relevant tools/materials?

I don't own particularly amazing equipment; the most refined stuff I own is my spiral mixer, which I do like. My fermentation chamber is falling apart and is all warped, sometimes it blows up, but it's an important part of most of my processes, as are my air-conditioning units. Poilâne used to say, "The better the oven, the worse the baker." I believe a real professional must extract the best results with the equipment they have, because it's the processes that must be mastered. Otherwise, you're just an expensive-equipment operator.

Tell me about your most memorable collaboration with another baker.

I'd say the consulting I provided Casa Nacre in Natal, Rio Grande do Norte; it was a great experience working with George Nacre and his crew and helping production become smoother, as well as helping him develop new recipes. But other than consulting or classes, I don't really like working with people; I enjoy working alone.

Brag about yourself a bit. What are your highest achievements and/or proudest moments as a baker?

My highest achievement was giving a sourdough made by me to a very accomplished French baker and hearing that it was a really great French-style bread. It helped that he was in Brazil for two weeks and was probably eating bad bread all that time. Making people happy with my products and getting to help other professionals or students is what make me proud of what I do.

WENDY SMITH BORN & JAMES BARRETT

METROPOLITAN BAKERY

PHILADELPHIA, PENNSYLVANIA

For Wendy Smith Born and James Barrett, the partnership came easily. While working together at the original White Dog Café in Philadelphia—Wendy as the managing partner and James as the pastry chef—the pair bonded over their shared love of the beautiful breads they'd enjoyed in Europe during their formative years. In 1993, though, those loaves were not so easily found in Philadelphia. So, they decided to do something about it, opening their flagship bakery at Rittenhouse Square that same November.

Things have changed considerably since then. Born and Barrett's labor of love has become a massive commercial success, found at locations all over Philadelphia and enjoying features in *Gourmet, Bon Appetit, O, The Oprah Magazine*, *Zagat*, and the *TODAY* show. They've also developed a substantial online store, where they sell cakes, pies, to-go meals, and even their own ice cream to customers nationwide. But in spite of all that, Metropolitan remains a Philly staple first and foremost. "For us, Metropolitan Bakery is about community," says Born. "In addition to all-natural high-quality products (locally sourced whenever possible), we're proud to be part of our customers' daily lives and proud that we've provided job training and skills to thousands of Philadelphians."

It may sound like a platitude, but Born and Barrett practice what they preach. Metropolitan partners with many organizations to help give back to Philadelphia, including schools, environmental sustainability groups, coalitions addressing homelessness and poverty, and local farmers. For this alone, Metropolitan is a bakery worth supporting. But there's a much simpler reason, too: its baked goods. Baguettes, sourdough and multigrain loaves, millet muffins, and sour cherry chocolate chip cookies all highlight their bestsellers, not to mention their granola, which was voted best in America by Epicurious.com. Even better, they make their own starter, usually referred to as "the chef" in-house. As Barrett says, "At Metro, it's all about the natural starter." This process (which Barrett explains in more detail below) helps create "loaves with rich, crackling, mahogany crusts and nutty, intensely fragrant interiors—the hallmarks of old-world bread."

Metropolitan Bakery walks the tightrope of success as well as any bakery in the country, maintaining a local presence in its community while delivering good food to as many people as possible. Whether you're close to Philly or not, this is a bakery you'll want to order from.

lemon bar

How and when did you get your start baking?

James: I first learned about baking from my Grandmother Tucci, who would gather my brothers, sisters, and I in her kitchen. It was from her that I learned the ritual of baking, and how certain recipes evoke a feeling or a memory.

Who inspired you to bake? Who inspires you now?

James: I get my inspiration from other chefs, customers, employees, and sometimes the ingredients themselves. Other times, I'll have a craving and the only way to satisfy it is to make something. That's how many Metro favorites, like our award-winning granola, came to be.

What is your golden rule of baking?

James: Always use the best ingredients, locally sourced if possible, and stay true to time-honored techniques. If you take the easy way out, you can taste it.

What is your favorite thing to bake? Why?

James: My favorite thing to bake is our miche. It takes almost *60* hours to produce from start to finish. It is awesome watching the loaves have their final oven spring and slowly bake to a rich dark caramel color. The smell is incredible and complex.

What are your most popular items?

Wendy: Our most popular breads are the levain, multigrain, sourdough, French baguette, and, when available, our chocolate cherry bread. We also sell a lot of millet muffins, sour cherry chocolate chip cookies, chocolate layer cake, French berry rolls, and handmade granola. Many of these products are available nationwide via our website.

Where do you get your tools/materials? What non-essential items should every baker have?

James: I get my tools from Fante's Kitchen Shop and various professional equipment companies.

What book(s) go on your required reading list for bakers?

James: Two great resources are *Advanced Bread and Pastry* by Michel Suas and *How to Bake Bread* by Michael Kalanty.

What outlets/periodicals/newspapers do you read or consult regularly, if any?

James: I like Instagram, *The New York Times* Food Section, and the Bread Bakers Guild newsletter.

Wendy: I also read *The New York Times*, plus *The Washington Post* and Food52.

Tell me about your most memorable collaboration(s) with another chef.

James: I have enjoyed working with Alice Waters, Nancy Silverton, Mark Peel, and Paul Bertolli, to name a few.

Do you follow any cooking shows or chefs? If so, which is your favorite?

James: I love PBS and Netflix cooking shows and series.

Where did you learn to cook? Please tell me about your education and/or apprenticeships.

James is a trained chef as well as a master baker. He graduated from the Culinary Institute of America, and has studied in Europe at the Ecole Française de Boulangerie d'Aurillac.

How do you make your starter, "the chef"? How long does this process usually take?

James: Wild yeasts in the air are allowed to feed on a mixture of flour, water, and catalysts such as mashed bananas, raisins, or Concord grapes. For two weeks, the mixture is fed a steady diet of breakfast, lunch, and dinner, allowing it to ferment and multiply. Eventually, it becomes the bubbly, pleasantly sour-smelling natural starter called the "chef." Then, over two days, the dough will be mixed, hand-shaped, and signed, before it's left to rise in rye-dusted wicker baskets in cool, dark rooms. Only after this "long-slow-cool" rise are the loaves ready to be baked in steam-injected, stone-deck Bongard ovens.

Where can people find more recipes, or buy products?

James: Metropolitan Bakery products are available at our three retail shops in the Philadelphia area, and throughout the United States via www.metropolitanbakery.com. Our site also features additional recipes, videos, and information for other retailers.

Baking enthusiasts can also follow us on Twitter at @metrobakes or on Instagram at metrobakesPHL.

JOSHUA BELLAMY

BOULTED BREAD

RALEIGH, NORTH CAROLINA

"Initially, Boulted Bread was a pretty selfish endeavor. A means to explore our own ideas of bread and pastry while indulging our own creativity. But that self-indulgence vanished pretty quickly once we opened our doors." The speaker is Joshua Bellamy. Alongside Fulton Forde and Sam Kirkpatrick, he owns and operates Boulted Bread in Raleigh, where the three men bake beautiful loaves and pastries for the local community.

Their original focus may have been bread experimentation, but Boulted has a new priority these days: "Doing right by the people who sustain it: our customers and our employees. This is the fundamental obligation of any bakery," says Josh, and it ties in nicely with their original goal. "Our products aren't pigeonholed by rigid morality, other than this quest for taste. We want our customers to be shocked at and to revel in the fertility of flavor in everything we make. This ambition toward a nebulous ideal keeps us honest and driven." In other words: creativity is still encouraged.

Boulted got its start in 2014, when Fulton and Josh met at the Asheville Bread Festival. They immediately recognized one another as "like-minded idiots," and it wasn't long before Fulton and his longtime friend Sam reached out to Josh with their plans to open a bakery; all three men are Raleigh natives themselves, and felt it was important to bake for the community they knew and loved. Boulted was soon up and running, establishing itself as a part of the community just as quickly. With its loaves, both chewy and crunchy, and its buttery pastries, it's not hard to see why.

With Boulted's success came a natural push away from the day-to-day baking duties, but Josh has held firm on that score. "I love to bake bread, and so far, thank goodness, the success and growth of Boulted Bread have not come at the expense of what I love." Members of the Raleigh community certainly agree—their products can be found throughout the city!

BOULTED BREAD

How and when did you get your start baking?

I've worked at bakeries and coffee shops since high school, but my first real urge to bake came later in life, after college. At the time, I was running an after-school program for at-risk middle school students, and it was a lot. I started baking bread at home to relieve the stress of it, and things snowballed pretty rapidly from there.

Who inspired you to bake? Who inspires you now?

Initially, my curiosity was piqued by Peter Reinhart's books. They gave me a window into a world of which I had such limited understanding, and I knew pretty quickly that I wanted to explore more.

Currently, no baker inspires me more than Jim Lahey of Sullivan Street Bakery. His continued evolution as a baker proves his persistent curiosity, which I find deeply impressive.

What is your golden rule(s) for baking?

My only "golden rule" for baking is that I only bake things I'd like to eat. Does it taste good? Despite other moral and ethical proclamations, I believe that's really the essential goal of baking.

What is your favorite thing to bake, and why? Least favorite?

Baguettes are the ultimate challenge for me: the purest expression of a baker's proficiency, focus, and ethos. A perfect baguette requires so many distinct skills and such precise execution. If you're even fractionally off your game, the whole thing can fall apart. For the same reason, baguettes are also my least favorite thing to bake. Nothing has caused me more stress, grief, and sleepless nights.

Where do you get your baking tools? What non-essential items should every baker have?

We purchased almost all of our equipment secondhand. We also did most of the build-out ourselves, asking friends and family to pitch in when our construction skills were found lacking.

And, bountiful, high-quality bench scrapers are an absolute must for us! We use these orange, hard plastic scrapers from King Arthur Flour exclusively. They're amazing.

What book(s) go on your required reading list for bakers?

Bread Builders by Daniel Wing and Alan Scott and all of the *Tartine* books played a role in informing our overall ethos toward baking. For technical knowledge, nothing beats *Advanced Bread and Pastry* by Michel Suas and *Bread* by Jeffrey Hamelman. *Practical Milling* by B. W. Dedrick is also great for an informative trip into the history and mechanics of milling.

What outlets/periodicals/newspapers do you read or consult regularly, if any?

The online forum for the Bread Bakers Guild of America offers an amazing, ongoing conversation on all things bread and pastry related.

Tell me about your most memorable collaboration with another chef.

It's always really exciting to see how Drew Maykuth of Stanbury (in downtown Raleigh) uses our bread. We've created some custom loaves for chefs in the past, and it's interesting to see how our vision of bread pairs with what chefs are accomplishing in their restaurants. Drew always finds a way to enhance and highlight the best qualities of our loaves. He's a real hero.

Where did you learn to cook? Please tell me about your education and apprenticeships.

After struggling to unlock some bread-baking mysticism at home, I moved to Vermont and got a Certificate of Professional Baking from the New England Culinary Institute. It was a short and wonderful experience. I worked with some really talented instructors, learned all the important fundamentals, and got a great taste of what it would be like to work in a production setting.

I completed my apprenticeship at Elmore Mountain Bread in Wolcott, Vermont, with Blair Marvin and Andrew Heyn. They were gracious enough to let me stick around after the internship and gave me an immense wealth of knowledge, ethics, and skills with which to grow my career. I am forever in their debt, and I'm lucky to count them as my friends.

Tell me about your milling process. How long have you been using a stone mill in-house? Why do you prefer it?

Our stone mill has been the focal point of our bakery, both physically and ethically, since our inception. It was designed and built by our very own Fulton Forde, as part of New American Stone Mills. We now fresh mill over 60% of our flour and plan to increase that number in the next few years.

We try to stay loose with our milling dogma and avoid sacrificing product integrity, identity, and flavor for the sake of fresh milling. That being said, milling most of our flour in-house gives us a number of distinct benefits. We have access to a wide variety of grain, directly from the farm, and the fresh flour has a sweeter aroma and fattier flavor than conventionally milled grains. We use our mill, in conjunction with several other techniques, as a tool to elevate and deepen the flavors in our products.

GRAISON GILL

BELLEGARDE BAKERY

NEW ORLEANS, LOUISIANA

One of the most respected bakers in New Orleans, Graison Gill has been featured on platforms such as *Saveur, Edible New Orleans*, and *The Wall Street Journal*. But his proudest moment took place on a different sort of stage: the Louisiana House of Representatives. A resolution he cowrote, aimed to protect and promote organic and local agriculture, passed with a whopping 92–0 vote. "My initial smug pride quickly buckled under a very humbling and empowering feeling that, really, it is possible to help change the laws in America," says Graison.

This larger awareness is not merely tangential to what Bellegarde does, but woven into the bakery's identity. Everything stems from Graison's own ethos, which he summarizes thusly: "I gradually had the epiphany that everything is inherently imperfect, but bread always proved to be a potential rubric of perfection. It *is* possible to make a perfect loaf of bread; realizing you have inspiration that, however ephemeral, achievement and fulfilment are possible. It proves that there can be a map between head and heart, between intention and experience. I found purchase in this belief. And to me the perfect loaf of bread became a medallion to be spent against everything else, to be spent against the things that didn't come out right."

If things didn't come out right in the beginning, they certainly do now. Producing only four loaves on regular rotation—ciabatta, country, baguette, and rye—has allowed Bellegarde to fine-tune their recipes to near perfection. To enhance their refinement process, the team at Bellegarde makes everything by hand for a more deliberate approach. And though plenty of world-class bakeries don't follow this method, one can certainly appreciate the personal touch at Bellegarde.

Graison Gill is a baker, first and last, but his poetic style is more than just a way of speaking. It shines through in his bread as well—each result a labor of love, representing his hope to, one day, create the sublime loaf.

How and when did you get your start baking?

I began baking in my first New Orleans apartment, on Royal Street, in 2009. I arrived in New Orleans on a Greyhound bus on April 15, 2009, and that summer I began sharing a commercial kitchen in the Bywater with local chefs and caterers. From there, I began selling bread to neighbors and at a farmers market. I was attracted to baking because of its nature: I was working with my hands. Bread baking is the manifestation of many metaphors: failure, exile and solitude, intimacy, nurturing, consistency, moderation. I was mesmerized by the ingredients, the history, the process. More than anything, I found the experience of a bad loaf—its hubris—humbling and necessary, especially as a young man. Loaves competed between my expectation and their reality.

How and when did the bakery get its start?

I began the bakery with an SBA loan. My best friends and I did some painting and assembling of used equipment in the rented warehouse. For about six months, I worked alone: baking, mixing, delivering, bookkeeping, cleaning. For about one and a half years I worked seven days a week; on Mondays, I woke up at 7 a.m., the rest of the week at 4 a.m.

Who inspired you to bake? Who inspires you now?

Sebastien Boudet (Petite France), Christophe Vasseur (Du Pain et Des Idées), Chris Bianco (Pizzeria Bianco), Nan Kohler (Grist & Toll), Mike Zakowski (The Bejkr), Scott Peacock (formerly of The Watershed), Glenn Roberts (Anson Mills)—these individuals and my family have been the strongest compasses and brightest stars in my life. When the bakery began, there was nothing but personal inspiration. I merely had the desire to create a place where I could do right.

What is your golden rule(s) of baking?

Chris Bianco once said, "Whether it's a tomato or a rumor, you must always consider the source." For me, baking is about terroir. Not only the terroir of the grain, but also of the salt, the water, the baker, the process, the style. Ninety-nine percent of American wheat products are made with white flour. White flour is a dead, inert product. It has little flavor, minimal nutritional value, and is entirely uninspiring. American bakers are groomed to work with this product for their entire careers; I certainly was. It really had no bearing upon who I was or what I was seeking. It's as if you were a musician and were asked only to play cover songs. There is not much inspiration or imagination in constantly performing the work of others. And so, my golden rule is that chefs and bakers need to be like midwives. We don't create, we don't parent, in the way a farmer or winemaker does. Instead, we merely facilitate a process, and we allow ingredients to speak for themselves.

What does Bellegarde represent to you?

At its best, Bellegarde is a manifestation of my life. Everything I've experienced, everywhere I've traveled, everything I've done, and most importantly, all the things I haven't done.

Where do you get your tools/materials? What nonessential items should every baker have?

We do everything by hand; we don't use tools at Bellegarde. The only machines we have are our mixer, our walk-in fridge, our oven, and our mill.

What book(s) go on your required reading list for bakers?

Jeffrey Hamelman's *Bread* is the most essential and critical text for every baker. It is exceptional, flawless, and graceful. No other book was more important to me. Chad Robertson's *Tartine* is also beautiful for its iconoclasm. I'd relate both of them, respectively, to The Beatles and Rolling Stones: but in order to break the rules, one must learn them first.

Tell me about your most memorable collaboration(s) with another chef.

I am working with Professor David Shields of USC and Glenn Roberts of Anson Mills to perform a tactile and historical review of heirloom Southern grains. The plan is for David to present on the narratives of certain grains and then for Glenn to discuss their horticultural experience. That discussion will include who grew them, why, where—all the interrogatives. And, if pertinent, how Glenn found those seeds.

The Judgment of Paris in 1976—when California wines usurped French wines—inspired this event. We have so many programmed expectations and qualifiers for breads; yet, as a culture, we have no emotional or literal vocabulary to speak about bread. Before 1976, the world thought only France could make great wine; those blind tastings disproved our cognitive bias. You don't have to be in Rome to be a priest.

Where did you learn to bake?

I trained at the San Francisco Baking Institute. My teachers—particularly Mac McConnell and Frank Sally—were incredibly influential to the character, ethics, and discipline of my career. What Michel Suas has done at SFBI is incredible. If it weren't for that foundation, I would not be who I am today.

Bellegarde uses its own stone mill. Why is this process so important to you, and what grains do you prefer to use? Do you ever experiment with more uncommon grains?

Milling our own flour has become the defining aspect of Bellegarde. I wasn't born into a baking family, nor was I raised with strong food rituals. My craft chose me and I practiced it constantly, often at the cost of other aspects and relationships in my life. Like athletes, a baker only gets out what they put in. Everything that goes around comes back again, like the tide; nothing is ever created, it is merely transferred. It is for this reason that we mill most of our own flour. Our baking process and its methods are incredibly intimate: on busy weeks, we make 5,000 loaves of bread. Every single aspect of the ceremony is performed by hand; I felt that it would be an awkward hypocrisy if we were doing all this work by hand while using store-bought white flour. Machines and technology went into creating that white flour; granite and soil went into stone milling our wheat flour. It is because of this desire for continuity and connection that we stone mill flour in-house. And of course, fresh flour tastes better.

AMY EMBERLING

ZINGERMAN'S BAKEHOUSE

ANN ARBOR, MICHIGAN

For bread enthusiasts, it's impossible to hear the words "rye bread" without immediately thinking of Zingerman's. Michiganders know the Deli for its overflowing, Jewish deli–style sandwiches, made with corned beef, pastrami, and several other traditional favorites. But the real magic happens at the Bakehouse nearby, where head baker Amy Emberling and Frank Carollo and their crack team whip up loaves and pastries from all over the world. Everything at Zingerman's is delicious, but even among their many standouts, the rye has received special attention. *Saveur* named it "America's best deli rye…no contest." *The Atlantic* champions their rye as well, calling it "one of the best" in the country, and the list of accolades only continues from there.

Of course, the bread from Zingerman's Bakehouse is not *literally* magic. Like all breads, it must be built, cared after, and baked to perfection—and that's where Emberling and partner Frank Carollo come in. Making delicious loaves since 1992, the Bakehouse has a singular goal: make the best bread possible. Carollo, who started the bakery with the support of Zingerman's founders, Ari Weinzweig and Paul Saginaw, was lucky enough to hire Emberling as one of the shop's original eight bakers, and the rest was history.

Emberling is not a perfectionist by nature, but one would be forgiven for thinking otherwise. When asked for her golden rule of baking, she can't help but list five. Her younger brother nicknamed her "Baker Woman" when she was only 10, and then there's the bread itself. Rustic Italian, German spelt, challah, even bagels—Zingerman's Bakehouse offers dozens of different loaves every week, each requiring its own specific precision and understanding. On top of it all, the Bakehouse manages BAKE!, a baking school that teaches the craft to hundreds every year. It adds up to a lot more hours in the kitchen than anyone would have time for, but Emberling and Carollo juggle their obligations with stunning composure.

At Zingerman's, growing fame led to an increased sense of community; the bakery has only become more entrenched in Ann Arbor as its notoriety spreads. As Emberling says, "What's most interesting about us is the continuing choice of all of Zingerman's partners (there are about 20 of us) to keep our businesses in the Ann Arbor area. We are deeply committed to our community and understand the reciprocal relationship between a business and its local community. We've been local in a very rooted physical way long before 'local' entered the food world's conversation." And the partners have done more than just stay put. "We also share with our community, giving 10% of our profits back to nonprofit organizations. We realize that we're nothing without our greater community."

SPAIN

DAILY·BREAD·BAKE
9:30 Challah.
New Yorkers, Frita
buns, New Jerseys,
French baguettes, hoagies
11:00 Jewish rye.
onion rye, caraway
rye, pumpernickel.
12:00 Rustic Italian,
Sesame Semolina,
Mt Chestnut baguette
1:30 Sourdough,
Chocolate Sourdough,
country wheat,
pain de montagne,
dinkel brot
4:00
5:00 Farm

How and when did you get your start baking?

I started baking at about age 10. I loved dessert. My mother hated to bake and we didn't have a traditional bakery in my hometown, so I decided to try it out myself. Even at 10 I loved looking through recipe books and daydreaming about what this list of ingredients and set of instructions would create. It all seemed mysterious and intriguing. I used recipes from *The Joy of Cooking* and from *McCall's* magazine. They had a section at the back of the magazine every month, and sometimes I was lucky and it was something baked. That was the beginning.

Who inspired you to bake?

I had many inspirations before I turned 20, somewhat because I was very drawn to anyone who engaged with food and baking, and would let me participate. My Nanny, my father's mother, was a very good cook and baker. She was a typical self-taught baker who didn't measure anything—so challenging to learn from but inspiring nonetheless. My other grandmother, my New York Grandma, only bought cakes and cookies. They were inspiring, though, because they introduced me to my first experience of professional baking. I was fascinated by checkerboard cakes. I remember wondering, "How did they do that?" And I loved the names—"Charlotte Russe," so fancy! And then there was our Italian babysitter/housekeeper, Elva Pezzarello, who made special cookies for us, and pizzas on Friday. She introduced me to yeast for the first time. The list goes on, but I have to come back to my mother. Although she was a reluctant baker, she did it from time to time. I now realize that some of her reluctance may have come from her perfectionism. If you're a perfectionist, baking can either make you very happy, or very crazy. Well, it made her crazy. But she inspired me to be more of a perfectionist (I'm not one by nature), because it's a valuable trait when you're trying to make truly great baked items, every time. Thanks, Mom!

Who inspires you now?

I am super appreciative of the many bakers and baking instructors in America (famous and little known) who do what looks like the same thing every day but continue to learn about the process and make their bread better and better. Examples of famous people are Jeffrey Hamelman, Frank Carollo (my partner at Zingerman's Bakehouse), Peter Reinhart, and Chad Robertson. They go deep in their study of bread making and bring progress to the field in important ways. I'm more drawn to world cuisines, and educating the public on breads that are not well-known, or on the verge of being forgotten. The work these other bakers do educates me and enables me to make better versions of these breads. It's a great relationship for me. I'm not so drawn to exploring the intricacies, but am happy to learn them from those who are and then spread the word.

What is your golden rule(s) for baking?

These are some of my rules:

• Bake in a neat and clean environment. I'm addicted to order and need it in my work environment. For me it allows for the possibility of a well-executed recipe. Disorder clutters my mind, distracts me, and leads to mistakes.

• Weigh ingredients. A scale is a must in my baking. Volume measures introduce too much variation.

• Measure everything prior to starting the process. This sets the stage for success. No missed items. No unexpected ingredients, and order because all of the bags and boxes can be put away where they belong prior to starting the work.

• Do a double check. Everything measured? Measured correctly?

• Always do a recipe as written the first time through, and then start to change it.

What does a bakery represent to you?

At Zingerman's Bakehouse we're very clear about what a bakery means. It's a community of people working toward an agreed-upon and documented mission and vision. Our Mission, created in 1994, is, "At Zingerman's Bakehouse, we are passionately committed to the relentless pursuit of being the best bakery we can imagine." As part of this "best," we are deeply engaged in our greater community. We are in daily conversations with our customers about what's going well and not so well, receiving at least 100 points of feedback every week.

Favorite thing to bake? Why? Least favorite thing to bake? Why?

I love baking things that have very few ingredients, but an involved process. That's where the skill of a baker comes into play for me. I find it super rewarding when the seemingly simple, nondescript ingredients are transformed into a tasty and multitextured treat. Examples of this are French baguettes and palmiers. They both use five ingredients or fewer, and are amazing in their complex end result.

On the other side, I like to stay clean when I bake, and there are some steps that can make that difficult, like using cocoa powder or cinnamon in large quantities. I'm a small person and am usually quite close to the mixing bowls when I work, so it's easy to get enveloped by the clouds of items like this as they enter the bowl. So, if they're in the recipe, I won't love that particular mix.

Why Ann Arbor? How did Zingerman's come to be?

Zingerman's Bakehouse is one of 10 food-related businesses that work together under the umbrella name "Zingerman's Community of Businesses." The bakery was opened in 1992, the second business after Zingerman's Delicatessen, which started in 1982. The founders of the Deli and the Zingerman's Community of Businesses are Ari Weinzweig and Paul Saginaw. They both went to university in Ann Arbor, love great food and the food business, and met working in an Ann Arbor restaurant.

Where do you get your tools/materials?

Oh, they come from all over our state, the country, and the world. We are most interested in great flavor and choose our ingredients based on that. We are fortunate to live in a state with a large agricultural community, so we are able to get great-tasting and fresh dairy, eggs, fruit, and vegetables. Grains are obviously critical to our bakery. We can get local rye and oats, and we're working on developing wheat with some local farmers. We then travel farther away when we want to use items not created here, like Parmigiano Reggiano cheese or vanilla.

BOB KLEIN & PHOEBE PLANK

COMMUNITY GRAINS

OAKLAND, CALIFORNIA

For 30 years, Bob Klein has owned and operated Oliveto, a renowned farm-to-table Italian restaurant in Oakland, CA. About 10 years ago, he started thinking about the gap between how much local produce they used and how little their flour varied. As Community Grains writer Phoebe Plank says, "As if wheat wasn't an agricultural product as well." Plank continues, "Thus Bob set out to source heirloom wheat seeds from friends in Italy, roped in a couple of the same local farmers that the restaurant had been buying vegetables from for years, and gave it a go! The resulting flavors were exciting and spurred the vision to build this alternative grain economy that would innovate toward flavor and nutrition rather than just efficiency and uniformity. What began as the Oliveto Wheat Project slowly developed into its own whole grain products company, Community Grains."

Community Grains doesn't grow itself, but its work with mills and farmers has reinvigorated the grain community in Northern California, and for good reason. "The change from thousands of local stone mills to a few hundred centralized, high-speed roller mills has had a significant effect on both the flour coming out of it and the industry behind it." And while Plank and Klein acknowledge the importance of modern roller mills, they also note that "[in light of the] renewed demand for whole grains, however, the roller mill is sub-par in that it inevitably separates the components of the kernel, which can arguably not be recombined in the same way."

Of course a focus on local, sustainable grains is essential to Community Grains' vision, but there is plenty of focus on quality as well. Their grains are grown in nutrient-rich soil on farms that have been organically building soil for 30 years—and it shows in the quality of the wheat. This allows farmers more flexibility in their planning and the option to profit off fields that would otherwise lie fallow and subject to erosion. Add Plank and Klein, "Everything we sell is 100% whole grain, so you get the whole thing. Wheat, when consumed whole, is actually a superfood in terms of the essential minerals and nutrients it contains. The problem is that the most nutritious parts of a wheat kernel—the bran and the germ—are completely sifted out to create white flour (leaving only the starchy gluten-protein-rich endosperm). Furthermore, the bran and the germ are often grossly underrepresented in most 'whole grain' flours on the market, so we offer grain that has been milled whole, and never sifted, to improve the health of our community."

Who—or what—first inspired you to begin working with locally grown whole grains? Who inspires you now?

Initially it was food historian William Ruble and Glenn Roberts of Anson Mills who opened our eyes to the possibilities of growing grain here. Since then, it has been the farmers we work with. They were harvesting such fantastic produce when we started out, and have continued to do so, inspiring us with their ingenuity, energy, and grit.

What is your golden rule(s) for growing grains?

Our golden rule really is to look at the whole thing; in the same way that a good farm is a whole system, a grain economy is a whole system. Good organic, sustainable farming is incredibly complex. We certainly agree with the farmers that believe you need to focus on building nutrient-rich soil, and then the crops will grow themselves. As a company that buys grain, we don't require farmers we work with to be doing anything in particular, just that they are completely transparent and excited to share with us all that they're trying out.

What does Community Grains represent to you?

A community of people excited about the potential for grains, executing on an alternative to commodity wheat, and creating exceptional whole wheat products.

Tell me a little bit about the different grains you grow. What's the importance of growing the grains sustainably?

Our farmers grow an array of different wheat varieties, some old heirloom varieties bred and cultivated in Europe, some preindustrial northern American varieties, and even some newer varieties adapted for our growing conditions here in Northern California. Besides needing to able to be grown organically, they have to be healthy, flavorful, and have pretty good yield. Right now we use a mix of hard red, hard white, soft white, and hard amber durum varieties.

Growing grains sustainably is of the utmost importance, because it is a virtuous circle that produces healthier, better-tasting food, a healthier environment, and healthier farm communities!

What is your favorite type of grain? Why? Least favorite grain? Why?

Dwarf modern varieties that can't survive without pesticides and herbicides and are essentially a product of all the wrong turns that the grain industry has made in regard to flavor and nutrition of grain. We like all the other ones.

What are your most popular items?

It's hard to say what our most popular items are—we have a lot of different types of customers, from grocery and online shoppers to restaurants and cafeterias. Perhaps our pastas and Red Flint polenta are the most beloved.

Where do you get your tools/materials? What mill(s) do you work with and why?

We work with a mill in Woodland, California, that has an air classifier mill, an innovative mill from Japan. We really like it because unlike a roller mill, which is what the vast majority of flour is milled with, it allows you to mill grains whole into very uniform flour particles. In addition, even though the whole kernel is together the entire time, the flour that comes out is shelf stable. Initially the kernel is cracked and we presume the endosperm coats the germ (which is the part that contains the nutritious oils that cause rancidity) and keeps it from going off.

What outlets/periodicals/newspapers do you read or consult regularly, if any?

Most often we're up on *Civil Eats, The Atlantic,* and *The New York Times.*

Tell me about your most memorable collaboration with another mill/farmer/etc.

Our friends at Full Belly Farm have experimented with a bunch of our odd wheat ideas over the years. When we were first starting out, the harvest analysis came back with a very low protein reading, and everyone (the farmer and the miller) simply thought the wheat was going to have to end up as pig feed. Bob disagreed, bought a bag of it and convinced the miller to mill it, convinced a few bakers to play with it, and it turned out to be a crowd favorite! It made delicious bread despite the fact that by "industry standards" it was of a quality below human consumption.

Please tell me about the type of mill you use.

The mill we use is an air classifier mill (ACM), which gives us true whole grain by milling it whole like a stone mill. Unlike a stone mill, however, the ACM consistently puts out very uniform granulation and is more efficient for the scale that we operate at. The ACM operates by blowing the kernels around at high speeds so they smash into themselves and metal pegs in the mill, until they are the desired size and are blown up and out.

Brag about yourselves a bit. What are your highest achievements and/or proudest moments in this industry?

We've put on two major conferences over the years, bringing together some brilliant minds in farming, nutrition science, plant science, history, journalism, and baking to discuss the future of wheat. Starting these conversations and executing on the vision they put forth is what it's all about.

Please tell me about your education and experience.

We don't grow grains ourselves, but have learned a ton about it from our farmer partners over the years. When Bob first got excited about growing grains, he learned from farmers and millers in Italy as well as in California.

Please tell me about the growing and milling processes.

The grain is planted in the spring or winter, grows green and heads-out as the kernels swell, and then is dried on the stalk (hopefully without getting too top-heavy and falling over). Once the wheat is thoroughly dried out in the hot summer, the wheat is harvested using harvesting machines that drive through the fields threshing the stalks and separating and cleaning the grain in rotating cylinders. Once the farmer has harvested and

cleaned the wheat, he'll have it analyzed by the California Wheat Commission for protein percentage, amongst other metrics. Our process is then to mill a small batch of it up in Woodland and distribute samples to the bakers we're closest with to get a good read on it. The grain is stored at the farm or chilled at our warehouse in 2,000-pound super totes and ultimately milled fresh to fill orders and stock inventory.

KEVIN MORRIS

DANTE'S PIZZERIA

AUCKLAND, NEW ZEALAND

How does *pizzaiolo* Kevin Morris (he of the Michelin-starred Dante's Pizzeria; host to prime ministers, adviser to celebrity chefs, television *pizzaiolo*) make such a brilliant Margherita? According to him, love. "The most important rule for me, before I start any recipe or idea, is that it has to come from the heart. Most bakers will tell you baking requires some luck. I choose to replace luck with love. When you put love and care into your baking, your finished dish will smile back at you with much more love when taken out from the oven."

Ah, if only it were so simple. But there's no denying Moriss's passion, which has been cultivated over years of experience in Italy and elsewhere. What began with him watching his Italian mother bake focaccia in London, and continued during frequent visits to his grandparents' home in Italy, has led him to become one of the Southern Hemisphere's most respected authorities on pizza Napoletana. And that's not just a platitude.

His was only the second pizza in the Southern Hemisphere to receive "La Vera Pizza Napoletana," a title that indicates his pizza (specifically, the Margherita) counts as true pizza Napoletana and is a legitimate member of the Naples pizza scene—protected by European law!

It is easy to lose track of the many achievements Morris has reached in his career. Dante's has been awarded "Best Pizza in Auckland" by *Metro* magazine four years in a row. In 2014, they also won "The Best Pizza in New Zealand" by Campionato Mondiale della Pizza. He has appeared on New Zealand television to spread his gospel, and received countless write-ups in local and national publications.

For Kevin Morris, though, it all comes back to his mother's focaccia bread in the kitchen all those years ago. Without it, he would have never fallen in love with dough—and the world would never get to enjoy his true pizza Napoletana.

PIZZERIA
Dantes
NAPOLETANA

How did Dante's come to be? What are your most popular items?

One afternoon at a friend's barbecue, I was talking about pizza Margherita and how I wished I could find one to eat. As a result, a friend suggested I open a pizzeria myself. So I did. At this time, Auckland's restaurant scene was growing, so I started my first pizzeria in Kumeu, and Dante's Pizzeria Napoletana was born. Later on, we moved to Ponsonby, Auckland. We are most famous for our Margherita, along with the sourdough Panuozzi (a Napoli Street sub sandwich) and our fried sourdough dressed in tomato sauce and mozzarella.

Who—or what—first inspired you to make pizza? Who inspires you now?

In 2008, I was invited by Associazione Verace Pizza Napoletana in Naples to experience their culture and advance my knowledge of pizza Napoletana. During this time, I was honored to meet and work at Pizzeria Gaetano along with Gaetano himself in Ischia. Even now, he is still the man who inspires me to uphold the art of the perfect "cornicione"—the perfect crust of the true pizza Napoletana.

What does Dante's mean to you?

Dante was my Italian grandfather. Every Christmas as kids, we would fly to Italy to visit my grandparents. All my memories of that time were always about food. As a result, I wanted to use my grandfather's name to tie in my Italian side when opening my pizzeria.

What is your favorite pizza to make? Can you talk a bit about your process?

When it comes to food, I like simple dishes done well, with the best ingredients you can get. Therefore, the pizza Margherita. It begins with the two-day sourdough base, after which the dough is stretched by hand. I then spread on hand-crushed San Marzano tomatoes imported from Italy, sprinkle with freshly picked basil, and buffalo mozzarella, and finish with a drizzle of extra virgin olive oil. It's important to remember that less is more. Finally, the pizza is cooked in a very hot wood-fired oven for just over a minute. During this time, I use the turning peel to turn the pizza in order to achieve an even cook. As the pizza arrives on the table, the aroma of the wood fire blended with the sourdough base and basil is what makes the Margherita a Michelin star–winning dish.

Where do you get your tools/materials? What non-essential items should every pizza baker have?

The oven is the most important item. We imported our ovens from Naples and pizza tools from different parts of Italy. Every Naples oven has a dome shape, which allows a swirling effect of intense heat to create the pizza Napoletana's signature blisters around the crust. In addition, a marble workbench is necessary to open (stretch) the pizza dough. Marble has a cool and even temperature all year, so the dough is always easy to work with. Last but not least, a good pizza peel and a turning peel are essential to place the pizza into the oven and help with even cooking. I also recommend a pizza stone for even cooking and to improve your crust.

What book(s) go on your required reading list for bakers?

One of my favorite books to read is *Bread* by Dean Brettschneider. Dean explains how simple baking can be as long as you prioritize the basic products. As we all say, practice makes perfect; once you have mastered the basics and understood the taste, texture, and feel of the dough, other baking will come easily.

Brag about yourself a bit. What are your proudest moments as a chef?

When I decided to open my own pizzeria, I started looking for the best pizza recipe. After days and days of trying different recipes, I made my mind up on pizza Napoletana. However, I kept practising and changing the recipe until I was able to achieve the light, fluffy, and chewy crust of the traditional pizza Napoletana. That was when Dante's Pizzeria was born. As I learned more about pizza Napoletana, I found AVPN, which is an organization that protects the art and craft of the true Naples pizza. After contacting them and discussing what I do with them, they invited me to Naples to advance my knowledge of "opening the dough."

In early 2008, New Zealand Prime Minister and National Party leader John Key visited Dante's. He was not just happy enjoying his pizza, he also rolled up his sleeves and joined me in my kitchen for a one-on-one pizza-making lesson. Key also made a joke that the chance to swap politics for pizza could also be tempting. I told him with a smile that if he ever wanted a part-time job, I'd happily employ him.

Favorite crust?

Napoletana crust is always the best. It's light, fluffy, crispy, and chewy, all at once. Since the dough is a two-day fermentation, the pizza base and crust can be digested easily and are light on your stomach, leaving room for your favorite dessert. Besides Margherita, my other favorite pizza topping is hot Calabrese salami, another must-have in my pantry.

MIKE KEON & ANTHONY ALLEN

OTTO PIZZA

MULTIPLE LOCATIONS IN MAINE & MASSACHUSETTS

Even if OTTO pizza was just so-so, owners Mike Keon and Anthony Allen would still deserve a spotlight for their desire to give back. Allen started Nantucket's first-ever pizza joint at age 17—before his senior year of high school—because he knew how badly his fellow islanders were clamoring for it. In 2012, Keon and Allen traveled to New York City in the wake of Hurricane Sandy, armed only with 600 pizzas and a grill. After hours of travel and coordinating, they spent five days handing out free pizza and rations to storm victims, leaving only once everything was gone. They've worked closely with local organizations to aid fundraising efforts in Maine and Massachusetts as well, and Keon once tried to cook a full Thanksgiving dinner on a fishing boat…during a storm. In other words: they're men of the people.

Of course, the pizza *is* good—good enough, actually, to be included in Food Network's "50 Pizzas, 50 States," where it was named one of the best pizzas in America. Good enough to have grown from one little shop in Portland in 2009 to 12 locations today. They have also been featured on the Cooking Channel and numerous local "best-of" lists.

"We had talked for many years about working together and made steps toward larger-scale restaurants in Boston. For many different reasons in many different locations, we never opened in Boston," says Allen. "Mike moved to Portland in '07 and was taken by the vibrant food culture. When a tiny space on Congress Street became available in '09, Mike called and asked me to come up and take a look. We agreed that rather than open a big restaurant in a big city, maybe starting a very small slice shop that focused on one thing had its upsides. Having never worked together, it made sense to start small and see how it went as a team. It went remarkably well from the very start."

And it continues to go well, as Allen and Keon feed the hungry masses from Boston to Maine.

OTTO

How and when did you get your start baking? Why pizza over other breads or pastries?

Anthony opened Anthony's Pizza, the first pizza shop on Nantucket, where he grew up. He was 17, and opened the shop at the start of the summer leading into his senior year in high school. Pizza was a much-needed commodity on the island. Anthony and his wife D. D. would later open a café in Gloucester, MA, where they would bake a daily array of fresh breads and pastries.

Who—or what—first inspired you to make pizza? Who inspires you now?

We continue to inspire each other with the passion from which we began in 2009, searching for the perfect pie: a combination of the best ingredients we can source (or produce ourselves), the art of making a balanced pie, and focusing on the quality of the ingredients rather than the quantity. It's prepping the dough so it's just the right temperature and elasticity before being topped and baked. And it's about using the right equipment—the Marsal oven, a brick-lined cavity with consistently high, intense heat that bakes an unusually even pie with a golden crown and crispy bottom. As a company, we're more inward looking, constantly asking how we can improve our consistency, process, and delivery of our product. We make sure to remain current with all things pizza, but it's our commitment to ourselves, to constantly challenging what we do and how we do it, that enables us to produce our pie with consistency.

What is your golden rule(s) for baking?

"Golden" is the key word—it marks that the dough is perfectly proofed (62°F), ready for the oven, resulting in an airy, open cell–structured, crispy bake. The optimal point of doneness for our product is golden with slight blistering or char. If it's pulled too early, it can be bland, flaccid, and unremarkable. Left in too long, it can take on bitter and unwanted flavors.

What does Otto's represent to you?

An interest in reengineering a ubiquitous food. Our studied approach to pie was one in which we transformed what is often blandly accepted into an exceptionally envisioned pie—one that ignites curiosity and a slow nod of approval as one begins to enjoy the often unusual combination of flavors, created and executed by a devoted and caring team.

What is your favorite pizza to bake? Why? Least favorite pizza to bake? Why?

Anthony: Plain cheese is the go-to for anyone in the business. It's the "vanilla" of pizza. If I can belt out a killer cheese slice, chances are we know what we're doing. If I've got company over, it's the sausage, Vidalia, and Fontina pie, with a little scallion and fresh herb.

Mike: Plain cheese with a little basil, because it is simple and perfect. My least favorite is any half-and-half—they're messy, busy, and slow down production.

What are your most popular items?

Our most popular pie is "The Masher"—mashed potato, bacon, and scallion.

Where do you get your tools/materials? What non-essential items should every pizza baker have?

Mike: Cornmeal to create a gap between the dough and the stone.

Anthony: Cornmeal is *absolutely* essential. Essential equipment for the home pizza chef: a pizza stone and hopefully a gas-fired oven that cranks to 550°F. We use Marsal ovens in all our shops; their brick-lined cavities allow for even heat distribution and recover exceptionally well.

What book(s) go on your required reading list for bakers?

My Pizza by Jim Lahey, *Flour Water Salt Yeast* by Ken Forkish, and *American Pie* by Peter Reinhart. We're also big fans of Zingerman's Training Seminars in Ann Arbor, Michigan.

What outlets/periodicals/newspapers do you read or consult regularly, if any?

Mark Bittman, *The New York Times*, *Food & Wine*, *Saveur*, and Anthony Bourdain's *Parts Unknown.*

Tell me about your most memorable collaboration with another chef.

OTTO's Master Baker, Alex Castiello, knows more about the history of dough, the science behind the dough, and industrial dough production than anyone we've ever met. We're lucky he sought us out, and we're lucky we listened to "the dough whisperer."

Where did you learn to cook? Please tell me about your education and apprenticeships.

Ant learned how to make pie on his own when he opened his first shop at the young age of 17. He was also inspired after a trip to Naples. Mike first started cooking on a fishing vessel in Alaska and then at a very busy restaurant in Boston. He opened his own bistro north of Boston in 2000.

JONATHAN GOLDSMITH

SPACCA NAPOLI PIZZERIA

CHICAGO, ILLINOIS

Chicago's Spacca Napoli Pizzeria produces not only some of the best Neapolitan pizza in that city, but some of the best in the world, thanks to certified pizzaiolo Jonathan Goldsmith. Recommended by the Michelin Guide and celebrated by local and international pizza aficionados, Goldsmith's reverence for tradition comes through in his team's commitment to turning out delicious uncut pies with beautifully blistered crusts. When he is not busy running the restaurant, Goldsmith is dedicated to educating aspiring pizza makers about why this culinary art form elicits so much passion.

What type of oven do you use to cook your pizzas? What temperature do you cook at?

We have two wood-burning ovens. Both built on-site by the Agliarulo family of Naples, fourth- and fifth-generation oven builders. The first oven built by the family is circa 1870 somewhere in Naples. The normal temperature range is 850 to 900°F.

If you use a wood-burning oven, what type of wood do you burn? Why?

We use locally kiln-dried oak. We have played with imported beech, as both give a clean, hot burn. Were we in Connecticut, we would be using beech. In Colorado or Arizona, something else.

What flour(s) do you use for your doughs?

Our principal flour producer is Molino Caputo of Naples. Our daily mix consists of Caputo Red, Caputo Blue, and a touch of tipo uno. We also use Caputo's gluten-free mix and one with a special selection of grains and seeds such as sunflower, rye, flax, barley, sesame, and wheat for our cuor di cereal (heart of cereal) dough.

Focaccia is new for us, but fun. A much wetter dough with 70 percent hydration; our usual hydration is 62.5 percent. We sometimes go out of the box, using a biga and incorporating quinoa, chia, and cracked wheat. Our usual method is more direct.

Do you primarily use locally sourced ingredients, or a combination of imported ingredients and local ones?

Produce is primarily local and from elsewhere around the US. During the warmer months in Chicago, we purchase as much as possible from the surrounding farms: tomatoes, peppers, beets, and squash blossoms come to mind. From Italy, we bring in tomatoes, olives, olive oils, vinegars, prosciutto, beans, anchovies, capers, salt, Vesuvian peaches and apricots, select beers and sodas, and all of our wines. The wines we offer are all from Campania, representing all of the region and all of its terroir. A few years back, we let go of marinated white anchovies, as some products are best enjoyed where they are produced.

There is no comparison between anchovies fresh out of the water and those packed in brine for six months.

A big move we made a few years back was our bringing in a mozzarella for our pizza (though not for our antipasti) that is working great. It's a blend of 85 percent cow's milk and 15 percent bufala milk. Less moisture, and lovely, gentle acidity. We are also making more use of a burrata we bring in from Puglia.

What's the most important factor to keep in mind when making pizza?

YOU HAVE TO MIND THE DOUGH. IF YOU HAVE NO DOUGH, YOU HAVE NO PIZZA! Some say the pizza maker is most important. Maybe so in a small shop where the pizza maker is doing everything—from making the dough, preparing ingredients, and opening, extending, and baking a pie. When you are a big operation, you are an ensemble with many moving parts—each one being important. I am the arrangiatore, the conductor, as well as the dough maker, menu planner, visionary, etc. I would be lost without my pizza makers, salad station staff, runners, wait, bus, and dish staff, managers, hosts, and office administrator.

Everyone is important!

Before you thought about being a pizza maker, and before you thought about entering the hospitality industry, you were fascinated by Italy. Why? What made you want to spend so much time in Italy?

Art brought my wife, Ginny, and me to Italy in 1988. We lived in Florence for 3½ years. My wife, who is a painter and mixed media artist, studied at the Cecil Graves atelier. I was the atelier's janitor in exchange for Ginny's tuition, and I was also dedicated to our daughter's care.

Not a bad life, to be a house husband in Florence. Three of our four summers were in Puglia. There, I was a bagnino on the beach. Our daughter, 20 months old when we arrived, was our passport to goodwill. We were embraced by our local communities, we were not tourists passing through. We were lucky to have had this opportunity early in our adult years.

We enjoyed the rhythm of daily life, the local culture and customs, shopping in the neighborhood, the spontaneous generosity and hospitality of new friends as well as strangers, the magic of a simple tomato with good olive oil and salt. We were surrounded by art, architecture, fashion, the beautiful countryside, artisans, and contadini (farmers).

The transition home was not easy, it took many years to settle back in. I longed for Italy. Luckily, we were able to continue our summers in the south, in Rodi Garganico. By the grace of a chance encounter, the pizza idea was born, and that renewed my connection to Italy. Through pizza we try to share all of the joy, wonder, simplicity, and generosity we experienced in Italy. We are a terzo posto, a third place, somewhere between home and work, that nourishes the soul as well as the stomach.

You are very involved with educating others about making pizza. What about your craft inspires you to share your knowledge with others? So many restaurants keep certain recipes and techniques closely guarded, but it seems you are happy to share all your pizza making "secrets."

There are many who keep their craft close to their vest. Not me. I learned, and continue

to learn, through others sharing with me. I did not invent this craft, but I can celebrate it. When we first opened, I would get nervous when I learned of a new place in town, but I soon realized that I would go crazy if I worried whethersomeone else's pizza was better than mine. I focus on my own work. More importantly, I realized that pizzerias can have the same formula, the same product, the same oven, but each one can produce a pizza and a culture that is unique unto itself, and that is a great thing for all of us.

CRAZY

DAN RIOS

CONSPIRACY PIZZA

TORONTO, CANADA

Dan Rios opened Conspiracy Pizza in 2017. The name comes into focus with menu items like the Jimmy Hoffa and the Grassy Knoll. Everyone knows how a good conspiracy theory can get folks worked up, and these pizzas, defined by big, bold, and at times surprising flavor combinations, elicit the same kind of opinionated excitement. The two Toronto locations are local favorites, though they do not supply plastic utensils or paper plates because "climate change is not a conspiracy."

What type of oven do you use to cook your pizzas? What temperature do you cook at?

We use a PizzaMaster electric oven with three cooking decks. We do a two-stage cook with the pizzas, first going in at 750°F for 1 to 2 minutes, and then finishing at 480°F for 3 to 4 minutes.

If you use a wood-burning oven, what type of wood do you burn?

For the smokers we cook our meat in, we use a 50/50 mix of red or white oak and sugar maple.

Oak is expensive but offers excellent flavor, and sugar maple is cheap and plentiful in Canada and burns well.

What flour(s) do you use for your dough?

We use Caputo Neapolitan pizza flour. We find it gives the best flavor and texture.

Do you primarily use locally sourced ingredients or a combination of imported ingredients and local ones?

We use local products as much as we are able, such as pork, beef, and produce, when in season. Due to our short growing season in Canada, we end up using American or Mexican produce in the fall and winter months. We use Italian pizza flour and tomatoes, as we find they both taste and cook better than the local alternatives.

What's the most important factor to keep in mind when making pizza?

I think attention to detail is the most important factor. Paying attention to your dough and changing factors as needed—like temperature, moisture, and yeast—to ensure a consistent product is critical. Secondarily, focusing on quality of ingredients and toppings is necessary to ensure the final product is high quality and good value.

What are your signature pizzas? Why do you think they are so popular?

Our signature pizzas are the Cowspiracy and Halifax Explosion. The Cowspiracy features a creamy garlic-and-Parmesan white sauce as the base; Emmental cheese; smoked beef brisket; red onions; pickled jalapeños; and barbecue sauce. The smoky, buttery brisket carries this pizza, and our tangy barbecue sauce cuts the richness.

Our Halifax Explosion is inspired by eastern Canada's donair pizza, and it is very popular. The base is tomato sauce and mozzarella, with donair-spiced ground beef, shredded pepperoni, and red onions, with fresh tomatoes added after cooking and a drizzle of sweet, tangy, and garlicky donair sauce. Transplants from Canada's East Coast love that they can find a taste of home, and people who have never had it are blown away by the combination of ingredients and the very addictive donair sauce.

Is it accurate to say that Conspiracy Pizza was able to happen in part because of the success of Adamson Barbecue? Barbecue is the art of low-and-slow cooking, while pizza is fired very quickly. Is there any crossover in terms of how to approach these two very different types of cuisine?

Conspiracy Pizza began as an offshoot of Adamson Barbecue and definitely benefited from the popularity of their top-quality smoked meats. We are fully inspired by barbecue in its many forms and feature pickles, mustard, barbecue sauce, pork, and smoke in all that we do. We took the idea of "low and slow" to heart and began experimenting with longer proofing times for our dough. Currently, we age our dough 5 to 7 days, allowing for a richer flavor to develop and a crispier crust to result.

Why do you think your pies are so often included on lists celebrating the best in Toronto?

Our unique dough and toppings are the main selling points for us. There are not a lot of places in Toronto where you can get smoked meat on pizzas. We work hard to constantly come up with new and interesting pizzas to keep our customers interested. We aren't afraid to take chances and experiment with new flavor combinations, such as our French onion soup–inspired pizza, the Tour de France, or our nacho pizza, the Roswell. We take what we do very seriously and always aim to offer excellent value and service to our customers.

MEXZA

ALEJANDRO SOUZA

PIXZA

MEXICO CITY, MEXICO

Declaring it "a social empowerment platform disguised as a pixzeria," founder Alejandro Souza started Pixza to help disadvantaged individuals and champion local ingredients, like blue corn, traditionally prepared meats, and grasshoppers.

What type of oven do you use to cook your pizzas? What temperature do you cook at?

A stone and gas oven, at 660°F.

What flour(s) do you use for your doughs?

High-protein flour and organic blue corn.

Do you primarily use locally sourced ingredients or a combination of imported ingredients and local ones?

Only locally sourced, 100 percent Mexican ingredients.

What's the most important factor to keep in mind when making pizza?

Getting the dough right.

Would you please explain the linguistic origin behind the name Pixza?

When Mexicans say pizza, they say "pixza." I am not sure why, or where this came from, but it is a cultural adaptation of the word that is uniquely Mexican. That being said, the x in the middle of the word is also representative and symbolic of the x in the middle of "Mexico." So that has a nice ring to it also. For us this worked perfectly because we have a very Mexican name for a pizza that is 100 percent Mexican.

What came first, the pizza joint or the desire to create a food-centric social empowerment platform? And why pizza? Why not a Thai restaurant or a traditional Mexican restaurant?

Since day one, Pixza has operated as a social empowerment platform. The idea of creating a 100 percent Mexican pizza came to me while I was studying for my master's degree in New York City. I was with a friend of mine at a bar and we were doing what Mexicans abroad do: reminisce and dream of Mexican food. We were remembering a traditional Mexican dish called a huarache, which is made out of blue corn and has a bean sauce as a base, a variety of different ingredients on top, and cheese. The idea of the huarache made me think of a pizza and I said to my friend, "Why is there no such thing as a blue corn pizza? Maybe it isn't possible." But I kept dreaming of my blue corn pizza and thought out loud how, instead of having pepperoni or other traditional pizza ingredients, it would have grasshoppers and other purely Mexican ingredients. And that's how I decided to call it Pixza, to make it blue corn–based and 100 percent Mexican.

I've always been a social entrepreneur, so making it a social enterprise was an automatic

calling. As a social empowerment platform, Pixza is dedicated to achieving the socioeconomically productive reintegration of young adults through a multidimensional empowerment program that drives them to achieve four objectives in 18 months. First, ensure and maintain formal employment and professional development at Pixza. Second, establish and implement a personal and professional life plan. Third, move out of the shelter and into their own apartment. Finally, take ongoing practical and professional courses. We identify young adults between the ages of 17 and 27 who contend with any of the following challenges: homelessness, abandonment by their family, no formal education, history of drug abuse, a criminal record, or being a migrant or refugee. Since starting Pixza, over 70 such individuals have graduated from our program.

ES
PIXZA
NO
PIZZA

TOM GUAGLIARDO

TANO'S PIZZERIA

CHICAGO, ILLINOIS

When you think of Chicago pizza, your mind probably jumps to deep dish. And for good reason—cheesy, thick, and gooey, the Chicago deep dish has long been an icon of the area. Which is why it's a surprise to find out that Tano's, which has been named on several best-of lists for its deep dish, makes more thin-crust pizza on a daily basis than any other kind.

"Our most popular item is a thin-crust pizza, which is not what you might expect in a deep-dish pizza town," says owner Tom Guagliardo. "But we cater to locals and neighborhood people, and, truth be told, locals don't eat a lot of deep-dish pizza. Buffalo wings are our second-best-selling item, and those two go hand in hand." Both styles of pizza have had a lot of local recognition, so it's a good idea to go with a big group and empty stomach to try some of each.

Tano's is a true neighborhood pizzeria, a descendent of the popular Manzo's down the street, which had been operated by Guagliardo's father for decades. "Tano's pizza is part of the community—we help find lost dogs, serve as a meeting place for friends and families, and have a voice in the neighborhood's future. But my proudest moments come from the customers. We had a chef come from Africa to try our deep-dish pizza—that blows me away. More than anything, I am proud to have regulars; I've watched children grow up and I have mourned the loss of family members. I hear about bad first dates and I watch couples fall in love."

If pizza is family, then Tano's is the truest pizzeria. Recipes passed down over half a century have remained largely unchanged, and Guagliardo still uses tools passed down from his father and grandfather. While Guagliardo's pizza speaks for itself, you would be crazy not to visit and experience a meal at Tano's in person. By the end, West Irving Park Road might even start to feel like home.

How and when did you get your start in this industry?

I grew up in restaurants. My father started in this industry when he was 16. He learned the business, and eventually opened up his own restaurant with the help of his brother and father. As I grew up, I helped out in the kitchen, first making bread baskets and then salads. Soon I was taking orders for delivery and routing delivery drivers. The real fun began when I learned the pizza station and then how to cook on the line.

Who—or what—first inspired you to begin baking pizza? Who inspires you now?

A restaurant kitchen is a magical place. It can be a hot, stress-laden environment, or it can be a beautiful dance of flying dough and sauté pans. It's hard not to fall in love with it. When you're young in the kitchen, you get stuck doing boring tasks like slicing bread or making side salads, but it helps move the show along, and can be a lifesaver when a server has five or six tables. Plus, you get to see what's going on in other stations. You get to watch flames fly from the sauté station and pizza sauce spiral out of the center of a pizza skin. It gives you a drive to "level up" in the kitchen. Nowadays I get a lot of inspiration from the internet; viral videos of bakers giddy over yeasty, bubbly dough bins and before-and-after shots of pizzas keep me excited about what I'm doing next.

What are your golden rules for baking pizza?

My golden rules are:

1. Never use water over 100°F. "You don't want to kill the baby!" Yeast is a living organism—you need to keep it alive so it can transform your dough into a beautiful product. If the water is too hot it will kill the yeast.

2. Consistency is key. You have to do everything the same way each and every time. Baking is a science. Every batch of dough is an experiment; if you change one variable you will get a different outcome.

3. Time cooks the dough, temperature browns the cheese. This is great to remember when trying out new recipes or working on a new oven. You have to find the right temperature and time for a recipe. That little sentence will help zero in on the perfect bake.

What does Tano's Pizzeria represent to you?

Tano's Pizzeria is my family legacy. My father and his lessons are the foundation of this place. Many recipes have remained the same for over 50 years. But we are also looking to the future, and always trying new things and updating others.

What is your favorite pizza to bake? Why?

Research and development for pizza are so much fun. Talk about a dream job! Who wouldn't want to make and eat pizza every day? When we have time, we test out new things. I'll hear about a new ingredient from a distributor or see something cool online. We jump on it and play around in the kitchen. It is a lot of fun.

What is your favorite type of pizza crust? Why? Least favorite crust? Why?

I have been into Neapolitan-style pizza for some time. I love the crispy exterior and the chewy interior of the crust. And, of course, the beautiful wood-fired ovens. I think it's great that they cook at such high temperatures—just 90 seconds and pizza is cooked! The blisters from the high heat give the pizza a great smokiness. I think it also has something to do with not being able to make it myself. My restaurant just doesn't have the right equipment for the job. My least favorite crust is something that's underdeveloped or overworked. Pizza dough needs time to ferment. The yeast does its thing, developing flavors and lightening the dough. Some places take shortcuts with fast rises or frozen dough, but nature cannot be rushed.

How did Tano's Pizzeria come to be? Why Chicago?

Tano's is a culmination of everything I have learned over the years. My father's last restaurant, Manzo's, was located only 3 blocks away from our location. That place raised my brother and me for 20 years. We celebrated and mourned inside those walls. The neighborhood was very good to my family, and when my father decided to retire, I knew I wanted to stay in the same neighborhood when I opened up Tano's.

Chicago is a world-class city, and the food here rivals that of anywhere else. We are lucky enough to have everything that makes a great pizza at our doorstep: flour from the Great Plains, Lake Michigan gives us the best water, and Wisconsin brings in the best cheese. Plus, Chicago is known as the sausage capital of the US, so it's no surprise we use a lot of it on our pizza. Our tomatoes take the longest trip—they come from California.

Where do you get your tools/materials? What non-essential items should every home baker have?

Most of the tools of the trade can be found online or at our distributors. Luckily I have some tools that are older than I am. I have a pizza peel that was made by my grandfather. And our oven, a beautiful stainless-steel carousel oven, is from the 1950s. The great thing about pizza is that you don't need many tools to create it. For the home cook, there are a few basic tools that can help, but nothing mandatory: pizza stones are great for keeping a constant temperature in the oven and on the crust. A rolling pin is useful if you're making Chicago-style thin-crust pizza. Dark metal pans work the best for deep-dish pizza. The dark finish brings more heat to the pizza.

What book(s) go on your required reading list for bakers?

The Pizza Bible by Tony Gemignani. It has just about everything you need to know about pizza, from different types of flour to the right kind of knife to use for pizza cutting.

What outlets/periodicals/newspapers do you read or consult regularly, if any?

There are a lot of great industry magazines. I like *PMQ Pizza Magazine* and *Pizza Today*.

Tell me about your most memorable collaboration with another chef.

I love to cook with my dad. Even at 65 years old, he is still one of the fastest pizza makers I know.

Do you follow any cooking shows or chefs? If so, which is your favorite?

I love *Chef's Table* on Netflix. It lets me nerd out on all things restaurant, from kitchen design to modern plating. I also love that it features chefs from all over the word and all different cuisines—from a farm-to-table chef in Colorado to a Jewish chef making ramen in the heart of Japan.

Where did you learn to bake pizza? Please tell me about your education and apprenticeships.

The restaurant business is in my blood. My father met my mother when she was waitressing at a restaurant; he used to close up shop and go out for breakfast, and that's where he met my mother. I learned everything from my father, and, as his friends would say, you got the best education from the school of West Irving Park Road.

Tell me about your pizza baking processes.

It all starts with the dough. Our dough is mixed and rests for 24 to 48 hours. It is sheeted out to a thickness of about ¼ inch and placed in a dark round baking pan that has been buttered. Any ingredients are placed directly on the dough, and that is topped with our mozzarella blend. A thin layer of dough is placed on top of the cheese, and our thick pizza sauce is ladled on over that. It is then baked in our oven at 450°F for 35 minutes.

VINCE MORENA

ST-VIATEUR BAGEL

MONTREAL, CANADA

Quite simply, St-Viateur Bagel is one of the most popular bagel shops in the entire world. Vince Morena's shop—first located in Montreal's trendy Mile End neighborhood but now found across Montreal—is known as the standard-bearer of the Montreal bagel scene. A scene, of course, that is unrivaled anywhere outside of New York—and even there it's hotly contested.

"We're the best because we still do it the old-fashioned way," says Morena (after a bit of prompting). "We really love what we do, and care about it, and the bagels are just different. Meaning that they're not as big and doughy and salty as the New York–style bagels. And there will be New Yorkers who argue the opposite. They'll call our bagels small and sweet. So, there is a division. But Montreal bagels are the best, definitely, because of the way we do it."

"We've grown to eight locations, we have an online store, we have three restaurants, a food truck, and we're at about 600 grocery stores, so we're still growing." After a trip to St-Viateur, it's not hard to understand the magic bakery's growth. In fact, there's a specific answer: the sesame bagel. Morena estimates that about 95 percent of their bagels sold are sesames—and if that's hyperbole, it's not as much as one might think. One bite of this iconic recipe justifies everything—the press, the longevity, and, yes, even the lines.

"When it comes to bagels, I have a master's degree; everything else I'm just a dummy. I always tell people I got two educations; I got one education in school, and I got another education in the bagel shop. Experience is everything. I've been making bagels for so long that when it comes to bagels I really know what I'm doing."

LA MAISON du BAGEL INC.
CHAUD
276-8044
OUVERT 7 JOURS
BOULANGERIE
BOULANGERIE
ST-VIATEUR
BAGEL
SHOP

How and when did you get your start baking?

My first shift in the bagel shop was in 1984, when I was 13 years old. I learned to roll bagels and make bagels the following year in 1985. My brothers all did the same thing. When we all finished our schooling, however, we all ended up back in the bagel business and we bought the whole thing in 1994.

Who—or what—first inspired you to bake?

My father, because he was in the business. You always look up to your dad, so when he started working in the bagel shop, it was just a natural progression. Coming out of the early '90s there was a bagel boom, so I felt that because I already knew the business and had a business background from my schooling, that I could expand the business that we already owned. At that time, all we had was two spots, and then in '94 we opened a third, in '96 a fourth, and then we kept on growing and growing.

Who inspires you now?

Well when it's your own business, you always care for it more than if you worked somewhere else. And there's always been, and there always continues to be, so much potential for us, because we do things differently. We're not any run-of-the-mill bagel company. We're trying to see how far we can take it.

What is your golden rule(s) for baking?

The golden rule is to get golden nuggets. When the bagels are perfectly cooked, we call them golden nuggets. That means that they're

perfectly golden and symmetrical in their cooking. That's not as easy as it sounds, because we are dealing with a wood-fired oven. Our goal is to always get those perfectly golden brown bagels.

We're only as good as our last bagel. So, our main goal is to keep the bagel consistent. There's people from all around the world who have heard about us, and we want them to have that great experience every time.

What does St-Viateur Bagel represent to you?

Well right now it represents my life. I've been here since I was a kid, and it's more than a bagel shop. It's part of the fabric of Montreal. Especially in the last ten years, we've really become a local landmark, and a tourist site. And, for me it really is my life. A lot of the other parts of my life revolve around the bagel shop.

What is your favorite thing to bake? Why?

Well, bagels are all similar to bake. The question would be what is my favorite bagel to *eat*. And, I would say the sesame is the golden standard. It's a different mentality from America. A lot of people come here from the States and say, "Our bagel shop has 32 flavors," whereas up until about 10 years ago we only had three flavors. Now, we have some of the other flavors, and we're up to about nine. But my favorite is still the sesame seed.

How did St-Viateur Bagel come to be? Why Montreal?

St-Viateur is a family business. It was started by a Holocaust survivor named Myer Lewkowicz. My father started working for Myer as a boy in 1962, and then in 1974 he became a full partner. They kept growing the business. There was just one shop back in the old days, and we didn't grow to two shops until 1984. In fact, there were only two bagel shops in all of Montreal at that time making bagels the way we do. So, we were the only game in town for a long time.

Montreal is the birthplace for Montreal-style bagels. So, now you'll see some Montreal-

style bagels popping up all around the world, but I think the way it happened here was with the immigration patterns. Montreal had a similar immigration pattern to New York City, where at the turn of the century there were a lot of Eastern European Jewish people that came over, and they brought their bagels. We get compared to New York all the time, because we're both bagel meccas, so to speak. And so, the main difference we tell people is that we never evolved.

At a certain point of time, bagels were made the same way everywhere, because it got brought over from Europe a long time ago. However, people, technology, and machinery got in the way. The American bagel is machine-made, and is made in gas or electric ovens, and with time it got bigger and bigger. Whereas our bagel, it fits in the size of your hand. We never changed. We make a lot smaller by batches, but they're tastier.

What tools/materials do you use?

Well the tools are easy. We build the brick ovens in-house. We make every bagel by hand, so you need your hands. Then, we have a boiler, a knife, and a shibba. A shibba is used to shift the bagels in the oven. That's about it. And a mixer, obviously. It's very simple!

Tell me about your most memorable collaboration with another chef.

One of the most memorable collaborations would probably have to be with Bob Blumer. He had this TV show called *Glutton for Punishment.* In that show, we had to teach him how to make bagels in five days. So, that was his challenge, and it was probably one of the more memorable TV shows we have ever done. He did it, and we're still friends today.

Brag about yourselves a bit. What are your highest achievements and/or proudest moments as chefs?

We just celebrated our 60th anniversary with a big block party. So, we're just proud of the fact that we've been around for so long. We're the furthest thing from an overnight success. My dad's been here for 50 years, and my brothers and I have been here for 30 years, so it's the long process that I'm proud of.

Where did you learn to cook? Please tell me about your education and apprenticeships.

I started as a boy. It's a simple process, but it takes some time to master. Once you learn to bake bagels, you can't unlearn—it's like learning to ride a bicycle.

Tell me about your bagel baking process.

We put the ingredients together in a mixer, and we make batches of about 100 pounds at a time. We take the large dough, put it on the table, and cut it in strips. Then we roll the strips by hand into bagels. The bagels all weigh about two and a half or three ounces each.

It's a five-minute cycle. So, every five minutes we put four dozen bagels into a large pot of boiling water, and in the boiling water there is some honey that gives the bagels a little bit of sweetness, a little glow, that helps the sesame seeds stick. Then, we take the bagels out of the water, and cover them in sesame seeds, and put them on these wooden boards and into the oven to dry. There's always 20 dozen bagels in the oven, because it takes them about 18–20 minutes to cook. Then, we pull the ones that are cooked out of the oven, and through a chute, and then we start the whole process over again five minutes later. 24 hours a day, 365 days a year.

CONVERSION TABLE

WEIGHTS

1 oz. = 28 grams
2 oz. = 57 grams
4 oz. (¼ lb.) = 113 grams
8 oz. (½ lb.) = 227 grams
16 oz. (1 lb.) = 454 grams

VOLUME MEASURES

⅛ teaspoon = 0.6 ml
¼ teaspoon = 1.23 ml
½ teaspoon = 2.5 ml
1 teaspoon = 5 ml
1 tablespoon (3 teaspoons) = ½ fluid oz. = 15 ml
2 tablespoons = 1 fluid oz. = 29.5 ml
¼ cup (4 tablespoons) = 2 fluid oz. = 59 ml
⅓ cup (5 ⅓ tablespoons) = 2.7 fluid oz. = 80 ml
½ cup (8 tablespoons) = 4 fluid oz. = 120 ml
⅔ cup (10 ⅔ tablespoons) = 5.4 fluid oz. = 160 ml
¾ cup (12 tablespoons) = 6 fluid oz. = 180 ml
1 cup (16 tablespoons) = 8 fluid oz. = 240 ml

TEMPERATURE EQUIVALENTS

°F	°C	Gas Mark
225	110	¼
250	130	½
275	140	1
300	150	2
325	170	3
350	180	4
375	190	5
400	200	6
425	220	7
450	230	8
475	240	9
500	250	10

LENGTH MEASURES

1/16 inch = 1.6 mm
⅛ inch = 3 mm
¼ inch = 1.35 mm
½ inch = 1.25 cm
¾ inch = 2 cm
1 inch = 2.5 cm

IMAGE CREDITS

Pages 9, 10–11, 22–23, 25, 30, 33, 39, 43, 45, 72, 112, 116, 158, 169, 170, 173, 174, 196, 199, 215, 222, 230, 251, 255, 258–259, 270–271, 275, 277, 278, 279, 282, 283, 284, 290, 301, 308, 313, 314, 318–319, 328–329, 346–347, 355, 356, 359, 374, 481, 494–495, 520, 551, 569, 591, 599, 600, 604, 621, 622, 625, 638–639, 688–689, 710–711, 730–731, 768–769, and 776–777 courtesy of Unsplash.

Pages 75, 130, 133, 139, 140, 178, 200, 208, 225, 233, 249, 264, 267, 269, 382, 497, 498, 531, 549, 570, 575, 596, 612, 632, 641, 655, 672, 674–675, 681, 682, 683, 686–687, 691, 692, 693, 695, 696–697, 699, 703, 704, 705, 707, 709, 713, 717, 718, 721, 722, 725, 726, 727, 729, 732, 734, 735, 737, 739, 741, 743, 744, 747, 748, 750, 751, 752, 755, 756, 758, 759, 760, 762, 763, 765, 767, 771, 772, 773, and 774 courtesy of Cider Mill Press.

All other photos used under official license from Shutterstock.

INDEX

ABOUT CIDER MILL PRESS BOOK PUBLISHERS

Cider Mill Press publishes exceptional books that combine creativity and craftsmanship. As an imprint of HarperCollins Focus, we specialize in premium cookbooks, cocktail and spirits guides, and illustrated gift books, all distinguished by compelling content, striking design, and a commitment to quality in every detail. Cider Mill Press sets the standard for books that inform, inspire, and elevate everyday moments. Learn more at cidermillpress.com.

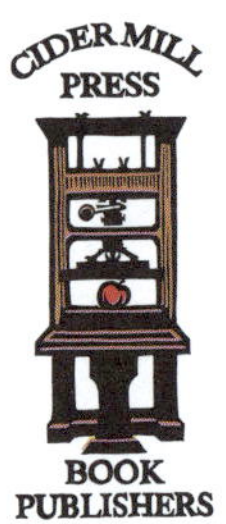

"Where Good Books Are Ready for Press"

501 Nelson Place
Nashville, Tennessee 37214 USA